CW00956751

HANDBOOK OF THE INTERNATIONAL POLITICAL ECONOMY OF PRODUCTION

HANDBOOKS OF RESEARCH ON INTERNATIONAL POLITICAL ECONOMY

Series Editors: Matthew Watson, *Department of Politics and International Studies, University of Warwick, Coventry, UK* and Benjamin J. Cohen, *Louis G. Lancaster Professor of International Political Economy, University of California, Santa Barbara, USA*

This highly original *Handbook* series offers a unique appraisal of the state-of-the-art of research in International Political Economy (IPE). Consisting of original contributions by leading authorities, *Handbooks* in the series provide comprehensive overviews of the very latest research within key areas of IPE. Taking a thematic approach, emphasis is placed on both expanding current debate and indicating the likely research agenda for the future. Each *Handbook* forms a prestigious and high quality work of lasting significance. The *Handbooks* will encompass arguments from both the British and American schools of IPE to give a comprehensive overview of the debates and research positions in each key area of interest, as well as offering a space for those who feel that their work fits neither designation easily. Taking a genuinely international approach these *Handbooks* are designed to inform as well as to contribute to current debates.

Titles in the series include:

Handbook of the International Political Economy of Governance
Edited by Anthony Payne and Nicola Phillips

Handbook of the International Political Economy of Monetary Relations
Edited by Thomas Oatley and W. Kindred Winecoff

Handbook of the International Political Economy of Trade
Edited by David A. Deese

Handbook of the International Political Economy of Production
Edited by Kees van der Pijl

Handbook of the International Political Economy of Production

Edited by

Kees van der Pijl

Fellow, Centre for Global Political Economy and Professor Emeritus, University of Sussex, UK

HANDBOOKS OF RESEARCH ON INTERNATIONAL POLITICAL ECONOMY

Cheltenham, UK • Northampton, MA, USA

Published by
Edward Elgar Publishing Limited
The Lypiatts
15 Lansdown Road
Cheltenham
Glos GL50 2JA
UK

Edward Elgar Publishing, Inc.
William Pratt House
9 Dewey Court
Northampton
Massachusetts 01060
USA

Paperback edition 2016

A catalogue record for this book
is available from the British Library

Library of Congress Control Number: 2014950765

This book is available electronically in the **Elgar**online
Social and Political Science subject collection
DOI 10.4337/9781783470211

ISBN 978 1 78347 020 4 (cased)
ISBN 978 1 78347 021 1 (eBook)
ISBN 978 1 78471 258 7 (paperback)

Typeset by Servis Filmsetting Ltd, Stockport, Cheshire
Printed and bound in Great Britain by TJ International Ltd, Padstow, Cornwall

Contents

Figures

Tables

Contributors

Joseph BAINES is a PhD candidate in the Department of Political Science at York University, Toronto. His research focuses on the impacts that the business operations of the major agricultural commodity traders have on global food security. He has presented some of his findings in an article entitled 'Food price inflation as redistribution: Towards a new analysis of corporate power in the world food system', published in *New Political Economy*. He has also published in the *Review of Capital as Power* and he was a 2013 winner of the Association for Institutional Thought Student Scholars Award.

Anannya BHATTACHARJEE is the President of the Garment and Allied Workers Union (GAWU) in North India and Executive Council Member of the New Trade Union Initiative (NTUI). She is the International Coordinator of Asia Floor Wage Alliance. She has helped build grass-roots labour-related collaboration between North America, Europe and Asia. Before, Ms Bhattacharjee was an activist based in the US in the women's, migrants' and the workers' rights movements. She was a Charles Revson Fellow at Columbia University and Activist-in-Residence at the Asian Pacific American Studies Program and Institute at New York University. She is the co-editor of *Policing the National Body* (2002).

Miriam BOYER received a joint PhD in sociology and political science in 2013 from Columbia University and the Free University of Berlin. Her dissertation develops a novel framework for studying living processes as part of nature–society relations by capturing the materiality of nature through the use of spatiotemporal categories. Areas of research include the history of science and technology, agriculture, theories of nature and interdisciplinary methods between the social and the natural sciences.

Davide BRADANINI holds a PhD in 'Political systems and institutional change' from IMT Lucca, where he defended a thesis on 'Common sense and national emergency: neoliberal hegemony in 1990s Italy'. His research interests in the field of International Political Economy are in the areas of European integration, Italian history and political economy and neo-Gramscian and Marxist theory.

Ulrich BRAND is Professor of International Politics at the University of Vienna. His interests are in critical state and governance studies, regulation and hegemony theory, political ecology, international resource and environmental politics; his regional focus is Latin America. He was member of the Expert Commission on 'Growth, Well-Being and Quality of Life' of the German Bundestag. His work in English has been published in journals such as *Antipode, Austrian Journal of Development Studies, Austrian Journal of Political Science, Globalizations, Innovation* and *Review of International Political Economy*. He recently co-edited books on Regulation theory, Political Ecology and Latin America.

Jenny CHAN joined the School of Interdisciplinary Area Studies at the University of Oxford in September 2014. She was Chief Coordinator of SACOM (Students and Scholars Against Corporate Misbehaviour) between 2006 and 2009. Educated at the Chinese University of Hong Kong and the University of Hong Kong, she went on to pursue her doctorate in sociology and labour studies as a Reid Research Scholar at the University of London. In finishing her PhD thesis (June 2014) she was assisted by a grant from the Great Britain–China Educational Trust. Her articles have appeared in *Current Sociology, Global Labour Journal, Modern China, The Asia-Pacific Journal, The South Atlantic Quarterly, New Labor Forum, Labor Notes, New Internationalist and New Technology, Work and Employment*.

Christine B.N. CHIN is Professor in the School of International Service, American University. Her research and teaching interests are in the political economy of transnational migration, South-East Asian studies and intercultural relations. Dr Chin's most recent book is *Cosmopolitan Sex Workers: Women and Migration in a Global City*. She is also the author of *In Service and Servitude: Foreign Female Domestic Workers and the Malaysian 'Modernity' Project*, as well as *Cruising in the Global Economy: Profits, Pleasure and Work at Sea*. Dr Chin has published in international academic journals such as *International Feminist Journal of Politics*, *Third World Quarterly* and *New Political Economy*. Her current research project examines human insecurities and immigrant communities in the Global North.

Matt DAVIES is Senior Lecturer in IPE at Newcastle University, UK. His research interests range from work as an issue for IPE, to the critique of everyday life in international relations, to popular culture and world politics. He is the author of *International Political Economy and Mass Communication in Chile* and co-editor (with Magnus Ryner) of *Poverty and the Production of World Politics*. His articles have appeared in *Global Society, International Political Sociology* and *Alternatives: Global, Local, Political* and other journals. His current research focuses on a critique of the notion of precarity and an extended study of the concept of everyday life in IPE.

Raúl DELGADO WISE is Professor and former Director (2002–12) of the Doctoral Program in Development Studies at the Autonomous University of Zacatecas, Mexico. He is general coordinator of the UNESCO Chair on Migration, Development and Human Rights; member of the advisory board of the UNESCO–MOST committee in Mexico; president and founder of the International Network on Migration and Development, and co-Director of the Critical Development Studies Network. Professor Delgado Wise has published or edited 22 books, and written more than 150 essays, including book chapters and refereed articles. He has been a guest lecturer in more than 30 countries on all five continents.

Radhika DESAI is Professor at the Department of Political Studies, University of Manitoba, Winnipeg, Canada. She is the author of *Geopolitical Economy: After US Hegemony, Globalization and Empire* (2013), *Slouching Towards Ayodhya: From Congress to Hindutva in Indian Politics* (2nd rev edn, 2004) and *Intellectuals and Socialism: 'Social Democrats' and the Labour Party* (1994, a *New Statesman and Society* Book of the Month) and editor of *Revitalizing Marxist Theory for Today's Capitalism* (2010) and *Developmental and Cultural Nationalisms* (2009). She co-edits the Future of Capitalism book series with Alan Freeman.

Adam FISHWICK completed an ESRC-funded PhD at the University of Sussex in 2014. He holds an MA in Global Political Economy and an MSc in Comparative and Cross-Cultural Research Methods. He published articles in *Capital & Class* and *Peripherie* and has co-authored two introductory books on economics. In the course of his PhD research he spent six months conducting archival and field research on workplace conflict and industrial development in Argentina and Chile. He has taught at the University of Sussex and worked for its Centre for Global Political Economy and as an intern at the International Institute of Social History in Amsterdam.

Alan FREEMAN is a former economist at the Greater London Authority, where he wrote *Creativity, London's Core Business* and was lead author for *London: A Cultural Audit* and *The Living Wage: Towards a Fairer London*. He is a Visiting Professor at London Metropolitan University and lives in Winnipeg, Canada. With Radhika Desai, he co-edits the *Future of World Capitalism* book series and with Andrew Kliman he founded the International Working Group on Value Theory (IWGVT), and co-edits the new critical pluralist journal *Critique of Political Economy*. He currently serves on the Board of the Winnipeg Symphony Orchestra.

Sam GINDIN spent most of his working life (1974–2000) on the staff of the Canadian Auto Workers – now UNIFOR – where he was Research Director and later Assistant to the President. He was subsequently (2000–10) the Packer Chair in Social Justice in the Political Science Department at York, where he is now an Adjunct Professor. He has written extensively on labour issues and in 2010 he co-authored, with Leo Panitch and Greg Albo, *In and Out of Crisis*. Most recently he and Panitch co-authored *The Making of Global Capitalism: The Political Economy of American Empire* (2012, Deutscher Memorial Prize, Davidson Prize).

Kevin GRAY is Senior Lecturer in International Relations at the University of Sussex, UK. He is the author of *Korean Workers and Neoliberal Globalization* (2008), *Labour and Development in East Asia: Social Forces and Passive Revolution* (forthcoming 2014), as well as co-editor (with Barry Gills) of *People Power in an Era of Global Crisis: Rebellion, Resistance and Liberation* (2012), and (with Craig N. Murphy) *Rising Powers and the Future of Global Governance* (2013). He is also the Assistant Editor of the journal *Globalizations* and co-editor of the *Rethinking Globalization* book series.

Jean-Christophe GRAZ is Professor of International Relations at the Institut d'Etudes Politiques et Internationales of the University of Lausanne, Switzerland, and co-founder of the *Centre de Recherche Interdisciplinaire sur l'International (CRII)*. For the last 15 years his research field has been on regulation issues in international political economy and the interplay of transnational and private patterns and agents of change in globalization. His latest book is titled *Services sans Frontières: Mondialisation, Normalisation et Régulation de l'économie des Services* (2013).

Yury GROMYKO is a Director of the consultancy and research company Shiffers Institute of Advanced Studies, based in Moscow. He holds a degree in psychology and is a Professor at Moscow State University and a visiting professor at Tamkang University in Taipei, Taiwan. His research interests lie in the sphere of international political economy, innovation politics and international cooperation in Eurasia. He has been one of the initiators of the international cooperation network 'Trans-Eurasian Belt of *Razvitie*' which embraces researchers, politicians and businesspeople from the European Union (Italy, Germany, France), Asia (Japan, China) and Russia.

Jeffrey HARROD is a writer and essayist and supervises research at the University of Amsterdam. He graduated in international law at UCL London and holds a PhD from the University of Geneva. His publications and online material relevant here are *Power, Production and the Unprotected Worker* (1987); 'The global poor and global politics: Neo-materialism and the sources of political action' in Davis and Ryner (2006); the 16-lecture online course 'Global political economy: How the world works'; and essays on 'Global Weimarism: Or why the centre cannot hold' and 'Corporatism: The 21st century political economic system', at www.jeffreyharrod.eu.

Otto HOLMAN is Reader in International Relations and European Politics in the Department of Political Science and a member of the Amsterdam Institute for Social Science Research at the University of Amsterdam. He has been a Visiting Professor at the University of Lausanne since 2009. His research focuses on EU enlargement, transnational governance in the EU and the role of transnational business, and on patterns of uneven development within the EU and its member states. His most recent project deals with the multidimensionality of crisis and core-periphery dynamics inside the EU and in its external relations.

Ryoji IHARA holds a PhD in Sociology from Hitotsubashi University. He is currently working as Associate Professor in the Faculty of Regional Studies at Gifu University in Japan. His books include *Toyota's Assembly Line: A View from the Factory Floor* (2007) and *Power, Politics and Culture in the Workplace: A Comparative Study of the Shop Floor at Toyota and Nissan* (in Japanese, forthcoming). His research interests are in Japanese-style management and workers' culture on the shop floor in the context of the global economy.

Youngseok JANG is Professor of Chinese Studies at Sungkonghoe University, South Korea. He is author of *Chinese Labour Relations in an Age of Globalization* (in Korean, 2007), and *Changes in the Contemporary Chinese Labour System and Transformations in the Functions of Trade Unions* (in Chinese, 2004). He is also co-author, with Seung-Wook Baek, of *Chinese Workers and the Politics of Memory: The Memories of the Cultural Revolution* (in Korean, 2007).

Sylvia KAY is a researcher at the Transnational Institute (TNI). She is part of TNI's Agrarian Justice team, working on issues related to land and resource rights, food politics and agricultural investment. She holds a BA in International Relations and Sociology from the University of Sussex and an MSc in Global Politics from the London School of Economics and Political Science. She currently lives in The Hague, the Netherlands.

David T. MARTIN is a PhD candidate in the Doctorate of Development Studies at the Autonomous University of Zacatecas in Mexico. Prior to his return to academia, he served as researcher for United for a Fair Economy and the Center for Migrant Rights, where he researched issues of inequality and migration. In 2011, he earned a Master's degree in International Development Studies from Saint Mary's University in Halifax, Nova Scotia for a thesis he wrote on US hegemonic decline in Latin America. His current research interests include global capitalist crisis, financialization, international migration and the commodities boom in Latin America.

Siobhán McGRATH is a lecturer in Human Geography at Durham University. She completed her PhD at the University of Manchester's Institute of Development Policy and Management. She is interested in work, labour and employment, particularly forced/unfree labour; degrading, precarious and unregulated work; and labour within Global Production Networks. She is part of a research project on addressing demand for trafficking, funded by the European Commission. She is also interested in Brazil's role as a rising power in the context of South–South globalization and development. She is on the Associate Board of *Work, Employment and Society* and the International Advisory Board of *Antipode*.

Jeroen MERK is David Davies of Llandinam Fellow at the London School of Economics where he works on a project 're-inventing corporate accountability after the Rana Plaza collapse'. His research interests lie at the crossroads of international relations, political economy, social movements and the governance institutions of global industrial relations. Since 2003, he has been a research and policy coordinator at the International Secretariat of the Clean Clothes Campaign, a labour rights NGO with branches in 15 European countries and an extended network of partners in production countries.

Phoebe MOORE is Senior Lecturer in International Relations at the University of Middlesex, London. Her research covers international employment relations, education and training policy, and the use of technology in workspaces and on working bodies. She is the author of *Globalisation and Labour Struggle in Asia* (2012) and *The International Political Economy of Work and Employability* (2010). She is on the Editorial Boards for *Capital and Class, Globalizations* and the *Journal for Critical Education Policy Studies*. She served as Convenor for the International Political Economy Group (IPEG) of the British International Studies Association (BISA) 2011–14 and is an elected BISA Trustee.

Leo PANITCH is Canada Research Chair in Comparative Political Economy and Distinguished Research Professor of Political Science at York University. For the past 25 years he has been the co-editor of the internationally renowned annual volume, *The Socialist Register*. His most recent books are *The Making of Global Capitalism: The Political Economy of American Empire* (with Sam Gindin, 2012, Deutscher Memorial Prize, Davidson Prize), *In and Out of Crisis: The Global Financial Meltdown and Left Alternatives* (with Greg Albo and Sam Gindin, 2010) and *American Empire and the Political Economy of Global Finance* (ed., with Martijn Konings, 2008).

Matthew PATERSON is Professor of Political Science at the University of Ottawa. His research focuses on the political economy of global environmental change. His publications include *Global Warming and Global Politics* (1996), *Understanding Global Environmental Politics: Domination, Accumulation, Resistance* (2000), *Automobile Politics: Ecology and Cultural Political Economy* (2007), and most recently *Climate Capitalism: Global Warming and the Transformation of the Global Economy* (with Peter Newell, 2010). He is currently focused on the political economy and cultural politics of climate change.

PUN Ngai is Professor in the Department of Applied Social Sciences at Hong Kong Polytechnic University. She is the author of *Made in China: Women Factory Workers in a Global Workplace* (2005), which received the C.W. Mills Award and was translated into French, German, Italian, Polish and Chinese. Her articles have appeared in *Modern China, China Journal, China Quarterly, Global Labour Journal, Work, Employment and Society, Cultural Anthropology, Feminist Economics, Current Sociology* and *Third World Quarterly*. She also co-authored three books in Chinese on construction workers, Foxconn workers and Chinese social economy.

Ashim ROY is founding General Secretary and currently Vice President of the New Trade Union Initiative, a left democratic, non-partisan national federation of independent trade unions. From the time of the anti-Emergency movement in the 1970s (when the then-Prime Minister, Indira Gandhi, tried to impose a police state in India) Roy has been a leader in the trade union movement nationally. He is also president of the Garment and Textile Workers Union in the state of Karnataka, president of several manufacturing unions in Gujarat, and member of the International Steering Committee of the Asia Floor Wage Alliance.

Saskia SASSEN is the Robert S. Lynd Professor of Sociology and Co-Chair, The Committee on Global Thought, Columbia University. Her recent books are *Territory, Authority, Rights: From Medieval to Global Assemblages* (2008), *A Sociology of Globalization* (2007), and *Cities in a World Economy* (4th rev. edn, 2012). Among older books is *The Global City* (1991/2001). Her books are translated into over 20 languages.

Her latest book is *Expulsions: When Complexity Produces Elementary Brutalities* (2014). She is the recipient of diverse awards, most recently the Principe de Asturias 2013 Prize in the Social Sciences.

Mark SELDEN is Senior Research Associate in the East Asia Program at Cornell University, Coordinator of *The Asia-Pacific Journal*, and Professor Emeritus of History and Sociology at Binghamton University. His books include *China in Revolution: The Yenan Way Revisited, The Political Economy of Chinese Development, Chinese Village, Socialist State* (with Edward Friedman and Paul Pickowicz), *Chinese Society: Change, Conflict and Resistance* (with Elizabeth Perry), *The Resurgence of East Asia: 500, 150 and 50 Year Perspectives* (with Giovanni Arrighi and Takeshi Hamashita). He is the editor of two book series.

Benjamin SELWYN is Senior Lecturer in International Relations and Development Studies in the Department of International Relations, University of Sussex, UK. He is the author of *The Global Development Crisis* (2014), and *Workers, State and Development in Brazil: Powers of Labour, Chains of Value* (2012) and has published articles in *Le Monde Diplomatique, Open Democracy* and *Global Labour Column*. He sits on the editorial board of *Development Studies Research: An Open Access Journal* and on the international advisory board of the *Journal of Agrarian Change*.

Mehmet Gürsan ŞENALP holds a PhD in economics from Gazi University. He works in the field of international political economy with a focus on transnational economic and political relations, social class formations and struggles. Along with a book in Turkish titled *Transnational Capitalist Class Formation in Turkey: The Koç Holding Case* (2012), he has published articles in academic, political and literary journals on the transnationalization of capitalism and capitalist classes, global governance, institutional economics and the political economy of Turkey. He is currently working as an assistant professor in the Department of Economics at Atılım University, Ankara.

Örsan ŞENALP is a transnational social justice and labour activist, political economist and Internet specialist. Previously he worked as a trade union expert and took an active role in international trade union–NGO alliances as part of both the global water justice movement and European convergence processes like the Joint Social Conference, Alter-Summit, and Firenze 10+10. Since 2010 he has been managing a Social Network Unionism blog project and actively took part in the 15M, Occupy and Gezi uprisings. In May 2013, he organized the Networked Labour seminar in Amsterdam and since then he has coordinated the networkedlabour.net website and social network.

Werner SEPPMANN studied social science and philosophy and worked for many years with Leo Kofler. His recent book publications include *Subjekt und System: Der lange Schatten des Objektivismus* (2011); *Die Verleugnete Klasse: Zur Arbeiterklasse heute* (2011); *Dialektik der Entzivilisierung: Krise, Irrationalismus und Gewalt* (2012); *Marxismus und Philosophie* (2012); *Ästhetik der Unterwerfung: Das Beispiel Documenta* (editor, 2013); *Kapitalismuskritik und Sozialismuskonzeption: In welcher Gesellschaft leben wir?* (2013); *Marx Kontrovers: Aktuelle Tendenzen der Marxismus-Diskussion* (editor, 2014), and (with Erich Hahn and Thomas Metscher) *Marxismus und Ideologie* (2014). Dr Seppmann is currently president of the Marx-Engels-Stiftung, Wuppertal, where he directs the Klassenanalyse@BRD project.

Beverly J. SILVER is Professor of Sociology and Director of the Arrighi Center for Global Studies at the Johns Hopkins University (Baltimore, USA). She has written widely on the historical dynamics of global capitalism. Her best known book, *Forces of Labor: Workers' Movements and Globalization since 1870*, has been translated into eleven languages and won several major awards including the Distinguished Publication Award of the American Sociological Association. She worked closely with the late Giovanni Arrighi, co-authoring numerous publications including *Chaos and Governance in the Modern World System*, 'Workers North and South' and 'The end of the long twentieth century'.

Kendra STRAUSS is a feminist economic and labour geographer and Assistant Professor of Labour Studies at Simon Fraser University. Her research interests include labour market change, pension reform, and new and evolving forms of unfreedom in contemporary labour markets. Prior to returning to Canada, she was an Urban Studies Postdoctoral Research Associate at the University of Glasgow, and University Lecturer in the Department of Geography at the University of Cambridge. Dr Strauss has published in the fields of geography, labour law and labour studies; her books include *Saving for Retirement* with Gordon L. Clark and Janelle Knox-Hayes (2012) and *Temporary Work, Agencies and Unfree Labour* (co-edited with Judy Fudge, 2014).

Kees VAN DER PIJL is Professor Emeritus in the School of Global Studies and Fellow of the Centre for Global Political Economy, University of Sussex. He studied law and political science in Leiden and taught International Relations at the University of Amsterdam where he also obtained his doctorate in 1983. His publications include *The Making of an Atlantic Ruling Class* (1984, new edn 2012), *Transnational Classes and International Relations* (1998), *Global Rivalries from the Cold War to Iraq*

(2006) and a trilogy, *Modes of Foreign Relations and Political Economy* (vol. I, *Nomads, Empires, States*, 2007, Deutscher Memorial Prize 2008; II, *The Foreign Encounter in Myth and Religion*, 2010; and III, *The Discipline of Western Supremacy*, 2014). Upon his return to the Netherlands in 2012 he was elected president of the Dutch Anti-Fascist Resistance, an offshoot of the wartime Communist underground and a member organization of the European *Fédération Internationale des Résistants*.

Markus WISSEN is Professor of Social Sciences at the Department of Business and Economics of the Berlin School of Economics and Law. He works on society–nature relations and the socio-ecological transformation of production and consumption patterns. Besides books and book chapters he has published articles in *Review of International Political Economy, Globalizations, Austrian Journal of Political Science, PROKLA* and other journals. In 2011 he and Ulrich Brand edited a special issue of *Antipode: A Radical Journal of Geography* on the internationalization of the state.

Joscha WULLWEBER is Assistant Professor in the Political Science Department, University of Kassel. He holds a PhD in political science, an MA in global political economy and an MSc in biology. His research interests concentrate on theories of IPE and IR; the global political economy of finance, critical security studies, and politics of R&D, technology and innovation. His recent publications include 'Post-Positivist Political Theory', in Michael T. Gibbons, ed., *The Encyclopedia of Political Thought* (2014); and 'Global politics and empty signifiers: The political construction of high-technology', *Critical Policy Studies* (2014).

Acknowledgements

In the composition of this collection I profited from the assistance of many colleagues, none more so than Magnus Ryner of King's College London, whose wise judgement helped me focus the project and draw up a first line-up of possible chapter titles and contributors. We would have edited this volume together had not his many current commitments been in the way.

Others who helped getting the project on the rails, identified potential authors, and/or made important suggestions include Alexander Kovriga, Jan Nederveen Pieterse, Marcel van der Linden, Christoph Scherrer, Masao Watanabe, Peter Waterman and Frido Wenten. Of the contributors, Ulrich Brand and Jeroen Merk played crucial roles in helping to get others on board.

All contributions have either been specially written for this collection or reworked from previous papers. An earlier version of Beverly Silver's chapter was presented at the International Conference of Labour and Social History, Linz, Austria, 11–14 September 2003 (Unfried et al. 2004). Leo Panitch and Sam Gindin's contribution draws on various chapters of their recent book *The Making of Global Capitalism* (Panitch and Gindin 2012). Jean-Christophe Graz's contribution takes further the argument in his chapter in a collection by Joerges and Falke (Graz 2011). Davide Bradanini's chapter includes material from an article in *Global Labour Journal* (Bradanini 2014). Jeffrey Harrod's chapter contains material from his contribution to a volume edited by Ryner and Davies (Harrod 2007). Matthew Paterson's chapter includes a section from his *Understanding Global Environmental Politics* (Paterson 2000), with licence granted by Palgrave Macmillan. Sylvia Kay's chapter includes sections from a working paper published by the Transnational Institute (Kay 2012).

One topic I wanted to include in the collection is the production of waste, one of the most striking consequences of how linear production violates the circularities of nature. Barbara Harriss-White and Sarah Hodges, whose commitments prevented them from contributing themselves, helped me in the search for a contributor but in the end the search was fruitless in spite of their assistance.

Finally I want to thank the series editors, Benjamin Cohen and Matthew Watson, for the confidence expressed in the invitation to edit this collection, and the publishers, Edward Elgar, for their support throughout the undertaking, and Yvonne Smith for the careful copy-editing.

Kees van der Pijl
Amsterdam, 3 October 2014

Introduction: the world of production and political economy

Kees van der Pijl

This volume provides a comprehensive overview of research, key concepts and debates on the international political economy (IPE) of production. It adopts an expansive approach to the topic, encompassing research that would not immediately be recognized by conventional definitions of the research area. Only thus can it cover key aspects of production as the transformation and exploitation of nature, the most fundamental and universal of human practices. This understanding of production necessarily includes the exploitation of the natural substratum of humanity itself. Marx formulated what remains the *locus classicus* of this when he characterizes the process of production in *Capital*, volume I, as

> a process between man [*Mensch*] and nature, a process in which man mediates, regulates and controls his metabolism with nature by his own action. He confronts the substance of nature [*Naturstoff*] as one of its own forces, setting in motion arms and legs, head and hands, the natural forces of his body, in order to appropriate what nature yields in a form useful for his own life. Whilst influencing and changing external nature in this movement, he simultaneously changes his own (*MEW* 23: 192).

Now if production is a 'unifying characteristic' of historical human existence (Harrod 1997: 108–9), the question arises why this is not evident in the social sciences today. In this introductory chapter I answer this question, first, by looking at the key mutations in the combination of mental and manual work, with special reference to the concept of the socialization of labour. Second, I briefly investigate how social science originated in the quest for controlling the labour process and the working class. Yet labour paradoxically disappeared again as a unifying concern once the disciplinary organization of the social sciences took shape in the nineteenth and twentieth centuries. I then address the issue that runs through the first two parts of the collection, the geographical and social bifurcation between mental and manual labour and the possibility of their coming together again. Finally, I briefly discuss those aspects of the anchorage of production in reproduction and nature that are not covered in detail in Part III.

MENTAL AND MANUAL WORK

From a broad historical perspective, labour, or production, which we today recognize as a general category, began as the ability to make and use tools. This then guided the further evolution of the human mind and body, as captured in Marx's definition above. In all pre-modern societies, the actual process of (manual) work was separated from activities usually considered worthier, such as magical-religious tasks and contemplative activities, in other words, 'mental work'. Hence in most societies labour was associated with low social status, if not actually assigned to slaves. Manual work was further divided in the most elementary menial tasks like cleaning and food preparation, often the preserve of women; and skilled work that made it worthwhile to try and control access to its legitimate performance, as by the medieval guilds. These passed on the specific skills of their craft through a closed system of apprenticeships. One of the achievements of the *Encyclopédie* of Diderot and D'Alembert, eventually codified by the French Revolution, was the divulgence of the secrets of the guilds.

Science early on developed separately from work. Like art, its magical and religious connotations kept it in the domain of contemplation as an activity for those not forced to work. Like mathematics for the natural world, systematic philosophy followed in the footsteps of art and religion in transcending the 'meso-cosmos' that our minds have organically developed in – thus exploring the macro- and micro-worlds that lie beyond our direct experience (Vollmer 2013: 147–50). In the Italian Renaissance an important step in applying such abstract projections back into the sphere of actual production happened when the builder of the dome of the cathedral of Florence, Brunelleschi, sought the advice of the city's leading mathematician, Toscanelli, to help him with problems his craft had no solution for (Sohn-Rethel 1970: 123). Galileo a century later took a step further into the macro-cosmos when he built his own telescope to verify Copernicus' hypothesis that the earth circles round the sun, widening the sphere of fruitful application of pure thought in doing so. But he also combined mental with manual work in a way that reversed the inherited hierarchy between the two (Meeus 1989: 48).

The genius of Galileo and contemporaries like Leonardo da Vinci was long interpreted in terms of 'universal humanity' (the late-nineteenth-century ideal of the *Übermensch* formulated out of unease over advancing mass society by Burkhardt and Nietzsche, cf. Deppe 1997: 11–13). However, universal humanity actually took a much less glorious road in achieving its miracles. Beginning in response to opportunities for wool exports to the Flanders manufactures, the enclosures of common lands in late-medieval England produced the mass of wage-dependent labourers on which the emerging capitalist mode of production relied, as it still does today. The Humanist, Thomas More, in his *Utopia* famously characterized the early process as 'sheep eating men'. English craft workers soon found themselves outpriced by the human surplus expelled from the villages and employed as unskilled day labourers. The craftsmen's defeat in the struggles against machine production and the backlash against the French Revolution in England eventually led to what E.P. Thompson calls 'a long counter-revolution', covering the twenty-five years after 1795 (Thompson 1968: 888). In the early nineteenth century, English wages were pushed so low as to make hunger the main regulator of the labour market. As Karl Polanyi infers (1957: 117), 'From the utilitarian point of view the task of the government was to increase want in order to make the physical sanction of hunger effective'. It entailed the degradation of humanity on which the Industrial Revolution was premised, a fate worse than slavery (see McGrath and Strauss, this volume, for these distinctions).

Capitalist industry produced miracles compared to which the boldest technical designs of Leonardo remain child's play – on one condition: that the mass of humanity brought under the command of capital can be operated as a single force. This control passed a critical threshold in the closing decades of the nineteenth century with the so-called second industrial revolution. Capitalists involved in the new, integrated iron and steel, heavy chemicals, shipbuilding and other large engineering industries looked to ways of raising labour productivity by intensifying work whilst keeping a close watch on how life evolved in working class neighbourhoods.

This quest was most acute in the United States and Germany, which did not enjoy the advantage of income from large colonial empires as did Britain and France. Scientific management, associated with Frederick W. Taylor's time-measurement experiments in the United States in the 1880s, devised a system of breaking down the worker's job into separate movements which could be streamlined into a more fluid, ergonomic series and paid by piece-rates – assuming the worker's core motivation was for higher pay. 'Taylor was guided by the concept of energy, a nodal point in the positivism and bourgeois culture around the turn of the century,' Vahrenkamp writes (1976: 15), 'and this guided his attempt to find out "how many metric kilos a worker can possibly achieve in one day at the lowest cost".' Or in Gramsci's words,

> Taylor is in fact expressing with brutal cynicism the purpose of American society–developing in the worker to the highest degree automatic and mechanical attitudes, breaking up the old psycho-physical nexus of qualified professional work, which demands a certain active participation of intelligence, fantasy and initiative on the part of the worker, and reducing productive operations exclusively to the mechanical, physical aspect (Gramsci 1971: 302).

Today, as documented in this collection, a differentiation has evolved in the context of the global political economy between locations where this process is still in full swing, such as in Asia, and a concentration of control functions in the metropolises, or heartland, of the capitalist world economy. Here too a measure of 'intelligence, fantasy and initiative' has also been allowed back into the labour processes immediately adjacent to 'tertiary' activities concentrated there. In addition, to varying degrees and again with huge regional disparities, the evolution of labour processes continues to require 'initiatives [that] have the purpose of preserving, outside of work, a certain psycho-physical equilibrium which prevents the physiological collapse of the worker, exhausted by the new method of production' (Gramsci 1971: 303).

Mental and manual labour thus are connected into a complex but ultimately single grid again. The process is captured by the notion of *socialization of labour* (more accurately, 'societization'); in the German original, *Vergesellschaftung*. Socialization of labour refers to the separation of tasks (mental/manual, and further sub-divisions) *and* their reconfiguration into a composite social labour process. Without the latter aspect, we are only looking at division of labour per se; with the control element added, there is actual socialization, the creation of mutual dependence and complementarity into a social bond, a *Gesellschaft*. In the Marxist tradition, the concept was anchored in the progress of production, and linked to the prospect of social transformation (e.g. Marx in *Capital*, I, *MEW* 23: 790, or Marx 1973: 832). The compensatory aspect of preserving an equilibrium outside of work that Gramsci refers to, on the other hand was theorized by Max Weber as *Vergemeinschaftung*, 'communitization'. Weber sees it as a factor compounding every rational process of socialization with emotional, affective bonding (Weber 1976: 21).

The mechanization of the labour process, applying science to the sphere of production, is an instance of mental and manual labour coming together in a specific format favourable to controlling the workers. 'Machinery is not neutral because the machine incorporates the dexterity and the skill of the individual worker who is henceforth deprived of [it] and subordinated. . . to the machine', writes Palloix (1976: 53); 'the separation of the mental from the manual part of work is materialised in the machines themselves'. The transformation of *homo faber* into *homo fabricatus*, by which Jürgen Habermas denotes the reversal of the relation between the producer and the tools into which the skills have been objectified (Habermas 1971: 82), hence is never a merely technical process, a matter of a subject-less artificial intelligence as in Stanley Kubrick's masterpiece, *2001: A Space Odyssey* (when the computer, HAL, takes over the space mission after discovering that the two pilots doubt its judgement).

Socialization of labour, both by dividing tasks between living labourers and by mechanizing their jobs through the objectification of skills into machines or work organization, always remains a social relation, premised on authority guiding the 'collective worker'. In capitalism, this guidance is provided by the discipline of capital over society and nature, which is passed on to each separate unit of functioning property by competition, both in the sphere of production and of reproduction. I have elsewhere (van der Pijl 1998: chapter 5) argued that this comprehensive process of socialization engenders a social stratum, or cadre, of functionaries entrusted with planning and supervisory roles in both spheres.

This takes us to our second theme in this introduction, the connections between the changes in the labour process and the growth of the social sciences including IPE.

LABOUR DISCIPLINE AND DISCIPLINARY SOCIAL SCIENCE

Disciplinary social science has its origins in the surveillance of populations: to monitor public health, keep a check on working conditions, or for other reasons. In the course of the nineteenth century this surveillance specifically came to focus on industrial workers, both on the shop floors of large-scale heavy industry and in the working class residential areas of the big cities. The original surveillance infrastructure of populations emerged in response to the French Revolution. The Anglo-Irish parliamentarian and writer, Edmund Burke, warned in his *Reflections* of 1790 (1934: 23, emphasis added) that 'a state without the means of *some change* is without the means of its conservation', and from 1815 onwards biannual reports to Parliament on the lower classes in England provided the information to make the necessary adjustments. This practice soon spread to the United States, notably in the state of Massachusetts (Derber 1967: 21).

In the English-speaking countries religion was initially seen as the best means of regimenting the workers outside of the factory. In Andrew Ure's *Philosophy of Manufactures* of 1835, Thompson writes (1968: 395), 'we find a complete anticipation of the . . .case for the function of religion as a work-discipline'. Ure saw in religious discipline a 'moral machinery', as important to the factory owner as his mechanical machinery. His fellow Utilitarian, Jeremy Bentham, by that time was beginning to think of alternatives to religion, which proved less and less effective in this respect. Bentham's calculus of pleasure and pain offers a different method of control of worker behaviour. Hence Foucault's claim (2004: 76) that 'the utilitarian philosophy has been the theoretical instrument which has supported the novelty of that period, the government of populations'.

The theory of the self-regulating market from the utilitarian perspective functioned as 'a mechanism of rewards and punishments that would ensure effective order in social relations' (Gammon 2008: 273), but the labour theory of value at its heart was becoming a potential liability. From Grotius and Locke to Smith and Ricardo this theory had served to legitimate property obtained through work (rather than by hereditary title). But what if the industrial workers would seize upon it as *their title* to a decent life? Hence from John Stuart Mill onwards, conceptions of political economy were being floated which played with the idea that wealth did not result from work, but from entrepreneurial initiative, or from property per se.

In the 1870s W. Stanley Jevons generalized this perspective into a different value theory altogether when he declared utility ('marginal', i.e., measured by the last unit added) as the source of value. After taking up the chair in Political Economy at the University of London in 1876, Jevons elaborated the axiom of self-interest into a deductive system. He also rebaptized the field 'economics', since 'erroneous and practically mischievous' ideas about political economy were circulating and were 'becoming popular among the lower orders' (quoted in Meek 1972: 88n, 90n). Thus labour was removed from the codex of understanding the economy at the same time that the field of 'political economy' was narrowed down to a psychology of choice modelled on entrepreneurial decisions – whether or not and where to invest (and 'give work'), what to produce, and so on; and the same for investor decisions and also, consumer decisions. Everybody thus is made into the equivalent of an entrepreneur, the human ideal of bourgeois economics.

In the Restoration on the European continent, the focus on social control inspired the separation of another branch of social science, sociology. In France, Auguste Comte and Émile Durkheim, and in Germany, the *Kathedersozialisten* ('socialists of the lectern') of whom Max Weber was the most renowned exponent, reflected on how the world of work might be disciplined through more or less subtle forms of class compromise. This made sociology into what Therborn calls (1976: 225), 'an investigative instead of a dogmatic guardian of the ideological community'. Thus after economics, a British field par excellence, a second field branched off from general political economy: sociology; although in Germany, it remained part of the *Staatswissenschaften* identified by Immanuel Wallerstein (2001: 192) as a 'current of resistance' to Anglophone liberalism.

In the United States the coming of monopoly capitalism with its scientific management of socialized labour, also resonated in the social sciences. When Taylor was called before a Special Committee of the US House of Representatives in January 1912, he explained his methods as 'a complete mental revolution' both for the working man and for 'those on the management's side – the foreman, the superintendent, the owner of the business, the boards of directors'. 'Without this complete mental revolution on both sides scientific management does not exist' (Taylor 1947: 27). Such a revolution would of course not leave the structures of higher education outside its purview. This did not so much take the form of a research focus on work, but of a Taylorization of intellectual labour itself through the academic disciplines as we know them today.

It is often forgotten that, as Andrew Abbott reminds us (2001: 123), 'the departmental structure appeared only in American universities' and was adopted elsewhere only much later. Indeed from the 1880s on, higher education in the United States was subjected to repressive control as businessmen began to replace clergymen on university boards. A series of spectacular dismissals and academic freedom cases led to a situation in which 'academic men in the social sciences found themselves under pressure to trim their sails ideologically' (Hofstadter 1955: 155). In addition, Henry S. Pritchett, president of MIT, a railway director and president of the influential Carnegie Foundation for the Advancement of Teaching, in 1909 commissioned Taylor to produce a blueprint for the scientific management of US universities. The report, by an associate of Taylor's, advised that the 'guild structure' of academic life be broken up and a labour market created for academics, with competition fostering 'greater research and teaching specialization by faculty as a condition for promoting more intensive mass production' (Barrow 1990: 71–3). Intimidated by attacks on socialist or otherwise socially concerned scholars, the disciplines, organized in national associations to watch over the definition of their fields and control access to expert knowledge, retreated into their own domains, 'shattered and torn from any holistic underpinning' (Harrod 1997: 108).

Intellectually, Taylorism was translated into a positivist social science methodology that took its cue from the functional psychology of William James and his fellow Pragmatists, and from the animal experiments of the Russian, I.P. Pavlov. This behavioural perspective no longer assumed a substantive consciousness but focused on controlling reflexes and responses to stimuli (O'Neill 1968: 133). In actual labour studies it was soon to be contested by the Harvard psychologist, Elton Mayo, who became the founder of the 'human relations' school of industrial psychology on the basis of his experiments at the AT&T telephone plant in Hawthorne, Illinois. These experiments brought out that team spirit, not economic or ergonomic stimuli, was the most important factor in raising productivity (Whyte 1963: 37). 'The battle between the Taylorist and the Human Relations schools,' Jeffrey Harrod writes, 'essentially that between two schools of thought on how to enhance labour productivity', would permeate all the social sciences including international studies. Actual labour studies also remained a separate discipline, a branch of sociology. Up to the early 1970s, this 'had the potential for, and was moving in the direction of, *connecting workplace to world order*' (Harrod 1997: 110, 112, emphasis added; Harrod, this volume).

However, if positivist Behaviouralism and interpretive approaches such as Constructivism today resonate across academia, this is no longer explicitly connected to the world of work. Economics has moved away from the world of production from the time of the Marginalist revolution; the discipline concerned with world order, International Relations (IR), had no interest in economics. Codified in the slipstream of Woodrow Wilson's intervention in Europe at the close of World War I, (political) IR specifically served to sideline the remaining bastion of historical materialist critique, the theory of imperialism. With it, 'IPE' disappeared from the academic radar screen.

One effect of the crisis of the Cold War order from the late 1960s to the mid-1970s, was the shaking up of the different branches of academic orthodoxy. Economic wisdom was being challenged by the monetary crisis and stagflation in the capitalist West; the oil price hike, Vietnam and other neo-colonial wars upset the balance of forces between the West and the dominated periphery. Comparable shocks in the state-socialist world, from the Czechoslovak experiment with democratizing and/or liberalizing socialism to the Chinese cultural revolution, highlight that this was a transformation not just of the world order, but of the deeper productive and reproductive structures of society on a world scale.

The student and worker revolts of the period also entailed a resurgence of Marxist ideas, both within and outside academia. Within the mainstream, business economists like Raymond Vernon addressed the challenge to national state sovereignty posed by transnational corporations (TNCs) (Vernon 1973). This in turn generated a debate as to whether TNCs made the realist analytical model of IR (in which states alone are seen to be the essential actors) implausible, and whether the international system should not be understood in more 'pluralist' terms (Gilpin 1975). Relative outsiders like former financial journalist Susan Strange, then teaching at LSE, also called for the emancipation of IR from the realist frame of reference. The states of the West in Strange's view (1972: 192) constitute an 'alliance of the affluent' waging a 'class struggle' against the Third World, only to find themselves locked in a simultaneous struggle with 'an invisible adversary, the unruly market economy which somehow they must subdue if they are not to risk social and political disruption'. In addition, this period saw the first, often dramatic calls for rethinking the human impact on the Earth's biosphere, such as the *Limits to Growth* report (Meadows et al. 1972).

International Political Economy (IPE) by then had established itself as a subfield within IR. Its boundaries, as Katzenstein et al. write (1998: 645), 'have been set less by subject matter than by theoretical perspectives'; in other words, IPE presumes an acceptance of different philosophical frameworks. Yet work and production were still largely absent from this opening; in the first major attempt to absorb and contain the intellectual disarray within the IR discipline, the Harvard conference on transnational relations convened in 1970 by Robert O. Keohane and Joseph Nye (Keohane and Nye 1973: xi), the labour movement was only one 'case'. The Roman Catholic church, revolutionary movements, the Ford Foundation, and of course the TNC in its relation to the state system, were the others, all in an obvious effort, perhaps more by habit than intentionally, to generalize the phenomenon (of transnational relations) away from its most contentious forms.

Certainly the rediscovery of Gramsci's notes on Fordism and the work of writers like Robert Cox (the author of the labour paper in the Keohane and Nye collection) taking this forward into the realm of a revitalized IPE, has brought back production as an area of study, connected to the study of world order (Cox 1987; Gill 1993). Actual labour relations studies, now conceived as 'human resource management' and once again unrelated to the structure of the global political economy, on the other hand have been shifted into the domain of business schools in the context of the neoliberalism that took hold in the 1980s. Yet today as never before, the connection between work as the transformation of nature and the structures of power in the world, requires urgent examination.

TWO TRENDS IN GLOBAL PRODUCTION AND THE OUTLOOK OF LABOUR

The socialization of labour in the early twenty-first century covers the entire globe; the product or commodity chains approach is one way of capturing the process theoretically (Gereffi and Korzeniewicz 1994; Selwyn, this volume). This is not a straightforward 'globalization', but a transnational process in which productive capital is necessarily nested in different 'human resource complexes' (Harvey 2006: 399). Such complexes are held together by cumulative class compromises cemented by religion and education, and hence are difficult to change. States, among other things, serve to demarcate one or more human resource complex(es) and through their trade and currency policies regulate their links with others; capital in turn seeks to exploit cost and regulation differentials between state jurisdictions. After several failed attempts to place TNCs under a system of controls (nationally, regionally or via various proposals to create a New International Economic Order under the United Nations), capital has recaptured the high ground. The NAFTA and EU common markets, to be merged in a projected and still contested Transatlantic Trade and Investment Pact (Bizzari and Burton 2013), are testimony to this.

The process of socialization of labour is thus modulated by human resource complexes fixated both in state territorialities (and in offshore enclaves through which host states commercialize their sovereignty, Palan 2003), and transnationally, across the world economy as a whole. As Charles Bettelheim puts it, the socialization of labour as a result evolves 'through a structure of specific complexity, embracing the structure of each social formation and the world structure of the totality of social formations' (Appendix I in Emmanuel 1972: 295, emphasis deleted). Or in Harvey's words, 'peoples possessed of the utmost diversity of historical experience, living in an incredible variety of physical circumstances, have been welded, . . . often through the exercise of ruthless brute force, into a complex unity under the international division of labour' (Harvey 2006: 373; cf. 404 and Milios and Sotiropoulos 2009).

Capital exploits this transnational structure by combining activities parcelled out across different human resource complexes, and different circuits of capital (money and productive capital in particular) into historically specific structures of socialization. Thus the 'working relationship' between the United States and China combines production for export in China with a flow of funds that keeps the United States, which consumes much more than it can actually pay for itself, afloat – paradoxically allowing it to lay siege on China militarily, a process that must sooner or later force the Chinese leadership to reconsider its political and economic strategy. This it can do as long as it keeps in place the state prerogative that limits the free circulation of capital (Arrighi 2007; Fingleton 2008).

Whilst high-quality manual labour in sectors associated with the most advanced production technology remains ensconced in the West, the most prominent component of the workforce in this part of the world is the cadre (managers, engineers, professionals). They are directing labour processes *across* the 'structures of specific complexity': both the metropolitan structures of socialization and the product/commodity chains connecting distant manufacturing with developed markets. This has resulted in a world map of productive and other paid work that shows a functional differentiation between cadre functions and circulation activities (clerical,

Table I.1 *Cadre, productive workers and workers in circulation activities in the economically active population, selected countries, 2008*

	United States	Germany	France	Japan	Mexico	Indonesia
Total in thousands	154 287	41 875	27 983.5	63 850	43 866.7	102 552.8
Cadre*	35.1%	38.7%	37.8%	17.5%	18.4%	7.4%
Productive workers**	23.0%	21.9%	22.0%	35.1%	37.0%	52.8%
Circulation workers***	41.3%	22.1%	22.6%	46.2%	25.4%	21.7%

Notes:
Not counted: elementary occupations, unclassifiable, army, unemployed.
Definitions (not identical in different national statistics): * managers, professionals, technicians; ** agricultural, craft, industrial workers; *** clerical, sales & service workers.

Source: Calculated from ILO *Laborsta*. Economically active population, by occupation and status in employment.

sales, etc.) concentrated in the West as mental labour; whereas productive activity as manual labour has a much greater weight in Asia and Latin America, both developed and underdeveloped. Table I.1 illustrates this for selected countries (China is not included in the ILO data from which the table was compiled).

Of course the share of agriculture in a country like Indonesia is much larger and productivity levels are much lower. But the point is that the people *producing* things are relatively more numerous outside the West, with Japan already showing a quite different structure of the workforce (more comparable to Mexico than to the US and EU). Production is therefore integrated on a world scale, but because of the different jurisdictions across which it extends, it is both global and local, a condition sometimes labelled 'glocalization' (Ruigrok and Van Tulder 1995). The chapters in Part I of our collection, 'Restructuring the global political economy', document in depth the driving forces of this process and the different forms it takes, not just at the lower-end extremes of the product chains spanning the globe, but also in the service sector.

As a result of the ability of capital to diversify across the global structures of socialized labour, production in the core economies has tended to abandon the integrated assembly lines of Fordist mass production favourable to labour. Sometimes these have been replaced by 'craft communities' organized around regional nodes and with a particular ethnic identity

(Piore and Sabel 1984: 265–6). The development of quality circles in large production complexes likewise has worked to parcel out the structures of socialized labour into separate entities again (Hoogvelt and Yuasa 1994; Ihara, this volume). The deepening of the impoverishment of many Third World and former Soviet bloc societies in addition has set in motion what Saskia Sassen calls 'a new phase of global migration and people trafficking', processes which 'used to be national or regional and today operate on global scales' (Sassen 2010: 32–3, and this volume; Delgado Wise and Martin, this volume). However, the evacuation of the traditional large-scale factory, premised on historic defeats of the labour movements in the West and Japan (documented in Part II), also poses new challenges to capital. One consists of the possibility that the global socialization of labour may give rise to what Jeroen Merk calls the emergence of the collective worker in the product chain (Merk 2004, and this volume). This is a reference to Marx's notion of a socialized workforce, 'whose combined activity expresses itself materially and directly in a comprehensive product' (Marx 1971: 226, emphasis deleted).

From the above it would seem that as far as production is concerned, the most urgent issue that will decide whether the destructive exploitation of society and nature by capital will be halted by something resembling such a collective worker, resides in combining the advancing labour movement in the periphery with the post-capitalist impulses animating the cadre in the West and Japan. Didn't Marx theorize how the forces immanent in capitalist socialization were laying the foundations of what he called, in *Capital* vol. III, the 'associated mode of production' (*MEW* 25: 485–6), along these lines? On the one hand, he argues there, governments will find themselves compelled to take control of the financial world, which by its increasingly fraudulent operations jeopardizes ongoing production; on the other, the 'collective worker' is seen to become a reality also in the consciousness of the producers as the socialization of labour within and between units of production demands a rational, planned structure liberated from the competitive hunt for profit. Thus in the garment-exporting countries in South-East and South Asia and Central America, complex forms of struggle take place in which workers, with the support of Western-based NGOs such as the Clean Clothes Campaign, have secured alliances with consumers and enlightened management of the branded companies organizing the chains (Merk 2009: 606). In this way at least a section of the cadre in the West have acted to mitigate excessive exploitation across the product chain, suggesting possibilities to turn the 'collective worker' into a conscious social agent.

So on the one hand, we have 'traditional strategies of labour to protect itself against exploitation, turning the global supply chain into a barrier both for organizing and collective bargaining' (Merk 2009: 605–6). Contemporary labour struggles in China (Chan, Pun and Selden, and Jang and Gray, this volume) thus feed into wider strategies, of which the Asian Floor Wage campaign documented in the chapter by Anannya Bhattacharjee and Ashim Roy, would be an example. This trend of an increase in worker militancy and social conflict, which as Beverly Silver argues in her chapter, historically accompanies the world market movement of capital, is one component of the current evolution of class struggles on a world scale.

There is a second trend, concentrated much more, but not exclusively, in the metropolitan centres of the capitalist heartland. This concerns the possibilities created by new technologies. Not only do new technologies facilitate the operation of global product/commodity chains as integral, planned processes, but they also enable new forms of production which may altogether transcend the commodity form on which market transactions and private appropriation are premised. Just as information technology suspends the separation of publishers and readers characteristic of print media, it works to destabilize the 'ownership of the means of production' once 'information' is no longer held exclusively by capital as a knowledge monopoly, but will tend to be shared with employees (Boccara 2008: 127, cf. 118).

The potentially greater autonomy of qualified professionals performing control functions as a managerial–technical cadre, has been responded to by 'knowledge management'. In this way capital seeks to re-establish discipline on mental labour by the 'identification, codification and application' of knowledge, in a 'quest to harness, monopolize and systematize' knowledge circulating and accumulating in a company (Chumer et al. 2000: xvi). Permanent auditing and self-assessment, as well as access to all communications including employees' emails, becomes mandatory to realize this (McInerney and LeFevre 2000: 15, cf. 11). Ultimately the aim is to gain hold of the socialized knowledge of these professionals so that it can be applied by less qualified personnel; for example doctors' diagnoses by nurses, professors' teaching by junior assistants, and so on. But even where the socialization of specialized knowledge into standardized packages (owned by the employer, like a Microsoft programme) succeeds, a complementary process is needed to keep knowledge workers under a market discipline. Regulatory standardization, as documented by Jean-Christophe Graz in Chapter 8, is one strategy; another is self-employment.

Self-employment has emerged as a major route towards creating market dependency but it also has brought to light profound contradictions. For unlike traditional factory workers, who are completely dispossessed of any means to make a living on their own, and whose labour therefore comes under the heading of what Marx calls *real subsumption to capital*, self-employed knowledge workers operate at arm's length from this discipline, under the regime of 'formal subsumption', which is inherently incomplete and unstable (Marx 1971: 197–8). Indeed whilst the fluidity of capital movements in money form and its derivatives evokes the postmodern concept of a universally mobile, all-sided functional human being who has cut him/herself off entirely from any inner constraints in order to be able to exploit any market chance (Harvey 1990), for the self-employed professional (maybe for all professional cadres), the question arises as to why this universality should remain only at the disposal of capital and the market.

From this inner tension, Oskar Negt deduces (1997: 16) that we are actually living in the twilight zone between two economies. One is the seemingly immutable rule of capital, under which living labour power must be manipulated into serving the needs of the system; the other instead evokes a 'second economy', the contours of which become visible as the irrationality of the system becomes ever-more apparent in financial swindle and in human misery, war and ecological degradation. In this second economy, necessary labour is enlarged by forms of activity that realize our humanity more profoundly, rewarding social-ecological responsibility and creativity (Negt 1997: 29). This points to a fundamental departure which at this stage can only be discussed in terms of potential and promise. In our collection this is covered by Yury Gromyko in the concluding chapter of Part I and Alan Freeman's in Part II. The Appendix to Part II by Mehmet Gürsan Şenalp and Örsan Şenalp serves to document the growing cohorts of those qualified knowledge workers left behind by the crisis who have been drawn into activist networks.

PRODUCTION, REPRODUCTION, NATURE

The self-employed, qualified worker-turned-liberated subject that Negt sees emerging as market constraints weaken, meanwhile remains captive of a political economy in which the escape hatches are still largely shut. Often the market discipline of capital has already taken hold of the human subject, mentally and bodily. The 'quantified self' analysed by Phoebe Moore in this volume denotes a subject submitting to a regulation that is formally at arm's length, but which has internalized the rule of the market entirely in practice. Thus the exploited become administrators of their own exploitation, apparently oblivious of their ability to resist it. Indeed because of its confusingly flexible imposition of discipline, 'the new capitalism,' writes Richard Sennett, 'is an often illegible regime of power' (Sennett

1998: 10). This regime reaches deep into the personality, where it removes attitudes of dependency by substituting a precarious freedom. Yet

> [t]he social bond arises most elementally from a sense of mutual dependence. All the shibboleths of the new order treat dependence as a shameful condition: the attack on rigid bureaucratic hierarchy is meant to free people structurally from dependence; risk-taking is meant to stimulate self-assertion rather than submission to what is given (ibid.: 139).

In the process the underlying mental–physical bonds are jeopardized and along with it, the integrity of the individual personality. For the process of socialization is a constitutive factor of one's ability to function in society. Whilst on the one hand, the extreme individualization and commodification of the self (as in sex work, cf. Chin, this volume) suspends honour and familial obligation, on the other it induces a general lowering of the level of civilization. For the 'de-socialized', affectively impoverished human subject, the neoliberal codex of behaviour ultimately leaves only two attitudes towards others: instrumentalization or elimination. Anomic, aggressive and destructive actions as a result become more widespread as the 'tension between a reduced capacity to act socially and the need for an active participation in social life' intensifies (Seppmann 2013c: 74, and this volume).

The exploitation of the human, social substratum by capital has all along been complemented by the exploitation of the soil. If we think of Marx's definition of human labour as anchored in the metabolism with nature cited earlier, exploitation occurs once the reproductive capacity of the medium with which metabolism takes place, becomes strained by the unsustainable degree of appropriation from it. In this sense the human/social substratum and the remaining natural world are not different. Marx, who studied the contemporary advances in agricultural chemistry of Justus Liebig and others, actually developed a theory of *metabolic rift* to make sense of the exploitation of the soil. This refers to the removal, along with the products of the land, of the soil's nutrients, leaving it bare and in need of artificial fertilizer, whilst in the cities, waste accumulates without regenerative, productive application. A socialist society would have to overcome this fatal separation of urban life without nature, and an impoverished, denuded hinterland from which food is to be procured nevertheless. Instead of the a-social existence under neoliberalism by the apparent suspension of social bonds, society for Marx was always the point of reference. 'Freedom,' he wrote in a rare reflection on the topic,

> in this sphere can consist only in this, that socialized man, the associated producers, govern the human metabolism with nature in a rational way, bringing

> it under their collective control. . .. accomplishing it with the least expenditure of energy in conditions most worthy and appropriate for their human nature (Marx in *Capital*, vol. III, as quoted in Bellamy Foster 2013: 7).

The large-scale acquisition of agricultural land for export monoculture by foreign buyers or lessees, notably in Africa, increases the 'rift' as crops are transported to far-away destinations by the corporations that invest in land abroad. The ensuing disruption of life on the land, discussed in the Conclusion to this volume by Saskia Sassen, is often aggravated by a second major aspect of the internationalization of agricultural production: the spread of genetically engineered plants.

Thus a country like India, whilst active abroad by investing (alongside German companies) in Ethiopia, is simultaneously targeted by US corporations like Monsanto. Monsanto has gained access for biotech products like genetically modified corn and cotton and hybrid seeds, with devastating consequences for the country's landed population – and, still largely hidden, for all of us. Between 1997, when corporate seed control started in India, and 2010, 200 000 but probably more farmers according to Indian government figures committed suicide, as they could no longer pay debts incurred to buy seeds. Vandana Shiva, the renowned agricultural activist, speaks of 'a negative economy, . . . an agriculture that costs more in production than the farmer can ever earn'; she singles out Monsanto's biotech Bt cotton as the major cause of suicides (quoted in Louv 2013: 20–21).

Certainly there are also positive developments such as the recourse to peasants' indigenous knowledge, or even entirely novel ways of organizing agriculture and overcoming metabolic rift (cf. Kay, this volume). Whether the various dislocating effects of the global reorganization of production under the auspices of capital will be brought under control remains to be seen. The present collection brings together insights on which such a reversal – towards a rational economic geography, the emancipation of labour, and the safeguarding of the biosphere without which human life cannot exist – will be premised. In the final analysis the fate of the Earth and its inhabitants will depend on the active engagement of those striving for a better society.

PART I

RESTRUCTURING THE GLOBAL POLITICAL ECONOMY

Introduction to Part I: restructuring the global political economy

The chapters in this part of the collection address the fundamental changes to the organization of the capitalist world economy that have come to characterize our epoch. This is never a merely economic process, but one that is profoundly imbricated with power politics. Beverly Silver's chapter, 'Labour, war and world politics', analyses the evolving interrelations between labour and war in light of past historical experience. She elucidates a 'vicious circle' of war and labour unrest in the first half of the twentieth century, before going back to the world-hegemonic transitions from Dutch to British and on to US hegemony in which comparable social convulsions were in evidence. Originally developed as an argument about the 2003 invasion of Iraq, Silver's conclusion that the decline of American hegemony will entail a period of war and social unrest, has lost little relevance today.

Whether we can actually speak of such a decline is challenged by Leo Panitch and Sam Gindin in Chapter 2. They argue that the material base of American empire, its productive capacity, remains under the sway of US capital. The hypertrophy of finance, often perceived as entailing a 'hollowing out' of production, in fact has allowed production to be restructured across the wider space, both in North America and globally. The authors maintain that the globalized economy remains anchored in national states, which is why class struggles at the national level have lost little of their importance.

This theme is taken up by Joscha Wullweber in his chapter on 'Innovation policies and the competition state: the case of nanotechnology'. In Wullweber's argument, states are not only the material drivers of real innovation, but equally serve to facilitate the restructuring of the state/society relation along the lines of a post-Fordist mode of regulation. Nanotechnology is an example of how a relatively vague field of potential applications is inscribed into a discourse of a society's success as dependent on being 'competitive'. Although both public acceptance and even actual economic potential remain in doubt, a veritable innovation race has been unleashed by the 'nano hype'.

In Chapter 4, Raúl Delgado Wise and David Martin introduce the process on which the entire restructuring of the world economy rests: global labour arbitrage. Over the last two decades, structural adjustment, the collapse of state socialism, and the insertion of China and India into the world market has doubled the man/womanpower available for exploitation to 3.3 billion people. Half of this number have insecure jobs and in 2009, 630 million were living on wages below $1.25 a day. A new nomadism of production, reproducing geographic asymmetries on an expanding scale, combines dispersed production and often involuntary labour migration with an increasingly centralized control by capital. Highly skilled technical work is not exempted from global labour arbitrage, as innovation systems are subject to restructuring too.

China today continues to operate as the 'workshop of the world' among low-wage production locations. In Chapter 5, Jenny Chan, Pun Ngai and Mark Selden discuss the outsourcing to China of the production of one of the most desired gadgets today, the Apple iPad. The Taiwanese-owned Foxconn Technology Group in the process has become the world's largest employer of industrial workers, with 1.4 million employees in China alone. Amidst protests and 'riots' at Foxconn factory complexes and the shocking incidence of worker suicides, a grim picture emerges of how transnational capital and the state collude in shaping the lives of rural migrant workers in Apple's China supply base.

Now labour is never a passive victim in the process of exploitation and global restructuring. In 'The grapes of wrath: social upgrading and class struggles in global value chains' (Chapter 6), Ben Selwyn highlights that the concept of social upgrading, introduced to deal with working conditions and derived from the International Labour Organization's Decent Work Agenda, still places too much confidence in the readiness of firms, national states and international organizations to improve the workers' lot. Taking Marx's understanding of capitalist exploitation and class struggle as its starting point, Selwyn argues that labour is always the decisive social force in bringing about real improvements, a thesis illustrated by the case of North-East Brazilian export horticulture.

The theme of worker resistance is explored further in Part II. Here we concentrate on the ways in which evolving labour relations react back on the process of global restructuring as such. In Chapter 7, Jeroen Merk discusses how globally dispersed labour processes paradoxically generate forces towards reintegration. The example of Nike's outsourcing of athletic shoe manufacturing to Asia highlights the political consequences of the socialization of labour. The need to coordinate production processes in distant locations, insulate the brand from reputational damage on account of employer brutality, and other aspects of planning value chains both technically and socially, lend credence to Marx's concept of the 'collective worker'. Covering the entire design, production and sales network from the centre to the extremes and back, labour as a result may obtain opportunities to restore a commensurate bargaining position.

One result of the process of socialization of labour is standardization. This in turn is not confined to actual production but fosters the growth of a burgeoning service industry. In Chapter 8, 'Standardizing services: transnational authority and market power', Jean-Christophe Graz discusses the common norms that standardization imposes on highly differentiated current practices, whether they concern the availability, provision or use of services. Accounting today for 70 per cent of GDP in the OECD countries and around 50 per cent in others, service standards are one aspect of the development of a transnational, 'hybrid' (public/private) authority that exercises a distinct form of market power in the reorganization of the global capitalist economy.

Whether the constraints imposed on individual corporations by the processes discussed in the two previous chapters are affecting them positively or negatively remains a matter of debate. But in the case of Wal-Mart, the world's largest retail concern, it would seem that global restructuring is far from a never-ending success story. As Joseph Baines argues in Chapter 9, after rapid growth in the first four decades of its existence, Wal-Mart's fortunes are apparently dimming. Discussing the company's expansion in terms of the theory of differential accumulation, Baines contends that as a result of resistance at multiple social scales, Wal-Mart has seen its global green-field growth running into barriers, while its cost-cutting measures are also approaching a floor both at home and abroad.

One myth concerning the restructuring of the global political economy is the BRICS thesis. The peripheral economies covered by this acronym are supposedly on the way of overtaking the West, but as Yury Gromyko argues in the concluding chapter of Part I, the creation of a new public wealth-generating pole in the world economy will have to break with finance-led liberal capitalism. He discusses the formation of a Trans-Eurasian development corridor (in Russian, *razvitie*) as a possible way out of the ongoing world recession, which would connect Russian fundamental science with Western European and Japanese technology. Establishing new cities in underpopulated spaces, connected by a high-speed rail, energy and data transmission grid, the project would provide a new way of life and steer clear of the ecologically disastrous and culturally destructive imitation of Western lifestyles implicit in the BRICS imagery.

1. Labour, war and world politics: contemporary dynamics in world-historical perspective

Beverly J. Silver

INTRODUCTION

During the last decade of the twentieth century, there was an almost complete consensus in the social science literature that labour movements worldwide were in a general and severe (some argued terminal) crisis. By the turn of the century, however, a growing number of observers were suggesting that labour movements were on the upsurge, most visible as a mounting popular backlash – from Seattle to Genoa – against the dislocations provoked by contemporary globalization. Yet, in the immediate aftermath of September 11, 2001, with demonstrations and strikes being cancelled around the world, questions were raised about the future of movements that had appeared to be on a strong upward trajectory. Then, on 15 February 2003, with war looming in Iraq, some of the largest demonstrations in world history – with strong labour movement participation – were held in hundreds of cities throughout the world.

Students of labour movements have focused much attention on world-*economic* processes in explaining both the global crisis of labour movements in the 1980s and 1990s, and their recent and partial resurgence. This continues to be an important line of inquiry. Yet, the ups and downs around the turn of the century also remind us of the central role played by war and world politics in the dynamics of global labour and social protest. This theme is the focus of this chapter, not only in terms of the impact that war and world politics have on labour movements, but also in terms of the ways in which workers and workers' movements have shaped the dynamics of war and world politics.

The central purpose of this chapter is to derive lessons for thinking about the contemporary link between labour and war from an analysis of past dynamics. The chapter proceeds in three steps. In the first section I draw on some of my empirical research on the world-historical dynamics of labour unrest (including a database on world labour unrest, cf. Silver 2003) to describe (what I call) the 'vicious circle' of war and labour unrest that characterized the first half of the twentieth century. The second section takes an even longer-term view by briefly comparing two periods of world hegemonic transition – that is, the period of transition from Dutch to British world hegemony in the late eighteenth and early nineteenth century and the period of transition from British to United States world hegemony in the late nineteenth and early twentieth century. By lengthening the time horizon of the analysis, we can begin to see aspects of both recurrence and evolution in the relationship between war and labour/social unrest (see Arrighi and Silver 1999a, especially chapter 3). In the final section I return to the more recent period by asking whether and to what extent the nature of contemporary warfare has changed, and what such changes mean for the way in which workers and workers' movements are now embedded in world politics.

LABOUR, WAR AND WORLD POLITICS IN THE TWENTIETH CENTURY

Figure 1.1 presents a time series of the number of annual newspaper reports about labour unrest worldwide from 1870 to 1996 (cf. Silver 2003: 126). The figure is based on the World Labour Group (WLG) database, which includes all acts of labour unrest (such as strikes and demonstrations) reported in either *The New York Times* or *The Times* (London) over this period. The database only includes the international reports from these two newspaper sources, so omitting reports on the UK in *The Times* and on the US in *The New York Times* (for a more extensive discussion of procedure and reliability, see Silver 2003, Appendix A).

The most immediately striking feature of Figure 1.1 is the interrelationship between world labour unrest and the two world wars – with labour unrest rising on the eves of both world wars, declining precipitously with the outbreak of war, and exploding in the aftermath of the wars. The two highest peaks in overall world labour unrest are the years immediately following the two world wars. The years 1919 and 1920 are the peak years of the series with a total of 2720 and 2293 reports, respectively. The next highest peak is 1946 and 1947 with a total of 1857 and 2122 reports, respectively. The early war years themselves are among the low points of the time series. There are only 196 reports in 1915 and only 248 and 279 in 1940 and 1942, respectively. Finally, the years just prior to the outbreak of the wars are years of rapidly rising labour unrest leading to local peaks in the time series. In the decade leading up to the First World War, the total number of mentions of labour unrest increases from 325 in 1905 to 604 in 1909 and 875 in 1913. Likewise, the total number of mentions of labour

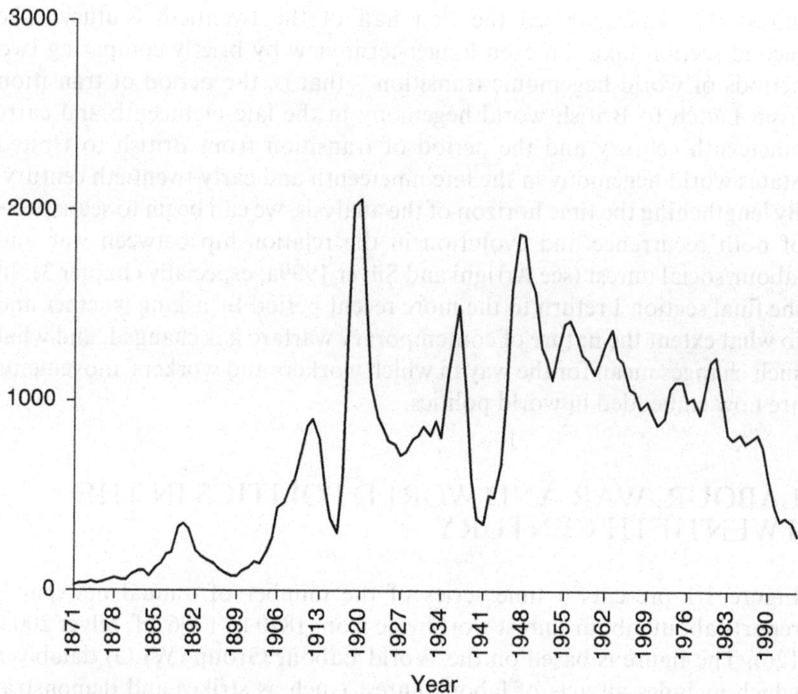

Source: World Labour Group.

Figure 1.1 World labour unrest, 1870–1996 (mentions of labour unrest, 3-year moving average)

unrest is rising in the decade leading up to the Second World War (from 859 in 1930 to 1101 in 1934 and 1186 in 1938).

If differentiated for metropolitan and colonial/semi-colonial countries (Silver 2003: 127, 128; for a more extensive discussion, chapter 4 of the same work), the connection is strongest in the former. Even in the colonial/semi-colonial aggregate the link is clearly visible, with labour unrest rising on the eves of both world wars; short-lived but major declines in overt unrest with the onset of war; and then major waves of unrest in the aftermath of the world wars. For these countries the pattern is visible for both world wars, but more pronounced for the Second World War.

This then provides striking *prima facie* evidence for the existence of a strong link between wars (or at least world wars) and labour unrest. Such an interrelationship among labour movements, war and world politics should come as no surprise to us. Indeed, there is a long established tradition within the labour studies literature (and in the social science literature more generally) linking domestic and international conflict (Levy 1989: 258–88; Levy 1998: 139–65; Stohl 1980: 297–330). The 'presumed nexus of civil conflict and international conflict', political scientist Michael Stohl suggests, is 'one of the most venerable hypotheses in the social science literature' even whilst there is extensive debate on its forms and spatial-temporal peculiarities (Stohl 1980: 297).

Stohl identifies three sub-variants of the civil/international conflict hypothesis in his review of the literature:

1. involvement in war increases social cohesion at the national level and thus brings about internal peace (sometimes known as the 'rally-around-the flag' hypothesis);
2. involvement in war increases social conflict at the national level including the chances of revolution (most famously formulated in Lenin's 1916 prediction that inter-imperialist war would intensify the contradictions of capitalism and lead to revolution); and
3. social conflict at the national level encourages governments to involve themselves in wars (sometimes also referred to as the 'diversionary' or 'scapegoat' hypothesis).

Curiously, the patterning of labour unrest visible from the World Labour Group data may be interpreted as providing support for all three hypotheses. Their apparently contradictory nature disappears if we see them as having different temporal relevance. That is, hypothesis 3 (the scapegoat or diversionary hypothesis) best describes the period leading up to the world wars; hypothesis 1 (linking war and social cohesion) is most relevant for the early phases of the hostilities; while hypothesis 2 (linking war and revolution) is most relevant to the aftermath of the world wars. Their combined effects helped produce the volatile and explosive character of labour unrest during the first half of the twentieth century that is visible in our figure.

Thus, on the one side, it has been widely argued that 'diversionary' tactics in part motivated decisions about war in the late nineteenth and early twentieth centuries. Rulers had learned that, at least in the short run, little victorious wars could bolster governments. The Spanish-American War (for the United States) and the South African War (for the United Kingdom) were two such examples. On the eve of the Russo-Japanese War of 1904, the Russian interior minister had openly stated that 'this country needs... a short victorious war to stem the tide of revolution' (quoted in Levy 1989: 264). Yet the revolutionary upheavals that shook the Russian Empire in the wake of its 1905 defeat by Japan showed the potential boomerang effect of lost (or otherwise unpopular) wars. The First World War brought both tendencies into sharp relief, with the initial 'rally around the flag' response of workers being followed by a wave of revolutions and revolutionary crises in the final years of the war and its aftermath.

Yet beneath the volatility of labour unrest was an important longer-term trend – that is, the strengthening of workers' bargaining power vis-à-vis their governments. By the late nineteenth century, workers in the main imperial powers had become critical cogs in war machines, not only at the front, but also in the factories and in allied transportation industries supplying the front. The growing industrialization of warfare (McNeill 1982: chapters 7–8) and the increasing size and centrality of industrial working classes, combined with the turn toward mass conscription armies, meant that rulers in Europe and North America were becoming more and more dependent on the active cooperation of their citizens for imperial expansion and war (Tilly 1990; Mann 1988).

The growing bargaining power of labour, in turn, contributed to a second important long-run trend beneath the volatility of the period – that is, the expansion of democratic and workers' rights (including welfare rights) or what might be called the increasing 'socialization of the state'. This extension of democratic and workers' rights came in fits and starts, with wartime itself often providing an especially propitious environment for advances. To be sure, increased government repression of labour militancy was characteristic of war periods, and is an important element explaining the decline in wartime labour unrest. Yet with the growing size and bargaining power of industrial working classes, simple repression was becoming an inadequate solution and had to be supplemented by active government efforts to secure the consent and cooperation of the masses. At the shop floor level, tripartite agreements between trade unions, employers and governments secured no-strike pledges from union leaders in exchange for government and employer recognition of trade unions and the establishment of collective bargaining and grievance procedures. For the union movement in many core countries (notably, the United States), the First World War marked the first time that employers relaxed their implacable hostility to trade unions (Hibbs 1978; Feldman 1966; Brody 1980; Dubofsky 1983; Giddens 1987).

Similarly, wartime proved propitious for the successful expansion of suffrage rights for both propertyless men and women (the latter were drawn into wartime factories in large numbers). The case of Belgium is illuminating: there had been mass strikes in 1886, 1888, 1891, 1893, 1902 and 1913 for which universal suffrage was a central demand; yet Belgium entered the First World War with a voting system in which older men owning property had three votes. By the war's end, however, Belgium had equal male suffrage (Markoff 1996: 73–4, 85).

This same period saw major advances in social insurance schemes such as old-age pensions and health and unemployment insurance (Abbott and DeViney 1992). These measures were, in no small part, responses to increasingly effective labour militancy. However, they were also part of a more general development of cross-class alliances in favour of a strong and activist state. The intense competition that characterized the late nineteenth century Great Depression prompted clamours for protection from all segments of the class spectrum and economy. By the 1878 Congress of Berlin, national bourgeoisies in continental Europe had joined agrarian elites in demanding that government action be oriented toward obtaining exclusive spheres of influence, protected markets and privileged sources of supply. Likewise in the United States, the depression of 1893, which hit both agriculture and industry, and moreover, produced widespread social unrest, prompted US business and government leaders to finally accept 'overseas expansion as the strategic solution to the nation's economic and social problems' (Williams 1969: 41; cf. Polanyi 1957: 216–7).

E.H. Carr has suggested that by the eve of the First World War the incorporation of European working classes into cross-class national projects was already quite real. In the nineteenth century, Carr wrote, when 'the nation belonged to the middle class and the worker had no fatherland', socialism had been 'international'. Yet, the 'crisis of 1914 showed in a flash' that things had changed dramatically. The 'mass of workers knew instinctively on which side their bread was buttered' – that is, on the side of their own state's power. During the first years of the war draft evasion was virtually non-existent, and labour and socialist agitation declined precipitously in the belligerent countries (Carr 1945: 204).

Whatever the extent to which workers were effectively incorporated into cross-class national hegemonic projects by the eve of the First World War, a central characteristic of the first half of the twentieth century was the extremely unstable nature of these projects. In part, the sheer brutality of industrialized warfare disabused many of the idea that successful formulas for protecting workers and citizens had been found. More generally, as would become increasingly clear, such national hegemonic projects – without a facilitating structure of global governance – tended to malfunction; and moreover, only further stoke the flames of inter-imperialist rivalry and war.

The world economic crisis of the 1930s prompted a large number of countries to pursue rapid industrial expansion as part of an effort to overcome the social and political crises caused by the failure of the market system (Polanyi 1957: chapter 2). But rapid industrial expansion relieved unemployment only by exacerbating other sources of domestic and international tensions. First and foremost, it increased pressures to seek out new markets and new sources of raw materials. These pressures, in turn, brought about a renewed escalation of inter-imperialist rivalries as the major powers sought out exclusive and protected overseas domains. As inter-imperialist rivalries re-ignited, the pressure to industrialize further intensified given the now intimate links between industrial and military capabilities. The vicious circle of international and domestic conflict thus resurfaced on a far greater scale and with wider geographical scope than that surrounding the First World War.

The labour unrest and revolutionary upheavals that followed the Second World War also engulfed the colonial and semi-colonial countries (Silver 2003: 128). Already on the eve of the Second World War, colonies and semi-colonies had become tightly interwoven into the supply structures of the imperial powers (as suppliers of both men and material). Workers in colonial export enclaves and allied transportation industries came to occupy strategic positions within the resource-needs structure of the imperial powers. At the same time, the long arm of the European state reached into colonies and extracted colonial subjects to fight as soldiers in imperial armies on faraway battlefields. Resentments against such mobilizations fuelled worker radicalism and anti-colonialism. Key nationalist leaders, most of whom made little effort to connect with the masses prior to the First World War, by the 1920s and later came to recognize the growing strategic importance of the masses, and consciously made efforts to mobilize workers and peasants in the struggle for independence.

To be sure, war did not everywhere lead to the strengthening of the working class. In Shanghai, which had been the centre of the textile industry, the war initially dissolved the working class as factories closed and workers returned to the countryside so as to be able to survive. But in the colonial and semi-colonial areas that were being incorporated into resource provisioning, rather than being plundered, the war strengthened the strategic bargaining power of workers.

Colonial powers, in an effort to keep labour unrest under control for the duration of the war, promised to expand workers' rights. One indicator of this tendency was Britain's decision during the Second World War to introduce trade unions and conciliation and arbitration mechanisms throughout its empire (Cooper 1996). During the First World War, tripartite agreements among trade unions, employers and states only emerged in metropolitan countries and were rapidly eliminated after the war. The tripartite agreements concluded during the Second World War were both relatively longer-lasting and broader in geographical scope (see Lichtenstein 2002, especially chapter 3, on the less than whole-hearted embrace of the labour–capital accord by US business).

Labour militancy and revolutionary upheavals peaked worldwide in the aftermath of the Second World War. With the Communist victory in China in 1949, the problem of repressing or accommodating the social revolutionary challenge from the non-Western world moved to centre stage in the global strategies of the new world hegemonic power (the United States). Until 1949, attention had been focused on Europe where, as a US undersecretary of commerce reported to President Truman in 1947, 'most. . . countries were standing on the very brink [of revolution] and may be pushed over at any time; others are gravely threatened' (quoted in Loth 1988: 137). By 1949, the social revolutionary threat was unmistakable. 'Instead of a single, weak and isolated USSR, something like a dozen states emerged, or were emerging, from the second great wave of global revolution. . . Nor was the impetus of global revolution exhausted, for the decolonization of the old imperialist overseas possessions was still in full progress' (Hobsbawm 1994: 82).

Nevertheless, by the 1950s the rising and explosive pattern of labour unrest in the first half of the twentieth century gave way to a far less volatile dynamic in the second half of the twentieth century, especially in metropolitan or core countries. This shift was in part related to the unprecedented concentration of military and economic power in the hands of the United States at the close of the Second World War, which brought an end to the great power rivalries that had fed the vicious circle of war and labour unrest. Of equal importance were deep institutional reforms at the firm, national, and especially the global levels, which sought to accommodate some of the demands that had been thrown up by the labour, nationalist and other movements of the first half of the twentieth century, and through which the US sought to respond to the global challenge posed by the Soviet alternative. The various elements of these reforms have been referred to as 'liberal corporatism', 'embedded liberalism', the 'globalization of the New Deal', the 'welfare–warfare state', and for the third world, 'decolonization' and 'development' (cf. Silver 2003: 149–61). Embedded in the reformed global institutions was the implicit recognition that labour is a fictitious commodity that needs to be protected from the harshest verdicts of an unregulated world market economy. It was only in the context of this reformed *international* institutional environment that cross-class national hegemonic compacts could find a *relatively* stable ground on which to stand.

WORLD HEGEMONIC TRANSITIONS COMPARED

From a world-systems perspective, the current period in world history not only has strong analogies with the first half of the twentieth century; it is also comparable to the late eighteenth and early nineteenth centuries. All three periods are times of deep 'systemic chaos' associated with the crisis and decline of world hegemonies: (1) the transition from Dutch to British hegemony in the late eighteenth and early nineteenth centuries; (2) the transition from British to United States hegemony in the first half of the twentieth century; and (3) the current period of crisis and decline of US hegemony. Limitations of space and time prevent me from defending the proposition that we are now in a period of crisis and breakdown of US world hegemony; an extensive defence of this proposition as well as of other arguments put forward in this section can be found in Arrighi and Silver (1999a).

Let's start by noting that there are strong links between interstate conflict and domestic conflict in the late eighteenth and early nineteenth centuries, analogous to those that we found for the first half of the twentieth century. We cannot draw on a database of global labour/social unrest similar to that used in the previous section. Nevertheless, a clear pattern emerges from the secondary historical literature. As argued in detail elsewhere (Arrighi and Silver 1999a: 159–76), the Seven Years' War marked the first step toward a late-eighteenth-century 'vicious circle' of war and social unrest. The dislocations of the boom–bust cycle caused by the Seven Years' War in North America were important in detonating the American Revolution. The immense costs of France's intervention in the American Revolutionary War, in turn, were crucial in bringing about the final collapse of the French monarchy and the French Revolution. The French Revolution and Napoleonic Wars simultaneously increased social strains and produced the intra-elite rift that opened the space for a full-scale slave insurrection in France's most profitable colony (Saint Domingue/Haiti), which, in turn, inspired further slave conspiracies and maroon rebellions throughout the Americas, as well as a second wave of abolitionist and reform mobilizations in Europe. The late eighteenth and early nineteenth centuries, like the first half of the twentieth century, was thus an age of 'global' war and revolution.

Yet differences are as important as similarities. My use of the word 'global' (and the fact that it is in quotation marks) points to a similarity, but also a first difference between the two periods of hegemonic transition. In the late eighteenth century, 'globalization' processes had advanced to the point where words and deeds in the Americas often had a rapid and resounding impact on Europe (and vice versa). Thus, it would be accurate to characterize the revolutionary ferment of the period as unfolding within the Atlantic world as a whole. Yet, if revolutionary contradictions largely diffused within the Atlantic world during the first transition, in the second transition such 'contagiousness' had become a truly global affair, interconnecting Africa, Asia, Europe and the Americas.

A second difference is the fact that interstate and intrastate conflicts were far more deeply intertwined in the second transition. In both transitions, wars produced social unrest. However, in contrast to the transition from British to US hegemony, there is no evidence that the reverse relationship also obtained – that is, neither the Seven Years' War nor the French intervention in the American Revolutionary War seem to have been motivated by efforts to quell social unrest on the home front. By contrast, not only was class and nationalist agitation escalating on the eve of the First World War; even the colonialist adventures in the late 1890s followed (and attempted to divert) increasing class antagonisms.

This is related to a third difference between the two world hegemonic transitions: over time, war produced mass social unrest far more quickly in the twentieth century. Put differently, we can detect a 'speeding up of social history'.

At the root of this 'speeding up of social history' is a fundamental transition in the organization of warfare. For as long as old-style armies of paid professional mercenaries and 'gentlemen' predominated, wars could drag on for years without provoking mass social unrest. However, as states came more and more to depend on mass conscription and the patriotic mobilization of their citizens in wartime struggles, great power rivalries and social conflict became far more intertwined, and the 'vicious circle' of war and social unrest was unleashed far more quickly. In this respect, the mobilization of citizen armies during the Napoleonic Wars was a first premonition of things to come – a premonition that led Europe's rulers to end experiments and restore old-style armies of 'paid professionals, mercenaries and gentlemen' after the war. As William McNeill has pointed out, the experience of warfare in the age of revolution convinced Europe's rulers that 'the fierce energy of the French conscripts in 1893–95, and the nationalist fervour of some German citizen soldiers in 1813–14, could challenge constituted authority as readily as it could confirm and strengthen it'. By restoring old-style armies, Europe's rulers 'refrained from tapping the depths of national energies that the revolutionary years unveiled'. But they also kept 'the spectre of revolutionary disorder at bay' (McNeill 1982: 221). Nevertheless, by the end of the nineteenth century, states once again were developing nationalism and patriotism as the new civil religion and as a basis for mobilizing soldiers as citizens.

Indeed, by the time of the First World War, military strategists were well aware of the close relationship between war and mass social conflict.

New military strategies, such as naval blockades aimed at cutting off food supplies and raising the threat of mass starvation among non-combatants, were designed to create domestic instability on the enemies' home front. Such strategies recognized the importance of retaining popular loyalty (and the danger of losing mass support) for success in war.

In sum, if prior to the nineteenth century rulers seemed to fight wars with little concern for 'public opinion', by the end of the century domestic politics and international politics were intimately intertwined.

INTO THE TWENTY-FIRST CENTURY

What are the implications of the preceding discussion for understanding the early twenty-first century? We have described a process in which war and labour/social unrest played out on an ever larger and more interconnected global stage; a process in which all three of Stohl's hypotheses linking domestic and international conflict became increasingly relevant as war and labour/social unrest became more and more intertwined; and a process of 'speeding up' of social history, with wars producing mass labour/social unrest more quickly. Another important question that arises is what role wage workers will play in the social unrest of the transition. If we interpret the evolution from the first to the second transition as a trend (increasing importance of wage workers, declining centrality of peasants and especially slaves), then we would expect wage workers to be even more central protagonists in the current transition. This is not totally far-fetched, but is an important argument to be developed later.

At first sight, the anti-war movement that emerged in 2003 in response to the threat of war on Iraq would seem to confirm these predictions, with mass protest *preceding* the start of the war. Nevertheless, there are important differences between the nature of warfare today and the nature of warfare in the first half of the twentieth century, and these differences have important implications for contemporary dynamics. With the establishment of US world hegemony and the Cold War world order, the scope for conventional inter-imperialist (North–North) wars was greatly reduced. The end of overt wars among the most powerful states, in combination with the relatively 'labour-friendly' institutional reforms at the national and international level that accompanied the 'global New Deal', accounts in large part for the less volatile pattern of labour unrest in the 1950s, 1960s and 1970s.

While the tendency towards North–North war was contained, North–South wars were not. In the US–Vietnam War we can see both a continuation of the trends discussed above as well as a significant turning point. The radicalizing effects of costly and unpopular wars were demonstrated once again with the emergence of a strong anti-war movement, the growing refusal of US soldiers to continue fighting (Appy 1993), and the 'contagion' between the anti-war movement and other social movements. Likewise, the propensity of states to respond to unrest through a further 'socialization of the state' (an expansion of workers' and citizens' rights) was once again in evidence. Here I have in mind the expansion of the Great Society programmes that went hand-in-hand with the escalation of the Vietnam War. Yet the intertwined fiscal, military, political and social crises produced by the Vietnam War also showed the limits of the combined guns *and* butter strategy.

The deep crisis of the 1970s led the United States government in the 1980s under Reagan to implement a series of major changes in its global economic and military strategy. The new economic strategy amounted to an abandonment of the domestic and global New Deals. In the military sphere, the new strategy involved the end of universal conscription and an increase in the weight of capital-intensive (as opposed to labour-intensive) warfare. The long-term tendency of the United States to rely on high-tech military methods increased still further with the application of 'information age' technologies to warfare. Tremendous energies were devoted to the automation of war (that is, the development of military hardware such as pilotless drones and cruise missiles that allow for the complete removal of the First World human from both the risk of being killed and *direct* contact with the process of mass killing).

Wars in the 1990s like the Falklands/Malvinas War, the First Gulf War and the Kosovo War were a very different type of war than that which radicalized workers and other citizens, and created the explosive pattern of world labour unrest in the first half of the twentieth century. Internal opposition to these late-twentieth-century wars within First World countries remained low because First World governments (the United States in particular) went to extreme lengths to keep casualties *among their own citizen-soldiers* to a minimum (tending toward zero). These wars inflicted tremendous damage on the generally poor countries on whom the high-tech explosives landed – destroying economic infrastructures and hence stable working classes and civil societies (indeed, it has been reported that not a single factory was operating in either Kosovo or Baghdad; Vargas Llosa 2003; author's own communication). But they have not (to paraphrase Durkheim) 'violently moved the masses' in the First World. If warfare continues to insulate First World workers (and citizens more generally) from its more horrifying aspects while destroying stable working classes and civil societies elsewhere, it is not likely to produce the kind of powerful and explosive labour and social unrest that characterized the first half of the twentieth century.

This type of warfare is also reversing the long-term trend in the relationship between states and the mass of their citizens discussed in the previous sections. For the more the United States and other First World countries move toward the automation of war, the more they emancipate themselves from dependence on their worker-citizens for success in war. As such, the growing bargaining power of workers and citizens vis-à-vis their states – an inadvertent by-product of the inter-imperialist and Cold War rivalries of the late nineteenth and twentieth centuries – is being reversed, along with many of the economic and social benefits achieved. It is an open question as to whether the major declines in workers' and citizens' rights in the 1980s and 1990s are causally related to the transformations in the military sphere, or are merely coincidental. There is, however, no doubt that the decline in social welfare benefits and the disappearance of union jobs with good wages and benefits along with rising tuition costs and declining scholarship funds, has made it much easier for the US government to recruit its 'all volunteer' army from the ranks of the poor and working class (Halbfinger and Holmes 2003).

I have argued that in the 1980s and 1990s, the global political–military context contrasted sharply with the global political–military context that produced radicalized and explosive labour and social unrest in the late nineteenth and first half of the twentieth centuries. However, the response of the Bush Administration to the September 11 attacks on the World Trade Centre and the Pentagon raised the question as to whether we were seeing another fundamental turning point in the nature of war and in the interrelationship between war and workers' movements. Indeed, the 2003 occupation of Iraq (and the developing military quagmire) was a fundamentally different operation than the routine bombing of Iraq that had been going on since the end of the First Gulf War.

The early signs of demoralization and open protest among US troops in Iraq and their families – resistance that burst into the open at a far earlier stage than it did in the Vietnam War – together with the global mass anti-war movement, suggests that the 'speeding up of social history' thesis continues to have some validity (cf. Harris and Franklin 2003). It is possible that unrest in the military ranks had already been building up in response to the high disability rates associated with service in the First Gulf War, combined with cuts in veterans' benefits implemented by the US government. Chalmers Johnson (unpublished) has suggested that the US casualties in the 1991 Gulf War are far higher than the wartime battle figures would suggest, given the 'potential toxic side effects of the [depleted uranium in the] ammunition now being widely used by [the US's] armed forces'. He estimates a death and disability rate of 29.3 per cent for the First Gulf War once one includes the deaths and disabilities linked to 'service-connected exposures' during the war.

Moreover, it is important to point out that the policy of simultaneously cutting the welfare state while expanding the warfare state constitutes a sharp reversal of the twentieth-century trend in which the two grew hand in hand. Indeed, this sharp reversal may in large part explain the passage of a (relatively timid but unprecedented) anti-war resolution by the AFL–CIO (American Federation of Labour–Congress of Industrial Organizations) in 2003 – a step that broke with the US labour federation's long-held practice of actively supporting US foreign policy (Letwin 2003; to be sure, many within and outside the labour movement, while acknowledging its unprecedented nature, have nonetheless emphasized the timidity of the US labour movement's anti-war mobilization).

Rather than respond to these signs of labour and popular unrest with a social policy that expands workers' and citizens' rights, the current US government strategy seems to be to further reduce its reliance on the mass of the population for fighting wars. Efforts to further automate war continue apace (Brzezinski 2003). At the same time, two 'new' strategies were already taking shape by the time of the 2003 war on Iraq. One was the growing reliance of the US military on private military contractors. The supply contracts awarded to Halliburton have been mainly commented on in relation to the odour of crony capitalism. Yet, they are also a way of privatizing military supply activities and thereby limiting the number of troops officially in the war arena. Employees of the Halliburton subsidiary, Kellogg Brown & Root (KBR), not only fed and housed troops and constructed, supplied and serviced military bases; they also maintained high-tech weapons and trained soldiers in how to use them. Other private military contractors (such as the Vinnell Corporation) were even more directly involved in combat activities.

The trend towards using private military contractors began in the 1990s, and has become central to the current Defence Department's strategy for limiting the number of active duty troops, even in the face of expanding military commitments. This strategy has the effect of further reducing the benefits that the working class and poor can derive from the existence of the military–industrial complex. As pointed out in an article in *Business Week*, aptly titled 'Outsourcing war', the supply and support jobs previously done by full-time soldiers receiving salaries and fringe benefits are now being done by 'flexible employees' working on a contract basis, including lower-cost 'host country nationals' and immigrant workers brought to Iraq from other low-wage countries (Bianco and Anderson Forest 2003). Training of foreign armies is another area outsourced to private companies. Thus Vinnell, on the basis of its previous contracts, including ones for training the Saudi national guard, was awarded a $48 million contract to train the nucleus of a new Iraqi army (ibid.).

Such privatization of warfare harks back to the period before the age of nationalism when states depended on paid mercenaries rather than their own citizens to conduct warfare. It also harks back to an even earlier age – to the age of discoveries – when the lines between business enterprises and war-making enterprises were far from clear (here I have in mind the chartering of the early British and Dutch East India Companies both to conduct trade and make war in the extra-European world, see Ortiz 2010: 19–24).

A second 'new strategy' – the concerted efforts to cajole, bully and/or bribe other countries (especially third world countries) into sending troops to Iraq – harks back to the age of colonialism. This strategy is in many ways reminiscent of the reliance of the imperial powers on colonial troops in the first half of the twentieth century. As discussed above, in the twentieth century this reliance on colonial troops had rather contradictory effects. On the one hand, the mobilization of the Indian Army meant that Britain could conquer and then run an empire that simply could not be run by British citizens alone. On the other hand, such mobilizations had an empowering and dislocating effect that increased the bargaining power of colonial subjects including workers, while simultaneously fuelling labour radicalism and nationalism. In the post-colonial era, it is still unclear whether the Indian army (or the armies of other post-colonial states) can be cajoled, bullied and/or bribed into playing the role of the 'iron fist in the velvet glove' of the new Anglo-American empire. The enormous popular opposition to suggestions that their citizens should play such a role is visible in places as diverse as South Korea, Turkey and India. Such opposition – *prior* to troop deployment – once again suggests that the thesis of a 'speeding up of social history' retains some contemporary relevance.

The above discussion suggests that there is a growing decoupling of the warfare and welfare states. This in turn has potentially important implications for labour internationalism. To paraphrase E.H. Carr, if workers in the twenty-first century are now finding themselves once again without a 'fatherland', will labour politics turn 'instinctively' internationalist once again? (Carr 1945: 20–21). To be sure, the persistence of the enormous North–South wealth divide is a significant (and perhaps insurmountable) barrier to any such development (Silver and Arrighi 2001; Silver 2003, chapters 1, 3 and 5). Nevertheless, the above discussion suggests that a sea change in the relationship between labour, war and world politics may be in progress.

In conclusion, what does the above narrative suggest about what is to be (and can be) done? How effective can social movements in general, and labour movements in particular, be in influencing the contemporary dynamics of war and peace? If we return to our comparison of world hegemonic transitions, we come to a rather pessimistic conclusion. For in the first half of the twentieth century, labour and other protest movements were *not* able to stop the slide into a long period of war and 'systemic chaos' (Arrighi and Silver 1999a; 1999b: 310). What they were able to do was to affect the nature of the new world order that emerged afterwards. To be sure, movements from below were far more effective in influencing the content of the newly emergent world order in 1945 than in 1815. At the outset of British world hegemony in 1815, Britain no longer faced a serious popular revolutionary challenge. France (the main great-power embodiment of the revolutionary challenge of the late eighteenth and nineteenth centuries) had suffered a decisive military defeat, as did the British labour movement domestically. Haiti won its independence, but was ostracized from the international community. The initial thrust of British domestic and international policy in the immediate aftermath of the Napoleonic Wars was repression at home and the restoration of the *anciens régimes* on the continent. Reform policies only emerged later. In contrast, at the outset of US hegemony, the Soviet Union (the main great-power embodiment of the revolutionary challenge of the first half of the twentieth century) emerged from the Second World War battered, but much stronger politically and militarily, and was shortly joined by a revolutionary China. Moreover, both labour and nationalist movements emerged from the twentieth-century world wars strengthened and radicalized. The *counter*revolutionary challenge of the Axis powers was defeated in the war, while the power and prestige of the revolutionary challenge was enhanced (Arrighi and Silver 1999a: chapter 3).

US hegemony from the start had to incorporate reformist policies designed to respond to the popular demands thrown up from below, including policies that recognized that labour is a 'fictitious commodity' that cannot simply be left at the mercy of an unregulated world market economy (ibid.: 202–3). Thus, in past hegemonic transitions both the strength and content of popular protest mattered in shaping the long-term outcomes.

However, as we stand on the eve of a new slide into systemic chaos, considerations about the eventual impact of labour and other movements on a future world order may not be particularly comforting. They may not even be relevant, for given the tremendous destructive powers that humans have at their disposal, there is no particular guarantee that most or any of the world's population would survive another long period of generalized war. Thus, the problem of avoiding the slide into systemic chaos takes on great urgency.

The analysis carried out here has tended to emphasize that labour is being weakened vis-à-vis states by the ongoing transformations. Moreover, 'the biggest demonstrations in world history' in February 2003 did not succeed in stopping the war. Nevertheless, the weakness thesis can be overstated. In the first half of the twentieth century, strikes by workers in the armaments, energy and transportation industries had a major impact on the military–industrial complexes of the belligerent powers. Today, transportation workers are still strategic actors, not only for the smooth operation of the world-economy, but also for the smooth operation of the world military–industrial complex. In this context, the announcement in early 2003 by railroad and dockworkers in countries around the world that they would refuse to move materials for war on Iraq is important, even if they were not able to materially affect the course of events (Letwin 2003). Second, the growth in the use of private military contractors notwithstanding, the refusal of worker-soldiers at the front to go on fighting has been key in affecting the course of events from the First World War to Vietnam and Iraq.

Moreover, it is important to point out that there is nothing inevitable about the slide into systemic chaos. The 'international system', writes David Calleo, 'breaks down not only because unbalanced and aggressive new powers seek to dominate their neighbours, but also because declining powers, rather than adjusting and accommodating, try to cement their slipping pre-eminence into an exploitative hegemony' (Calleo 1987: 142). The neoconservative Project for the New American Century was in large measure an attempt by the United States to convert its declining hegemony into an exploitative empire through the use of military force (a point anticipated in Arrighi and Silver 1999a, especially the concluding chapter; cf. Arrighi 2007, chapters 7–9). The mass anti-war protests in 2003 appear as an almost intuitive recognition by people around the world (including many in the United States) that what amounted to a new US imperial project risked precipitating major worldwide chaos. Indeed, since 2003, the likelihood that we have already entered a long and deep period of global systemic chaos has grown. It remains an open question as to whether the forces identified in this chapter (and others not discussed here) will be sufficiently strong to put a break on the slide into mounting systemic chaos and to facilitate a transition to a more peaceful, just and equitable world order.

2. Rethinking production, finance and hegemonic decline in IPE

Leo Panitch and Sam Gindin

IPE as a field in the academic International Relations discipline was born at a time when the breakdown of Bretton Woods and the growth of economic nationalism in the third world appeared to signal not only the downfall of the dollar but also the erosion of US hegemony. It indeed took a whole decade to realign the balance of class forces both domestically and internationally so as to exit the crisis of the 1970s in a way that, in contrast to the 1930s, accelerated the globalizing dynamic of capitalism, and did so, moreover, under continuing US leadership. This occurred as the process of market liberalization to promote greater economic competition was beginning to be registered, aided by the US Treasury's efforts in particular (including the creation of the G7 as 'a vehicle for providing support and endorsement for US-generated initiatives and ideas') to sustain and develop a common purpose and solidarity along these lines (Baker 2006: 11, 26). And this would soon be followed by the Treasury's no less successful efforts in turning back the challenge of third world economic nationalism.

What was significant about the way the 1970s crisis was resolved was that rather than *displacing* US postwar hegemony, it opened up the space for both the renewal of the material foundations of American leadership and the further integration through the course of the century not only of the Western European and Japanese states, but for a good many 'emerging market states' in Eastern Europe, Asia and the 'Global South'. To grasp all this properly requires an understanding of the relationship among production, finance and the American state that has too often been missing from IPE.

US HEGEMONY FROM THE BRETTON WOODS CRISIS TO THE VOLCKER SHOCK

The growing centrality of the American state's role in global capitalism through the crisis of the 1970s showed that whatever problems and frictions US balance of payments deficits might produce, they did not have the same implications for the US as they would for any other state. Far from necessarily representing a diminution of American power, the outflow of capital from the US and the balance of payments deficits that had so concerned economic and political elites through the 1960s had actually laid the basis for further dollar-based credit expansion and financial innovation both domestically and internationally in the 1970s. The capacity to achieve this, however, still rested not only on the international activities of the American state but also on the material base of the American empire at home. For example, US expenditure on research and development at this time was about four times that of the countries of Western Europe combined (Kindleberger 1970). In the newly developed business computer market (with the personal computer market, initially fully dominated by the US, still to come) US firms accounted for one-third of the computers in Japan, half of those in the UK and France, and more than three-quarters of those in West Germany (Hart 1992: 14; Olegrio 1997: 354–5; Lecuyer 2006: 25). Moreover, the US also retained its competitive advantage in agriculture. Alongside the enormous expansion of US agriculture, with its productivity continuing to outpace that of non-farm industries though the 1970s, the US not only benefited from high commodity prices, but saw its overall agricultural exports increase between 1972 and 1980 by an average annual rate of 8.9 per cent (Clayton 1981: 75).

This technological lead reflected a distinctive American combination of supporting factors: new commercial opportunities emerging from the military–industrial complex; university research serving private innovation; early access to venture finance, alongside secure property rights; a base of skills in engineering, optics, chemistry and metallurgy, as well as sales; and the mobility of managers across firms and regions, which helped to disseminate and further commercialize the new technology. The direct role of the American state itself was especially important: agencies from the Pentagon to the Department of Health ensured that 'government funding and infrastructure played a key role in such technologies as computers, telecommunication satellites, jet planes, civilian nuclear energy, lasers and ultimately bio-technology' (Block 2008: 174–5). European capital now flowed to the US (where half of all global total FDI was located by the end of the 1970s), not so much to avoid protectionist measures as to have access to the wide range of research, productive, financial and sales capacities that were constitutive of the richest market in the world (McCulloch 1991).

The significance of all this was recognized in an April 1973 memorandum prepared for Treasury Secretary George Shultz by Bill Casey, who had just moved from chairing the SEC to become Undersecretary of State for Economic Affairs (he would later become Reagan's CIA Director).

Casey argued that 'the dollar's problem comes from a failure to properly assess the solid assets which lie below the surface. . . The US is still dominant in computers, photography, pharmaceuticals, medical technology, aerospace, nuclear power, home building, heavy industrial machinery, off shore drilling utility operations and so on.' So in direct contrast to the State Department's traditional position for so much of the twentieth century, Casey presciently argued that 'trade need no longer be the only source of major gains in our balance of payments'. It was precisely because the US could instead make 'securities an export' that it had 'such a large stake in the creation of better capital markets and in a better interrelationship of capital markets around the world. Fortunately know-how is one of our great assets and the securities markets of the world are becoming increasingly internationalized.' All this would allow US financial institutions, Casey insisted, 'to take the leadership in the developing global securities market' as long as there was also extensive action by other states to establish 'common rules of the road in the various capital markets' (Casey 1973).

Immediately after the collapse of the Bretton Woods system of fixed exchange rates, the Chicago Mercantile Exchange (CME), the world's central futures market in livestock long after the slaughterhouses were gone from Chicago, gave birth to the financial derivatives revolution by inventing a futures market in currencies. The Chicago Board of Trade, which was also still the world's centre of futures trading in wheat, corn and soya even though grain was no longer stored in Chicago, soon followed by launching a futures market in US Treasury securities. The key role state regulation played in the process was indicated by the creation in 1974 of the Commodity Futures Trading Commission (CFTC) to regulate derivatives in a way that facilitated their development. The head of the CME, Leo Melamed, explicitly recognized that the CME's plans for derivatives 'were ambitious and could be greatly assisted by a federal stamp of approval' (Melamed 1992: 108). The CFTC proved keen to promote the spreading and hedging of risk, including by the many non-financial corporations which invested in derivatives to protect themselves from volatile commodity prices, floating exchange rates and fluctuating interest rates. The derivatives revolution was also intimately linked to the internationalization of the US bond market, which was occurring at the same time as the development of the separate Eurodollar bond market. The financial uncertainty that followed the collapse of the fixed exchange rate system amid the inflationary conditions of the time actually enhanced the attractiveness of Treasury bills to international investors, who recognized the depth and liquidity of the US bond market despite all the hand-wringing about declining US power and economic strength (Aquanno 2009).

In addition to the creation of new agencies like the CFTC, a new interdepartmental Council on International Economic Policy was created, designed to operate along the lines of the National Security Council in terms of pulling together 'domestic economic developments and our broad foreign policy objectives' (Shultz 1974: 7–8). It was headed by the Secretary of the Treasury, which in this period considerably advanced its claims to play, right across the policy spectrum, 'a leading role in the international as well as the domestic sphere' (Simon 1975). With very few exceptions, the Treasury's consistent and effective opposition to the use of countervailing duties in relation to investigations of unfair trading practices by other states through the crisis of the 1970s permitted it not only to fend off the implementation of domestic protectionist measures but to use the threat of these as lever for the liberalization of foreign markets, including in relation to what were increasingly being identified as 'non-tariff barriers' associated with other states' domestic regulations (Chorev 2007; Dryden 1995; Essex 2007).

The more immediate challenge that the Treasury still confronted, if the dollar's new role as the anchor of global capitalism was to be made secure, was its incapacity to cope with the continuing impact of domestic inflationary pressures on global financial markets. This involved, above all, breaking the power of American trade unions. An attempt to do this had been made at the end of the Johnson administration and the beginning of the Nixon one. As the Bretton Woods crisis came to a head, the Treasury undertook fiscal restraint and the Federal Reserve pushed interest rates up to 10 per cent. This attempt collapsed by early 1970, not only in the face of a strike wave that involved one out of every six unionized workers, but also because the high interest rates induced a crisis in the commercial paper market through which investment banks raised funds for corporations (Panitch and Gindin 2012). With the realization that a tightening of monetary policy was having the effect of inducing a financial crisis, the central bank's role as lender of last resort to keep the financial system afloat overrode the commitment to defeating inflation. This already showed how far the deep structural relationship between Washington and Wall Street could not but be affected by the new volatility of financial markets, all the more so since major non-financial corporations were also increasingly embedded in those markets.

The decade of crisis appeared to come full circle when President Carter appointed Paul Volcker, who had overseen the US Treasury's response to the dollar crisis of the late 1960s, to head the Federal Reserve. What was now required to resolve the dollar crisis, Volcker insisted, was to 'discipline ourselves', by which he meant that the Fed had to discipline *itself* this time to see through a policy of pushing interest rates to such 'painfully high' levels as would prove that beating inflation trumped all other policy goals (Volcker and Gyohten 1993). By the end of the 1970s most industrial sectors of capital had come to accept the need to give priority to fighting inflation and defeating labour, and agreed that the strengthening of financial capital that this would involve was in their own interest. This was crucial for the new age of US finance that took off in the 1980s, as well as for making the US Treasury bonds that covered the Reagan administration's fiscal deficits seem as good as gold (indeed, since they paid interest, better than gold). Many critics at the time insisted that high interest rates would not only block economic growth but expose US industry's vulnerability to competition from Europe and Japan. In fact, the imposition of class discipline to break the great inflation and the wage militancy of US labour, strongly confirming the American state's commitment to property, the value of the dollar and the inviolability of its debt, laid the basis not only for the new age of finance but also for the broader restructuring of the US economy.

RENEWING THE MATERIAL BASE OF US HEGEMONY AT HOME

Four specific transformations in the last two decades of the twentieth century were especially important in this restructuring. The first of these was the relationship between industry and finance. The new age of finance was often portrayed as diverting corporate funds from potentially productive investment to speculative activity, forcing corporations to look for high immediate rates of return rather than longer-term growth in order to maximize 'shareholder value' (Orhangazi 2008). The new age of finance certainly did involve enormous speculation, and was accompanied by much economic irrationality. Yet, as was proved in the following decade's remarkable productivity growth in manufacturing, amidst an expansion of unprecedented length, it is a mistake to see the dominance of finance in terms of speculation displacing productive activity. The greed that lay behind the assertion of shareholder value, and that drove so many of the corporate mergers and industrial closures, should not blind us to the way in which the broadening and deepening of US financial markets, including their ability to attract so much capital from abroad, expanded the availability of relatively cheap credit for US firms. This was seen not only in the enormous growth of the commercial paper and corporate bond markets, but also in what has been called the 'financialization' of non-financial corporations. Without this generally becoming the foundation for their central activities or their profits, large corporations increasingly engaged in financial arbitrage themselves, using both the credit subsidiaries they had developed to attract consumers and their own bond and equity portfolios.

As for the impact of financial discipline on corporate governance, this was not so much imposed on managers as used by them to facilitate and accelerate restructuring within firms and across industries. Moreover, the massive reallocation of capital that was involved in restructuring the US economy would have been inconceivable without the role financial markets played not only in pushing so-called 'inefficient' firms out of business and funding mergers but also in supporting risky but innovative start-ups through the US's unique venture capital markets, whose disbursements grew ten-fold in the 1980s alone (Gompers and Lerner 1999: 13). The development of derivatives products was also important, not only for limiting exchange-rate and interest-rate risks for corporations but also for assessing and comparing alternative accumulation strategies across both space and time; risk management, like transportation and marketing, should not necessarily be seen as a drain on the productive sectors of the economy, even if it does increase systemic volatility.

The second transformation, the one most associated with the thesis of US decline, occurred in the core industries that had fuelled American economic dynamism in the postwar era. The old labour-intensive sectors like shoes, textiles, food and beverage had seen a sharp contraction well before the 1980s, but it was rising imports and the corresponding loss of jobs in steel, auto and machinery that occasioned alarm about the state of American manufacturing. But more was going on here than the word 'decline' could adequately capture. By the end of the century, a major restructuring had occurred within these industries. In the auto industry there were 18 assembly plant closures between 1988 and 1999, but 13 new plants also opened, while the 66 auto-parts plants that closed over these years were more than offset by 184 new parts plants. Moreover, the number of plant expansions greatly exceeded the number of downsizings (Aschoff 2009; 2011). The direct foreign investment flowing into domestic US auto production, primarily from Japanese companies, expanded rather than diminished the US industrial base. The spatial relocation of the industry involved not only Japanese (as well as some German and South Korean) corporations concentrating their production in the states of the US south, but also saw GM and Ford opening plants there (they also opened new plants in the mid-west states, sometimes just a few miles away from where old plants had closed).

This was accompanied by the reorganization of workplaces everywhere in the US to facilitate 'lean' production and outsourcing. The emulation of Japanese firms in this respect was enhanced by the possibility of outsourcing to non-union plants, decreases in transportation and communication costs, and the logistical coordination that computerization facilitated. Outsourcing was also directly promoted by the state, as was seen when federal loan guarantees to Chrysler were made conditional on it. Alongside the relocation and reorganization of production, the 'Big Three' US auto companies responded to foreign competition by shifting output towards truck and SUV production in the 1990s, where they retained a strong competitive advantage. This too was at least indirectly promoted by the state, whose commitment to low interest rates and low energy prices sustained the market for such expensive and fuel-hungry vehicles. This shift restored the Big Three's profitability through the 1990s – and it was this, not pressures from financial capital, that led them to close their eyes to the implications of oil price hikes for future car sales, let alone the environmental costs to society. A significant indicator of the transformation going on in the automobile industry was that through the 1990s US auto firms (including the Japanese transplants) were the leading purchasers of high-tech equipment. In steel, where US firms had lost their technological leadership, they carved out new market niches in high-quality steel while a series of mergers, especially with Japanese companies trying to escape quotas on steel imports, generally narrowed the technology gap with US competitors (Fine et al. 2005). And the machinery sector responded to the increasing competition it faced from abroad, including increasingly from Asia, as it led the world in the move to computerized equipment and software.

All this brings us to the third transformation: the shift to high-tech manufacturing production. This new industrial revolution – which soon spread globally and encompassed computer and telecommunication equipment, pharmaceuticals, aerospace and scientific instruments – was largely American-led in terms of its origins, concentration and the mechanisms of its subsequent diffusion abroad. The new computer and information technologies that had emerged in the 1960s really proved their worth to industrial and service corporations in the 1980s and especially in the 1990s. With labour resistance now greatly diminished, corporations were more willing to undertake the heavy additional investments that were needed to accompany the employment of the new technologies, in terms of the reorganization of work, management systems and relations with component suppliers. And US financial markets stood uniquely ready to finance budding high-tech commercial ventures. Financial institutions were, at the same time, themselves early and crucial players in the information revolution, providing the major market for computers and software, and developing key information technologies and systems for themselves and others (Klein et al. 2003; Berger 2003).

US high-tech firms also benefited from public subsidies, sometimes indirectly, as in the case of military procurement, but often directly in the form of government laboratories linked to particular departments (defence, energy, health, agriculture); and increasingly through the growing commercial role of American universities, aided by legislation expanding the property rights of university researchers. Indeed, Congress's general bias in favour of corporate interests was reinforced by its concern for US security interests in the high-tech arena. Congress showed great flexibility in lowering standards geared to public protection, especially in pharmaceuticals, as its interest moved 'from the safety issues of the 1970s to the upcoming "bonanza" of biotechnology' (Loeppky 2004: 503). With these supports American capital proved capable of expanding even further into new research-intensive sectors, often inventing entirely new sectors for accumulation. At the turn of the century, even not counting the extensive high-tech production by US TNCs abroad, some 35 per cent of global high-tech production took place within the US – the same as the share of all global manufacturing held by the US in the early 1950s. The EU as a whole had a share of 24 per cent, Japan 21 per cent and China 3 per cent (National Science Foundation 2010). Shored up by its high-tech sectors, during 1983–99 US manufacturing output grew faster (4.2 per cent annually) than overall GDP (3.7 per cent) (Economic Report of the President 2002). The restructuring led to manufacturing productivity actually growing faster in these years (3.3 per cent annually) than it had in the 'golden' 1950s and 1960s (when it averaged 2.4 per cent) (US Bureau of Labor Statistics 2012). This enormous productivity growth was reflected in an increase in overall manufacturing volume of 90 per cent over the samc period, while manufacturing employment showed virtually no increase at all (Economic Report of the President 2002).

The fourth structural transformation in the economy revolved around the growth of a diverse range of 'professional and business services' that ranged across consulting, law, accounting, market research, engineering, computer software and systems analysis. Here, the number of jobs increased dramatically. In 1983 employment in this broad sector was less than half that in manufacturing, but by the turn of the century employment – growing even faster than in financial services – had doubled, and matched total manufacturing employment. Not all of these jobs were 'knowledge-intensive', nor were they all new – many were clerical, and had previously been done by corporations in-house. Nevertheless, they brought a new set of strategic economic relations into play. Specialization in such activities by American firms spanned many countries as their services were sought out by foreign companies anxious to operate more 'efficiently' along neoliberal and 'new public management' lines. They were sought out too by foreign governments concerned to navigate the new currents of international trade treaties and commercial law. At the end of the century, the US's global share of professional and business services, measured by revenue generated, was close to 40 per cent (National Science Foundation 2010).

The development of this sector was closely related to the accelerating expansion of finance from the 1960s onwards, through which major changes occurred in the nature of what financial institutions did, taking them beyond credit provision and directly into the heart of the accumulation process. The American Dream has always entailed promoting popular integration into the circuits of financial capital, whether as independent commodity farmers, as workers whose pay cheques were deposited with banks and whose pension savings were invested in the stock market, or as consumers reliant on credit – and not least as homeowners subsidized by the tax deductions allowed on mortgage payments. But in the context of intensified competition, stagnant wage income and more sophisticated financial markets, this incorporation of the mass of the American population now took on a more comprehensive quality. Gains through collective action gave way to individual adjustments in lifestyles, from young couples moving in with parents to save for a down payment on a house, to a family decision to cancel a vacation and use the money to buy a 'home entertainment system'; while longer hours of work stole from workers even such time as they had once had for self-education and social and political activity. Workers reduced their savings, increased their debt and looked to tax cuts to make up for stagnant wages; they cheered rises in the stock markets on which their pensions depended and counted on the inflation of house prices to serve as collateral for new loans, provide some added retirement security and leave a legacy for their children. All this, along with increasing inequalities among workers themselves, left a working class more individualized and fragmented, its collective capacity for resistance more severely atrophied than at any previous time in the century.

These transformations – the new age of finance, the restructuring of manufacturing, the explosion of high tech, the ubiquity of business services and the profound defeat of labour – reconstituted the material base of American hegemony. This was crucial for the way global capitalism was 'made' in the final decades of the twentieth century. A truly global financial system based on the internationalization of the US financial system became 'neither a myth nor even an alarming tendency, but a reality' (Grahl 2001: 44). American TNCs, expanding much faster globally than at home, transferred technology abroad (yet comfortably maintaining their home research and development base), while high-tech manufacturing came to both encourage and depend on global networks of competitive production that drew on expanding pools of newly-proletarianized labour (cf. Delgado Wise and Martin, this volume).

RENEWING THE MATERIAL BASE OF US HEGEMONY ABROAD

The defeat of US labour in the early 1980s corresponded not only with the defeats suffered by the Left across Western Europe and the demise of the sclerotic Communist regimes in the East, but also with the defeat of radical nationalist and socialist forces in the developing world where, in the midst of the widespread debt crisis of the 1980s, many states now adopted strategies compatible with their integration into global capitalism. Import-substitution strategies were abandoned, export-oriented strategies in East Asia succeeded in breaking with capitalist underdevelopment, and the regions of the globe that had been closed to capital accumulation under Communist regimes were added to the global capitalist economy.

The creation of the European Union, so widely interpreted as constituting a challenge to American hegemony, turned out to be something altogether different. Especially significant in this respect, and indeed for the overall shift in the balance of class forces in Europe, was the transformation of European financial markets along US lines. The City of London, which had since the 1960s served US banks 'as a laboratory for financial innovation' at the centre of the Euromarkets, was the leading site of this Americanization (Moran 1994: 169). As one experienced City insider put it:

> The triumph of American values and American ways provided an ideal background for the Wall Street investment banks. What more powerful message can there be than: 'If you want to compete in an American-style market place and secure access to the vast pool of American capital who better to service you than an organization that is imbued with these practices and epitomizes these values?' (Golding 2001: 26).

The most influential European banks and corporations emulated American practices, while at the same time substantially increasing their investments in the US. US TNCs as well as Wall Street investment banks were themselves major players in the corporate mergers and acquisitions in Europe which were so important to regional integration. The capital expenditures of US TNCs in Europe more than doubled in value within the first five years following the passage of the 1986 Single European Act, and continued to rise through the 1990s. At the same time the two-way flow of FDI, incorporating as it did networks of production (components flowing in both directions before being assembled into final products for diverse markets), made the economies on both sides of the Atlantic more and more interdependent and pushed the free trade agenda well beyond European regional integration. The training of European managers was strongly linked to the leading US business schools, ensuring that the management practices that made the most impact were first 'validated' in the US (Carpenter and Jefferys 2000: 166). Even Japanese methods like Just in Time and Total Quality Management were only adopted in Europe after American corporations had embraced them. By the 1990s American IT corporations such as Apple, Hewlett-Packard, IBM and Microsoft were supplying over 80 per cent of Europe's software and computer market, and Europeans were 'increasingly working with technologies and tools originally designed for the American marketplace' (Carpenter and Jefferys 2000: 119). While this certainly demonstrated the importance of European markets for leading US corporations, it also showed Europe becoming more rather than less integrated with the US as the information technology revolution proceeded.

Economic and productivity growth in the major European countries, which had already slowed considerably relative to the US in the 1970s, lagged behind the US in the 1980s and 1990s, and European unemployment rates were persistently higher. This did not write *finis* to the European variety of capitalism, embedded as it was in the deeply entrenched corporatist arrangements of 'coordinated capitalism' throughout the postwar era. But these arrangements were now more and more attuned to competitiveness as the overriding goal. Motivated by a concern that 'business and citizens in the European Union have been slower in embracing [the] new economy than in the United States', the European Commission wanted Europe to 'become the cheapest and easiest place to do business in the world' (European Commission 2001). Thus having started with the seductive promise in the mid-1980s of a European and Monetary Union based on a 'social charter', by the time the euro was launched in 1999 it was clear that regional economic integration was, in effect, 'the antechamber to broader liberalization'. As John Grahl went on to note: 'Not only financial reforms, but also labour market and social protection policies, liberalisation and privatisation of public services, the promotion of venture capital and other such measures were all put forward in a completely uncritical attempt to mimic the growth process of the US in the late '90s' (Grahl 2004: 293).

At the end of the twentieth century the advanced capitalist countries accounted for 90 per cent of all financial assets, 65 per cent of world GDP, and almost 70 per cent of global exports of manufactured goods; not only did 85 per cent of global FDI emanate from these countries, they were also the recipients of over two-thirds of it (Kose et al. 2006; Dicken 2003: 34–42). Over half of all US FDI was located in Western Europe (up from 45 per cent in 1983) while Western Europe accounted for two-thirds of FDI in the US (WTO 2012; UNCTAD 2001; US Survey of Current Business 2012). But these statistics mask what was going on in the rest of the world. The major shift across so many developing countries to export-led manufacturing production meant that their place in global capitalism was no longer that of mere suppliers of raw materials to the advanced capitalist states. In fact, this transformation in the international division of labour involved a reconfiguration of social relations in one country after another, yielding not only new capitalist classes which became more and more linked to international capital accumulation, but also a massive expansion of the global proletariat – which in turn had a profound impact on the restructuring of production and on classes and class relations in the advanced capitalist countries.

Even in those regions where the political relationship with the American empire was to become ever more fraught there was still nothing like an economic rupture. This was all the more remarkable given that it was states in these regions who figured so prominently in the passage of the UN General Assembly's Charter of Economic Rights and Duties of States in 1974, which asserted the right to 'nationalize, expropriate or transfer ownership of foreign property'. Even if the US Treasury was well aware as early as 1975 of the need to 'discount the rhetoric', few in Washington would have been so bold as to predict that by the 1980s the expropriations would largely become a thing of the past. Having already declined from 83 in 1975 to 17 in 1979, the number of expropriations fell to one each year from 1984 to 1986 and zero for the rest of the decade (Minor 1994: 180). The question of how to fashion political and legal frameworks through which such a diverse array of states could be integrated into international capital accumulation, while sustaining order and containing economic crises in the face of the contradictions that the realization of global capitalism simultaneously gave rise, was an immense challenge. The recognition of this was seen in the World Bank's call by 1997 for transcending 'the sterile debate of state and market' and addressing the issue of 'state effectiveness' in developing the kind of public rules and institutions that 'allow markets to flourish' (World Bank 1997: 1, 25). The constitutionalizing of free trade under the rubric of the WTO, alongside the restructuring of states in the South under IMF and World Bank conditionalities as well as a host of bilateral treaties usually modelled on the United States Trade Representative's model treaty (wherein states guaranteed investor rights above all), provided the political carapace for a fundamental change in TNC relationships with the South.

The integration of developing states into global capitalism was of course extremely uneven, taking very different forms according to the nature of the state and class alignments in individual countries, and the extent to which the integration was sponsored (or occasionally blocked) by the advanced capitalist states. Throughout the debt crisis of the 1980s the US Treasury focused on ensuring that the strict lending conditionality the IMF attached to its loans required not just immediate measures of fiscal austerity but long-term structural adjustment programmes designed to protect and guarantee financial assets through the economic and political liberalization of each recipient state. This changed the dynamics of international financing. Developing state borrowers were increasingly forced to turn to international securities markets where risks could be more fully diversified and absorbed. They could no longer rely on their relationships with foreign and domestic banking syndicates and could now only attract capital if they submitted fully to the discipline of impersonal global financial markets.

The administrative and technological capacity of the TNCs to centralize the crucial functions related to control (planning, research and development, allocation of investment), while decentralizing the use of technology and selected manufacturing operations, allowed them to take advantage of local conditions such as cheaper and abundant labour supplies. This finally opened the door to significant manufacturing taking place within the developing countries, with a high proportion of them being in such technologically-advanced sectors as electronics, transportation and machinery. This did not mean, however, that global hierarchies in the division of labour did not persist. Most strategic activities (research, development, engineering and capital-intensive high valued-added production) were concentrated in the first world as were newly emerging products and processes. Moreover, as TNCs picked and chose where to go, the distribution of FDI was very highly concentrated in a few countries of the South, with some regions, especially large parts of Africa, largely left out.

FINANCE, PRODUCTION AND US HEGEMONY IN THE NEW MILLENNIUM

If one of the key features of global capitalism at the beginning of the twenty-first century was the continued centrality and even dominance of the US, there could be no mistaking that another hardly less important feature was the rapid rise of China within global capitalism. Especially in the wake of the 1997–98 Asian financial crisis and China's admission to the WTO in 2001, the East Asian economic integration initiated by

Japan four decades earlier was now increasingly reoriented around China. Yet this regional integration was still primarily directed to maintaining and expanding ultimate export markets in the US, and an unprecedented spate of bilateral trade agreements that were now made within the region also served this purpose. But the pace was now largely determined by the growth of China's exports and by related changes in production processes in other countries, all of which 'were linked and collectively shaped by broader *transnational* capitalist dynamics, in particular by the establishment and intensification of transnational corporate-controlled cross-border production networks' (Hart-Landsberg and Burkett 2006: 4). As the Asian Development Bank emphasized, 'an open, rules-based global system of trade and investment remains a high regional priority'; and since 'Asia's continued success depends on access to global markets', the main goal was to 'move faster towards global integration' (Asian Development Bank 2008: 8, 16, 23).

The largest capital outflows from the developing world took the form of far larger purchases of US Treasuries as central bank reserves than ever before. Especially in the context of the Asian crisis and the further liberalization of capital markets, these purchases served as an insurance policy against future runs on local currencies, as well as a means of maintaining exchange rates relative to the dollar. This was not simply a costly transfer of wealth from the South to the North; it was also a necessary condition of successful export-oriented capitalist development. What the emphasis on building up their reserves to insure against another run on their currency now implied, however, was that exports should significantly surpass imports. Since the requirements of neoliberal free trade meant they could no longer protect their domestic manufacturing markets from foreign imports, the concern with restraining consumer imports while accelerating export competitiveness in turn required limiting working class incomes.

By 2000, manufacturing as a portion of GDP was higher in the developing countries (23 per cent) than in the developed ones (18 per cent) (Kozul-Wright and Rayment 2004: 32; US Bureau of Labor Statistics 2012; Lett and Bannister 2009). Far from the shift of productive activity from the developed core leading to a fragmentation of production, it was part and parcel of a much greater global coordination of production through a broad range of subsidiaries, suppliers and distributors (Sturgeon et al. 2008: 297–321; Merk, this volume). Transnational corporations increasingly outsourced many operations, now purchasing from other companies much of what they had previously performed 'in house' (from accounting to janitorial services, and a great deal of production itself). Although this often led to a greater concentration of corporate power on a global scale, it also intensified competition in each sector (and indeed among divisions within each firm) as well as between nominally independent suppliers and distributors across the world, bidding for entry into global networks of integrated production. The result was a more interdependent global capitalism that required more than ever the consolidation of 'free trade' to facilitate borderless production.

Despite all the anxiety on the one hand and *Schadenfreude* on the other about the productive capacity of American capital, US corporations were able to take special advantage of the open world they had been so central to creating. The measure of this success was not the proportion of global production that took place in the US (this had clearly fallen over time as a by-product of the successful promotion of capitalist social relations abroad), but rather the *strategic* importance of American capital in the global economy. This was most obvious in key new areas of economic activity such as information technology, where a 'powerful research infrastructure' put the US 'at the forefront of major breakthroughs. . .It remains undisputed leader in software technology. US venture spending far outstrips international spending' (Cowhey and Aronson 2009: 15). To a substantial degree, the 'commanding heights' of global accumulation had shifted to these high-tech sectors, and to a range of business services (management, legal, accounting, engineering, consultancy and financial) in which American corporations overwhelmingly dominated.

As of 2007, the top three or four global firms in such diverse sectors as technological hardware and equipment, software and computers, aerospace/military, and oil equipment and services were American, as were 14 of the 16 top global firms in health care equipment and services. In global media, four of the top five corporations were American, as were two of the top three in each of the pharmaceuticals, industrial transportation, industrial equipment and fixed-line telecommunications sectors. And five of the top six corporations in the general retail sector were American. These included Wal-Mart, which used its application of computerized information systems to become one of the world's most strategically important corporations (*Financial Times* 2010). It is wrong to see these US TNCs as transnational rather than American. Not only were their controlling shareholders and headquarters located in the US, so was 70 per cent of US TNCs' global value-added, and 85 per cent of their research and development (Barefoot and Mataloni Jr 2010: 208–9). Even for the most internationalized US manufacturing TNCs – that is, those with more than 50 per cent of their sales and employment outside the US, such as General Electric, Ford, IBM and Procter & Gamble – the most significant locale by far remained the US, their foreign activities being distributed among a wide variety of countries (UNCTAD 2009: 225).

To top it all off, nine of the top ten corporations in global financial services were American, a dominance that went beyond that in any other sector. Of course, non-financial US corporations themselves were directly involved in financial markets. This was the case not only in the myriad ways they used financial markets as described above, and the proportion of profits they earned from doing so, but also in terms of the proportion of compensation paid in stock options to executives, managers and sometimes even other employees. Moreover, non-financial firms became especially involved in hedging foreign exchange and interest rate risks via the derivative markets, treating these as necessary costs, similar to expenditures on transportation and telecommunications. These developments blurred the old lines between financial and non-financial activities. Yet this should not be taken too far. For all the greater complexity of the interactions between finance and industry, they each retained their distinct characteristics.

Most US job losses stemmed not from foreign outsourcing but from the impact of the sustained increases in manufacturing productivity at home, which in the boom of the 1990s was compensated for by job creation in other sectors. The investment abroad was primarily about capturing *new* markets for manufactured products (the bulk of what US TNCs produced abroad was not exported back to supply the US domestic market). A great many American jobs were of course lost – in some cases, like textiles, entire sectors were wiped out – but to the extent that this was part of American capital's capacity to move on to new manufacturing sectors, it reflected not a hollowing out of manufacturing but a restructuring (Rowthorn 1997). Alongside the outsourcing abroad, there was often outsourcing *within* the US (e.g. auto suppliers going to the southern states or call centres established in prisons).

And while US manufacturing job losses were indeed heavy after 2001 (especially in auto and electrical appliances as well as the long-suffering textile and apparel sector), the US was still producing more manufactured goods and receiving more foreign investment before the global economic crisis that began in 2007 than all the BRICs (Brazil, Russia, India and China) combined (World Bank 2004). Rather than taking the US trade deficit as a measure of industrial decline, it is instructive to consider US exports and imports separately. The growth in the volume of US exports in the two decades up to 2007 – even as the trade deficit accumulated – averaged a very robust 6.6 per cent, leaving it only marginally behind Germany and China, the world's largest exporters; it was the relative expansion of US imports that was the source of the growing deficit (UNCTADSTAT, Statistics; OECD, International Trade Balance). It was in good part US consumer spending that maintained effective global demand into the first years of the twenty-first century.

The average annual real rate of growth of the American economy in the quarter century after the resolution of the crisis of the 1970s (i.e. from 1983 to 2007) was 3.5 per cent. This was higher than in any similar period from 1830 to 1950, and was only marginally less than during the so-called postwar 'golden age'; and, unlike then, US GDP growth in the quarter century after 1983 surpassed that of the other advanced capitalist countries (Maddison 2001). Similarly, though US manufacturing productivity growth had averaged 2.5 per cent from 1950 to 1973, well below that of the other advanced capitalist countries, between 1983 and 2007, it increased quite dramatically to 3.5 per cent, running ahead of all the other G7 economies. In terms of attractiveness as a place for capitalists to invest, the US was still, despite the wide dispersal of FDI to Europe and Asia by 2007, the largest single recipient of FDI inflows and the rate of US manufacturing productivity growth ran considerably ahead of the growth in labour compensation at home (Fleck et al. 2011). As a result, the share of after-tax corporate profits relative to US GDP earned by American corporations in 2006 was at its highest level since 1945.

Moreover, US TNCs' operations abroad consistently contributed about 30 per cent to total US profits in the new millennium, as compared with less than 20 per cent in the 1980s (Barefoot and Mataloni 2010). It was largely the failure to take sufficient account of the dominance and integration of American production and finance that led to the misreading of what US trade deficits signalled by way of undermining the value of the dollar and its place as the world currency. It was the balance of capital flows more than the balance of trade that now determined the dollar's value. The issue of US 'imbalances' that so many observers were fixated on in the first years of the new millennium failed to appreciate this central point. Far from the capital inflows signalling the dollar's weakness, and being significant mainly in offsetting US trade deficits, they highlighted the central role of US banks and TNCs in the global economy, and the extent to which the integration of the third world was dependent on the pull of both US consumer and financial markets.

US HEGEMONY IN THE FIRST GREAT ECONOMIC CRISIS OF THE TWENTY-FIRST CENTURY

Given the severity and duration of the latest crisis in a global capitalist economy that the American state had been so central to constructing, it was hardly surprising to see a resurgence of pronouncements that US hegemony was coming to an end. While the American empire is certainly not always able to control the spirits it has called up from the deep, it nevertheless remains critical to the system's survival. The continuing centrality of the American state in the global economy was in fact reinforced as the crisis unfolded, with virtually no trace of such inter-imperial conflict that a century earlier had given rise to world war. This is not to say that the problems of crisis management became any less acute, not least because the conflicts that emerged in the wake of the greatest capitalist crisis since the 1930s took shape much less as conflicts *between* capitalist states and their ruling classes as of conflicts *within* capitalist states.

The crisis that started in 2007 in the American heartland of global capitalism was not caused by either domestic under-investment in production or US trade and capital flow imbalances but rather by the volatility of finance. The crisis that erupted in the US in 2007 was not caused by a profit squeeze or collapse of investment due to general over-accumulation in the economy. In the US, in particular, profits and investments had recovered strongly since the early 1980s. Nor was it caused by a weakening of the dollar due to the recycling of China's trade surpluses, as so many had predicted. On the contrary, the enormous foreign purchases of US Treasuries had allowed a low interest rate policy to be sustained in the US after the bursting of the 'new economy' stock bubble at the beginning of the new century. While this stoked an even greater real estate bubble, after a brief downturn there was a resumption of economic growth and non-residential investment. Indeed, investment was growing significantly in the two years before the onset of the crisis, profits were at a peak, and capacity utilization in industry had just moved above the historic average.

The roots of the crisis, in fact, lay in the growing global importance of US mortgage finance, a development which could not be understood apart from the expanded state support for home ownership, a long-standing element in the integration of workers into US capitalism. Since the 1980s wages had stagnated and social programmes had been eroded, reinforcing workers' dependence on the rising value of their homes as a source of economic security. Crucially important in explaining why the financial crisis turned into such a severe economic crisis was that the collapse of housing prices also undermined workers' main source of wealth, leading to a dramatic fall in US consumer spending. The bursting of the housing bubble thus had much greater effects than had the earlier bursting of the stock market bubble at the turn of the century, and much greater implications for global capitalism in terms of the role the US played as 'consumer of last resort'.

It was also because US finance had become so integral to the functioning of global capitalism that the ultimate impact of this crisis throughout the international economy was so profound. Given the role of US financial assets and consumer spending in global capitalism, illusions that other regions might be able to avoid the crisis were quickly dispelled. But the centrality of the American state was at the same time made clearer than ever. The American state's key role in terms of global crisis management was confirmed as the 2007–08 crisis unfolded, from the US Federal Reserve directly bailing out not just American but also foreign banks and providing other central banks with much needed dollars, to the Treasury's coordination of stimulus policies with other states. The enormous demand for US Treasury bonds right through the crisis reflected the extent to which the American state continued to be regarded as the ultimate guarantor of value, and demonstrated how much the world remained on the dollar standard. Even while international tensions surfaced, what was so striking when the G20 leaders were gathered together to meet for the first time in late 2008 in Washington was the consensus on avoiding protectionist measures. The establishment of the G20 was not a matter of shifting effective decision making powers from the national to the international level, much less from the American state to an international body. The G7 had never been about this in any case, and US hegemony within it was even further enhanced by the turn of the century. But it did symbolize the growing importance, and at the same time the difficult challenge, of integrating the leading developing states into the management of the global capitalist system.

CONCLUSION: THE MEANING OF HEGEMONY

The massive growth of the global proletariat that has been the *sine qua non* of capitalist globalization produces tendencies towards the equalization of wages and conditions at a global level, and the continuing travail of trade unionism in the developed capitalist countries has partly been a reflection of this. The very financialization through which global capitalism was realized was also the means by which workers were disciplined and was closely linked to the recovery of corporate profitability – albeit a recovery characterized by new vulnerabilities, above all that so much consumption was dependent on credit. And given the political and organizational defeats working classes had suffered since the 1980s, the vast growth in inequality during the neoliberal decades was further aggravated by the way the financial crisis of 2007–08 and the subsequent great recession was addressed.

In employing the term 'hegemony' to characterize the staying power of the informal American empire, we must be careful not to imagine that this must depend on the continued prosperity of the US working class. The aspiration to achieve US standards of living was certainly an important factor in the postwar era, and even today this remains the dream of a great many of those being drawn into capitalist development. But just as the declining fortunes and prospects of US workers have more often led to fatalism or right-wing populism, let alone socialist consciousness, so the image abroad of an America where the streets are not paved with gold does not necessarily undo the powerful economic and political structures underlying the American empire's central role in global capitalism. To undo this – abroad no less than at home – will require the creation of trade unions and working class parties of a new kind, capable of putting forward alternatives to the neoliberal integration of states into global capitalism, and also capable of building the international solidarities needed to sustain new attempts to socialize capital and foster genuinely democratic economic planning in each state.

3. Innovation policies and the competition state: the case of nanotechnology

Joscha Wullweber

INTRODUCTION: 'INSERT THE PROBLEM, NANOTECH IS GOING TO DO IT'

Technological development has always been the linchpin and the driver of human development in general, and of profit-driven, market-based economies in particular. For this reason, states give special attention to technology research and development (R&D) policies. However, the form of technology R&D policies has changed. (West) Germany, for example, started large-scale technological programmes like nuclear technology, aerospace technology, data processing technology and micro-technology at the end of the 1950s. At that time, technology R&D policies were mostly planned top-down. After the 1980s, however, technology R&D policies became increasingly understood as generic innovation policies to support the capacity of firms to compete internationally. Simultaneously, technology R&D policies were reoriented from large-scale technologies and top-down programmes (although these still exist) towards incentive-driven, flexible and bottom-up ones. These changes mirror the transition from Fordism to the post-Fordist era and the transformation of the nation-state towards a 'competition state'.

Nanotechnology as a broad innovation strategy serves to assist the reconstruction of the industrialized states along the lines of competitive criteria. There meanwhile exists a burgeoning body of literature and analyses on nanotechnology in the humanities and social sciences; the realm of nanotechnology has been widely explored. Yet the political and economic aspects of how it was introduced remain hazy. While many studies highlight the fantastic, visionary and rhetorical character of nanotechnology and discuss the expectations, hopes and fears associated with various utopian scenarios (e.g. Coenen et al. 2004; Lösch 2006; Kaiser and Kurath 2007; Selin 2007), the global politics of nanotechnology is largely under-scrutinized and lacks an explanatory framework. For in the words of Rodney Loeppky, 'Such an explanation would require us to identify the critical social, political and economic forces that historically condition the trajectory of science policy, and how this policy, in turn, has been able to interact with science itself' (Loeppky 2005: 3). In the case of nanotechnology, the lack of politico-economic analysis is surprising, given that 'nanotechnology has become a symbolic subject of international competition, much like the Cold War space program' (Schummer 2004: 67; Wullweber 2010; 2014a).

Nanotechnology has been approached from diverse angles by scholars across the humanities and social sciences. But rather than coming closer to elucidating the relevance of nanotechnology in global politics, they all struggle, explicitly or implicitly, with its definition. No generally agreed definition exists and the concept of nanotechnology still remains highly debated. It has even proven impossible, so far, to agree on the appropriateness of the term 'nanotechnology' itself. Most definitions of nanotechnology make reference to the nanoscale, which (usually) varies between 1 and 100 nanometres (10^{-9} to 10^{-7} metres). But even the range of scale is under debate. The most restricted definitions are those which refer to molecular manufacturing, the ability to understand, control and manipulate matter at the level of individual atoms and molecules and to construct greater structures atom by atom.

The question therefore arises: Why is nanotechnology so difficult to define? In this chapter I propose that nanotechnology is neither a specific technology or method, nor an array of applications or a research field. Rather it must be understood as a comprehensive political project or, more precisely, as a complex of diverse political, economic and technological projects bound together by the term 'nanotechnology'. Nanotechnology works as a kind of 'carrier force', as a techno-socio-political innovation strategy for techno-economic expansion in general. In short, it is an innovation strategy to solve current socio-economic problems. Or, as Patrick Reinsborough from the NGO smartMeme expressed sarcastically: 'Insert the problem, nanotech is going to do it' (interview with the author, March 2007).

The chapter begins with an exploration of the transformation of the nation-state after the crisis of Fordism. This analysis is based on Regulation theory and theories of the state. Drawing on this framework, I will then scrutinize the politics of nanotechnology by locating these politics analytically within the notion of contemporary industrialized states as competition states. This analysis focuses mainly on nanotechnology policies from the 1990s to the mid-2000s. Finally, I will connect innovation politics with different discourses, to wit, the narratives of 'the high-technology market', 'the knowledge-based economy' and 'the pressure of international competition'.

THE CRISIS OF FORDISM AND THE ROLE OF TECHNOLOGY

Many studies have explored the transformation of the nation-state in the era of globalization following the crisis of Fordism (Lipietz 1987; Strange 1996; Cameron and Palan 2004; Jessop 2007). In this context, the notion of the internationalization of the state refers to different and often contradictory policy answers formulated by state administrations to handle this new situation. In the following, I will argue that the prevailing discourse in the advanced industrialized countries to reconstruct the nation-state emphasizes a state that has to become streamlined by reference to competitive criteria. Technological innovation in general and nanotechnology policies in particular play an important role in supporting this discourse.

Fordism can be described as a macro-economic regime sustaining expanded production, a cycle of growth based on mass production and mass consumption. It involves a rising level of industrial productivity based on economies of scale in mass production, rising incomes linked to productivity, and increased mass demand due to rising wages (Lipietz 1987: 14; Desai, and Brand and Wissen, this volume). Accordingly, macro-economic coherence is institutionally embedded in a *mode of regulation*. Fordism, as a specific mode of regulation, can be understood 'as an ensemble of norms, institutions, organisational forms, social networks and patterns of conduct which sustain and "guide" the Fordist accumulation regime and promote compatibility among the decentralized decisions of economic agents despite the conflictual character of capitalist social relations' (Jessop 1991: 2).

Robert Boyer (1990: 42–5) sums up three characteristics of the mode of regulation: the reproduction of the fundamental social relations; the reproduction of the regime of accumulation; and the dynamic reconciliation of decentralized decisions of individuals and institutions. The state is conceptualized as the institutional nodal point of regulation or, according to Alain Lipietz (1992), as the *first force of regulation*. Accordingly, the state is not conceived as an entity that acquires power for itself, nor as an instrument of power wielded by a dominant class. Rather, the state is the material condensation of social relations of force (Poulantzas 1978). Drawing on Foucault (1991: 102), one may even take this further and conceive the state itself as a technology of governance. It is the *tactics* of governance that make possible the definition and redefinition of what is within the competence of the state and what is not, public versus private sphere, and so on. The *strategy* of governance defines the policy fields and, simultaneously, offers specific strategies for managing them.

From the 1940s to the 1970s, Fordism was founded upon an intensive regime of accumulation, based upon a specific Fordist accumulation regime. In return for rising real wages, the workers did accept the profit-oriented market relation of production and the Taylorist organization of work (Alnasseri et al. 2001: 169–70). This spatio-temporal fix has been described as a *Keynesian welfare national state* (Jessop 2002). It is Keynesian in so far as it is supposed to secure full employment in a relatively closed economy, mainly through demand side management. It has a welfare orientation, and it is national, because the economic and social policies are being pursued through the historically specific matrix of a national economy. And it is statist because the state institutions are the chief supplement to market forces in securing the conditions for economic growth and social cohesion. But then, as Jessop and Sum (2006: 68) point out: 'Fordism à la Henry Ford was not widely diffused and was never fully realised even in Ford's own plants in North America – let alone those in Europe'.

In the 1970s this mode of socio-economic regulation landed in a crisis. The Taylorist way of work organization, for example, lost its effectiveness and had already run up against its limits at the end of the 1960s. Thus, among other things, the rate of productivity growth declined (Lipietz 1992: 14). Taylorism was not able to react adequately to the adoption of new technologies and *just-in-time* methods of managing the production cycle. Hence the demand for a *lean production process*, which led to a more horizontal way of organizing production. But this was not just a matter of shop-floor relations; the period also witnessed intense social struggles, to which state apparatuses responded with open repression. It was this response that highlighted that a crisis of a mode of development will also tend to generate a comprehensive crisis of hegemony. In Regulation theory, the core component of the crisis is defined as an insufficient dynamic of accumulation; at the same time it entails an extensive economic, political and ideological crisis. Hence new technologies have always played an important role in the quest for new forms, both of accumulation and political hegemony. Thus according to Joachim Hirsch (1978: 94), the 'systematic generation of science and technology . . . becomes an important area of the functions of the state administration.' The advent and spread of nanotechnology in this sense are inscribed into a post-Fordist restructuring process.

Bob Jessop (1990) emphasizes that the nation-state is a social relation of which the unity has to be constructed actively. In addition, a state is characterized by selectivity, in so far as 'the state is not equally accessible to all social forces, cannot be controlled or resisted to the same extent by all strategies, and is not equally available for all purposes' (Jessop 1990: 317). But then, 'structures rarely have a simple, unequivocal relation to a single strategy' (Jessop and Sum 2006: 66). Rather, the state accommodates and articulates the relatively stabilized spatio-temporal, socio-political and selective structure of a specific society, including general concepts and values of social order. Hence it is always a terrain of struggle over political hegemony, fought in terms of competing definitions of the general interest. Within the process of permanent reconstruction since the mid-1970s, the constitution of the state moved from the Keynesian welfare national state to something that is still not entirely fixed and might be defined as the *post-national Schumpeterian workfare state* (Jessop 2002), or alternatively, as a *competition state* (Cameron and Palan 2004).

The competition state articulates a paradigm of competitiveness, in which technological policies, trade policies and social policies jointly function as mutually reinforcing practices (Jessop 1990: 119–20). Social behaviour under this paradigm is aligned with specific criteria such as efficiency, the ability to compete, an orientation towards global market scale, and so forth. But 'capitalism per se produces no spatial fix' (Alnasseri 2003: 165). Therefore this process of restructuring, or *neoliberal reconstruction*, has to be politically and socially regulated and secured by coercion. According to Jessop (2002), the (ideal-typical) Schumpeterian workfare post-national regime can be described as follows.

First, it is *Schumpeterian* in so far as it tries to promote permanent innovation and flexibility in relatively open economies by intervening on the supply-side and strengthening structural competitiveness. The protection of the accumulation of value and private property rights plays an important part in this respect. Second, it is a *workfare* regime because it subordinates social policy to the demands of labour market flexibility and structural competitiveness; it is concerned with providing welfare services that benefit business. The subjects are expected to serve as partners in the innovative, knowledge-driven flexible economy. Third, it is *post-national*, because of the increased significance of different spatial scales and horizons of action other than the national state. This is associated with a transfer of policy-making decisions upwards (to the IMF, WTO, EU, OECD and so on), sideways and downwards (to the regional, urban and local levels). Jessop explains this as a shift from states entrenching in sovereignty to a role in which they focus instead on controlling the levers of multilateral relations with other states: 'Paradoxically, this can lead to an enhanced role for national states in controlling the inter-scalar transfer of these powers–suggesting a shift from sovereignty to a *primus inter pares* role in intergovernmental relations' (Jessop 2002: 253). Fourth and finally, it has a *regime* form, because of the increased importance of non-state mechanisms in compensating for market failures.

Cameron and Palan (2004: 110–14) argue that the modern competition state is engaged in a process of (re-)negotiating a social structure and a set of political institutions inherited from the period of the nation-state. The process of reformation and adaptation can be understood at the macro level as a process of destruction and construction, in which international competition plays the key role. The notion of *comparative* advantage – the notion that each nation is unique and endowed with particular resources and characteristics – is replaced by the notion of *competitive* advantage: the idea that natural endowment and culture are unimportant and that all states are in principle the same. States are now placed on a sliding scale of global indicators on account of their supposed *competitiveness*. In the process of trying to reconstruct the social and political order, national competitiveness 'has become . . . a central ideological defence for far-reaching socio-economic restructuring' (Palan and Abbott 1996: 4).

A competition state, then, aims at securing economic growth within its borders, while ensuring competitive advantages for investors on its territory. This can be achieved by promoting the economic and extra-economic conditions that are perceived as vital for success. It emphasizes strategies to create, restructure or reinforce the competitive advantages of its territory, social capital, social institutions and economic agents. A competition state highlights certain 'Schumpeterian' characteristics, 'because of its concern with technological change, innovation and enterprise and its attempt to develop techniques of government and governance to these ends' (Jessop 2002: 96). For Schumpeter, entrepreneurial innovation can proceed in different ways (Schumpeter 1934: 129–35; Lim 1990): via the introduction of a new good or a new quality of a good, via the introduction of a new method of production, via the opening of a new market, via the conquest of a new source of supply of raw materials or semi-finished goods, or via the implementation of the new organization of an industry.

Schumpeter himself leaves the politico-economic circumstances that work to boost certain sciences and technologies largely in the dark (Loeppky 2005: 33). Yet his approach is useful to describe certain characteristics of the competition state. It highlights the set of guiding ideas concerning the ways in which society should be transformed in light of a paradigm of innovation and competition. Jessop (2002: 124) identifies certain tendencies in this respect: the emergence of entrepreneurial localities, cities and regions; increased efforts in all three growth poles of the Triad (the United States, the European Union and Japan) to promote their systemic or structural competitiveness on an international, pan-regional and/or supranational basis; and the propagation of a self-image of states as proactively engaged in promoting the competitiveness of their respective economic spaces (including a region, as in the case of the

European Union). The discourse also creates a specific link between the industrial future of advanced industrialized states and a new technology such as nanotechnology.

THE COMPETITIVE ADVANTAGE OF NANOTECHNOLOGY

From the perspective of 'competitiveness', nanotechnology is understood as a technology which is *the* pre-eminent factor for achieving a nation's innovation. Not only does it introduce new goods but it also offers a new quality of goods, it ushers in new methods of production, and it opens up new markets. Last but not least it offers a new source of supply of raw materials. Nanotechnology is preordained as the magic tool leading to the production of ever smaller, faster and more efficient products with an acceptable price-to-performance ratio. This has come to be seen as an increasingly important success factor for many industrial branches in international competition.

Hence, nanotechnology serves as a techno-economic innovation strategy. Thus a dedicated supplement to the US President's budget for 2004 states that 'because nanotechnology is of such critical importance to US competitiveness, both economically and technologically, even at this early stage of development, it is a top priority within the Administration's R&D agenda' (NSET/NSTC 2003: 3). In a similar way, the European Commission argues that:

> advances across a wide range of sectors are being enabled through R&D and innovation in N&N [Nanotechnology and Nanoscience]. These advances can address the needs of citizens and contribute to the Union's competitiveness and sustainable development objectives and many of its policies including public health, employment and occupational safety and health, information society, energy, transport, security and space (European Commission 2005: 2).

The hope that nanotechnology will lead to generic innovation and competitive advantage has triggered a veritable, global nanotechnology race among the industrialized nations to win monopoly control of the expected huge nanotechnology market and a share of the two million nanotechnology workers that are said to be required by the nanotechnology industry (Roco 2003). States play a crucial role in promoting innovative capacities, technical competence and technology transfer. They hope that as many corporations and economic sectors as possible may benefit from the assumed new technological opportunities created by nanotechnology R&D activities. The nanotechnology discourse, combined with the narratives of the nanotechnology race and of a knowledge-based economy, also supports the (re-)construction of the competition state. The competition state has to 'focus upon . . . knowledge-based industrial innovation ("nanomanufacturing"), integration at the macro–micro–nano interface and interdisciplinary ("converging") R&D. Appropriate synergy with the European Strategy on Life Sciences and Biotechnology may also be beneficial' (European Commission 2004a: 8).

All this does not mean that the nanotechnology race is a fact of life all by itself. Rather, the creation of the discourse of a nanotechnology race is the outcome of political practices and struggles in which the actors in the nanotechnology race take their positions not on an imaginary starting line, but within a discourse on competitiveness. This discourse in many ways shapes the worldview of these actors, defines their goals and structures their actions. The perception of 'a highly competitive global economy' and the prevailing analysis that only those nations will thrive 'that can compete on high technology and intellectual strength' (Her Majesty's Government 2005: 1) supports the discourse of the nanotechnology race.

NANOTECHNOLOGY AS A HEGEMONIC PROJECT

The *nano-hype*, then, provides an important pointer to how nanotechnology is part of a larger political strategy and plays an important role in its political contextualization. Both scientists and politicians promise revolutionary breakthroughs generated by nanotechnology: new ways of detection and treatment of diseases, in drug development, in the monitoring and protection of the environment (e.g. water decontamination), in the production and storage of energy, or in enhanced information and communication technologies. In their view, nanotechnology will enable complex structures to be built as small as an electronic circuit or as large as an aeroplane but with much stronger and lighter material (Royal Society/Royal Academy of Engineering 2004; Department of Trade and Industry 2002). Nanotechnology can be understood as an all-embracing technology, including fields such as nanomaterials (e.g. nanoparticles, nanotubes, fullerene, nanosurfaces), nanobiotechnology, DNA nanotechnology, nanomedicine, nanoelectronics, nanotoxicology, and so on.

To understand the promise of nanotechnology hype, it is also necessary to take into account the most utopian expectations concerning future applications of nanotechnology. According to these visions, the most promising applications will stem from processes called 'self-assembly' or 'molecular manufacturing'. Self-assembly refers to the tendency that some materials are spontaneously 'able' to arrange themselves into ordered structures (Antón et al. 2001). The aspiration is to build desired structures from atomic scratch. Not only is the idea to manufacture individual particles with useful properties, but also to manufacture complex and useful structures made from multiple molecules. Hence, the desired outcome of nanotechnology is the manipulation and assembly of nanoscale particles into supramolecular constructions and even larger structures. Some scientists believe that one day, molecular manufacturing will be possible by controlling atomic positioning so precisely that any object of which the atomic composition is known can be assembled from its basic units (Drexler 1986).

Thus nanotechnology is perceived as a universal technology with the ability to solve the world's most pressing problems: the provision of clean water worldwide, the satisfaction of global energy needs (and with 'clean' solutions at that), the maximization of agricultural productivity, the creation of new jobs, and so on and so forth. Hence, nanotechnology can be seen as a comprehensive innovation strategy – a strategy that offers a technological solution for socio-political problems. This strategy is intimately connected with the emerging narrative of a nanotechnology industry and the fantastic expectations surrounding the nanotechnology market. They all construct the narrative of a technology that will bring wealth to the people and at the same time serve as a competitive advantage in the global struggle for market shares. It follows that nanotechnology can therefore not be reduced to a definite technology or method, nor even to an array of applications or a research field. It rather has to be understood as an encompassing hegemonic project or, more precisely, as different political projects that are kept together only by the term 'nanotechnology' itself. Nanotechnology, as an ensemble of different technologies *and* as a hegemonic project, potentially changes the material livelihoods of many people (Wullweber 2006: 106–12). However, there is no *one coherent strategy* that we can ascribe to a certain group supposedly guiding the nanotech project. Quite the contrary, there are different interests involved and, to a certain extent, also conflicting strategies engaged in competition with each other.

For a political analysis the question arises why certain hegemonic projects are able to prevail. With regard to nanotechnology, its success as a hegemonic formula would require that nanotechnology becomes widely accepted as a technology producing wealth for society. For Gramsci hegemony means the ability of certain political groups to pursue their interests in ways that lead other political groups and the people in society at large to regard these interests as common or general interests. Hegemony in that sense is understood as the active consent of the ruled (Gramsci 1971: 180–82). Neo-Gramscian approaches to international political economy in turn have introduced a concept of power that primarily rests on the ability to universalize the particular interests of a group as a socio-economic and political structure. A certain group is hegemonic, rather than just dominant, if it succeeds in securing approval for its authority among members of other social groups. Of course the ruling groups have to be responsive, at least to a certain degree, to the respective interests of other groups as well. This can be achieved by taking into account the interests of other groups in the formative processes of political institutionalization. These interests have to be merged, so that they become equated with the institutions as such (Cox 1996: 99–100).

From a post-structuralist point of view, the concepts of discourse and hegemony are inextricably linked and mutually conditioned. Hegemonic practice shapes discourse, which in turn provides the conditions of possibility for hegemonic articulation (Laclau and Mouffe 1985). Framed like this, hegemony is a type of social relation. It can be described as the widening of a particular discourse to give it the form of a socio-political and economic project pointing towards a horizon of social orientation and action. The ambit and the limit of a particular discourse-formation are constituted by the exclusion of competing social practices and truth claims, and this exclusion of alternative practices is a substantial element of hegemonic practices. To be successful, that is, to become hegemonic, a socio-political project has to be articulated in relation to the common good. Since the common good only exists as an imaginary common good, and hence as an empty space, there are only particular interests, which are engaged in the attempt to try to occupy this space through strategic articulations (Jessop 2007: 11). Thus, a hegemonic project has to be articulated in a specific way: for it to become a reality, a multiplicity of subjects, actors and relevant social forces must base their actions on the assumption that implementation of the project is a prerequisite to achieve the common good (Wullweber 2014b).

Besides its embeddedness in global political economy structures, the success of a hegemonic project therefore depends heavily on its public acceptance. Indeed, 'public trust and acceptance of nanotechnology will be crucial for its long-term development' (European Commission 2004a: 19). In the 2000s, the majority of people in the advanced industrialized states did not have much knowledge about nanotechnology (and still today, public knowledge about nanotechnology remains limited). This poses a problem for protagonists of nanotechnology, because 'without a serious communication effort, nanotechnology innovations could face an unjust negative public reception' (European Commission 2004a: 19). Accordingly, in many countries that run nanotechnology programmes, advocates of nanotechnology have initiated public debates, because 'an open public dialogue with citizens and consumers is absolutely necessary as a basis for an objective judgement on nanotechnology and to avoid baseless fears' (Luther 2004: 94). Apparently, the overall goal of all these programmes is not to discuss possible problems but to achieve acceptance for nanotechnological development. It is not the risk of nanotechnology that is at stake, but its 'smooth' development (Wullweber 2010: 233–98).

HIGH-TECHNOLOGY MARKET, KNOWLEDGE-BASED ECONOMY

The nanotechnology project as we see it is supported by different strategies. One is the narrative of the nanotechnology market, others are the knowledge-based economy and the nanotechnology race. Between 1997 and 2006, governments' investment in nanotech R&D worldwide increased more than tenfold from US$432 million to about US$4681 million a year (Roco 2007: 30). In 2007, industry and governments invested an estimated US$13.9 billion in nanotech R&D worldwide. Global nanotechnology funding for 2010 is said to have reached approximately US$17.8 billion, with corporate investment (US$9.6 billion) accounting for a majority of funding for the first time (Sargent 2013: 1).

Coherent nanotechnology policy strategies have been developed, for example, in the USA, Japan, South Korea, Germany, Taiwan, China, Australia, Canada and by the European Commission. In 2010, more than sixty countries supported nanotechnology programmes. The most extensive and comprehensive programme is the US National Nanotechnology Initiative (NNI). From 2001 to 2013, the US government has funded nanotechnology research with approximately US$17.9 billion (Sargent 2013: 1). In 1999 the White House Office of Science and Technology Policy decided to make the development of nanotechnology a national priority; in 2000, NNI was launched with a press release entitled: 'Leading to the next Industrial Revolution' (The White House 2000). At first there were six participating agencies in the NNI: the Department of Defense, the Department of Energy, the National Science Foundation, the National Institute of Health, the National Institute of Standard and Technology and the National Aeronautics and Space Administration. Later on, the network expanded rapidly (see Table 3.1).

With every year NNI's budget increased by between 35 and 50 per cent. The proposed NNI budget for the fiscal year 2012 amounted to US$1.857 billion (NSTC/NSET 2013). Besides the Department of Health and Human Services, the National Science Foundation, and the Department of Energy, the Department of Defense was one of the most important departments involved in nanotechnology research (US$425 million in

Table 3.1 Most important NNI R&D institutions and networks

Name	Institution
NATIONAL SCIENCE FOUNDATION – 9 Networks	
National Nanofabrication Infrastructure Network (NNIN) – 13 nodes (user facilities)	Cornell University – central node
Network for Computational Nanotechnology (NCN) – 7 nodes (user facilities)	Purdue University – central node
National Nanomanufacturing Network (NNN)	University of Mass., Amherst – central node
Nanotechnology in Society Network (NSN)	ASU– central node
Nanoscale Center for Learning and Teaching (NCLT)	Northwestern University – main node
Nanoscale Informal Science Education (NISE)	Museum of Science Boston
Nanoscale Science and Engineering Centers (NSEC)	University of Columbia
Materials Science and Engineering Centers (MRSECs)	Distributed
Center for Environmental Implications of Nanotechnology (CEIN)	Distributed
DEPARTMENT OF ENERGY	
Center for Functional Nanomaterials	Brookhaven National Laboratory
Center for Integrated Nanotechnologies	Sandia NL and Los Alamos NL
Center for Nanophase Materials Sciences	Oak Ridge National Laboratory
Center for Nanoscale Materials	Argonne National Laboratory
Center for Molecular Foundry	Lawrence Berkeley National Laboratory
NATIONAL INSTITUTE OF HEALTH	
NHLBI Program of Excellence in Nanotechnology	Four centres
Nanomedicine Development Centers	Eight centres
Centers of Cancer Nanotechnology Excellence	Eight centres
Nanotechnology Characterization Laboratory (user facilities)	NCI Frederick
NATIONAL INSTITUTE OF STANDARDS AND TECHNOLOGY	
Center for Nanoscale Science and Technology	NIST Gaithersburg

Source: Roco 2008: 239.

2011). In terms of global top ten governmental nanotechnology spending in 2010, the United States is still leading the race, followed by Japan, Russia, Germany, France, China, South Korea, the United Kingdom, the Netherlands and Canada. In relation to the percentage by country of worldwide citations for nanotechnology articles in Web of Science the USA is followed by China, Germany and Japan. Regarding priority patent applications the ranking is almost the same.

If popular acceptance remains uncertain, economic interest in nanotechnology is not automatically given either. After years of basic research it is still unclear whether nanotechnology will actually produce substantial goods for the market. In spite of this there are countless studies that assess the possible impact of nanotechnology for future markets. Some market analysts argue that the simple reduction of the microstructure in already existing materials could lead to a whole set of new applications (see also Gromyko, this volume). Nanotechnology is perceived as a technology that has incentives for practically all sciences, and the increasing proliferation of classic disciplines, fields of technology and branches of the economy, makes nanotechnology interesting for industry and governments alike.

The convergence of different technologies, methods and research approaches at the nanoscale entails that investment in nanotech R&D is not restricted to a certain branch of industry either. Here the example of the life sciences industry is illuminating: it played such a crucial part in the 1990s because it was knowledge-based, generating and appropriating the results of scientific research. Today, this role is being complemented and has been taken over, at least partly, by nanotechnology. Immense expectations regarding the new technology are evoking an image of vast future markets. Yet this is only achievable if industry branches move up the technological ladder and align their R&D policies with the nanoscale. For this reason, all advanced industrialized countries, almost all Fortune 500 companies and two-thirds of the companies in the Dow Jones Industrial Average, are active in nanotech research, development and investment in some way.

At the same time, critical voices express concern about the social impact of nanotechnology. Thus the Canadian Action Group on Erosion, Technology and Concentration (ETC) warns that 'with the depth and energy of a tsunami, nanotech will have a powerful impact on every industrial sector. Every commodity used in industry today, including food, will potentially be displaced' (ETC 2005a: 7). ETC also argues that the significance of nanotechnology resides in the fusion of the basic units of transformative technologies – bits, atoms, neurons and genes, so they call it BANG. The bit is for the operative unit in information science; the atom in nanotechnology; the neurons in cognitive science; and genes in biotech (ETC 2003a).

Since technological competence in nanotechnology is allegedly a necessary condition for competing successfully in the markets of the future, with better procedures and products, a view has become hegemonic that does not allow any alternative to the development of nanotechnology. Those nations which fall behind in this development will inevitably miss the chance to enter these markets too. Nanotechnology in this way becomes a synonym for innovation within competition states. As nanomaterials and processes are applicable to many manufactured goods, and in almost all sectors of industry, control and ownership of nanotechnology is deemed decisive for virtually all governments and for the competitiveness of industry, whether it concerns attracting initial investment or ensuring future revenues. With certain patents it would be possible to control complete chains of production. Nanotechnology is the first research field in which the basic ideas and applications are being patented right from the outset: the most fundamental concepts and components of nanotechnology 'are either already patented or may well end up being patented' (ETC 2005b: 10). Hence, intellectual property rights are a key element in both the knowledge-based economy and the global competitive struggle for global market shares, since 'companies that hold pioneering patents could potentially put up tolls on entire industries' (Regalado 2004: 1). The 'race' for the nanotechnology patent 'gold rush' (ETC 2003b: 24) has started among transnational corporations, leading academic labs, start-ups and universities.

Within a competition state, the factor 'knowledge' has generally become more important for international competitiveness. As the EU Commission writes, 'To create wealth and new employment in a globalised market and within a knowledge-based economy, the competitive production of new knowledge is essential' (European Commission 2004a: 9). The narrative of the 'knowledge-based economy' (Jessop 2002: 96) constitutes an important discourse in the context of the competition state, supporting and articulating contemporary processes of primitive accumulation. The knowledge-based economy is widely taken for granted as a focal point of economic strategies, flagship projects and hegemonic visions.

Clearly the nanotechnology project fits seamlessly within the narrative of knowledge generation and the knowledge-based economy in policy speeches, documents and programmes. Philippe Busquin, then European Commissioner for Research, thus states that 'nanotechnology provides a golden opportunity for the creation of new knowledge-based enterprises and has a "revolutionary" potential that can open up new production routes' (European Commission 2004a: 1). In the same vein the EU Commission declares on its research homepage: 'Nanosciences and nanotechnologies are crucial to the establishment of a knowledge-based EU society and economy' (European Commission 2004b). According to this logic, 'Europe must . . . transform its world-class R&D in N&N [Nanosciences and Nanotechnologies] into useful wealth-generating products in line with the actions for growth and jobs' (European Commission 2005: 2). Together these narratives frame nanotechnology as a competitive advantage for the industrialized countries.

CONCLUSION

Today high-technology policies are overwhelmingly characterized by an accelerating commercialization. From this perspective, nanotechnology is *the* pre-eminent factor for achieving innovation and competitive advantages. It introduces new goods and offers a new quality of goods, it ushers in new methods of production, it opens up new markets, and it offers a new source of supply of raw materials. Instead of a definite technology, nanotechnology denotes an encompassing hegemonic innovation project. However, the adoption of new technologies is not an automatic, self-evident process. Rather, it is embedded in social relations and has to be backed by political measures. Nanotechnology has to be embedded in modified governance structures, which have materialized in the political form of the competition state. For this new mode of socio-economic regulation the consent of the people will be required. Therefore, many governments try to invoke different discursive elements in order to strengthen the perception that nanotechnology is indispensable for an economically viable society.

The analysis of the nanotechnology project in this chapter presupposes that we see it in the context of power struggles and interests, just as contingent and accidental events must be taken into account as constitutive of particular routes of technological development. This implies a critique of the notion that technological development is a matter of the inevitable and automatic progress of science, as well as challenging the assumed progressive character of scientific development. Neither the 'truth' of nanotechnology as the technology of the twenty-first century, nor the policy problem of 'nanotechnological risks', or again, the 'high-technology gap', are simply given. Rather, the question is what constitutes 'high-technology', whose interest is served by this kind of framing, and what social forces can be seen trying to articulate such tropes. That is why science and political power must be conceptualized as intimately interconnected phenomena, and the existence of stable boundaries between economy, politics and science questioned.

The perspective outlined in this chapter makes it possible to delineate political interests and strategies within the process of nanotechnology development. Likewise we may distinguish the different discourses and policy strategies that have been associated with nanotechnology. While the discourse of international competition is fostered through the trope of an ongoing nanotechnology race, nanotechnology itself is presented as one of the most important strategies of innovation to win the battle for global market shares. The success of the nanotechnology project derives from an alignment with the competition state in general and the specific arenas of the knowledge-based economy, the nanotechnology race and the immense future markets for nanotechnology. These elements are mutually reinforcing. In this light, the nanotechnology project encompasses not just an array of policies reshaping research and development policies. Even more importantly, these are being instrumentalized to serve the process of reconstructing the nation-state into a competition state. There is no need to emphasize here that such a reconstruction of the state will necessarily be a conflict-ridden process of which the outcome is uncertain.

4. The political economy of global labour arbitrage

Raúl Delgado Wise and David T. Martin

INTRODUCTION

The strategy of global labour arbitrage, pursued by the large transnational corporations, has become a major component in the neoliberal restructuring of the international political economy. The neoliberal era has opened a new phase in the history of contemporary capitalism and imperial domination, based on the exploitation of cheap, flexible labour, principally from the Global South. Facilitated by the revolution in information and communication technologies, the massive expansion of global reserve army of labour – particularly as a consequence of the dismantling of the former Soviet Union and the incorporation of China into the global capitalist labour market – and the imposition of structural adjustment programmes on the Global South, monopoly capital has found an easy, and yet apparently inexhaustible, source of extraordinary profits: the polarization and intensification of wage differentials along the North–South axis.

The purpose of this chapter is twofold. First, to disentangle the theoretical and practical foundations for understanding global labour arbitrage from a Marxist political economy perspective; and second, to analyse some of its main implications in shaping the context of neoliberal globalization. These include: (a) its relevance in the configuration of global networks of production as a predominant corporate strategy; (b) its dialectical relationship with the intensification of uneven development; (c) its crucial role in the emergence of a new international division of labour and the concomitant advent of novel modalities of unequal exchange; and (d) its relevance for reframing the labour question today.

WHAT IS GLOBAL LABOUR ARBITRAGE?

For the purposes of our analysis, it is necessary to remember that in the capitalist mode of production, the worker is dispossessed of the means of production and subsistence, and labour power is converted into a commodity. However, labour is not just another commodity; it has the capacity to create value, and, through unequal exchange, uniquely enables the owner of the means of production, the capitalist, to appropriate a significant part of the value generated by the worker in the production process: surplus value. The secret to this unequal exchange, the most fundamental in capitalism, is that workers, in exchange for the value they generate (i.e. the product of their labour), receive a wage that equals the cost of reproduction of labour power, or as Marx puts it, 'the value of the necessaries required to produce, develop, maintain, and perpetuate the labouring power' (Marx 1969: 17). This fundamental premise to the analysis of capitalism is presented by Marx in the first volume of *Capital* (1867) on a level of abstraction that does not yet take into account modifying conditions, the level of *capital in general* (Moseley 1995). In the first section of Chapter 17 of *Capital*, Marx states:

> The value of labour-power is determined by the value of the necessaries of life habitually required by the average labourer. The quantity of these necessaries is known at any given epoch of a given society, and can therefore be treated as a constant magnitude. What changes is the value of this quantity. There are, besides, two other factors that enter into the determination of the value of labour-power. One, the expenses of developing that power, which expenses vary with the mode of production; the other, its natural diversity, the difference between the labour-power of men and women, of children and adults. The employment of these different sorts of labour-power, an employment which is, in its turn, made necessary by the mode of production, makes a great difference in the cost of maintaining the family of the labourer, and in the value of the labour-power of the adult male. Both these factors, however, are excluded in the following investigation (Marx 1990: 362).

To understand the notion of labour arbitrage, it is necessary to transcend this level of abstraction and to remember that wages, or the cost of reproduction of labour power, have two dimensions: one, material and the other, cultural; and that these are defined historically and nationally, depending on the type of labour in question. In his text, *Value, Price and Profit*, Marx notes: 'Besides this mere physical element, the value of labour is in every country determined to by a *traditional standard of life*. It is not merely the physical life, but it is the satisfaction of certain wants springing from the social conditions in which people are placed and reared up' (1969: 27). In the wage differences between countries and within them, an important element emphasized by Marx is the wage pressure exerted by the reserve army of labour. Another point highlighted by Marx, which reinforces the recognition of wage differentials between countries is the following: 'By comparing the standard wages or values of labour in different countries, and by comparing them in different historical epochs of the same country, you will find that the value of labour itself is not fixed

Table 4.1 Labour cost differentials

Average compensation per hour for production workers in US dollars	
Country	2009
Indonesia	$0.70
China	$1.27
India	$1.68
Thailand	$2.78
Mexico	$3.28
Czech Republic	$3.28
South Korea	$5.47
Spain	$13.01
France	$14.29
United Kingdom	$20.01
Canada	$21.38
Japan	$22.61
United States	$25.34
Germany	$34.46

Source: Boston Consulting Group.

but variable, even supposing the values of all other commodities remain constant' (1969: 28). Thus, the costs of subsistence and reproduction vary widely depending on historical, cultural and national conditions, and therefore wages between countries can vary widely as well.

What is important to emphasize here is that throughout the long history of capitalism, and in particular with the advent of imperialism in the advanced stage of capitalism, the asymmetries between countries – as a result of the tendency toward uneven development inherent in this mode of production – tend to grow and expand. Under neoliberalism, this trend, as discussed below, is exacerbated to new heights. In turn, the explosive growth in the global reserve army of labour and its unequal spatial distribution have generated and deepened the enormous wage differentials between countries, as shown in Table 4.1.

This situation, coupled with favourable technological, demographic, economic and political conditions, has enabled large transnational corporations to shift a significant part of their production, trade, finance and other services to peripheral regions of the global economy to take advantage of extreme wage differentials. In essence, this is a new route for imperial expansion, which continues to widen and deepen asymmetries between both countries and regions, as well as polarizing social inequalities on a global scale.

In addition, this strategy not only has consequences for the working class of the peripheral countries, but also has had a wider impact on the working class in general. In effect,

> As developing nations provide an increasingly skilled workforce, developed nations' ability to differentiate themselves is dissolving, and the companies operating in those countries no longer need to pay their workers a premium. The most widespread and long lasting impact of the global labour arbitrage is the decline of real wages in developed nations (Hansen 2005: 7).

Thus, the massive expansion of the global reserve army of labour through the incorporation of labour forces in the former socialist countries and the imposition of structural adjustment in the Global South has combined with the increasingly polarized social inequalities on a global scale as well as the variations of wages due to historical, cultural and national standards of life to produce highly profitable conditions for the transnational corporate strategy of global labour arbitrage.

IMPERIALISM TODAY: THE RESTRUCTURING OF MONOPOLY CAPITAL

While the monopoly position of the labour aristocracy in the Global North has been eroded in the neoliberal era, the commanding heights of global capitalism remained solidly entrenched there with increasing monopolization of finance, production, services and trade, leaving every major global industry to be dominated by a handful of large transnational corporations. In the expansion of their operations, the agents of corporate, or monopoly, capitalism have created a global network and process of production, finance, distribution and investment that has allowed them to seize the strategic and profitable segments of peripheral economies and appropriate the economic surplus produced at enormous social and environmental costs. Thus, while labour faced increasing global competition, it also confronted an increasingly centralized and concentrated capital, fundamentally altering the balance of class power in the favour of capital. In the international political economy, monopoly capital has become, more than ever, the central player. Through mega-mergers and strategic alliances, this fraction of capital has reached unparalleled levels of concentration and centralization: the top five hundred largest transnational corporations now concentrate between 35–40 per cent of world income (Foster et al. 2011a). More important is the fact that, in the neoliberal era, monopoly capital has undergone a profound restructuring process rooted in the 'comparative advantage' provided by global labour arbitrage. This process has been characterized by:

- *Global networks of monopoly capital* created by a restructuring strategy led by the large transnational corporations, which through outsourcing operations and subcontracting chains extend parts of their productive, commercial, financial and service processes to the Global South in search of abundant and cheap labour as well as the extraction of natural resources. This strategy is exemplified by the export platforms that operate as enclave economies in peripheral countries. This turn toward global production chains has been impressive: 'the top one hundred global corporations had shifted their production more decisively to their foreign affiliates [mainly in the South], which now account for close to 60 per cent of their total assets and employment and more than 60 per cent of their global sales' (UNCTAD 2010). This represents a 'new "nomadism" [that] has emerged within the system of global production, with locational decisions determined largely by where labour is cheapest' (Foster et al. 2011a: 18). Moreover, an outstanding feature of contemporary global capitalism is the degree of network articulation and integration with the operations of large transnational corporations dominating international trade: at least 40 per cent of all global trade is associated with outsourcing operations, including subcontracting and intra-firm trade (Andreff 2009), an estimated 85 million workers are directly employed in assembly plants in the Global South, and over 3500 export processing zones have been established in 130 countries (McKinsey Global Institute 2012). This restructuring strategy has transformed the global geography of production to the point that now most of the world's industrial employment (over 70 per cent) is located in the Global South (Foster et al. 2011b).
- *The restructuring of innovation systems* involves the implementation of mechanisms such as outsourcing the scientific and technological innovation process (including offshore), which allows transnational corporations to benefit from the research of scientists from the Global South. This restructuring reduces labour costs, transfers risks and responsibilities, and capitalizes on the advantages of controlling the patent process. Four over-arching aspects characterize this restructuring process:
  a) the increasing *internationalization and fragmentation of research and development activities*. In contrast to the traditional innovation processes occurring 'behind closed doors' in research and development departments internal to large transnational corporations, this trend is known as *open innovation*. This denotes the sharing of knowledge-intensive corporate functions within a growing network of external partners, such as suppliers,

clients, subcontractors, universities, etc. to create 'ecosystems' of innovation (OECD 2008);

b) the creation of scientific cities – such as Silicon Valley in the United States and the new 'Silicon Valleys' established in peripheral or emerging regions, principally in Asia – where collective synergies are created to accelerate innovation processes (Sturgeon 2003);

c) the development of *new methods of controlling research agendas* (through venture capital, partnerships and subcontracting, among others) and *appropriating the products of scientific endeavours* (through the acquisition of patents) by large transnational corporations; and

d) the rapidly expanding highly skilled workforce, particularly in the areas of science and engineering, in the Global South is being tapped by TNCs for research and development in peripheral countries through recruitment via partnerships, outsourcing and offshoring (Battelle 2012). In fact, this spatial restructuring of R&D has crystallized into a *new geography of innovation*, in which, following the pattern of industrial production, R&D is shifting to peripheral economies. In fact, this trend can also be conceived of as a higher stage in the development of the global networks of monopoly capital, as the New International Division of Labour moves up the value-added chain to R&D and monopoly capital captures the productivity and knowledge of a highly skilled workforce in the Global South.

Closely related to these changes in the international political economy – the increasing concentration and integration of global networks of monopoly capital, and the rise of a new geography of innovation and 'scientific maquiladoras' – are the following trajectories of contemporary capitalism (Foster et al. 2011a; Gallagher and Zarsky 2007):

- *Financialization* refers to the ascendancy of finance capital over other fractions of capital (Bello 2005: 101). Finance capital began this ascendancy with the onset of an overproduction crisis in the late 1960s, when German and Japanese capital recovered from the devastation of World War II and began to compete with US capital on world markets (Brenner 2002). With the lack of profitable investment in production, capital began shifting into financial speculation. Another response to the overproduction crisis was the reduction of labour costs through global labour arbitrage. The centripetal force of centralization of command and control through management and finance countered the centrifugal force of geographic dispersion of production. According to Saskia Sassen, 'the spatial dispersal of economic activity made possible by the [information and communications technology revolution] contributes to an expansion of territorially centralized functions, if this dispersal is to take place under the continuing concentration in corporate control, ownership, and profit appropriation that characterizes the current economic system' (Sassen 2007: 108).

Moreover, with the downward pressure on real wages through global labour arbitrage, a finance-led debt explosion sustained purchasing power for the realization of production. The end result has been the financialization of the capitalist class, of industrial capital, and of corporate profits (Foster 2010).

- The *environmental degradation and the ecological crisis* have intensified due to the continuing over-consumption of the world's natural resources and the expansion of carbon-based industrial production. The increasing urbanization and industrialization in Asia, particularly China, has increased demand for raw materials, which, combined with the shift towards transforming commodities from a hedge asset to a speculative asset for finance capital, has created a commodities boom since 2002. High prices for commodities have driven the exploration for and production of non-renewable natural resources into remote geographies, deeper into the oceans and the jungles, in the process exacerbating social conflicts over land and water (Veltmeyer 2013). This new extractivism has worsened environmental degradation, not only through an expanded geography of destruction, but also by global extractive capital's strategy of environmental regulatory arbitrage (Xing and Kolstad 2002). Moreover, despite 25 years of increasingly dire warnings from the Intergovernmental Panel on Climate Change, the global consumption of fossil fuels continues to rise, 'triggering a cascade of cataclysmic changes that include extreme heat-waves, declining global food stocks and a sea-level rise affecting hundreds of millions of people' (World Bank 2012a: xvii). Given that the revenues of some of the world's most powerful and profitable transnational corporations depend on fossil fuel consumption, this pattern is likely to continue, setting the world on the path toward a deepening ecological crisis.

The cumulative effect is that neoliberal capitalism is facing a profound multi-dimensional crisis (e.g. financial, economic, social, ecological crises) that undermines the main sources of wealth creation – labour and nature – to the point that it can be characterized as a civilizational crisis with a potentially catastrophic outcome. It is crucial to realize that it demands both engaging in a radical social transformation process as well as constructing a social transformation agent capable of confronting the current power structure. Unfortunately, this power structure has responded to this multidimensional crisis with desperate attempts to maintain this unsustainable and unstable form of capitalism.

THE MUSHROOMING OF UNEQUAL DEVELOPMENT AND THE EMERGENCE OF A NEW MODE OF UNEQUAL EXCHANGE

A major and inescapable feature of the current form of capitalism, neoliberal globalization, is *unequal development*. The global and national dynamics of capitalist development, the international division of labour, the imperialist system of international power relations, and the conflicts that surround the capital–labour relation and the dynamics of extractivist capital have made economic, social, political and cultural polarization more extreme between geographical spaces and social classes than ever before in human history. A conspicuous result of this development is the disproportionate concentration of capital, power and wealth in the hands of a small elite within the capitalist class. Nowadays the richest one per cent of the world's population concentrate 40 per cent of total global assets (Davies et al. 2008). Moreover, 'from 1970 to 2009, the per capita GDP of developing countries (excluding China) averaged a mere 6.3 per cent of the per capita GDP of the G8 countries' (Foster et al. 2011a).

In fostering the above trend, global labour arbitrage has become a key pillar of the new global architecture. As previously mentioned, arbitrage refers to the advantage of pursuing lower wages abroad. This allows capital to 'earn' enormous monopolistic returns, or imperial rents, by taking advantage of the relative immobility of labour and the existence of subsistence (and below) wages in much of the Global South, a differential documented in Table 4.1. Through the mechanism of global labour arbitrage, social and geographic asymmetries are reproduced on a global scale. Social inequalities are one of the most distressing aspects of this process, given the unprecedented concentration of capital, power and wealth in a few hands while a growing segment of the population suffers poverty, exploitation and exclusion. Increasing disparities are also expressed, ever more strongly, in terms of racial, ethnic and gender relations; reduced access to production and employment; a sharp decline in living and working conditions; and the progressive dismantling of social safety nets.

A fundamental mechanism in the promotion of this new global architecture and its underlying trend toward unequal development has been the implementation of *structural adjustment programmes* in much of the Global South and former socialist economies. These programmes have been the vehicle for disarticulating the economic apparatus in the periphery and its re-articulation to serve the needs of core capitalist economies, under sharply asymmetric and subordinated conditions. In particular, these programmes served the needs of capital through the export of labour in its two modalities, indirect and direct, which are key to conceptualizing this process. On the one hand, the indirect, or disembodied, export of labour is associated with the configuration of global networks of monopoly capital through outsourcing, offshoring and subcontracting operations to the Global South, as described in the previous section (Delgado Wise and Márquez 2007; Delgado Wise and Cypher 2007). In this case, the main input of domestic origin in the exported commodities is the labour used in the assembly, service or commercial process. On the other hand, the *direct* export of labour refers to international labour migration, mainly composed of South to North and South to South flows. In fact, 156 million of the existing 214 million migrants, or 72 per cent, come from the periphery (World Bank 2011).

It is crucial to realize that the export of the workforce, that is the export of the most critical commodity characterizing the capitalist mode of production, labour power, underlies the materialization of a *new international division of labour* along the South–North axis. This, in turn, implies the advent of new and extreme modalities of unequal exchange. Regardless of the centrality that the concept of unequal exchange had in past decades in explaining the dynamics of unequal development, the nature of the ties between developed countries and emergent or peripheral countries (as conceived by the Economic Commission for Latin America, ECLAC, as well as among dependency theorists) demands its inclusion in the analysis of contemporary capitalism. It is important to keep in mind that most of the debate on unequal exchange was and remains limited to an analysis of the international division of labour that places the periphery in the role of source for raw materials and the developed countries as the providers of industrialized goods. And although this division remains relevant for a significant number of peripheral countries, it has stopped being exclusively a feature of new North–South relations. Some recently-industrialized peripheral countries – principally in Asia – ever more frequently play the role of providers of industrialized goods. Even more important is the fact that, to this classic mode of unequal exchange, a new factor has been added in the age of neoliberal capitalism, and one that is increasingly taking centre-stage: the direct and indirect export of the labour force.

To enter into the analysis of this factor, with its dual fronts, it is important to note that these mechanisms of unequal exchange are more disadvantageous to the periphery than those of the exchange of raw materials for manufactured goods. On the one hand, the indirect export of the labour force, associated with the participation of peripheral nations in adding value to global commodity chains, carries with it a net transfer of profits abroad. This represents an extreme form of unequal exchange, which implies a transfer abroad of practically the total surplus generated by the labour force employed in the *maquiladoras*, or assembly plants, in the export processing sector. This mechanism, which revives the logic of the export enclave, inhibits any economic growth and development derived from the labour process performed, under the guise of manufactured exports, by the peripheral nation. In fact, its key contribution to the process of national accumulation is limited to a meagre income flow from low wages that, in the best of cases, contributes to a small multiplier effect by way of consumption. Even more, the installation and operation of assembly plants in peripheral countries is usually supported through generous subsidies and tax exemptions, which put the weight of reproducing the labour force on revenue-strapped governments of the Global South, while imposing collateral damage through precarious labour markets and environmental degradation.

Another aspect of the indirect export of labour power, which has begun to gather force in the context of peripheral or emerging countries, is the creation of joint scientific-technological complexes, as we have seen, in the restructuring of innovation systems in some of the more developed countries, with the United States in the lead role. By way of these complexes, which function under subcontracting arrangements, associations or other forms of partnership, intangible benefits are transferred abroad that have a value and a strategic significance beyond the net profits accruing from the *maquila* and assembly plants. We refer to the transfer of knowledge and technical capabilities, which takes the form of competitive advantages and extraordinary profits, from South to North. The knowledge and technical skills that have historically played a central role in the transformation of peripheral economies to developed ones are now captured by the Global North through the new geography of innovation.

On the other hand, the direct export of the labour force, via labour migration, implies a transfer of the anticipated future benefits that arise from the costs of training and social reproduction of the workforce that emigrates. These costs – as the case of Mexico has shown – are not compensated for by the flow of remittances (Delgado Wise et al. 2009). In demographic terms, this results in the transfer of their demographic dividend from the Global South to North – particularly for peripheral countries that are in the advanced stage of the demographic transition, when declining birth rates create a large working age population relative to the pre-working age and retired seniors. Thus, in a profound sense, this transfer implies the loss of the most important resource for capital accumulation in the country of origin: its labour force. Furthermore, the export of the highly skilled labour force exacerbates this problem by seriously reducing the sending country's capacity to innovate for its own benefit and drive its own technology-intensive development projects.

To analyse these new modes of unequal exchange presents theoretical, methodological and empirical challenges, which require changes in the perception and characterization of categories typically used to interpret contemporary capitalism. Without disregarding the significant contributions of ECLAC to advance the understanding of these new modes of unequal exchange (above all in regard to the central role played by scientific and technological progress), it is important to bring to bear Marxist theories of unequal exchange in its dual aspects. In both a strict and a broad sense, these theories provide a solid and fertile conceptual basis upon which to advance the conceptualization of the emergent modes of unequal exchange, implied by the direct and indirect export of the labour force (Emmanuel 1972). On the one hand, unequal exchange, in the strictest sense, places wage differentials (or differentials in surplus value) derived from barriers to population mobility at the centre of the analysis. On the other hand, unequal exchange, in the wider sense, expands those differentials to include value emanating from diverse compositions of capital, such as the differentials arising from scientific and technological progress (*Críticas de la Economía Política* 1979). We take into consideration that the internationalization of capital in the framework of neoliberal globalization seeks incessantly to lower labour costs – including those relating to the highly skilled labour force – whilst maximizing the transfer of surpluses generated from that labour from peripheral to developed countries, which is the purpose in taking advantage of wage differentials in the first place.

THE LABOUR QUESTION TODAY

One of the main engines of neoliberal capitalism, then, is cheap labour. Costs of labour are lowered by any and all means, as capital takes advantage of the massive oversupply of labour, reflected in growing levels of unemployment and precarious employment the world over. With the dismantling of the former Soviet Union, the integration of China and India into the world economy, and the implementation of structural adjustment programmes (including privatizations and labour reforms) in the Global South, the supply of labour available to capital over the last two decades has more than doubled from 1.5 to 3.3 billion, in what Richard Freeman calls the 'Great Doubling' (Freeman 2006). This rapid expansion of the *global reserve army of labour* has occurred most dramatically in the Global South, where 73 per cent of the 'reserve' global workforce can be found (ILO 2008b).

The size of the reserve army of labour is dialectically related to the abysmally low wages and chronic insufficiency of 'decent' employment that characterizes contemporary capitalism, since this global oversupply of labour has scaled down the global wage structure and increased the overall precariousness of labour. According to estimates of the International Labour Organization (ILO), the number of workers in conditions of labour insecurity rose to 1.5 billion in 2009 – encompassing more than half of the world's labour force – with 630 million receiving a salary of less than US$2 per day and nearly half of those finding themselves in situations of extreme poverty, while the global number of unemployed continues to rise (ILO 2011). This, in turn, has led to growing structural pressures to emigrate internally and/or internationally under conditions of extreme vulnerability.

Neoliberal capitalism has restructured labour markets and reconfigured the global working class in the following ways (Márquez and Delgado Wise 2011a):

- *The creation of a dispersed and vulnerable proletariat available to the global networks of monopoly capital.* The social and productive fabric of the TNCs covers strategic and profitable economic sectors, such as agriculture, mining, industry, services, trade and finance. The neoliberal restructuring of labour markets has dismantled labour protection and imposed a 'new labour culture' based on competitiveness, while creating a regime of job insecurity characterized by labour flexibility and precariousness. Outsourcing stands out as the main corporate management strategy to cheapen labour costs and thereby generating a permanent threat of layoffs. Business requirements have also led to a new profile of labour: desperate young workers without union experience and willing to work under insecure and poorly paid conditions. The new proletariat is compelled to subject itself to high levels of exploitation in order to access a source of income. This labour becomes increasingly alienated from its sense of class belonging, and its place in the socio-economic and geographic fabric, given the predominance of what resembles abstract forms of capital – that is, global capital that depersonalizes, even more so than in the past, the relationship between capital and labour in the transnational arena. These abstract expressions of capital leave the proletariat without a human referent for their exploiters, only a faceless, mobile and de-territorialized corporate entity that, if necessary, can quickly shift production to other factories. This abstract form of capital undermines the development of a consciousness of what happens in the work process and prevents workers from building long-term relations necessary for cooperation and solidarity when confronting employers; the daily struggle to earn a livelihood occupies their vital energies with little social cohesion.

- *The covert proletarianization of the highly qualified scientific and technological worker.* The large transnational corporations have managed to absorb scientific and technological labour into an innovation system, protected by patents, that generates extraordinary profits for the TNCs. In this way, the fruits of technological progress are directly appropriated by monopoly capital. Scientists and technologists constitute a privileged segment of the working class, and do not conceive of themselves as workers, but, rather, as part of the global ruling class, and even as promoters of social transformation inasmuch as their innovations affect everything from production patterns to the daily lives of ordinary people. This highly qualified workforce has gradually lost, directly or covertly, its relative autonomy and control over the means of knowledge production and the tools of their labour (laboratories, research agendas, etc.). In this sense, scientific and technological labour is subsumed by the large transnational corporations, while researchers' awareness of the work process is progressively lost. One of the strongest forms of scientific and technological labour appropriation and subsumption is that of the disguised proletarianization of this type of worker under forms of outsourcing and offshoring, embedded in the dynamics of the restructuring of innovation systems, as previously described. Given the precariousness of their labour and lack of control over the means of knowledge production, TNCs drive R&D research agendas and appropriate the products of the research.
- *The real or disguised proletarianization of the peasantry.* A global agribusiness system dominated by large transnational corporations controls all stages of the productive, financial and trading processes, leaving practically no room for small-scale agricultural production (cf. Kay, this volume). Like other economic sectors, agribusiness employs subcontracting schemes that degrade peasant autonomy and entail visible, or covert, forms of proletarianization with a high

degree of precariousness. 'Accumulation by dispossession' (Harvey 2007) dismantles the peasant subsistence system and expands the presence of large-scale agribusiness production for export, annihilating political attempts at local food sovereignty, appropriating nature and biodiversity, blocking public resources from being channelled into the peasant sector, and 'freeing' the workforce from the land so that it can, in turn, be employed in precarious and unsafe conditions in manufacturing, trade or services. In order to subsist within the new institutional framework of neoliberal capitalism, peasants are forced to: (i) become a proletariat working for agribusiness, even on lands they might have formerly owned; (ii) migrate to the cities in search of precarious jobs, many of them offered by the large transnational corporations, and in areas such as the *maquiladora* industrial zones; (iii) survive within the ranks of the lumpenproletariat, through black market or criminal activities; or (iv) migrate abroad to work in vulnerable social conditions and in degraded, poorly paid jobs. These processes of overt or covert proletarianization and sub-proletarianization have further exacerbated the dynamics of semi-proletarianization already in place before the neoliberal onslaught. Despite the social decomposition of the peasantry as a subaltern class that lies even below the proletariat, it is worth noting that some of the most visible and consistent anti-globalization movements come precisely from the ranks of the peasantry and indigenous groups (i.e., *Via Campesina*, the Zapatista Army of National Liberation in Mexico, CONEI in Ecuador, and the Landless Workers Movement in Brazil), which demonstrates that many of these groups retain the social and geographic space necessary to develop counter-hegemonic ideologies and bases of resistance (Scott 1992).

- *The semi- and sub-proletarianization of migrant workers.* Neoliberal capitalism has accelerated mechanisms of social exclusion and dispossession. The most evident result of this is the creation of a population that has no means of earning a living and whose livelihood is precarious at best. These social groups are forced to migrate domestically or internationally in order to access any source of income that will enable family subsistence. Migration in this context is far from being a free and voluntary movement; rather, it is a structural imperative. A wide range of social subjects are forced to move from their places of origin: peasants deprived of land or unable to make a living from it; unemployed or poorly paid workers; youths with no employment prospects; professionals without access to social mobility; women lacking access to the labour market; skilled workers with few or no opportunities for work and income. Those who participate in forced migration are placed in relatively more adverse conditions than native counterparts; they become a highly vulnerable proletariat, or sub-proletariat, facing social exclusion, wage discrimination, the lack of social and labour rights, loss of citizenship (or a precarious citizenship status), and if undocumented, criminalization. This massive contingent of the labour force works under conditions of insecurity, vulnerability and considerable risk; as a proletarian subclass, they are often subject to conditions of over-exploitation of labour which hark back to pre-capitalist features of coercion, bordering on new forms of slavery (Márquez and Delgado Wise 2011b; Harrod, and McGrath and Strauss, this volume).

- *The expansion of the reserve army of labour* and with it an increase in new forms of poverty and an underclass of workers without any hope or possibility of any, let alone, decent work; some are even disabled or incapacitated through the process of capital accumulation and economic growth. These surplus workers suffer from the worst living and employment conditions, and are found in the lowest social strata; they constitute a highly degraded and large segment of the global population. To survive, the poorest of the poor work on the margins of society and, often, on the margins of legality, participating in petty crime, organized crime, human trafficking and prostitution. They also carry out activities in public spaces, working as mendicants, shoe-shiners, announcers, vendors and street musicians, among many other things. This group also includes door-to-door vendors and informal workers. The dysfunctional nature of their work, their detachment from the institutional framework and the discrimination they endure prevent these groups from developing a class identity or interacting openly with power, capital or other categories of the proletariat.
- *The subordination and resistance of the intellectual worker*. This sector of the intelligentsia, one that enjoys greater visibility and privileges, is bound to intellectually support the expansion of large transnational corporations and the powers behind them. Critical thinking is seen as *passé* or is associated with the populist defence of irrelevant social sectors. There is a drive to impose a singular form of thought regarding the neoliberal project: the free market, electoral democracy and the so-called end of history (i.e., the elimination of alternatives) pervade various fields of academia, the media, parliaments, governments and political parties, until they eventually inoculate the popular mind or construct a 'common sense'. The educational system is pressured into privatization or, at least, the commodification

of its services. According to this rationale, the teaching and learning process is conceived as skill formation, for the student has to dispense with ethical and humanistic concerns and become human capital ready to enter and compete in the labour market. For this reason, curricula are moulded according to the needs of employers rather than to social needs. In line with this pseudo-intellectual trend, the conformism imposed by dominant modes of thought, and its attachment to corporate interests and power elites, portrays critical thinking as banal, and unproductive. In contrast, critical thought cultivated by artists, scientists, politicians, journalists, researchers and academics has been a source of creation and social innovation. The development of knowledge and ideas meant to understand the contemporary world and the detection of possibilities of transformation is the primary task of this sector, which historically has engendered an interest sympathetic to those of the subordinate classes, resistance movements and social struggles.

Under the circumstances fostered by neoliberal capitalism, then, working conditions are eroding the social wage, whilst the social welfare system excludes the subordinate classes from accessing basic social needs to such a degree that wages no longer ensure subsistence. This engenders a trajectory of capitalist development tending towards the impoverishment and/or super-exploitation of labour. The violation of basic labour and human rights creates a situation of *systemic violence* and *human insecurity* affecting the majority of the world's population, whereby the Universal Declaration of Human Rights has been evidently and flagrantly infringed by the economic and political forces of neoliberal globalization.

CONCLUDING REMARKS

The notion of global labour arbitrage provides a vital tool for understanding and exploring the nature of contemporary capitalism (i.e., neoliberal globalization). This notion relies on basic categories for comprehending capitalism from the perspective of Marxist political economy, beginning with the capital–labour relation and the value of labour power, particularly in surplus generation. By descending from the abstract to the concrete in its dialectical conception, global labour arbitrage deepens our understanding of how capital creates its own geography, by taking advantage and reproducing the wage differentials arising from historical, social, political, economic and cultural contexts, and from the dynamics of unequal development inherent to capitalism. Such has been, at its root, the history of imperialism, which in its current phase, the neoliberal one, is characterized, among other things, by a brutal and uncompromising attack on the living and working conditions of the working class on a global scale. This process, marked by an intensification of asymmetries between countries and regions as well as an unprecedented social polarization, has been the background of an, until recently unimaginable, exacerbation of contradictions of the capitalist system, provoking a profound civilizational crisis affecting the whole of humanity.

Global labour arbitrage has become a key part of the international organization and restructuring strategy of large transnational corporations, and of imperialist domination, raising serious theoretical and conceptual challenges concerning the operation of the law of value in the new world order (or disorder). The enormous wage differentials between countries and regions seem to indicate that we are witnessing the reign of super-exploitation of labour (i.e., the wages of the labour force are well below its value necessary for its social reproduction). The issue here is simple: we have moved to a different mode of capitalist production. Even recognizing that the workforce can have different and contrasting values at distinct latitudes, given the legacy of colonialism, neo-colonialism and extreme forms of imperialist domination, many questions still remain. Among them, how do we understand the laws of capitalism characterized by the domination of monopoly capital, which penetrates all levels of social life, while promulgating the myth of the free market? How do we understand the logic of price formation within dynamics of financialization (fictitious capital) and the resurgence of rampant resource extractivism to levels that threaten to destroy the foundations of our ecosystems? These and other contradictions demand an enormous theoretical and analytical effort of the progressive intelligentsia to unravel the complex reality in which we are living and contribute to the very organizations and movements leading the social transformation for the benefit of the working class and popular sectors.

Finally, it is not noted often enough, that, in this task, it is vital to understand the recomposition of the social classes under the rule of neoliberal globalization. As we saw, neoliberal globalization is distinguished by generating many forms of disguised proletarianization within and between countries, particularly along the North–South axis. This situation tends to produce multiple divisions within the working class, making it ever more urgent to move strategically toward the construction of an agent of social transformation with the capacity to overcome the current regressive/parasitic/predatory and ultimately unsustainable form of capitalism for the sake of humanity.

5. Apple's iPad City: subcontracting exploitation to China

Jenny Chan, Pun Ngai and Mark Selden[1]

INTRODUCTION

Many image-conscious technology companies, probably none more than Apple in our digital age, have professed ideals of corporate citizenship, environmental, labour and social responsibility in their supplier codes of conduct. This is in part a response to the growing anti-sweatshop movement in the electronics industry from within the United States, Europe, and more recently Greater China (Smith et al. 2006; Litzinger 2013). Violations of factory workers' fundamental rights in export-oriented industry nevertheless remain intractable, prompting scholars and practitioners in corporate responsibility to promote the leverage of private and public power to create 'just supply chains' (Locke 2013; Mayer and Gereffi 2010; *Boston Review* 2013). The main effort of public–private partnerships is to call on a shared commitment of the national governments, transnational corporations and non-governmental labour organizations to better protect workers.

This chapter assesses the direct impact of Apple's outsourcing practices on manufacturing workers' conditions in China. We focus on workers' lives at the world's largest supplier of Apple products, Taiwanese-owned Foxconn Technology Group (hereafter Foxconn), which are shaped by both *state policies* and *global capital* played out inside the factory. The consolidation of high-tech electronics production in China and elsewhere potentially strengthens state regulation or 'public governance' of transnational firms (Mayer and Gereffi 2010: 15–17). In our close study of the Apple–Foxconn relationship in China, however, we have not observed the 'positive role' of the Chinese government 'in promoting collaborative buyer–supplier relations' (Locke 2013: 19), even when international capital is concentrated at the national, local and firm levels. Instead,

[1] The authors wish to thank Debby Chan, Jeffery Hermanson, Pauline Overeem, Scott Nova, Isaac Shapiro, Michael Burawoy, Peter Evans, Richard Appelbaum, Nelson Lichtenstein, Jeroen Merk, SACOM (Students and Scholars Against Corporate Misbehaviour), and the University Research Group for their support.

workers face foreign giants such as Apple and Foxconn that enjoy the full backing of the local state. We document for China the ways in which the integration of the electronics manufacturing industry in a global division of labour has intensified labour conflicts and class antagonism.

Foxconn has risen to become the largest employer of industrial workers, with 1.4 million employees in China alone. Between 2010 and 2014, we collaborated with an independent University Research Group to carry out fieldwork on Foxconn's labour practices and production systems in twelve major Chinese cities, where Foxconn runs giant manufacturing sites and research and development centres (Pun et al. 2014). Foxconn has more than 30 factories across China; the surveyed factories are based in eastern, central and western China, from Shenzhen in Guangdong, Chongqing, Shanghai, Tianjin, Beijing and others, to the 'iPad City' in Chengdu (Sichuan). Because Apple is the world's most profitable electronics company, Foxconn the largest employer of workers, Apple its largest client, and China the largest producer and exporter of electronic goods, this study concentrates on the seminal Apple–Foxconn relationship in order to chart its consequences for labour.

With government officials prioritizing economic development rather than advancing labour and human rights, we highlight a range of abuses resulting in a wave of suicides among Foxconn workers in 2010 and a deadly industrial explosion at one of the new Foxconn factory complexes in May 2011, as well as continuing worker abuses including illegal overtime and forced student labour to the present. External monitoring of Foxconn conditions by the Fair Labor Association, we show, provided public relations cover for Apple and other firms that pay for its surveys, but failed to curb flagrant corporate abuses or strengthen workers' rights.

The next section reviews the changing geography of manufacturing and the growth of Asian electronics contractors in global outsourcing. It follows with an account of Foxconn's high-speed expansion across China. We enter the iPad City where workers producing this signature Apple product are struggling for fundamental rights to a work–life balance, decent wages, and a safe and healthy working environment. As production requirements tighten under intense market competition, and the speed of the line relentlessly increases, labour crises have also intensified. The conclusion sheds light on the social movement forces for justice.

LABOUR, OUTSOURCING, AND THE RISE OF ASIAN ELECTRONICS CONTRACTORS

Capital concentration and consolidation are inherent to capitalism. As Karl Marx wrote in *Capital* (1990: 929), 'one capitalist always strikes down many others'. Corporations exploit spaces of uneven development at home and abroad to maximize profit. Capital transforms favoured rural and urban sites for industrialization, while excluding 'other regions of the globe' from 'new waves of economic transformation' (Webster et al. 2008: 1). From the 1980s, with the demise of central planning in the Soviet Union, central and eastern Europe and China, and the promotion of 'free trade' in other emergent economies, the global structure of industrial production has fundamentally shifted. Through corporate outsourcing, restructuring, mergers and acquisitions, large companies expand market share at home and abroad. Leading firms such as Apple and IBM, known as the 'chain drivers' or 'market makers', once produced many of their products in-house in their own countries. In recent decades they have preferred to set up hierarchically structured networks of independently-owned suppliers to produce their commodities (Hopkins and Wallerstein 1986; Gereffi 1994; McKay 2006). Offshore mass production increased by leaps and bounds. By 2000, 50 per cent of global manufacturing production was in developing countries with production organized through global supply chains, and the trend accelerated thereafter (quoted in Mayer and Gereffi 2010: 3).

Transnational giants seek to partner with a small number of highly efficient and strategically located contractors, while diversifying risks and minimizing costs through supply chain management. 'Global supply bases' have emerged in India, Brazil, Mexico, South Africa, Vietnam, and other rapidly developing economies, but above all in China, where production activities and market transactions are taking place at competitively low price, high speed, and in huge volumes (Sturgeon et al. 2011; Bonacich and Hamilton 2011; Henderson and Nadvi 2011).

Large contract manufacturers have been upgrading and growing in size and scale. Richard Appelbaum (2008) finds that East Asian contractors, ranging from footwear and garments to electronics, have been integrating vertically in their supply chains. Joonkoo Lee and Gary Gereffi (2013) explain the co-evolution process that capital accumulation of smartphone leaders have advanced alongside the innovation within their large assemblers. Electronics manufacturers provide value-added services, component-processing and final-assembly in 'one-stop shopping' to technology firms such as Apple (Dedrick and Kraemer 2011) and retail giants.

Giant manufacturers, rather than small workshops, are better able to 'respond to shortening product cycles and increasing product complexity' (Starosta 2010: 546), thus becoming powerful players in just-in-time production networks. They serve multiple clients to climb the global value chains. Not only production tasks, but also inventory management and logistics, are being concentrated in strategic factories, resulting in ever stronger mutually dependent relations between buyers and suppliers.

Boy Lüthje (2006: 17–18) observes that in recent decades brand-name firms have focused on 'product development, design, and marketing', gaining a larger share of the value created in trade even as they abandon hardware manufacturing. Subject to strong demands from global brands, manufacturers and electronics service providers in China and other countries compete against each other to meet production speed, pricing and quality goals, shaving profit margins (Ross 2006).

As we show in the case of Apple and Foxconn, it is Apple that dominates the relationship and imposes its will on its contractors. Given its considerable market share, Apple dictates price-setting and the timing of product delivery, at times resulting in intense pressures for Foxconn and other workers, and above all, health and safety hazards (Chan and Pun 2010; Pun and Chan 2012; 2013; Chan 2013; Chan et al. 2013). At the industry level, facing strong competition, Apple seeks to lower costs, strengthen control over suppliers, and speed up to release newer products. The *buyer-driven* pattern is characteristic of numerous American, European, Japanese and South Korean transnationals that dominate the electronics industry (Lüthje et al. 2013).

Searching for cheaper, disciplined and more pliant labour, global buyers – in Western and Asian countries alike – have exported capital (thereby circumventing tighter labour regulatory systems within certain nations). The resulting 'successive geographical relocation of capital' has been facilitated by efficient transportation and communications technologies, regional and international financial services, and access to immigrants and surplus labour (Silver 2003: 39; Harvey 2010; Harrison 1997). The 'race to the bottom', however, has rarely proceeded without labour, social and/or environmental challenges at sites of new investment (Cowie 2001; Silver 2003; Chen 2011; Jang and Gray, this volume). China, in its opening to foreign capital and international trade since the early 1980s, well exemplifies all these processes – and in an extreme form, where hundreds of millions of workers are being drawn into global production chains. Some aggrieved workers have taken aim at reputation-conscious large companies to defend their rights and interests. The question remains whether, and under what conditions, workers can effectively challenge the combination of corporate and state power to raise labour and social standards.

THE FOXCONN EMPIRE

Foxconn – the name alludes to the corporation's ability to produce electronic connectors at nimble 'fox-like' speed – supplies components and finished products not only for Apple, but also for IBM, Microsoft, Google, Intel, Cisco, GE, Amazon, HP, Dell, Motorola, Nokia, Panasonic, Sony, Toshiba, Fujitsu, Nintendo, Samsung, LG, Sony Ericsson, Acer, Huawei and Lenovo, a Who's Who of global electronic producers including two of China's own leading tech companies. Its parent corporation, Hon Hai Precision Industry Company, was founded in Taipei in 1974. In these four decades, Foxconn has successfully integrated production processes from raw material extraction to component manufacture to final assembly (Foxconn Technology Group 2009: 10). In July 2013, *Fortune* Global 500 ranked Foxconn 30th on the list, up 13 places from the previous year, with annual revenues of US$132 billion, far higher than most of its corporate customers, with the notable exception of Apple (which had US$156.5 billion in sales).

In outsourced production, Foxconn competes on 'speed, quality, engineering service, efficiency, and added value' to maximize profits (Foxconn Technology Group 2009: 8). In the 1990s, Apple, Lucent, Nortel, Alcatel and Ericsson 'sold off most, if not all, of their in-house manufacturing capacity – both at home and abroad – to a cadre of large and highly capable US-based contract manufacturers, including Solectron, Flextronics, Jabil Circuit, Celestica, and Sanmina-SCI' (Sturgeon et al. 2011: 236). In 2002, Apple contracted Foxconn to assemble Macs, and established the long-term business relationships that continue to the present (Interview, 7 March 2011). Since 2004 Foxconn has led the electronics manufacturing sector in market share, surpassing long-time rival Flextronics to become the world leader (Pick 2006).

Currently Foxconn captures more than 50 per cent of the world market share in electronics manufacturing and service (Dinges 2010). Under the leadership of founder Terry Gou, Foxconn has ridden the waves of successive revolutions in information and communications technology to vastly expand its '6C' product lines. Their products are computers (desktops, laptops and tablets), communications equipment (mobile phones and smartphones), consumer digital (music players, cameras, game consoles and TVs), cars (automotive electronics), content (e-book readers) and health-care products. In all of these, Foxconn has achieved state of the art technologies while simplifying production processes to reduce workers to repetition of simple motions throughout ten to twelve-hour days.

Industry analysts note that 'manufacturing operations in China were responsible for more than 75 per cent of aggregate [electronics manufacturing services] industry growth in 2010 [US$347 billion], and the country is expected to continue carrying the burden of driving worldwide growth' (Dinges 2011). Foxconn boasts that 'China is not the only one globalizing' (*Bloomberg Businessweek* 2010). The sprawling industrial empire has more than 200 subsidiaries around the globe,[2] but the overseas Foxconn operations are dwarfed by the mega factories in China. Working outside of China enables Foxconn's customers to get quicker turnaround on orders, reduce labour and transportation costs, and avoid some import taxes (Andrijasevic and Sacchetto 2013). Nevertheless, the enterprise's most extensive operations by far are in China.

Facing fierce competition, Foxconn strives to tighten labour processes, control costs, and expand engineering and manufacturing technologies to maintain its position as 'the most trusted name in contract manufacturing services' (Interview, 25 October 2010). It recruits mostly teens and young adults to run the assembly lines. 'Over 85 per cent of Foxconn's employees are rural migrant workers between 16 and 29 years old', a Chinese human resources manager said (Interview, 14 October 2011). Foxconn in this respect is emblematic of the national pattern. Official data in 2009 showed that of all rural migrants, 42 per cent were between 16 and 25 years old and another 20 per cent were between 26 and 30 (China's National Bureau of Statistics 2010).

From the 1980s, rural migrants have moved from constituting a marginal part of the Chinese industrial labour force to dominating it in numerical terms, reversing the situation prior to market reform in which their movement had been severely limited by state restrictions on rural-to-urban migration. They are the mainstay of the new urban industrial labour. In Shenzhen, the rapidly growing city just across the border from Hong Kong in southern coastal China, Foxconn's more than 500000 employees (Foxconn Technology Group 2010a; 2010b) were churning out a wide array of electronic devices, day and night. It was here that in the first five months of 2010, at least 12 'jumps' – attempted and completed suicides of Foxconn workers who leaped from high-rise factory dormitories – were reported by local and international media.

The Foxconn 'campus', as the managers like to call it, organizes production and daily labour reproduction activities in a self-contained environment. The Longhua complex of 1.75 million square metres – larger

---

[2] Foxconn has worldwide production facilities in Taiwan, China, Japan, South Korea, Australia, New Zealand, Malaysia, Indonesia, Singapore, Vietnam, India, United Arab Emirates, Russia, Finland, Sweden, Denmark, Germany, Czech Republic, Slovakia, Hungary, the Netherlands, Austria, Turkey, Ireland, Scotland, Brazil, Canada, Mexico and the United States.

than the entire new 'University City' in Shenzhen – includes factories, warehouses, dormitories, banks, two hospitals, a post office, a fire brigade with two fire engines, an exclusive television network, an educational institute, a library, soccer fields, basketball courts, tennis courts, track and field, swimming pools, cyber theatres, shops, supermarkets, cafeterias and restaurants, an employee care and support service centre, and even a wedding dress shop. The complex is equipped with advanced production facilities since it is the model factory for customers, central- and local-level governments, and visitors from media organizations and other inspection units.

Foxconn has manufacturing complexes not only in Shenzhen and all four major Chinese municipalities of Beijing, Shanghai, Tianjin and Chongqing, but also in fifteen provinces throughout the country (see Figure 5.1). Below we look beyond its gleaming facilities to the daily lives of its workers.

Foxconn is building a production network in which vertical integration, flexible coordination across different facilities and 24-hour continuous assembly bolster its market competitiveness. Its expansion has been intertwined with the Chinese state's structural reforms since the 1980s, and in recent years, the company has kept pace with the Chinese state's call to prioritize inland development in the lagging western region (Hung 2013; Selden and Perry 2010). In 1988, Foxconn launched a small processing factory in Shenzhen, the first special economic zone opened up to foreign trade. In the 1990s, Foxconn diversified its production lines and locations in step with Deng Xiaoping's 1992 call to prioritize the coastal regions to spearhead export-oriented development. Major production clusters were established in two coastal regions: the Pearl River Delta in the south and the Greater Shanghai Delta in the east. In 2001, the company became one of China's leading exporters following the country's accession to the World Trade Organization and further liberalization of international trade, and it has maintained and strengthened this position ever since (Foxconn Technology Group 2009: 6).

During the global financial crisis in 2008, Chongqing municipal government, the only municipality directly under the central government in inland China and the gateway to consumer markets in south-western regions, launched a Warm Winter stimulus plan to subsidize 1500 businesses (Dreyfuss 2009). Going west, Foxconn swiftly set up a computer assembly plant in the Xiyong Microelectronics Industrial Park in Chongqing, where the corporate tax rate was slashed from 25 per cent to 15 per cent (Interview, 15 March 2011). Despite the contraction of American and European demand for consumer electronics, in 2009, Foxconn generated a solid NT$1.96 trillion (US$67 billion) in sales (Foxconn Technology

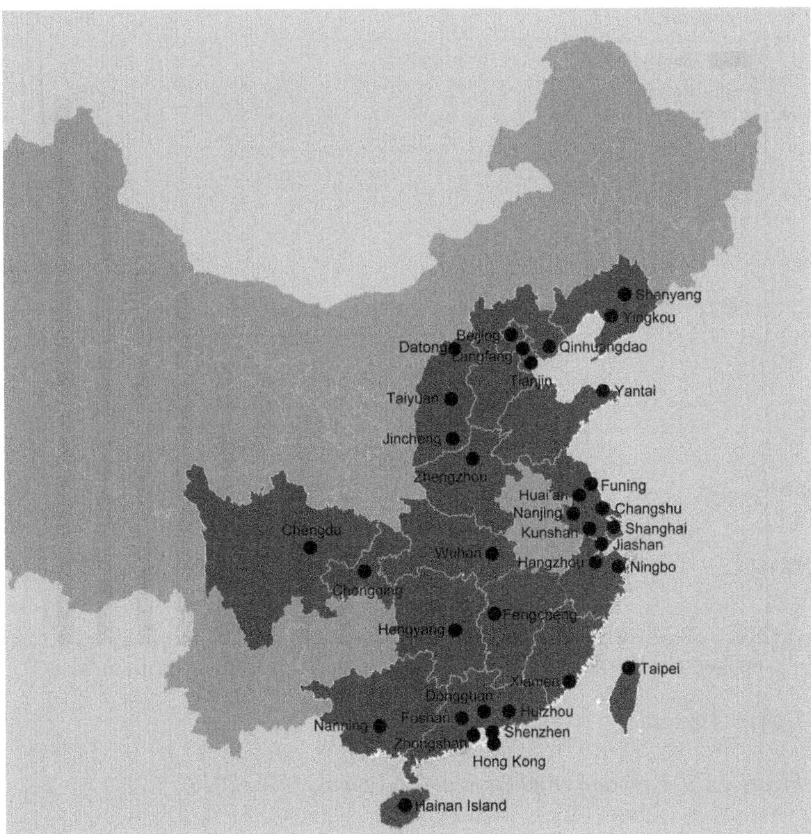

Source: Foxconn.

Figure 5.1 Foxconn's locations in Greater China

Group 2010b: 5). Following the economic recovery, the company reported a stunning 53 per cent year-on-year increase in revenues to NT$3 trillion (US$102.5 billion) in 2010 (Foxconn Technology Group 2011: 4). The employee suicides at Foxconn's China facilities that year, and the subsequent pay rise, did not seem to impact on revenues.

'In twenty years,' some business executives suggest, just two companies will dominate global markets, 'everything will be made by Foxconn and sold by Wal-Mart' (Balfour and Culpan 2010). A wild exaggeration that ignores the central fact of Foxconn's dependence on Apple and other international electronics firms, but the hyperbole is emblematic both of the changing character of the world economy and consumption patterns,

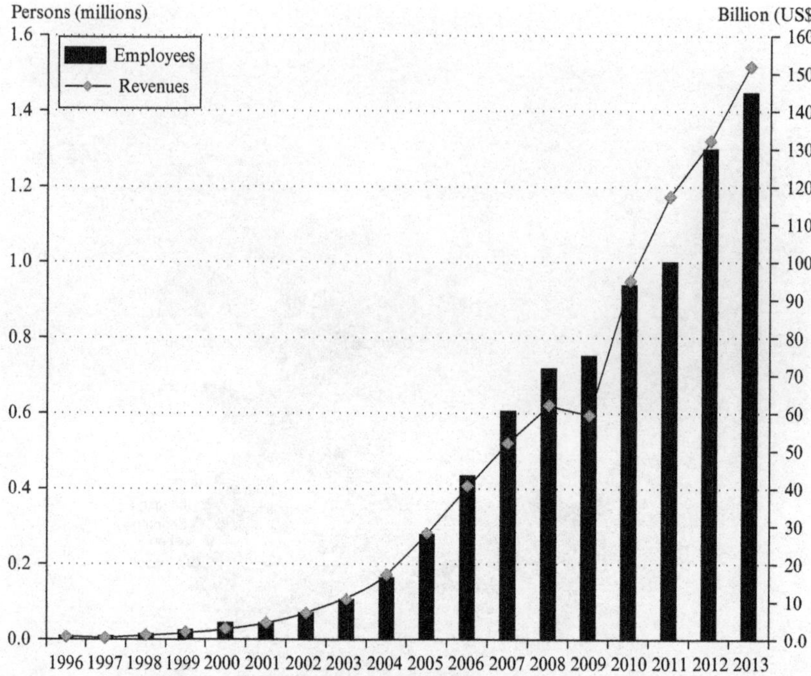

Source: Foxconn.

Figure 5.2 Foxconn employees and revenues, 1996–2013

and of the manufacturing company's startling rise in scale of employment and revenues in China, East Asia and the world.

While Apple's profit margins are far higher than Foxconn's (Chan et al. 2013), as of fiscal year 2013, Foxconn's revenues reached an unprecedented high of US$133.2 billion (*Fortune* Global 500 2014), thanks to the large orders of Apple and other clients. Figure 5.2 shows the increase in number of employees and annual revenues of Foxconn since 1996, according to the earliest publicly accessible company data, to 2013.

Foxconn's astonishing expansion across geographic regions was predicated on its ability to secure contracts from Apple and other international brands, an outcome facilitated by its ability to forge an alliance with the Chinese state at both central and local levels. The company's access to labour, especially young productive workers in low-wage regions, has enabled it to achieve economies of scale. Recent Chinese government statistics show that the eastern coastal region is still the primary destination for rural migrant workers nationwide. However, as enterprises build new factories in regions with lower wages, central and western China have narrowed the gap: in 2009 more than 90 million migrants worked in the eastern region, around 24 million in the central region, and nearly 30 million in the western region (China's National Bureau of Statistics 2010). This trend has since continued.

THE APPLE–FOXCONN RELATIONSHIP

Apple leapfrogged Google in 2012, and Samsung in 2013, to become 'the world's most valuable brand' (Brand Finance 2013). In recent years, 'approximately 40 per cent of Foxconn revenues are from Apple, its biggest client', a Foxconn production manager reported (Interview, 10 March 2011). Another 20 per cent come from HP, while the remainder is provided by multiple customers (Interview, 21 March 2011). Foxconn's heavy dependence on Apple has been a source of its rise and profit, but the company remains vulnerable as Apple retains the option to employ other contractors as well to squeeze Foxconn's profits. Our group interviews with two mid-level production managers reveal that during the 2008–09 global financial crisis, Foxconn was forced to cut prices on components, such as connectors and printed circuit boards, and assembly, to retain high-volume orders. 'Margins were cut. Still, the rock bottom line was kept, that is, Foxconn did not report a loss on the iPhone contract' (Interviews, 10 November 2011; 19 November 2011). How did Foxconn manage to stay in the black while cutting its margins? By charging a premium on customized engineering services and quality assurance. The upgrading of the iPhones since 2007 has in part relied on Foxconn's senior product engineers' research analyses and constructive suggestions. Foxconn's edge in technology and services served the company well in the crisis.

In 2009, in the wake of the global recession, the Chinese government froze the minimum wage across the country for one year. Foxconn accommodated Apple's and other corporate buyers' squeeze while continuing to reduce labour expenditures, including cuts in wages (overtime premiums) and benefits (productivity bonuses and quarterly prizes). Nevertheless the pressure was on the manufacturing company and frontline workers and staff.

'Apple tightened the control over Foxconn by splitting iPhone and iPad orders with Taiwanese-owned Pegatron, a manufacturing unit spun off from Asustek, in the aftermath of the spate of worker suicides [in 2010]' (Interview, 15 December 2011). By pitting its suppliers against each other, and investing in research, design and marketing, the American giant reaps

Table 5.1 Apple's revenues by product segments, 2010–12

	2011 (ended 24 September)		2012 (ended 29 September)	
	Millions (US$)	%	Millions (US$)	%
iPhone	45998	42.5	78692	50.3
iPad	19168	17.7	30945	19.8
Mac	21783	20.1	23221	14.8
iPod	7453	6.9	5615	3.6
iTunes/Software/Services[a]	9373	8.7	12890	8.2
Accessories	4474	4.1	5145	3.3
Total	108249	100	156508	100

Note: a. Includes revenue from sales on the iTunes Store, the App Store, the Mac App Store, and the iBookstore, and revenue from sales of licensing and other services.

Source: Adapted from Apple's (2012a) reclassified summary data.

very high profits and commands a leading position in the consumer electronics market. Table 5.1 shows Apple's revenues generated from sales of its branded products and services. The signature Mac computer has now been far surpassed by the iPhone, with the iPad following in second place.

From keyboards and mice to touch-based controls, *Time* magazine immediately recognized the iPad as one of the '50 best inventions' of 2010. A cost and profit analysis of an iPad reveals the economics and corporate power relations underlying Apple's global business model. Where profit margins are often in the single digits in the low-end computing market, Apple retains 30 per cent of the sales price of the US$499 iPad, even more if it is sold through Apple's retail outlets or online store. In contrast, labour cost for the iPad in China is estimated at only 1.6 per cent, or US$8 (see Figure 5.3). Although Apple does not disclose its contracts with Foxconn, there is no doubt that Chinese workers who assemble much of the iPad receive a small share of the value it generates, while Apple enjoys extraordinary profit margins.

The iPad has bolstered the profit margin for Apple in the worldwide tablet market, placing it ahead of strong competitors like Samsung. Incredibly, Apple (2012c) sold three million upgraded 'new iPads' in the first three days of its release in March 2012 – that is, one million iPads a day in the American market – making it dominant in global tablets. For Christmas shoppers, in December 2012 Apple introduced the fourth-generation iPad running on a new operating system iOS 6 (competing with Google's Android application system), and the lighter and thinner 7.9-inch

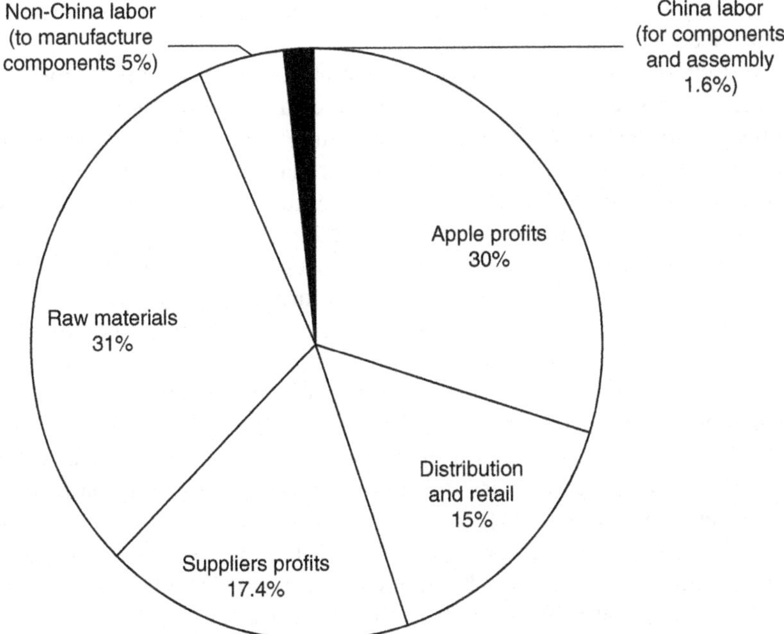

Source: Adapted from Kraemer et al. (2011: 11).

Figure 5.3 Distribution of value for the iPad

iPad mini in white and silver or black and slate. 'Few brands are as loved in China as Apple', exclaims *The Economist* (2012). Shoppers flocked to visit Apple's three-storey store, the largest in Asia, on the Wangfujing shopping street in the heart of Beijing. In this era of the mobile technologies revolution, the production cycle and delivery schedules are shorter than ever, the pressures on workers higher.

INSIDE IPAD CITY

Foxconn Chengdu, legally registered as Hongfujin Precision Electronics (Chengdu) Ltd and known as iPad City, began operation in October 2010. All workers at this new production site are responsible for making iPads, serving only Apple. The factory labour force grew to 50 000 employees in March 2011, making it one of the city's biggest employers in its first half-year of operation in the provincial capital of Sichuan, south-western

China. As of December 2012, it expanded to 165000, and recruitment continued (Interview, 29 January 2013).

Andrew Ross (2006: 218) noted that in Chengdu 'it was impossible not to come across evidence of the state's hand in the fostering of high-tech industry'. In the years since the 7.9 magnitude earthquake struck Sichuan in May 2008, the provincial government has made efforts to attract investments to fund reconstruction. In the autumn of 2010 the officials subsidized the construction of the gigantic Foxconn Chengdu production complex and high-rise 18-storey dormitories, designating it as 'the Number One Project'. Foxconn CEO Terry Gou returned the compliment, praising the government: 'I'm very much impressed by the efficiency of local government departments that led to the start of the project. Foxconn will add investment to make the [Chengdu] factory one of Foxconn's key production sites in the world' (quoted in *Chengdu Weekly* 2011).

Village, township, city and provincial-level governments in Sichuan all offered Foxconn free labour recruitment services. A worker commented (Interview, 23 March 2011), 'Foxconn is hiring, and the whole city has gone crazy. Local officials grab people and ask if they'd be willing to work at Foxconn. The government has made it an official task. Officials at every level have a recruitment quota. Isn't this recruitment crazy?'

Many workers are taking advantage of job opportunities opening up in or near their native place, rather than moving to distant provinces. Clearly the inland city of Chengdu is the new frontier for Foxconn and the electronics industry generally. Factory management, facing stiff procurement orders and tight shipment deadlines, turns again and again to overtime work. Posters on the Foxconn workshop walls read (our translation):

> Value efficiency every minute, every second.
> Achieve goals or the sun will no longer rise.
> Execution is the integration of speed, accuracy and precision.
> There is no best way, but always a better way.
> The devil is in the details.

Apple and other buyers want their tablets fast to meet Chinese and global demand. Apple CEO Tim Cook, who succeeded the late Steve Jobs in August 2011, put it this way: 'Nobody wants to buy sour milk' (quoted in Satariano and Burrows 2011). And elsewhere, 'Inventory. . .is fundamentally evil. You want to manage it like you're in the dairy business: If it gets past its freshness date, you have a problem' (quoted in Lashinsky 2012: 95). Tracking demand worldwide, Apple adjusts production forecasts *daily*. Streamlining the global supply chain on the principle of market efficiency and 'competition against time' is Apple's goal.

Frontline workers in outsourced factories frequently pay the price. If a target is not fulfilled, Foxconn Chengdu workers have to stay on the production line to finish it, sometimes working an entire twelve-hour shift. Worse yet, workers frequently report that overtime is not fully documented, with the result that overtime wages are unpaid or under-paid. This happened when line leaders under-reported extreme (and illegal) overtime hours, fearing punishment by higher-ups. In another situation, workers were often required to work on Saturdays and Sundays during the production peak season. While they should be paid double in accordance with the law, they were instead given rest days during low seasons to offset the overtime premiums. Grievances about pay, work stress and unreasonable production demands sometimes culminated in open conflicts.

In holding Foxconn and other suppliers responsible for the problem, Apple ignores its own purchasing practices, such as order specification and sales forecasting, and the direct impact of its production deadlines on suppliers' capacity to schedule working hours (Ruggie 2012).

Louis Woo, special assistant to Foxconn's chief executive, explained to the journalist in an American Public Media programme (*Marketplace* 2012) the kinds of pressures that Apple or Dell applies:

> The overtime problem – when a company like Apple or Dell needs to ramp up production by 20 per cent for a new product launch, Foxconn has two choices: hire more workers or give the workers you already have more hours. When demand is very high, it's very difficult to suddenly hire 20 per cent more people. Especially when you have a million workers – that would mean hiring 200000 people at once.

Foxconn continues to hire more workers, including teenage student interns in the name of skills training and business-school cooperation, and at the same time imposes compulsory overtime on the labour force during the peak production months.

SELLING LABOUR OR SELLING LIFE?

During the spring of 2011, at the still-under-construction Foxconn Chengdu plant, shimmering aluminium dust often filled the air. The iPad's casing is aluminium, and polishing creates a large amount of dust. All around the factory area was not only metallic dust but also piles of sand, stones and soil, and the roads were uneven. The entrance to the factory had some crudely placed wooden boards creating a small path between two uneven sand piles for workers who daily passed through the makeshift pedestrian thoroughfare to enter the factory. Construction materials such as steel bars and cement were stacked everywhere. Some factory floors in Zones A, B and C had already been put into production, even though auxiliary facilities such as toilets and canteens were not fully accessible.

In the entire month of March 2011, most production workers in Foxconn Chengdu logged long hours of overtime with only two rest days. Fan Chunyan (interviewees' names have all been changed), a 22-year-old female worker, attended compulsory unpaid work meetings every day: 'I report to the line leaders 15 to 20 minutes earlier for roll call. Leaders lecture us on maintaining high productivity, reaching daily output targets and keeping discipline.' On the factory floor, 'toilet breaks during the working hours are also restricted. Meal times were occasionally shortened or even cut to finish the production quotas of the day' (Interviews, 18 March 2011; 20 March 2011). Machinery was never left idle. The well-lit factory floor was visible throughout the night from afar.

Apple, by introducing myriad changes in the design of its sophisticated devices, each with multiple variations to suit consumer tastes, relentlessly drives the pace of production with each new model and holiday season.[3] Not long after the original iPad was introduced in April 2010, Apple reinvented the iPad to boost sales. A company press statement dated 2 March 2011 reads, 'While others have been scrambling to copy the first generation iPad, we're launching iPad 2, which moves the bar far ahead of the competition and will likely cause them to go back to the drawing boards yet again' (Apple 2011).

'When we have work,' Duan Dong, a 19-year-old male worker said, 'half of our income is from doing overtime' (Interview, 5 March 2011).

> I didn't go home during the Spring Festival holidays in early February [2011] even though my village was nearby. Instead I did 78 hours of overtime work that month [more than double the 36-hour legal limit for overtime under the Chinese Labour Law], thereby earning an additional 1090 Yuan, which added to my base pay of 1060 Yuan, gave me a total of 2150 Yuan [US$338].

Excessive overtime was the norm. Dong's co-worker, Ouyang Zhong, married with a one-year-old daughter, had returned from home after a brief family reunion. That same month, he worked 44 overtime hours.

---

[3] Apple (2012b: 8) describes two major sources of production-time pressure, which are transferred to outsourced suppliers, in its annual financial report filed to the United States Securities and Exchange Commission: 'The Company has historically experienced higher net sales in its first fiscal quarter [from September to December] compared to other quarters in its fiscal year due in part to holiday seasonal demand. Actual and anticipated timing of new product introductions by the Company can also significantly impact the level of net sales experienced by the Company in any particular quarter.'

Zhong emphasized that 'without overtime, it's hard to get by' (Interview, 6 March 2011). Many workers are eager to maximize overtime as the only way to send home money. Others, however, are hard pressed to survive the long hours and intense pace but have no choice other than to accept overtime assignments. Day and night, they toil under dangerous conditions, risking health and safety.

Workplace hazards monitoring, more specifically ductwork inspection and ventilation system review, had largely given way to meeting impossibly high iPad production targets. Foxconn's polishing workers are responsible for transforming raw aluminium into shiny stainless iPad casings. Each polishing machine produces metallic dust as it processes and grinds with ever greater refinement. Microscopic aluminium dust clouds the air. It coats workers' clothes. A young female polishing worker described the situation, 'I'm breathing aluminium dust at Foxconn like a vacuum cleaner.' The polishing workshop windows were tightly shut so that workers 'felt as if we were suffocating' (Interview, 24 March 2011). 'Some tearing and pain also occur as the tiny solid aluminium particles are rinsed from my eyes by tears', Ma Quan, a 20-year-old worker, explained to us in Sichuan dialect (Interview, 23 March 2011). He added: 'Everyone in the workshop is wearing a thin gauze mask, with a centre section of activated charcoal, but it doesn't have an airtight seal and provides no protection. Some of us are suffering from shortness of breath.'

If the masks are useless for preventing the aluminium dust's toxic effects, they do help Foxconn pass factory inspections. Although workers were constantly coughing and complaining of a sore throat, Foxconn managers and Apple engineers and product development teams dispatched to the Chengdu factory apparently prioritized the hourly production figures.

'Apple is committed to ensuring that working conditions in Apple's supply chain are safe, that workers are treated with respect and dignity, and that manufacturing processes are environmentally responsible': the very first commitment made by Apple (2012e: 1) in the opening line of its Supplier Code of Conduct rings hollow. Four colleagues of Quan had already quit their jobs long before their six-month probation was over. In the polishing workshop, workers put on cotton gloves, but the finest particles penetrate through the flimsy material to their hands. Workers simply wash their hands and bodies with soap and water, without knowing the exposure level of aluminium dust in their workshop. After work Quan took off his cotton gloves and looked helplessly at both his hands covered in aluminium dust. Encouraged by other workers, he relayed their shared health concerns to his line leader, only to hear words that left the workers feeling distraught (Interview, 27 March 2011): 'The factory conditions are absolutely safe!'

SPEED-UP, FIRE AND EXPLOSION

Repeated warnings from workers and labour activists about the dangers of aluminium dust on the eyes, lungs and skin of human beings had fallen on deaf ears (Students and Scholars Against Corporate Misbehaviour 2011a, 2011b). Instead, a Foxconn media statement dated 7 May 2011 reads:

> We have made tremendous progress over the past year as we work to lead our industry in meeting the needs of the new generation of workers in China and that has been confirmed by the many customer representatives, outside experts, and reporters who have visited our facilities and openly met with our employees and our management team (quoted in *IDG News* 2011).

This and numerous other public relations statements, ignore the deep concerns of workers and make no mention of pressing grievances, demonstrating Foxconn's failure to conduct a comprehensive risk assessment of its workplace health and safety conditions, or even to recognize the need for such an assessment. On one point, the company statement is all too accurate: 'customer representatives', that is, Apple, visited the facilities and raised no significant issues concerning health and safety.

Two weeks later, on 20 May 2011, an accumulation of aluminium dust in the air duct on the third floor at Foxconn Chengdu Building A5, Zone A, provided fuel for an explosion (Duhigg and Barboza 2012). The metallic dust was ignited by a spark in an electric switch. Dense smoke filled the workshop. 'We barely escaped with our lives. It's terrifying,' the workers told us as they recalled the 'black Friday evening' (Interview, 23 May 2011). Firemen arrived at the scene around 7:30 p.m. Ambulances and company vans brought male and female victims who were either seriously burnt or had lost consciousness to the emergency units at the Sichuan Chengdu People's Hospital and other hospitals. In the midst of lightning and thunder that night, some workers could not hold back their tears in the rain.

The hectic daily work schedule was only disrupted by the Foxconn Chengdu aluminium-dust explosion that killed four workers and severely injured at least eighteen others (Apple 2012d: 15). Apple's statement reads (quoted in Branigan 2011): 'We are deeply saddened by the tragedy at Foxconn's plant in Chengdu, and our hearts go out to the victims and their families. We are working closely with Foxconn to understand what caused this terrible event.'

But where, before or since, has Apple stepped in to ensure that Foxconn take steps to protect the health and safety of workers, or accepted its own partial responsibility for death and injury? It was business as usual. On

17 December 2011, only seven months after the Foxconn Chengdu explosion, combustible aluminium dust fuelled another blast, this time at a Shanghai-based supplier to Apple, injuring 59 workers (Apple 2012d: 15). In the blast, young men and women suffered severe burns and shattered bones, leaving many permanently disabled.

HOW DO THE CHINESE STATE AND COMPANIES UNDERMINE WORKERS' RIGHTS?

Immediately after the aluminium-dust explosion at Foxconn, government officials and the police took control of the hospital wards. China's State Council Information Office moved swiftly to curb the media. 'In regard to Foxconn's Chengdu plant explosion [on 20 May 2011], all media and websites are to wait for an official report. No independent reports, re-posts, or recommendations will be allowed' (*China Digital Times* 2011). Similarly, the Sichuan Provincial Propaganda Department announced: 'With regard to Foxconn's Chengdu iPad 2 plant explosion, no independent reporting can be conducted. Unauthorized reports will be immediately deleted' (*China Digital Times* 2011). The blackout on the Chinese press was complete. There could be no more graphic indication of the coordination between the party-state and the corporation at the expense of workers' occupational health and lives.

The clash between worker safety and high pressure production targets was evident at iPad production sites. Foxconn closed the polishing workshops for one week to 'cooperate with government investigation' (Interview, 29 May 2011). Under mounting social pressure, Apple sent its Supplier Responsibility management team and 'external experts' to check 'all suppliers handling aluminium dust and put stronger precautionary measures in place before restarting production', as publicly communicated in its January 2012 annual report (Apple 2012d: 15). Fast-paced production of iPads resumed shortly. Despite the establishment of new safety guidelines, Apple's ordering, pricing and delivery demands directly conflict with their own supplier compliance programmes and local legal requirements, while maximizing profits.

Just three months after the deadly explosion, local government officials launched a large-scale recruitment campaign to support Foxconn in ramping up the iPad exports. Between September 2011 and January 2012, Foxconn Chengdu recruited more than 7000 'student interns' to work on the assembly line, making up approximately 10 per cent of the company labour force (Interview, 13 December 2011). Contrary to our research findings, the Fair Labor Association (2013: 5), which received funding from Apple for its investigation of Foxconn, 'found *no interns* had been engaged at Chengdu since September 2011' (our emphasis).[4]

Sichuan municipal and local-level governments directed full-time vocational school students under their jurisdiction to perform 'internships' at labour-hungry Foxconn Chengdu factory complex. To spur schools, governments disbursed funds to schools that fulfilled company target numbers of student interns. If schools failed to meet the human resources requirements, education bureaux would hold up funds for the schools (Interview, 12 December 2011). In this way, Foxconn enlarged its labour recruitment networks with schools, drawing on the assistance of local government officials and teachers to utilize student labour, rather than hiring new workers.

The interns have become a huge source of cheap and disposable labour in China. In the summer of 2010, for example, Foxconn hired as many as 150000 student interns, 15 per cent of its 1 million workforce at the time (Foxconn Technology Group 2010a). Even though interns and entry-level workers have the same starting wage at the company, unlike employees, interns enjoy none of the insurance protections regulated by local government. Nor are they eligible for productivity bonuses, regardless of how well they do their jobs. They are subject to the same treatment as regular workers including alternating day and night shifts monthly, and extensive overtime, defying the letter and the spirit of the national education and labour laws as well as Apple's own labour code. A 17-year-old student intern told us (Interview, 4 March 2011), 'Come on, what do you think we'd have learned standing for more than ten hours a day manning the machines on the line? What's an internship? There's no relation to what we study in school. Every day is just a repetition of one or two simple motions, like a robot.'

Apple claims to exercise its power of 'private governance' to improve workers' lives involved in outsourced electronics production (Locke 2013: 6–9), which is based on the asymmetric power structure in its global supply chain, either on its own or in partnership with the Fair Labor Association and other non-governmental organizations. 'The same leverage [of large

---

[4] In the absence of financial independence from companies that support it, we raise questions about the Fair Labor Association's (FLA) ability to fulfil its mission to protect workers in the global economy. Between 2012 and 2013, the FLA received from Apple membership dues of US$250000, plus 'well into the six figures' audit fees for conducting its investigation at Foxconn Chengdu (and two other Foxconn factories in Shenzhen) (Weir 2012). The FLA ostensibly scrutinized Apple's corporate behaviour, including its purchasing practices and supplier code enforcement. In practice, the systemic abuse of student workers at Foxconn factories in Chengdu and other cities (such as Yantai in north-eastern Shandong province) were not mentioned, let alone ended.

firms] that can be used to demand lower prices and better quality from suppliers,' in the analysis of Frederick Mayer and Gary Gereffi (2010: 8), 'can also be used to press for better labour practices.' Foxconn workers and interns, however, testify that iPads are produced under unethical and unsafe conditions. The promises of corporate care and responsibility, again and again, are broken.

In a capitalist global labour regime, Garrett Brown (2010), coordinator of the Maquiladora Health and Safety Support Network, emphasizes that the corporate social responsibility policies 'have been fatally undermined by the "iron triangle" of lowest possible per-unit price, highest possible quality, and fastest possible delivery times.' At the same time, the Chinese state, despite its strong capacity of regulating labour markets and workplace conditions, has colluded with capital in the race of economic globalization. Notwithstanding China's significant legal reforms in recent decades, workers confront managerial despotism at the point of production (Gallagher 2005; Lee 2007; 2010; Friedman and Lee 2010). Foxconn's unions, even when they are largest in the industry, remain extremely weak. Not unlike their peers in the foreign-invested enterprises, Foxconn workers are not institutionally represented, while student interns are not even eligible for union membership. Attempts in reorganizing grassroots unions have been proceeding at a snail's pace (Pringle 2013; Butollo and ten Brink 2012). In the face of explosive labour unrest, in Foxconn and beyond, the government has been compelled to accommodate some worker demands in the interests of securing a measure of social stability (Lee and Zhang 2013; Lee and Hsing 2010; Selden and Perry 2010). But worker grievances and collective resistance are widespread.

CONCLUSIONS

'Taiwan's history of economic growth is also a history of technological catastrophes.' Thus Hsin-Hsing Chen (2011: 563) highlights the suffering of 1395 former workers of RCA (Radio Corporation of America), who were poisoned by trichloroethylene at the workplace and diagnosed with cancer. In response, RCA shut down the Taoyuan factory and migrated elsewhere, without compensating the terminally ill. This worker tragedy is not an isolated example. With American, Taiwanese and international capital entering China, workers are similarly subject to life-threatening risks of globalized electronics production.

Apple, together with other firms, has created a global consumer class with its products and through Foxconn and other subcontractors it has simultaneously contributed to the creation of a new Chinese working class.

Foxconn, given its corporate power and intricate ties with the Chinese government at all levels, has manufactured not only signature electronic goods for global brands, but also occupational injuries and deaths, while refusing to accept even minimal responsibility. Chinese workers, through popular writings on micro-blogs, open letters, videos, poems and songs, as well as in growing numbers of walkouts, strikes, riots, sit-ins and legal protests, unveil the harsh reality behind the mainstream discourse of 'corporate ethics' and 'social harmony'. The following lyrics convey the sense of the heavy human cost behind transnational manufacturing.

A Worker's Requiem

My body stretches long
lying within a bare building
obstructing the cityscape,
sealed tightly in cement
burying my story

With each mouthful of toxic dust inhaled
profit is exhaled
following prices' rise and fall
each annual fireworks squander
burning my breath

Back bent I furtively twitter
computers nibble away life
backpack heavy on shoulder
muscles and bones strained to the limit
concealing my hardship

My body conveys a message:
reject this false prosperity
leave the corner of darkness—
strained body and soul embrace each other
still you and I will not yield

Teardrops accumulate,
collecting sediments of months and years of weight
of course, dreams are repeatedly shattered
but spirits always sing in the wind
of a worker's story.

Mininoise, Hong Kong grassroots folk band
(Translated by Gregory Fay and Kyoko Selden)

In the course of our ongoing research and support work, some Foxconn workers have joined hands with students, scholars and independent labour rights groups to pressure brands to respond to their demands. An important goal is to 'create a sense of moral accountability' to urge the target corporations (Seidman 2007: 32), in this instance particularly Apple and Foxconn, to live up to their professed global corporate citizenship ideals. In a tightly integrated production supply base, such as China, 'the potential geographical ramifications of disruptions' can be extensive (Silver 2003: 6). The new international division of labour and the growing realization of worker precarity creates 'opportunities for counter-organization', as attested by the rise of transnational labour movements and anti-sweatshop campaigns (Evans 2010: 352; Webster et al. 2008).

The young cohort of Chinese workers are calling for dignified treatment and economic justice. The forms of labour resistance will change as workers find employment closer to their native place and can draw on local social networks. With new factory operations in booming inland cities, a substantial proportion of rural workers are being recruited from within their home province and even their home prefecture or town. Foxconn, with its large-scale operations in China's west, well exemplifies the trend. With a greater sense of entitlement associated with belonging to a place, and perhaps more social resources to bring to the fight for their interests, working-class power could emerge in factories and in worker communities.

6. The grapes of wrath: social upgrading and class struggles in global value chains

Benjamin Selwyn

INTRODUCTION

Over the last three decades there has been an enormous expansion of the global labouring class – from 1.1 billion people in 1980 to 3.05 billion in 2005 (Kapsos 2007: 13). Increasing numbers of workers work within globalized production systems. A core question for those concerned with the IPE of production is the extent to which employment within these globalized systems can yield meaningful work, and contribute to sustainable and thriving livelihoods for the expanding global working class. This chapter investigates this question through an interrogation of two interlinked conceptions of better work: the concept of 'social upgrading' and the International Labour Organization's conception of 'Decent Work'.

The concept of social upgrading has been proposed by leading practitioners within the global commodity chain, global value chain and global production network frameworks (GCC, GVC and GPN, respectively; Barrientos et al. 2011; Milberg and Winkler 2010). Prior to this conceptual innovation, most analysis within these frameworks understood 'upgrading' as an outcome of increased firm-level competitiveness, and questions regarding labour were of secondary importance, at best. The social upgrading concept attempts to place labour at (or at least close to) the centre of GPN research. It seeks to identify how workers' conditions in chains and networks can be improved. It brings to the fore and problematizes the relationship between increased firm-level competitiveness and workers' conditions. By highlighting labour questions, ranging from remuneration to rights and conditions, the social upgrading concept represents a welcome development within the chain and network approaches. The concept of social upgrading is derived from the ILO's Decent Work Agenda (see, for example, ILO 1999), which seeks to comprehend and contribute to processes whereby workers can benefit from increased firm-level competitiveness.

Whilst the social upgrading concept and the Decent Work Agenda frame benefits to labour and capital as potentially positive sum, it is argued here that they contain serious analytical and political ambiguities and weaknesses. Their primary *analytical* weakness is their inability to comprehend the nature of capitalist exploitation and indecent work. Their primary *political* weakness is their argument that improvements to workers' conditions are to be delivered by collaboration between elite bodies, in particular firms, states and international organizations. They thus represent 'top-down' conceptions of social upgrading and Decent Work. This chapter argues, by contrast, for a 'bottom-up' conception of social upgrading and Decent Work, rooted in analysis of the capitalist labour process, where changes to workers' conditions are determined, fundamentally, by the balance of power between labour and capital and how this balance is institutionalized by states.

Prior to the social upgrading concept, upgrading within the chain and network literature referred, primarily, to the process of enhancing firm-level competitiveness. Upgrading was also assumed to contribute to broader human development. A number of paradoxes and tensions characterize this assumed causal relationship that advocates of social upgrading are now attempting to transcend.

- First, the causal relationship implies a situation of mutual gains for capital and labour. It will be argued in this chapter that this assumption is untenable.
- Second, a focus on firm-level innovation reflects an elite conception of development where the actions of a minority of entrepreneurs, firm managers and/or state agencies engender progress for the majority of workers. Within this elite perspective, beneficiaries of upgrading are relegated conceptually to secondary analytical importance (Palpacuer 2008).
- Third, it will be argued that the form and content of the labour process and broader class relations represent both a determinant of successful firm-level innovation and whether these are subsequently translated into improved conditions for workers.
- Fourth, there is little theoretical conception within the majority of the chain/network literature of how firm-level upgrading can also be achieved through *worsening* workers' conditions within and beyond the workplace.

Evidence from the author's research into the horticulture commodity chain in Brazil will be utilized to illustrate how, under appropriate conditions, worker and trade union action can be central to delivering meaningful social upgrading. The chapter concludes by drawing these arguments together and suggesting how they might inform new areas of research.

UPGRADING LABOUR FROM ABOVE IN GLOBAL PRODUCTION

In its original formation (Gereffi and Korzeniewicz 1994), the GCC framework lacked a comprehension of labour as a constitutive factor of global commodity chains. Its core conceptual innovations, 'governance' and 'upgrading', were firm-centric as they focused on lead firm actions in governing commodity chains and supplier firm attempts to increase their competitiveness through upgrading within these chains (Gibbon et al. 2008; Selwyn 2012a). As Smith et al. (2002: 47) noted, 'insofar as "workers" are present in this literature, they appear as passive victims as capital seeks cheap labour'. This perspective has continued within GCC and GVC analysis as it subsequently developed. For example, in his discussion of the developmental impacts of garment production in the Dominican Republic, Kaplinsky (2005: 60–61) notes how initially low labour costs were a major attraction to US firms, but once these firms found cheaper regional sources of labour they restructured their commodity chains and terminated their contracts with the Dominican producers. In their discussion of the fate of sub-Saharan African commodity producers, Gibbon and Ponte (2005) do not consider workers or broader social relations between capital and labour.

There have been attempts to remedy these limitations. Smith et al. (2002: 47–8) argue that there is a 'need for a more systematic analysis of the relations between capital, the state and labour in the production, circulation and realization of commodities'. Rainnie et al. (2011: 161) concur, but also argue that 'labour, as the ultimate source of value . . . must lie at [GPNs'] heart' (see also Taylor 2010). The central divergence between GCC, GVC and GPN approaches are that the former two are conceptualized as 'essentially linear structures' and 'focus narrowly on . . . governance and inter-firm transactions', whereas GPN approaches 'strive to . . . incorporate all kinds of network configuration' and 'all relevant sets of actors and relationships' (Coe et al. 2008: 272). Indeed, the GPN approach emerged, in part, in reaction to what its practitioners viewed as a 'network essentialism' (Taylor 2007) of the GCC/GVC tradition (see Henderson et al. 2002). GPNs are conceived of as being 'embedded' within broader, multi-scalar structures and institutions of the global economy. The most ambitious formulation of the GPN approach is by the Manchester School of Economic Geography (see, for example, Hess and Yeung 2006; Hess 2008), which explicitly attempts to integrate workers and trade unions into its conceptual framework. However, Cumbers et al. (2008: 369) note how, within the GPN literature, 'little has been said about labour as an active constituent of the global economy, rather than the passive victim of restructuring processes'. Levy (2008) also argues that, despite its stated objectives of transcending the limitations of GCC and GVC approaches, most GPN literature is very similar to these earlier modes of conceptualizing processes of global economic transformation.

A much more successful attempt to conceptualize labour within global systems of production is provided by Cumbers et al. (2008), for whom labour constitutes a 'fundamental component of GPNs'. They argue that:

> From the perspective of capital, the labour problem sooner or later reasserts itself into the logic of accumulation. That problem . . . is threefold: first, the need to successfully incorporate labour into the production process; second, the need to exercise control over labour time in the production process and third . . . the imperative to exploit labour as part of the process of commodification to realize surplus value. In other words, capital comes up against the reality of labour agency and resistance (Cumbers et al. 2008: 370).

In a complementary vein, in his investigation into the call centre value chain, Taylor (2010) emphasizes the indeterminacy of labour power, that is, the difficulties faced by managers in ensuring that, once employed, workers carry out the tasks allocated to them as efficiently as possible (see also Smith 2006). Whilst much chain/network research tends 'to view the firm as a black box' (Coe et al. 2008: 284), highlighting the indeterminacy of labour power means that the capital–labour relation within the firm becomes an important area for investigation, particularly when trying to identify causes of successful or unsuccessful upgrading. Taylor (2010) also argues for conceptually and empirically connecting the 'inner workings' of workplaces and the multiple contexts within which they exist, with a view to understanding the extent of labour's ability to shape these contexts. Herod (2001), Castree et al. (2008) and contributors to McGrath-Champ et al. (2010) investigate and theorize how workers are constitutive actors in economic development, through gaining improvements in wages and conditions and in the spatial formation of economic zones through, for example, pressuring municipalities to construct housing and infrastructure that facilitates workers' social reproduction.

Other studies within the GCC/GVC and GPN literature show how, whilst capitalist managers may initially conceive of workers as sources of cheap and disciplined labour, through their actions the latter have been able to alter the most exploitative firm practices (see Appelbaum 2008 and Barboza 2010 on Chinese industrial relations). In a complementary vein, Herod (2001), Dunn (2005), Feeley (2008) and Selwyn (2008) show how, while just-in-time systems of production and delivery are designed by firms to reduce their inventory costs and potentially increase their ability to source 'flexibly' from a large number of suppliers, they simultaneously give workers the ability to disrupt the functioning of supply chains through short bursts of strike action at strategic 'choke points' of the chain. Quan (2008) argues, however, that for such strategies to succeed, workers need to be educated by trade unions as to their strategic power within the chains (see also Taylor and Bain 2008).

These studies reflect in various ways what Wright (2000) labels workers' structural and associational power. Structural power accrues to workers on the basis of their position in the production process and their ability to disrupt it. Associational power comprises 'the various forms of power that result from the formation of collective organization of workers' (ibid.: 962). Whether or not workers' structural power is exercised in order to achieve concessions from capital depends on the politics of their organizations. That such studies have emerged suggest that the sidelining of labour within much of this literature is not necessarily a problem of conceptual incompatibility (between chain/network concepts and 'labour').

Upgrading is represented within most of the chain/network literature as a process of innovation where firms raise their competitiveness through enhancing their use of technology, skills and knowledge (Kaplinsky and Morris 2001; Humphrey and Schmitz 2002). Such a focus on firm-level innovation often leads to a situation where 'labour is considered primarily as a productive factor' that will benefit from a firm's enhanced competitiveness (Barrientos et al. 2011: 324). As Milberg and Winkler (2010: 345) put it, 'the presumption in the literature is that economic upgrading brings both improved export performance and social upgrading'. This presumed causal relationship, however, derives from neoclassical economics rather than real-world empirical observations (Bernhardt and Milberg 2011).

SOCIAL UPGRADING AND THE 'DECENT WORK' AGENDA

As a reaction to the limitations of the upgrading concept and its trickle-down assumptions, leading scholars have proposed that greater firm-level competitiveness and profitability be termed 'economic' upgrading, whilst the betterment of workers' conditions and remuneration be termed 'social' upgrading. Milberg and Winkler (2010: 361) contrast neoclassical and institutional comprehensions of economic development. For the former, 'the link between economic and social upgrading is automatic, while [for institutionalist approaches] there are a variety of norms and regulations that mediate this relationship'. The nature of the institutional arrangement between capital, labour and the state will determine the extent to which gains to capital from greater competitiveness (economic upgrading) translate into gains to labour (social upgrading). Advocates of social upgrading do not assume that the former automatically translates into the latter. Rather, they problematize how to achieve such mutually beneficial processes and outcomes. As Barrientos et al. (2011: 320) note, the key challenge is 'how to improve the position of both firms and workers within GPNs'.

The concept of social upgrading derives from the International Labour Organization's Decent Work Agenda. The ILO's conception of Decent Work (see Ghai 2006) comprises four aspects: employment, social protection, workers' rights and social dialogue. The Decent Work Agenda 'promotes work performed under conditions of freedom, equity, security and human dignity, in which rights are protected and adequate remuneration and social coverage are provided' (Barrientos et al. 2011: 324; ILO 1999). Following the Decent Work Agenda, social upgrading is defined as: 'The process of improvements in the rights and entitlements of workers as social actors, which enhances the quality of their employment. . . . This includes access to better work, which might result from economic upgrading. . . . But it also involves enhancing working conditions, protection and rights' (Barrientos et al. 2011: 324).

The benefits of social upgrading may not only accrue to the direct employees, but 'can also help their dependents and communities' (ibid.). Mayer and Pickles (2011) conceptualize social upgrading as a potential counter-movement to profit-driven economic upgrading. They argue, following Polanyi (1957), that the disembedding of the market from society 'results in struggles over the appropriation and distribution of social surplus'. On the other hand, they also suggest that '[t]his movement of the market . . . generates a counter-movement to re-embed the economy' (ibid.: 3–4). Whilst neoliberal globalization has created a 'global governance deficit' the latter has, in turn, 'generated a counter-movement, as governments, NGOs, organized labour groups and other social actors strive to create new institutional arrangements to re-regulate work, sourcing practices and the movement of factories in the global economy' (ibid.: 4). The argument here is that 'appropriative and distributive struggles' occur under disembedded markets. It is not unreasonable to suppose, on the basis of this argument, that such struggles would not occur under embedded markets.

The adoption of the Decent Work Agenda by leading chain/network scholars reflects its broader appeal. It became part of the Millennium Development Goals in 2006, the majority of the world's governments have signed its core conventions, and international institutions, including the World Bank and IMF, have incorporated the Decent Work Agenda into their development discourse (Lerche 2012). Pruett (2005) documents how supplier firm integration into ILO-led auditing programmes in partnerships with buyers, governments and trade unions can have selective positive impacts, in particular over issues such as child and forced labour and health and safety. Miller (2009) confirms this perspective in his research on Cambodian export textile manufacturers. However, he also notes the limited impacts of such campaigns on workers' remuneration, freedom of association and ability to pursue collective action.

LIMITATIONS AND GAPS

The Decent Work Agenda is based around a number of assumptions arguably derived from an institutionalist political economy framework. These are that, contrary to the neoclassical position, benefits to capital do not necessarily translate into benefits to labour. However, given the right institutionally mediated relations between capital and labour, mutual gains are possible. Also contrary to a core neoclassical precept, it is held that strong worker representation can contribute to successful resource allocation, leading to rising firm profitability and more rapid economic development. Finally, in agreement with neoclassical economics, most institutionalists and the ILO hold that capital does not systematically exploit labour within the production process. Rather, exploitation, when it occurs, takes place within the sphere of exchange, where workers receive below-market rates for their labour power. Neither neoclassical nor institutional approaches define with any precision the mechanisms and processes of exploitation or how to measure it. The following discussion highlights three significant problems for the Decent Work Agenda and advocates of social upgrading.

The first problem is the extent to which the Decent Work Agenda can be realistically implemented and, relatedly, the dangers of its cooptation by elite institutions. It may be encouraging for proponents of Decent Work that international institutions and many governments have either signed up to its agenda or adopted its discourse. For example, it is notable how the World Bank's position (as articulated in its World Development Reports) on labour markets has changed over the last three decades. In the mid-1990s the World Bank's (1995) World Development Report, *Workers in an Integrating World*, took the position that trade unions and employment-related institutions, rather than constituting 'distortions' in the economy, could potentially contribute positively to economic growth and efficiency. Hence,

> In many jobs workers are better informed than management about how to improve productivity. They will be more willing to share this information if

> they are confident of benefiting from any resulting change in organization. The presence of an agent on the workers' behalf, the union, may make them less suspicious that any information they reveal will benefit only management. If the union involves workers in activities that improve efficiency, unionism can be associated with a more productive organization (World Bank 1995: 74–80).

This extract may appear to contradict the above claim that a core precept of neoclassical economics is that trade unions detract from economic efficiency, growth and welfare gains. However, as Fine (2006) notes, the international financial institutions' shift from Washington to post-Washington consensus represents a continuation of these organizations' conceptual methodological individualism, but also a recognition that markets require various support mechanisms if they are to function properly. From this perspective, then, trade unions that complement capital's objectives of profit maximization, through facilitating the regulation of relations between employers and workers, are conceived of as 'market-friendly' actors.

There has been further, perhaps quite significant, convergence between the ILO and World Bank recently. While the Bank's 'Doing Business' publications have held, consistently, to an openly pro-capital perspective, arguing that labour market regulation (whether by states, or generated by trade unions) hampers economic growth (see below), in its 2013 World Development Report (WDR) (World Bank 2012b), entitled 'Jobs', it suggests that job creation is a developmental policy, that employment protection legislation and minimum wages contribute to reducing income inequality (p. 262), that higher trade union densities also reduce wage inequality (p. 264), and that voluntary labour standards are insufficient to protect and enhance the quality of jobs in an economy (pp. 306–7). The 2013 WDR represents a significant shift by the Bank towards the ILO's Decent Work Agenda (even if it is not conceptualized as such). Indeed, the 2013 WDR has been welcomed critically by organizations such as the International Trade Union Confederation, and the British TUC. Notably, however, the report does not discuss strategies of trade union mobilization, and discounts the effects of trade unions on poverty reduction (p. 263).

However, even before this shift by the Bank, the dangers of the cooptation of the ILO's Decent Work Agenda had been recognized by those who advocate social upgrading. Mayer and Pickles (2011: 9) record how since 2006 the World Bank's International Financial Corporation has required adherence to the ILO's core labour standards in all of its funded infrastructure projects, but they also note how its Doing Business benchmarking programme defines 'almost all labour regulations–such as hours of work, minimum wages, advance notice of mass dismissals and protection against discriminatory practices–as undue impediments to "doing business"'. The possibilities of the Decent Work Agenda being coopted by elite international institutions, states and firms reflect a fundamental weakness of the ILO:

> It has no powers of enforcement at its disposal, apart from 'naming and shaming' those in breach of conventions. Compared to the economic and political power of capital and of neoliberal governments, and even compared to the sanctions available to the WTO . . . the solely discursive powers of the ILO are extremely weak. (Lerche 2012: 20).

A second problem for the Decent Work Agenda is that it is relatively devoid of analyses of the causes of indecent work and processes contributing to its amelioration. Rather, as Miyamura (2012: 105) argues in his discussion of labour market institutions literature, the ILO's presentation represents a focus on best case labour market outcomes, 'rather than the social processes and mechanisms to achieve them'. It is assumed that combinations of incorrect policy choices and inappropriate micro-institutional arrangements are the cause of bad work. Consequently, the ILO, like the World Bank, promotes good governance and the tackling of corruption as prerequisites for the generation of decent work (see Lerche 2012).

A third problem in the Decent Work Agenda is its weak conceptualization of class relations and its inability to identify the systemic processes of exploitation characteristic of capitalist social relations. This problem derives from its assumptions that, given the right institutional context, capital does not exploit labour. For example, Mayer and Pickles argue that struggles over appropriation and distribution of social surpluses occur in contexts of the disembedding of the market, rather than when markets are 'embedded' in society. Their argument represents the conceptual denial of the source of capital's existence in the exploitation of labour. This conceptual denial, by Mayer and Pickles and by the ILO, perhaps explains why 'the development of . . . outright political mobilization is not part of the ILO Decent Work Agenda'. Consequently, however, this 'leaves [it] without transformative power' (Lerche 2012: 27). As Miyamura concludes:

> The 'decent work' agenda must open up space for class focused struggles and arguments that not only demand redistribution of surplus through the state, but also focus on the causes and processes of socio-economic inequalities. . . . It must also secure legal, political and social conditions which enable exploration of commonalities in the struggle of labouring classes. (Miyamura 2012: 118).

The next section discusses the nature of capitalist exploitation and resistance to it. It is suggested that these, rather than institutional arrangements between state, capital and labour, should be placed at the heart of attempts to conceptualize and realize Decent Work and social upgrading.

THE CAPITALIST LABOUR PROCESS

In their contribution to debates about the labour process, Smith and Meiksins (1995) note how the globalization of production is facilitating a rapid diffusion of managerial techniques across the globe. Lead firms' governance of their supply chains enables them to regulate supplier firm production and labour processes to meet their demands. These observations complement GPNs' emphasis upon the multi-scalar constitution of the labour process, distinguishing local, national and global moments of capital accumulation.

The capitalist labour process exists within two sets of mutually conditioning relations: competition between firms and the employment of labour by capital. It consists of two sub-processes. First, the production of use and exchange values and second, and simultaneously, the generation of surplus value (Marx 1990). Because firms relate to each other through constant competition, the labour process is characterized by an endless productivity drive designed to maximize the speed and intensity of the performance of tasks and the 'precision, predictability and quality of transformations being worked' (Brighton Labour Process Group 1977: 13). The productivity drive is technical and sociological. Once the employment contract has been signed and workers enter the workplace, managers attempt to ensure that they work as effectively as possible. However, as Smith (2006) observes, labour power is 'indeterminate' in that there is often a disjuncture between the expectations of managers and of workers of what exactly needs to be done, how and how fast. Capital must therefore continually reorganize 'a system of power relations the function of which is to define and enforce the discipline of the labour process' (Brighton Labour Process Group 1977: 13).

Ownership, control and organization of the production process, the means of production, workers' labour power and the final commodity by capital are all indispensable in the process of exploitation and are guaranteed by capitalist property relations backed up by states. These social relations, which co-constitute the imperatives of competitive accumulation, explain why capital will seek to reduce to a minimum, if not eliminate altogether, activities by labour that might limit the valorization process, often including those associated with social upgrading. The kernel of truth in institutional analysis is that, without arrangements that commit capital to providing benefits to labour, there is no reason why individual capitalists would choose to do so (even if they wanted to) as their actions would represent a cost, thus potentially handing competitive advantage to their rivals in the market. However, what the Decent Work Agenda and, so far, the social upgrading framework ignores, is that such institutional arrangements are themselves often outcomes of and/or responses to real or potential struggles between capital and labour.

An example of the interaction of capital–labour relations and institutional norms is provided by Smith and Meiksins (1995) in their discussion of TNCs' attempts to diffuse 'best practice' workplace relations along their supply chains. They note that, since 'nodes' of each chain are geographically located within distinct national territories, the process of diffusion is mediated by national political economies, rather than determined solely by lead firm requirements. They also argue that the institutional arrangement within national political economies, between capital, labour and the state, is itself partially determined by the balance of power between capital and labour. For example, they note differential forms of best practice diffusion in the UK-based car industry. When American firms located in the UK in the 1950s and 1960s they faced a relatively strong trade union movement and a state committed to Keynesian economic demand management, meaning that firms had to 'conform to [the UK's] multi-union environment . . . [and] industrial relations customs'. In contrast, when Japanese auto firms began directly investing in the UK in the 1980s, in the context of faltering trade union power and a neoliberal (anti-labour, pro-foreign capital) state, they were able to force through major changes in workplace industrial relations and extract significant concessions from labour. These examples suggest how trade union strength in relation to capital and the state is constitutive of the institutional environment within which globalizing capital seeks to operate and thus represents a determinant of the relationship between economic and social upgrading.

WORKERS AND SOCIAL UPGRADING: UNION ACTION IN BRAZILIAN EXPORT HORTICULTURE

A central argument of this chapter is that workers' ability to transform their structural power into associational power in order to extract concessions from capital constitutes a core determinant of the relationship between economic and social upgrading. Put differently, if workers are able to organize in the face of capitalist management systems designed to raise the rate of exploitation, then they raise, significantly, the possibilities of achieving some form of social upgrading. This argument is derived, in part, from the present author's research into capital–labour relations in north-east Brazil (Selwyn 2007; 2012a; 2012b).

The São Francisco valley in the interior of the Brazilian north-east is home to a fast-expanding region of export horticulture. Thousands of hectares of irrigated land enable the production of high quality grapes and mangoes for Northern markets. The valley is but one of many zones of export horticulture production that have emerged across the global South over the last three decades and that operate within tightly coordinated retailer-dominated supply chains. There are numerous cases, for example in South Africa and Chile, where profitable export horticulture is characterized by domineering farms and precarious conditions for labour: temporary contracts, low pay and limited union recognition or presence (Barrientos 2001). Such cases represent examples of economic upgrading without social upgrading.

In the São Francisco valley, however, the local rural workers' union, the Sindicato dos Trabalhadores Rurais (STR), has been able to mobilize the workforce in the export grape sector and has contributed to significant social upgrading. As part of their competitive strategies and within the context of the global 'retail revolution' Northern retailers have, since the 1990s, been ramping up requirements across their proliferating supplier base. Suppliers to Northern supermarkets need to produce grapes according to strict size, shape, colour, weight and sugar-level requirements, and are strictly regulated by buyers, importers and third-party certification agencies.

Meeting such standards requires farms to oversee an increasingly complex labour process. For example, while export grape producers require over 30 operations per harvest cycle to meet retailer standards, producers selling onto 'traditional' (street) markets within Brazil perform as few as nine operations per harvest cycle. In order to carry out these operations, exporting farms rely on an increasingly skilled and hard-working labour force, of which a large percentage is female.

Initially, working conditions in the valley's export grape sector were very poor, characterized by low and often ad hoc pay, lack of employment security and even the use of child labour. As a lawyer from the STR described it:

> Before we had the collective agreement, working on grape farms could be very dangerous. Workers were transported to the farms on top of lorries, they had to apply insecticides without using protective clothing, they might hurt themselves at work and not be able to continue working, and then the boss would sack them. Lunch breaks were not specified, with workers sometimes being forced to work throughout the day without a break, and safe drinking water was not provided. (cited in Selwyn 2007: 545).

However, in the mid-1990s, the STR began an ongoing campaign which has led to significant improvements in workers' pay and conditions. These improvements have been codified or 'institutionalized' within a collective convention between the employers' organization (VALEXPORT) and the STR, overseen by the Ministry of Labour. Employers' obligations to workers are negotiated and, in some areas, heavily contested by either side during the annual negotiations for the renewal of the convention.

At the heart of STR's strategy of pressurizing employers to ameliorate workers' conditions has been the threat, or use of, strike action. In order to meet retailer demands, exporting farms must implement a strict and precise production calendar and any delays reduce fruit quality. This represents a strong reliance by farms on dedicated and skilled labour input. It also represents, for workers, a source of structural power, that is, the ability to disrupt production through suspensions of work. Short strikes by workers on exporting farms have deleterious consequences for fruit quality and its sale price. This structural power, which has been augmented by rising retailer demands, has been realized through workers' associational power – their ability to organize through the STR. Early gains made by the STR included commitments by farms to employ only registered workers, leading to pension and other social security contributions, such as the right to paid maternity leave for female workers, specified working hours, payment above the minimum wage, higher pay for overtime and the provision of protective clothing, and the right for the STR to represent, organize and visit workers on farms during the working day. Subsequent gains have included the provision of crèche care, safe transport to and from work and the rights of workers to pursue an education outside work, implying the need for workers to be able to leave the farms on time.

The STR pursued these tactics from the mid-1990s to the mid-2000s. Workers represented by the trade union enjoy substantially better conditions than prior to the STR's mobilization and better conditions than unrepresented workers elsewhere in the fruiticulture sector. These victories do not mark the end-point of the STR's campaign for ameliorating the pay and conditions of its members. They do, however, demonstrate how workers' collective action can bring about social upgrading.

Farms have responded in various ways to STR gains. On the one hand, they have tried to reduce non-wage costs, such as their commitments to crèche care and maternity leave for women, by restructuring the rural labour force and reducing their reliance on women workers, leading to a stratification of the female workforce between a small core of permanently employed women, enjoying relatively good pay and conditions, and a larger periphery of temporarily employed women, enjoying fewer benefits. On the other hand, they have tried to substitute themselves for the STR as workers' principal benefactor, thus reducing workers' associational power, by providing benefits to workers directly, such as free or very cheap on-farm housing and some health care. However, whilst many attempts by farms at holding the STR at arm's length have been successful, they have come at a cost, of having to provide real, material benefits to their workforces.

BROADER IMPLICATIONS

Does the above example have any broader implications for conceptualizing sources and processes of social upgrading? Barrientos et al. (2011: 337) do acknowledge that 'independent trade union representation of workers' can contribute to social upgrading. However, they do not specify the causal weight they give to trade unions and their activities in relation to the actions of 'benign' states and capital. This recognition and arguments like those advanced in this chapter should encourage advocates of social upgrading to consider how they conceptually incorporate the labour process, class relations and in particular workers' movements and actions into their broader developmental objectives. There are at least three reasons for them to do so.

First, there can be a gulf between the adoption of Decent Work principles and their practice. The example of Cambodia is instructive. In 1999 the governments of Cambodia and the United States signed a three-year, quota-based trade agreement covering textiles and apparel exports, on the basis of improvements to Cambodian workers' conditions. The governments jointly requested ILO oversight and assistance to implement this 'social clause'. Miller (2009: 14) notes that the resultant Better Factories Cambodia project 'is arguably the most comprehensive and systematic monitoring effort governing any national garment supply base in the world'. The Better Factories Cambodia project has been hailed as a success (Polaski 2003) as working conditions across the sector have improved in some important ways, with, for example, no more reported cases of forced or child labour. Payment of wages also became regularized across much of the sector. The value of exports has boomed – from US$26 million in 1995, to US$1.6 billion in 2004, to over US$2 billion by 2006 – and employment in the sector numbered around 265 000 by the mid-2000s.

This case study appears to lend credence to arguments by advocates of the Decent Work Agenda that simultaneous economic and social upgrading is possible. Miller (2009) advances an alternative interpretation, however. He documents the above-mentioned improvements, but notes that other much-needed improvements to workers' pay and conditions, such as freedom of association, collective bargaining and reduction in excessive working hours, remain distant hopes, with numerous cases of unfair dismissal of workers and harassment of shop stewards, leading to widespread discontent, manifested in strikes, across the sector. He also notes how, despite not being part of the ILO's objectives in the Better Factories Cambodia project, the demands for a 'living wage' lay at the heart of many of the strikes. This is because 'in an economy where the monthly living wage is estimated at US$82, garment workers earned an average wage equivalent to US$65 per month in 2005, including overtime and bonuses' (ibid.: 22).

Workers' productivity (or the rate of exploitation) has increased across the sector as it has expanded. For example, one worker cited by Miller described her situation thus: 'Before . . . I had to finish 300 pieces per eight hours and worked only on one machine. But now I am assigned 550–600 pieces to finish in eight hours and operate two machines' (ibid.: 26). Miller concludes by noting the 'real changes in working conditions and working environments' that have been brought about through Better Factories Cambodia, but also that 'factory owners continue to mount dogged resistance to the establishment of collective bargaining in the workplace and demand excessive overtime from their workers for less than a living wage' (ibid.: 27). His conclusion should serve as a corrective to the excessive focus on institutional agreements by the ILO and advocates of social upgrading and suggests the need to investigate more closely processes of exploitation and resistance to it that characterize the capitalist workplace.

Second, it is arguably problematic to conceptualize the institutionalization of capital–labour relations as analytically prior to those relations themselves. But this is what the ILO does by conceiving of workers' actions as secondary to the institutional arrangements between capital, labour and the state. An important seam of political economy illustrates how changing class relations determine differential patterns and trajectories of capitalist development (Brenner 1977; Byres 1991; Kay 2002b). These authors highlight how the outcomes of class struggles constitute historical moments which, once stabilized, determine the form and content that national institutional arrangements take, which in turn subsequently influence the nation's developmental trajectory. Whilst this literature is concerned with the world-historical transition to and diverse developmental trajectories within capitalism, there are also similar insights to be had from scholarship addressing more recent transformations. For example, Seidman (1994), Moody (1997) and Silver (2003) document how rapid industrialization and high rates of capital accumulation occurred in dictatorial Brazil and South Korea and Apartheid South Africa, respectively, during the 1970s. Under these regimes, rapid economic upgrading occurred, based upon high rates of worker exploitation and social downgrading. These authors also show, however, that through collective action workers' organizations were able to gain concessions from state and capital and, further, that they represented the essential component of movements that contributed to the installation of democracy in these countries.

Third, by analytically prioritizing institutional arrangements over workers' self-activity, advocates of social upgrading risk demobilizing the very actors that can bring about the kinds of improvement that they wish to see. An alternative approach, suggested here, is to analytically prioritize workers' attempts to ameliorate their conditions and to understand that institutional arrangements between capital, labour and the state are, in part at least, outcomes of these struggles from below.

CONCLUSIONS

What are the implications of the above discussions for critical chain and network conceptions of social upgrading? Clearly, a focus on workers' actions and trade union representations and how these achieve or fail to achieve improvements in their members' conditions, would constitute an important avenue of research. Also, from the perspective of the Decent Work Agenda, it is important to investigate processes whereby class relations become institutionalized in such ways that contribute to/detract from the possibilities of social upgrading. Such investigations would examine strategies of organized and unorganized labour and of capital in its many forms, in their respective attempts to enhance their positions within the accumulation process. Such examinations and theoretical reflections would also seek to shift the intellectual agenda of critical chain and network approaches towards a constructive engagement with labour movements, as advocated by Quan (2008), and would therefore be highly political in seeking to legitimate workers' actions as contributing to social upgrading and broader human development.

By analytically discounting systemic exploitation of labour by capital, current conceptions of Decent Work and social upgrading leave a central feature of the capital–labour relation – the labour process – relatively untouched, empirically and conceptually. As has been argued here, following Cumbers et al. (2008), Taylor (2010), Rainnie et al. (2011) and Selwyn (2012a), a closer focus on the labour process and its multi-scalar dimensions (how it is constituted at local, national, regional and global 'levels'), places greater analytical weight on workers as actors in the constitution of the global economy. In the analysis of the labour process and of the wider labour regime we can, if we look beneath the surface ideology held by both neoclassicals and institutionalists of a 'fair day's pay for a fair day's work', detect means of economic upgrading, processes of exploitation and of labour's resistance to it and possibilities of what might be termed 'labour-led' social upgrading.

This shift in emphasis, from the institutional arrangements prioritized by advocates of social upgrading and Decent Work to the labour process, also leads to a different political perspective. While advocates of social upgrading and Decent Work represent a 'top-down' approach to addressing problems of labour's maltreatment by capital, a more critical chain/network framework, rooted in an analysis of the labour process, represents a 'bottom-up' approach to these issues. The first perspective allocates labour a subordinate 'partnership' role to capital's profit orientation and states' attempts at regulating the capital–labour relation. The second perspective analytically prioritizes workers' struggles to ameliorate their conditions through collective action. There may be some situations where both perspectives are complementary – where class alliances are formed when workers' struggles complement capital's and states' attempts at regulating employment practices. But it would be a mistake for advocates of a more critical chain/network analysis to intellectually and politically subordinate their commitments (the primacy of workers' collective action) to objectives of capital and the state. As Wright (2000) and Selwyn (2012b) observe, class compromises, alliances and the institutionalization of these relations emerge out of processes of collective action by workers as they pursue their own goals, demonstrating to capital their collective strength.

7. Global outsourcing and socialization of labour: the case of Nike

Jeroen Merk

INTRODUCTION

In this chapter I look at the athletic shoe as a microcosm of social relations. Taking the Nike sportswear company as a case in point allows us to uncover a small node in a worldwide set of interconnections, which we can deconstruct as a 'multiplicity of social dynamics operating at different levels' (Perrons 2004: 26; Korzeniewicz 1994: 261). With its design, components production and sourcing, assembly, transport and eventual purchase spread across countries in all corners of the globe (Vanderbilt 1998: 84; DMG 1998), deconstructing a mundane article like a Nike sneaker shows us a capitalist system not only global in reach, but also 'globalised in terms of the functional integration of the production process itself' (Dicken 2003, cited in Lier 2007b: 816).

What little we know of those who produce the shoe we buy in a shop easily recedes behind its immediate appearance, the features that make us consider owning a pair. The world of objects appears to us as autonomous and independent from the subjects which produce it. As Marx put it, 'from the taste of wheat it is not possible to tell who produced it, a Russian serf, a French peasant or an English capitalist' (Marx 1977: 6; cf. 1976: 290; Miller 2005). Likewise, wearing a pair of Nike shoes does not reveal the labour conditions under which it was assembled either. It may have been assembled, as Donald Katz notes in an otherwise friendly biography of Nike (1994: 172), by a young Indonesian woman worker suffering management by 'terror and browbeating', or by a fellow worker in one of the rare unionized footwear factories operating under a collective bargaining contract. In a market economy social relations among people take on the 'fantastic form of a relation between products', as Marx famously put it (1976: 165), a phenomenon he labelled 'commodity fetishism'.

The global anti-sweatshop movement has made an effort to bring this invisible world into the open, not just to express solidarity with labour struggles in distant corners of the world but also to raise the issue of how the global economy operates more generally (Ascoly and

Zeldenrust 1999: 11). Stories on substandard working conditions are easily picked up by foreign news services, NGOs that operate on a global level and trade union federations, and may trigger picket lines at corporate headquarters or demonstrations at retail outlets. Worldwide commodity production ensures that local events are increasingly affected by distant processes and events (Giddens 1990), allowing their politicization through demands for better working conditions or, for that matter, 'clean clothes'.

Like many other industrial and service industries, the outsourcing system dominant in footwear and garments creates a 'social distance between the worker and the entity for which the productive activity is ultimately performed' (McIntyre 2008: 34–5). Jane Wills (2009: 444) speaks of 'subcontracted capitalism', which denotes that

> increasing numbers of the world's growing workforce, and particularly those connected to the global economy, face constant pressure on their wages and conditions of work. The nature of short-term contracts and increased competition means that contractors are forced to cut back on employees' pay and standards of work. Moreover, given that they are no longer directly employed, these workers have no industrial relations contact with their 'real employer'.

Nike is a prime example of this trend towards outsourcing, fragmentation and distancing. The company never owned factories and has become a world famous brand through outsourcing all labour-intensive production, which allowed it to amass huge profits and extend its market reach. Nonetheless, we argue that industrial production always relies upon a set of integrative, regulatory mechanisms at the level of a particular commodity group. Even if production and consumption have become spatially and organizationally fragmented, as they have over the last decades, what is equally at work is a process of *socialization of labour* that turns the process of marketization, or *commodification* (the historical process through which capitalism expands), into a contested terrain again and potentially transcends it. Nike is no exception here. From its viewpoint as an organization, outsourcing therefore has a contradictory aspect: the drive towards a global dispersion of production sites disconnects the unity of company direction into a range of potentially conflicting centres and confronts the company with a range of coordination and planning problems. Hence it will seek to restore a degree of unity by allowing various non-market linkages to develop. In other words, even neoliberalism cannot undo the ongoing process of socialization of labour.

COMMODIFICATION AND SOCIALIZATION OF LABOUR

Commodification refers to the transformation of ever more aspects of society into exchangeable commodities. It denotes that 'goods produced, services rendered, but also the raw material of nature and human beings as such, are . . . subjected to an economic discipline which defines and treats them as commodities' (van der Pijl 1998: 8). As a result individuals increasingly depend on the (world) market for their basic needs, whilst capitalist production 'expands on an ever greater scale until it has become the generally prevailing social condition' (Marx 1981: 117). As an *intensive process* in an already existing market economy, commodification incorporates ever-more human activities previously outside the market logic, like, for example, culture, sports, healthcare or education; as an *extensive process*, it replaces pre-capitalist or non-capitalist forms of production (Robinson 2004: 6).

Nike operates on both dimensions. In terms of intensive commodification, it has specialized itself in aestheticizing everyday products by way of marketing, promotion and branding. In this process it seeks to destroy 'all traces of production in their imagery, reinforcing the fetishism that arises automatically in the course of market exchange' (Harvey 1990: 102). By associating its products with sports events like the Olympic Games or with well-known athletes, a sportswear company like Nike seeks to evoke the 'magical' quality of its products that unbranded commodities lack. 'Commodity spectacles' are organized or sponsored along with other activities aimed at 'defining and fixing cultural and artistic standards, fashions, tastes, consumer norms, and more strategically, public opinion' (Lazzarato 1996: 132). Images that appeal to social and cultural values thus become attached to particular brand names (Goldman and Papson 1998: 24) whilst physical aspects of the product such as manufacturing are outsourced. This has 'freed' branded companies from the surveillance of workers, instead allowing them to focus 'on the terrain outside of the production process: sales and the relationship with the consumer' (Lazzarato 1996: 140; Hardt and Negri 2004; Gorz 2010). Or in the words of the former CEO of Nike, Phil Knight, 'The most important thing we do is market the product. We've come around to saying that Nike is a marketing-oriented company, and the product is its most important tool' (quoted in Klein 2000: 22). Thus the material utility of a pair of athletic shoes becomes secondary to the consumption of experience, lifestyle, attitude, reputation and image, satisfying 'imaginary appetites' with symbolic values.

The extensive moment of commodification resides in geographical expansion. In the case of Nike, more than a million workers in hundreds of garment and footwear supply operations located in dozens of countries, serve a company which itself directly employs about 38 000 workers. Phil Knight, Nike's founder, proudly told a journalist that whilst 'Puma and Adidas were still manufacturing in high wage European countries. . . we knew that wages were lower in Asia, and we knew how to get around in that environment' (cited in LaFeber 1999: 104). Thus Nike escaped the regulated labour markets of industrialized countries by leaving management control over large labour forces to third parties. Meanwhile, the mostly young (teenage) female workers in the factories in China, Vietnam, Bangladesh or Indonesia typically belong to the first generation of employees to work outside of their home villages. Most of them have only recently migrated from rural villages to industrial production zones, where their fate comes to depend on the global investment decisions of corporations located far from their communities and workplaces – decisions over which the affected workers typically have no, or very little, influence.

Now if commodity exchange 'fosters an impression of self-sufficient atomism' (McIntyre 2007: 50; cf. Marx 1973: 157; 1976: 163), the market connection, even if it is made anonymous by the vast distances between producers and consumers, nevertheless binds all of them into a single productive/reproductive web of social relations. Commodification thus implies the simultaneous socialization of labour, in the sense of an increased interdependence of individuals under the social division of labour. Capital in the process manifests itself as a social force, one that is not bound to nation-states once it gains access to others. Far from seeing capitalism as a closed system, a view sometimes ascribed to Marx (Hettne 1995: 9; Gilpin 1987: 3), it instead represents a set of 'relational complexes that exist neither merely "inside", nor merely "outside", the state borders' (Patomäki 2003: 361). And whilst commodification is the deep, structural dimension of transnational relations across the divide (van Apeldoorn 2004: 161; Postone 1996), socialization of labour refers to the 'steady emergence of collective organization within capitalism' (Brick 2006: 41; Gill 1995).

INTEGRATION OF DIVIDED LABOUR PROCESSES

There exists an important qualitative difference between a social division of labour in society, which is coordinated *ex post* through the exchange of commodities, and a detailed division of labour at the level of the workshop, which nowadays is commonly referred to as a technical division of labour. A technical division is coordinated *ex ante*. In a social division of labour, different production processes blindly connect via the exchange of commodities. Marx actually gives the example of how this occurs in the production of a shoe:

> The cattle-breeder produces hides, the tanner makes the hides into leather, and the shoemaker makes the leather into boots. Here the product of each man is merely a step towards the final form, which is the combined product of their specialized labours. There are, besides, all the various trades which supply the cattle-breeder, the tanner and the shoemaker with their means of production (Marx 1976: 474–5).

The bond between the independent labour of the different crafts here is organized via the purchase and sale of commodities, via market exchange. Various kinds of specialized work are performed independently of one another by private producers. There is no overall conscious coordination guiding the exchange process. Despite the myopic motivations, the different activities somehow become integrated. The social costs of this 'blind' integration are of course immense. Overproduction and other crises resulting from disproportionalities, mass unemployment and idle capacity, social dislocations affecting entire regions and countries, famines and wars, all have to be brought into the picture to avoid ending up with an idyllic account of the market 'mechanism' as a failsafe invisible hand. But certainly, economically speaking, the market unites the various production processes into a single process.

By contrast, a technical division of labour takes place within a single organizational unit (workplace, factory, transnational corporation). Here, labour is organized or coordinated according to plan as the different activities carried out by labourers within this organization are immediately linked. Each worker performs a specialized task that fits into a single production process associated with a particular commodity (or set of commodities). On the shop floor, it is not competition but cooperation between different labourers that prevails, although under vertical relationships of management and control. A conscious agency 'ensures that labour, semi-finished objects and raw materials are spatio-temporally distributed in accordance with the technical requirements of the various stages of the productive processes' (Fleetwood 2002: 80). Within these organizational boundaries, production processes are prepared, supervised and regulated by management. The distinction between both types of division of labour can be described as follows: 'Division of labour within the workshop implies the undisputed authority of the capitalist over men [while the] division of labour within the society brings into contact independent producers of commodities, who acknowledge no other authority but that of competition' (Marx 1976: 476–7).

Marx thus argues that the social division of labour is ruled *anarchically*, for example, without a single coordinating centre, while the technical division of labour is ruled *despotically*. The distinction points at two very different or even contrasting modes in which the reunification of divided tasks is achieved. The first is a result of blind interaction, or spontaneous integration, via the invisible hand of the market. The various activities connect without previous collective regulation or design. Here, as Steve Fleetwood observes, 'labouring activities are indirectly co-ordinated via the systematic exchange of the products of these very activities, commodities' (2002: 81). The second, however, is a result of an *a priori* plan developed by management within a particular capital (company), which operates as a single coordinating centre and where conscious decisions dominate. The contrast between these two different ways of integrating fragmented activities 'illuminates capitalism's extraordinary and perhaps contradictory combination of spheres of rational organization and spheres of anarchy, a combination which structures both the world economy and the texture of everyday life' (Sayer 1995: 45).

However, such clear-cut, stylized distinctions in which the technical division of labour negates the social division of labour (and vice versa), do not correspond to the way production is organized today. An important aspect of today's socialization of labour is that the production of commodities is already subject to more ambivalent processes, in which coordination and planning are often pushing beyond the boundaries of legal (corporate) ownership. Planning and anarchy do not stand in straightforward opposition to one another but merge in various combinations. Instead of an absolute dichotomy between planning versus market forces, a plurality of hybrid forms can be distinguished.

COORDINATION AND CONTROL IN GLOBAL PRODUCTION

The global value chain approach highlights how corporations manage to steer or control production processes even if they have little direct relation to the actual production of goods made on their behalf (Gereffi et al. 2005; Bair 2005; Selwyn, this volume). Thus, even though we can speak of vertically disintegrated and spatially dispersed production, the various activities remain subject to coordination. The commodity, even the pedestrian sneaker, is 'the product of gradual sophistication of the social coordination of production' (Duménil and Lévy 2011: 94). In fact, companies like Nike are constantly trying to limit the anarchical aspects of the market. They have dissociated themselves from *strategic* control over labour-intensive production and control over large labour forces, but maintained *operational* control over production through the processes of conceptualization, design, quality control and so on (Ietto-Gillies 2002: 54).

The drive to global dispersion of production sites disconnects the different units in which production is broken down (the process of the extensive commodification of labour, which disconnects the unity of company direction into a range of potentially conflicting centres of direction). The company will therefore be confronted with coordination and planning problems and for obvious reasons will seek to restore a degree of unity in the dispersed production processes. This has resulted in numerous technical and managerial innovations to achieve functional unity, to speed up flow processes and to promote collaboration among corporations in order to restrict market anarchy and to strengthen (or re-introduce) the planning aspects of production. Far from an aspect alien to the liberal, capitalist economy, regulation and private governance are already an integral part of market exchange. For example, in order to limit the number of 'blind buys', Nike has spent hundreds of millions of dollars in its global supply chain to improve inventory management and to reduce sourcing lead times. The company is even buying 'materials on behalf of the entire manufacturing base, rather than having its individual factory partners go and source the material separately' (Citigroup 2005: 44). This shows us that the 'distinction between "making" and "marketing", which once structured so much business thought and praxis, has transformed itself into a dialectical unity' (Appelbaum and Lichtenstein 2006: 113–14).

It also indicates that the search for increased control over the market does not necessarily lead to a concentration of production 'under one roof', as many (orthodox) Marxists thought. Instead, large-scale production can be understood as a reaction to a low degree of the socialization of labour, driven for example by the high costs of transportation and communication, the lack of agreed-upon standards, or the absence of developed (world) markets (Shamsavari 1991: 277). Hence the spatial fragmentation, decentralization and restructuring of production processes through subcontracting, outsourcing arrangements or 'lean' organizational methods does not reflect, as sometimes argued (e.g. Carnoy 2001; Piore and Sabel 1984), a reversal of the trend towards socialization of labour (production), back to increased 'anarchy of the market'. Rather it expresses the more complex organizational forms of inter-firm cooperation on an increasingly transnational scale. What has emerged, as the World Investment Report puts it, is a 'cross-border *non-equity mode of TNC operation* [wherein] a TNC externalizes part of its operations to a host-country-based partner firm in which it has no ownership stake, while maintaining *a level of control* over the operation by contractually specifying the way it is to be conducted' (UNCTAD 2011: 127, emphasis added). Instead of defining the corporation in terms of ownership of assets, the firm is here conceptualized in terms of control over its external linkages, which include both market and non-market activities (Peoples and Sugden 2000: 177; Dicken 2003; Gereffi et al. 2005: 81).

Every advanced social division of labour requires objectified knowledge, logistics, standards, rules, benchmarks, training materials, guidelines, trust, and so forth, in order to merge the inter-firm division of labour into a coherent sequence of activities. This has resulted in numerous technical and managerial innovations to achieve functional unity, to speed up flow processes and to promote collaboration among corporations in order to restrict market anarchy and to strengthen (or re-introduce) the planning aspects of production. Regulation and private governance are already an integral part of market exchange. These managerial instruments and regulatory institutions remain an integral element of the process of socialization of labour. The concept of governance as developed in the global value chain approach certainly captures the idea of non-market forms of coordination that accompany these processes, but it often fails to grasp the transformative nature of capitalist production, or the historical dimension of social processes for that matter.

An example of the socialization of labour in global footwear production is offered by UNIDO leather expert Ferenc Schmél. He argues that:

> The ever broadening international cooperation gradually *eliminates* technical differences among different countries and regions, the technology . . . implemented in different parts of the world is very much the same today. Consequently, there is no reason for having different training programmes in industrialized and developing countries, so the creation of a uniform syllabus for the leather, footwear and other leather products is not only an opportunity but also a necessity (Schmél 1997: 2, emphasis added).

The creation of a uniform syllabus for training programmes may seem like a trivial example, but it shows how the socialization of labour imposes itself on daily production processes. It reflects that productive activities do not function in an isolated, local context, but are part of a larger system of production (e.g. Marx 1973: 705; 1976: 1024). It reflects that 'production itself changed from a series of individual into a series of social acts' (Engels 1880). Footwear production, like other industrial commodities, is no longer based on tacit experience-based knowledge transferred from generation to generation by craftsmen, or within families. It is increasingly dependent on knowledge produced 'elsewhere' and taught at management schools and incorporated into standardized machinery. Foreign customers may also demand new technologies, which imposes a socializing logic on the production processes in the form of product convergence or industry convergence (Graz 2006b). The importance of standardization for production is expressed in the following remark by a Nike manager confronted with production problems at a Chinese supplier in the early 1980s:

> We are educating factory managers that Korean, Taiwanese, and Chinese shoes are sold as equals and must, therefore, meet international standards. We are also getting the China Trading Company to understand the Nike production and marketing concept. The trading company staff and factory managers don't communicate enough with each other. Nike's people are physically in each of the factories almost daily. Our role is quality control, but we're looked on as educators. We prepared lots of manuals to define our methods (cited in Austin and Aguilar 1988: 9).

This underlines Nike's aim of total substitutability of the production of its merchandise ('shoes are sold as equals') among a fragmented set of suppliers operating in Korea, Taiwan and China. In turn this requires various kinds of non-market relations of planning, education, communication, coordination, cooperation and governance, activities that promote the industrial upgrading of supply chain 'partners'. Nike certainly found out that when there is a failure to do so, as was the case in China in the early 1980s, it results in delays, cost overruns and inferior products (Austin and Aguilar 1988).

Thus we observe how the manufacturer, even though formally independent, de facto becomes an integral part of a flow of activity encompassing multiple geographical locations and capitals, just as it is governed by various private as well as public actors. Taiwanese footwear company Feng-Tay, operating in mainland China exclusively for Nike, was an early example of this. As Lu-lin Cheng writes,

> Nike has its Asian Research and Development Centre located in Feng-Tay. The Nike R&D Centre, although a joint investment of both companies, is organisationally a unit of Feng-Tay, and not an independent company controlled by Nike. There are, in total, about forty engineers in the unit. Ten of them are from Nike. Its operation is fully independent from other units of the company and under the twin management of Nike's Asian R&D head and a chief technician from Feng-Tay. It is, in a sense, an overlapping territory of the two companies (1996: 178).

Here we may insert the concept of the *collective worker*, which emphasizes 'the necessarily co-operative character of the capitalist labour process in which valorisation depends on the collective functions of individuals' (Martinez Lucio and Stewart 1997: 49; Gough 2003; Merk 2004). In 'Fordist' factories, the division of labour between conception and execution, or mental and manual work, takes place within the various departments of one factory. Here, production units operate, as Braverman puts it, 'like a hand, watched, corrected, and controlled by a distant brain' (1974: 124–5). Or as Marx puts it, 'in order to labour productively, it is no longer necessary for you to do manual work yourself; [it is already] enough, if you are an organ of the collective labourer and perform one of its subordinate functions' (1976: 643–4). In today's decentralized environment, the same process takes place on a global level. In the words of one athletic footwear designer working at headquarters of a Western company, 'The biggest eye opener for me was coming out this way [to Asia]. When they say that a thousand hands touch these things before they reach the customer–you don't really understand that. But coming here you see this is like a city. Changing one line affects so many people' (quoted in Mamic 2004: 73).

While competition between different capitals is the main factor that compels producers to heed this socializing logic of harmonization, it is often assisted by state or semi-state agencies (the UNIDO leather expert providing standardized training programmes), as well as by various kinds of private forms of *ex ante* collaboration aimed at transcending the limits of the separate (localized) structures of socialization of labour. Nike and other sourcing companies do not find their merchandise on the *market* but train and educate their suppliers, usually located on the periphery of capitalist production, to meet international standards and to ensure that a particular type of shoe (say, the 'Nike Air Alpha Force' or 'Nike Terminator') assembled in Indonesia is identical to one made in China. The establishment of these connections between Nike and its suppliers, which is a common strategy for how most branded corporations organize their production, introduces coordination and planning into the production process, thus imparting a flow logic that in turn requires a 'structural conformity to socialised labour' of the different units (Sohn-Rethel 1976: 31).

The transnational fragmentation of productive processes therefore does not signal the end of planning, direction or coordination, even if the different owners of capital – Nike, its Taiwanese manufacturer, the retail outlet and so on – remain subject to competition. This in turn creates a situation in which the shoe producer in faraway China is no longer hidden behind the horizon, but enters into almost direct relationships with management in the West. As a result the (managerial) systems that accompany global production reflect not only a growing capacity to consciously plan and manage large-scale, interdependent operations (Adler 2007); they also erode the separation between technical division of labour within a company and the social division of labour within society (Rupert 1995: 37).

Although standards remain largely invisible in daily life for consumers, corporations – who buy and supply products to each other – rely crucially

force. Their struggles, however disparate and isolated from one another, nevertheless have an impact on the dynamics, practices, institutional structures and relationships that make up Nike's supply chain (cf. Selwyn, this volume; Amoore 2002: chapter 5). From this perspective it is warranted to speak of the emergence of the 'collective worker' as a conscious political movement that reaches out across space and time 'to confront the universal and transnational qualities of capital' (Harvey 2001: 390).

NIKE AS A SITE OF STRUGGLE, CONTESTATION AND RE-REGULATION

During the first few decades of its existence, Nike could afford to ignore the poor working conditions prevalent throughout its supply chain. Stories of extreme forms of exploitation remained local and unnoticed by a larger public. This started to change in the early 1990s when accounts of poor working conditions began to provide ammunition to transnationally organized anti-sweatshop campaigns that were picked up by the global media. Nike started to be confronted with an ongoing stream of publications of sweatshop practices, in 'an endless series of local crises' (Knight and Greenberg 2002: 558). Numerous reports, scandals and campaigns have revealed violations of ILO Convention no. 29 (forced and compulsory labour), Convention no. 98 (the right to organize and bargain collectively), Convention no. 100 (equal remuneration), Convention no. 105 (forced labour), Convention no. 111 (discrimination) and Convention no. 138 (minimum age of employment), which all came into the spotlight. Frequently observed substandard working conditions included extremely long working weeks (often over 70 hours), poverty-level wages (often lower than national laws allow), verbal and physical abuse by management, authoritarian style of management, dangerous working conditions, lack of environmental standards, short-term contracts, or no contracts at all.

Nike responded in different ways. Its first response was to deny responsibility: 'We don't pay anybody at the factories and we don't set policy within the factories: it is their [the subcontractors] business to run' (company statement cited in Brookes and Madden 1995). This position was soon abandoned and the company instead opted for a code of conduct in 1992. This represented the first step through which social instructions and directives began to play a role in the planning and organization of production. In the years following, Nike adjusted the language of its code to match the guidelines of the ILO core labour standards, whilst setting up an internal compliance team called SHAPE (Safety, Health, Attitude, People and Environment). Today SHAPE employs about 100 people responsible for social and environmental issues across the Nike value chain. By benchmarking and rating systems, SHAPE assumes responsibility for the implementation and monitoring of labour standards by suppliers. They are now obliged to produce payroll records indicating that employees are paid the legal minimum wage, whether they work for Nike or other companies. Timecards trace how many hours employees actually work.

Nike was one of the first brand-named companies to publicly disclose the names and addresses of all of their suppliers. The company argued that disclosure 'is key to unlocking greater collaboration among brands and the creation of the incentives necessary for factories to turn their CSR [corporate social responsibility] performance into a point of differentiation' (Nike 2005). Nike's learning process, Simon Zadek (2004) argues, meant that the company evolved from denying responsibility for labour conditions at legally independent suppliers (early 1990s) towards assuming greater responsibility, promoting collective responsibility and industry change (after 2000). Of course, this dynamic between Nike and its critics should be understood in a dialectical fashion, or, as Ronen Shamir argues, as a 'case of governance-in-action' (2010: 533). It suggests that there is a dynamic at work that potentially exceeds the originally envisaged, very limited targets of auditing by paid consultancies.

Of course, these CSR instruments are being introduced by Nike without the meaningful participation – let alone bargaining – of trade unions or worker representatives. While workers are the stated beneficiaries of Nike's code implementation and monitoring programmes, their influence on these programmes remains marginal (at best). It assumes that improved working conditions, as Selwyn puts it, 'can be delivered by collaboration between elite bodies, in particular firms, states and international organisations. It thus represents a "top-down" conception of social upgrading' (2013: 76). In addition, these privatized systems of labour monitoring largely fail to 'challenge embedded social relations or business practices that undermine labour standards in global production systems' (Barrientos and Smith 2007: 727). Labour rights advocates have long pointed out that the underlying problem is that brands and retailers neglect to factor in the compliance costs associated with decent working conditions when they negotiate the pricing structures with their suppliers (Bhattacharjee and Roy 2012, and this volume). Lasting improvements to worker rights violations require an empowered workforce, which can only come about when workers are able 'to extract concessions from capital' (Selwyn 2013: 83). Yet while it is highly unlikely that CSR and codes of conduct will deliver these changes by themselves, they can provide a fertile ground for more meaningful forms of negotiations and bargaining.

Below we provide a number of examples of labour rights advocates who are pushing in this direction, eroding the distinction between 'direct' and 'indirect' employers further.

At PT Nikomas, a giant Indonesian-based footwear manufacturer, over 70 000 workers assemble shoes for several brands, of which about 18 000 work exclusively for Nike. Research by Educating for Justice, a US-based NGO, found that PT Nikomas workers were 'told by their supervisors to punch out on the time clock [and then] forced . . . to get back on the production line for one hour of unpaid overtime'. In addition, workers were required to come in 15–20 minutes before 7 a.m. and to stay for 15–20 minutes after work. Following an investigation by Nike, 4500 workers were compensated for close to 600 000 hours of overtime clocked up over two years (the practice had existed for 18 years, but Indonesian law allows redress only for the last two). In a statement Nike said it 'commends the factory on their action plan and efforts to correct inadequacies in current policies designed to protect the rights of workers. Nike will continue to monitor and support their efforts to remediate the situation' (*The Guardian*, 12 January 2012).

Another example is the international campaign around two Nike suppliers from Honduras: Hugger and Vision Tex. Both factories closed in 2009 without paying severance payments and health care benefits, a form of wage theft common in the garment and footwear sector. Initially Nike refused to pay back wages on behalf of the subcontractor, but following a transnational campaign the company negotiated an agreement with the local union 'that resulted in a package of measures that benefit workers, including a relief fund, vocational training programs, hiring priority, and health coverage' (Fair Labor Association (FLA) 2010a). In the agreement, Nike took responsibility to provide $1.54 million to a worker relief fund. It also arranged for workers to receive health care for one year (Adler-Milstein et al. 2014: 30). As two US labour rights activists conclude,

> In signing this agreement, Nike took financial responsibility for correcting a violation committed by a supplier factory and set an example by addressing a significant case of one of the most common forms of wage theft in the industry. While the Nike agreement does not prospectively address ongoing factory conditions, it set an important precedent and provides another example of the potential of agreements directly between labour unions and international brands (ibid. 2014: 30).

For all the difficulties of cross-border campaigns, including collective bargaining demands, positive results have already been booked in this area. A good example is the Indonesia Protocol on Freedom of Association (FoA), negotiated by an alliance of Indonesian unions, global sportswear brands (including Nike) and four major Indonesian footwear manufacturers. Negotiations started in 2009 – as a direct result of the pressure generated by the Play Fair campaign targeting the Beijing Olympics in 2008 – which attempted to address the gap between global codes of conduct and auditing processes and the persistent violations of workers' rights in Indonesian sportswear supplier factories. After two years of negotiations, a protocol was finally hammered out that provides companies with a practical set of guidelines on how to uphold and respect workers' rights such as the right to join a union to achieve decent pay and better working conditions. The agreement establishes specific guidelines to ensure that factory workers in Indonesia are able to organize and collectively bargain for better conditions in their workplaces. The protocol's scope encompasses all tier-1 manufacturers of the brands signed on (Nike, Adidas, Puma, New Balance, Pentland and Asics), whilst also incorporating a national oversight committee and a dispute resolution process.

These mechanisms are designed to promote sustainable solutions to freedom of association disputes and strengthen constructive dialogue processes between worker representatives and factory management. It ensures, among other things, that unions have the right to distribute information to their members, to hold union meetings at the workplace, to have a space at the factory for union activities, to collect union dues, and so on (Gardener 2012). The content of the protocol goes beyond the standards granted in codes of conduct and is much more concrete than current Indonesian labour laws. Sixty-eight footwear manufacturers have signed the FoA protocol. The document has been used by Indonesian unions to successfully vindicate the freedom of association (Siegman et al. 2013). As a result, the effective distance between workers at an Indonesian supplier and at Nike has been reduced. As one participant puts it: 'Before, it was impossible for workers to contact brand name companies directly. But now, if there is a case at factory level, they can call direct to Nike or Adidas and complain or send a letter' (cited in Jacobsson 2013: 21).

These examples show a trend towards a more consensual logic of power sharing which might in turn open the way for negotiated social compromises. Although these systems are far from adequate, the contours of a transnational capital–labour constraint across the entire circuit may be emerging and it is in this context that we use the notion of collective worker. Denoting not an organization, but a plurality, a complex matrix of forces in movement (cf. Gill 2003: 157), the collective worker takes shape on a continuum that runs from local labour struggles to, potentially, a conscious, political movement. Its diverse constituency, ranging from worker organizations, labour rights NGOs, women's organizations, consumer associations, anti-sweatshop activists, students, fair trade organizations and so on, challenges substandard working conditions and corporate power from different geographical locations and political perspectives.

CONCLUSION

It has often been argued that the logic of socialization of labour sets in motion a process of integration, interdependence, conscious planning, technical coordination and large scale cooperation, which ultimately will come to challenge its specific capitalist nature. Clearly, as long as we stick to a purely sociological concept of a class of manual labourers, the 'collective worker' would appear to be a phenomenon that moves from the centre to the periphery of the global political economy. If we take a broader view of all those who in one way or another are involved in the planning, execution and regulation of the labour process, the collective can be visualized as occupying positions all along the circuit of capital. Although these non-market linkages are established first of all for technical and/or organizational reasons, under managerial control, and are necessary to guarantee the flow-logic of fragmented production processes, political struggles across them often reveal the inner connection captured by the notion of the collective worker. In the process, they will tend to generate pressures for the re-regulation of capitalist relations. This in turn can be argued to promote the self-consciousness of the collective worker, transforming 'objective' connections mediated by the market, and enforced by management, into 'subjective' social relations, which in turn feed back into all kinds of political negotiation (Merk 2004).

In this chapter I have looked at a single commodity group, athletic footwear, but similar processes of bottom-up contestation and struggle can be identified throughout the global political economy. In various ways they crystallize a field of local, national and transnational counter-hegemonic movements and coalitions, 'all seeking to smooth down the rougher edges of what seems to be a largely self-regulating global capitalist system' (Lipschutz 2005: 2). The case of a labour-intensive commodity category such as athletic footwear demonstrates how the transnationalization of production, based on extreme forms of exploitation, through these struggles has not only created a space for workers' concerns to be heard beyond the local or national levels. It has also helped raise awareness of their working conditions to a wider audience, such as consumer organizations, which in turn can be mobilized to increase the pressure on brand-named companies to ensure workplace improvements. Thus the athletic footwear industry has become a site (actually a multiplicity of sites) of regulatory intervention as well.

There is a real risk in celebrating these privatized systems of labour monitoring as the solution to poor working conditions. Corporate Social Responsibility (CSR) is a testing ground where divergent interests intersect, representing different and, frequently, conflicting agendas. Yet however imperfect, the evolution of these systems challenges capitalist relations of production and creates opportunities for labour. In a globally organized industry, the future of decent working conditions depends critically on confronting capital mobility as well as on including distant powerholders into systems of accountability. This would also make them subject to a consensual logic of power-sharing that has the potential to allow negotiated social compromises and create opportunities for a 'worker-driven social upgrading process' (Selwyn 2013: 83, and this volume). That these processes are characterized by controversy and conflict will ensure that each outcome is again the object of political contestation between different social forces searching for ways to fill the regulatory vacuum (Bartley 2003: 437). Discussing new accountability trends affecting companies like Nike, Adidas and H&M, one business analyst expresses his dismay at this process thus: 'Nothing is a private transaction between buyers and sellers any more. Over the past ten years all sorts of groups once considered outsiders are now given an influence over how goods are bought and sold' (Flanagan 2012). *The Economist* (20 January 2005) also recognizes the threat when it writes,

> Particular CSR initiatives may do good, or harm, or make no difference one way or the other, but it is important to resist the success of the CSR idea—that is the almost universal acceptance of its premises and main lines of argument. Otherwise bones may indeed begin to snap and CSR may encroach on corporate decision-making in ways that seriously reduce welfare.

Nike and its supply chain have turned into a 'contested terrain' embodied in different initiatives – compromised, disputed, contested – that can be understood as a trial-and-error search to build regulatory institutions at a level that matches the scale of today's globalized productive operations and to re-establish labour as a representative force within them.

8. Standardizing services: transnational authority and market power

Jean-Christophe Graz

INTRODUCTION

When asked in 2007 which fields of standardization will be the most active in the coming years, Alan Bryden, former Secretary General of the International Organization for Standardization (ISO), was straightforward in stating that 'one of our biggest challenges is precisely how to address the service sector' (interview with the author). While standards supposedly lead to greater rationality and coherence in distinct industries and services, all of them also give rise to ongoing struggles in complex configurations of power involving multiple actors including multinational corporations, organized interests and state regulators. This chapter relies on global political economy approaches that uncover the power relations exercised on a transnational basis in the area of service standards. It assumes that the process of globalization is not opposing states and markets, but a convergence of processes involving both of them, with new patterns of formal and informal power and regulatory practices arising at the intersection of the two. Of these, standards are a key aspect.

The availability, provision and use of services all rely on social constructs with intrinsic limits as to the extent to which they can be disembedded from society. Some rely on public services, others raise concerns of consumer protection or relate to security matters involving liability issues for users and providers alike. Yet both the ambivalent status of the private and public actors involved in the setting of standards, and the tendency to blend physical measures with societal values, are likely to reinforce the commodification of services and their disembedding from societal concerns. Thus service standards reflect the development of a form of *transnational hybrid authority*, which undermines the functional differentiation between the different spheres of society, and reinforces the potential of political capture in the deliberative process of regulatory practices in contemporary capitalism.

The chapter begins with some background on the service sector, service standards, and, more generally, the international standardization in goods and services. It then fleshes out a theoretical framework for analysing service standards as a form of transnational hybrid authority, with a particular emphasis on how the rise of standards impinges upon bureaucratic practices and state law. Finally, the chapter examines the emerging power of service standards in the ISO context and at the European level.

OFFSHORING SERVICES AND THE RISE OF STANDARDIZATION

The significance of the service economy is a prominent feature of the shift towards a so-called knowledge-based global economy. Services now account for around 75 per cent of GDP and employment in the advanced economies of the OECD, and for more than 50 per cent in developing countries and emerging economies. The significance of services goes beyond their growing share in the economy and their close connection to technology and knowledge. It is also closely related to an expected surge in their internationalization resulting from sustained regulatory reforms triggering global integrated models of services outsourced to affiliates and client companies on a worldwide basis. Services previously provided by the state in the form of public utilities and social services can now increasingly be supplied on a global commercial basis.

The institutional environment enabling a globally integrated supply of services has gradually emerged with the establishment of the General Agreement on Trade in Services (GATS) in 1995 and the adoption in 2006 of a new EU directive (2006/123/EC) on services in the internal market. Negotiations are also underway at the World Trade Organization (WTO) and new initiatives for highly ambitious preferential trade agreements such as the Transatlantic Trade and Investment Partnership (TTIP) and Trans-Pacific Partnership (TPP). Despite such developments supporting the internationalization of services, sectoral coverage remains narrow and no upsurge of total trade in services has apparently taken place for the last two decades. As Tables 8.1 and 8.2 show, it continues to represent around 20 per cent of world trade. Yet a significant shift has occurred in the distribution between developed and developing countries. During the same period, developing countries have almost doubled their share in the world trade of services to reach more than 30 per cent in 2010.

If we look at foreign direct investments (FDI), the overall share of services has not considerably changed either. According to figures presented with some caveats by UNCTAD (Table 8.3), their share increased by less than 10 per cent over the last 20 years, of which trading and finance still count for more than half. However, here again it is worth noting an important shift in composition: while developing countries accounted for less than 20

Table 8.1 Exports and imports of goods and services, 1990–2012 (US$ at current prices and current exchange rates, in millions)

	1990	2000	2012
Total trade in services	831 345.2	1 521 347.0	4425784.8
Total trade in goods	3443 139.8	6431 490.3	18214680.9
Share of services (%)	19.4	19.1	19.6

Source: UNCTAD, UNCTADSTAT2013.

Table 8.2 Share (%) of developing/developed/transition economies of services exports, 1990–2012 (US$ at current prices and current exchange rates)

	1990	2000	2012
Developing economies	18.1	23.1	30.4
Transition economies	2.0	1.6	2.9
Developed economies	79.9	75.3	66.7

Source: UNCTAD, UNCTADSTAT2013.

per cent of all FDI inward flows in services in 1990–92, they now account for more than 40 per cent, with the share of business services having almost doubled. Consulting, accounting, auditing, customer relation centres, all belong to these new types of business services easily established in developing countries and attracting massive volumes of foreign direct investments. Interestingly, sectors such as health or education, although often making headlines, remain marginal in comparison, with worldwide inflows of $391 and $814 million, respectively, in 2009–11. Certainly data on services are notoriously complex to gather, let alone data on their international trade. A recent joint OECD/WTO initiative has attempted to address this issue by producing data disaggregated by the value added in the exchange of goods and services consumed worldwide. According to these figures, the service sector contributes over 50 per cent of total exports from countries such as the United States, the United Kingdom, France, Germany, Italy, and even close to one-third in the case of China.

Against this background, it is obvious that the offshore diversification of services represents a powerful and significant trend (Graz and Niang 2013). The shift began in the 1980s with outsourcing contracts in data processing and call centres at the bottom of the value chain. Today, it has

Table 8.3 Estimated world inward FDI flows, by sector and industry, 1990–92 and 2009–11 (US$ millions)

Sector/industry	1990–1992				2009–2011			
	Developed economies	Developing economies	Transition economies	World	Developed economies	Developing economies	Transition economies	World
Total	134419	39779	1530	175728	729143	613772	82593	1425507
Primary	10215	4211	911	15337	43994	75884	14733	134611
Manufacturing	37422	14457	279	52158	161241	155722	14528	331491
Services	77605	17918	208	95732	475660	369913	52830	898403
of which: Trade	16735	2474	22	19232	61126	51463	13803	126392
Finance	25745	2575	15	28335	194735	77595	9322	281652
Business activities	17107	4257	130	21494	154803	149066[a]	18029	321898[a]
Share of services (%)	57.7	45.0	13.6	54.5	65.2	60.3	64.0	63.0
of which in trade and finance (%)	54.7	28.2	17.9	49.7	53.8	34.9	43.8	45.4
of which business activities (%)	22.0	23.8	62.4	22.5	32.5	40.3	34.1	35.8

Notes:
a. A considerable share of investment in business activities is in Hong Kong (China), which accounted for 37% of developing economies and 17% of the world total during 2009–2011. Hong Kong (China) data include investment holding companies.
Data should be interpreted with caution. The world total was extrapolated on the basis of data covering 79 countries in 1990–1992 and 116 countries in 2009–2011, or the latest three-year period average available. They account for 83 and 90 per cent of world inward FDI flows respectively in the periods 1990–1992 and 2009–2011.

Source: Adapted from UNCTAD, *World Investment Report 2013*.

moved into much more advanced sectors with activities such as legal, fiscal or medical services, financial consulting, and all sorts of other services enabled by information technology, from the entertainment industry to security-related activities. Although it was still embryonic then, UNCTAD already emphasized ten years ago how the outsourcing of services had reached a tipping point: 'the cutting edge of the global shift in production activity [gives] rise to a new international division of labour in the production of services' (UNCTAD 2004: xxv). Companies have not been shy of innovating in many areas to increase their internationalization, but at the same time, many of them have become aware of the difficulties that need to be overcome.

Conventional explanations of the barriers to internationalization of services focus on various factors hindering trade transactions in this area. A particular instance is the fact that some service activities cannot be stored and thus require direct co-production between clients and suppliers. Similarly, the more services tend to be immaterial, the harder it is to provide them at distance. Moreover, most firms providing services are SMEs and are thus more likely to face additional difficulties to project their activity at an international level. More generally, cultural barriers, distinct legal frameworks and the weight of institutions are time and again identified as additional hindrances to the internationalization of services (OECD 2000; World Trade Organization 2012).

In the light of this observation, it is important to understand the influence of mechanisms that go well beyond intergovernmental cooperation and trade transactions. Indeed, a greater global integration in the supply of services hinges upon a number of informal, non-state processes challenging national regulatory arrangements. It is in this context that international voluntary standards come into play.

The promise of a knowledge-based economy is largely made on the assumption that, as services become intertwined in manufacturing processes on a global scale, expertise and innovation enabled by a standardization of such high-skilled services will pervade the economy as a whole. As Boden and Miles (2000: 258) point out, 'the service economy is not merely an economy in which service sectors are quantitatively dominant. It is one where "service" is becoming a guiding principle throughout the economy'. The ability to develop a global market of services is not just a matter of technology or economic logic. It also supposes an ability to define the gradual decomposition of complex work into sequences of more simple work. The more fragmented the nature of the labour and consumption processes, the more requirements to codify them. This is why services are often described as intrinsically resisting relocation (Dossani 2006: 245). Intangible and interpersonal services, such as teaching, consulting, on standards or processes covering quality, safety, reliability, efficiency and interchangeability. As 'external points of reference' (Hawkins 1995, cited in Nadvi and Wältring 2002), standards facilitate the international exchange of goods and services and widen the social division of labour (Elam 1990). An important institution here is the International Organization for Standardization (ISO), the world's largest developer of standards, and well-known for the certification of quality management systems (ISO 9000) and environmental management systems (ISO 14000). The importance of standardization and certification also indicates that today the institutional forms that support these activities are increasingly of a private, non-state, nature. Various scholars have pointed out that this represents a wider shift in society from a politically negotiated system of rules towards neoliberal, privatized systems of negotiations in which business plays a more important role (see, for example, Cutler et al. 1999; Graz 2006b and this volume). In this shift, regulatory tasks are delegated from state bodies to private specialists. Market-based and private voluntary strategies are presented as an alternative or a supplement to traditional state regulation. Neoliberalism has created a political context highly conducive to the rise of private regulation in which reporting, standard-setting, auditing, monitoring and certification have become central elements (Utting 2000: 74).

So far from being alien to a liberal, capitalist economy, regulation and private governance are already an integral part of market exchange. Rules, regulations, codes, standards, benchmarks, networks and a range of state institutions and other specialized agencies such as coordination service firms remain necessary for social, functional and normative reunification of fragmented productive activities. 'At first sight diametrically opposed to the drift of the 1970s planned interdependence, global governance under the discipline of capital in fact also signifies a further advance in global planning' (van der Pijl 1998: 160–61). For capital, regulation always carries the risk of eroding the core principles on which the mode of production rests (principles such as private property and free contract). Because of this risk, corporations will not easily yield to regulations not written by themselves or backed up by an authority other than their own.

Given that socialization of labour is a structural accompaniment of worldwide commodification processes leading to wider circles of social interdependence, advocacy groups have attempted to turn this dynamic to their advantage and press an agenda for restoring the social fabric and create opportunities for collective action and social improvement (Merk 2007: 118; 2004). By challenging substandard working conditions and corporate power from different geographical locations and political perspectives, these forces are increasingly coming together as a unified social health and personal services, are conventionally seen as the most difficult services to move offshore, industrialize and standardize. According to Blind, it is precisely 'because of the intangible nature of services and the information asymmetries thus caused between management and service provider, [that] the need to introduce quality standards for each stage of the service production is especially high' (Blind 2004: 167).

According to research inspired by the French regulation school, the uncertainty inherent in the intangible and relational nature of many service activities should not be apprehended as a problem of information asymmetry distorting the price mechanism, but as the logical consequence of the actual conditions in which wage relations and forms of competition are implemented in a post-Fordist regime of accumulation. Uncertainty as to the quality and usefulness of a service goes to the heart of what a service is – its pronounced relational and immaterial component. Understanding the potential of standardization enabling a globally integrated supply of services thus presupposes a focus on the contested nature and the great diversity of labour processes involved in services. According to Du Tertre (2013), production of the service always goes hand in hand with a 'social relation of accessibility', defined as a 'historic and institutional construct' characterized by considerations such as geographical proximity, temporal synchronization, and cultural and social understanding.

From this perspective, the internationalization of services with high relational and intangible contents is rather unlikely, contrary to those non-service activities whose logic remains close to manufactured goods. Such a restrictive hypothesis with regard to the internationalization and standardization of services would imply that the nature of the service is the main determining factor in its propensity for standardization. In our view, however, this hypothesis is too restrictive. It does not fully do justice to the great variety of responses that international standardization is likely to provide to the immaterial and relational dimensions of many types of services and the issues involved in terms of transfers of authority on a transnational basis. By linking the global marketplace to distinct national economies, service standards can respond in various ways to the conflicting understanding of quality and security uncertainties. On the one hand, they can promote a broadening and deepening of minimal market rules; on the other, they can include a number of provisions with the aim of defining a number of socially or environmentally based specifications likely to be crucial for the production or usage of distinct services. In Polanyian terms, they relate to overlapping moments in which disembedding and re-embedding forces diverge in their response to the role of market mechanisms in society. This prompts us to explore further the extent to which international standards reflect a distinct form of market power in the reorganization of the global economy towards services.

THEORIZING THE POWER OF INTERNATIONAL STANDARDIZATION

The power of standardization epitomizes one of several new forms of non-state authority that have evolved over the past decade in the global political economy. The scope of international standards pertains not only to their potential worldwide reach, but also to the broader organization of the capitalist system (Murphy and Yates 2009). The rise of international standardization as a privileged form of devising technical specification typically encroaches upon two core issues which give rise to social struggles in capitalism: the opposition between labour and capital, and the separation of the economy from the state. Thus standards intervene in the struggle between capital and labour in various ways. Workers may look to technical standards to ensure a safer workplace (for example, standards on machine safety or maximum noise pollution) or to obtain quality guarantees on the goods which they purchase. In contrast, entrepreneurs, merchants and financiers will equate standards with risk reduction, technological progress, strategic competitive behaviour and profit. With regard to the separation between the economy and the state, the voluntary market-oriented dimension of standards may reinforce free market claims to keep economic constraints and appropriation separated from politico-legal coercion.

At the same time, the authority conferred on standard-setters by state agencies and intergovernmental agreements may narrow down the conventional Weberian view of state autonomy. The larger scope of standards in the organization of transnational markets substitutes, to a certain extent, the role of bureaucracies in the foundations of authority and the domination of modern states in capitalism. A central assumption of Weber's analysis of modern state power is that any legal rational form of domination relies on functional differentiation in order to exercise its power and claim to legitimacy. To a large extent, such a functional differentiation was understood as constituting the basis of the state bureaucracy. The supposed autonomy of the bureaucracy was identified as a guarantee against state capture by ruling elites or otherwise by all sorts of organized private and associative interests. In contrast, Weber's disenchanted view on modern life and capitalism highlights on numerous occasions how the search for efficiency through rational calculus leads to the darker side of bureaucratization and reification of human activities (Weber 1995; 2004).

However tricky the analysis of the 'iron cage' of modern bureaucracy and capitalism may be (see, for example, Löwy 2013), standardization challenges the conventional Weberian legal-rational view of organizing state bureaucracies along distinct functional tasks typical of the rationalization of modern societies. Support for industry-based and flexible, market-friendly voluntary standards is, indeed, often made on the basis of such claims as the lack of knowledge and expertise attributed to regulatory practices on the part of state agencies. Standards are therefore identified as valuable instruments, based on rational calculation, to clamp down on cumbersome intergovernmental regulatory agreements. From a more critical perspective, standards display a 'technical authority' belonging to the rise of global hybrids, the power of which resides in a sustained ambiguity between technical and societal issues, and an intertwining of private and public spheres that reinforces a de-politicization and de-territorialization of authority (Porter 2004; Best 2012).

According to Hibou, this reflects the extent to which the governance of modern societies is driven by a neoliberal bureaucracy which 'seeks to transform a complex reality into abstract categories, norms, and general rules . . . formulated from the perspective of the market and the corporation' (Hibou 2012: 37). Yet rather than demonizing standards as instances of a reified homogenization and dehumanization of social life across the globe (a neoliberal 'iron cage'), standards remain inherently contestable and politically contested (cf. Merk, this volume). Battles regarding standards are not confined to technological choices underpinning monopolistic rent-seeking behaviour in high-flying cases such as the DVD format war between Blu-ray (Sony and Disney) and HD-DVD (Microsoft and Universal). They also convey social values, influence people's day-to-day work experience and contribute to defining the private/public divide – as the 2013 decision of the ISO to develop a standard for occupational health and safety demonstrates.

From this standpoint, standardization looks like a comprehensive process that plays out in various normative contexts and on different levels of governance in order to provide structural coupling between fragmented social systems. It constitutes one of the pillars of a 'global law without a state'. Kessler and other system theorists stress that the concept of functional differentiation should thus help us identify 'structures and processes that are constituted on a global level and thus–by definition–escape the logic of the inter-state system' (Kessler 2012: 78). Yet, far from coupling fragmented and differentiated social systems into a tentative world society, the proliferation of standards and their growing influence first of all, and far more likely, work to undermine the functional differentiation of politics. The wide range of very distinct actors promoting standards reinforces the lack of distinction between an authority founded on scientific knowledge, technical expertise and market power, on the one hand, and an authority built upon a formal mandate and establishing procedures for delegating the sovereign power of political subjects, on the other. This leads rather to a *functional in-differentiation,* in which the authority of non-state actors, founded on their expertise as well as on their market power, intermingles with the authority claimed by professional civil servants. The decline of the functional differentiation born with modern state power gives way to undifferentiated private and public bodies in charge of setting rules on issues indeterminately related to the sphere of hard science or societal values. This clearly challenges the assumption made in most of the literature on the regulatory practices of non-elected bodies and private actors, which underestimates their ability to capture the state (Egan 2001; Majone 2001). As capture relates to a control of resources, access and the capacity of actors to durably modify the environment of their practices for their own benefit, non-elected bodies and private actors can take advantage of this by setting and certifying standards. Standards definition, implementation and monitoring may thus well be privileged vehicles for exercising structural power.

The rise of non-state actors as standard-setters reflects a new form of transnational authority in international relations, which I have elsewhere referred to as the rise of global hybrids (Graz 2006a). Global hybrids are instances of a form of authority that blurs the different nature and legitimacy of subjects involved in it, pertains to objects undermining the distinction between science and society, and pursues a fragmentation of social space so that the endogenous logic of territorial sovereignty gives way to an exogenous logic emanating from transnational capitalism.

The distinction between the private and public spheres in which standardization practices take place may, therefore, be seen as located on an *institutional continuum* that defines *who* can standardize. Both market mechanisms and policy choices affect the agents involved in the field, although they do so in different ways. Technical specifications belong to the private sphere of economic activities governed by market constraints, and affect social and technological change from that angle. They nonetheless remain related to the public sphere of political action directed at the general interest of society – for instance, by determining a certain level of risk or by setting principles of liability. Hence, even in the narrowly circumscribed field of technical specification, norms relate as much to capital accumulation and technical progress as to social improvement or the various instruments of the welfare state.

Whereas the private/public nexus of the actors involved in defining standards can be located on an institutional continuum, a second dimension maps out a *material continuum* delineating what can be standardized. This dimension covers the relation between human beings and nature, for so-called technical specifications range from natural and invariable physical measures to constructed and historically bound societal values. This sheds light on the increase in scope of international standardization. If standards were initially confined to 'physical' standards like screw thread, they are now covering more 'societal' topics and so-called generic issues. Corporate social responsibility standards, quality and energy management system standards, occupational health and safety guidelines are emblematic in this regard. Applied to the standardization of services, this aspect raises questions about what a service standard actually is. In other words, do service standards concern the material support enabling service provision (protective equipment used in the leisure sector, the IT interface of a call-centre, etc.) or do they concern common intangible aspects of services (like billing, complaint redress, information provisions)?

Summing up, the growing integration of services is a prominent feature of a worldwide knowledge-based economy. This process rests on formal and informal regulatory practices of a wide range of non-state actors. Among them, service standards are likely to play a crucial role. They reinforce the deterritorialization of regulatory practices in contemporary capitalism. Their significance can be situated along an institutional and a material continuum blending private and public actors, as well as physical measures and societal concerns. The remainder of the chapter provides an overview of the institutional setting of service standardization within the ISO environment and the European Union.

PRODUCING AND STANDARDIZING SERVICES ACROSS BORDERS

The entry into force of the WTO Technical Barriers to Trade (TBT) Agreement and the revision of the Sanitary and Phytosanitary Measures (SPS) Agreement in 1995 validated a formal devolution of power to international standard-setting organizations. Unlike the loose provisions regarding technical regulation of the old GATT, the TBT and SPS Agreements, like some provisions of the General Agreement on Trade in Services (GATS) and the 'plurilateral' Agreement on Government Procurement (GPA Article VI:2b), grant international standards a major role in harmonizing the technical specifications of goods and services traded on the global market. State regulation in this domain must comply with 'legitimate objectives'. With regard to goods, such concerns are related to health, safety and environmental issues. In contrast, as we have seen, conflicting understandings of market uncertainties about quality and security are the major issues in the sphere of services; they encompass a wide range of expectations regarding, in particular, competence and professional skills, the capacity to deliver and business continuity, data protection and privacy, and consumer protection and information, as well as larger societal and environmental concerns.

Since the WTO is not a standard-setting body, its promotion of regulatory convergence is made by prompting its members to use international standards. GATS article VI:4 thus assigns to the Council for Trade and Services (through its Working Party on Domestic Regulation) the largely market-inspired task to develop 'any necessary discipline' to ensure that such regulation by states is not 'more burdensome than necessary to ensure the quality of the services'. Article VI:5b specifies that in this respect, 'account shall be taken of international standards of relevant international organisations'. The WTO in this regard considers that cooperation in regulation affecting trade in services would have much to gain from improving 'regulators' understanding of, and confidence in, standards and requirements with which they may not be familiar'. Yet existing provisions still grant a wide range of international bodies the ability to define standards affecting the internationalization of services. The following overview of the ISO and the European institutional frameworks will show us how standards can affect the demand and supply of services worldwide.

As the world's largest developer and publisher of international standards with a membership of over 160 mixed private and public national standardization bodies, the ISO represents a core arena for assessing current developments of service standardization. The move into the standardization of services began in 1995 with a Committee on Consumer Policy (COPOLCO) workshop in Beijing. Lawrence Eicher, then ISO Secretary General, emphasized that the manufacturing industry was already changing with the move towards generic management system standards, and, from there on, 'the emphasis could change even more to take into account the needs of the burgeoning service industries'. Six workshops were held in the following years with various focuses, such as tourism, exhibition management, banking and insurance, engineering consultancy, as well as multi-sectoral methodological issues for developing service standards. In 2001, a new working group was established to draft a guide on the use and development of service standards from a consumers' perspective (ISO/IEC Guide 76:2008, Development of service standards – Recommendations for addressing consumer issues).

According to the UN international classification system, 27 technical committees have been set up so far to develop service standards at ISO, with 348 international standards published and 193 under negotiation by the end of 2011. These are still few compared to the 220 or so technical committees and more than 19 000 international standards of the ISO. Moreover, standards labelled as belonging to services include domains far removed from what is usually understood as services, such as transport infrastructures, laboratory techniques and construction engines. The broad inclusiveness of the UN classification system highlights the uncertainties in defining and classifying service standards, which can never be taken for granted. Cross-border service providers also rely on more generic standards, which may indifferently be applied in the production and exchange of goods and services. Among the most widely used are the quality, environmental and information security management system standards ISO 9000 (with more than one million certificates since 2012), ISO 14000 and ISO 27000 series, as well as the guidance on conformity assessment provided by the ISO 17000 series or the ISO 31000 guidelines and principles on risk management. As a result of the size of its market and its dependence on global value chains, China is in the top ten countries for six out of the seven standards covered in the yearly ISO survey of certifications in such domains and is the uncontested leader in the number of certificates issued to ISO 9001 and ISO 14001 (International Organization for Standardization 2013). While some developments have taken place in domains epitomizing core intangible and relational features of services, such as personal financial planning used in countries with individual funded pension schemes (ISO 22222: 2005) or the vocabulary and service requirements for market, opinion and social research (ISO 20252: 2006), those standards remain marginal in terms of the global service economy. Obviously, large parts of the economy, such as in finance and insurance, use instruments developed within their own sectors. For instance, Basel III for banks and the European Solvency Directive II for insurance recognize internal company models as valid prudential standards of self-regulation. Such sectors are highly organized and internationalized and face complex regulatory issues. Fearing to be blamed for the economic crisis, they have joined forces to keep sufficient leeway to ensure the autonomy gained by self-regulation even if such a shift to private authority has been seriously challenged (Helleiner and Pagliari 2011).

Why has so little progress been made in the ISO, two decades after the launching of the institutional process? The autonomous regulatory environment of sectors as large as finance, accounting and insurance is a first answer. A second is the lack of public support, which is often the driving force behind transnational private authority. A further explanation is provided by the large number of private actors and industrial consortia setting specifications directly sold on the consultancy market for company and individual certifications. A case in point is the Capability Maturity Model Integration (CMMi) developed by the Software Engineering Institute (SEI) that includes a detailed management model of over 700 pages with quantified capability and maturity targets. This is a widely used standard setting market access for business processing services such as those offshored to India (Graz and Niang 2012). In any case, quality issues pertaining to relational and immaterial services prompt the development of standards that encroach upon the business operating procedures to deliver such services. In the ISO, the latter are understood as management system standards (MSS) and require dedicated procedures. A final explanation therefore is that such requirements hinder the development of ISO service standards in many domains. Overcoming this difficulty will only be possible by setting ISO standards based on a very narrow understanding of procedural and generic aspects of services. In turn, this will impair the ability to set standards affecting more substantial issues such as the co-production of services and related to societal values and cultural contexts.

More developments are taking place at the regional level, especially in Europe. The European Union is a prime example of the public support enabling both service integration and international standardization. In 1985, Council Resolution 85/C 136/01 on a 'New Approach' to technical harmonization and standardization instigated a completely new regulatory technique and strategy. The resolution was a response to the growing role of the European Court of Justice in solving conflicting regulatory policies in the internal European market, especially since the 1979 *Cassis de Dijon* case securing the principle of mutual recognition in the absence of harmonized legislation or technical standards. It was also an early move towards the completion of the Single Market by devising procedures to avoid turning technical specifications into structural impediments to trade. Although member states were suspicious about seeing regulation in this domain transferred to the European authorities, they did acknowledge the threat of a race to the bottom in public purpose standards, should standardization remain in the national domains whilst market integration was deepening.

The New Approach provides a framework for the harmonization of EU public law only on the general and essential requirements of goods and services traded on the European market. This concerns in particular the fields of health, the environment, safety and consumer protection. Depending on the sectors affected, technical specifications, performance criteria and quality requirements are either based upon mutual recognition of national standards, or delegated to European standard-setting bodies. In most sectors, the procedure for monitoring standards is a matter of business self-regulation, since products put on the market are granted a presumption of conformity, solely based on the declaration of the manufacturer (the CE marking). Thus, the European New Approach has done more than strengthen the importance of voluntary standards in the Single Market. By avoiding costly third party testing and certification, and providing the procedural means for a simultaneous adoption of European standards as international ones (through the so-called Dresden and Vienna Agreements), the EU has also included third countries in its standardization system. This has led to a powerful strategic positioning of European standards in the global market (Vogel 1995; Egan 2001).

The European Commission was well aware that the emergence of an increasingly dense and extensive European standardization complex with global reach could also support the 2000 Lisbon Agenda. Services were a core feature of the plan to make the EU 'the most competitive and dynamic knowledge-based economy in the world'. Service standards were given new emphasis after 2005 and the adoption of Directive 2006/123/EC on services in the Internal Market, the so-called Bolkestein Directive, eventually agreed upon at its second reading in December 2006 and fully implemented since the end of 2009. At the centre of this directive lies a horizontal approach to the harmonization of different regulations at European level, which aims to minimize the limitations on the free movement of services and service providers by discrimination based on nationality or local residence. The controversial 'country of origin' principle that prompted the so-called Polish plumber controversy has now been substituted for the formula 'freedom to provide services'. The service must conform to the regulations of his or her 'place of establishment'. But, in order to further unify the internal market for services, the Directive sees the promotion of quality as a key objective. To this end, it explicitly encourages the work of professional independent or community bodies of standard-development and certification (such as CEN, CENELEC and ETSI) in order to develop voluntary quality marks and labels (Preamble 102 and Article 26).

Actually, in 2003 DG Enterprise and Industry of the European Commission had already awarded a first programming mandate (M340) to European standardization bodies in the field of services to identify priority sectors of intra-community trade in services. Issues were to include horizontal cross-sectoral generic standards and vertical sector-specific standards, as well as service providers or end-users. A second programming mandate (M371) in the field of services was published in 2005. Half a dozen European standardization bodies responded with 11 projects.

The CEN Horizontal European Service Standardization Strategy

(CHESSS) is the largest project responding to EU Mandate M371. It includes a consortium of national standards bodies led by the British Standards Institution (BSI), with those from Spain (AENOR), Germany (DIN), Denmark (DS), Estonia (EVS) and the Netherlands (NEN), as well as Capgemini, one of the world leaders in IT services consulting and management. Its final report published in 2009 examined the feasibility of taking a generic approach to European service standardization across multiple service sectors, as opposed to a sector-specific approach (CEN/Cenelec Management Centre 2009). By taking a generic approach, it seeks to establish the underlying principles for an ongoing programme of European service standardization capable of facilitating the delivery of services across the EU, unimpeded by national borders. The topics expected to be included in a future single horizontal standard are confined to the design of the service, information provision to customers, billing, complaints and redress, as well as innovation and review.

Unsurprisingly, the report points out the likely difficulty of involving a wide range of stakeholders. This clearly bodes no good as far as the expected deliberative quality in the production of such a standard is concerned. It is worth noting, however, that throughout the modules, significant differences exist with regard to the approach to horizontal standards. Some favour multiple horizontal standards as opposed to a single horizontal one; others prefer horizontal standards completed by vertical standards; while still others remain sceptical about the capacity of any generic standards to deal with the distinctiveness and diversity of the service economy. By and large, it remains unclear whether such a generic approach will be successful. The interest in a single horizontal generic standard with a certification scheme is clearly an attempt to promote services standards on a par with the worldwide achievement of the ISO 9000 series. Standards supporting a globally integrated supply of services would narrow down their specifications to sheer managerial procedures excluding substantial definitions of what is involved in co-producing relational and intangible services. Only such substantial vertical standards are likely to have emancipatory potential with detailed expectations regarding labour processes, environmental impacts and consumers' protection.

The ten other projects responding to EU Mandate M371 address the specificity of distinct markets of services. AFNOR, the French national standardization body, a pioneer in setting national standards in well-defined service sectors, initiated those projects in consultation with some European partners, in particular from the Netherlands and Denmark. The recommendations identify a number of service activities likely to be standardized at various levels, whether European standards per se, or at a lower level, guidance materials and so-called workshop agreements

(CEN/Cenelec Management Centre 2009). The advantage of a vertical and sectoral approach is seen in the ability to better address the distinctiveness of services in sectors of activities highly relational and immaterial. However, the ambiguous mixture of private and public actors involved in standardization processes privileged by this approach remains important. Similarly, the issues concerned do not clearly distinguish between societal or more strictly technical objects of reference. A proper differentiation of actors among stakeholders and issues spanning physical measure to societal values, as well as clear-cut incentives to mitigate representation biases would be necessary to ensure a fair, substantial and thorough representation in standardization processes.

A swifter development of service standards at the national instead of the European level and fears concerning barriers to intra-EU trade in services have prompted the Commission to initiate a reform of the European standardization system, known as the 'standardization package'. A better inclusion of service standards in the regulatory framework is one of its key objectives. As a result, the entry into force in 2013 of the new regulation on European standardization (1025/2012) extends the New Approach to services and forces European national standardization bodies to notify services standardization activities. This clearly supports further developments at the European level. Moreover, the new regulation reinforces the support granted to European stakeholders and SMEs. However, the new regulatory framework has not overcome the divide between supporters of vertical sector-specific standards such as AFNOR and advocates of horizontal cross-sectoral generic standards such as the BSI. This probably explains the compromise reached in the new Mandate M517, addressed by the European Commission to the European standardization bodies in January 2013. The objective is still to foster the standardization of the generic attributes of services. Yet, in contrast to a single, all-inclusive horizontal service standard, the target is now '"narrower" horizontal service standards for particular aspects/parts of a full service provision'.

CONCLUSIONS

The picture emerging from the ongoing institutional developments at the European and worldwide ISO levels suggests that the transnational hybrid authority of international standards in the service sector is likely to have a growing influence on the regulatory environment of the economy and society at large. Such developments remain, however, more difficult than commonly expected, and are supported by two sets of competing profiles. Those in favour of horizontal standards endorse the development of generic specifications cutting across distinct sectors and disembedding transnational markets thanks to narrow definitions of requirements such as transparency and quality. In contrast, supporters of vertical standards claim that the internationalization of the service economy should remain embedded in concrete market practices, labour processes, and, arguably, the biosphere and society at large. In their view, services can only be standardized according to the specificity of the production configuration in which they are provided and the context of their usage.

These conflicting claims reflect opposing types of relationships between standards and society at large in globalizing the delivery of services. International standards can be used either as driving forces for broadening the domain of market self-regulation, or as alternative instruments for embedding markets within society. The direction in which the balance will tilt depends on the degree to which public and associative actors increase their awareness of the comprehensive political implication potentially raised by standards and claim a fairer and more substantial role in standardization processes. This would be one additional avenue of what Selwyn (this volume) refers to as a 'labour-led' social upgrading. It is also subject to the differentiation of issues likely to be appropriate for such alternative tools of market organization. In the meantime, the ambivalent status of actors involved in standardization processes and the tendency to intermingle physical measures with societal values are likely to reinforce a commodified understanding of services standards disembedded from societal concerns.

9. Encumbered behemoth: Wal-Mart, differential accumulation and international retail restructuring

Joseph Baines[1]

INTRODUCTION

Wal-Mart is a behemoth. The retail giant has garnered greater annual revenues than any other firm for seven of the last ten years. And with 2.2 million employees, it has about as many people in uniform as the People's Liberation Army of China. The enormity of Wal-Mart's operations has made the company the focus of much attention from journalists and scholars alike. In particular, the social effects of its model of 'everyday low prices', in which very cheap products are sold in very high volumes, have been hotly debated. Economic geographers, labour historians, business analysts, neoclassical economists and sociologists have all weighed in on the discussions (cf. Basker 2007; Bianco 2006; Gereffi and Christian 2009; Lichtenstein 2006). While some have pointed to the savings that Wal-Mart offers to cash-strapped consumers, others have sought to highlight the deleterious effects Wal-Mart's cost-cutting strategies have on its own employees, on local communities and on the workers that toil in sweatshop conditions for Wal-Mart's suppliers.

Much of the research done on Wal-Mart is very instructive for those who seek to make sense of the company. However, what all of the analyses appear to lack is a systematic quantitative means of actually gauging the changes in Wal-Mart's power. And without a clear conception of Wal-Mart's power trajectory, it is difficult to make sense of the wider significance of the insights that existing analyses offer. This chapter seeks to make up for this deficiency by drawing on, and developing, aspects of the capital as power (CasP) framework propounded by Jonathan Nitzan and Shimshon Bichler. The CasP framework offers a method of analysing relations of control and resistance as they redound across every social

[1] The impetus for this research project was sparked by a post by D.T. Cochrane entitled 'Wal-Mart: Stagnant since 1999' on the forum page of capitalaspower.com. I am very grateful to Cochrane and Jonathan Nitzan for their invaluable support at every stage of the research and writing of this chapter.

scale (Nitzan and Bichler 2009). As Nitzan and Bichler argue, these disparate and heterogeneous power dynamics can be empirically investigated because their effects are encoded into the universal metric of capital.

This chapter explores Wal-Mart's power trajectory with reference to the company's relationship with labour. More specifically, it examines how dynamics of control and resistance between Wal-Mart and workers employed within Wal-Mart stores have impacted the pecuniary development of the company. The argument is divided into three sections. The first section elaborates on the CasP approach and demonstrates how it can help the researcher chart the development of Wal-Mart's power in the last four decades. The second section seeks to make sense of this power trajectory by offering a new quantitative measure of the company's relative control over its workers. Moreover, I draw on some qualitative analyses of the growing resistance Wal-Mart has faced within the US. The third section surveys Wal-Mart's attempts to spread its operations in 'human resource complexes' abroad to compensate for declining differential earnings in the US (Harvey 2006: 399). As I show, the retail behemoth has been encumbered by labour resistance in many of its foreign ventures, just as it has been encumbered in the US.

CAPITAL AS POWER

The CasP framework suggests that capital is the central power institution of contemporary society. But how is this power measured? Nitzan and Bichler point to capitalization, the formula through which risk-adjusted future earnings are discounted to their present value. As the first chapter of any corporate finance textbook testifies, this formula constitutes the generative grammar for the language of business. Nitzan and Bichler's theoretical innovation lies in recasting the discounting formula from the perspective of what they call 'dominant capital': the major firms and government entities at the core of the accumulation process. Capitalization is all-encompassing. Any social process that may bear on the future earnings of any given asset is factored into the capitalization formula. And since dominant capital actively seeks to shape and re-shape social processes in a manner that augments future income and curbs risk, capitalization is itself the central algorithm of business power. This insight has far-reaching implications. Instead of being a mere tool that enables owners to reactively measure the value of their ownership claims, capitalization is the means through which dominant capital appraises its capacity to actively restructure society in ways that boost future earnings and reduce volatility (Nitzan and Bichler 2009).

Moreover, from the CasP perspective, power is not an entity itself. Just as force only exists where there is counter-force, power presupposes resistance. As such, power should be understood in relative rather than absolute terms. This relativity has both quantitative and qualitative dimensions. On the quantitative side, it is indicated by the fact that corporations do not seek to reach a conceptually indeterminate 'profit maximum'. Instead they benchmark their own performance in relation to an average. On the qualitative side, it is indicated by the fact that different groups of corporations constantly seek to transform the manifold institutions of social order, against resistance, so as to augment their power over and above other business groups. Thus, capitalized power is manifest in its redistributional effects. Nitzan and Bichler call the quantitative dynamic of power redistribution between corporate groupings *differential accumulation*. By conducting a quantitative–qualitative analysis of the dynamics of differential accumulation on the one hand and the contested processes of institutional restructuring on the other, the researcher can begin to map out transformations in the power of dominant capital over society (Nitzan and Bichler 2009).

With the bare essentials of the CasP theory outlined, we can now begin to trace the power trajectory of Wal-Mart. Figure 9.1 offers the starting point of the analysis. It depicts the firm's differential capitalization and differential profit as set against the average corporation within dominant capital, both plotted against a logarithmic scale. The proxy I use for dominant capital is the Compustat 500 – the 500 largest firms by market capitalization listed in the US. Two major observations can be made from the chart. First, the differential capitalization and differential profit of Wal-Mart are very tightly correlated. This strong correlation underlines the importance of understanding current earnings as driving the long-term increases in the capitalization of the company.

Second and most importantly, the figure gives a very good insight into the differential trajectory of Wal-Mart. In 1975, the market capitalization of Wal-Mart was just one-tenth of the average firm in dominant capital. But in less than two decades the relative capitalization increases almost one-hundredfold, so that by 1993 Wal-Mart's capitalization is over nine times larger than the average dominant capitalist firm. The period from the late 1970s to the early 1990s thus represents a true golden age for Wal-Mart. However, from the early 1990s onwards Wal-Mart's capitalization has just been growing more or less at the same pace as the average firm within dominant capital. As such, it appears that the retail behemoth has reached a differential ceiling.

In what remains I investigate why Wal-Mart appears to be reaching a differential ceiling by linking a qualitative appraisal of Wal-Mart's

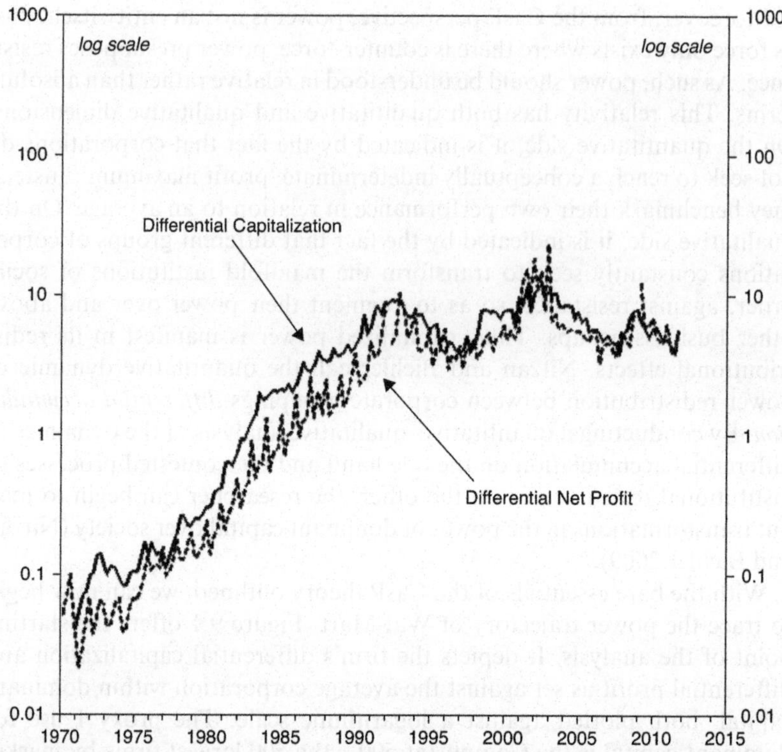

Note: Differential capitalization is the ratio of Wal-Mart's market value to the market value of the average corporation in the Compustat 500. Differential net profit is the ratio of Wal-Mart's net income to the net income of the average corporation in the Compustat 500. The Compustat 500 is the top 500 firms by market value listed in the United States.

Source: Wal-Mart, Compustat.

Figure 9.1 The differential capitalization and differential net profit of Wal-Mart

development to a quantitative analysis of the company's relative profit growth. Now according to Nitzan and Bichler, the differential accumulation of dominant capital as a whole is achieved primarily through mergers and acquisitions and price rises. Moreover, these two regimes of differential accumulation have become increasingly countercyclical. However, for much of Wal-Mart's history, the key propellants of its pecuniary development have been cost-cutting and greenfield investment. And rather than operating counter-cyclically, they operate in a coeval and symbiotic manner. This self-reinforcing dynamic between cost-cutting and greenfield investment is explained by the fact that Wal-Mart can only control its workers if it is large enough to reshape local labour markets in the ways it deems necessary; and it can only exert meaningful pressure on manufacturers if it can promise, in return for low supplier prices, access to a significant portion of US consumers.

Such a relationship between Wal-Mart's political economies of scale on the one hand, and control over labour and supply chains on the other, gave rise to a 'virtuous cycle' of profit growth in which high sales volume finances low-margin pricing and low-margin pricing drives high sales volume. In the next section I show how the virtuous cycle propelled Wal-Mart's rapid ascent in the 1970s and 1980s. In the section after that, I show how the symbiosis between cost-cutting and greenfield investment has become less and less effective as Wal-Mart has become larger in size and as it has encountered more and more resistance. In order to continue accumulating differentially, Wal-Mart will either have to engage in inflationary price increases and thus betray its founding retail principle of 'everyday low prices' or it will have to conduct more cross-border mergers and acquisitions. As I argue in the last section, the evidence so far suggests that Wal-Mart is principally opting for the latter strategy, but with mixed success.

THE CONTESTED DEVELOPMENT OF WAL-MART IN THE UNITED STATES

Wal-Mart's Golden Age of Accumulation: 1960s to Mid-1990s

Wal-Mart's model of lean retailing took shape in its early development during the 1960s in Bentonville, in Northwest Arkansas. At that time, agricultural production was getting belatedly mechanized in these rural backwaters and this caused the displacement of tens of thousands of workers from the region's farmland. In this context, Wal-Mart was able to draw upon surfeits of cheap labour (Lichtenstein 2006). And the company's founder, Sam Walton, wanted to keep things this way. Unlike the executives of other retail giants, such as Kmart and Sears, which accommodated unionization in the post-war era, Walton took a zero-tolerance approach to organized labour. He viewed unions as an intrusion upon managerial control and an impediment to his hallmark cost-cutting strategy. While the first reason for Walton's anti-unionism was perhaps born out of his idiosyncratic paternalism, the second reason had a more direct pecuniary logic. The retail business is very labour-intensive. Supermarkets, for example, pay as much as 70 per cent of their operating budget on labour costs (Lichtenstein 2009: 135). Thus, the benefits that Wal-Mart accrued from keeping wages low by keeping unions out were significant. Wal-Mart's animus towards unions was manifest in the geography of the company's early expansion. For the first two decades of its existence, Wal-Mart built almost all of its stores in small towns in the south-east and midwest where organized labour has historically been weak. It largely avoided the 'archipelago' of union strongholds stretching from the District of Columbia to the metropolitan areas of New York, Boston, Minneapolis, Seattle and San Diego (Lichtenstein 2009).

Wal-Mart expanded through small-town America through a process of market saturation: gaining commercial dominance in one region and then moving onto the next. With this market saturation strategy in place, Wal-Mart expanded its retail dominion throughout rural America virtually unimpeded. By the end of the 1980s the company became the third largest retailer in the US, even though it operated in only half of the American states (Vance and Scott 1994). Wal-Mart was almost becoming a vast state in itself. It even developed its own nomenclature. The company's precariously employed workers were christened 'associates'; the company's human resources department was termed 'the People Division'; the company's founding father was known by the sentimental moniker 'Mr Sam' and his multimillionaire directors were named, in true Orwellian fashion, 'Servant Leaders'. The firm went so far as to invent its own rallying cry – 'the Wal-Mart Cheer' – that its retail clerks and shelf stackers are still expected to sing with gusto at the beginning of every morning shift (Vance and Scott 1994; Lichtenstein 2009).

However, it would be wrong to attribute Wal-Mart's early pecuniary success solely to the corporation's own agency. There were political-economic developments beyond the company's control that had a significant bearing on its pecuniary trajectory. For one thing, the decline of organized labour in the US was highly propitious for Wal-Mart's expansion. Indeed, although Wal-Mart avoided a head-on clash with unions partly because of its rural location strategy, the company also benefited from the fact that the morale of union organizers within the retail sector was sapped by a series of defeats suffered by the American labour movement as a whole. Chief among these defeats was the failed passage of the Labour Law Reform Act in 1978 and Reagan's hugely symbolic quashing of the Professional Air Traffic Controllers Organization strike in 1981 (Lichtenstein 2009). Against this backdrop of union retrenchment, Wal-Mart was enjoying relative pliancy from its workers.

Moreover, the declining role that the manufacturing sector in the US has played in the generation of income in the US coincided with the increasing significance of service industries. This shift has been accompanied by a profound transformation in American society: the feminization of labour. On the one hand, this transformation is reflected in the massive influx of women into paid work, with employment rates of adult females shooting up from 48 per cent in 1973 to over 67 per cent in 1997 (Richard B. Freeman 2000: 5). On the other hand, the transformation is constitutive of the degradation of wage labour along lines associated with the subordinate gender roles of women. Indeed, the burgeoning service sector has opened up a new segment of the labour market characterized by more casualized, more 'flexible' and less secure work. Women in general, and women from ethnic minorities in particular, became disproportionately represented in these new jobs. Wal-Mart capitalized on this process, and at the same time reinforced it, by filling its lowest labour ranks with predominantly female workers, while keeping its managerial staff overwhelmingly male. In fact, from the company's foundation, around 70 per cent of its low-ranking employees have been female. Yet even to this day women receive far less pay for the same work that their male counterparts carry out, and they only gain around one-third of all promotions to managerial positions (Seligman 2006: 237). As such, hierarchical social relationships outside of Wal-Mart stores have been reproduced and reaffirmed within them.

The company's initial success in marrying worker discipline and wage repression is registered in Wal-Mart's changing differential selling and general administration (SGA) expenses per employee as presented in Figure 9.2. This measure calibrates the relative efficiency of Wal-Mart's internal operations and thus can be seen as a rough proxy of the company's differential control over its workers. The data are weighted relative to the corresponding SGA expenses per employee of the average firm within the Compustat 500. Thus, we can surmise that the lower the indicator gets, the more intensively Wal-Mart is projecting its power on its employees relative to dominant capital as a whole. In measuring Wal-Mart's cost-cutting performance in this manner we can build a richer understanding of the differential profit and differential capitalization data presented in the previous section.

Figure 9.2 clearly shows how Wal-Mart dramatically reduced its relative internal expenses in the 1970s and 1980s. In 1970 Wal-Mart's SGA expenses per employee were 17 per cent higher than the average firm in dominant capital, but twenty years later they were 60 per cent lower than the average. This massive drop in Wal-Mart's relative internal expenses testifies to the early success of Wal-Mart's disciplinary control over its workforce. The company's sales motif of everyday low prices was undergirded by a ruthless regimen of everyday low labour costs (Roberts and Berg 2012).

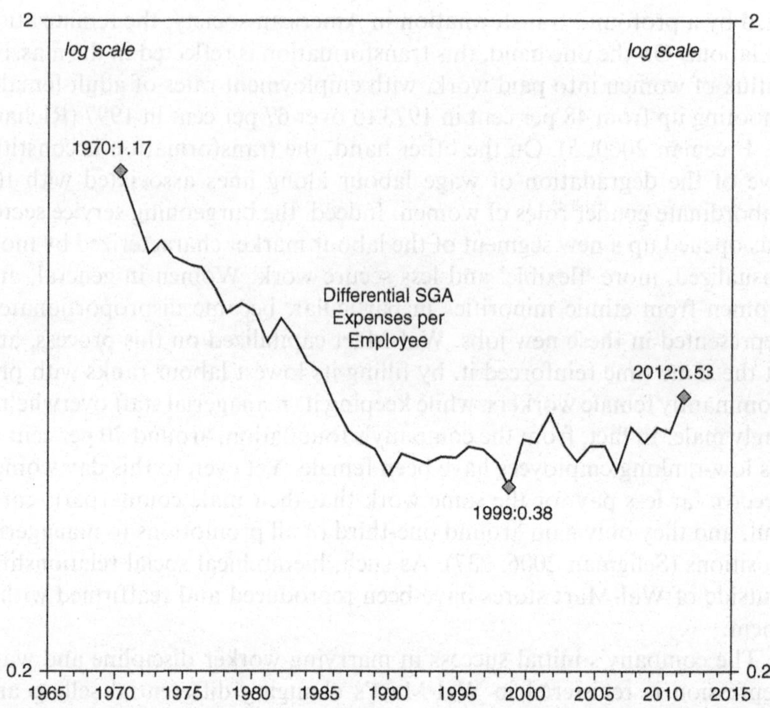

Note: Wal-Mart's SGA expenses per employee are weighted relative to the corresponding SGA expenses per employee of the average firm within the Compustat 500 to yield differential measures. These data are plotted on a logarithmic scale to highlight rates of change.

Source: Wal-Mart, Compustat.

Figure 9.2 The differential cost-cutting of Wal-Mart

The Mid-1990s Onward: Wal-Mart's Differential Accumulation Model Runs into Limits

By the late-1980s Wal-Mart had enveloped much of rural America. And by the early 1990s Wal-Mart had come to dominate the discount sector along with its two major rivals Kmart and Sears. As such, there was little room for Wal-Mart's continued expansion within its existing pecuniary ambit, both in sectoral and geographical terms. Wal-Mart began to extend its business interests from rural to metropolitan areas, and from non-food retailing to food retailing. However, by extending its dominion in this manner, Wal-Mart was impinging on the territorial domains of its retail rivals. Moreover, by entering the union strongholds in the north-east and the west coast, it was also setting itself on a collision course with organized labour. The over one million strong United Food and Commercial Workers (UFCW) union was particularly keen to defend existing workers within the grocery sector against the outgrowth of Wal-Mart's lean retailing model (Lichtenstein 2009; Roberts and Berg 2012).

Wal-Mart continued expanding into grocery retailing and by 2001 it had become the largest food retailer in the US. During this period of rapid expansion, the company sought to quash the intensified union threat by ramping up surveillance of its employees. Wal-Mart installed a nationwide anti-union hotline for store managers to use if they felt suspicious of any errant workers and it put in place a rapid response team, complete with its own special corporate jet, committed to taking over a store at a moment's notice when incipient unionization efforts were identified (Lichtenstein 2009). At face-value, Wal-Mart's sectoral expansion into food retailing and its geographical expansion into metropolitan areas has been a triumph. Up until the time of writing this chapter, not one of its workers in the US is represented by a union. And perhaps more impressively, 96 per cent of the US population now lives within 20 miles of a Wal-Mart store (Zook and Graham 2006: 20). Notwithstanding Wal-Mart's success in expanding its network of stores in union strongholds, the company has experienced massive worker desertion rates. By 1999 the annual labour turnover reached an astonishing 70 per cent as low-ranking employees were buckling under the pressure of harsh work conditions and poverty-line wages. The constant need to find replacements was very costly for Wal-Mart because of the huge expenses incurred in training new employees. Indeed by the early 2000s, it was estimated that Wal-Mart was spending $1.4 billion annually to replace the 600 000 to 700 000 workers that were leaving the company each year (Hopkins 2007).

Moreover, despite the fact that it has quelled unionization efforts, by becoming so ubiquitous within America, Wal-Mart has become subject to broader forms of social resistance. Lawsuits against the company have offered one avenue of contestation for disgruntled employees. Indeed, by 2004 Wal-Mart was involved in a total of 8000 ongoing legal cases (Olive 2004). The cases were launched in regard to a whole gamut of complaints such as gender and race discrimination and violation of state and federal regulations on overtime, lunch breaks and health and safety. The most famous of these was the 'Duke versus Wal-Mart' case – the largest class action attempt in history, involving 1.6 million female plaintiffs who were allegedly discriminated against when working for Wal-Mart. The Bentonville giant successfully appealed to the US Supreme Court to revoke the class action status of these legal efforts and, in so doing, the

the slated store opening. Although Wal-Mart eventually prevailed in this struggle, the protests against Wal-Mart's incursion into downtown LA are illustrative of the latent resistance that the company now faces in parts of the US that lie beyond the retailer's imperium.

To make matters worse for Wal-Mart, there has been a recent upsurge in struggles waged by employees working directly for the company. In October 2012, over seventy Wal-Mart retail clerks engaged in walkouts in Los Angeles. The strike – the first ever by retail workers in Wal-Mart's history – spread to 28 Wal-Mart stores in 12 different states. These actions were taken because Wal-Mart allegedly harassed and cut the hours of workers who became affiliated to OUR Wal-Mart (Organization United for Respect at Wal-Mart), a non-union campaign group supported by UFCW that seeks better pay, more affordable healthcare and improved working conditions for Wal-Mart workers (cf. www.forrespect.org). On Black Friday, the day that follows American Thanksgiving and the busiest shopping date of the year, Wal-Mart workers rose up again, with over 1000 individual actions and strikes reportedly taking place in over one hundred cities (Hines and Miles 2012). But in spite of the unrest, Wal-Mart triumphantly declared that it was their most successful Black Friday ever. Among other things, 1.8 million towels, 1.3 million dolls and 1.2 million televisions were sold by the company within just 24 hours (Wohl 2012).

One day later, 112 workers died in a fire in a cramped garment factory owned by one of Wal-Mart's suppliers in Bangladesh. Such is the strange, global algebra of everyday low prices, with rabid consumption on one end of the equation and inhuman labour conditions on the other. On the Sunday of that week, thousands took to the streets of Dhaka, the capital of Bangladesh, to protest against the lax health and safety standards that precipitated the factory inferno. And on the Monday, Wal-Mart sheepishly announced that it was severing ties with the supplier that owned the factory (Chalmers 2012). This episode points to the broader issue of whether Wal-Mart might be encountering the social limits of its cost-cutting model, not only within its own stores, but within the supply chains that furnish these stores with cheap commodities.

WAL-MART EXPANDS ABROAD

To summarize the argument so far, Wal-Mart's expansion in the American retail market has been slowing down in part because of intensified social resistance. In the face of this problem, Wal-Mart increasingly turned to international expansion as a means of augmenting its earnings growth.

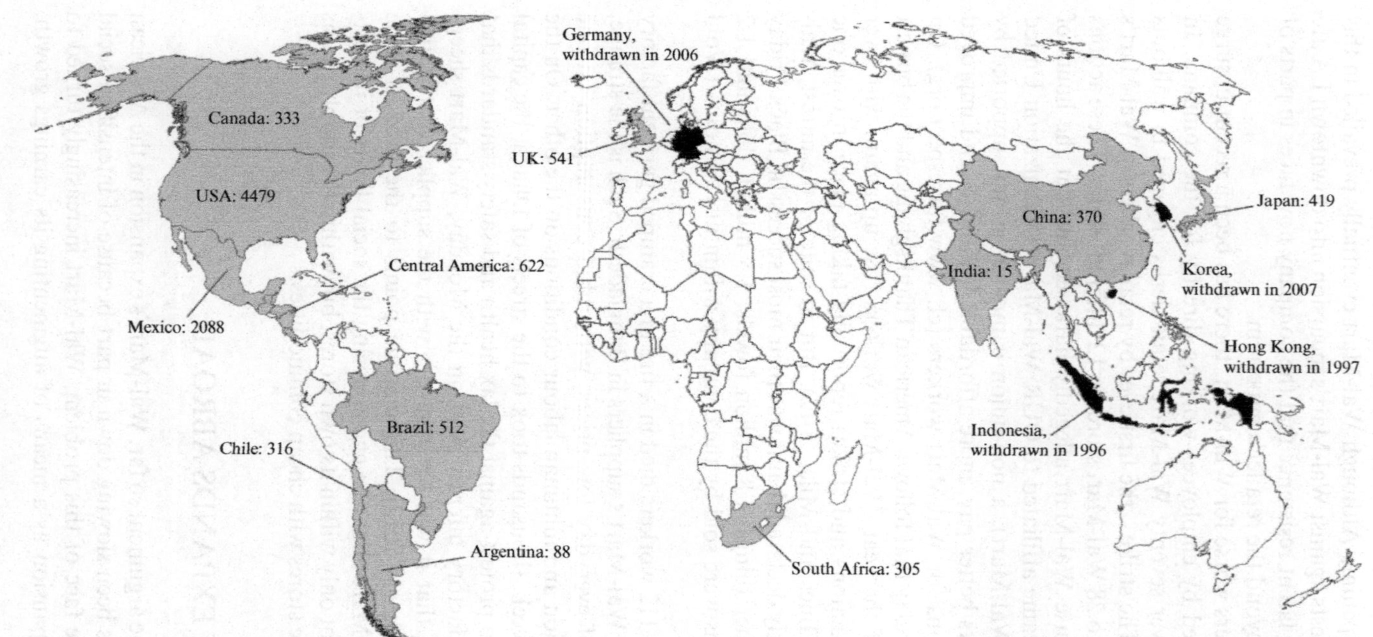

Note: Wal-Mart has a presence in countries shaded in grey. Data labels for the countries shaded in grey indicate the number of stores that Wal-Mart has within their borders. Wal-Mart withdrew from the countries shaded in back.

Source: Wal-Mart; Digital Maps.

Figure 9.3 Wal-Mart's would-be retail empire 2012

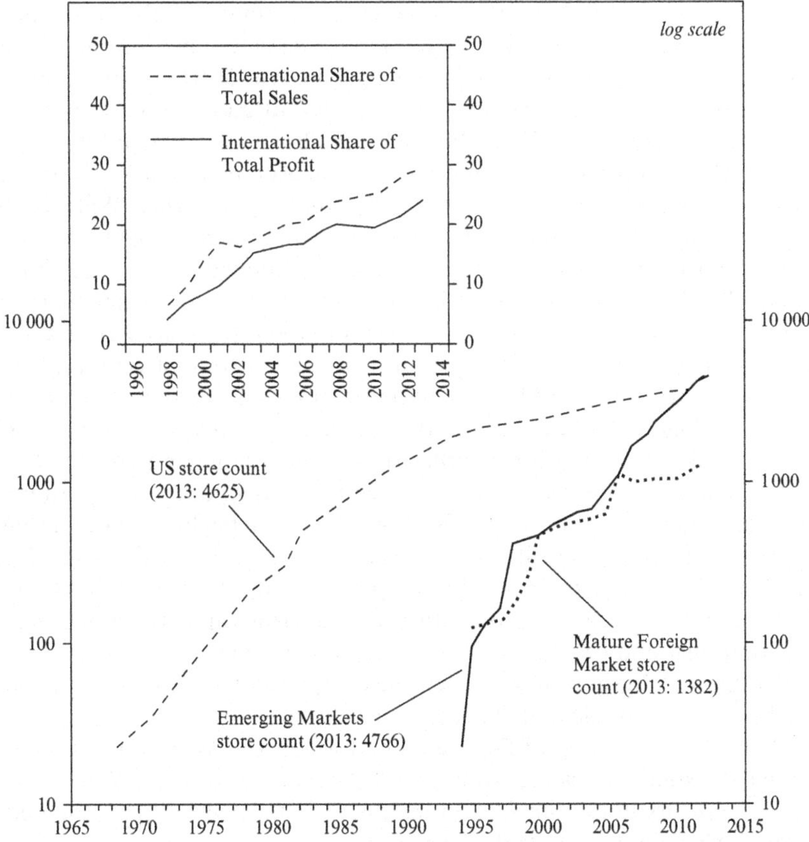

Note: The 'emerging markets' category comprises the following countries in order of Wal-Mart's year of entry: Mexico (1994); Argentina, Brazil (1996); China, Indonesia (1997); Costa Rica, El Salvador, Guatemala, Honduras (2007); Chile (2009); India (2010); and South Africa (2012). The 'mature foreign markets' category includes the following countries, in order of Wal-Mart's year of entry: Canada (1995); Germany (1998); South Korea (1999); UK (2000); and Japan (2005). The store count data are plotted on a logarithmic scale to highlight rates of change.

Source: Wal-Mart; SEC; Mergent Online.

Figure 9.4 Wal-Mart's store count in the US and abroad

Figure 9.3 depicts Wal-Mart's would-be retail empire. The company has a presence in the countries shaded in grey and it has withdrawn from the countries shaded in black. The data labels indicate the number of stores Wal-Mart has in each national territory.

While Figure 9.3 shows the spatial configuration of Wal-Mart's international division, Figure 9.4 shows how it has developed through time. More specifically, it presents the changes in Wal-Mart's store numbers within the US market, mature markets abroad and emerging markets. The chart confirms that Wal-Mart sought to break the 'national envelope' once opportunities to expand in the US domestic retail market began to dwindle (Nitzan and Bichler 2009: 390). Indeed, just when Wal-Mart's long arc of growth in the US began to flatten in the mid-1990s it started to extend its pecuniary ambit elsewhere. Additionally, the chart shows that while Wal-Mart experienced very rapid expansion in foreign markets in the early years of its internationalization, the rate of store growth has slowed down somewhat since the turn of the twenty-first century. Two other proxies for Wal-Mart's internationalization are presented in the insert of Figure 9.4: the share of the company's total sales and the share of its total operating income garnered by its international division. These are admittedly imperfect measures given the vicissitudes of international exchange rates and transfer pricing; however, it still might be worth noting that although the majority of Wal-Mart's stores are outside of the US, the company's foreign operations account for only 29 per cent of its total sales and 23 per cent of its operating income. This gap between the share of total sales and the share of total operating income held by Wal-Mart's international division suggests that the company's US business continues to be more profitable than its operations abroad.

How do we account for the overall performance of Wal-Mart's international division? One can see from Figure 9.4 that the growth in Wal-Mart's store numbers in mature foreign markets has tapered off since the mid-2000s. This trend suggests that the group of advanced capitalist countries that Wal-Mart has entered only offer a limited outlet for Wal-Mart's expansion. Indeed, among the mature consumer markets, Wal-Mart has attained unalloyed success in just two countries: the UK and Canada. As the UK and Canada have social compacts and cultural heritages that are comparable to that of the US, it is perhaps no surprise that their respective human resources complexes have been broadly receptive to the 'Wal-Mart Way'. However, even in these two countries Wal-Mart has encountered pockets of resistance. In the French-speaking province of Quebec, the norms of the Anglosphere, or what Kees van der Pijl calls the 'Lockean heartland' (1998: 65), have not permeated so deeply into the social fabric. Perhaps partly as a result, Quebecois workers were at the forefront of the Canadian labour struggle for unionization in Wal-Mart stores in the early to mid-2000s. When one Wal-Mart store in rural Quebec was successfully unionized, Wal-Mart quickly responded by closing the store down. Similarly, when Wal-Mart acquired the British supermarket giant Asda in

1999, it got embroiled in a battle with a union representing one-quarter of the employees working at Asda's distribution centres (Tilly 2007). After a protracted struggle, Wal-Mart ceded substantial organizing rights to the union. As such, given the residual worker resistance in the UK and Canada, and given their saturated retail markets, it appears that the Anglosphere only offers a temporary outlet for Wal-Mart's international growth.

Outside of the Lockean heartland, Wal-Mart has encountered even more pronounced worker resistance. Most notably, Wal-Mart's attempts at penetrating the German retail market ended in ignominious defeat. In the eight years that Wal-Mart did business in Germany it lost around $200 million annually and it cost the company one billion dollars to finally divest itself of its operations in the country in 2006.

What explains the failure of Wal-Mart's operations in Germany? For one thing, the Bentonville giant was hamstrung by Germany's restrictive land use regulations and strict store-hour regulations – a legacy of the *Mittelstand*'s successful mobilization against big retailers in the 1950s. These spatial and temporal limitations made it difficult for Wal-Mart to differentiate itself from its competitors with its low-cost, out-of-town box store expansion strategy that it honed in the US (Christopherson 2006; 2007). And perhaps more importantly, Wal-Mart had immense problems managing its German workforce. Although Germany has undergone dramatic changes in recent decades which have shifted the balance of power away from labour towards capital, the institutions that undergird a collaborative and coordinated system of engagement between workers and management remain partly intact. Moreover, the Bismarckian, insurance-based features of the German welfare system militated against Wal-Mart's preferred practice of shifting the costs of employee social reproduction to the public sector at large. This clash between Wal-Mart's disciplinary labour practices and prevailing social norms in Germany was cast in sharp relief when the retail behemoth attempted to introduce its employee code of conduct in the country. This code formed the core of Wal-Mart's private labour regulations and was a key tool for workplace discipline in the US. Among other things, the code forbade flirtation between Wal-Mart workers. Such overbearing and intrusive rules were widely taken to be an affront to retail workers' autonomy. Amid growing worker disdain for Wal-Mart's strictures, a German Labour Court struck down many features of the code. In short, the hierarchical relation that Wal-Mart prided itself in having with workers in the US did not meld well with the dilapidated, but nonetheless deeply embedded structures of German corporatism (Backer 2007).

Given the marked slowdown in Wal-Mart's expansion in mature

markets, emerging markets appear to offer the greatest possibilities for the company's future accumulation. Of these ventures in emerging markets, Wal-Mart's Mexican operations have been by far the most successful. Like Wal-Mart's Canadian operations, Wal-Mart's venture in Mexico has benefited from the fact that the country borders the US and can thus draw on the extension of the company's pre-existing US supply chain infrastructure. Since 2003 Wal-Mart has been the largest private employer in Mexico, with well over 200 000 people currently on its payroll. However, Wal-Mart has been less successful in other emerging markets. For example, in China – the largest emerging market of all – Wal-Mart has been experiencing major problems. Aware of the importance of China's burgeoning middle class for its own international sales drive, Wal-Mart's directors have assiduously sought to forge linkages with the Chinese Communist Party (CCP). In the early to mid-2000s, the then CEO of Wal-Mart, Lee Scott, went on five visits to China to meet high-ranking government officials, including the then president of the country, Jiang Zemin. Notwithstanding these overtures, the Chinese government and Wal-Mart have differed in their views on the extent and pace of liberalization in the country's retail sector.

Government-led resistance to Wal-Mart's expanding presence in the country's retail landscape was clear to see in 2004, when the ruling Communist Party's ostensible organ of labour representation, the All China Federation of Trade Unions (ACTFU), threatened to take Wal-Mart to court if it did not allow the formation of a workers' union for its stores. ACTFU then launched a unionization drive amongst Wal-Mart workers. The company caved in and accepted ACTFU's demands. The significance of this episode lies in the fact that by getting Wal-Mart stores unionized, the Chinese government could install intelligence-gathering capabilities within the company itself. Given the size of the potential retail market in China, Wal-Mart of course could not refuse this measure, but it did represent a defeat for the company (Wang and Zhang 2006).

Clearly, there is much work that still needs to be done to harmonize the operations of Wal-Mart's retail segment with the agenda of the Chinese government. Partly as a result of the disjuncture between the machinations of Wal-Mart and the priorities of the CCP, the retail giant's sales growth in the country still lags behind many of China's domestic supermarkets (Chuang et al. 2011). If Wal-Mart is to close the gap with its rivals in China, it will probably need to continue to attain prime real estate in the saturated property markets of major cities such as Shanghai through the process of acquisition. But so far, Wal-Mart's experience has shown that this approach to penetrating metropolitan areas is tough and often protracted (Tacconelli and Wrigley 2009). Taken as a whole, the prospects for Wal-Mart in the world's largest emerging retail market are shrouded in uncertainty.

CONCLUSION

Wal-Mart's pecuniary success has been based on a reinvestment strategy of rapid greenfield growth and rigid control over workers throughout its supply chain. In the first two decades of its existence, Wal-Mart could grow largely 'under the radar' of organized labour. It expanded at a dramatic pace in the relatively un-unionized and hence uncontested retail landscape of the south-east and midwest. Moreover, although it was not the first major retailer to source goods from East Asia, by the 1990s it had the largest network of suppliers in the region (Gereffi and Christian 2009). And whilst the development of the back-end of Wal-Mart's supply chain has not figured prominently in this analysis, it has been integral to the company's differential accumulation trajectory. Wal-Mart's suppliers filled their sweatshops with masses of underpaid female workers who had migrated from rural areas, just as Wal-Mart had filled its own stores with underpaid female retail clerks who had been displaced by agricultural transformations within the US. The success of this explicitly gendered nexus of corporate power is undeniable. Perhaps no other firm in history has harnessed the energies of feminized labour more effectively and on such a colossal scale.

However, the retail behemoth has become increasingly encumbered. As Wal-Mart expanded into the metropolitan areas of the north-east and the far west in the 1990s, the company found it harder to apply its distinct model of retailing, because in these parts of the US unions are more active and municipal zoning rules are more heavily contested. As such, soon after Wal-Mart moved into these areas it became subject to increased resistance. Now Wal-Mart's model of lean retailing is facing stern opposition at all levels of its supply chain: from its workers involved in the OUR Wal-Mart campaign and from the suppliers' employees who at times are engaging in a life and death struggle for humane work conditions. Moreover, as the data in this chapter indicate, the internationalization efforts have failed to increase the company's differential capitalization and differential profits. In fact, in 2012 Wal-Mart announced that it would cut store openings for its international division by an astounding 30 per cent (Jopson 2012). The massive downsizing of expansion plans was motivated by the desire to attain satisfactory levels of profitability and assuage outstanding bribery claims made against the company. Bribery allegations first broke out after revelations that Wal-Mart bribed government officials in Mexico to expedite zoning approvals and planning permits for its new stores, but it now encompasses alleged breaches in US anti-corruption laws in its operations in Brazil, China and India. With opportunities for frictionless growth characteristic of the first few decades of its existence long gone, Wal-Mart seems to have been pushing the limits of legality in its bid to expand further (Barstow 2012). If no transformative upsurge in foreign investment takes place, Wal-Mart will perhaps experience relative stagnation or even differential decline. In short, the paragon of rapid business growth in the late twentieth century may become the exemplar of the limits to corporate power in the twenty-first.

10. Beyond the 'BRICS': new patterns of development cooperation in the Trans-Eurasian corridor

Yury Gromyko

INTRODUCTION

In this chapter we analyse the initiative of Russia with Kazakhstan, Belarus and also Ukraine, to design and develop an integrated system of production in the Trans-Eurasian belt, or corridor. This futuristic project, under its Russian label of *razvitie* ('development'), projects a new type of platform for investment and economic development with a potentially planetary impact. Its primary aim is to create a new wealth-generating pole on Russian territory (to begin with, West and East Siberia and the Russian Far East), based on cooperation with Western European countries and on mutually profitable trade with China, India, Iran and other countries. At the core of this project is the challenge to create a science-intensive, industrial development pole embedded in next-generation infrastructure. It will provide a qualitatively new connection between production and transport, on which will rely, on the one hand, the provision of new resources (energy, information, materials, technology), and on the other, the process of new settlements and actual cities. The specific mission of Russia consists in conceiving and taking the first steps in the design and organization of this project.

The projected Trans-Eurasian Development Corridor (from the Russian 'belt of *razvitie*', TEBR) gives a modern twist to the notion of the Great Silk Road, but it is not just a transport route (Gromyko 2012). Unlike a 'land bridge' or a mere 'development corridor', it combines a new geo-economics that departs from the current practice of global political economy, with a new geopolitics. This geopolitics is based on the cooperative establishment of new human settlements and the accompanying geo-cultural notion of a dialogue of civilizations, derived from Eurasian ideology. New forms of finance and law will also be part of it, all in an effort to create a communicative super-infrastructure in which different states, religions and civilizations interact.

The notion of development, *razvitie*, is used to contrast the project with traditional concepts of economic growth. The idea of 'emerging economies' such as the BRICS, the rise of which is based on the relocation of existing industries such as automobiles or electronics, was formulated with an eye to profiting from fast-rising stock market prices in them. The TEBR on the other hand is conceived to meet the current planetary crisis by projecting a scale of production of social wealth (goods, devices, infrastructures, dense energy flows) that goes beyond current practice and presumes qualitative changes in the way of production, in forms of knowledge, forms of social organization and life, and also the structure of identity.

PRODUCTION AND THOUGHT-ACTIVITY IN THE DESIGN OF A NEW ECONOMIC SYSTEM

The commonly used concept of 'sustainable development' falls short of capturing the notion underlying the TEBR project. Sustainable development, translated into Russian as steady, persistent, stable development (*ustoychivoe razvitie*) rules out qualitative change as it relies on linearity of quantitative fluctuations instead of a quantum leap; and then we cannot speak of progress if it remains unclear what exactly we are trying to sustain. Sustainable development can be understood in a long tradition of *auto-poesis*, used already by Fichte as *Selbsttätigkeit, Selbst-Betätigung*, self-activity. Auto-poesis is not necessarily about production, and today it is rather connected with notions of individual self-realization, even with a Bohemian lifestyle.

Production, on the other hand, denotes transformative, creative action in which a certain way of life and the human being itself are being (re-)produced. However, the perverse dynamics of capital accumulation have degraded work in industrial systems into routine, partial tasks, executed under conditions of submission and disconnected from any creative aspect. From the separation of mental from manual work, via Taylorism and Fordism and the appearance of Toffler's 'prosumer' figure (producer + consumer, Toffler 1970; 1990), this got us to the concept of a post-industrial society, which claims that the most advanced forms of production are not associated with industry at all and instead are confined to knowledge work and handling information. Yet the power of the developed world has remained critically dependent on dual-use high-technology, both for sophisticated consumer goods and for weapons of mass destruction. The ideology of post-industrialism in the USA would rather seem to be an expression of the erosion of production capabilities and the slowing down of the development of the know-how needed to produce new materials, devices and technological components (Fingleton 1999).

A true IPE of production, then, requires a return to a proper understanding of what development means. Marx's understanding of labour as a human essence (cf. Introduction, this volume) opens up a perspective in which production is not identical to 'activity' in opposition to 'passivity'. Rather it refers to the German *Tätigkeit*: sensory, substantive (*gegenständlich*) activity, which is at the core of the social creation of an objectifiable totality. Thus the production of things, knowledge, instruments, machines, abilities and competences, as well as services, cannot be reduced to the grid or 'lattice' of production, distribution, exchange and consumption and reproduction, and the cycles through which each of them operate in the economy. It demands, in addition, an anthropological understanding of productive activity, connected to creativity and hence, to education and the social-cultural conditions of life. This is what *autopoesis* refers to. It includes interaction with other communities and with nature, and allows us to design not only products in the form of things but also forms of activity that allow the self-realization of the human being. It is this human substratum that remains the foundation of production, however much it is spread across the 'lattice' defined by the cycle of capital.

The so-called emerging market economies offer the most striking examples of the distortions produced by financial capitalism in this respect. Here capital and market dynamics have not been socialized to the same degree as in the existing capitalist core countries. Thus in Russia or even in apparently successful China, there is a disjunction between the financial sphere dominated ultimately by the financial centres in the United States, and their own social systems (Arrighi 2007; Fingleton 2008). This expresses itself in the destruction of nature, huge injustices and a distortion of demographic reproduction. The emerging economies are inserted into a global finance-led world economy without a corollary restructuring of the global productive economy; on the other hand the existing centres of capitalist reproduction will not be able to digest a new, planetary productive system as envisaged by the TEBR project.

So how can we imagine that a truly new productive system arises? For this to be realized it would have to display the features that the Russian philosopher, G.P. Shchedrovitskiy, calls the process of 'thought-activity' (Shchedrovitskiy 2005). It comprises three processes: *thinking; thought-communication*; and *thought-action*, which must be integrated into one through fusion. Such fusion and integration are achieved through reflection, in which the participants in practical interaction understand the full thought-activity system in which they find themselves. This, we contend, is impossible in Fordism–Taylorist production systems, it is necessary to design a novel, productive planetary economy.

Shchedrovitskiy's three-step thought-activity process in turn is a concretization of the concept of *noösphere*, the sphere of human thought, as applied by V.I. Vernadskiy, the Russian-Ukrainian founder of geo-chemistry, bio-geochemistry and radio-geology. Vernadskiy was a representative of Russian cosmism, a philosophical-cultural movement that proposes an all-embracing, planetary vision of the evolution of life. For our purpose, Vernadskiy's idea of a noösphere, which he borrowed from the French philosopher and mathematician, Édouard Le Roy, is of special relevance. This concept, in analogy to Vernadskiy's idea of the biosphere, in the twentieth century has come to represent the equivalent of a new geological force (Vernadskiy 1998). Just as the biosphere had previously transformed abiotic, geological minerals and planetary material into elements of the Earth's life-world, the noösphere, which was an aspect and a result of biospheric evolution, has transformed the planet's biosphere and material systems. Here we are talking about the planetary effects of human thought (first of all, scientific, disciplined thought that produces technologies and a new system of production, in the spirit of Marx's idea of a 'transformation of science into a direct productive force of society'). So how can this thought-effort be turned into a new practice of development?

TOWARDS A PLATFORM FOR NEW DEVELOPMENT

Today the world economy is facing an 'investment pause', since there is neither a new generation of technologies for mass consumption, nor a new general-purpose technology in sight (Bresnahan and Trajtenberg 1995; Lipsey et al. 2005; Ruttan 2006). The idea that information technology would provide this has been proven wrong by the 'post-industrial' fallacy (Prestowitz 2010). A truly innovative class of technologies will have to be connected with new energy systems, new materials, new instrumental systems and new means to cultivate and sustain living organisms (for example, bio-photonics devices detecting and imitating ultra-weak emission of light). The currently paramount fields of technological innovation, nano, bio, info and cogno (from 'cognition'), the so-called NBIC technologies (Empereur 2007; 2008), have not been able to generate profit by operating in conjunction, as suggested by Rifkin (2011). To reconnect investment finance with technology, we may think of the model proposed by Carlota Perez, who theorizes a cycle that passes through: (a) investment into new technology; (b) overinvestment and ensuing bubble; (c) decoupling of productive from financial capital; and (d) renewal of the cycle as finance directs 'idle money' to search for new spheres of technological investment (Perez 2002; 2006). How then can we expect that this time, a re-coupling of techno-dynamics and the dynamics of finance be achieved, so that a transition to a new techno-industrial, social-cultural formation and to new forms of property becomes possible?

This takes us back to the Trans-Eurasian Development Corridor project. Our assumption is that this vast project, with its planetary implications, requires a long-term perspective which cannot be expected to fit into the time horizons of capital accumulation as it operates today. Nor would it chime with the interests of property-owners involved in it. But the TEBR cannot be reduced to strictly national initiative either. It will only become a reality by dedicated networking aimed at increasing connectivity and by integrating the capacities of different states, mobilizing a variety of pools of investment finance, and engaging different professional communities, in order to develop the infrastructure and the technologies required. Also, a 'territorialization' (in the sense of Deleuze and Guattari's dialectic of territorialization and de-territorialization, Deleuze and Guattari 2004a; 2004b) will have to occur in the sense of obtaining the space for its realization.

Only by establishing a viable platform in which the necessary conditions for the new technological programme can be created, will investors (expecting profit) and the population (demanding employment) be convinced of the TEBR's ability to deliver on its promises. The core project would have to be oriented to the so-called emerging markets, where so far, financialization and social reproduction have failed to become integrated into a functioning structure of socialization. For these countries, the two aims of the TEBR, modernization of the existing industries using new technologies, and the creation of joint international technological systems not yet available today, would have the greatest impact. The creation of the infrastructure of the Trans-Eurasian Development Corridor on the basis of transport, energy and telecommunication corridors is the first step in this process.

The elimination of customs barriers among the participating states is a step to facilitate transfers among them and allow large-scale industrialization, using Soviet and international experience in the sphere of producing new goods, services and technologies from the perspective of redesigning a planetary productive system. Yet the TEBR is not a strategy of catching up with the advanced economies of the West and Japan, but a project oriented to advancing and developing innovative industrialization based on breakthrough technologies. New settlements of a type not yet in existence, 'future-zones' in which researchers, inventors and architects collaborate to design and develop innovations aimed at overcoming current crises, are at the heart of the project. Density of research and development activity in clusters will produce series of interconnected discoveries.

Crucially, to be put into practice, these must then be linked to the industrial economies of the European Union and Japan. Ingenuity and design cannot function without existing productive capacity if they are to lay the groundwork for the next techno-industrial formation, organized around technologies such as thermonuclear and solar energy, nanomaterials (cf. Wullweber, this volume), laser machine-tool equipment, space engines, biophotonics systems, and magnetic levitation ('maglev') transport systems. In the scientific centres of Kazakhstan, Belarus and Russia, inherited from the USSR, technological solutions for a large spectrum of industries have been found. However, as a consequence of institutional weakness and the collapse of project and applied research, post-Soviet applied science lacks the ability to create experimental equipment and prototypes of new technological devices, and even lags behind existing mass production industrial systems. Hence the need to integrate Russian, Belarusian and Kazakh scientific research with European industrial systems, if these technologies of the future are to become a reality. There are already nodes of such integration, for instance between the Russian Academy of Sciences and the Italian network of industrial enterprises, *Fabbrica del Futuro* (Ceracchi 2013). The conditions for a transfer of scientific research and new discoveries into new technologies that can be deployed into mass production as turnkey technologies, are created through such innovative networks and groups.

Now it is obvious that the TEBR should meet the needs of Russian society as well. With its vast territory but relatively small population, a demographic impulse is needed, and the new technologies would have to serve a biopolitical function for the Russian and neighbouring populations – one that is different from the demographic explosions that are occurring elsewhere. This takes us back to our understanding of development, *razvitie*, which can be summed up under the heading of five basic principles:

- The creation of a multiple infrastructure composed of at least three, flexibly integrated systems: transportation, energy and telecommunications (cf. Figure 10.1).
- International, joint creation of a platform from which new technologies and dense energy flows radiate to create a new techno-industrial and socio-cultural formation.
- Organization of a zone for industrial revolution connected with comprehensive implementation of breakthrough technologies on the basis of new fundamental knowledge by the creation of new industrial clusters and scientific cities and new settlements.
- Design and organization of a consortium of future consumers for multi-infrastructure services.
- Creation of new types of long-term investment instruments.

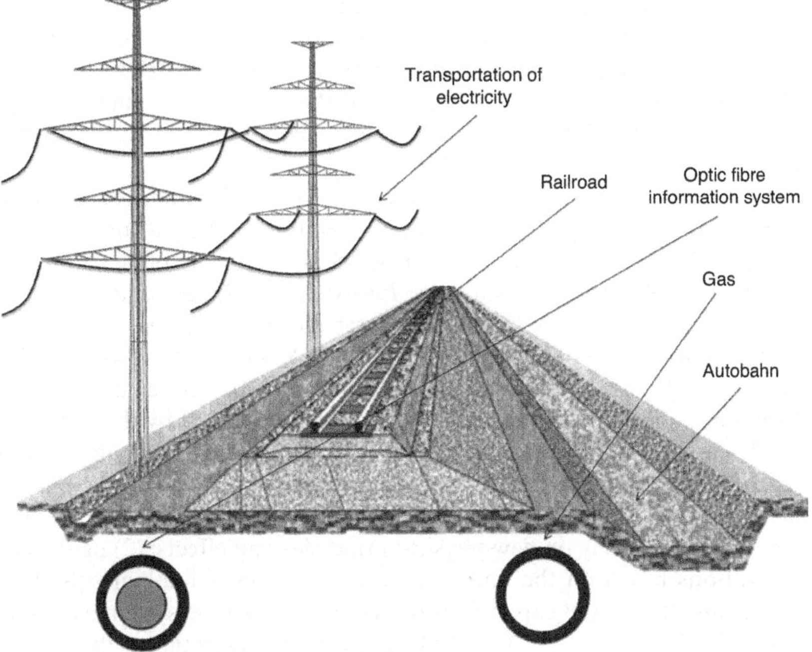

Figure 10.1 *Energy, information and transport at the basis of a development corridor*

The basic axis running through a corridor, referred to in the first principle, is shown in Figure 10.1 (Paz et al. 2011).

This takes us to how we can expect that such a project can be realized.

ORGANIZATIONAL FRAMEWORK: REALIZATION OF THE INITIATIVE

A group of Russian, Italian, Brazilian, Kazakh and German scientists, administrators, financial experts and social activists has been formed to elaborate the concept of a TEBR. In November 2012 an international conference on the Trans-Eurasian Development Corridor was held in Milan at the University Luigi Bocconi. At this stage, Russian specialists representing the Russian Railways (OJSC), the Russian Federal Electricity Grid company, other corporations, and various scientific experts from multiple disciplines met with members of the Italian Research Institute for International Politics. On this occasion the *Cassa Depositi e Prestiti* proposed to link the issue of constructing a transcontinental infrastructure with identifying new instruments of long-term investment, some of which have been developed by the Long-Term Investors Club (Bassanini and Reviglio 2010; *La Finanza* 2013). Out of this conference came a memorandum and a book published in Moscow (Baidakov et al. 2012; Sergeev et al. 2012).

In July 2013, the combined efforts of OJSC, Lomonosov Moscow State University, and the reorganized Institute of Social and Political Studies of the Russian Academy of Sciences, led to the publication of a report titled *An Integrated Eurasian Infrastructure System as a Priority of National Development* based on the aforementioned materials and signed by the heads of the named bodies, Vladimir Yakunin, V.A. Sadovnichiy and G.V. Osipov, respectively (Osipov et al. 2013). On behalf of OJSC, Yakunin established a dedicated working group headed by the chairman of the board of the Millennium Bank, M. Baidakov. It was agreed that given the crisis, implementation of the project had to aim beyond existing arrangements and technologies. Thus the creation of: (1) technological devices that can rely on new physical principles and effects; (2) new social institutions based on the implementation of these technologies; and (3) new competences and capabilities of people through the systemic integration of different kinds of knowledge, are seen as essential to the success of the TEBR. In October 2013, finally, a Russian–Italian conference was held in Verona organized by the bank Intesa San Paulo and with the participation of the *Cassa Depositi e Prestiti* and its president, Franco Bassanini, who highlighted the importance of the TEBR concept and its possibilities (Gromyko 2013).

The present author's notion of an 'integrative multi-infrastructure' (or 'integrated infrastructure system' as it was adapted by the leadership group) envisages the integration of infrastructures of a new type, capable of producing non-linear effects through flexible, oscillating fusion of different components in one integrative pattern. In contrast to the classical definition of infrastructure, the integrated infrastructure system replaces the classical notion of an economic basis by highlighting the synergetic effects of the participants in the project. These exchange different production dynamics which, in combination, have the potential of creating a new wealth-generating pole. Obviously this is not a rigid, motionless centre, or a fixed point on the map, but a dynamic process of organizing cooperation and integrating different possibilities for production and investment.

The idea to organize the corridor envisages the deployment of new, advanced manufacturing systems on Russian territory in cooperation with domestic technological, scientific, industrial and financial groups, jointly with neighbouring countries. Thus the elementary grid of an advanced transport system will function as a productive value chain along its track. The proposal to construct an integrated 'maglev' train/electricity grid in Russia is under discussion at the time of writing. Likewise there is a Russian–Chinese initiative to construct a railway line from Zabaikalsk to Tiksi, which Chinese investors are keen to use with an eye to shortening, via the Northern Sea Route, transportation time needed to connect Chinese urban centres to Scandinavia. For Russia this proposal opens up the possibility to reclaim a vast landmass with permafrost, which holds rare earth metals on which electronics production can be based. Clearly the various possibilities offered by opening up this landmass through smart grid development, are enormous – and not only because, unlike Thomas Friedman's assessment in *Hot, Flat and Crowded* (Friedman 2009), we are looking at a space that is 'cold, multi-dimensional and empty'.

For collaboration to succeed, there will have to be a shared understanding of the spatial factor involved for specific projects to be undertaken in concrete joint initiatives. This raises the question of the material factors determining the communication among different countries. What will be the common cultural, civilizational and, finally, economic space in which interactions will evolve? The assumption here is that the definition of this space, which will serve as the operational basis, will not merely be a matter of the political, geographical, geo-logistical, infrastructural, technical, corporate and demographic characteristics of the participating entities, but also a semiotic one. This implies that the space of interaction will also be the space in which meanings, symbols, common problem formulations and knowledge are produced and exchanged in communication between different international actors. In this context we may recall the Japanese concept of *ba* (place of knowledge creation) which would have a counterpart in the concept of 'semiosphere' developed by Y.M. Lotman (Lotman 2001: 683–4).

The Japanese concept of *ba* functions in a model of knowledge creation built around the spiral-like interaction between explicit and tacit knowledge, as formulated by I. Nonaka in 1998 (Nonaka and Konno 1998). The concept of semiosphere was coined in the early 1980s, again with reference to Vernadskiy. A text, from this perspective, is seen not as an isolated, reified cultural 'thing', but in conjunction with the terms and procedures of its production in a concrete situation. Thus a methodology for inter-state and inter-cultural collaboration, involving thought-activity in the noösphere, can be developed into a comparative meta-cognitive analysis. Ultimately, finding possibilities for real investment projects, finding investors and creating conditions for their implementation is also an epistemic procedure in which new knowledge is created along with the technological knowledge on which the concrete projects rely.

Returning to the material aspect, we should not forget that this is a mega-project. A Trans-Eurasian Development Corridor would involve, for a populated zone of 200 to 300 kilometres wide on each side of the track, an estimated minimum of 1.5 trillion euros to realize, to fund around 12 million jobs. Its real promise is the potential for expansion: by 2035 ten new cities are projected to emerge. A mega-project of this size requires the identification of sources of investment capital, which will only be available if political risks are secured and legal procedures cover international contracts to ensure investment returns. Concessions, access to new technological solutions, external social effects such as a decrease of the unemployment rate in the EU, the mitigation of ecological risks, spatial development of underpopulated areas, and so on, here would have to combine in mobilizing the required investment. The theoretical platform is provided by the TEBR documentation, which has been elaborated into a more detailed Russian–Japanese platform, Russian–Chinese, Russian–EU, Russian –Kazakh platforms, and so on. These were worked out during the 11th Annual Session of the Rhodes Forum, 'The Age of the World Picture' by participants of the Plenary Meeting, 'Alternative Visions of the World: Geo-Economics' (Rhodes Forum 2013).

In these sessions, the key tenets of a new language of development (*razvitie, sviluppo, fāzhǎn-*发展*. . .*) were reaffirmed once again. It was stressed that the reformulated concept is necessarily opposed to the currently hegemonic category of 'growth', which it must replace in light of the present crisis. We need a paradigm change including new approaches to economics, management, finance and business administration, as well as a new, practical philosophy and a new language, or semantics. Breakthroughs in fundamental knowledge and technology will enable new forms of energy and materials, mastery of near-Earth and outer space, a transmutation of chemical elements, and an isotope economy. As a future-oriented mutation in the quality of life and the level of consciousness, it is the opposite of a nostalgic return to village life, which would not provide a solution to demographic problems. Instead the project aims at the renovation of material well-being and spiritual values, replacing the materialism and consumerism of capitalist society.

To achieve this ambitious goal a clear and fundamental change is needed in the economic principles of designing, building and managing infrastructure systems. That applies not only to the construction of the physical infrastructure itself, but also, and above all, to its financing mechanism. We need a 'finance for development' that is inherently long term and based on just, rather than speculative returns on investments. This means renouncing monetarism and abandoning the economical doctrine of neoliberalism. This is not merely an ideological gesture but an effort to combine the most important technical principles of infrastructure construction with a new system of financing, which includes new approaches to the life-cycles of projects, contracts and land leases, and project financing. In this new environment, a stronger public sector will support the financial engineering mechanisms needed to make such large projects viable and economically sustainable in the long term.

Appropriate accounting principles replacing those attuned to short-termism and speculation will be part of this comprehensive mutation. The nature of transcontinental infrastructure projects dictates a move away from simple, fixed monetary metrics, since the projects themselves change the value of money. The implementation of such projects therefore entails totally new and different metrics. Instead of a dollarization of all payments, a basket of currencies reflecting relative values and costs of different resources in the countries participating in the projects will be in order. This would allow judging the viability of projects on the basis of what the Russian scientist Malenkov calls the 'comprehensive economic result', in the form of real infrastructural services provided by the future system (Malenkov 2008; 2011).

THE RUSSIAN AXIS IN A TRANS-EURASIAN DEVELOPMENT CORRIDOR

The TEBR project combines re-industrialization, the allocation of new industrial clusters and settlements, and development of integrative multi-infrastructure. It challenges the currently dominant social-economical model of production in Russia. Instead of conceiving production as an ancillary of a resource-based economy, and infrastructure as an auxiliary factor for industrial policy, in the TEBR infrastructure becomes the key factor, the locomotive pulling other economic activity forward.

For Russia, the project implies the creation of physical infrastructure with an overall capacity several times existing ones (first of all, energy and transport infrastructure). This includes ultra-high-speed trains that can attain twice the velocity of current high-speed trains (i.e. 500–700 km/h); and energy systems which will allow a reduction of CO_2 emissions and harmful effects for the environment, whilst raising flow density. To achieve next-generation industrialization, it is not enough to increase energy efficiency but also to qualitatively raise the level of horsepower. Only thus will currently available, turnkey German technologies find the energy supply they require (Tennenbaum 2001: 206–16; Tennenbaum et al. 1997). Petrochemicals, coal chemistry, natural gas utilization, laser and machine-tools production, biotech, engine-building development: all are dependent on a particular ratio of horsepower per worker. It is no coincidence that Japan, an industrial and technological superpower, is also the world leader in energy consumption per head of the population.

Clearly the construction of such vast infrastructural works should not repeat the mistakes of USSR-era *dolgostroy* (unfinished and delayed construction), with its changes in deadlines and cost increases during the construction period (Flyvbjerg et al. 2003). Instead a cascade system of launching projects should ensure that technology and expertise are recycled from project to project and avoid the experience of large tunnel construction on the BAM railway (Baikal–Amur Mainline), in which the unique expertise of the workers was not exploited on a subsequent project and valuable competences were made redundant. Hence sophisticated planning is required, which in turn will be premised on a different organization of society. Current corporate practice in Russia falls short of meeting these requirements. New productive systems are in order, in which innovative productive units operating outside rather than inside existing corporations are brought into a matrix structure designed to bring forth an entirely new energy and transport infrastructure. Existing corporations basically use the technologies of the previous techno-industrial and social formation, and they are not interested in innovations that change the power balance in the corporation. In addition, Russian corporations are sector-specific, a legacy of Soviet economic organization, whereas the TEBR is dependent on cross-sector organization. Also, managements have not abandoned the bureaucratic routines inherited from the past.

At the same time, the neoliberal monetarist ideology to which current large corporations are committed rules out the insertion of certain territories into the interconnected social spaces projected by the new infrastructure. For example, according to the monetarist paradigm all the supplementary industries and settlements in the basic infrastructure corridor are regarded as incidental assets or else as additional costs that should be reduced. But the TEBR looks at these in the context of new settlements, zones of future living space with a potential for large-scale expansion. Such expansion is not given by the natural growth of population and the trek to the big cities; this only results in increased consumption as can be seen in countries such as India, Vietnam, Indonesia, Bangladesh, and partly also in China.

The pattern of development in Russia projected by the TEBR instead is premised on the creation of next-generation, capital-intensive infrastructures that reorganize the space for communities of professionals, who would live next to infrastructure nodes and ensure its operation. Pioneer technological towns and scientific settlements along the Trans-Siberian and Baikal–Amur mainline would follow in the footsteps of the proposal of Russian architect Iliya Lezhava to turn new conurbations along these lines into a single, integrated urban agglomeration. This is also why from a Russian point of view, the TEBR should not be a mere transportation tube for cheap goods from China to Europe, with no socio-economic development in the territories it traverses. It must include the creation of new industrial centres on Russian land, zones of experimentation with advanced technologies that clear the way for the next socio-cultural and techno-industrial formation. Magnetic-levitation train technology, laser-based energy transfer (including electric discharge), and superconductivity technologies developed to intensify energy flows and smart grid systems would be among the innovations on which the TEBR will rely. These technical parameters already imply profound socio-political changes. Ultra-high-speed and ultra-high-power capacity cannot be wasted, so their use should be made strictly dependent on need. This would require a civilization shift including more advanced institutional systems (Baidakov and Gromyko 2013).

What is the essence and the inner structure of this new techno-industrial and socio-cultural formation? On the one hand, we are looking at a society operating high-density energy flows, with an advanced power capacity; on the other, one that avoids wasteful energy use and minimizes environmental damage. This will require urbanization of a completely different type from the Moscow-type of agglomeration, which is an attempt to imitate a 'global city' as they have developed in financial capitalism (Sassen 1991). Instead a dispersed system of one or two-storey buildings will be created, set in the natural landscape and spread through the corridor along the high-speed landline, connected by new types of transport.

At the heart of this new techno-industrial and socio-cultural formation is not the concept of the machine (typical of the eighteenth and nineteenth centuries and the first half of the twentieth century; cf. Freeman, this volume), but the notion of *device*. The device is a special tool to regulate machine tools and mechanisms based on new physical principles and/or effects, used in a new form of human activity. Such devices, used within existing technological complexes, advance the processes of modernization and transformation in functioning productive industries by the utilization and replacement of outdated sets of components by more sophisticated ones. The organization to retool and reorganize existing industrial complexes, or *meta-industry*, will constitute the socio-economic core within the new civilizational cluster (Baidakov et al. 2011). Russia in our view needs meta-industrialization, not a secondary, catch-up industrialization to connect it into the existing world-economic and technological landscape. The Trans-Eurasian Development Corridor offers the opportunity for such a meta-industrialization.

TRANSCONTINENTAL EXTENSIONS

We now turn to possible extensions of this system beyond Russia. Potential participants are, on account of their geographic locations, the European Union, China, Japan, the Koreas and Mongolia. Figure 10.2 gives as an example how a smart grid with a 'maglev' train can be projected around the Sea of Japan, connecting Russia with China, the Koreas and Japan, and back across Sakhalin. Attached to it would be an electricity grid, as depicted in Figure 10.1. To design such vast infrastructure projects and manage them on the envisaged scale, a dedicated agency would have to be established (Baidakov et al. 2012), not least to secure the participation of the partner states and mobilize their particular contributions.

The idea of a TEBR as a transcontinental project can be traced to discussions at a conference in Beijing in May 1996, in which a group of American economists associated with the politician/futurologist, Lyndon LaRouche, also participated. Here the idea of a 'land bridge' or, as Chinese geopolitics experts labelled it, 'continental bridge', led to the formulation of the notion of a development corridor. This was then taken forward by a series of research papers by Jonathan Tennenbaum (Tennenbaum et al. 1997). In Japan, the same idea was labelled the 'Iron Silk Road', by Katsuhide Nagayama, with reference to a railway construction plan linking Japan and Korea (personal communication). At the time, the idea of a development corridor was interpreted by leading American geo-strategists as an attempt by China to project a territorial expansion beyond the borders of the country, if not seize the whole continent, and to make the Chinese economy the dominant centre of a logistical network (Brzezinski 1997: 158–85). Chinese geo-strategists and logistic groups in turn proposed to develop a southern continental bridge from China to Europe (on the basis of a railway) through Kazakhstan, Uzbekistan, Turkmenistan, Iran, Iraq and Turkey. Due to the invasion of Iraq, the entire idea was shelved. But now that US troops have pulled out, the discussions on a Southern Silk Road are resurfacing, and president Xi Jinping has identified a New Silk Road as a key geo-economic project for China.

From a Russian point of view, there is no doubt that modernization and development of its railway land bridge is vital. Its two main axes are the link between Urumqi (China) via Almaty to Astana, Petropavlovsk and Ekaterinburg; the second, a modernized Trans-Siberian railway including the use of the BAM and the construction of a tunnel or bridge to connect Sakhalin Island with the mainland. This connection may also be used to connect it further with Hokkaido, thus involving Japan in the railway transportation infrastructure of the BAM and the Trans-Siberian railway, as in Figure 10.2. But as argued above, the idea of a development corridor company saved itself from the possibility of paying billions of dollars in damages. However, Wal-Mart has not been able to avoid all of the legal repercussions of its draconian labour practices. To illustrate, in 2008 alone Wal-Mart agreed to pay $352 million to settle 63 suits across the US over charges that it did not provide its employees with meal breaks and proper rest (Seligman 2006; Banjo 2012). The increased employee resistance is probably complicating Wal-Mart's hallmark cost-cutting strategy. As Figure 9.2 shows, Wal-Mart's differential SGA expenses per employee have grown since 1999. This uptrend indicates that Wal-Mart may be increasingly disinclined to enforce retrenchment on its evermore restive workforce.

But skirmishes with Wal-Mart have not only been fought in the law courts. They have also been taking place on the streets. Bernstein Research, the Wall Street-based investor advisory firm, produced a report in 2005 warning shareholders that Wal-Mart's growth 'is under siege in several regions of the country from growing opposition by local communities'. The report concluded that the 'heightened resistance' could slow down the company's square footage growth rates, which in turn could negatively impact Wal-Mart's stock price and earnings per share (cited by Norman 2007).

Community resistance has been most pronounced in the 'site fights' headed by local activists and labour unions who have sought to lobby local and municipal governments to change zoning and land-use laws so as to thwart Wal-Mart's planned store openings. When viewed on a case-by-case basis, these grassroots mobilizations can be derided as exhibiting little more than 'not-in-my-back-yard' parochialism. However, when considered on a nationwide level these local struggles appear to bc part of a sustained and expansive movement of resistance against Wal-Mart. The site fight phenomenon climaxed in 2008, when 70 of Wal-Mart's planned store openings were blocked or postponed. Given the fact that the average Wal-Mart store makes over $50 million in annual sales (author's own calculations), each community victory represents a considerable blow to the company. Partly in response to the intensified resistance, Wal-Mart revised its domestic expansion target in 2007 from 265–70 new super-centre openings per year to 170 super-centre openings per year for the three following years (Norman 2007).

Yet despite there being fewer new targets for community activists, site fights still rage on. In 2012 and 2013, Wal-Mart engaged in a protracted battle over plans to open a new store in Los Angeles' historic Chinatown. In late June 2012, thousands of Angelinos – ranging from union organizers to Chinese owners of small family-run shops – joined together in the largest anti-Wal-Mart march to date, to express their opposition to

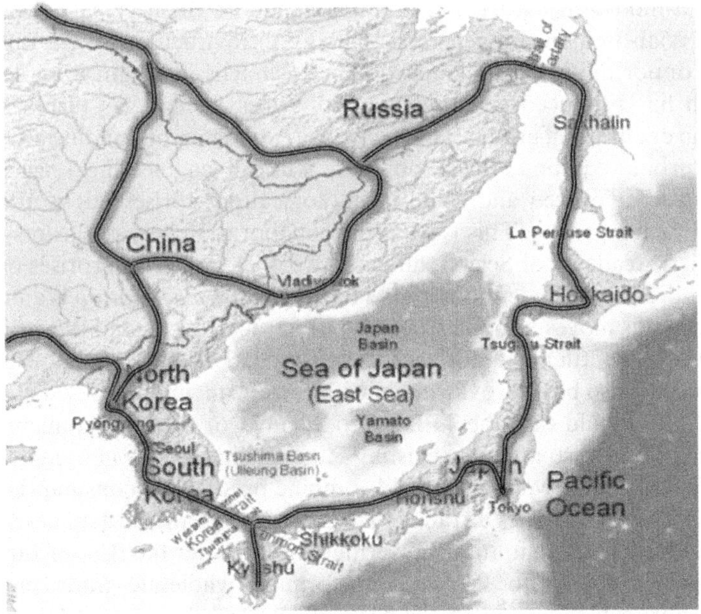

Figure 10.2 Railway ring around the Sea of Japan

implies much more than transporting Chinese products to Europe. From a Russian perspective, the EU is not just a market but a technological platform. To transform ideas generated by Russian basic science into practical applications, European technological capabilities are indispensable for the TEBR to succeed. There is an obvious mutual interest, which combines employment opportunities at the European end and technology transfer to Russia, coupled with the establishment of new, advanced manufacturing systems; a move away from an economy dominated by financial speculation; and opportunities for middle-sized and small enterprises via participation in a large project.

Again there is a difference with the current practice of, for instance, German high-tech corporations collaborating with Chinese business groups. This type of interaction is oriented towards the transfer of modern production lines and delivering turnkey factories to China. In the case of Russian–European interaction, however, the aim would be a collaboration between high-tech centres as well as small and medium-size enterprises in EU countries, with science centres in Russian universities in the perspective of creating next-generation technologies and infrastructures, with financial participation geared to long-term investment projects of a meta-industrial nature. An example would be the necessary transition from coal-fired, steam-generating energy infrastructure to gas turbines. Here opportunities for collaboration between Russian engineering science, which has produced experimental prototypes of new gas turbines, and Italian engineering groups which have the experience of building advanced gas turbine equipment, are obvious. Russian engineering science and Italian middle-sized and small technological enterprises might also link up in such a project. This is what the collaboration between teams of the Russian Academy of Science and a network of Italian enterprises operating under the aforementioned label of the *Fabbrica del Futuro* is aimed at.

Once this moves into the stage of 'infrastructure 3.0', and the establishment of new settlements and techno-cultural cities comes within reach, the aim would also be to provide them with European, high-level social standards. This would turn the TEBR into a conveyor belt for producing new social capital, also affecting existing Russian cities. Thus new cities along the Baikal–Amur Mainline would combine productive, consumption and socio-cultural activities attracting Russian, European and Japanese investors, whilst a Sakhalin tunnel or bridge would foster the flow of Japanese high-tech goods into Russia, transforming wholesale trade practices into short-run exchange on the basis of intensified transport logistics. A second axis in the extension of a TEBR might point southwards, towards the Indian Ocean, in collaboration with Indian and Iranian financial and engineering groups and involving Russia, Kazakhstan, Kyrgyzstan, Turkmenistan and India. Yuri Krupnov has proposed an India–Siberian railway as an element of TEBR in this connection (Krupnov 2013).

This takes us to the geo-economical structuring of a Eurasian Union. Founding a Eurasian Union was first proposed by the Kazakhstan president Nursultan Nazarbayev in 1994, and made a political project by then-prime minister of Russia, Vladimir Putin, in 2011. Its main difficulty so far has been that this initiative covers vast territories but that the allies, whilst certainly eager to cooperate, still have different ideas about what such cooperation might consist of. This is perhaps again best approached in the context of a TEBR, and in terms of connecting macro-regions through it. Thus Ukrainian opposition to a customs union with Russia should not obscure the obvious complementarity between the Belgorod and Kharkov regions in both countries. Likewise macro-regional development cooperation suggests itself between the south Tyumen and Kazakh Petropavlovsk regions. This has the potential of becoming an arena of cooperation between the Russian Federation and the Republic of Kazakhstan, paralleling cooperation with Belarus and Ukraine. From the TEBR perspective, these are not anti-EU projects because they depend, for the full realization of the innovation potential contained in the Trans-Eurasian Development

Corridor concept, on collaboration with European high-tech centres, corporations and institutions.

For Kazakhstan, a first step would involve obtaining technology from abroad to explore and apply the most advanced technologies in raw material processing, transportation, petro-chemistry, coal chemistry, the chemical industry as a whole, the energy sector and metal industry. To attract as many advanced technology companies as possible from the West, the Russian strategy here would be to cooperate with Western partners in developing new technological applications and solutions based on previously unknown devices, to determine the process of generating new industrial sectors (laser production, chrome-lithography, production of catalytic agents, etc.). The simultaneous realization of two strategies – modernization of resource-oriented, non-sophisticated manufacturing industries (the strategy 'from below') and technology transfer from the West, together with joint elaboration of new devices from the next techno-industrial formation (the strategy 'from above') – would then lead to a revolution in mechanical engineering, engine construction, robotechnics and machine tool building.

For the modernization of the entire machine tool production sector in the Eurasian Union, the role of Belarus and Ukraine with their machine tool capacities, construction tradition and scientific and engineering schools from the Soviet period, should also be seriously evaluated and included in overall plans. Innovative industrialization at the current level of development cannot be reduced to the localization of industrial complexes into small complexes via application of 3D and 4D printers (*The Economist* 2011), or simply to the substitution of human machine labour by robotechnics and automatic machines. The next step in innovative industrialization is to create previously non-existent smart-devices: chips, lasers, scanner-steppers, nano-diamonds, nuclear mini-reactors with helium cooling, protonic oscillators and so on. These applications then become the components of the new infrastructure. As instruments for the transformation of existing industrial systems in the energy sector, petro-chemistry, machine tools building and instrument making, they will have to bring forth the technologies for production of new goods, thus sidestepping the need to buy goods ready for use in Japan or Germany.

This is a question tied up directly with global leadership. The world leader is the one capable of creating newly elaborated and sophisticated gadgets. Thus the United States succeeded in upping the ante in the arms race with the USSR by the creation of electronic memory chips, a move that remained without response. Leadership emerges from the ability to create new devices and apply them to the most advanced, integral technological systems. The TEBR aims at nothing less. In Russia, a strategy along these lines would centrally involve overcoming the mono-sectoral management system inherited from the Soviet period. New applications (new 'units' of infrastructure) would have to be deployed simultaneously across different sectors and branches of industry. This task can be fulfilled only if new innovative groups emerge to ensure the transfer and implementation of the new technological solutions.

Finally, the new way of life which will utilize the technological breakthroughs of the TEBR for its own prosperity and for guiding the world out of the current existential crisis, must have a collective subject, a social force capable of shaping it into its most efficacious line-up. Here we must think of a regrouping of the forces that in the Cold War were welded together into a Transatlantic community, combining a North-American 'super-ethnos' with its Western European counterpart. Now that this community is unravelling, a tentative Eurasian community, likewise combining a European super-ethnos with its counterpart in the former state-socialist zone, linked by the TEBR, may be thought of as taking its place. Just as the Transatlantic community derived its attractiveness from mass consumption on the basis of Fordist mass production, the new way of life of a meta-industrial alternative will have to generate a life-world that pulls people towards it.

A first step would be to organize new cities attractive for young people on the territory of the newly formed Eurasian Union. New modern settlements must become centres for attracting young people from all over the world. Beautiful and convenient science-intensive towns, with a comfortable life environment, populated by highly qualified, well-paid professionals, would arise along the multi-track infrastructure of the TEBR. They must be a new type of settlement, engaged in servicing the new industrial megalopolises and science-intensive plants under construction. As argued above, instead of an urbanization fed by the overflow of rural populations, the artificial neo-urbanism of the Trans-Eurasian Development Corridor will provide an alternative form of territorial reclamation. Young people for whom the future is becoming bleaker and bleaker by persistent unemployment (such as Italians, Greeks or Spanish, cf. Holman, this volume), may want to reclaim the land of Siberia, Yakutia and northern Kazakhstan, and Russians and Kazakhs will follow.

CONCLUSION

The weakness of high-tech development in Russia today and the weak representation of its corporations on the global market of high value-added products forces us to think of the deeper causes of the crisis and to propose solutions. Having a detailed understanding of current world problems and sharing this understanding with an open-minded international community, allows Russia to claim a leadership role in proposing a collaborative project like the Trans-Eurasian Development Corridor and the society projected to arise around it. Only by embracing this ambitious undertaking can Russian society hope to find a way forward.

It is evident that such an approach contradicts the pillars of economic monetarism. From such a starting point, it cannot be expected that non-standard proposals for reorganizing society would be possible. As long as people think that Russians must follow decisions made by the financial centres in the developed economies, and that their manoeuvring space is confined to delicately moving between the US position and the claims of the ascendant geo-economic giant, China, no original and responsible agenda of its own can be expected to take shape. Russia would forever remain a geo-economic periphery that doesn't have much influence in the international arena.

This also explains why a transformation of the world financial system is a prerequisite for a new Russian role in the world. The TEBR approach breaks with traditional notions of linearity and with concepts of growth as the exclusive variable of economic success. It boldly projects the creation of a new pole of social wealth-generation, taking its place in a succession of world economies that did the same from other centres. This new pole of production of social wealth will be based on new technologies and industries and is connected with a new organization of space, in the form of new technological cities and settlements that will be the basis of a new socio-cultural formation.

PART II

LABOUR AND THE POLITICS OF WORK

Introduction to Part II: labour and the politics of work

In this part of the collection, the chapters deal with the labour process, labour markets and working class formation, and the evolving politics of the labour movement.

In the opening chapter, Radhika Desai contrasts the analysis of Fordism by French Regulation theory with its most systematic critique, Robert Brenner's understanding of the 'Long Boom'. Regulation theory, in particular Aglietta's foundational text, is found to be largely vindicated because it identifies the two aspects of labour – productivity and workers' consumption – that underpinned the class compromise of the post-war 'golden age'. Yet both approaches, Desai argues, overlook the central role of decolonization in launching the golden age. Only thus can we grasp the geopolitical multipolarity on which our understanding of world order today must be based.

The next four chapters illustrate the political–economic fate of labour from high hopes in the 1960s and early 1970s to defeat henceforth. In Chapter 12, Adam Fishwick analyses how the Chilean working class in the twentieth century has struggled to become a true political subject, a 'class-for-itself'. This trajectory, which he documents in detail for the country's textile industry, culminated under Salvador Allende's *Unidad Popular* government. Starting from a critique of the New Economic History approach, Fishwick demonstrates how in the *cordones industriales* the contours of a democratic, worker-controlled economy became visible until the Pinochet coup brutally ended it in 1973.

The Italian Communist Party (PCI) drew the conclusion from the Chilean debacle that an ascendant Left should not become locked in a frontal confrontation with its own bourgeoisie. In Chapter 13 Davide Bradanini highlights how this fitted into a longer PCI practice of unilateral sacrifices in exchange for political legitimacy, on the assumption that only in socialism would real working class gains come within reach. Employing Gramsci's concept of *trasformismo* to explain how the Italian ruling class has throughout sought to prevent the formation of a counter-hegemonic bloc, Bradanini argues that the PCI allowed a fatal demobilization of its working class base just when the strategy of tension and neoliberal austerity policies were beginning to be deployed against it. Thus one of the bastions of European labour slipped into a protracted meltdown.

In northern Europe the social democratic, Fordist class compromise struck deep roots. Yet as Otto Holman argues in Chapter 14, the flexibilization of labour in the European Union would not have been achieved without the German assault on wages in the reunification process with the defunct German Democratic Republic. This created the neoliberal benchmark that, after the establishment of the eurozone, became the norm for pushing through labour market reforms. Interpreting this as a Kaleckian 'political business cycle' in which class interests trump full employment goals, Holman demonstrates how in several steps, 'structural reforms' targeted remaining social protection and union strength across the EU and, after the credit crunch, peripheral eurozone economies in particular.

The claim that Japanese employment relations had meanwhile prepared a post-Fordist alternative is contradicted by Ryoji Ihara in Chapter 15, 'Globalization and Japanese-style management: image and changing reality'. Challenging the cultural stereotypes often adduced to explain the success of Japanese capitalism on the basis of a review of the management literature and his own shop-floor experience, Ihara argues that even in its heyday the protected lifetime employment and reciprocal worker commitment were always buttressed by reliance on peripheral, unprotected workforces. Even for core workers, extreme work pressures have throughout characterized Japanese production at home and abroad.

The downscaling of workers' rights and labour conditions in the course of the global restructuring of production once again raises the question of where we must look for the origins of workers' consciousness. In Chapter 16, 'Work, power and the urban poor', Jeffrey Harrod reminds us that categories like 'the poor' or 'the underclass' provide insufficient guidance here. Situating himself in the tradition that he co-founded with Robert Cox, the social relations of production or 'power in production' approach, Harrod explains that the relations of strength in work and production are a key determinant of political power. Amongst others they differentiate the outlooks of various categories of unprotected workers depending on the particularities of their employment, a circumstance of great importance given that much current political turbulence can be traced to the growing number of people in unprotected work.

Approaching the same issue from a different angle, Siobhán McGrath and Kendra Strauss in Chapter 17 argue against isolating the phenomenon of 'modern slavery' from other forms of unfreedom in labour relations. Comparing the experiences of workers in Brazil engaged in sugar and garment production, they highlight how mobility restrictions, workplace disempowerment and racialization combine to keep workers in bondage without necessarily representing slavery. Whilst there is no denying that more than 20 million people today are in outright forced labour, the quest for emancipation cannot be confined to them. Not vulnerability, but workers' rights should provide a starting point of the improvement of employment conditions for all.

The concluding chapters of Part II and the appendix highlight that real opportunities for restoring the power of labour can be identified. Thus Youngseok Jang and Kevin Gray in Chapter 18 question whether in China, the global 'race to the bottom' in the exploitation of labour has not actually reached its limit. Using the Gramscian concept of a passive revolution, they argue, on the basis of a detailed analysis of the strike at the Honda factory in Nanhai, that the Chinese state must adjust its policies to mounting worker militancy. This may usher in a medium-term shift towards a more domestically focused political economy. Whilst the more mobile elements of transnational capital may seek to relocate production to the interior of the Chinese mainland or to low-wage production sites elsewhere in Asia, such fixes to workers' resistance are likely to be only temporary in scope. This would draw a line under the series of defeats that run through the episodes discussed in previous chapters.

In Chapter 19 two prominent Indian trade union activists, Anannya Bhattacharjee and Ashim Roy, take this further. Drawing on global value chain and related approaches, Bhattacharjee and Roy document the struggles waged by the Asia Floor Wage Alliance for a general minimum wage as a counterstrategy against untrammelled labour arbitrage. Whilst this campaign aims to secure an existence minimum for those at the bottom level of the labour market in the most ferociously exploited continent today, Alan Freeman in 'Twilight of the machinocrats' (Chapter 20) raises a different and for the long term, even more fundamental issue, that of the content of labour itself.

Freeman argues that technological progress has reached a point where purely mechanical revolutions in productivity can no longer provide the impulse for the kind of radical transformation of technology and society that has previously been associated with periods of accelerated capitalist growth. Creative work in the context of a general trend to the predominance of service provision opens up the possibility of a revolution of labour. It also refocuses thinking about the economy to the qualitative expansion of the human content of the product.

This part of the collection concludes with an overview by Örsan Şenalp and Mehmet Gürsan Şenalp of current networks of labour research, in which they specifically focus on those networks which adopt an activist attitude towards the topic.

11. Look back in hope? Reassessing Fordism today[1]

Radhika Desai

The recent financial and economic crises have landed the world in unknown territory. Old maps no longer work. The crises have discredited not only neoclassical economics and neoliberal policy prescriptions (Independent Evaluation Office 2011), but also (as I argue, Desai 2013a) recently dominant conceptions of the capitalist world order, like 'globalization' and 'empire', which assumed a single world economy. For the crises were neither 'global' nor 'imperial', neither imposing the same misery on all economies nor imposing more on the peripheral economies than the core ones. Instead, they widened the divergence between the stagnating advanced industrial world and the still fast-growing emerging economies even more.

If the world is 'not in Kansas anymore', if it needs to find new political and policy bearings, one promising line of inquiry is to investigate the 'golden age' (Marglin and Schor 1990), the two postwar decades that created greater and more broadly based welfare in the advanced capitalist world than ever before or since. We attempt this here by revisiting the most systematic attempt to understand the golden age, the Regulationists' broadly Marxist theorization of 'Fordism' within their 'theory of capitalist regulation'. It has today achieved a currency so wide as to blur its chief arguments and conceptual distinctions, and we no longer speak of a Regulation theory but only an 'approach'. We therefore return to the original theorization proposed by Michel Aglietta in *A Theory of Capitalist Regulation* (1979[1976]) and confront it with the most systematic Marxist critique of it by the most prominent contemporary Marxist historian, Robert Brenner (Brenner and Glick 1991). This engagement has important implications for progressive national and international economic policies in the post-neoliberal, multipolar world as I understand it within the geopolitical economy of multipolarity I have recently proposed (Desai 2013a), in particular the hitherto unrecognized relationship between decolonization and Fordism which this engagement reveals.

[1] Thanks to Robert Chernomas and Alan Freeman for their helpful comments on previous drafts of this chapter. They are not, however, implicated in its remaining inadequacies.

MARX VERSUS SCHUMPETER

While neoliberal policies in the West led to crisis and many hailed the 'return of the state', the growth of the emerging economies underlined its importance further. Though they were not entirely untouched by neoliberalism, their growth was largely the work of interventionist states directing economies to contest the international division of labour which had hitherto consigned them to being producers of low-value goods, whether agricultural or industrial. The result in China, the most spectacular instance of such development, is the greatest industrial revolution humankind has yet witnessed.

The contrast between neoliberal austerity in the West and the state-directed growth in emerging economies is, however, far from being noted in public discourse. True, the 'return of the state' was briefly hailed. Yet, neoliberalism hangs on in a 'strange non-death' (Crouch 2011) because financialized capitalist classes have not been dislodged from power.

The resulting impoverishment of public debate is glaring. Some confine themselves to occasional euphorias about this or that titbit of good economic news amid interminable stagnation. Others, whether positioned to the right or left of the narrow political spectrum, suggest that the only new asset bubbles will generate even the most anaemic growth (Summers 2013; Krugman 2012 respectively). And central bankers keep assuring us that renewed growth is just around the corner of the next monetary policy innovation, principally, it would appear, to keep us awaiting it vainly rather than getting on with demanding the fiscal activism that is in fact necessary to end it (Desai 2013b).

However, contemporary Marxists too have tended to overlook both 'the materiality of nations' (Desai 2013a) and their role on the 'grandest terrain' on which the contradictions of capitalism play out, that of the 'world market' (Marx 1973: 886–7). The reaction against 'economic determinism' among Marxists who had come unmoored from working class politics and increasingly concerned with philosophy and sociology rather than political economy (Anderson 1976), and 'Marxism without Marx' (Freeman 2010), which, since the early twentieth century has attempted to fit Marx's political economy into the mould of the antithetical neoclassical economics (Desai 2010 and Desai 2013a), has resulted in a conception of capitalism just as free-market and free-trade, free of contradictions and thus from state intervention, imperialism or state-directed 'contender' development to resolve them, as any neoliberal ideologues could dream up. This supports the assumption that the Anglo-American form of capitalism is somehow purer, featuring less state intervention, though this is contradicted by history (see Chang 2002: 19–22; Desai 2013a: 31–3).

Such a capitalism is not Marxist but Schumpeterian: a Promethean system which ceaselessly develops the productive forces, contains no inherent contradictions and has practically miraculous self-correcting capacities when it nevertheless runs into crisis for entirely contingent reasons (of this conception and its relation to Marx's, see Freeman 2014) rather than one in which the development of the productive forces is not guaranteed, which is inherently prone to crisis and can break down. Such a view of capitalism had already prevented Marxists from explaining the Great Depression (Howard and King 1992: 19) and today Marxists have ended up diagnosing the greatest crisis since the Great Depression as merely crises of 'financialization' (Lapavitsas 2009, for a critique see Desai and Freeman 2011) or 'neoliberalism' (Duménil and Lévy 2011).

Politically, such a conception of capitalism cannot see the state's role in handling capitalism's contradictions and making concessions to working people as the lever for reforms to strengthen them for stronger, potentially even revolutionary, action. It cannot appreciate how such demands have already modified the workings of capitalism to make it serve the needs of working people better – whether through the welfare state or the sensitivity of most governments of capitalist countries to employment levels. Instead, contemporary Marxists subscribe to one of two equally unrealistic beliefs. One is a purely voluntarist and apocalyptic revolutionism in which working people take power through the sheer force of a collective will *formed independently of any objective foundation for it*. Guy Bois identified this problem with Robert Brenner's historiography early on while giving it the label it wears today, 'political Marxism'. While agreeing that some reaction against economic determinism and its devaluation of the role of class struggle was warranted, he objected to the 'summary and purely ideological manner in which it is implemented' as a 'voluntarist vision of history in which the class struggle is divorced from all other objective contingencies' (Bois 1985: 115). The second position is that networked activists taking control of decentralized production units without challenging the overall market organization of the economy or capitalist control over the state will usher in the millennium (for a critique see Desai 2011 and 2013c).

The Regulation School's analysis of Fordism emerged when Marxism and working class politics retained some vestigial connections, the trend towards Marxism without Marx was yet to mature and the reaction against 'economic determinism' lay in the future. In the 1950s and 1960s mainstream scholarship was dominated by discourses in which the mixed economies, welfare states and full-employment economic policies amounted to a transcendence of capitalism, if not the advent of socialism itself (Bell 1960; Crosland 1956), while in critical circles, Paul Baran and

Paul Sweezy's *Monopoly Capitalism* had dropped key Marxist categories altogether. It was only when the reality of the underlying capitalism asserted itself in the form of capitalist crisis in the late 1960s and early 1970s, an emerging neoliberalism aimed only to denounce the 'statism' of the golden age to advance its marketist agenda, that Marxist scholarship was renewed by two major works. Ernest Mandel's *Late Capitalism* (1975[1972]) was distinctive for its theorization of the postwar dynamics of imperialism while Aglietta (1979[1976]) founded the Regulation approach by concentrating on capitalism's domestic dynamics.

Immediately these works were published, however, trends towards Schumpeterian Marxism – the installation of a significant number of Marxists, some who were neoclassical economists first and Marxist second and others who did not study political economy at all and would soon mount the attack on 'economic determinism' – were set in train. If nevertheless Brenner's critique is valuable enough to discuss here, it is because his scrupulous historiography, in his account of late twentieth-century capitalism as much as that of the origins of capitalism, so often escapes the limitations of his theoretical commitments.

THE SUCCESS OF 'FORDISM'

Among concepts of Marxist provenance, Fordism is probably unique in enjoying wide currency, indeed ubiquity, beyond Marxist circles. Formed through a critique of neoclassical economics (Aglietta 1979: 9–13), rounded and inter-disciplinary, it captured so wide a range of the distinguishing elements of postwar capitalism that it spoke to the lived experience of the times. Fordism involved the mass production of standard goods for mass consumption through the assembly-line organization of de-skilled labour in large, vertically integrated corporations. It needed large markets and they were provided by the success of working class struggles in instituting full employment, counter-cyclical demand management and welfare states to sustain the consumption of non- or un-employed members of society.

The culture of Fordism was the mass culture of expanded working class consumption. Now including items – consumer durables such as refrigerators and washing machines, holidays and above all, automobiles and comfortable, clean and bright owned or rented homes – once beyond the reach of the working class, it featured a vastly expanded role for advertising to promote their use. The high culture of Fordism coincided with the peak of aesthetic modernism and was followed by the 'post-modernism' of the neoliberal age. David Harvey (1990) and Stuart Hall and Martin Jacques (1989) theorized this transition using the Regulationist conception of Fordism (while Mandel's *Late Capitalism* formed the basis of Fredric Jameson's rival theory; cf. Jameson 1991). The end of domestic work was less commented upon but very meaningful for the dignity of working people. Large, centralized unions became a fixture on the political landscape, and corporatist arrangements kept wages and the social wage rising and unemployment low. 'Fordism' became an icon, as likely to appear in journalistic as in scholarly writings, whether in political economy, geography, sociology, political science or cultural studies.

Of course, greater currency incurred costs. The theory originally proposed by a handful of French originators such as Michel Aglietta, Robert Boyer and Alain Lipietz became a school, and a multitude of these schools were established both within France and beyond. Today, the Regulationists constitute an approach. And this appeared to peter out. Though much was said about flexible specialization replacing assembly-line production and niche markets replacing mass markets, Fordism had no successor as a regime of accumulation. At best, it was 'still in the process of formation'. Many decades after the crisis of Fordism, it did not and probably never would, 'constitute a "stable mode of development"' (Brand 2006: 237). Educated at the prestigious École Polytechnique, economic bureaucrats and technocrats in the *dirigiste* tradition though they may have been (Husson 2001), the original Regulationists' theorization was unmistakably Marxist. Against neoclassical economics as well as Althusserian Marxism, they emphasized two things. First, capitalism's 'distortions' (Aglietta 1979) or contradictions: in capitalism 'crisis is the normal, natural state and non-crisis is a rather chance event' (Lipietz n.d.). Regulatory structures were needed to stabilize it (Lipietz 1992). Paucity of consumption demand and a consequent tendency to overaccumulate capital, particularly in Department I, the producers' goods department, were the key contradictions. Second, political agency was critical and the class struggle produced the 'norms and laws which form the object of a theory of social regulation' and was 'itself beyond any law' (Aglietta 1979:67).

REGIMES OF ACCUMULATION

To Marx's history of humankind as a succession of modes of production corresponded the Regulationists' account of capitalism as a succession of 'regimes of accumulation'. This was an 'intermediate' concept, less abstract than capitalism's laws of accumulation. Aglietta originally identified two regimes, the extensive followed by the intensive, defined by four key elements.

From Absolute to Relative Surplus Value

Surplus value, absolute and relative, is value produced in excess of the value of labour power. It was increased in its absolute form by making workers work longer and harder and in its relative form by developing the productive forces and increasing productivity. Since the latter became necessary when the limits – temporal, technical or social – of the former were reached, the two were 'indissociable from one another' (Aglietta 1979: 51). Though capitalism was compelled to 'continuously revolutionize the conditions of production', the necessity of relating production and consumption asserted itself periodically, whether in regimes of accumulation or crises when they failed. In this way, 'technical progress . . . is subordinated to the extension of capitalist relations of production' (ibid.: 51–2). While they always co-existed, absolute surplus value predominated in the extensive and relative surplus value in the intensive regime of accumulation.

From Craft Production to Taylorism and Fordism

Before Taylorism workers still possessed their craft skills and exerted considerable control over the labour process. Taylorist time-and-motion studies enabled scientific managers to appropriate workers' knowledge and skills to transform work into repetitive and mechanizable tasks. Designed to 'accelerate the completion of the mechanical cycle of movements on the job and to fill the gaps in the working day', Taylorism was 'a capitalist response to the class struggle in production' (Aglietta 1979: 114–15). It was superseded by Fordism, in which 'semi-automatic assembly-line production' (ibid.: 117) increased mechanization, work intensity, labour discipline and the separation of manual and intellectual labour and 'turned scientific progress against [workers] as a power serving the uniform expansion of value'. It was based on two 'complementary principles', the assembly line, which integrated the labour process 'by a system of conveyors and handling devices ensuring the movement of the materials to be transformed and their arrival at the appropriate machine tools', and by 'the fixing of workers to jobs whose positions were rigorously determined by the configuration of the machine system', robbing them of all autonomy and possibility of resistance (ibid.: 118–19).

With the Fordist labour process increasing production and productivity to new heights, new norms of working class consumption became necessary and, most fundamentally, Fordism was 'the principle of an articulation between process of production and mode of consumption' (ibid.: 117). However, richer consumption came at the cost of impoverished politics. The labour movement's hitherto broad concerns with working conditions, self-organization, self-help and self-education, and its rival scale of values and mode of life were replaced by a focus on 'monetary gains from capitalist production' while collective bargaining became centralized (ibid.: 195).

From Traditional to Fordist Consumption

Though initially capitalism took 'traditional' modes of consumption as given, it eventually replaced them with one specific to itself (Aglietta 1979: 152). Traditional modes, characterized by 'extreme poverty and total insecurity' of the working class prevailed in the extensive regime. Consumption was 'either totally destructured or else organized in the context of the extended family, with a strict division of domestic labour and a great expenditure of domestic labour time' (ibid.: 158). Fordism, by contrast, was the first fully capitalist mode of consumption with 'increasing . . . individual use of commodities and a notable impoverishment of non-commodity interpersonal relations'. It entailed a new 'social consumption norm', much as Gramsci has foreseen (Gramsci 1971), 'in which the capitalist class seeks overall management of the production of wage-labour by the close articulation of relations of production with the commodity relations in which the wage-earners purchase their means for consumption' (Aglietta 1979: 117).

Consumption in Fordism centred on standardized production and mass consumption of, in particular, housing and the automobile. It also relied on 'a vast socialization of finance, and a correlatively very strict control over workers' resources and expenditures' and 'the small family unit and household'. Maintaining the continuity of consumption and repayment also required limiting working class material insecurity and this was accomplished through 'legislative arrangements, a homogenization and socialization of wages and the establishment of social insurance funds against the temporary loss of direct wages' (ibid.: 159). Full employment macroeconomic policies were critical to this set of institutions (in reality, not so much full employment, which, as Kalecki (1943) had foreseen, was politically unpalatable to capital, but relatively high employment levels compared with the past; cf. Holman, this volume).

The new social consumption norm meant that the working class was now entitled to greater costs of its generational reproduction including the education of its children, pensions, and insurance against illness, temporary unemployment and so on. It was 'the *keystone of that socialization of consumption that prevents a cumulative shortfall in effective demand* when the conditions of surplus-value production deteriorate' (Aglietta 1979: 181–2, emphasis in original).

From Competitive to Monopoly Regulation

Modes of regulation are essentially forms of competition through which individual capitals 'adjust themselves to the general rate of profit'. Indeed, competition is 'a process of unification of the capitalist class' (Aglietta 1979: 289). Competitive regulation is conceived in classically Marxist terms. First movers investing in a new cost-reducing technology garner surplus profits by selling below prevailing prices but above their own costs. Thus they corner a larger share of the market and profits until the process of competition forces others to invest in the new techniques, bringing prices down to the new value and thus re-equalizing the rates of profit (ibid.: 289–97), at least among firms who have survived this ferocious process. It puts strict upper limits on profits, with a considerable number of firms operating at below the average profit rate, and generates insecurity among firms threatened with elimination unless they 'interrupt their current process of valorization and go into massive debts to acquire the new and very expensive means of production required for the new methods . . . by a more or less brutal devalorization of a portion of their capital presently immobilized in productive functions' (ibid.: 294).

Monopoly regulation did not imply monopoly so much as the replacement of price competition for stagnant markets with a 'set of procedures of social regulation' to increase demand so that innovating capitalists could 'improve their market shares by capturing the *increase* in demand at a given price' (ibid.: 304). In these conditions, planned technical progress met fewer obstacles because 'output increased by new and more efficient methods can be sold at a market price equal to the former social value'.

Together forms of surplus value, types of work processes and modes of consumption and of competition comprise a regime of accumulation defined, most generally, as 'a form of social transformation that increases relative surplus value under the stable constraints of the most general norms that define absolute surplus value' (ibid.: 68). These general norms are instituted by national states when they define the wage relation by specifying things like working age, length of working day and so on. Beyond the limits set by such laws, increases in surplus value must become relative. Accumulation under these conditions typically leads to overaccumulation in Department I, the sector producing producers' goods, because consumer demand remains well short of production in Department II, the consumer goods producing sector, and, though capital can flow into Department I for a while, eventually, thanks to low demand for investment goods from Department I, that investment will prove excessive. This tendency can only be overcome if '*capitalist production revolutionises the conditions of existence of the wage-earning class*'. That is why, for the Regulationists, there is 'a social rather than a technical content' to the development of the forces of production (ibid.: 60, emphasis in original).

The two regimes of accumulation, though conceptually distinct, typically co-existed, with one predominating. So the

> *predominantly extensive regime of accumulation* is that in which relative surplus value is obtained by transforming the organization of labour; the traditional way of life may persist or be destroyed, but it is not radically recomposed by the logic of utilitarian functionalism. Only agriculture is affected, by the formation of the agricultural-foodstuffs complex . . . The combined development of the two departments of production is achieved only with difficulty, the pace of accumulation encountering recurrent obstacles (ibid.: 71, emphasis in original).

On the other hand, the

> *predominantly intensive regime of accumulation* creates a new mode of life for the wage-earning class by establishing a logic that operates on the totality of time and space occupied or traversed by its individuals in daily life. A social consumption norm is formed, which no longer depends in any way on communal life, but entirely on an abstract code of utilitarianism. . . . The intensive regime of accumulation accomplished an integration of the two departments of production that makes possible a far more regular pace of accumulation and a far more rapid increase in the rate of surplus-value (ibid.: 72, emphasis in original).

Variants of these regimes could be seen in all capitalist countries but, for the Regulationists, the US case was paradigmatic because there capitalism had developed without the encumbrance of 'archaic social structures' (ibid.: 23). As 'the final act in the struggle against colonial domination' (ibid.: 77), the Civil War inaugurated the extensive regime and it lasted until the end of the First World War. The 'intensive' or Fordist regime (1945–66) did not emerge until after the Second World War and had run into crisis by the late 1960s. The inter-war period, considered by some a separate regime of accumulation with intensive production but without mass consumption (ibid.: 93–5), was the crux of the Regulationist explanation of the Great Depression.

Working class struggles of a uniquely American sort effected the transition from extensive to the Fordist regime. An immigrant working class attached to norms of 'individualism, stable family life and monetary gain as the mark of social success and the spur to labour discipline' also faced 'extremely harsh . . . economic exploitation'. The combination generated bitter class struggles against the degradation of living conditions by the 1890s. 'Conducted on a strictly economic basis' and gaining support from 'new bourgeois strata', these struggles helped transform the mode of consumption (ibid.: 83) through four waves of urban infrastructure development, including public housing: in the early twentieth century, one each after the world wars and in the early 1960s. The resulting expansion of working class consumption led capitalist dynamics to 'dramatically quicken': 'Advances of productivity in Department I find their outlets in the expansion of Department II. The fall in unit exchange-values in this department sufficiently increases the production of relative surplus value to enable real wages to rise' (ibid.: 86).

The virtuous circles of Fordism came up against three distinct limits by the late 1960s: in production, public consumption and private consumption. There were

> the limits to the saving of living labour and the extension of surplus labour in the frame work of current labour processes, the increasing difficulties in further revolutionizing the conditions of existence of the wage-earning class in the direction of an ever more total dependence on commodity production, and the significant rise in social overheads that is linked with the generalization of commodity relationships (ibid.: 87).

This takes us to Brenner and Glick's critique.

MAY THE BEST MARXIST WIN?

The nub of Robert Brenner and Mark Glick's critique, which focused primarily on Aglietta's 'founding statement', was to question whether capitalism could be periodized at all. It had to be 'comprehensible in terms of a single set of laws that remain unchanged from its inception until its eventual suppression' (Brenner and Glick 1991: 46). These laws turned out, however, to define a Schumpeterian capitalism featuring 'development on the basis of relative surplus-value' ceaselessly developing the forces of production; 'long-term capital accumulation bringing about rises in wages and aggregate consumption; and investment and cost-cutting technical change leading to, but not necessarily conditioned by, growth of the mass market' (ibid.: 54), ruling out contradiction and crisis. While Brenner and Glick raised questions about modes of surplus value and regulation, their arguments about production concentrated on the labour process while on the realization side, of course, they disputed the idea of a transition in the mode of consumption.

Production

Brenner had long insisted on the inherently promethean nature of capitalism (1977) and he and Glick now questioned, first of all, whether absolute surplus value ever dominated in the US. It may have done so in France, for instance (1991: 110), but only because pre-capitalist relations of production persisted. By contrast in the US, according to Brenner and Glick, a 'fully established' capitalism emerged, like Athena from the head of Zeus, and in such a capitalism absolute surplus could never have dominated. Incredulity is not an argument, however, and Brenner and Glick failed to show that US capitalism before 1914 was not reliant on 'intensifying labour, a spectacular increase in the labour force and a dramatic expansion of the system in geographical space' (ibid.: 50): technical conditions of early industry in the US were not notably different from those in Europe, immigration expanded the labour force continuously and the US's internal colonialism even accelerated after the Civil War.

The Regulationists are mistaken, Brenner and Glick also claim, in regarding competition as a fetter upon increased productivity and investment: for Marx, it was the spur to investment (ibid.: 55). They forget, however, that Marx also argued that eventually the same competitive mechanisms could lead to declining profits and eventually a decline in investment, as Brenner himself would later argue (Brenner 2009: 73).

Brenner and Glick also question whether craft control over production acted as a constraint on investment in the extensive regime and was entirely removed in the Fordist. Against this view, which relies on Braverman's (1974) thesis about the 'degradation of work in the twentieth century', Brenner and Glick argue that both deskilling as well as reskilling occur throughout the history of capitalism. Mechanization may displace older skills, but requires new ones (Brenner and Glick 1991: 60, relying particularly on Elger 1979 and Stedman-Jones 1975). However, they cannot deny that craft work dominated in the extensive regime of accumulation or that craft workers are 'more difficult to exploit' (Brenner and Glick 1991: 60), only insisting that capitalists cannot always choose who to employ.

Brenner and Glick argue further that the Regulationists do not credit how much technical change depends on scientific advances 'beyond the production process itself', for example in computers or biotechnology (ibid.: 101–2), rather than on the appropriation of workers' knowledge. So the crisis of Fordism cannot be attributed to problems in the Fordist labour process. Such an explanation cannot, moreover, 'account for the *simultaneous and general* character' of the fall in profitability 'on an international scale, the *suddenness* of its onset, and the extreme *sharpness* and *depth* of the fall, marking a clear discontinuity with previous trends' (ibid.: 102, emphasis in original). While these aspects of falling profitability would form Brenner's explanandum in his account of the Long Boom (Brenner 1998), he and Glick also question the Regulationist finding of declining productivity setting in in the later 1960s.

However, Brenner and Glick misunderstand the Regulationists here. Far from assuming that all productivity increases arise from appropriation of workers' knowledge, they argue that the introduction of science into the production process 'radicalized the separation between manual and mental labour, rigorously subjected workers to the law of accumulation and turned scientific progress against them as a power serving the uniform expansion of value' (Aglietta 1979: 117–18). The crisis in productivity was rooted in the worker's involvement in the labour process: it had 'to remain "informal", "hidden" and even "paradoxical" – the engineer or the supervisor will deny that the operative has to think, and will simply give the order to follow the correct drill . . . but they are counting on the operative's initiative to make sure all goes well' (Lipietz 1992: 4). Increases in delays due to non-synchronization of the assembly line, the negative effects of repetitive work on workers and the tendency of assembly-line work to unify workers (Aglietta 1979[1976]: 120–21) initially slowed down productivity increases and caused the famous 'blue collar blues' in the late 1960s. This was when, despite the persistence of high employment levels, the advanced capitalist world witnessed a 'wave of revolts or "micro-conflicts" in firms and offices by workers stripped of their initiative and dignity by Taylorism . . . an increasingly open revolt against the denial of personality by the starkest forms of separation between those who designed and those who performed tasks' (Lipietz 1992: 15). However, if '[p]roductivity gains had virtually disappeared; investment was more costly with each year; [and] profit margins remained depressed' even after higher unemployment quelled such revolts,

> The reason went deeper than the fact that Taylorist principles had led to revolt: the principles themselves, by separating 'the scientific organization of work' from its unskilled performance, had in the end dried up the source of productivity gains. Since most workers were formally excluded from the fight for productivity and product quality, and since even the idea that they were subjectively involved was rejected, an increasingly small number of engineers and technical staff found themselves with the task of improving collective skills; *but they could only raise workers' productivity by means of increasingly complex and costly machines which they designed for them.* (Lipietz 1992: 15–16, emphasis added)

While undoubtedly Lipietz's later tendency to think that the solution lay in the enhancement of workers' involvement through Japanese-style production methods (Brenner and Glick 1991: 116–19; cf. Ihara, this volume) could be questioned, this sort of understanding continues to inspire a rich body of literature (see Spencer 2009 for a recent survey).

Though Brenner and Glick think otherwise, productivity trends in the US economy vindicate the Regulationists' general point about the crisis of productivity and associated crisis of profitability in Fordism. More than four decades into the crisis of Fordism, productivity continues to increase markedly more slowly, computers or biotechnology notwithstanding. The reason, according to Robert Gordon, the most widely recognized expert on productivity trends in the US, is that for about a century to 1970 a group of 'great inventions' associated with the second industrial evolution – electricity, the internal combustion engine, plumbing and central heating, advances in (petro) chemistry and electronics – transformed life but, and here is the catch, '*many of the improvements could only happen once*'. Additional improvements could only be marginal. Productivity measured as output per hour slowed after 1970 because 'all that remained . . . were second-round improvements, such as developing short-haul regional jets, extending the original interstate highway network with suburban ring roads, and converting residential America from window-unit air conditioners to central air conditioning' (Gordon 2012: 6–7).

Computers, the central technology of the 'third industrial revolution' fit this overall pattern: they increased productivity through labour saving in both industry and services greatly until 1970. Since then, though personal computers, email and the Internet were responsible for small productivity increases, innovation shifted to entertainment and communication devices, enhancing consumption rather than making production more efficient.

To be sure, computer technology still transforms lives and even the economy: investment in it is compulsory for firms seeking control over markets against competitors in a zero-sum game and over inventories, employees and customers (Gordon 2000: 69). Moreover, in economies increasingly dominated by services, Jeff Madrick's speculation that computer technology could well be leading to 'a high-technology version of a crafts economy, based on worker skills, thinking, and inventiveness, rather than on the muscle of large-scale factories and distribution networks' is very plausible. Such an economy 'may simply not be able to remove human beings from the production process as rapidly as the old standardized economy of the mass production age' (Madrick 1998; see also Graz, Freeman, this volume).

Declining productivity despite large state investments in research and development (Block 2008) due to the exhaustion of the potential of one-off improvements in production; the exhaustion of the potential to increase productivity amid the separation of mental and manual labour except among extremely 'traumatized workers'; the increasing domination of services in which productivity increases through labour saving are replaced by product enhancement and differentiation through the input of more, and more intensified (because highly skilled and 'cultural') labour providing qualitatively different sorts of satisfactions than the mass-produced commodities of the machine age; and the decline in hours worked all point to the possibility that the most advanced economies may be transiting towards structures which are less and less amenable to the sorts of increases in welfare that capitalist competitive cost-cutting had introduced over the previous two centuries. While such a transition was only partially anticipated by the Regulationists, it is certainly antithetical to any Schumpeterian conception of capitalism.

Realization

As Brenner and Glick recognize, changes in consumption provide the key to the Regulationists' 'entire historical conception of capitalist evolution' (Brenner and Glick 1991: 52). Adequate consumer demand is important not only for the realization of surplus value of Department II goods but also for the smooth and robust development of Department I: without it, capitalists would not invest in production goods.

On restricted consumer demand in the extensive regime of accumulation, Brenner and Glick essentially restate Say's Law that supply creates its own demand. They claim that there are 'powerful mechanisms for pushing up working class consumption that are built into the normal processes of competition and capitalist accumulation over the medium term . . . [which] . . . create inexorable upward pressures on both aggregate consumption and the real wage' (1991: 64–5). So '[a]ggregate consumption increases simply because the investment of surpluses entails the employment of additional waged workers'. Mass consumption does not require class struggles. Instead, 'changed conditions of supply lead . . . to a reduction in price: *the rise of mass production does not require, but rather issues in, mass consumption*' (Brenner and Glick 1991: 66, emphasis added. Desai 2010 discusses this and other modern forms Say's Law takes).

Neither Marxist party notices, however, the international dimension of restricted working class consumption. Aglietta did not discuss imperialism, he said, because extant theories thereof were inadequate (Aglietta 1979: 32–3). However, the theories he dismissed were theories of postwar imperialism, not the extensive Marxist literature on imperialism in the period up to the First World War which centred on the importance of colonies as markets and investment outlets. For his part, as patron saint of 'political Marxism', Brenner must deny contradictions such as the systematic danger of gluts of commodities and capital and subscribe to the associated belief that though imperialism 'can and does happen and it does aid capitalist accumulation when it does happen, . . . *it is not required by the logic of capitalism*' (Zarembka 2002: 8, emphasis added).

Considerable debate had focused on whether and to what extent working classes of imperial countries *benefited* from imperialism, and undoubtedly such benefits were never inconsiderable. However, the social liberal, John A. Hobson, a precursor of Keynes on whom Lenin also relied for his more famous pamphlet on imperialism, in 1902 identified quite a different relationship between imperial markets and the much-needed expansion of working class consumption which anticipated the transition to Fordism.

> If the consuming public in this country raises its standard of consumption to keep pace with every rise of productive powers, there could be no excess of goods or capital clamorous to use Imperialism in order to find markets: foreign trade would indeed exist, but there would be no difficulty in exchanging a small surplus of our manufactures for the food and raw material we annually absorbed, and all the savings we made could find employment, if we choose, in home industries. (Hobson 1965: 81)

That the simultaneous destruction of colonial economies through the dumping of surplus products of the advanced/ imperial countries and restriction of working class consumption in them came to be substantially alleviated after two world wars, working class mobilizations in the advanced industrial world and nationalist movements in the colonies had done their work, is broadly indicated by many developments associated with decolonization. Newly independent economies posted considerably higher rates of growth than they had as colonies. The non-settler colonies' importance to the trade of the imperial advanced industrial countries declined (on the British case, see Hobsbawm 1968: Diagram 28). Also there was a one-time increase in the share of wages and salaries in national income from less than 50 per cent in 1914 in Britain to above 70 per cent in the postwar period (Deane and Cole 1962: 247). The US may have lacked a formal empire but other forces worked to expand markets: the powerful expansionist impulse that drove its internal colonialism until 1890, the subsequent fast growth of its exports, continuing immigration, the practically unique development of consumer credit from at least the 1920s, and the centrality of wartime allied demand in producing the most powerful bursts of growth in the US economy. And the US too witnessed a one-off increase in the share of wages in the national income in the postwar period.

The exact connections between decolonization and the increase in the share of workers' income and national variations in them must be further investigated but the connection is unmistakable.

In the Regulationists' understanding of the inter-war period and the Great Depression, an intensive regime of accumulation had emerged but the mode of regulation remained competitive and the mode of consumption insufficiently transformed to match the increased capacity to produce. Such an 'underconsumptionist' account is tantamount to heresy in Brenner and Glick's Schumpeterian view of capitalism in which insufficient demand in the consumption goods sector is always compensated by increased demand in the producers' goods sector (1991: 80–81) and cost-cutting averts demand problems by reducing the value of the goods produced. Empirically, Brenner and Glick claim that the index of real wages in the US manufacturing sector rose 'dramatically' after the First World War and profits, as a share of national income, and the rate of profit, correspondingly fell (1991: 83–4). However, their own figures (they rely on Glick 1987 and Duménil et al. 1987), raise questions. Did wages rise enough to absorb the increased production at a time when consumer durables had become the leading edge of economic growth? And did they rise in the economy as a whole? If they did, why was there an explosion of consumer credit during the 'roaring twenties', an explosion that soon assumed bubble proportions and burst in the run-up to the stock market crash? Moreover, Brenner and Glick make no comment on standard accounts of income inequality in the inter-war period, according to which it reached a peak in 1929 unequalled for the rest of the century, and the associated view that the Great Depression was caused by 'a fundamental shift of income shares away from wages and consumption to corporate profits' (Livingston 2009: 37).

Brenner and Glick attack the Regulationist account of 'monopoly regulation'. Competition is irrepressible, they argue. Firms will invest wherever profit rates are high enough and monopoly is only possible where firms have political leverage. What is really interesting, however, is that Brenner himself accepts a version of monopoly at the national level in explaining the 'Long Boom'. With 'giant banks mobilizing much of the world's capital' and capitalist states which, particularly in developing countries, invest vast amounts even or particularly where low rates of profit normally deter private investment and improved modern transportation, 'competition can now emerge from such a multitude of points throughout the international system' that 'stable monopoly [becomes] massively more difficult to establish' (ibid.: 89). In this account, competition is displaced to the international level, a matter between nationally organized blocs of capital, effectively conceding that some version of monopoly exists nationally.

Finally we turn to Brenner and Glick's apparently frontal attack on the core of the concept of Fordism, that the development of a social norm of consumption alleviated the problem of demand. The Great Depression was 'transcended well before' the structures of Fordism were put in place and the profit rate in the wartime and postwar boom, '*adjusted for capacity utilization*' was twice that of the inter-war decades. 'Growth in consumption, in demand, is incapable in itself of explaining such dramatic movements in this fundamental economic variable' (1991: 92). Further, Brenner and Glick claim that consumption as a share of GNP in the US was not only 20 per cent lower than it had been in the 'ostensibly underconsumptionist twenties, but perceptibly lower than at any other time since 1890 (outside of brief periods during the two World Wars)' and that the Japanese economy grew through the stimulus provided by rising investment (ibid.: 94). They also doubt whether, in the US at least, a 'so-called capital–labour accord' to keep up the working class's share of GDP ever existed and whether 'capital ever resigned itself to the principle of maintaining labour's share or failed to fight tooth and nail to limit the degree to which wages kept up with the cost of living or with productivity' (ibid.: 93). The result was that real wages failed to keep up with productivity and fell in relation to productivity increases from 1948–70 and, with Aglietta himself admitting that this was so for most of the period, 'the epoch of "Fordist collective bargaining", if it existed, thus lasted for a few years in the 1950s' (ibid.).

True, it was not the New Deal but the onset of the Second World War, which brought an enormous increase in demand for US goods, making it the chief supplier of war materiel, that really ended the Great Depression, and the Regulationists would not disagree. However, is it valid to lump together the Fordist period with the war when the state more or less eclipsed private investment and powered growth of a scale and extent not witnessed before or since? As for the rate of profit, Brenner and Glick do not explain why they adjust it for capacity utilization here and are silent on the difference between the postwar profit rate and the much higher one that prevailed before 1914.

Even more interestingly, they smuggle in demand as a factor explaining the recovery of the profit rate if only to insist that it does not originate in working class consumption demand but in 'massive deficit-spending on armaments' which continued at a high rate, 'amounting to 80 per cent of federal government purchases of goods and services and 9 per cent of GNP through 1960' (ibid.: 92). When they complain that the Regulationists fail to note that 'the share of state expenditures in national income rose precipitately in the post-World War II period' (ibid.: 92n) they ignore the reliance of the Regulationist argument on increases in government (not just federal government) expenditure. In the US it rose from 1.2 per cent of GDP in 1930 to a wartime high of 48.4 per cent in 1944, declining thereafter to a postwar low of 16 per cent in 1947 before rising to 25.8 per cent in 1953. Certainly postwar economic managers were conscious of the need to keep demand levels high, if necessary by government expenditure and high wage settlements (Desai 2013a: 97).

Later on, Brenner would concede in his explanation of the Long Boom that workers' consumption demand did expand across the advanced industrial world if only to point to the distinctive geography of the Long Boom. Since domestic demand expanded in all major capitalist states, Brenner averred, it did not explain why the Long Boom's growth was concentrated in the recovering economies, while the US growth lagged in the 1950s and enjoyed only a brief and highly inflationary boom in the 1960s (Brenner 1998: 91).

CONCLUSION

Working class consumption demand has been central to the fate of capitalism, both when it was restricted and when it expanded after the wars. Restricted working class consumption initially was the domestic face of imperialist expansion and, as long as it could provide markets, the expansion of working class consumption could not be a systemic necessity. The elevation and stabilization of consumption demand at the higher levels that would power growth in the postwar period therefore required not only working class struggles, as the Regulationists rightly insisted, but also that complex combination of weakening imperialism and strengthening nationalism which led to decolonization. The golden age was their combined creation. While it is undoubtedly easy to overstate the strength of both these movements, it was the increase in domestic consumption demand among working people in both the advanced industrial world and the ex-colonial world that explains such dynamism as the golden age possessed.

From our twenty-first-century vantage point, it is critical that we understand that the golden age was, therefore, a function of the replacement of a world of imperial and colonial economies by national ones in which working class consumption had increasingly become a systemic necessity. For, thanks to the increasing prominence of states' economic management in today's multipolar world, the possibilities for reversing the decades-old dominance of neoliberalism are greatest. The most promising path of growth for all economies lies in expanding domestic markets, thus resuming the trend towards increasing political control over the power of capital that neoliberalism attempted to reverse, ultimately vainly. Not only was Fordism not replaced by any stable regime of accumulation under neoliberalism, the 'Long Downturn' was not ended by it. These overlapping diagnoses underline the possibility that the present crisis is not so much a crisis of neoliberalism or financialization but *the end of the long, painful and ultimately vain neoliberal effort to resolve the crisis of Fordism on capitalist terms*. While Brenner and Glick were not successful in demonstrating that capitalism should not be periodized, they may have inadvertently made a case for not thinking about capitalism in cyclical terms – whether as successive regimes of accumulation or periods of boom interrupted by contingent crises from which it must rejuvenate itself by 'slaughtering capital values' (indeed one may question whether, historically, such an eventuality ever ended a capitalist crisis). Trends in consumption demand or in productivity or profitability (Freeman 2012b) indicate continuous rises or declines. It may be better to think of capitalism in linear terms.

This might imply that the growth slowdown since the 1970s, whether we call it the crisis of Fordism or the end of the Long Boom, was a more profound crisis of capitalism than hitherto appreciated. In retrospect, all the three main crisis trends that the Regulationists pointed to appear to have played a role. Perhaps organized workers had indeed become too strong by capitalist standards by the early 1970s. That would certainly explain the worldwide attack on them that ensued in following decades. Perhaps the state social expenditures did indeed reach levels that capital again found intolerable and attacked with the weapons of neoliberalism. And perhaps the limit of capitalism's signature method of increasing human welfare, by increasing productivity by displacing labour in the production of standard goods for mass consumption was indeed reached in Fordism. Increases in welfare must now come in other ways, including the production and employment of high-end labour to produce high value goods and services with a high cultural content, all economic activities which are peculiarly resistant to capitalist cost-cutting competition over markets for standardized mass produced goods. Therefore, we must be willing to countenance the possibility that a resolution of the crisis on capitalist terms is no longer possible and we are faced with the Rosa Luxemburg Question: socialism or barbarism? Do we have the political will and organization to build socialism?

12. Paternalism, Taylorism, socialism: the Battle for Production in the Chilean textile industry, 1930–1973

Adam Fishwick

INTRODUCTION

Under the socialist Popular Unity (UP) government of Salvador Allende that ruled Chile from November 1970 to the military coup of General Pinochet of 11 September 1973, the country's workers engaged in a 'Battle for Production', a campaign for vigilance and resolve in the factories against sabotage and efforts by domestic and foreign capital to limit supplies of primary materials and machinery. Pursued most vigorously by the country's communist party, the Battle for Production marks the culmination of the formation of the working class as a political subject. Workers interpreted it as a mandate not just to protect their workplaces, but also to defend past gains and demand an extension of nationalization and liberation from the stranglehold on the economy by foreign capital. In addition, the campaign fuelled a drive to expand nascent forms of worker control in the 'industrial belts' (*cordones industriales*). Thus the Battle for Production came to symbolize the radicalization of a working class seeking to transform both their workplaces and the political order.

This chapter will explore the industrialization of Chile during the twentieth century by dissecting the strategies of capital and the state to discipline and control the working class in production. However, these strategies, originating in the period of import substitution industrialization (ISI), have been contested throughout by those who most directly experience the changes that they bring about, more particularly the attempts to fragment and weaken the working class both on the shop-floor and politically (Lebowitz 2003). The response to this fragmentation induces a counter-process of socialization (*Vergesellschaftung*), in which the collective experience of discipline in the workplace leads to shared grievances and opens up new spaces for politicization. Thus the working class may find ways to contest the trajectory of industrialization and develop into a self-conscious political subject.

CONCEPTUALIZING INDUSTRIALIZATION AND THE ROLE OF LABOUR

The idea of political conflict in the process of industrialization is one pillar of the recent New Economic History (NEH) of Latin America, whilst the exploitation of labour by capital, and the tensions this has generated, has been an important concern of labour historians from the 1970s to today. NEH builds on various institutionalist approaches to reinterpret the history of industrialization in Latin America, notably the new institutional economics of Douglass North (1995). This in turn arose from dissatisfaction with the deductive reasoning of neoclassical economics, bringing instead historical and interdisciplinary perspectives into the 'hard' science of economics (Gootenberg 2004: 253). As a result, economic history on the region is now paying attention to long-run processes and to 'connections between social stratification, political power and economic strategy, and about the relative impact of structures, endowments and institutions on economic growth and development' (Coatsworth 2005: 126).

One of the most important debates to which NEH has contributed concerns the influence of the Great Depression. In Chile, it is argued that there is evidence of industrial growth from the late nineteenth century onwards. Much of this can be seen as deriving from the success of exports. Nitrates, for example, induced backward linkages in infrastructure and food production (Palma 2000a: 227). But as Palma shows (2000b: 50, 63), after 1914 there is no link between the growth of manufacturing and the export cycle. Industry was able to embark on a relatively autonomous accumulation as the 'engine of growth' after 1930, for which the tariff revisions of 1897, 1916 and 1928 had provided the protective framework. This then enabled ISI (Palma 2000a: 240; Palma 2000b: 48).

NEH, then, offers important insights into industrialization in twentieth-century Latin America. Its adherents argue that, despite the continuities, the process of 'accelerated industrialization' was 'accompanied by a thorough transformation of the particular economies and societies' (Cárdenas et al. 2000d: 2). The cumulative processes already underway were accentuated and consolidated during the turmoil of the 1940s. Despite the increased importance of industry during the early decades of the twentieth century, it was only after 1945 that it became the leading sector in the major economies (Bulmer-Thomas 2003: 270). Growth continued along a similar path, but with an increasing bias toward capital goods and basic inputs as the state and capital sought to deepen industrialization (Thorp 1992: 185). This was the result of the relative success of earlier efforts to respond to dislocations caused by breakdowns in international trade and the new institutional frameworks that had been developed and consolidated during the preceding decades.

The portrayal of the Chilean experience thus has shifted from seeing ISI as a failure with primarily 'internal' economic contradictions, to an emphasis on the evolution of social and political problems facing it. The attempt to create, through policy and institutional innovation, a 'new' industrial framework characterized by a proliferation of small, relatively backward firms, high levels of vertical integration and protected inefficiencies, went hand in hand with a new 'industrial culture', the expansion of human capital and increasing linkages between raw material production and industry (Ffrench-Davis et al. 2000: 117–18). The unwillingness of Chilean business to invest is ascribed to distrust of the leftist tendencies of successive governments; the Christian Democrat government of the 1960s was in fact stymied by the tension between strong conservative forces and a radicalized Left (Thorp 1998: 180–81). Accelerated industrialization was the outcome of state and firm strategies to overcome distortions within the economy shaped by prior economic development and contemporary institutional constraints and opportunities alike.

Now for all its merits, the theoretical underpinnings of the NEH approach are problematic by their combination of orthodox macroeconomics and historical research. Taylor's widely-cited article of 1998 is indicative of how this can lead towards a static conception of history, in which change is attributed either to some radical external stimulus, or occurs within the confines of a narrow set of relatively inflexible institutional constraints. Taylor (1998: 5) tends toward the former; others instead emphasize a steady cumulative process of social change buttressed by a relatively stable political–institutional context (Thorp 1992: 188). As actors respond to historically contingent circumstances, social pressures are mediated through this institutional matrix, which unlike 'mono-economics' allows historical diversity to be recognized (Kuntz Ficker 2005: 159). But replacing mono-economics with mono-institutionalism tends to marginalize actors beyond the institutional frameworks of industrialization, obfuscating the conflicts it generates within relatively stable 'pathways' of economic development. If the working class is discussed at all, organized labour is presented as an obstacle or object on the trajectory of industrialization. Thus Thorp sees two main prerequisites for ISI (1998: 133–4): adequate foreign financial flows and political control over militant labour movements.

BRINGING LABOUR BACK IN

The role of conflict and contestation in and around the workplace is central to understanding not just the limitations on strategies of industrialization, but also the nascent alternatives that were available to capital, the state and the working class. Struggles provoked by changes in the labour process had an important formative effect not just on the working class, but also in determining their influence in shaping the trajectory of industrialization. Early efforts by Latin American labour historians to return the working class to the forefront of analyses of industrialization have focused on the structural location of labour as a commodity input into an abstract process of production, highlighting the actions and formation of the political institutions of labour. Examples include Ian Roxborough's (1984) perspective on 'two-sided' historical models and Charles Bergquist's (1986) study on the role of labour in shaping the initial conditions for industrialization in Latin America. Both of these authors, however, overemphasize the structural determination of labour and the significance of organized labour as a political actor. They offer a limited understanding of the importance of the working class, focusing primarily upon structural determination and failing to move past the institutions that represent it.

To remedy this overemphasis on the structural determinants of labour's influence, as well as the overemphasis on the political institutions of labour, new labour historians have sought to move towards an understanding of the workers. Examples include Jeremy Adelman's (1991) critique of 'essentialism' that focuses on the multiplicity of struggles and identities manifested beyond the abstract category of labour and Joel Wolfe's (2002) argument in favour of moving away from the 'macro-politics of "labour"' and toward a more nuanced understanding of the worker as 'the social subject'. Not only are workers to be considered as existing within multiple spheres of determination, in which their interests are not simply defined by structures of capitalism; they are also seen to be acting on these interests in a variety of ways. This perspective is significant in moving away from a reliance on abstract notions of working class identity and interests, but when taken to its logical conclusion it focuses upon workers as individuals and leads away from the potentially fruitful similarities in experience, through the mediations of production that shape the political subject that is the working class.

To overcome these dichotomous positions of workers as labour and workers as individuals, it is necessary to return to the significance of work and the workplace in the formation of the working class. Harry Braverman (1974) offers one of the most famous accounts of how the modern factory heralded a new form of social power and exploitation under capitalism. He shows how the capacities of human labour power are exploited through changing technologies and managerial practices; the 'technological-scientific revolution' that expanded and transformed capitalism throughout the twentieth century, he argues, served primarily to extend the exploitation of the 'infinitely malleable character of human labour' through new and changing methods (Braverman 1974: 55).

The labour process, however, is not simply the domain of capital and neither are workers its passive objects. Braverman arguably has too little to say on the dynamics of the working class, as contestation is limited to dissatisfaction, rather than concerted opposition (Elger and Schwarz 1980: 361–2). Workers' engagements with the processes and practices imposed by capital offer important insights into these contested relations. Michael Burawoy (1985) argues that workers are active subjects in the imposition of discipline in the workplace. Subsumed beneath the labour process, workers reproduce their own conditions of exploitation and construct a form of implied consent to the strategies of capital and the state (Burawoy 1985: 10–11). Workers are active subjects within the particular production processes in which they are located, the relations *in* production, rather than abstractly connected to the domination of capitalist relations *of* production.

This may be taken one step further by considering how workers are also active in contesting the imposition of particular relations in production. One important notion is Chris Smith's (2006) 'double indeterminacy of labour power' in which it is argued that workers contest their incorporation into disciplinary relations in production around effort and mobility. Workers challenge the strategies of firms to intensify work processes under the guise of 'productivity' and place limits on the level of exploitation by the ability to quit and remain mobile across workplaces. Whilst firms employ managerial strategies to ameliorate and weaken these two aspects of indeterminacy (both of which give the worker power in the workplace), the nature of the capital–labour relation means that these elements always persist to some degree. As a result, workers are able to contest strategies of industrialization where they are experienced most directly – in the process of production and the workplace.

Contestation in and around the production process is central to the formation of the working class as a political subject. Not only does it create objective conditions of shared experience, it also allows for a collective subjective interpretation of these experiences that extends beyond the workplace and permits the articulation of coherent and salient political interests as a class. This process of class formation is best captured in the work of E.P. Thompson (1968), who argues that to understand the making of a working class it is necessary to consider not only the objective conditions that locate individuals within particular class situations, but also the subjective influences of experience that provide the raw material with which their identities in historically specific class formations can be constructed. Lived experience acts as a vital mediation between workers' social being in the workplace and their social consciousness as it is manifested politically (Wood 1995: 96). The working class should not be understood merely as influential in pursuing its own interests, but rather is influential in political conflicts in which historically specific interests are formed in society as a whole.

For Michael Lebowitz (2003), there are two important aspects to this process: one whereby capital mediates the 'social' product of labour and the other, the social construction of subjective needs. Strategies of discipline and control in the workplace fragment workers within the production process, but still require the mobilization of the social productivity of labour. As such, shared experiences of fragmentation are a source of grievances around which workers can mobilize collectively. The dynamic and contingent formation of 'needs', or political interests, is then shaped by the subjective interpretation of these grievances through a contingent process of appropriation, interpretation and politicization. Struggle transforms specific historical conflicts into the redefinition of the particular political interests of the working class acting for itself (Lebowitz 1992: 143–9). This not only transforms distinctive constellations of capitalist social relations, both of and in production, but in doing so it transforms the working class as a political force in pursuit of its own interests. Starting from contestation in the workplace around the imposition of particular production processes, the working class comes to constitute a subject mobilized around the politicization of this discontent. At particular conjunctures in this ongoing process of struggle, mobilizations then place constraints on the strategies of capital and the state and open up opportunities for alternatives.

HISTORICIZING THE BATTLE FOR PRODUCTION IN THE TEXTILE INDUSTRY

Drawing on the insights from the foregoing discussion I now turn to the experience of textile industrialization in Chile. Here I argue that prior to 1970, paternalism and modernization within the industry represented two forms of enforcing discipline and control in the workplace. The limits of the former led it to be replaced by an impersonal form exercised through the import of modern machinery and reorganization of the workplace.

How workers throughout the sector experienced these changes will be our primary concern, for in contesting the constraints imposed by these forms of workplace discipline, the working class came to constitute a salient political force with an influence well beyond the established political institutions of labour. Workers not only placed limitations on the strategies of industrialization, but their struggles for the pursuit of their own political interests also opened up space for alternatives. This culminated in the experiences of 1970, when the Battle for Production manifested itself in the contested interpretations of the slogan by the newly elected socialist government and the working class. The latter mobilized within and against the strategies of the state and came to construct a nascent form of production that offered a vision of a new future.

Paternalism and the Personalization of Discipline

The textile industry became a leading sector in Chile after 1930 under the tutelage and protection of the state. Import restrictions, new technologies, growth of domestic demand and, later, the immigration of technicians and businesspeople stimulated its rapid growth (Frias et al. 1987a: 23–5). For example, between 1929 and 1935 it increased its share of overall manufacturing output from 6 per cent to 13.7 per cent, whilst the share of local products rose from 30 per cent to 77 per cent (Palma 2000b: 60–62). This growth was divided between large modern factories and small workshops located in family homes or in the back of commercial premises (Toledo Obando 1948: 47). Large factories possessed relatively advanced industrial technology, yet smaller firms were still able to accrue substantial profits and purchase some newer machinery (ibid.: 43). The internal dynamics of market growth and state support, moreover, prevented the undercutting of production costs and enabled it to flourish. Despite these changes, production processes were characterized by relatively backward workplace organization, high levels of labour-intensity and low wages (Frias et al. 1987b: 24; Toledo Obando 1948: 9). The import of modern machinery was not complemented by the dissemination of modern production processes. Instead, personalized discipline and control was necessary to sustain this early growth.

These strategies were at the forefront of the emergent discontent in the workplace, constituting the main grievances expressed by the nascent working class in the sector. For example, one former worker at the La Continental silk factory writes at length of her experiences as an 'ex-victim' in which the owners would 'pass by with a watch in hand. . . applying arbitrary fines with each step' in a factory where 'only apprentices work. . . for the simple reason that they can be paid miserable wages'

(*Obrero Textil* 1936).[1] By the end of the decade immigrant factory owners, mainly from the Middle East, controlled a significant proportion of the textile industry. Primarily focusing their interests in the cotton-weaving sector, they brought relatively advanced technology along with a strict paternalist management style and a strong disdain for working class struggle (Winn 1986: 31–7). The strategies of firms in these early years of rapid growth centred on exerting a strict discipline within the workplace, symbolized by the paternalistic management styles of owners.

In contesting the extension of this personalized discipline throughout the industry workers began to mobilize as a political subject in the sense outlined in the previous section. They contested the terms of their incorporation into the low-wage, labour-intensive and disciplinarian production processes, undermining the strategies pursued by capital. Workers in the silk weaving sector attained significant victories against employers through strikes and other forms of industrial action, as well as forming a 'vanguard' around which workers from across the sector could mobilize (Frias et al. 1987b: 25). At Sedatex and Kattán they mobilized to challenge attempts to impose the 25 per cent wage reductions that were being imposed throughout the industry (*Obrero Textil* 1937). Moreover, at El Salto and Lourde, a series of strikes between 1934 and 1937 culminated in indefinite strike action over the dismissal of the lowest paid, and most militant, workers in the sector with a mobilization of over 1000 workers (*Obrero Textil* 1937). Thus they sought to contest the disciplinary strategies that were imposed to sustain the low-wage and low-technology processes of production.

By the end of the 1930s, there was an increasing process of institutionalization in response to these struggles. For example, following the failure of negotiations between workers and owners in sack manufacture, calls were made for state mediation to ensure the honouring of agreements to redress the demands of the workers (*Obrero Textil* 1937). Moreover, denunciation of abuses at Sedería Chile and justifications for large-scale strike action at El Salto and Lourde emphasized that it was the workers who were acting in defence of the laws that capital 'laughs at' and 'makes a mockery of' (*Obrero Textil* 1936; 1937). Increased levels of mobilization throughout the 1930s reflected the experiences of the workplace in this expanding sector and the increasing significance of the institutionalization of this struggle. As a result, FENATEX was formed in 1938 in the 'heat of political struggle . . . to unify the struggle around common problems'. It was a

---

[1] Citations from this source and other textile industry, factory and trade union journals are by reference to volume only. Like other sources in Spanish they have been translated by the author.

manifestation of the politicization of collective grievances experienced and contested within the workplace (Fernando Bombilla cited in Frias et al. 1987b: 27). The increasingly radical conflicts and political institutions of labour being established reconfigured the influence of the working class as a nascent political force.

Relatively spontaneous and isolated strike actions were displaced by organized negotiation through enforceable labour laws (Pizarro 1986: 104–5). As a result, the militant radicalism of the working class was mediated within its political institutions. In the largest factories in the industry, however, this process of institutionalization occurred outside FENATEX, with workers following their own independent routes (Frias et al. 1987b: 26, 28). On the one hand, this reflected the strategies of capital in terms of efforts to impose disciplinary relations in production and maintain a fragmented working class. On the other hand, they provided an important space in which the earlier radical politicization of workers' grievances could persist. For example, despite the efforts of capital, workers in these large factories tended to retain socialist political ideas (ibid.: 22). This incomplete institutionalization of working class struggle facilitated the mobilization of the working class and shaped the politicization of their grievances. The emergence of these institutions placed limits on the strategies of capital, but also on the capacity of the working class to pursue its own interests politically.

The ostensible political ascendancy of the working class at the turn of the 1940s consolidated a trajectory of industrialization guided by the alliance between firms and the state (Moulian 2009: 32). By 1944, for example, textiles were the second largest sector in manufacturing in terms of the total value of production, but there was a persistent underutilization of installed capacity (Frias et al. 1987a: 25; Toledo Obando 1948: 51; CEPAL 1962: 35). To address these problems, the strategies of capital turned to increasing exploitation through a relatively uncontested intensification of disciplinary relations in production. Wages remained low due to inflation (Pinto 1945: 18; Abarca 1943: 13). Moreover, large plants such as Yarur hired workers who had recently moved to the cities from the countryside and also women, who made up the majority of the workforce and received 30 per cent lower wages than men (Salazar and Pinto 2010: 178). These strategies maintained the profitability of labour-intensive production despite the problems pervading industrial structures and production processes.

Within the workplace, discipline remained strict. Pamphlets to be signed by workers at two textile factories provided long lists of prohibitions and obligations. Moving between sections, leaving the establishment 'for whatever reason', undertaking or forming social organizations within the workplace, and even holding conversations that may 'disrupt the complete development of the working day' were all banned. Discipline and order in undertaking tasks and protecting the 'better culture' in the workplace are all obligations for workers (Mazzei y Piovano Ltda 1941: 6–8; Visonet Ltda 1942: 7–8). These demonstrate the strict discipline within the factory, as the political institutions of labour marginalized the combative tendencies that had once prevailed (Frias et al. 1987b: 28).

Rationalization, Taylorism and Disciplinary Modernization

The second phase marks a shift in the means by which discipline and control were exerted. Personalized discipline had a limited efficacy and relied primarily on the support of a repressive state apparatus and weak, or poorly enforced, labour legislation. In response to these limitations, capital and the state began to pursue a strategy of disciplinary modernization. Its main feature was the rationalization of the workplace, transforming the socio-technical relations in production through the import of modern machinery and workplace reorganization. In 1947, the state began supporting this process through Decree 952, which restricted imports and removed foreign competition, and Law 8732, which permitted the import of low-cost machinery (Ortega et al. 1989: 90–91; Toledo Obando 1948: 59, 71–4). The disciplinary elements of these imports were explicit in their use. Centralized monitoring of production, features that allowed workers to attend more than one machine, and 'scientific control' over the production process were deemed particularly important by firms (*Chile Textil* 1946; 1947). The dissemination of these new production processes using modern machinery clearly focused on discipline and control in the workplace rather than ostensible gains in productivity or output.

Three examples demonstrate how this was implemented throughout the 1940s and 1950s: (1) an automatic production line in a sack-making factory saw employees reduced from 350 to 206, without having to change the machinery; (2) new methods and incentives in a textile spares workshop saw a 40 per cent rise in production with a 20 per cent reduction in personnel, with a further 12 per cent increase in production coming from a redistribution of machinery; (3) a cotton spinning factory saw a 13 per cent production increase with a minor personnel decrease. Rationalization was constructing a new 'nexus between man and machine' (*Chile Textil* 1956). Productivity increases were crucial not only in addressing stagnation, but also weakened the working class politically through workplace discipline and control.

These strategies reached their zenith in the 1960s. The sector was still riven by the problems including high costs, low productivity, excess and obsolete equipment, and excess and poorly distributed personnel. Producing 100 yards of cotton fabric required 2.33 hours of work in the United States, 2.74 hours in Japan and 12.85 hours in Chile (Frias et al. 1987a: 26; CEPAL 1962: 5). Despite this, however, foreign machinery was increasingly easy to access. In the cotton sector, 81 per cent of spinning and 83 per cent of weaving establishments possessed modern machinery, with Chile possessing the second highest proportion of automatic weaving machines in Latin America (ibid.: 4, 35). It is clear that this import of machinery and implementation of disciplinary relations in production was aimed at constraining the formation of a political working class.

For example, the implementation of Taylorist production processes and workplace organization at Yarur in 1962 led to the dismissal of over 1000 protesting workers (Winn 1986: 44–6). Moreover, demands of the new Taylorist methods meant that Yarur workers could not even speak to one another during working hours (ibid.: 80). By restricting the ability to communicate, the factory became an increasing site of discipline and control. These strategies also entailed a transformation of the worker. To address the limits of technical changes in the workplace, the 'professional formation' of workers was made increasingly prominent (*Chile Textil* 1962). Disciplinary modernization necessitated not only the import of advanced machinery, but also the reconfiguration of the workplace and the workers themselves.

By the mid-1960s, this strategy was firmly embedded in the practices of the state and capital. CORFO, the public industrialization body, supported the renewal and improvement of technological capacity (Ortega et al. 1989: 196). Advanced machinery was not the problem in the industry, according to OECD statistics; it was already considered capital-intensive. Instead it was the persistence of under-utilization that remained a problem in large factories (*Chile Textil* 1966; Winn 1986: 25–7). New machinery would not solve the industry's problem, so its import demonstrated the disciplinary motivations of these strategies. At Yarur, for example, new strategies that would enable the 'perfection' of the worker in his or her role were to be implemented alongside productivity-linked pay, relocation of workers within the production process, and a scientific reorganization that would maximize productivity (*Revista Yarur* 1968). However, as a strategy targeted specifically at placing constraints on the pursuit of the political interests of the working class, disciplinary modernization engendered an intensification of conflict.

Changes in the workplace had important implications for the formation of a political working class and the conflicts around which it would contest these strategies. One prominent campaign was over the 40-hour week. Cuts to the working week were not opposed to the rising production requirements of the industry, but rather workers engaged in the more modern 40-hour working week would contribute to rising productivity (*Tribuna Textil* 1947). Demanding more reasonable working hours demonstrated the articulation of political interests against the strategies of firms. Early mobilizations reflected these concerns. For example, workers across the silk sector spent 42 days on strike from 3 November 1946 as factory owners sabotaged production, persisted with the under-utilization of machinery and forced workers to work longer hours (*Tribuna Textil* 1947). The contradictions within the strategy of disciplinary modernization were increasingly clear to workers mobilizing against it.

The locus of conflict in the late 1940s shifted toward the cotton sector, which had taken the lead in implementing these strategies. Successful mobilizations were undertaken at Kallin Kattán, Dunay, Comandari and Hilandería Nacional to contest the disciplinary relations in production, arbitrary dismissals and squeezes on wages (*Tribuna Textil* 1947; 1948; 1951). Strikes were also held at larger plants like El Progreso over a daily minimum wage, attacks on workplace organization and arbitrary firings; at Sumar over pay and working conditions, and at Yarur throughout the 1940s over working conditions, widespread dismissals and the limits on workplace organization imposed by employers (*Tribuna Textil* 1947; 1948; 1951; Winn 1986: 39–40). These conflicts mark an important period of transition in the formation of the working class. From contesting the personalized discipline of the 1930s and early 1940s, workers were increasingly exposed to strategies that, whilst fragmenting production processes, created collective experiences across small and large factories.

This culminated in a renewed unity of the working class. At Sumar, for example, the strike that had continued from 1951 saw 1500 textile workers walk out and occupy the factory for several days. Workers at these plants and others had limited formal political experience, but mobilized around collective political interests (Vitale 2011: 569). Moreover, workers across the sector mobilized against the Prat Plan in 1954, which included an anti-inflationary programme to eliminate wage readjustments equivalent to the cost of living, the outlawing of strikes, and the imposition of arbitration to resolve disputes (Hernández 1954: 1–5; Moulian 2006: 164). In the textile workers' press, it was argued that this Plan was severely detrimental to their interests and that an alternative set of issues had to be tackled to address the ongoing problems in the industry (*Unidad Textil* 1954). Growing discontent in the workplace was articulated against the strategies of capital and the state, and alternative strategies were being proposed favouring the political interests of the working class.

Despite the institutionalization of these struggles after 1953, with the establishment of the United Workers' Confederation (CUT) and the affiliation of FENATEX, the radicalism and militancy of textile workers was sustained. For example, many of the problems facing workers were associated with the 'anti-national' monopolies, with calls for their regulation and the extension of credit to the smaller 'national' industries (*Unidad Textil* 1954). Institutional and ideological tools were mobilized to politicize these grievances and give a growing salience to the working class. This was reflected in the large strikes that occurred at Hirmas in 1961 and 1962 and at Yarur in 1962 over Taylorist relations in production. Over 1800 workers came out on strike at Hirmas in 1961, whilst at Yarur in 1962 it was over 3500 (Frias et al. 1987b: 31; Winn 1994; *Central Única* 1961). Workers from the large firms were taking the lead as the politicization of grievances against the strategies of disciplinary modernization consolidated an increasingly radicalized and politically salient working class.

By the mid-1960s workers from this industry constituted a significant part of the membership of the CUT, representing 24 per cent of affiliated manufacturing workers, with larger establishments making up the highest proportion (Zapata 1968: 48). Efforts to expand the political institutions of labour had not marginalized their radicalism, but instead further politicized their interests. Protests continued at Sumar in 1965 and at Yarur in what was described as a 'rebellion without a cause' by the firm's own magazine (*Central Única* 1965; *Revista Yarur* 1968). Moreover, there were mass protests in the silk industry that reflected similar grievances, but saw mobilizations beyond those that had occurred previously (*Central Única* 1965). The working class emerged from its conflicts over disciplinary modernization as an increasingly coherent political force. The accumulated experience of work, repression and mobilization, coupled with their politicization through the prevailing political institutions and ideas, produced a radicalized working class that contested the constraints imposed on the pursuit of its political interests.

State Socialism and the 'Battle for Production'

This third phase marked an unprecedented shift in the strategies of industrialization guiding production in the textile industry. The most important strategy of Salvador Allende in 1970 for the sector was the 'reactivation' of industrial production that sought a rapid increase in output and the nationalization of monopoly production and its integration into the Area of Social Property (APS). Textile firms made up a significant proportion of those firms that were incorporated into this state-run sector. Eighteen of the 90 firms originally on the list drawn up by Allende and his government were textile factories. Overall, 19 firms were eventually incorporated, the majority from the original list (Yarur, Sumar, Hirmas,

Tejidos Caupolican, Rayón Said, Textil Progreso, Paños Oveja Tomé, Rayonhil, Lanera Austral, Textil Comandari, Paños Continental, Pollak) and six from outside it (FIAP, Bellavista Tomé, Fabrilana, Sedamar, Hilanderías Andina, Confecciones Romitex) (Frias et al. 1987b: 35). These firms had dominated production and shaped earlier strategies of industrialization. As such, their nationalization had a profound impact, materially and symbolically, on the Battle for Production.

Transformations undertaken in this process encompassed changes to the structure of the sector and to the workplace. The takeover of the leading firms meant that, after 1970, the APS controlled 48.8 per cent of output and 43.2 per cent of employment in the industry (Frias et al. 1987a: 27). This meant that the strategies guiding industrialization were beholden not to the interests of capital, but rather to the socialist project of UP. This was reflected in the experiences in the workplace at Yarur. Since 1968, production had been in decline in the factory, but following the takeover by the state and its incorporation into the APS, this decline was reversed. By September 1972, the plant, now named Ex-Yarur, was held up as *the* example of how socialism could work in the industry. For example, the maintenance division was transformed into a spare parts factory producing three-quarters of previously imported spare parts. Moreover, worker initiative drove many changes on the factory floor: new ventilation systems, production processes and accounting systems were developed, whilst production was reoriented to serve the demand of the workers themselves (Winn 1986: 212–14). Workers and the state thus shaped socio-technical relations in production to pursue the Battle for Production. It was a crucial component of the political project of the UP, as well as for the workers whose experiences and struggles were reinterpreted through it.

The slogan of the Battle for Production brought workers into the project aimed at increasing output and defending the production process from direct and indirect attacks by former and present owners of factories throughout the sector (Santa Lucia 1976: 136). However, in the context of the struggles and experiences in the formation of the working class, these calls were taken as a rallying cry for seizing control of the production process in its entirety. The slogan was reinterpreted as a call to increase the pace of the factory occupations that had been occurring in previous years and as a call for 'direct revolutionary action' (Gaudichaud 2005: 97; Winn 1986: 237). On the one hand, in *FENATEX* (1972), published by the organization of the same name, there is a detailed outline for mobilizing and organizing Production Oversight Committees (*comité de vigilancia de la producción*) to monitor production and guard against sabotage and deliberate stoppages by employers. On the other hand, *Hombrenuevo* (1971), published at the worker-controlled El Progreso factory, identifies the Battle for Production with directly advancing the worker's role beyond that of 'one more machine', incorporating economic, social and even cultural advancement with control over processes of work. The Battle for Production was a symbol around which the long history of struggle over the strategies of industrialization culminated around the formation of a revolutionary working class.

This was demonstrated by the factory occupations that preceded and were further inspired by the appropriation and reinterpretation of this call for mobilization. These seizures began at some of the largest firms in the sector. By 1971, eight of the major firms in the sector, including Yarur, Sumar and Hirmas, had been taken over by the workers and then incorporated into the APS. One of these, Sedamar, was transformed into the most profitable textile firm controlled by the state (Sigmund 1977: 148; Espinosa and Zimbalist 1978: 41–2). The most symbolic seizure, however, was at Yarur. Workers at this plant were not only the first to occupy their plant after 1970, but they were also the first to force the socialization of their enterprise and to implement worker participation (Winn 1986: viii). The experience of workers in the smaller plants was also indicative of the deeper shift in the working class. Strategies led by the state did not include these, forcing them to submit to the alliance with 'progressive' industrialists and not to question the prevailing relations in and of production. As a result, they 'generated a popular movement that adopted its own dynamic, distinct from the process led by the government and Popular Unity' (Gaudichaud 2005: 87; Castillo 2009: 81). Workers were mobilizing in the construction of an alternative trajectory of industrialization that met with the political interests engendered throughout the previous decades of struggle and the expectations created in these years of potentially revolutionary transformation.

The most significant manifestation of the accumulation of historical experience and its autonomous mobilization in a contemporary context by a radicalized working class political subject was in the *cordones industriales*. The role of these organizations remains controversial and relatively sparsely researched. For those who have focused their research on the labour movement as a whole, they were a defensive mobilization against the sabotage of employers and a means of coordinating the fragmented unions that persisted throughout Chile (Angell 2010: 48). However, for those who have studied them in depth, through interviewing participants or through documentation produced at the time, their deeper significance is in terms of the formation of the working class as a radical and autonomous political force. Frank Gaudichaud (2005: 97), for example, argues that whilst the *cordones* were acting primarily to defend the government of the UP, they also encompassed far more radical aims, including the unification of the working class across all sectors of the economy. For Sandra Castillo (2009: 158–9), moreover, these organizations represented a 'new popular organization, with specific characteristics that gave it its own internal dynamic and that would be the model to follow for the formation of other similar structures'. They demonstrated a dynamism and autonomy that belies the notion that they were beholden to the state, to the political institutions of labour, or to any narrow defensive interests.

Whilst defending the UP, it was their autonomy that was most significant. Although linked to the state-run APS, the majority of the firms that participated in the *cordones* were small and medium-sized enterprises. Workers in these firms, within the textile sector and beyond, had little experience of the political institutions of labour, but came to represent the 'most radicalised fraction' of the working class (Castillo 2009: 180). The influence of this sector of the working class translated into the reshaping of production within the *cordones* and the APS. Production in the former continued without owners, and relations in production were transformed as questions were raised within the workplace over the divisions of labour, factory hierarchy and the legitimacy of ownership itself (Gaudichaud 2005: 95). Moreover, in the large firms of the APS, which were linked politically to the working class within the *cordones*, there were pressures to go beyond the reforms led by the state. The textile workers on 14 and 15 July 1973, for example, criticized the 'superstructural' character of worker participation, whilst mobilization at plants like Sumar and Yarur led to trade and credit relations being set up between the worker-run firms (Castillo 2009: 245–6, 234–5; Winn 1986: 238). The working class was transforming relations in and of production within the workplaces of the textile sector through radical and autonomous mobilizations within and against state-led strategies of industrialization.

It was only with the military coup of 11 September 1973 that the autonomy and radicalism of the *cordones* was destroyed. There were efforts to institutionalize these nascent formations within the political institutions of labour by both the CUT and the Communist Party (Castillo 2009: 213), but it was only the savage repression of the military, backed by foreign and domestic capital, that cut short the experience of the *cordones*. They should not be mythologized as Soviets, as was claimed by political activists, or as the alternative army referenced in the propaganda of the new regime, but they were a nascent form of an alternative future (Gaudichaud 2005: 105). Following decades of experience of disciplinary relations in production and contesting their implementation, workers constituted themselves politically within the workplace, backed and coordinated by autonomous political organizations in pursuit of their interests as a working class acting for itself.

CONCLUSION

The Battle for Production in the textile industry in Chile represents an unresolved, contingent and shifting process that shaped the trajectory of industrialization. It placed limits on this trajectory, as well as shaping the limits on the expression of the working class as a political subject. After 1930 the textile industry embarked upon a strategy of industrialization that focused on extending and expanding the low-wage, low-technology production processes that relied on a combination of personalized workplace discipline and state repression. In response, workers became increasingly active in contesting their shared experiences in the workplace, culminating in militant action and the institutionalization of struggle around new political institutions of labour. Although formed in the context of radical mobilization, these placed constraints on the pursuit of working class political interests, whilst simultaneously forcing capital to intensify and transform its strategies of industrialization.

From the 1940s and 1950s, firms turned to strategies of disciplinary modernization that relied on the import of advanced technology and its utilization in establishing a new form of socio-technical relations in production. These centred on workplace rationalization and the exertion of discipline and control through the production process itself, particularly through work processes associated with Taylorism and scientific management. In response, workers' struggles also intensified as the limited institutionalization of their struggle allowed for an increasing radical politicization of grievances that were increasingly extended beyond the workplace. The increasingly sophisticated strategies of discipline engendered increasingly sophisticated strategies of contestation in the workplace and beyond. As firms and the state sought to enforce the fragmentation of the working class in and around the workplace, workers' shared experiences of modern technology and increasing work rhythms led to targeted protests against these strategies.

Such struggles over discipline and control in the workplace culminated in the contested experiences of socialism after 1970. Whilst workers supported the state-led strategies of industrialization that included increasing output and nationalization of the largest firms, they also interpreted these through the lens of their own experiences of struggle across the sector. The Battle for Production that had played out over the previous decades in factories throughout the sector climaxed around the mobilization of the working class within the *cordones*. These were a manifestation of a radical and coherent political subject not only placing limits on the strategies of industrialization pursued by capital and the state, but also pursuing strategies to transform relations in and of production coordinated by the working class acting 'for-itself'.

The historical experiences in Chile have important implications for understanding the political economy of production. The nexus between production processes and the worker for understanding the working class is one; also, the fact that strategies pursued by the state and capital focus on a transformation not of relations of production, but of relations in production. It is at this level that workers most directly experience these strategies and it is at this level that they are first contested. The formation of the working class proceeds from within the subjective interpretation of these objective conditions of the workplace. Strikes and protests provide the starting point in this process, once grievances in the workplace are politicized. Mobilizing within and against the institutions of labour allows workers to come together as a working class to contest the discipline enforced in the workplace and the wider strategies of industrialization of which they are part. These struggles not only lead to changes in the workplace, but also in the working class. They not only create the potential for the construction of limits against the trajectory of industrialization, but also create space for the articulation and pursuit of radical alternative trajectories that can meet their contingent political interests. Starting from the battle for production in the workplace, the political influence of the working class can spread beyond the factory walls, beyond the limits of its political institutions, and manifest itself in forms that can produce a revolutionary future.

13. *Trasformismo* and the defeat of the Left in Italy

Davide Bradanini

How to make sense of the demise of the largest communist party in Western Europe and its subsequent transformation? How was this trajectory conditioned and shaped by the dynamics of the capitalist system and the production process in Italy? These are the questions addressed in this chapter. By using the Gramscian notion of *trasformismo* I will reconstruct the strategy of the Italian ruling classes to prevent the emergence of a counter-hegemonic historic bloc based on the autonomous political culture of the working class. In the postwar years the formation that might have built such a bloc was the Italian Communist Party (PCI).

Ever since the country's unification in the mid-nineteenth century the development of the Italian political economy and its insertion into European and global capitalism included a specific political *and* productive settlement. The particularities of this settlement prevented the Left, epitomized by the PCI, from obtaining the advantages of capital–labour compromise typical of postwar Western Europe. The PCI in most areas of the country was electorally confined to the industrial working class. It was unable, or perhaps unwilling, to expand its base of support to include all wage earners, as pursued by Social Democratic parties in central and northern Europe. The party's strategy instead was based on the assumption that there existed a fundamental incompatibility between a capitalist economy and any significant advances by labour. As I will argue in this chapter, it was this stance that made the party and Italian Left in general defenceless against neoliberalism in the 1990s.

THE DEVELOPMENT OF ITALIAN CAPITALISM

In Gramsci's famous analysis, the Italian *Risorgimento* was not a liberal bourgeois revolution, but a *passive revolution* on the basis of a compromise between the northern industrialists and the southern landowners (Gramsci 1949; 1972). The weak legitimacy of the Italian state implied opposition to it of many social forces, but during Giovanni Giolitti's rule (intermittently from 1892 to 1921), these were co-opted in a clientelistic fashion. Thus the policy of *trasformismo* was inaugurated that has since characterized how the Italian ruling class has sought to integrate the centrifugal forces in society and prevent the emergence of a counter-hegemonic bloc. It combined the task of promoting capitalist development in order to catch up with the expanding liberal heartland, with maintaining social control within a weak and fragmented nation-state.

Trasformismo, in Gramsci's interpretation (Gramsci 1971; Paggi and D'Angelillo 1986; Liguori and Voza 2009), is nevertheless a profoundly *modern* process. It is a form of development in which the active elements of diverse social and political groups – including those potentially hostile – are incorporated and co-opted through a strategy of *negative* integration. From Giolitti's rule up to the 'soft' hegemony of the Christian Democratic Party (DC) in the postwar years, and including the fascist period, the Italian ruling class and 'its' state (and dominant party) continually negotiated particularistic settlements with several social groups. These differentiated exemptions, 'privileges' and other settlements prevented the state from attaining the clear demarcation between the private and public sphere, or the 'level playing field' in the domain of the market, that would have qualified it as a Weberian state. In this respect Italy differs not only from the liberal state/society complexes of the Anglo-Saxon world, but also from Western nation-states such as France and Germany. On the other hand there are many similarities with a country like Spain (Gallo 2009).

Trasformismo has often been equated with clientelistic practices of political co-optation (from patron–client relationships to outright corruption, see Marshall 2007), but this neglects its class content and its modern characteristics. Indeed Gramsci argues that *trasformismo* is not a deviation from some 'natural' modernization path, but a response to challenges arising from the modernization of the economy and society and from the transformations in transnational capitalism. It acknowledges the existence of a mass society and the need to integrate interest groups with a mass base, albeit without making significant concessions, such as increasing domestic demand. This is how the administrative apparatuses try to neutralize social conflict preventively (Paggi and D'Angelillo 1986: 65; Liguori and Voza 2009).

Trasformismo, then, aims at preventing the rise of a working class political subject with hegemonic aspirations, as outlined for Chile by Adam Fishwick in the last chapter. In the final instance, the central point of hegemony is the *material* subsumption of the subaltern classes in the labour process, combined with their *cultural–ideological* subordination. As Paggi and D'Angelillo put it, 'The problem at the root of *trasformismo* is not that of governing in the absence of modernity, but of *modernising against the labour movement*' (1986: 67, emphasis added). Thus the ruling class tries to avoid 'that the main social partner . . . can obtain full and definitive legitimacy, hence equal dignity, within the political system.'

The dominant political party until the early 1990s, the DC, based both its political legitimacy and its economic policies on a historic bloc essentially drawn from the commercial petty bourgeoisie; small and medium enterprises (SMEs); large sectors of public employees (recruited also thanks to clientelistic practices in the South and owing their position to the party); the white-collar bourgeoisie (professional cadres such as lawyers and doctors); the landowners in the countryside; and sectors of labour itself, organized in the Catholic trade union confederation CISL (Amyot 2004: 96–105; Allen and McLennan 1971; Rhodes 1997). As Amyot argues,

> For a party which owes its strength to its control of the state, the most natural social basis is the petty bourgeoisie. This class, though it often espouses anti-statist ideologies, today depends on the state for its very survival as a class: without subsidies, protective legislation, tax exemptions, and other types of assistance, it would be defenceless against the tendency towards concentration inherent in modern capitalism. And in Italy, the self-employed petty bourgeoisie are particularly numerous – they still represent 29 per cent of the employed population, far more than in any other G7 country (Amyot 2004: 98).

In the *Mezzogiorno* (the South), a sprawling clientelistic network emerged based on institutions such as the *Cassa per il Mezzogiorno* (the funding agency for infrastructural and industrial projects in the South), the *Coldiretti* and *Federconsorzi* (associations of farmers). All these organizations distributed funds and benefits based largely on political links and thus generated support for the DC regime, whilst alleviating the huge social problems of the Southern regions and the tensions generated by a restrictive economic policy not geared toward full employment (Vianello 1979: 22–3). Moreover, many public employees were recruited on account of party affiliation. Paggi, referring to the Italian state's fiscal revenue deficit and the problem of tax evasion (see Barba 2011), argues that it 'must be placed within a larger picture, it is a problem of the lack of legitimacy of the state, not a problem of the lack of control, it is something deeper. The Italian state was born weak. Everyone bargains and negotiates with it since the beginning' (interview with the author).

Here one may discern a dynamic that has profound roots in the Italian political economy: the role of the state has tended to result from the most diverse corporatist interests and pressures, rather than from grand ideological projects (such as the Attlee–Beveridge Welfare State or the German Social Market Economy). The only state institution that has asserted itself as a strategic decision-making body has been the Bank of Italy (Fodor 2004: 201). In fact it is significant that during the neoliberal 'reformist' season of the 1990s political leaders coming from the Bank of Italy were hegemonic.

Crucially, the strategy of *trasformismo* was reflected in a socio-economic policy at odds with the prevailing Keynesian orthodoxy. The latter implied the state's so-called 'command over money', but also the recognition that the assertion of working class interests is politically legitimate and economically functional, inscribed in a settlement geared towards maintaining adequate effective demand and low unemployment. The Italian economic miracle of the 1950s and 1960s, on the other hand, was based to a large extent on low wages, low internal demand and high unemployment (for which emigration was conceived as the main solution). This implied the marginalization of the largest trade union (the communist CGIL) in the political economy and of the PCI politically, as well as paternalism within the firm and the prevalence of pre-Keynesian economic policies. The composition of the DC's historic bloc made it impossible to develop a comprehensive universalistic welfare state and Keynesian demand management techniques.

Tarrow aptly characterizes the DC regime as a 'soft hegemony' characterized by 'a pattern of political relationships based on a flexible centrist governing formula, an interclass social base, closeness to business but solicitousness to marginal groups and a governing style heavily based on distributive policy' (Tarrow 1990: 308). As he also notes, 'Italy's political economy was not organized along the classical lines of business versus labour, because such an alignment would have been disastrous to the DC's hegemony, and second because the party was trying to contest many sectors of social terrain with the Left for votes' (ibid.: 319).

The interclass nature of the dominant parties, as well as the perception of the autonomous position of the working class and industrial conflict as inherently subversive of the established balance of social forces, thus was a constant in national history. The state was weak, even under fascism. Indeed according to Cesaratto this weakness extended to the Italian bourgeoisie itself, which was 'incapable of reaching maturity'.

> Beccaris,[1] fascism, the strategy of tension, Berlusconi: this has been the response of the Italian bourgeoisie to any demand for change, systematically. In turn, it has prevented a maturation of the Left as well. On the left there is this perennial oscillation between moderation and extremism that is also part of Italian history (interview with the author).

This takes us to the role of *trasformismo* in the sphere of production.

---

[1] Army general responsible for a massacre among rioters in Milan in 1898.

TRASFORMISMO AND THE PRODUCTION PROCESS

Like any other form of class rule, *trasformismo* is to be understood as a historical structure constituted by ideological elements, material capabilities and institutions (Cox 1981). The realm of production thus both shapes and is shaped by this particular form of hegemony. In fact, it can be argued that *trasformismo* is the specific form that capitalist modernity has taken in a semi-peripheral latecomer capitalist state such as Italy, characterized by a strong territorial dualism, a weak legitimacy of the state (coupled with its weak fiscal capacity) and an entrenched network of petty bourgeois elements resisting capitalist centralization and concentration (Becattini 2000).

Italy's insertion into the international sphere is considered by economic historians to be weak and particularly vulnerable (Graziani 1989; 1998: Vianello 1979; Fumagalli 2006). As capitalist development remained highly dependent on the import of raw materials and technology, a constant in the economic culture of the postwar ruling classes has been their readiness to unreservedly adhere to international agreements favouring trade liberalization. Ever since the early postwar years, the country has extensively liberalized trade, more deeply and rapidly than most other European countries (Barba 2011), whilst the goal of monetary stability served as the cornerstone of the Bank of Italy's policy whenever wage increases (as in 1963 or 1969) threatened to disrupt the equilibrium in the balance of payments (Paggi and d'Angelillo 1986: 134). Whenever there was a wage push generating inflation, a strong deflationary move (either monetary or fiscal) was the response. This phenomenon, coupled with the failure to create a formal industrial relations system, signals the marginalization of working class interests from the political mainstream. Indeed the Italian ruling class, in contrast to most other countries in continental Europe, considered the working class (both politically and in industrial relations) as an inherently subversive social force.

The origin of the much-debated *external constraint* of the Italian economy is the idea that the country must maintain an equilibrium in its balance of payments because of its 'natural' vulnerability in the international economy. The objective was to enhance exports in order to pay for much-needed imports of raw materials and technology (Vianello 1979: 21–2). Barba argues that the political technique of referring to the 'external constraint' was a 'constant in the life of the Republic, in which internal conflicts are resolved, or better avoided, by making use of an external constraint, which depoliticizes them transforming them into non-choices, "facts of life" beyond our control' (Barba 2011: 67). This highlights that the domestic use of the *vincolo esterno* was an important aspect of the dominant 'common sense' assumptions concerning Italy's insertion into the international sphere (Bradanini 2012), and a key tenet of the strategy of *trasformismo*, aimed at keeping the balance of class forces under control.

In the absence of a technologically advanced industry, an export market can be conquered only by price competition, which requires productivity increases to offset wage increases (Graziani 1998: 9). This element was at the root of the Italian economic miracle of the 1950s and 1960s, characterized by a strong currency, high capital-intensive investments, price stability and equilibrium in the balance of payments (until the shock of the late 1960s). On the other hand stability was ensured by the strict containment of wage rises, repression in the workplace, exclusion of the Left from government, and the marginalization of trade unions (Graziani 1998: chapters 1 to 3). The low wages of Italian workers, the high propensity to save and the corporatist and non-universalistic nature of the welfare state had a detrimental effect on the growth of the internal market; the country's reliance on the international economy was enhanced by making growth dependent on the dynamics of external instead of domestic demand (Fumagalli 2006: 61; Amyot 2004: chapter 2). Hence the 'common sense' assumption regarding the country's insertion into capitalism was that Italy suffered from a structural economic vulnerability and, so the argument went, as a result laboured under the perennial imperative of keeping wages low lest the country face a disequilibrium in the balance of payments (Bradanini 2012). Thus the state's anti-Keynesian bias was rooted in the composition of the DC's 'historic bloc'.

The weakness of the trade unions and their marginalization, a distribution of income unfavourable to labour, the clientelistic distribution of state spending by the DC regime, and the nature of the balance of payments, Vianello points out, were factors that must be understood as *internally* linked. Low wages, the lack of a comprehensive welfare regime and the alienation of large sectors of the working class were compensated by clientelistic state spending as an instrument of social control. What crystallized as a result was a view of Italian capitalist development in which its key characteristics were seen as, 'on the one hand, openness to foreign trade and the quest for the maximum "efficiency", neglecting the problem of unemployment; on the other, the control of social tensions through the clientelistic use of public spending' (Vianello 1979: 23).

As wages systematically lagged behind productivity growth and the fiscal system operated in an inequitable fashion, general economic growth did not translate into significant real wage growth. Profits increased, and other forms of income also benefited from economic growth: in particular, the traditional middle classes supporting the DC regime (the petty bourgeoisie, notables and landowners) were granted considerable privileges (in addition to tax evasion, a widespread tolerance towards the breaching of laws concerning employment and the environment). In this sense the strategy of *trasformismo* was at the core of the settlement. Again in the words of Vianello,

> Large-scale participation of the middle classes benefiting economic development not only was made possible but also made indispensable by the 'heavy hand' used against the working class (both in the work relationship and in the fact that its political representatives were confined in opposition). Precisely because consent could not come from the working class, it had to rest upon the mass of farmers on the one hand, and on the urban middle classes on the other. What has been called the distortion of consumption was the outcome of a distribution of income that was equally distorted (ibid.: 28).

This point goes to the heart of what is argued here. The strategy of *trasformismo* was not only the *political* means by which to maintain the power of a specific historical bloc, but also lay at the base of the *economic* strategy of the dominant classes.

This logic reflects a specific political economy of production. In contrast to most European countries, Fordism – as a particular configuration of the capital–labour relation and a cycle of development based on high wages, unions incorporated into the regulation of the political economy, and relatively rigid employment conditions – only partially developed in Italy. It was largely confined to the industrial north-west and to capital-intensive industries: steel, the engineering and automobile sectors, as well as the state-controlled IRI (*Istituto di Ricostruzione Industriale*), through which public investment flowed to the centre and the south of the country.

As a result Italian capitalism, unable to develop an internal cycle of effective demand management, has been consistently more dependent on the international market than on the domestic one. As Tarrow notes, 'the economy had a small internal market that made it susceptible to recession at every international downturn' (Tarrow 1990: 319). The productive structure reflected this dependence: parallel to a small number of large firms (in the steel, engineering and automobile sectors, the 'Fordist' component of Italian capitalism), there was an extensive network of small enterprises based on a flexible employment structure. Here, national employment contracts were often not respected, workers were scarcely unionized, a paternalistic firm culture remained intact, and there was a constant circulation of workers between industry and countryside, so that most of the family continued to depend on independent agricultural production and wages could be kept low. In addition this ensured flexibility in case of a downturn, as workers could easily be laid off and return to work in the fields (see Roccas 2004). Crucially, it was again the strategy of *trasformismo* that managed to keep this phenomenon of early industrialization alive: tax evasion, lax enforcement of employment laws and clientelistic practices protected these sectors from the tendency towards centralization and concentration inherent to capitalism.

Thus, in major respects the Italian economy was *not* Fordist (on Fordism, see Lipietz 1987, and Desai, this volume). The automation of production in large-scale industries, a typical Fordist–Taylorist phenomenon and one that tends to generate a particular form of worker consciousness (which of course can still be canalized politically in different ways) was therefore not very developed in Italy, crucially affecting the political strategies available to the Left.

Extensive trade liberalization, the lack of an autonomous internal demand, and dependence on the international economy for raw materials and export markets were seen as dictating narrow 'limits of the possible': wage deflation and the fight against inflation per se (and not against its social origin in class conflicts – see Streeck 2011) were seen as the main goals by all political forces, including the Left. The 1960s were the turning point: in 1963 a first wave of strikes erupted in the north. The Italian working class was largely politically alienated and in contrast to other European countries, was still committed to a radical transformation of society. The bourgeoisie in turn reacted to class struggle in a defensive way, inaugurating a 15-year-long 'investment strike' that began right in 1963 (De Cecco 2004: 32).

There was no attempt (apart from a belated and unsuccessful proposal in the mid-1970s by Giovanni Agnelli of Fiat) to develop an incomes policy based on what Streeck (2011) calls a 'political exchange' – one between welfare protection and policies geared to full employment on the one hand, and wage moderation on the other. Here one can see how a constant in the culture of the Italian ruling classes presents itself at key turning points: industrial conflict is considered to be inherently 'subversive' and there is no attempt to incorporate it into well-defined 'rules of the game', as in West Germany for instance. The political reaction of Italian capital in the 1960s and 1970s tended to express itself in the continued exclusion of the Left and the 'strategy of tension', the use of terrorism, presumably by the state apparatus and the secret services, and aimed at maintaining social control and isolating the Left. Meanwhile the economic reaction was a process of restructuring that sought to undermine working class power.

In the late 1960s a process of fundamental industrial restructuring set in. With investment falling, large industries were gradually dismantled. The strength of the industrial working class in the Fordist sectors of the economy was more and more seen as a threat to the established order, to which a fragmentation of production in more complex product chains, involving networks of SMEs, was deemed the appropriate response. In fact the origin of the often praised Italian model of 'industrial districts' and of 'diffused industry' resides in a capitalist strategy to dismantle the entrenched power of industrial workers in the large factories. This was carried out in a decade (the 1970s) that witnessed the surge of leftist political terrorism in Italy, expressing the profound alienation of sectors of the working class from the political system and thus confirming the ruling class perception of the inherent subversiveness of the Italian labour movement – a perception that was belatedly incorporated within the culture of the main Left party itself.

The move to neoliberalism in 1980s Italy as a result was characterized by a particular twist, with the logic of *trasformismo* reproducing itself under different circumstances. Clientelistic spending (coupled with the low fiscal capacity and hence, limited redistributive capacity of the state, Barba 2011) was maintained as a strategy to help enterprises lay off large parts of their labour forces (for example through the extensive resort to premature retirement, so-called 'baby pensions') and decentralize production, thus promoting the jobless growth that is a key feature of the turn to neoliberalism.

Italy emerged from the 1970s as a unique case among Western political economies. The strategy pursued by Italian capital in the subsequent decade was that of coupling an aggressive post-Fordist decentralization with currency devaluation. While large enterprises, controlled by the ruling parties, the DC and the PSI (Italian Socialist Party) lost ground, SMEs producing niche products blossomed, most notably in the northeast, thanks to a permissive tax and labour standards regime. These firms based their success on a strong product innovation, low labour costs, an aggressive export strategy and post-Fordist product chains (Roccas 2004: 115). Thus the core of the organized working class diminished in size and strength, as the formal industrial relations system was applied only in the large enterprises (itself a feature of *trasformismo*, De Cecco 2004: 33). In the 1990s the remaining state-owned large firms were privatized and sold either to foreign investors or to important Italian industrial groups, maintaining the essentially family character of Italian capitalism (the national highways, for instance, were sold to Benetton, who were able to reap extensive profits from this natural monopoly).

TRASFORMISMO AND THE DEFEAT OF THE LEFT

Let us now turn to how the logic of *trasformismo* played out in the culture of the Italian Left itself. Here it is important to understand the dynamics that were at the origin of the peculiar interpretation of the country's political economy developed by the PCI. As noted, the Italian bourgeoisie, unlike other national bourgeoisies in Europe, has tended to react in a conservative, if not outright reactionary way to demands for social reform. The political marginalization of the PCI went hand in hand with the 'economic' marginalization of the CGIL and the deflationary and anti-Keynesian bias described above.

The exclusionary logic of *trasformismo* in turn generated a culture on the Left that was marked by the combined and contradictory elements of *hyper-identification* and *economic moderation* (Paggi and d'Angelillo 1986). Hyper-identification refers to the role played by the myth of socialism embodied by the Soviet Union in a national political context in which the PCI did not enjoy political legitimacy and was constantly attacked on account of its loyalty to the Soviet model. The lack of mutual recognition among the main parties made the constant re-affirmation of this identification a necessity; which in turn contributed to putting in doubt the democratic credentials of the PCI (ibid.: 101). Economic moderation was one of two elements in the PCI's political–economic culture; it refers to the tendency to exchange unilateral wage concessions for political legitimacy. This stance was legitimated by the second element, the idea of a fundamental incompatibility of gains by labour, wider welfare entitlements and full employment, with a capitalist economy. This then lay at the heart of the transformation of the Left, and the party's readiness to accept 'sacrifices' on behalf of its social base in times of 'economic emergency'.

There is thus an important difference between the PCI and the Social Democratic parties in other European countries, one I consider central to the argument developed here. In the words of Paggi and d'Angelillo, 'While the social-democratic trade-off tends to exchange moderation in social conflict with direct or indirect increases of the real salary, the communist one always tends to see a broader recognition of its legitimacy as the adequate compensation' (1986: 102). In the PCI's dominant culture, the labour movement's autonomous claims were perceived as subversive and menacing, potentially triggering reactionary tendencies of the bourgeoisie. Thus the party at key moments in Italian history promoted restraint, domesticating class struggle in order not to 'provoke' the bourgeoisie. This stance was gradually internalized into the party's culture. Hence, instead of the contractual perspective of the social-democratic tradition, the idea of the necessity of sacrifices on the part of the working class was seen almost as inevitable – *as long as the capitalist order remained in place*. Under these circumstances a political contract, exchanging the acceptance of capitalist social relations for wider welfare entitlements, was basically rejected. The party was thus unable to develop an autonomous programmatic position and has been available to be co-opted in large coalitions whenever it was called on to share 'national responsibility', in national unity with other parties.

Looking at the political responses to the crisis today, one cannot avoid a feeling of *déjà vu*. It is certainly not the first time that political representatives of the Left and organized labour have identified the need for 'sacrifices' as the necessary solution for economic recovery in order to 'save the country' (a peculiar anti-Keynesian logic if one thinks about it, cf. Mazzetti 2012a; 2012b). In fact, at two other crucial turning points in recent Italian history, the main party of the Left *and* the trade unions together approved and accepted tough policies of wage restraint and fiscal rigour in the name of 'national unity' and in the face of 'economic emergency'.

The first episode came at the end of the 1970s, when in the face of mushrooming inflation, economic crisis and terrorism, the PCI entered into the governing orbit (the governments of 'national emergency'). The literature underlines that, notwithstanding major concessions on the part of organized labour in the form of wage restraint and guarantee of social peace, the 'political exchange' was heavily skewed in favour of capital (Golden 1988: chapter 3). Yet Trentin, the secretary of CGIL in those years, argued that the importance of the unilateral wage moderation of the late 1970s resided in the union's 'clear dissociation from the previous, basically contractarian philosophy, which inspired the relations between the union and political power and which is still dominant in most countries in Europe'. The important fact about this stance is the overcoming of a logic by which 'the unions, in order to become protagonists of a new economic policy, believe that certain compensations are to be demanded from capital' (Trentin 1980: 182).

In the course of the 1970s, Enrico Berlinguer, the general secretary of the PCI, introduced terms like *rigour, tough effort, exceptional strain* and *austerity* into the lexicon of the Left. The president of the Republic at the time of writing, Giorgio Napolitano, was a convinced supporter of Berlinguer's line, which climaxed in a famous speech given in 1977 entitled 'Austerity: a chance to transform Italy'. In it Berlinguer presented austerity as a 'forced yet enduring choice, the condition for the "salvation" of the people of the West and, in particular, the Italian people'. For him, invoking austerity meant 'abandoning the illusion that it is possible to perpetuate a model of development based on the overblown and artificial expansion of individual consumption that is the source of waste, parasitism, privileges, profligacy of resources, financial disarray' (Berlinguer 1977). He also proclaimed, in an almost messianic tone: 'we, thus, take on the flag of the fight against inflation!' (cited in Paggi and d'Angelillo 1986: 20). Giorgio Amendola, leader of the 'social-democratic' current of the PCI, went so far as to argue that 'sacrifices are demanded by the state of affairs and are not negotiable. They are a necessary condition which transcends the interests of single social groups' (cited in ibid.: 11).

The second episode of moderation for the sake of national unity occurred at the beginning of the 1990s when, in the face of a deep recession and a speculative attack on the Italian currency, the lira, the social partners signed a tripartite deal institutionalizing for the first time a system of collective bargaining, incomes policy and the inclusion of the trade unions in a system of shared decision-making (Mania and Orioli 1993; Carrieri 1997; Baccaro 1999; Ciampi 1996). Yet in this instance too, the compensations offered to labour were disproportionately small and there was little 'political exchange' (Regalia and Regini 2004; Negrelli 2000). Social peace was guaranteed (see ISTAT 2003 for data on the significant decrease of strikes) and wage restraint was locked in, producing the largest wage slump in Italian postwar history, with labour losing 7.5 per cent of its share of GDP between 1992 and 1998 (Brancaccio and Passarella 2012: 48; a compression, and even *decrease* of real wages has been confirmed by economic analyses such as Tronti 2005, Ghiani and Binotti 2011, and Stirati and Levrero 2002). Crucially when this happened, the PCI supported the government in parliament, and its heir in the 1990s, the PDS (Democratic Party of the Left), would actually be part of the governing coalition.

The interpretation that the strategy of *trasformismo* pursued by the dominant parties in Italy signals a lack of hegemony and bourgeois weakness and backwardness was all along the dominant view of the PCI (see Michelini 2008). Yet according to Paggi and d'Angelillo, this view not only fails to acknowledge the inherently exclusionary dynamic of *trasformismo* vis-à-vis the working class (in the sense of both co-opting working class groups and denying it political legitimacy); it also does not recognize its modern nature. The strategy of *trasformismo* in the perception of the PCI leadership flowed from a supposed lack of bourgeois hegemony, which the ruling classes compensated by trying to contain a working class movement that, compared to other European states, was much stronger. However, this interpretation neglects the fact that in Italy the main party of the labour movement never joined the government, unlike what happened elsewhere in Europe.

Likewise clientelism, and corruption as its extreme manifestation, were interpreted on the Left as illicit political manipulation of economic development in a situation of lack of hegemony. Hence, it was argued, the government's punitive politics in matters concerning the welfare state and labour interests generally. But within this frame of reference, as Paggi and d'Angelillo explain, the 'harsh moral critique of the dominant party coupled with the support for a politics of "recovery" (*risanamento*)', were bound to backfire. For such a moralistic stance, 'although intentionally aimed at "cutting the enemy's nails" (shrink the DC), inevitably [had] the effect of weakening the contractual force of the labour movement' (Paggi and d'Angelillo 1986: xiv). Thus,

> the PCI . . . was never a proponent of easy money, inflation, devaluation and large deficits. It recognized that inflation tended to favour business and the petty bourgeoisie and that deficits financed DC patronage schemes. Hence it is possible to understand the commitment of the PDS to meeting the Maastricht criteria as the product of the party's history. It is indeed ironic that the PDS demonstrated a firmer resolve on this issue than the parties of the Right (Amyot 2004: 113).

A further element that must be noted here is the affinity of the PCI with the Bank of Italy. This can be explained by the fact that the Bank was one of the few institutions not controlled by the DC regime. Thus the party was inclined to accept that the financial balance must take precedence in the management of the state, whilst the welfare state was seen as a system of clientelistic management of the social consensus by the DC. The PCI's sympathy for liberal economic thought was also due to the lack of qualified Marxist economists in the party (Amyot 2004: 158). The 'general interest' thus becomes equated with the conservative figure of the 'tax-payer', seen as vulnerable to and potentially harmed by the demands of special interests like the trade unions or other interest groups. As Paggi and d'Angelillo argue, within this framework the critique of the 'economic Right' blends with a condemnation of the 'classic collusion between plutocracy and worker oligarchies' (1986: 128). This position was in fact at the heart of the liberal critique of the DC regime carried out by a generally liberal, centre-left public opinion, epitomized by the figure of Eugenio Scalfari and his magazine *Il Mondo*, and later the newspaper *La Repubblica* (starting from 1978) (Paggi 2003: 86–8).

Another aspect of the PCI's culture we need to underline is the notion of 'progressive democracy' (Curiel 1973). The way the PCI interpreted the relationship between socialism and democracy was to conceive of the battle for democracy as a progressive path that would lead to socialism. 'Democracy' and 'socialism' in the eyes of the party cadres went hand in hand. Certainly there was also, in the background, a persistent idea that democracy and capitalism are fundamentally incompatible, inherited from the Third International (and paradoxically resurfacing in the 1970s in the discussions about the crisis of democracy and the contradiction between capital accumulation and its legitimation: see Crozier et al. 1975).

Democracy was thus consistently understood as a 'subversive' element within a capitalist society. Indeed in the discussions in the PCI during the 1940s, Togliatti opposed economic planning, arguing that this could be done only in an *already* socialist country under workers' control. The dissociation between democracy and the market thus generated a non-contractual perspective on the relations between classes in the politics of the PCI, and thus 'an idea of the general interest as something necessarily opposed to conflict' (Paggi and d'Angelillo 1986: 113).

In the 1980s, the PCI gradually came to accept all the tenets of a liberal critique of the First Republic and of the *cattocomunista* constitution of 1948 (catholic-communist, hostile towards the market; Paggi 2003). This critique was developed most prominently within the PSI, which not by chance was also the leading neoliberal party in Italy in that decade and the cradle from which Silvio Berlusconi emerged. Together with the fall of the First Republic and the transformation of the PCI in the early 1990s, the discourse of an Italian political system marked by clientelism, corruption and political interference imposed on a decent and honest civil society took hold. Seeing civil society in these terms was obviously an organic accompaniment to the neoliberal drive of the 1990s (marked by privatizations, a restrictive monetary regime and the rise of unemployment), a decade under the political hegemony of centre-left governments. Politics increasingly became perceived, also on the Left, as the sphere of corruption. 'The sphere in which consensus is organized is that in which the process of *lottizzazione* [distribution of slices of the state apparatus among the parties] takes place' (Paggi 2003: 81. On the liberal attack on the PCI in the 1980s, apart from Paggi, see Michelini 2008). Thus emerged the emphasis in the new culture of the Left on the importance of strengthening civil society vis-à-vis the parties and the state. There was no reflection on the evolution of parties as such; it was not by chance that initially, the new political formation taking the place of the PCI was informally labelled 'the thing' and that the term 'party' was altogether removed from its name, re-emerging only in the late 2000s in the 'Democratic Party'.

In the early 1990s the 'perfect storm' broke loose, in a destructive climax of different social processes. Civil society *against* the state: that was the main thrust of the neoliberal revolution. In Italy, at the ideological level, the process obtained its key rallying cries in *giustizialismo*, of which the *Clean Hands* season of the early 1990s was the obvious manifestation; the culture of the referendum and direct democracy *against* the political elite; anti-party ideology, as well as the success of new anti-establishment forces such as the Lega Nord. The post-communist party leadership chose to exploit this ideology.

However, the liberal anti-party ideology under whose aegis the PCI dissolved has had deep consequences in terms of the very concept of the Left in a transformed national political competition and international context. The post-communists abandoned the central issues that had been inherited from the 1970s crisis: the exhaustion of the kind of party organization built by Togliatti's generation of party cadres, the organization of social demands within a modern welfare state, a redefinition of the very concept of socialism in changed historical circumstances. In its place came a view of the crisis of Italian politics largely based upon a critique of political corruption of the political parties and of the institutions of the First Republic (including, crucially, the proportional electoral system). Thus, a critique of *political* society instead of *civil* society, which obfuscates the power relations inherent in a capitalist political economy.

Finally, the demise of the PCI must be seen also through the lens of a molecular transformation of the post-1968 culture of the Left. The 1991 turning point was both the consequence and a further propellant of a liberal–anarchic ideology that exalts a form of possessive individualism geared to the immediate realization of increasingly marketized needs and an instantaneous enjoyment devoid of any form of shared responsibility (Recalcati 2010). All those that attacked the PCI from the Left (from the *giustizialisti* around the monthly *Micromega* to the new social movements, and including the daily, *Il Manifesto*) were paradoxically giving birth to a form of culture that underlined the intellectual critique of the so-called bourgeois domination, in the name of a liberation from the prohibitions and the oppressions that have haunted the impulsive authenticity of individuals. In a typical practice of co-optation, the discourse of 1968 was incorporated into capitalist ideology.

However, the material forms of domination in Italian society are *not bourgeois* – if what is meant by this term is the cultural practice of the bourgeoisie as a social class, with its conservative and patriarchical elements – but *capitalist*, referring to the objective and impersonal social force which imposes its logic of accumulation, 'production for production's sake', on society's reproductive needs. Once neoliberalism had succeeded not only in deflecting the critique of 1968, but also in incorporating it as an active element of its own ideology, the liberation of the individual from bourgeois domination becomes one of the hegemonic notions of a society conceived as an atomized world of individuals. Each one of them is cast as free to pursue his/her life project unhindered by others, or by the oppressive power of state bureaucracies, or by traditional moral norms. It is an increasingly unstable and crisis-prone 'market' which functions as sole arbiter of each individual's 'freedom' – once again conceived almost exclusively as consumer freedom rather than freedom to collectively control the means of production and the social relations developed anarchically through the market mechanism.

This stance has been entirely internalized by the Italian Left, also in many of its radical manifestations. The critique of capitalism all too often becomes a critique of authority in general, attacking any form of social constraint in the name of a liberated anti-Oedipus. As Tony Judt remarks, in the 1970s 'the angry protests of the proletariat against capitalist exploiters gave way to light-hearted and humorous slogans calling for sexual freedom' (Judt 2011: 67), a sort of aesthetic critique of bourgeois society, one that, moreover, is increasingly incorporated into the restored ideology of possessive individualism, instead of a reasoned diagnosis of the new forms of exploitation and economic domination.

Once the Left has internalized a critique of its own party tradition in the name of post-1968 liberalism and has distanced itself from an understanding of capitalism as a totality, all that remains is to liberate the individuals' potential within the market. Thus, it is perhaps not by chance that of the four 'technical' or centre-left prime ministers of the 1990s (all of them supported by the Left in parliament), two came from the Bank of Italy (Ciampi and Dini), one was an economics professor (Prodi) and the fourth (Amato) was a staunch critic of the 'consociational' political system of the First Republic and of the political interferences into civil society (see Amato 1992). As the former centre-left minister of the economy, Padoa-Schioppa, has argued, the goal of centre-left governments is to

> let the market do its job, limiting public intervention to what is strictly necessary in order to achieve that goal and to what is required by public compassion . . . attenuate the gamut of protections that were constructed in the course of the 20th century and that have progressively distanced the individual from direct contact with the harshness of life, from the ups and downs of fate and from the sanctions and rewards to his flaws or qualities (*Corriere della Sera*, 26 August 2003).

CONCLUSION

The dominant economic tradition of the Italian Left has generated the long-standing idea that the labour movement with its autonomous claims and demands can represent a subversive element within a harmonic view of the 'general interest' and the logic of 'national unity' in government. The PCI thus found itself defenceless against the strategy of *trasformismo* aimed precisely at its political marginalization and cyclically accepted a compromise of unilateral sacrifices in exchange for political legitimacy.

In the PCI this stance co-existed with the socialist myth. The reasoning, according to the dominant economic culture within the party, was that substantial advances of labour were fundamentally incompatible with a national capitalist order, and would only be possible under socialism. In the meantime, so the argument went, 'we' must swallow the bitter pill. Abjure the socialist myth, and what remains is today's neoliberal Left. The party dissolved under the assault of liberal culture, and internalized that very culture, leaving the door open to anti-political populism *à la* Beppe Grillo (a tendency bred, strangely enough, by the very Left when it chose to ride the 'justicialist' corruption-bashing but essentially liberal culture of the 'clean hands').

Thus, in the new ideological stance of the Left, civil society is increasingly seen as an autonomous realm, the sphere of liberty vis-à-vis the world of formal politics. The logical outcome of such a fluid view of social relations in civil society is that political competition becomes increasingly void of social antagonism. The utopia of democracy is precisely the idea of competing 'for' something without fighting 'against' someone. The maximum form of conflict that was carried out was the temporary personification of that someone in the part of the 'evil one' (i.e. Berlusconi).

In the new culture of the 1990s Left, *Berlusconismo* has taken the place of fascism and obscured the transformations of real social relations. The narrative is now that against a pre-modern Right, one has to answer with a modern Left. Arguably, however, what has emerged is a *post-modern* Left that has abandoned the claim to represent a *part* of society and unambiguously embraces the 'general interest' understood in a novel, neoliberal way. In its quest for 'the new', the post-communists in the 1990s have attempted to reset the past to zero and start all over again, with a so-called new beginning. Having internalized a liberal-democratic critique of their own tradition, the post-communists appear to be in the process of re-interpreting the sedimented history of their political party as a liability to be discarded as soon as possible.

The liberal economic positions and the policies that followed from them have likewise been a consequence of this choice. Gramsci's historical lesson concerning the need to organize politically in civil society with a view to conquering political society has been forgotten: the goal now is to separate a vicious and corrupt political society from a virtuous civil society. What has been relegated to the background is an entire trajectory of the Left that – organized in a political party – proposed an alternative modernity on the basis of a 'scientific' analysis of reality, one that refused abstract notions of freedom and justice and instead deployed on the battlefield of class struggle.

14. Flexibilization of labour in the European Union

Otto Holman

STRUCTURAL UNEMPLOYMENT AND THE POLITICAL BUSINESS CYCLE

Labour market flexibilization has been at the heart of the 'extended relaunch' of European integration (the completion of the Single Market and the introduction of the euro in 2002) from the start in the 1980s. Yet the parallel Europeanization of labour market policies, via the European Employment Strategy and the Lisbon strategy, has been non-binding, which has contributed to its partial failure. This chapter argues that the 2008 banking crisis, turned into a sovereign debt crisis, has triggered structural reforms at the member state level which otherwise would have been impossible. In what is best understood as a Kaleckian political business cycle, the austerity crisis today is being used to impose further neoliberal reform, euphemistically referred to as a 'Europe 2020 Growth Strategy'.

The dominant explanation of structural unemployment has long been one in terms of a lack of labour market flexibility. However, this has been contested time and again, even by mainstream commentators. In a 1996 study for the Dutch Ministry of Social Affairs and Employment by the *Deutsches Institut für Wirtschaftsforschung* (DIW), a Berlin-based research institute with Social Democratic credentials, it was argued that institutional and legal labour market rigidities cannot account for the post-1970s rise of structural unemployment. The so-called 'institutional rigidities thesis' wants us to believe that national labour markets have been structurally unable to adjust to changing product markets fast enough and that only a reduction in employment protection (by flexibilization at both the macro-economic and enterprise levels) can guarantee a return to full employment. But the DIW report argued that these rigidities 'have not significantly increased but rather declined since the 1970s, and the pace of structural change has not accelerated in the 1980s, compared to the previous decade' (DIW 1996: S5, 24–7).

This conclusion is even more true today. Blaming labour market rigidities for structural unemployment and expecting that national flexibilization programmes will provide a panacea for the European unemployment crisis does not add up (Grahl and Teague 1990: 186ff; Overbeek 2003). Indeed, as Gregg and Manning argued in 1997, deregulation of labour markets might even result in higher unemployment, 'primarily because they are likely to be monopsonistic in nature for those groups of workers who are most prone to unemployment' (Gregg and Manning 1997: 419).

So why did the European Commission initiate a European Employment Strategy (EES) based on a comprehensive labour market flexibility programme nevertheless? Here it is worth remembering that the Europeanization of labour market policies coincided with the austerity race triggered by the EMU convergence criteria formulated at the Maastricht summit of 1991. In order to be eligible for eurozone membership, member states had to bring down inflation rates, fiscal deficits and state debts to agreed levels. The slackening of growth that would result from this convergence race should then be accompanied by a decrease in employment protection. To explain this mechanism of imposing discipline on labour through austerity we may recall the famous essay of 1943 by the Polish Marxist economist, Michal Kalecki.

Kalecki here introduces the notion of 'political business cycle' to denote the relationship between government economic policy and the development of the economic cycle. According to this theory, a Keynesian policy of deficit spending may in principle establish full employment even in a slump, but the ensuing boom would conflict with the interests of business, as the disciplinary effect of unemployment gradually subsides and the power of the labour movement accordingly increases. Wage increases will put pressure on profits and business will react by raising prices and/or reducing output. Politically, a bloc of big business and *rentier* interests would therefore put the government under pressure to engineer a recession by means of a restrictive policy. Thus excessive wage and price levels can be brought back into equilibrium with productive capacity: 'The pressure of all these forces, and in particular of big business, . . . would most probably induce the Government to return to the orthodox policy of cutting down the budget deficit. A slump would follow in which Government spending policy would come again into its own' (Kalecki 1943: 330).

Of course Kalecki's analysis reflects the time in which he lived. Apart from a touch of economic determinism and perhaps an overemphasis on intentionality, Kalecki wrote about national government. In today's Europe, business has moved across borders, and government is better understood as transnational governance. National governments must deal with external European pressures as well as with domestic business demands, and 'Europe' largely stands for the demands of transnational business. Also, Kalecki's focus was on the artificial creation of unemployment; his analysis predated the comprehensive labour protection schemes of the postwar period. What is at stake today is labour market flexibilization rather than unemployment per se, which is a precondition to it. Finally, Kalecki's analysis rested on the assumption of a strong labour movement, whereas today's dismantlement of employment protection is enabled by a spectacular, indeed historic decline in the negotiating power of trade unions. Yet the current crisis may very well turn into what Klaus Dräger calls a 'political business cycle revisited' (Dräger 2011: 31ff).

The political business cycle Kalecki referred to was the one starting with the Great Depression of the 1930s. It laid the foundations of the subsequent New Deal and the Fordist mode of regulation (see Desai, this volume), developments he could not have foreseen; ditto, the postwar 'reconstruction of Europe'. In the contemporary European world the disciplining of labour can be realized through a wide variety of measures, with different components of the European welfare state key among them. Keynesian demand management opened up the epoch of political business cycles; Kalecki was the first to highlight that by utilizing monetary and fiscal operations, the state had the means to actually create a situation of stable full employment. However, the fact that states occasionally used monetary and fiscal instruments pro-cyclically, to deepen a slump, suggests that they were inclined to prioritize class discipline over short-term profits and to ensure that labour would not be able to use full employment to put upward pressure on wages, and hence structural downward pressure on profits.

Today, the Keynesian state in this respect has been merged into a European structure of governance. National states are entrusted with the execution of neoliberal regulation prescribed by the EU – with the dismantlement of welfare state structures in general and labour flexibilization in particular at the heart, even though resistance against abolishing social security proved more resilient than expected in most member states including the southern eurozone countries. It took the credit crunch and subsequent sovereign debt crisis for a Kaleckian political business cycle to really take off, or better, to spill over from Germany to the so-called peripheral eurozone states of southern Europe. Under the banner of austerity, a veritable 'assault on an entire social contract' ensued. According to Malcolm Sawyer, the 'argument for dealing with budget deficits has provided cover for attacking wages and benefits' and indeed for attacking the last among the 'rigid' labour market structures to the benefit of European competitiveness (quoted in Chakrabortty 2013).

I first turn to the earlier strategy to structurally reform European labour markets, introduced ten years before the outbreak of the credit crunch.

THE EUROPEAN EMPLOYMENT STRATEGY: THE PRIMACY OF COMPETITIVENESS

The Luxembourg Extraordinary European Council Meeting on Employment in November 1997 for the first time introduced a coordinated strategy. Four broad guidelines lend structure to the EES (European Council 1997, passim).

- Improving 'employability', among others by moving from passive to active labour market policies and promoting lifelong learning. Active labour market policies include reforms of tax and social security policies (aiming at an increase of the gap between minimum wages and unemployment benefits), making it 'more attractive' for the unemployed to take up jobs.
- Developing 'entrepreneurship' by making it easier to start up and run businesses and making the taxation system employment-friendly.
- Encouraging adaptability of businesses and their employees by modernizing the organization of work, including flexible working arrangements, and by incorporating into national law more adaptable types of contract.
- Strengthening the policies for equal opportunities: tackling gender gaps, reconciling work and family life and facilitating reintegration into the labour market. This objective seemed first and foremost directed at increasing employment rates in Europe.

These guidelines were supposed to be followed by the member states in their respective employment policies and to function as a framework for policy convergence. Each member state should provide the Council and the Commission with an annual report, the so-called National Action Programme on Employment, which was supposed to take into account the guidelines while allowing for national particularities. The European Commission was tasked with making best-practice comparisons and distilling specific (but non-binding) recommendations. Two years later, a Peer Review Programme was launched to disseminate best practices of member states in labour market policies. This was aimed at enhancing transferability and mutual learning processes and promoting greater convergence towards the main EU goals (for an early assessment, see Casey and Gold 2005).

Taken together, the Luxembourg guidelines boil down to an attempt to break up national systems of social protection by setting benchmarks for member states. Benchmarking (and related concepts such as best practice, mutual learning, etc.) formally became an integral part of EES through the adoption of the Open Method of Coordination (OMC) at the Lisbon

European Council meeting in 2000 (Zeitlin and Pochet 2005). The origins of this new governance structure can be traced back to previous proposals by the European Commission, which developed them in close partnership with the European Round Table of Industrialists (ERT), the planning body of the leading transnational corporations in the EU (van Apeldoorn 2002). The ERT outlined the method of the subsequent EES and comparable proposals in a 1996 report entitled *Benchmarking for Policy-makers*. It defined benchmarking as 'scanning the world to see what is the very best that anybody else anywhere is achieving, and then finding a way to do as well or better'. Benchmarking, the report holds, is a simple, flexible and above all dynamic process.

> It helps companies and governments to compare their own performance with the best in the world, and to motivate everybody concerned to do better. . . . No organisation today can afford to rest on its laurels in a world where last year's achievements are already gathering dust, remote and irrelevant. . . . Benchmarking succeeds because it works with human nature. It doesn't simply tell people to do better, it shows them how to do so by demonstrating what other people are doing. . . . Benchmarking is non-stop. It is a tool to bring about the continuous improvement and adaptation which are the only means to survival in a continually changing world (ERT 1996: 5).

In practice, 'scanning the world' led to the recommendation to introduce Anglo-Saxon practices of internal and external labour market flexibilization, to motivate workers by reducing social protection, to enhance individual competition (supposedly inscribed in human nature), and to continuously adapt, leading to the 'survival of the fittest'.

The resemblance between the direction of the EES and the proposals of the ERT is hard to miss. The ERT has persistently stressed the need for deregulation and flexibilization of labour markets, ascribing structural unemployment to institutional rigidities and excessive social protection (cf. Holman 2006). Time and again the need for micro-economic, supply-side structural adjustment has been emphasized and legitimized by stressing the need to strengthen European competitiveness. The New Public Management method, aimed at privatizing public services, was, again, to be disseminated with the help of benchmarking. In line with this the ERT on two occasions proposed a European Competitiveness Advisory Group (CAG). The CAG was established in 1995 and was tasked with formulating a 'clear, unambiguous political advice . . . on the major policy priorities that must be carried out in order to improve the European Union's competitiveness' (European Commission 1995).

The composition of the successive CAGs reflects the supply-side thrust. The first, chaired by former Italian prime minister Carlo Ciampi, had seven representatives of transnational business against four trade unionists. CAG-II started in 1997, chaired by the former OECD Secretary-General, Jean-Claude Paye, and again with a majority of business representatives (five) against three of the trade unions (in both cases the group was completed with a small number of representatives from the public sector). In fact, several members were directly recruited from the ERT itself or were former ERT members.

The eight reports of CAG-I and II published between 1995 and the end of 1999 all stress the need to modernize/reform social protection systems. The first report of CAG-II, *Competitiveness for Employment*, for instance, postulates a negative correlation between laws to protect existing jobs and job creation, with only an endnote recording that the trade union representatives were 'not convinced of the evidence of this assertion on the effects of labour laws' (Competitiveness Advisory Group 1997: 210). Even so, this did not keep them from signing the recommendations aimed at dismantling social protection systems, considered an essential part of Europe's ambition to return to the top rank of the world economy. The final report of CAG-II, published in September 1999, summarizes previous recommendations in a list of 20 priorities, including the reform of the 'European social model' in general, and labour market flexibilization in particular. It concludes that 'the Commission must develop high-level benchmarks, with associated targets, to monitor Europe's place in internationalisation and European competitiveness' (Competitiveness Advisory Group 1999: 20).

Thus the CAG's 'operational conclusions', aimed not only at internal competitiveness but also at competitiveness in the global economy, can be read as a blueprint for the strategy launched at the Lisbon European Council meeting of March 2000. Apart from the aforementioned OMC, this summit introduced 'a new strategic goal for the next decade: to become the most competitive and dynamic knowledge-based economy in the world capable of sustainable economic growth with more jobs and greater social cohesion'. The Lisbon strategy, as it came to be known, would follow 'a method of benchmarking best practices on managing change' (European Council 2000).

THE GERMAN *ALLEINGANG*

Let me now turn to the role played by German reunification, first as a lever to achieve a comprehensive overhaul of the corporate liberal class compromise of *Modell Deutschland*, and second, as a neoliberal benchmark for the EU. The transition may be interpreted also as the resurrection of a German *Alleingang* in Europe. This was largely the result of the incorporation of the defunct state socialism of East Germany, which by its sheer scale has come to dominate the further course of European integration. The decision to bankrupt East German industry by a differentiated exchange rate of the two German currencies (1 on 1 for households, 1 on 2 for business) marked the beginning of a downward slide for German labour overall. Unification increased the country's labour force by roughly one-third, with many inadequately trained or otherwise ill-prepared for immediate employment in a capitalist economy (Jacobi and Kluve 2006: 3). In addition, the transformation in Central and Eastern Europe triggered a net capital outflow of DM 234 billion between 1990 and 1997 as German business sought to tap into newly available reservoirs of low-wage labour (Silvia 1999: 84).

The Kohl government's scope for an expansive economic policy was simultaneously reduced by the Maastricht criteria and by the high interest rate policy of the Bundesbank. There was a sustained high level of unemployment in Germany through the 1990s and 2000s (in 2005 the rate peaked at 11.3 per cent and even rose above the peripheral eurozone countries, as in 2006). Only in 2007 did the unemployment rate begin the decline to a level below 50 per cent of the Euro area average (in 2012, Eurostat 2012). This can be largely explained thus from the collapse of the GDR, developments in Central and Eastern Europe and EMU-induced austerity. The initial aim of wage equalization between western and eastern Germany was postponed in 1994, creating a low-wage reserve army of workers that exerted downward pressure on the general wage level (Bruff 2010: 414). In the same period, German union density declined by six full points to 29.8 per cent in 1997 (Silvia 1999: 80).

It was this political business cycle in one country, triggered by the unique external shock that was the collapse of state socialism, which created the prototypical Kaleckian, pro-cyclical fiscal and monetary policy of the Kohl period; the subsequent dismantling of *Modell Deutschland* during the Schröder years, and finally, the Europeanization of German austerity policy to the rest of the eurozone, amplifying the Kalecki cycle on a European scale. As we will see further down, it would take yet another external shock, the credit crunch, to make German Europe the reality that it is today.

Back in 1999 Chancellor Schröder, yielding to pressure from German business (both directly and through the ERT), removed a key barrier to further capital mobility when he announced the abolition of capital gains tax. This tax had so far made it extremely expensive for German capital to divest itself of its corporate holdings, thus hampering its diversification into global markets (van der Pijl et al. 2011: 399).

As a result of these cumulative, mutually reinforcing changes, the position of German labour by the turn of the millennium had weakened to such an extent that the Red–Green government was able to launch the neoliberal Agenda 2010 programme, coinciding with the aforementioned EU Lisbon 2010 strategy. Named after the chairman of the commission that worked out the reform package (the personnel director of Volkswagen, Peter Hartz), the resulting package completely overhauled the postwar West German welfare state. In late 2002 the ministries of labour and economic affairs were merged into a new super-ministry under Wolfgang Clement, a member of the employers' think tank *Initiative Neue Soziale Marktwirtschaft* both before and after his term as minister. This robbed German labour of one of the institutional pillars of the postwar class compromise.

Four neoliberal labour laws were implemented on 1 January 2003 (Hartz I and II), 2004 (Hartz III) and 2005 (Hartz IV). Their different components were all directly borrowed from the benchmarks set by the ERT: labour market 'efficiency' by privatizing employment services; introducing labour flexibility in the form of part-time jobs, 'mini-jobs' and 'midi-jobs' (i.e. low-wage jobs with reduced social security contributions); and a shift from passive to active labour market policies, among others by widening the gap between wages and unemployment benefits (by lowering the latter; Jacobi and Kluve 2006: 7 and passim). Importantly, the Hartz reforms did not include an attack on existing employment protection schemes for core workers in German industry. In fact, Germany maintains one of the most protected permanent (or regular) job markets in the OECD area today (OECD 2013: 86, figure 2.6). At the same time, Germany clearly performs below OECD average when it comes to regulation on temporary work agency or fixed-term contracts (OECD 2013: 92, figure 2.9). This points to the emergence of a dual labour market structure in Germany too, particularly since the 1990s.

Labour market duality, a cornerstone of the Hartz reforms (Jacobi and Kluve 2006: 12–13), is one of three interrelated parts of the more comprehensive reform of *Modell Deutschland* set in motion by Agenda 2010 and continued by the Grand Coalition after the 2005 elections. The second part was the renewed resort to *Kurzarbeit*, a scheme whereby workers of an individual firm accept to work fewer hours and are partially compensated for reduced income by government subsidies (Brenke et al. 2011). In return they may keep their jobs. The third part consisted of a comprehensive wage restraint at the company level. Germany was the statistical outlier when it comes to real wage development in the EU during the period 2001–09; it was the only country experiencing a negative growth of 6.1 per cent (Schulten 2013: 595; cf. Reisenbichler and Morgan 2012).

According to some, this combination of labour market measures has turned Germany from the 'sick man of Europe' into a success story or 'miracle', exemplified by the spectacular decrease of unemployment during the crisis years. A closer look shows a different picture, however. First, the Hartz reforms did not have a significant effect on bringing unemployment down themselves, but they did dramatically increase the amount of precarious jobs and they did contribute to a widening of the income gap, while significantly increasing the percentage of Germans living 'at risk of poverty' (Statistisches Bundesamt 2013). Second, neoliberal reforms were made possible not only in the traditional Kaleckian sense of disciplining labour through unemployment; in the case of Germany, as the short-time work schemes suggest, it was the *threat* of unemployment that could do the job, a clear instance of the structural power of capital. *Kurzarbeit* has been referred to as 'Keynes in *Lederhosen*' because of the government subsidies to compensate for a loss of income (Silvia 2009). It would perhaps be more appropriate to call it 'state support in *Unterhosen*'. One is left wondering how the German government got away with this given the so-called level playing field of the EU Single Market.

Finally, wage restraint did give a boost to German exports at the expense of domestic demand. Current account surpluses then were translated into structural deficits elsewhere, in the process Germany beggaring its eurozone neighbours in the South. All in all the German social market economy has moved 'from social to market' in a relatively short period of time and, strikingly enough, under three different coalition governments. In other words, 'the system of political representation proved sufficiently elastic to ensure *both* the implementation of Agenda 2010 *and* the establishment of the long-term basis for the continuing neoliberalisation of the German political economy' (Bruff 2010: 419). Clearly during the German political business cycle of the 2000s it was the primacy of big business over party concerns that made the massive overhaul of the postwar class compromise possible.

The triple strategy of Hartz reforms, *Kurzarbeit* and wage restraint has been rightly referred to as 'a German answer to the Great Recession' (Brenke et al. 2011). It was obviously not a recipe that could simply be followed by the EU as a whole. On the eve of the planned mid-term review of the Lisbon strategy in 2005, there was in fact general agreement that the targets had not been met. A high-level group chaired by the Dutch Social Democrat and former prime minister, Wim Kok, was expected to once again prioritize European competitiveness. For the 'open method of co-ordination', whilst keeping alive the illusion of the 'persistent plurality of national citizenship regimes', in fact had not managed to empower national governments against domestic social forces defending welfare state achievements. The question of who would lead the process especially concerned labour market flexibilization, because it is both a key component of the neoliberal EMU process and an area of subsidiary member state adjustment. In an 'integrated market governed by fragmented sovereignty', Wolfgang Streeck argues, 'the wielders of that sovereignty compete with one another, in part for the respect of their citizens . . . but most importantly for the allegiance of mobile production factors' (Streeck 1997: 3). In this process the European Commission seeks to subordinate national political and social relations to the exigencies of European capital, removing employment and labour market policies from political accountability and making national governments more responsive to the discipline of market forces. But at the time of the mid-term review, the results of the referenda on the Constitutional Treaty in France and the Netherlands for the time being ruled out any further steps to curtail national sovereignty in the name of 'Europe'.

'ASYMMETRICAL REGULATION' BEFORE THE CREDIT CRISIS

In pursuing a neoliberal strategy, the European Commission, with the ERT in the background, theoretically had the upper hand thanks to a process of asymmetrical regulation. This concept denotes the process in which some policy areas are moved to the supranational, EU level, while others remain reserved to national authorities (see Holman 2004). It implies that the instruments to operate the political business cycle are being shared at these two different levels too. Concretely, this concerns the free market regulation at the EU level through the Single Market and Economic and Monetary Union, and social policy at the national level. However, national governments can no longer use interest rate adjustment to counteract slackening growth because of the primacy of eurozone price stability. The same goes for government spending to manage demand. Needless to say that competitive devaluations through the exchange rate mechanism are past history as well. *Austerity measures, tax regime competition and micro-economic supply-side structural adjustment are the only policy areas left to national governments to correct macro-economic imbalances.*

Labour market flexibilization, which as we saw was an integral part of the attempt to make Europe 'the most competitive economy' under the Lisbon strategy and the Europe 2020 strategy (to which I come back later), is central to the national adaptation to EU exigencies. Just as monetary integration from the 1978 European Monetary System onwards was used in Italy to break up the country's postwar social and political system (Della Sala 2004 and Bradanini, this volume), it has been the strategy of transnational business to modernize the 'rigid' social systems across the EU. With national governments in charge of reforming labour markets, supranational institutions like the European Central Bank (ECB) and the European Commission were to force compliance by governments and, more importantly, domestic social forces. This division of labour depended on a number of postulates to work properly, but precisely in this area EMU proved defective right from the start in 2002. The 'one size fits all' interest rate policy of the ECB led several states to flout the Stability and Growth Pact whilst the Single Market was malfunctioning. In the absence of binding and enforceable agreements, the benefits of deceit were obviously too substantial to resist. By the perverse operation of the common currency covering very different social formations with diverse class balances, the deficits occurring in eurozone economies with a lower productivity came to be financed by banks, mostly from the core EU countries. With labour market regulation one of the last remaining instruments available to states for improving competitiveness, the chances of a common European social policy were obviously minimal.

Thus the idea of 'flexicurity', in which job security is replaced by employment security following the Danish example (Fink 2011; Heyes 2013), was doomed from the start. Flexicurity was to be realized by career guidance, active labour market policies and lifelong learning strategies and the like; in short, the Hartz programme. In exchange for employment security the worker should accept less regulatory rigidity, which must be read as a euphemism for less social protection. In the words of the former Dutch Prime Minister, Jan Peter Balkenende, we should no longer talk about unemployment but refer to 'in between jobs' (Balkenende 2005). However, if in the Netherlands, Germany, or Austria and Finland, flexicurity might still be a realistic format of flexibilization, particularly for highly skilled workers, in the peripheral countries this was a much less feasible policy, if only because of persistently high levels of structural unemployment. Equally the formula worked for some occupational groups, but not for others, and employment security could not be guaranteed for all in a similar way either. The suspicion that flexicurity was a response to slackening labour market reforms at the national level, that is as an ideological device to convince social forces to accept flexibility while promising future security, was confirmed when it faded into oblivion in the wake of the 2008 credit crunch (Heyes 2013).

THE EURO-CRISIS AND THE ASSAULT ON LABOUR IN THE EUROPEAN PERIPHERY

From the above, then, we may conclude that Germany led the way in EU 'reform' because the country had been more successful than other eurozone member states in squeezing workers' pay and conditions. This applies in particular to the 'peripheral countries with weak welfare states, lower real wages, and well-organised labour movements [which] have been unable to squeeze workers equally hard' (Lapavitsas et al. 2012: 23). However, when the credit crisis struck in 2007–08 and the mountain of doubtful securities began to collapse amidst a crisis of confidence in existing financial institutions, most were saved at public expense. It was this bailout operation that set the stage for a concerted assault on the remaining bastions of labour strength in the European periphery.

The system of asymmetrical regulation, already weakened by persistent non-compliance since 2002, was the first victim of the crisis. States have re-appropriated the prerogative of managing their own financial affairs, and bank rescue and bailout operations were conducted by each government separately. Stability and Growth Pact rules were breached without exception, particularly with respect to fiscal deficits and total governments debts. European Central Bank decisions were no longer guided by price stability concerns alone, partly because inflation subsided, partly because saving the system became the overriding objective. Yet these exemptions to the mechanisms of asymmetrical regulation proved temporary. In the course of 2010 a consensus re-emerged on macro-economic austerity and monetary stability, if necessary by applying sanctions. A rapid return to neoliberal practice from before the credit crisis was the aim, this time with less lenient enforcement practices.

The transition from the 2007–08 credit crunch to the 2010 austerity consensus also reveals the full impact of a Kaleckian political business cycle in the EU. By taking on a large slice of bank losses and translating them into sovereign debt, the states involved helped transmute the crisis of speculative *transnational* banking into a *sovereign* debt crisis. The average fiscal deficit of the then 16 eurozone countries rose from 1.5 per cent of GDP in 2008 to 6.9 per cent in 2009 (IMF 2011: 21), with obvious outliers in Southern Europe and Ireland.

The political thrust of bailing out the peripheral states was made clear from the start. When Jean-Claude Trichet, the outgoing president of the ECB, gave his farewell press conference on 6 October 2011, he summed up the programme to be executed to deal with the financial crisis as follows:

> Fiscal consolidation and structural reforms must go hand in hand to strengthen confidence, growth prospects and job creation. The Governing Council therefore urges all euro area governments to decisively and swiftly implement substantial and comprehensive structural reforms. This will help these countries to strengthen competitiveness, increase the flexibility of their economies and enhance their longer-term growth potential. In this respect, labour market reforms are key, with a focus on the removal of rigidities and the implementation of measures which enhance wage flexibility. In particular, we should see the elimination of automatic wage indexation clauses and a strengthening of firm-level agreements so that wages and working conditions can be tailored to firms' specific needs (Trichet 2011).

The unified bloc of big business and *rentiers* that Kalecki spoke about in his paper, in today's political business cycle obtains representation on a European supranational level, with member states obeying the same neoliberal logic. As early as the mid-1970s, intellectuals like Samuel Huntington were addressing the issue of the ungovernability of Western democracies due to the equation of democracy with equality, on the one hand, and the uncontrolled rise of welfare expenditure on the other (Crozier et al. 1975). Both threatened to destabilize 'bourgeois democracy' *from within*. The extended relaunch of European integration, from the Single Market to EMU, together with unfolding patterns of transnational governance and regulation, has turned out to be instrumental in restoring bourgeois democracy *from without*. Business and governments, represented by a unique public–private partnership at the European level, in the process have been able to successfully bypass organized labour and national parliaments. Thus they have managed to structurally reaffirm a class society based on ownership and control of the economically relevant and/or income-generating productive assets in the hands of a small minority in society and unequally distributed across society (Wright 1996). Yet the attack on national welfare systems was never complete, as they proved more resistant to change than the architects of 'multilevel governance' Europe ever imagined. It took an external shock to trigger the final round of 'structural' reforms.

The application of the Trichet programme, then, is taking shape in two different ways. At a generic level, top-down control of national budgets and national reform programmes has become part of the so-called 'European semester', EU jargon for a mechanism that helps to enforce the political business cycle in Europe. Under the heading of 'Strengthening Economic Governance' as part of the Europe 2020 Growth Strategy, a new system is created that is beginning to approximate supranational government. As a direct result, in every member state measures are implemented to boost competitiveness through so-called structural reforms. A closer look shows that these structural reforms boil down to reducing public deficits, further flexibilization of labour markets, and restrictive wage policies (Schulten 2013: 596 and EU Crisis 2014). Thus the eurozone crisis is used to legitimize the current, all-out attack on labour market 'rigidity' and governments certainly appear more successful this time than during the previous two decades. The reduction of Employment Protection Strictness (EPS), as the annual Employment Outlook of the OECD calls it, a.k.a. the relaxation of national 'hire and fire' regulation, has started to affect regular (as opposed to temporary) employment too. Wherever we look – at the ongoing reforms in Spain, at the government of 'technocrats' headed by Mario Monti in Italy (who successfully reduced the difference in legal position between the *precari* and established *posto fisso* workers to the detriment of the latter), or at the Dutch Liberal–Labour coalition preparing an across-the-board reduction of employment protection – we see the same set of reforms, dictated by the sovereign debt crisis. In its latest assessment of EPS in the EU, the OECD is quite explicit in stating that particularly between 2008 and 2013 EPS relaxation has been 'concentrated in countries with the most stringent provisions at the beginning of the period' (OECD 2013: 67).

Second, and even more specifically targeting peripheral members of the eurozone, an externally imposed structural adjustment programme is being applied without reservations or exemptions. Thus the (IMF–EU–ECB) 'troika' is telling the Greek government exactly what has to be done in terms of austerity measures. Again the Trichet programme sums up all the elements of this consensus and it is not difficult to trace it to the German neoliberal reform package discussed above: fiscal austerity, with the implied reduction of public sector employment, labour market flexibilization and private sector wage restraint. In the words of Trichet 'this will help these countries to strengthen competitiveness'.

Spain offers a striking illustration of the perverse operation of asymmetrical regulation in a eurozone established between structurally unequal partners (on Spanish integration into the EU, cf. Holman 1996). Ever since 2002, the Spanish economy experienced above-average annual growth rates. As a result, unemployment fell well below 10 per cent and fiscal deficits turned into surpluses. However, the economic boom was first and foremost based on property and real estate development. The availability of cheap credit following the introduction of the euro fuelled economic growth through deficit spending, creating the proverbial bubble that had to burst sooner or later. Those sectors profiting most from this virtuous circle of deficit-based growth (private banks, construction firms, utilities and telecom companies) were among the sectors hit most severely as a result of the banking and euro crises (López and Rodríguez 2011).

Afterwards, the sovereign debt crisis in Spain (and not only in Spain) was explained by referring to the so-called competitiveness gap within the eurozone. Structural reforms should be implemented in the deficit countries in order to balance trade flows and hence put an end to the German beggar-thy-neighbour policy. Among the structural reforms most often suggested, labour market flexibility and fiscal austerity figured prominently. And this is exactly what the governments in deficit countries have done since 2010. In the case of Spain, this austerity policy was further legitimized by referring to global rating agencies like Standard & Poor's. The 2011 lowering of Spain's long-term rating according to S&P 'reflects. . . the incomplete state of labour market reform, which we believe contributes to structurally high unemployment and which will likely remain a drag on economic recovery' (Standard & Poor's 2011: 2).

CONCLUSION

Most economists will agree today that the real reason for structural adjustment in the eurozone and the EU at large is not the ambition to create more jobs, as business leaders and politicians (and rating agencies) still have it. The real reason is to increase labour market flows and hence productivity (Martin and Scarpetta 2012). This in turn may result in the firing of older employees (the 50+ generation), who then at a later stage of the reform process may have to accept demotions and lower wages and delayed pensions. In the short term, the question whether young entrants will proportionally profit from this development can only be answered by looking at the skyrocketing youth unemployment rates throughout the eurozone, but notably in Greece and Spain (Table 14.1).

As long as the current austerity race among EU member states continues, the prospects for job creation will remain gloomy. Certainly the project of Ever Closer Union will remain an empty shell if labour is isolated and excluded from it. Class and class struggle may have become past history, but it is not unlikely that the next round of struggles in Europe will be fought under the banners of euroscepticism and populism. The EU is in crisis, but it is above all the *social* crisis that is most damaging both for an entire generation of young people and for the process of European integration as a whole. Labour and European integration are intrinsically related, and mediated by what is commonly referred to as *social cohesion*. According to David Mayes, social cohesion is 'the political tolerability of the levels of economic and social disparity that exist and are expected in the European Union and of the measures that are in place to deal with them' (Mayes 1995: 1). One can only speculate about how far this political

Table 14.1 Unemployment, youth unemployment and labour costs in the original six EEC states and the Southern European eurozone states and Ireland, 2008 and 2011

	2008			2011		
	Labour costs in euros	Unemployment		Labour costs in euros	Unemployment	
		General	Youth*		General	Youth
Germany	28.4	7.5	11.2	30.1	5.9	8.6
France	31.8	7.8	23.9	34.2	9.7	22.9
Netherlands	29.2	3.1	7.7	31.1	4.4	7.6
Belgium	35.6	7.0	21.9	39.3	7.2	18.7
Luxembourg	30.8	4.9	16.5	33.7	4.8	15.6
Italy	24.5	6.7	25.4	26.8	8.4	29.1
Spain	18.9	11.3	37.8	20.6	21.7	46.4
Portugal	11.5	7.7	24.8	12.1	12.9	30.1
Greece	16.5	7.7	25.7	17.5**	17.7	44.4
Ireland	27.2	6.3	24.4	27.4	14.4	29.4

Note: *2009 **2010.

Source: Eurostat.

tolerability can be stretched given the increase in economic and social disparity.

A recent report of the European Commission in this connection has drawn alarming conclusions. Divergence between member states is going hand in hand with social polarization within countries; since 2010 the poorest quartile has been affected most by the deepening economic and social crisis in Europe. Long-term unemployment and the risk of long-term exclusion have increased, as well as poverty rates (European Commission 2012). However, political tolerability not only depends on existing or expected rates of polarization and divergence, but also on measures taken both at the national and European levels. The social consequences of austerity in Europe are now discussed beyond the social sciences. Suicide rates are rising because of the financial crisis, and austerity cuts are dismantling healthcare systems everywhere (cf. Chan, Pun and Selden, and Ihara, this volume). Medical journals currently are publishing articles with alarming messages in this connection. Thus preliminary findings of an international group of scholars predict immediate rises in suicides (and a decline in road-traffic fatalities) in response to 'early indicators' of crisis (Stuckler et al. 2011). A more recent article in *The Lancet* confirms this prediction. The findings show a strong correlation between fiscal austerity, the absence of strong social protection mechanisms and the rise of suicides and infectious diseases, particularly in those eurozone countries most affected by (externally imposed) structural reforms such as budget cuts, labour market flexibilization and welfare state retrenchment in healthcare (Karanikolos et al. 2013; see also Brand et al. 2013; for a general assessment of austerity, Blyth 2013).

In today's Federal Republic, supposedly the 'engine of European growth', 16 per cent of the population, or 13 million people, are at 'risk of poverty' (Statistisches Bundesamt 2013). If as I have argued in this chapter, austerity policies 'made in Germany' are being amplified across the EU, this evokes the grim spectre of what lies ahead for all if the trend is not stopped. Otherwise we will have to accept that poverty is back in Europe.

15. Globalization and Japanese-style management: image and changing reality

Ryoji Ihara

Japanese-style management has attracted widespread attention from the period of high economic growth in the 1960s to the zenith of the bubble economy in the 1990s. However, with the slackening of the Japanese economy, the same management style has become a target for criticism and has declined in relevance. The evaluation of how Japanese companies manage their workforces has accordingly fluctuated, depending on general business conditions. Most critical assessments meanwhile are based on a stereotypical image of Japanese behavioural patterns and society, and have therefore failed to grasp the true reality of the workplace. With this in mind, this chapter reviews and assesses studies of Japanese-style management in order to separate fiction from fact. In addition, the chapter will look at those changes that have affected the Japanese workplace in the epoch of globalization, in part based on the author's own direct experience.

JAPANESE-STYLE MANAGEMENT AS COMPETITIVE ADVANTAGE

Research on Japanese-style management began immediately after World War II, with labour relations and social policy scholars focusing on what was distinctive about Japanese work practices. In the prevailing atmosphere of democratization after the war, these practices were typically criticized as pre-modern and regressive. However, James Abegglen (1958), a pioneer of Japanese-style management theory, drew a different conclusion from his investigations into the features that distinguished Japanese labour relations from those of the West. It was from his work that terms like 'lifetime commitment', 'seniority wages' and 'enterprise union' spread among the general public, where they became known as the 'three sacred treasures' of Japanese-style management. If other scholars had already highlighted some of the aspects that made Japanese management practice special, Abegglen's originality resides in his appreciative evaluation of it. His findings and more particularly, his assertion that the peculiarity of

Japanese (or Asian) culture served as the impetus for Japan's economic progress and the modernization of its society after 1945, gained wide resonance, not least in Japan itself, where the positive evaluation of the country by a foreigner was most welcome to a people that had lost much of its self-confidence following the defeat in World War II.

As Japan's economy passed the phase of restoration and entered that of high economic growth, an increasing number of people concerned themselves with Japanese-style management. Thus emerged a broad consensus that the deeper source of the development of Japanese firms resided in Japanese culture. Commentators like Reischauer (1977) and Vogel (1979) concluded from their studies that labour–management cooperation engenders employees' loyalty to *their* company, whilst lifelong employment and the recognized seniority system induce diligent work. This employment system, it was argued, is based on the Japanese mentality that values collectivism, harmony and consensus, each strengthening the others. In that sense the particular mentality born from a long cultural tradition and the system of labour relations came together, reinforcing each other in a virtuous circle.

Whilst early management studies in the slipstream of Abegglen's pioneering work ascribed the features of Japanese labour relations to culture, subsequent research slowly shifted the focus of attention to technical aspects. Indeed Abegglen himself in the 1970s formulated a multi-dimensional matrix of Japanese business strategies. In his model, the government, the business community and individual firms collaborate at the macro-level, whilst labour harmoniously cooperates with management at the level of the company (Abegglen 1970). Peter Drucker (1971) also resisted the cultural approach to Japanese-style management, focusing instead on the economic rationality underlying the employment system and labour practices in Japanese firms, which differed from those in European and American companies. Likewise Ronald Dore in a comparative study observed what he thought was the key difference, illustrating it for Hitachi and English Electric, respectively. The former was characterized by lifetime employment, a seniority-plus-merit wage system, an intra-enterprise career system, enterprise training, enterprise unions, a high level of enterprise welfare, and the careful nurturing of enterprise consciousness. Dore identified each labour practice separately but understood each as an element of an integrated and internally consistent system; Hitachi in his analysis was characterized as an 'organization-oriented' company, whereas English Electric was 'market-oriented' (Dore 1973: 278). Looking towards the future, Dore saw signs that there was a pervasive convergence towards the Japanese pattern across business organizations everywhere.

In the same year that Dore's study appeared, the Organisation for

Economic Co-operation and Development in its assessment of Japan's economy listed high economic growth within a short period and a low unemployment rate as the main factors of its success (OECD 1973). In addition, the OECD indicated that the Japanese employment system was an effective guide for the economic development of other countries struggling with sluggish growth and high unemployment rates. Cole (1981) ascribed the reasons for Japanese car manufacturers' strength to the quality control that all employees, including blue-collar workers, participated in, as well as to information sharing among workers across divisional and hierarchical boundaries. Kenney and Florida, finally, proclaimed the superiority of the Japanese production system over the Fordist production system in terms of productivity and job satisfaction. 'The social organization of Japanese production has overcome many of the institutional rigidities associated with Fordism. Self-managing teams, just-in-time production complexes, and learning-by-doing have replaced the functional specialization, deskilling, and linear production lines of Fordist mass manufacturing' (Kenney and Florida 1993: 49). Hence they pasted the label of *post-Fordism* on the Japanese production system.

Obviously, researchers in Japan also entered the discussion concerning Japanese-style management practices. Their analyses highlighted that the cooperation of workers with management originally depended on the security of employment, and that workers would even accept a worsening of conditions if the company faced adversity. As a result, cooperative labour relations in the long run worked to secure the co-existence of high economic growth and price stabilization. Even after the 1973 oil crisis, when Japan, like other developed countries, faced serious economic difficulties, labour and management joined hands in the effort to overcome them.

This was facilitated by the fact that all regular employees, both blue-collar and white-collar workers, would be organized into a single union that cooperated to overcome the obstacles faced by *their* company. Of course, from a workers' perspective, enterprise unionism could as easily be denounced as failing to meet the criteria for a proper trade union and dismissed as a company tool. Shirai, for one, dismissed this line of critique by arguing that Japanese workers freely choose enterprise unionism and are successful in maintaining their independence and autonomy in representing the interests of workers.

> The enterprise union in Japan, as a single organization of employees of a particular firm, functions in two ways. As the workers' organization, it confronts and resists the employer in order to protect the employees' interests when they conflict with those of the employer. It also cooperates with the employer in promoting the mutual interests of the parties in a particular enterprise (Shirai 1983: 121).

Koike in turn explained the reasons for Japanese companies' competitive advantage from the perspective of developing the skills of blue-collar workers. Factory workers in large Japanese firms acquire important skills that enable them to perform a wide range of jobs. 'Rarely is a worker confined to only one job during his working life with a company. Rather, he would have a series of closely related jobs, and this series would determine the breadth of his skill and how much his wages would increase' (Koike 1983: 50). He further asserted that Japanese blue-collar workers in large firms profited from internal career patterns allowing for promotion into the advanced stages of a working life, and at a high level of remuneration, thus making them similar to white-collar workers in the West – a process therefore called 'white-collarization'.

Asanuma (1985, 1989) looked at Japanese-style management from the angle of stable, long-term transaction patterns linking parent firms and subcontractors. Whilst these relations have conventionally been regarded as a form of exploitation of subcontractors by parent companies, Asanuma evaluated them positively by taking efficiency and interdependence as his criteria. Since parent companies are involved in their subsidiaries' production operations and subcontractors commit themselves to continuous technological improvement, persistent cost reduction and accumulation of 'relation-specific skills', both parent companies and subsidiaries are concerned not only with market price but also with the design process and technological investment, thus sharing the production risk.

Aoki (1988) developed an economic model of Japanese companies based on the studies of Koike, Asanuma and other researchers. The Japanese 'main bank system' stabilizing the financial system promotes long-term business growth. A business relationship based on mutual 'trust' encourages mutually beneficial cost competitiveness and technical improvement. Within an organization with stable labour relations, a 'horizontal information structure' leads to efficient coordination between divisions and workers and 'rank hierarchy' serves as a powerful long-term incentive for hard work. Aoki constructed this Japanese model with reference to an American model, which depicts features of market-oriented organizations.

Finally, Nonaka and Takeuchi (1995) explained the competitive edge of Japanese firms from the perspective of 'knowledge creation'. Corporations trust workers, delegate authority to them and empower them to improve the workplace (*kaizen*). Workers in turn convert the 'tacit knowledge' of the shop-floor into 'explicit knowledge' made available to the corporation, knowledge that can then be shared across the organization. It was this mechanism of creating knowledge, Nonaka and Takeuchi assert, that ensured the competitiveness of Japanese companies in the global market.

In the 1980s, the cultural aspect of Japanese-style management again became the focus of attention. This time round it was not the previously mentioned, Japanese societal culture, but its specific organizational culture. A competitive company by developing a strong corporate culture secures complete employee commitment; Japanese firms with a substantial international presence were found to have precisely such strong corporate cultures. Management consultants and business scholars concerned about the recession in the United States at the beginning of the decade, and studying what made Japanese companies so much more resilient, thought that they discovered the secret of success in the strong corporate culture. This culture worked to integrate employees into an organization comprehensively and closely, whilst representing a source of competitive advantage to Japanese enterprises in their domestic market as well (Ouchi 1981; Pascale and Athos 1981; Deal and Kennedy 1982; Peters and Waterman 1982).

Thus writers debated Japanese-style management from various viewpoints, some treating the peculiarities of the system from a macro-level perspective, others focusing on the shop-floor from a micro-level perspective. And whilst particular authors adopted a technical approach to what makes Japanese enterprises tick, others put the emphasis on the Japanese culture that either secures harmony between labour and management generally speaking, or as a specific corporate culture elicits the commitment of all employees – the one obviously not excluding the other. Yet for all these differences in analytical perspective and the strategic goals animating the research, what practically all authors agreed was that Japanese-style management was radically distinct from conventional management methods. By contrast, the Fordist production system, with its combination of mass production and a mass consumption lifestyle bringing affluence also to the working class, relied solely on assembly-line production. By keeping workers tied to repetitive, dull labour routines, it provoked chronic labour discontent, union resistance to management and high labour turnover. Hence the claim that Japanese-style management was post-Fordist, superior to its competitors on account of the productivity gains made by raising the skills of workers, by allowing them to participate in *kaizen* activity, and by encouraging initiative in a spirit of shared interest.

However, amidst a broad consensus stressing the merits of the system, voices of dissent were noticeable as well. Those researchers who examined Japanese companies from the inside in greater detail, found that the benefits of their management systems tended to be greatly overrated. Thus it was found that work teams were not managed on the basis of egalitarianism at all, and that a majority of factory workers were as exclusively tied to tedious and repetitive assembly-line labour as those in the worst Fordist factories. Many Japanese workers in fact found themselves excluded from 'Japanese-style management' to begin with – indeed the majority of Japan's workforce do not work under that system. Most female workers, non-regular workers, workers in small and medium-sized enterprises (SMEs), and foreign workers do not enjoy anything like the famed secure lifetime employment or the fringe benefits supposedly tied to it. Instead many of them are overtly discriminated against in terms of pay and promotion, and they do not have the opportunity to join a labour union. Instead they face the prospect of abrupt dismissal whenever the corporation's performance no longer warrants their employment.

This broad and diverse category of secondary workers in fact serves an 'efficient buffer' for business fluctuations, and this is also how they see themselves – as peripheral members of the company. Studies based on participant observation, and focusing on the realities of employment conditions and workers' on-site mentality, concluded that these workers do not feel a strong sense of belonging to the organization and neither are they inclined to dedicate their life to a company (Kondo 1990; Roberts 1994; Ogasawara 1998). In this respect a clear division of labour is evident among male workers in large enterprises. At Toyota, Kamata (1993) found a prevalence of arduous, repetitive work persisting at the bottom of the occupational scale. Indeed by its way of subdividing the labour process and in terms of work density, Japanese-style management even takes a step back from the Fordist production system. Thus according to Kato and Steven, 'it is a move back to more primitive forms of social control which are only possible in the context of greatly weakened trade unions and increased divisions among workers' (Kato and Steven 1993: 49). Nomura investigated the division of labour between 'specialists' and 'production-line workers' among blue-collar workers in mass-production workshops. Whereas the former 'are responsible for tasks requiring high skill levels, such as maintaining equipment, inspections, die production, prototype production and so on', the production-line workers are typically engaged in simple, repetitive operations (Nomura 2004: 109–10). Hence his conclusion that the skills of production-line workers have been systematically overestimated by mainstream Japanese-style management theory.

But then, even male college graduates employed in large enterprises do not always work at their own discretion. For all Japanese workers, long working hours and unpaid overtime work are the norm. Undoubtedly, certain employees are satisfied with their jobs and will voluntarily work for long hours without pay. But this does not hold for workers who are being compelled to do so owing to harsh job competition through merit ratings and personnel evaluations, as well as peer surveillance in the office (on the pretext of mutual help). If Japanese employees work diligently, they do so partly because of compulsion, and only partly at their own initiative. At worst, excessive effort has resulted in the notorious 'death from overwork' (*karoshi*) (Kumazawa 1996: 83). That Japanese performance appraisals would be conducted fairly (the shared view among Japanese economists and business administration scholars) has therefore been criticized. Thus Endo has established that 'employees do not have the right to know their assessment results' and that Japanese companies use personnel assessment as a tool for employment discrimination (Endo 2004:14–18).

If one examines so-called lifetime employment more carefully, then, it becomes clear that this term does not accurately reflect real employment practice. Not only are peripheral workers excluded from this regime, as indicated above; also, most white-collar workers in large organizations find themselves outside its purview. Instead they feel compelled to obey instructions issued by the company, whether they concern job reallocation within the firm, temporary transfer to a subsidiary or an associated corporation, permanent transfer, or *voluntary* early retirement before the mandatory retirement age (generally 60 years). Certainly salaried employees ('salaryman' in Japanese) appear to be meek and obedient to their superiors and to management, but in reality, most do their jobs whilst feeling ambivalent toward them (Rohlen 1974; Clark 1979; Graham 2003).

Upon closer examination, Japanese organizations reveal what is surely the essential shortcoming of the renowned Japanese-style management: the weakness of labour unions. True, an enterprise union holds advantages for both the management and workers during high economic growth. But if during a period of slack business, management decides to rationalize an organization and drastically reduces manpower, enterprise unions are powerless and will not prevent it. This highlights to what extent *discretion* and *autonomy* remain management prerogatives, beyond the reach of workers. There is no doubt that Japanese society, rising from the ashes of a devastating war, achieved an amazing economic recovery, just as its companies demonstrated remarkable growth in the global market. Yet Japanese workers were not able to attain the sort of working life that must be deemed worthy of an advanced country (Ihara 2013). This takes us to the spread of Japanese-style management abroad.

JAPANIZATION: THE DIFFUSION OF 'LEAN PRODUCTION' ABROAD

Regardless of academic controversies surrounding the question of whether Japanese-style management constituted a post-Fordism or instead points backwards, the practices associated with it diffused into the field of business outside Japan. Following the Plaza Accord in 1985, the yen rapidly appreciated and export-dependent Japanese manufacturers felt compelled to engage in local production in their target markets, while adaptation to foreign locales became an urgent need for them. Simultaneously foreign firms lagging behind their Japanese competitors were forced to consider the introduction of Japanese-style management, and its application in their factories became a pressing need. At this juncture it was not the cultural aspect of Japanese-style management but its practical techniques that factories attempted to introduce overseas. In these circumstances the production system of the automotive industry, and more particularly, the Toyota Production System (TPS) sparked worldwide interest and it soon enjoyed ascendancy.

By the end of World War II the automotive industry in the United States had cultivated a large market. In contrast, the Japanese automotive industry had to rebuild from scratch. Toyota's top management believed that if the company adopted the same mass-production methods as US companies, it would stand no chance against them. Therefore, Toyota began developing a new production system immediately after the war to produce cars efficiently with limited resources and for a small market. This system rests on two pillars: 'just-in-time' (JIT) – which means that workers make and deliver what is needed, when it is needed and how much is needed – and 'automation with a human touch' – which involves an automatic stopping device attached to machines to prevent the production of defective parts, to detect faulty parts and to halt production in emergencies. Taiichi Ohno, a Toyota plant manager at the time, was central to the development of TPS. In 1977, he published a book explaining the details of this system in Japan; later, several handbooks on TPS were printed both in and outside Japan (Monden 1983; Imai 1986; Shingo 1989). Other enterprises were thus able to mimic the system, and many business scholars made it the subject of their research.

Among research conducted on TPS, a large-scale survey by the Massachusetts Institute of Technology was especially influential. Womack et al. (1990), who participated in the MIT project, compared Japanese automotive enterprise systems (especially TPS) with the Ford production system, rating the former highly in terms of productivity. Under TPS, factory workers are delegated authority and responsibility under reciprocal labour relations, and they work as members of a team, cope with on-site emergencies, and eliminate any waste of inventory, overproduction, motion and transport at the shop-floor level.

> The truly lean plant has two key organizational features: It transfers the maximum number of tasks and responsibilities to those workers actually adding value to the car on the line, and it has in place a system for detecting

> defects that quickly traces every problem, once discovered, to its ultimate cause (Womack et al. 1990: 99, emphasis deleted).

Whilst a production line with minimal inventory can easily come to a stop, this can be handled by workers applying *kaizen*. Thus, the production line continues to evolve through their initiative. This type of production system came to be referred to as a 'lean production system', implying that it is a system that eliminates waste. Hence it is no wonder that TPS found itself being gradually adopted globally, starting from North America and Europe and expanding to South America, Asia and Africa. In particular, its introduction into Chinese factories is remarkable. The rationalization of the 'workshop of the world' by TPS has well advanced. TPS has diffused into various types of businesses and occupations such as electrical appliance manufacturing, clerical work and work done by public institutions and non-profit organizations.

As TPS was being applied on a global scale, its impact on the workplace became the focus of labour process theorists. Early in the labour process debate, critics analysed workplaces using Marx's writings on the subject and notably, the framework developed by Braverman (1974). These depict the workplace within the analytical frame of control versus resistance. But once enterprises introduced sophisticated personnel administration and elaborate shop-floor management systems, overt defiance and protests ceased. To account for this, mainstream labour process theorists turned towards Foucault's analytical framework, with its depiction of close surveillance and self-disciplined or self-motivated workers. Researchers investigating Japanese-owned businesses more specifically found that work environments were transparent, so that employees are conscious of being subject to surveillance and as a result work autonomously and yet in accordance with management intent.

Foucault's analysis of power and subjectivity in modern society is inspired by the *panopticon*, a prison designed by Jeremy Bentham in the late eighteenth century. Its concept comprises the following. A watchman is stationed in an observation tower in the central portion of the prison, whilst prisoners are stationed around the perimeter of the tower. Though the monitor can minutely observe the appearance and motion of inmates, the latter cannot see the former. This arrangement and building structure enables effective surveillance of prisoners at a minimal cost. Even if inmates are not monitored by a watchman, they obey the rules of the prison and demonstrate self-discipline at all times owing to the possibility of being monitored (Foucault 1975).

It was this analytical framework that was applied by labour process theorists to factories introducing state-of-the-art management techniques.

Thus Knights and Collinson (1987) analysed a large-scale car manufacturer employing Foucault's idea of knowledge/power. This company aimed at disciplining workers by applying two management strategies. One was a human relations programme to achieve psychological discipline through communication, and the other was a programme for large-scale redundancy dismissal to strengthen discipline by creating financial hardship for workers. In their investigation, the authors found that control by using financial levers resulted in credible managerial power over the workforce, whereas psychological discipline through team pressure only fuelled worker suspicion and distrust.

Foucault's analytical framework has also been applied to human resource management (HRM) (Townley 1994). This is based on the assumption that the content of work is not necessarily spelled out clearly in a finalized employment agreement so that a gap will exist between the work that management expects workers to perform and the work that workers will actually accomplish. To bridge this gap, management must apply HRM, converting workers from abstract entities to real-time human resources for the company on the basis of manageable data obtained through recruitment techniques, examinations, appraisals and so on. Thus the personnel management division obtains the knowledge with which the company can control workers. But not only does employee information serve as a tool for management; since the workers are aware that this information is being obtained and centralized, they will behave accordingly and do their work properly. This control mechanism can be characterized as an 'information panopticon'. Indeed in Townley's words (and Foucault's terminology), 'HRM techniques are micro-technologies for producing a known and calculable subject, enhancing governmentality through constructing the individual as a more manageable and efficient entity' (Townley 1994: 139).

Foucault's conceptualization notably has served as an analytical framework for investigating workplaces of foreign subsidiaries of Japanese companies or foreign companies that have introduced Japanese-style management. Thus Sewell (1998) observed the just-in-time/total quality control (JIT/TQC) regime at a Japanese-owned electronic equipment manufacturer in the United Kingdom. Two complementary disciplinary forces were being exercised in this factory: discipline derived from 'peer group scrutiny' and discipline derived from a 'management information system'. According to his analysis, these control systems created a vertical and horizontal disciplinary force, whilst a web of close surveillance maximized employees' positive 'creativity', thus minimizing negative 'deviance' from management-defined norms. The manager reviews the workplace, obtaining knowledge about the workers to ensure their manageability, and in the process weaves the net of close supervision. Those working under such conditions are aware of the scrutiny by peers, and they improve their self-discipline, commit to their team and restrain co-workers' behaviour. This analysis became the mainstream labour process theory for workplaces introducing Japanese-style production systems. However, we may ask the question whether worker discontent, workplace deviance and resistance to management were actually eliminated in these factories.

To this question Parker and Slaughter reply by noting the stressful workplace and worker dissatisfaction under the JIT regime and team concept. As foreseen in this regime, each manufacturing process is tightly connected, and inventory and manpower are reduced to the minimum. As a result the production line easily comes to a halt and requires constant improvement by workers. Certainly, some workers will be fascinated with the team concept and *kaizen* at the opening of the factory. However, after the line begins operating normally, factory workers tend to concentrate on 'their duty' on the assembly line; they become more tightly connected by *kaizen* and face intense peer pressure not to halt the line. In this way, the introduction of lean production systems has tightened management control and increased pressure on workers. These authors thus characterize the JIT regime as 'management-by-stress' (Parker and Slaughter 1988: 16–30).

Likewise, researchers studying Japanese joint ventures in the United States and Canada found that the introduction of a different production system led to dissatisfaction with the new working conditions and actual protests against the introduction of Japanese-style labour relations (Fucini and Fucini 1990; Babson 1995; CAW-CANADA Research Group on CAMI 1993; Garrahan and Stewart 1992; Graham 1995; Besser 1996; Rinehart et al. 1995, 1997). Even though new workers were recruited for these plants, and who were then given on- and off-the-job training, the new cooperative labour–management relations ran into serious opposition. Traditional Fordist work practices in the field of collective bargaining and shop-floor representation practices were being challenged by the new methods, disrupting Fordist labour practices and union organization alike as a new hegemonic control regime was introduced in their place (Yanarella and Green 1996). As a result factory workers did not in fact commit themselves to their team, acquire high skill levels or work diligently without direct control. Lean production systems therefore failed to bring about the complete subordination of the workers to the lean production system, however sophisticated the web of control and in spite of the intensified pace of production.

Whether the Japanese-style management model was introduced through Japanese-managed firms investing abroad, or as a technique adopted by non-Japanese corporations, did not make much of a difference either. Thus Danford studied Japanese manufacturing subsidiaries in Wales (United Kingdom), as well as the effect of similar management techniques in British firms emulating the Japanese pattern, only to discover the gap between the ideal model of Japanese-style management and the realities of shop-floor practice. 'Although a number of plants displayed some of the salient features commonly associated with Japanese management practice,' he writes, 'not one conformed with the idealized "Japanese model", which stresses multi-skilled labour processes, self-managing work teams, total flexibility, and opportunities for full worker participation in job design and process improvement' (Danford 1999: 43).

Thus the assumption that the features of factories based on Japanese-style management would be the empowerment of workers, a democratic workplace or the enriching work intended to serve as an alternative to the alienation and degradation of work associated with Taylorism, was challenged. In fact, on the basis of his investigations of how Japanese-style management of labour processes influenced the micro-dynamics of factory politics, Danford concluded that although

> the new forms of shop-floor regulation in capitalist production exact from labour a more complete subordination to management and, through this, an intensification of its exploitation, this new despotism still cannot suppress the worker resistance and conflict which remain inherent to the capitalist labour process. The dynamic of class struggle in capitalist factory organization – including too, struggle initiated from above – ensures that the restructuring of work and employment relations will always be problematic (Danford 1999: 228).

Certainly not all companies that introduced Japanese-style management have failed. Despite having similarly applied new management practices, the actual conditions of their implementation differed depending on region, industry and company. Ultimately, workers have displayed varied and complicated responses in regard to these management systems. These responses have included, in the case of France, strikes at the Toyota factory which management had planned to close, and which were organized around the demand for full payment during temporary layoffs. But not only have Japanese-style management practices provoked strikes; after Renault joined forces with Nissan in 1999, the French company was confronted with a series of suicides. Thus in the course of four months in 2007, three engineers committed suicide at Technocentre, Renault's base for new vehicle development, as they failed to cope with the pressure of reducing the development period for new prototypes.

Lean production systems have also found their way into newly developing nations and have in a number of cases equally faced intense resistance from workers. Thus in the Philippines a major labour conflict erupted after the unceremonious dismissal of trade union members at Toyota Motor Philippines Corporation. Following legal action against the company, the dispute exploded into a major struggle that eventually led to military units entering the factory grounds. Such labour struggles are not limited to Toyota either. The strike for better pay at a Honda joint venture in China (see Jang and Gray, this volume) and riots at a Suzuki subsidiary in India are recent examples of labour unrest affecting Japanese-run operations in low-wage economies. Of course, not all of these social clashes were solely due to Japanese-style management. Political unrest, the class system, ethnic issues and so on, were also responsible for the turmoil. Nonetheless, the labour control practices of lean production, introduced and propagated by Japanese companies, have in many cases been implicated in the power relations and political dynamics that produced worker revolts in overseas locations.

In the course of their global dissemination, Japanese-style management and production systems have no doubt contributed to cost reduction and quality improvements. Indeed the 'Toyota way' has been praised as giving a critical edge to competition in world markets (Liker 2003). But latent discontent with lean production systems lingers, and sometimes explodes into protest. At its most tragic, this includes the cases where employees have been compelled to work themselves to death or have committed suicide owing to exhaustive labour practices and overwork. From a workers' perspective, therefore, the Japanese production system has left a grim legacy of serious problems, both in Japan itself and overseas. For the essence of Japanese-style management as it became apparent in the process of its global diffusion, has never been just a matter of a purely organizational or technological methods introduced to enhance competitiveness; and neither have its problems their root in cultural habits from which certain frictions arise. The key element in lean production has been management's intent to destroy and transform traditional labour relations by using the opportunities created by the introduction of a new production system. The aim of Japanese-style management has all along been to completely divest workplace control from workers – even if it has not always been entirely successful in the attempt to do so.

THE IMPACT OF GLOBALIZATION IN JAPAN: CHANGES IN JAPANESE-STYLE MANAGEMENT AND WORKPLACE DISORDER

As noted before, Japanese firms never managed all workers under a single pattern of working conditions and hence were not able to integrate their workforces into the organization as tightly as often assumed. Yet Japanese-style management did strengthen competitive power in the global market. However, as Japan's economic performance declined in the early 1990s, assessment of its management success formula also changed drastically. The prolonged downturn of the country's economy provoked severe criticism of the management style, and from a competitiveness standpoint at that. Indeed the tables now appeared to be turned against Japanese-style management, as methods based on market mechanisms were hailed as the global standard, to which 'old-fashioned' Japanese management techniques had to adapt. Given that the stable pattern of labour relations that had underpinned Japan's economic 'miracle' after World War II was no longer effective, but was in fact hindering its resurrection in the changed circumstances, the argument turned against the Japanese system (Katz 1998; Grimes 2001; Lincoln 2001).

In the barrage of criticism levelled against the Japanese economic system, Porter et al.'s (2000) were especially vehement and sweeping. Thus they challenged the industrial policy of the 'convoy system', under which government regulation protected and developed weak companies and embryonic industries, and which is widely seen as having supported their survival. In the view of Porter et al., however, this system not only impedes progress in mature markets. In fact it had not even contributed to the earlier industrial development of Japan: for success in industry is underwritten by 'similar underlying principles' and these can all be brought under the heading of competition in the market (Porter et al. 2000: 14–15).

The most virulent criticism of Japanese-style management meanwhile focused on the concept of lifetime employment. The call for labour mobilization based on the principles of neoliberalism intensified. Thus a prominent Japanese advocate of employment deregulation, Yashiro, argues that in the traditional employment system, young new hires were recruited directly out of college or high school, and male employees continued progressing up the promotion ladder until the mandatory retirement age. However, since non-regular workers and most female workers were always excluded from these traditional employment practices, confrontation and disparity between workers were the result. For Yashiro, the solution is to find a middle way between the two: 'time has come for a new lifestyle, based on more flexible employment and a better work–life balance, with fewer working hours and [more frequent] relocations of workplace' (Yashiro 2011: 152).

Nikkeiren, the Japanese Federation of Employers' Associations,[1] in 1995 published *'Japanese-style Management' in a New Era*. It advocated making the labour market more flexible and spoke out in favour of diversity in employment. Workers were divided into three types. The first type are long-term employees, who continue working in the same organization. These are the workers characteristic of the Japanese-style management practice of the past. The second type are specialists, who are independent professionals with expertise and who are recruited as consultants only when necessary. The third type are non-regular workers, who choose diverse employment according to their lifestyles. Applauded by the government, business leaders and individual companies' managements alike, these reforms of the employment system were seen as rooted in an acceptance of diversity of lifestyles, and were credited with reinvigorating the country's economy.

Thus, the evaluation of Japanese-style employment practices shifted from positive appreciation to a stark negative assessment. In fact, Japanese employment laws have steadily been deregulated as well. For example, non-regular workers can now work in fields previously prohibited by the Manpower Dispatching Business Law (such as manufacturing and medical treatment). Employment policy and employment structure in Japan are in transition. But if we overemphasize the shift, we fail to grasp the realities of the current employment situation, for the labour practices of Japanese firms did not drastically change from lifetime to short-term employment. First, as noted previously, those actually covered by Japanese-style management and labour practices were always limited, with discrimination and disparity based on company size, sex, academic background and nationality. But neither has security of employment been completely lost for those enjoying it. Core company staff continue to enjoy long-term employment. Given that the practice was institutionalized through long protracted struggles between the government, managers and workers, it will not easily disappear (Jacoby 2005; Moriguchi and Ono 2006). Therefore the current reforms to the employment system are not so much advancing in a direction opposite to past practice, but rather are a selective extension of it. For what has changed is that employment today is more flexible than ever and the peripheral layer of irregular workers continues to thicken.

---

1 In 2002, the Federation of Economic Organizations (Keidanren) merged with the Japan Federation of Employers' Associations (Nikkeiren) to form the Japan Federation of Economic Organizations (Nihonkeidanren).

So whilst management techniques have not significantly changed, employment deregulation seriously impacts the social structure. Non-regular employees now comprise more than a third of Japan's workforce; the working poor have become a feature of public life. The unemployment rate has risen from a low 2 per cent to about 5 per cent, and those who have lost any desire to work have come prominently into view. The number of young people that remain uneducated, unemployed or not in training (NEET) has multiplied. Income polarization is a major issue and the number of recipients of public assistance has reached 2 million people. Fluidization of the labour market is considered to promote 'fair competition' and energize a society. In fact employment deregulation has exacerbated economic disparity and the fossilization of social class distinctions. Moreover, in addition to the macro-level impact, effects in the workplace should not be disregarded either. Employment uncertainty radiates across society, and the reliance on organization is being reduced. As the spirit of mutual help diminishes, the office or workplace becomes a hostile environment. Hence the managerial ideology focusing on 'the company as family' or 'team fellowship' becomes difficult to sustain and the workplace suffers serious damage, leading to workplace disorder. The malfunctioning concept of a team has even permeated the shop-floor at Toyota.

The author himself had the opportunity to engage in participant observation at a Toyota factory (Ihara 2007). Working on the production line as a non-regular worker, he discovered a marked deterioration of order in the workplace. Toyota at that point in time was considered to be in the forefront of global competition, with the mass media reporting at the time that 'There is no contender'. Although as noted above, in academic discussion the pros and cons of work practices at Toyota were acknowledged, there was consensus that from a management perspective, TPS had few faults. From his position within the organization, the author, however, found a workplace on the verge of chaos.

This had its origin in the growing reliance on the peripheral workforce whilst keeping the lean production system with its teamwork requirements in place. Thus the number of casual workers in the factory rapidly increased from around the year 2000: in peak periods, they would number more than 10000 workers and accounted for 30 to 40 per cent of all workers in the factory. The majority of the non-regular employees no doubt put in their best to fulfil their production quota. Yet the production process, which under the principles of JIT relies on a tight connection with each worker, would nevertheless malfunction; it only needs a few workers not engaging in 'mutual help' to come to a halt. Even with the low skill requirements needed to keep the production line going at the bottom end, fine-tuning between different stages of the labour process and concern for operatives further down the line are indispensable. The increase in the number of workers lacking a sense of responsibility and a 'spirit of cooperation' thus weakened the team cohesion necessary to maintain a high-density assembly line. The result was frequent large-scale product recalls, ultimately reflecting the workplace chaos at this Toyota factory. The introduction of a performance-based wage system only disrupted workplace order further. Management introduced this system in order to enhance workers' motivation. However, the Japanese workplace, characterized by mutual assistance and unclear task demarcation, will not function if this wage system is implemented without reforming the work organization.

Bankruptcy of big businesses has also worked to reduce employees' reliance on organizations. Investigating a Japanese life insurance company ruined in 2000, Graham (2005) observed how employees' reactions to the bankruptcy were based on a calculated risk-to-reward ratio. Interviewees thus wagered on whether or not to remain with the organization (under a new company) or leave. On the verge of the company's collapse, the realities of the Japanese mentality, masked by 'collectivism' and 'selflessness', thus surfaced, leaving little of the supposed culture intact. Certainly the probability of a big enterprise going out of business is small, and yet the fact that it is not a zero probability has greatly diminished the sense of security within organizations, to which the mass media have added by spreading distrust. Even so, large corporations remain popular among applicants, because working conditions in SMEs have deteriorated much more.

Now if organizations are being affected by the spread of feelings of anxiety and distrust, the 'devoted worker' has not completely vanished from Japanese companies. There are employees who willingly perform the jobs necessary to maintain team and workplace order, including on-the-job training for younger colleagues, friendly advice for associates, voluntary assistance to bosses, and team coordination and negotiations with other divisions. Yet this culture and the informal practices in which it is expressed, and which previously would have been formally evaluated by a boss and informally respected by team-mates, are nevertheless disappearing. The introduction of individualistic, performance-based evaluation systems and the rapid turnover of workers are to blame for this. As a result, the 'self-sacrificial worker' finds him/herself continuing to hold a job that is not financially and emotionally rewarding. The occasional burn-out, depression, and in the worst case, suicide owing to overwork, are among the results. Indeed not only the unemployed, but also 'the diligent workers' have been driven into a corner.

Increasing suicide rates in Japanese society have become a matter of public concern. After the bubble economy, the number of suicides rapidly increased and has remained high for at least the last decade. About 30000 people commit suicide each year. The suicide rate among males in the prime of their working lives, between 45 and 55 years, is especially high when compared with the rate in other countries. In addition, as the employment environment has worsened and working conditions have deteriorated, an increasing number of people suffer from mental illness. Enterprise unions however continue to cooperate with management, and typically do not show strong opposition to workplace rationalization. Since the rank and file no longer expect help from the union, the ratio of organized labour to the total labour force has fallen below 20 per cent, as workers try more and more to fend for themselves, but also in response to unjust treatment or unjustified dismissal, no longer remain silent. An increasing number of workers are now appealing to the company through individual labour dispute solution systems (Ihara 2012).

The features of Japanese-style management, including trust, cooperation, consensus, harmony and commitment, which were the hallmark of the country's economic success, were long covered by elaborate business administration and widespread managerial ideology. These served to conceal Japanese employees' disagreements with management, internal conflict and occasional clashes with other workers. Today they have come out into the open. Workers no longer trust management, and in turn, employees become a liability for the company. In the workplace, confrontations arise, morale declines, responsibility is shirked, whilst mental health deteriorates and cynicism spreads. This chapter has evaluated Japanese-style management as a source of competitive advantage, highlighting that it was long seen as a preferable labour practice for workers too. However, the reality of Japanese workers significantly differs from its representation. Not only have Japanese companies not applied this management style to the peripheral workforce, but the business community discriminated against them and thus gave the disparity among workers a structural quality. In addition, core members of the community put up with, or felt compelled, and occasionally volunteered, to put up with a stressful working environment and long hours. As we saw, Japanese-style management has also greatly influenced labour processes outside Japan. Organizations that introduced TPS thus strengthened their competitive power, but because the system does not require workers' participation in shop-floor management or require high skill levels, whilst exerting high pressure on workers, it causes dissatisfaction and occasionally provokes resistance to management.

Japan itself is meanwhile under pressure to adapt in the global economy, jeopardizing the eponymous management style on its home ground. But even if business leaders seek to reduce personnel expenses and increase the fluidity of the labour market, they have not drastically shifted from lifetime to short-term employment. There is no doubt, however, that managerial ideologies such as 'the company as family' and 'team fellowship' have come under strain. The conflict and confrontation masked by these ideologies has increasingly come to light, and confusion today permeates the organization whilst worker morale diminishes. In line with the secular trend in the country's economic fortunes, the discourse concerning Japanese-style management has undergone massive changes from the glory days of the postwar economic miracle to the neoliberal critique today. From the viewpoint of the workplace, the gap between this discourse and the actual conditions of shop-floor management has widened accordingly.

16. Work, power and the urban poor

Jeffrey Harrod

INTRODUCTION

Throughout most of the twentieth century social unrest, political turbulence and politics were seen to originate in the conflicts between different power groups surrounding production. Even ethnically or religious based movements were couched in material terms – peasant wars of liberation were also peasant wars against landlords. In the industrialized countries politics were considered the result of the capitalist–worker relations in various disguises. During this period workplace power relations were routinely discussed under the headings of 'industrial relations' or in terms of Marxist class war. These constructions in turn were based on the presence of overt social organizations capable of representation. Trade unions were key in the century-long development of the idea of tripartite (state–union–employer) power relations. At the same time revolutionary political parties were said to be leading the working class, which was in a subordinate position in production.

However, these configurations eclipsed power relations in places of work which were less formally organized, as well as the groups within them judged as not suitable for collective representation. Unionists ignored the unpaid work of women and often bargained exclusively on behalf of their members; Marxist-based parties and organizations were only interested in the social relations of production in industry, whilst describing certain forms of work as a petty bourgeois mode of production and those without work and not in revolutionary movements as lumpenproletariat.

This situation changed dramatically in the last quarter of the twentieth century. The power of trade unions declined and as a result industrial relations evacuated its position in high politics. The European social democratic parties then moved to the centre to serve a broader base than those associated with work and union, and employment conditions changed in the direction of less structured and more flexible, part-time and casual work. While these changes removed the structured workplace power relations from the focus of attention, they did not usher in a revised consideration of the political importance of less structured and less formal workplace relations. Despite the greater presence of working conditions outside the scope of easy social organization and within a pattern of totally asymmetric power held by employers, these production patterns have not been examined as a possible source of politics and social conflict. Indeed for decades now the social sciences have not generally considered the power relations within work and production as a source or determinant of politics and political power.

This chapter presents an approach which may help restore the emphasis on the connection between work and politics through consideration of *the human power relations that surround different work situations and the consciousness and attitudes they create*. In the first part of the chapter, it is argued that such an approach is needed to help restore the importance of work and production in general in the analysis of politics and social conflict. To this end it is necessary to consider a departure from conventional definitions. This is especially important as almost anything connected with power, production, class and consciousness in the past decades has been dominated by Marxist concepts and debates. The approach presented here, which I label the *power in production* approach, is a neo-materialist approach in the sense that it based on a materialism (the world of production), but not entirely the Marxist version of materialism (Harrod 2007).

The second part of the chapter applies the power in production approach to some contemporary developments involving the expansion of work in which the direct employer has in past decades dramatically increased workplace power to help produce increased returns (to the employer as well as to indirect beneficiaries). The result has been a greater presence of what are called the 'urban poor' and the 'underclass', amongst other such names for poverty found in urban environments throughout the world, and to which the power in production approach can be fruitfully applied as a contribution to the study of political and social change.

PATTERNS OF POWER IN PRODUCTION

The approach presented here observes that there are different patterns of (power) relations which surround the most important activity of humankind: work and production. This approach to politics and society was originally launched in 1987 in two free-standing but linked volumes which elaborated a theory of social forces in the process of change in global society. Obviously these volumes provide a more complete view of the power in production approach than can be presented here. Part 1 of Cox's *Production, Power, and World Order* outlines the power in production approach which he had already partially developed in the early 1970s (Cox 1971). The 1987 study, however, was deservedly received as a seminal work, especially for Part 2 of the book, in which the focus on world orders associated it with the neo-Gramscian approach. This made it a core text in international political economy. The broader approach to society, change and its comprehension found in Cox 1987, Part 1, and the statement, elaboration and application of it in my own *Power, Production and the Unprotected Worker* (1987), were then again revised and updated in Harrod (2007).

The argument developed in these works is that world views or patterns of consciousness of individuals are developed from, and influenced by, power patterns in work and production, and that these world views are important to mobilization and political action. This means that the preferred method for disaggregating the global labour force is the criterion of power relations surrounding production, and not the conventional criteria of occupation, skill, sector, ethnicity or gender.

The origin of the power in production approach was developed through a process of surveying the world labour force, defined as those engaged in expending energy for socially valued output. The purpose was to discover identifiable and distinguishable patterns of power relations surrounding work and production. Thus the power relations between an entrepreneur and a non-unionized employee are different from those between an indebted peasant and the moneylender, or between those with a secure contract of employment and those casually employed. The basic uniformity of all the power relations resides in varying degrees of domination, subordination and authority within production. The differences in degrees of power and authority combined with different types of power-holders and subjects of power then create different patterns of power relations. These patterns are to be observed universally and thus the identification of them is not contingent upon country, region or other socio-political variables.

Some of the patterns of power and authority in work are dominant in that the groups and actors within them, and the dynamics of their particular power relations, substantially affect the nature of other patterns, while subordinate patterns are guided by events and outputs from the dominant patterns. The combination of dominant and subordinate patterns in any identifiable cluster is considered as a distinct political economy, which may or may not be an existing, recognized nation state. Currently at least eight patterns can be identified (see below). Each of the patterns is dynamic, that is, power relations are dynamic and the patterns may be transformed or eliminated. More importantly, persons within one pattern may find themselves moving from one pattern to another and may be in several patterns at the same time. For example, the power relations surrounding the work of a self-employed person, defined as someone producing without employing other people, is affected by four different forces: the suppliers of needed materials or services, the regulations governing the conditions of production (which are often state agencies), the customers, and the competitors. The level of the return to work is determined by the nature of the engagement of the self-employed person with these powers. If, however, someone is employed by the self-employed person, then a new actor in the power relations is introduced and the pattern becomes more typical of a small enterprise – and the previous self-employed person becomes an employer with power over the employee. The four-faceted pattern has now become a five-faceted pattern and the roles and attitudes of the persons involved will change.

It is also suggested that the power relations in production are the source of 'rationalities'– ideologies, world views or institutionalized practices – which enable, disguise or psychologically mitigate the acceptance of the inherent authority, domination and the inequalities within and resulting from these power relations. The strength of such rationalities and the internalization of them by subordinate producers affect the nature and direction of change originating in these relations. The development of world views or counter-rationalities and the political action which they precipitate or determine is then an essential part of social change.

In the period from the mid-1970s to the mid-1980s, twelve patterns were discerned (Cox 1987: 32–50; Harrod 1987: 14–19), but over the last quarter of a century, confirming the dynamic nature of the approach, some patterns have become less important (Ryner 2002) and some (notably, those associated with command economies) have been eliminated. In addition, the original nomenclature of some of the patterns has meanwhile become inappropriate. Currently, then, eight patterns can be discovered by considering the world labour force, the status of employment, the occupational changes and the changes in structures of different political economies. It should be emphasized that these patterns can be numerically named, but for purpose of image and identification, an attempt has been made to use words which help capture the core relationship or the most important persons, groups or organizations in the pattern. The current patterns, then, may be referred to as tripartite; corporate; state corporatist; peasant; casual; enterprise; self-employed; and household. Within these different patterns there is also a divide between workers or producers who are protected by worker organizations, state structures and corporate practices; and those who have less protection from the power and authority surrounding their productive work. The patterns of power involving the latter, the unprotected worker, or more accurately the less protected worker, are examined in detail in Harrod (1987) and are again the concern in the second part of this chapter.

There are three basic elements to this approach: production, power and consciousness. Each of these differs from both their use in traditional materialism or Marxist materialism, and their use in the power in production approach differs also from current conventional political sociology. Yet it is useful, in presenting a different approach, to elaborate it in relation to the conceptual frameworks and structures of knowledge with which it is supposed to interact.

Production for Marx had a specific and rather narrow meaning associated with capitalism and the theories of alienation and surplus value. On the basis of that definition Marx and his glossators built a huge and sophisticated philosophical, sociological, political and economic theory concerning capitalism. Apart from the divisions made in production under capitalism, it was seen to be largely divided between two classes: the capitalist and the working class. The focus on capitalism as a society-wide, so-called mode of production becomes problematic once societies which display only limited characteristics of capitalism become the subject of analysis.

Like all constructs, capitalism has to be a relative concept but it is relative only to the past (feudalism) and to a non-existent future (communism). It appears, then, that only the present is capitalist. Generations of non-European revolutionaries and intellectuals struggled with what would today be called a Eurocentric idea that the industrial present in Europe and even possibly more exclusively, in the United Kingdom in 1850, would be the current end of extant history. Indeed such ethnocentrism was expressed in communist and Marxist literature of the times. Cox in a long footnote (1987: 406) notes that

> The term capitalist is not used in this study to apply to a single mode of production. Indeed, the capitalist mode of development has spawned several distinctive modes of social relations of production. To bracket these all together as a single capitalist mode of production confuses things that are significantly distinct (see also Harrod 1987: 29).

The unsatisfactory nature of the narrowness of the Marxist view has been made explicit by three different developments. The first was by European intellectuals in the 1970s seeking to explain the contemporary scene in Marxists terms, that is, a century after Marx's view of his period; second, by revolutionaries and thinkers outside Europe and in circumstances where industrialization was in its infancy; and the third concerns the contemporary difficulty in expecting that capitalism will be disturbed or ended by the collective efforts of those said to supply labour power. Nicos Poulantzas writing in 1971, Mao Tse-Tung writing in 1926 and Nitzan and Bichler in 2009 can be taken as representative of these various angles and may been seen as representing three forms of analysis which can accommodate different patterns of power in production.

Poulantzas set himself the task of modernizing Marxism, essentially emphasizing the importance of the so-called capitalist state. Poulantzas' book *Political Power and Social Classes* contains many elements of a neo-materialist approach – a plurality of 'modes of social relations of production', dominant and subordinate modes comprising a 'social formation', power blocs within the capitalist state, and so on. It can be considered the most important and thoughtful of such books at that time. However, his refusal to leave the confines of Marxist literature and the overall domination of the 'capitalist mode of production' means that, despite his view of a plurality of modes in social formations, he never specifies other modes or formations unless they are historic. Eventually the potential of flexible analysis and greater scope in the plurality of modes in social formations is abandoned as he concentrates on the capitalist social formation. One mode thus becomes the formation (Poulantzas 1973: 15–16). The unresolved problem of being unprepared to depart too far from Marx's theory of capitalism causes even greater problems when it comes to class, and especially the bourgeoisie. 'Fractions' of the bourgeoisie present even greater problems, for while fractions connected with production – industrial and commercial – are acceptable, there is no place, for example, for the state bureaucracy (Poulantzas 1973: 84–5).

Mao Tse-Tung in his 1926 pamphlet *Analysis of the Classes in Chinese Society* laid the ground pursued by Poulantzas, but from a concern with the lower classes rather than the bourgeoisie. Mao was faced with a 'social formation' which no European Marxist had been forced to consider from the standpoint of revolution, and certainly not from strategies involving war and casualties. Informed by a Marxist focus on production, Mao listed categories, if not ideal types, of subordinate workers in different classes and situations in contemporary China. Within the so-called 'petty bourgeoisie', he distinguishes the self-employed artisans and owner-peasants; under the heading of the 'semi-proletariat' he sees renting peasants and small handicrafts workers; and finally, the lumpenproletariat. Missing from this account were household production and the role of women within it, which Mao corrected in a further publication in 1927. 'As for women, in addition to being dominated by these three systems of authority, they are also dominated by the men (the authority of the husband). These four authorities – political, clan, religious and masculine – are the embodiment of the whole feudal-patriarchal system and ideology, and are the four thick ropes binding the Chinese people, particularly the peasants' (Mao Tse-Tung 1926–27: 43).

Mao examined the consciousness these power relations produced in these groups of subordinate workers, using the yardstick of their potential attitude towards the revolutionary movement. At that time he noted a development relevant to the current Chinese situation, which was that peasants who had lost their land and handicraftsmen who were unable to get work joined in mutual aid societies which became secret sects with cult overtones.

Nitzan and Bichler, finally, in their *Capital as Power* (2009) argue that the production orientation of Marx is misplaced as the central ordering phenomenon. Rather, capital is the symbolic representation of power, whilst capitalization and its logic – especially contemporary corporate capitalization – is the central and totalizing logic. Corporate capitalization generates earnings and limits risk by exploiting all aspects of social life, and not just the productivity of labour or the industrial artefacts associated with it (2009: 8–9; and Baines, this volume). From this standpoint the Marxist division of labour into productive and unproductive, as well as the aggregate labour time necessary for sustenance of the system do not figure significantly in either the construction or the possible destruction of capitalism (Nitzan and Bichler 2009: 87–90).

Both Poulantzas and Mao dismembered the capitalist class and working class of Marx. They each devised new modes, forms or patterns of production; they elevated class fractions to dominant classes or distinguishable subordinate groups; they countered the Eurocentric and workerist bias, and thus they laid the groundwork for a new, eclectic and more encompassing materialism than that of the Marxist theory of capitalism. But both of them, Poulantzas intellectually and Mao practically, also attempt to square the circle by refusing to admit or declare their essential deviance from Marx. Poulantzas disguises his deviation by resorting to high theory and refinement of definitions; Mao, at least in 1926, declared that despite his profound and expert assessment of the revolutionary potential of various groups, the almost non-existent industrial proletariat was to be 'the leading force in our revolution' (Mao 1926–27: 14). Nitzan and Bichler do not have a focus on Marxist concepts of the working class or labour power, and for them, writing in a different era, it is not necessary either to disguise any deviation because their work is represented as a reconsideration of Marxist theory in order to generate a new approach. Thus they open the possibility of multiple points of opposing power, or a diversity of production forms all essentially incorporated, but not necessarily eliminated by the totality of the power of capital.

The power in production approach adopted here can be characterized as neo-materialist because it understands production and work to be a universal activity by all human beings. Second, the forms of work and production are different and the people in the various forms have very different attitudes and patterns of consciousness relating to political action. This approach therefore contravenes a whole range of structures of organization, conventions and specializations found in the academic practices of social science. For example, the argument that subordinate producers in different power patterns occupy different positions relative to the larger system challenges the concept of 'working class', which is rejected as a universal pattern and national categorization; and finally it considers that occupation, gender, economic and ethic divisions of the global labour force are not *by themselves* useful and meaningful categories to study the processes of social change.

Instead I proceed from the assumption that power in the workplace is the power which allocates work and production, configures the distribution of the product, disciplines the producers, and results in different and specific forms of consciousness and world views. There have been three basic entries or approaches to the study of power. The first concerns the power of large organizations at the apex of societies, such as the state, the church and the corporation. The second has been that of class or group power in which the organizations are seen as vehicles for such power; and third, there is the more diffuse power found in forms of discipline and authority which result in regularity of behaviour.

The first approach is the traditional approach in political science. Power in this purview essentially resides in the state. This entry into power either ignores or discounts the more primary uses of power which may indeed support state power.

The second entry point, of group or class power, which was closer to production and materialism, can be found in the works of most sociologists and political philosophers in the nineteenth and twentieth centuries. Putting class power and its material objectives in the supreme position resulted in a theoretical contradiction between state and class power which has never been fully resolved. The problem encountered here, however, was that the focus is on an extremely limited number of classes or groups based on an excessive variety of criteria for membership.

The third entry point into the discussion of power begins with the smaller units of power and, perhaps, only inductively building an understanding of the larger, more abstract exercise of power. This is the initial focus of the power in production approach. The Foucauldian view of power is relevant here, without necessarily accepting his complete typology (Bevir 1999). Foucault is scathing concerning the idea of a centralized and mechanistic, material power of the capitalist class and sees no virtue in studying it (Foucault 1976: 236). Instead he distinguishes between what he calls the power of sovereignty that is exercised over the earth and its products; and that which is exercised over human bodies and their operations, including labour, which he called disciplinary power.

The focus of the approach under discussion in this chapter, then, is on the disciplinary power found at the point of production. This is the power most global citizens in their wakeful state experience directly and daily. Conventionally it is the power most intensely studied in the sociology of work, labour relations, industrial relations and human resource management. The understanding of such power and its impact on consciousness, and therefore on politics, poses a challenge to any different approach and is also at the base of the contribution it can make to the more traditional concerns of political scientists. For in the power in production approach, consciousness is used not in the classical Marxist sense of class consciousness, consciousness of a class of itself. It is argued instead that each pattern of power relations has a 'rationality', which is used by the dominant groups in order to assuage the resistance of the subordinate group within production. Current research suggests that human beings suffer stress from authority and greater stress when there is perceived injustice (Crescentini et al. 2012; D'Aquili and Newberg 1999; Harrod 1999). The reaction to the stress produces a consciousness of the nature of the rationality, power position, and a world view relating to the position of the pattern in the social formation and within current political viewpoints.

THE URBAN POOR AND THE UNDERCLASS

Let me now turn to current discussions concerning the increase in work variously described as flexible, precarious, part-time or non-standard. The purpose is to consider what type of political action and mobilization might be expected from the people engaged in such work. The nomenclature used is relative to the type of work which predominated in the period approximately between 1950 and 1980. Work during this period would be, by implication of the current nomenclature, permanent (not flexible), stable (not precarious), full-time (not part-time) and standard (not non-standard).

From the perspective of the power in production approach, the reason for the permanent, stable, full-time and standard employment available in the last half of the last century would reside in the nature of the power relations which surrounded the work. These were the power relations of the tripartite, corporate or state corporate patterns. In each of these the employees or workers enjoyed a certain protection either through the state labour law in state corporatism, through bargaining and representative actions by trade unions in the tripartite pattern, or through achieving an established status within an organization such as the civil service or large corporation.

In the tripartite pattern the nature of the work was determined by the interplay of powerful unions facing employer and state organizations. The consciousness it produced was solidarity. In the corporate pattern the employment conditions were achieved by an internal coherence, a promoted loyalty to the corporation, profession or service, and a differential reward between those within the corporate confines and those without. Thus civil servants everywhere in the world enjoyed better conditions of work. At the beginning of the twentieth century in Switzerland and the USA, large corporations started to experiment with privileges awarded to permanent and differentially rewarded employees. This arrangement was also introduced in postwar Japan through the life-time employment system and corporate-based organizations of employees. Under state corporatism, finally, the governing system of one-party states with a low level of industrialization, the workers covered by the corporatist umbrella enjoyed protection derived from an often elaborate labour code which contained clauses preventing independent worker organizations.

In each case the workers and employees had some form of protection. The mobilizing consciousness in the tripartite pattern, the loyalty in the corporate pattern and the privileged perception in the state corporatist pattern were all sufficient to secure relative protected conditions. This was the cost incurred by the corporation and state corporatist governing elites for preventing the emergence of solidarity which could challenge their established power. In the long term this strategy was not successful, at least in state corporatism, as 'unofficial' unions developed and eventually challenged the system (Harrod 1989).

What should be noted in this trajectory is that the portion of the working population involved in these patterns was almost always a minority. Only in a very few countries of northern Europe did union density figures rise above 50 per cent. In Japan the workers covered by the so-called 'life-time' system was roughly 30 per cent (see Ihara, this volume), while in most state-corporatist social formations the system only covered the industrial workers and civil service employees, who were always less than 25 per cent of the labour force. These workers were considered as protected; they are the ones with whose working conditions the current 'non-standard' work can be compared. But then, these more protected workers and employees were always accompanied by a mass of people not so protected. Those in the production of household services (usually women), those in self-employment or casual work or unemployed, as well as peasants, always comprised the bulk of the labour force in most countries and certainly if the whole world labour force is taken into consideration.

The unprotected workers, then, were in the majority throughout, but their powerlessness rendered them less than visible (Harrod 1987). Only in 1972 did the International Labour Organization recognize the presence of such workers, when it launched the 'informal sector' concept considered to be characteristic of less industrialized counties (International Labour Office 1972; Harrod 2008). The core definition used in the studies involving the informal sector is that of Portes et al. (1989). It holds that the informal sector is based on the household and concerns income-producing activities not derived from contractual and legally regulated employment. From this definition proceed case studies of countries and informality, disaggregated often on the basis of space, gender, ethnicity, labour market and occasionally on vague occupational grounds.

The blanket nature of the informal sector means that the variety of production relations in it (self-employment, enterprise, casual) were never disaggregated. Furthermore, it did not promote the need to consider the political attitudes and actions of those within it. However, in 2008 the ILO introduced a new concept in its lexicon: 'unprotected work'. In the *ILO Declaration on Social Justice and Fair Globalization* it argues that global economic integration causes 'the growth of both unprotected work and the informal economy, which impact on the employment relationship and the protections it can offer' (ILO 2008a: 5). This may be a tacit admission of the difficulties with the concept of the informal sector, but more importantly the 'unprotected work' designation finally creates a space for the ILO to begin considering the differences in 'employment relationships', here seen as power relations, and the impact on mobilization and political action.

The power relations of tripartite, corporate and state–corporate patterns and the accompanying consciousness and mobilization were the driving force of social movements and conventional politics in the last half of the twentieth century, despite the fact that the people directly involved were always a minority. The question inherent in the current massive increase in the number of unprotected workers is then: how will the consciousness of these workers, derived from the workplace power relations, emerge in political form?

To answer this question, it is necessary to consider the discourses concerning two categories which (unlike the notion of 'informal sector'), and although they do not distinguish type of work within them, do have some political implications. The first of these is the 'urban poor'; the other is the so-called underclass. These two categories rely on space and levels of material income to distinguish them from others.

In the discussions of the urban poor there is usually a clear assumption that political action and social unrest arise from material deprivation: the poor are politically volatile because they are relatively materially deprived. Typically Nichiporuk (2000: 20) singles out the urban poor and notes that

> The squalid living conditions in the rings of slums that now surround many third world cities are becoming a fairly permanent condition. Many of the recent migrants live in these areas and their desperate straits can prove to be fertile ground for radical and revolutionary groups that seek new recruits for battle against the existing regime.

Similarly the writers of the UNDP *Human Development Report* for 1999 (UNDP 1999: 36) are unequivocal as to the source of global unrest.

> Social tensions and conflicts are ignited when there are extremes of inequality between the marginal and the powerful. Indonesia shows what can happen when an economic crisis sets off latent social tensions between ethnic groups – or between rich and poor. Recent research on complex humanitarian emergencies concluded that 'horizontal inequalities' whether ethnic, religious or social are the major cause of the current waves of civil conflicts.

Similarly material poverty and space are again used to distinguish the designation of an underclass. This concept, unlike poverty, recognizes both class and power. People in the underclass are said to be the poorest and are 'ghettoized' in segments of cities. However, the definition and use of the term 'underclass' is controversial and its use represents a deliberate deviation from social and political reality (Tyler 2013). There are two basic views concerning the members of the underclass. The first (and the one which is now current in sociology) almost exclusively relies on the criterion of poverty and couples it with social exclusion (Murray 1997). The second is much larger and includes the temporary unemployed and even sometimes the 'working poor'. In popular accounts the term is sometimes used to include all those in low-waged work (Florida 2012b).

As with the informal sector and the poor, the underclass concept is work-empty. In the more restricted definition of the underclass, the population included by implication do not work at all, as in the conventional definition of unemployment. Yet, for example, a high proportion of the designated underclass are single mothers who are working to produce household services for their children. 'Not working' in the underclass is then defined as being outside waged work: it is not about production. In the broader definitions, which include the working poor, there is recognition of the nature of work, which is low-waged, intermittent and uncertain. The observation that the areas of urban poverty have ethnically distinguishable populations in addition has produced a strand of studies attaching ethnicity to the underclass concept. In each case, the argument made is that the underclass are poor and they are poor because of discrimination in employment, making them unemployed or unemployable. Work then is seen entirely in terms of the material rewards and not as a determining factor in attitudes, consciousness and life history.

In summary, the informal sector, the urban poor and the underclass are concepts which usually do not carry with them any consideration of the work that is performed by people within them, nor the power relations which surround their work. This is part of the reason why they do not easily offer the possibility of analysing any conflicts or coalitions among them, the appeals mobilizing them, or the social demands they make. It is a different matter once we recognize that among the urban poor and in the underclass are the unprotected workers, who are best seen in that light rather than through sector, income or class.

APPLYING THE POWER IN PRODUCTION APPROACH TO THE URBAN POOR AND UNDERCLASS

If instead of using the disaggregation by sector, space, gender, religion or ethnicity, the nature of work and its power relations is used, a more nuanced and complex picture of political mobilization and action can be achieved. Of course it is always entirely possible that special social characteristics coincide with sector, gender and/or ethnicity. Thus casual work may be disproportionally supplied by minority groups or those with the least power in a social formation. But this does not make these categorizations the primary source of political mobilization.

Of the eight forms of power relations identified in the first part of this chapter, there are three distinctive patterns in which least protected workers are hidden in such categories as the informal sector, the urban poor, or the underclass. These are the self-employment, enterprise and casual patterns.

Self-employment Pattern

The self-employment pattern is ubiquitous in that it appears in all conventional categorizations, and the self-employed indeed are spread throughout the whole range of income groups. Thus a highly paid professional as well as low-paid service provider are subject to the interplay of power between their competitors, customers, suppliers (when value added is involved) and state agencies as tax collectors and regulators of activities (Ross 2008). Self-employment relations exist among the poor and the underclass when an individual takes work on his/her own account from several customers. Avoiding the power of tax authorities or competitors increases the return to work.

The multiple constellations of power involved here produce high degrees of insecurity. In turn this generates a fear of change; resistance to change is a noticeable characteristic of those involved in self-employment relations. Self-employment in the underclass would include, for example, individuals working outside of employment and tax regulations, or the productive work of single parents in child-rearing. A coping or survival strategy, once established, helps reduce the insecurity of changes introduced by other power holders in the pattern. One study notes that the own-account workers in the wider European Union tend to refuse paid employment when it is being offered (Millán et al. 2010).

Enterprise Pattern

The enterprise pattern is the transformation path when a self-employed or own-account individual becomes an employer. The power relations now come to include, besides the power configuration of the self-employment pattern, also the ways in which the employer must now deal with the power of the individual worker, and vice versa. Employer and worker may not be of the same religion, ethnicity or gender. So as with all power relations, any resentment of authority or injustice may be enhanced by previous generalized attitudes towards differences within the immediate society.

The changes which have produced more precarious work have substantially affected enterprise power relations over the past decades. Small enterprises could offer stability of employment more easily before the dismantling of general employment stability in the period after 1980. Employers previously had sought to reduce costly labour turnover by securing a core of workers socially attached to the enterprise – if not to the employer. The enterprise power pattern has within it a dynamic for the creation of workplace organization of the subordinate to redress the employer's power of dismissal. This dynamic was weakened when the presence of worker organizations in larger enterprises diminished.

The declining presence of unions in general and the increase in precarious work exposed to the power of employers were accompanied by the decline in conditions and returns to work. The 'working poor' were one result of this change in the power relations. The rationality governing them was always the market and social cohesion with other workers. The market explanation for precarious work or for reductions in pay have, under the wider ideology of market fundamentalism, acquired more force, while the fear of a downward trajectory into unemployment and the underclass increases the risks associated with expressions of solidarity and concerted action. The small enterprise workers amongst the urban poor and underclass therefore find their power to redress injustices in the current period heavily constrained.

Casual Pattern

The casual pattern of power relations predominates in most populations designated as urban poor or underclass. The power relations governing work and production are, like the work itself, time-limited, often fragmented and usually unstructured. This is evident in the sort of relations exemplified by temporary domestic servants, bag-carriers, itinerant shoe cleaners, or the temporary but structured employment dealt out at the gates of an enterprise employing casual workers. Amongst these populations there is always work and there is always production and there are always power relations according to the definitions provided in the first part of this chapter. These power relations do indeed produce the poorest of the poor that occupy the spaces of shantytowns, *bidonvilles* and *favelas*, ghettos and inner-city slums. Spatial aspects and ethnicity are increasingly used as distinguishing criteria. Thus Sultany (2012) argues that a large percentage of the Palestinian citizens in Israel who constitute at least 20 per cent of the total population, comprise an underclass. A similar situation in Istanbul is said to be the result of 'conflict-induced migrant Kurds' (Yılmaz 2008), while Massey and Pren (2012) talk of a new 'Latino underclass'. In the United Kingdom McDowell et al. (2009) report competition between different groups for the most casual and poorest paid work.

It is not uncommon for constructed social and biological disadvantages to be used in increasing the power over the workers with those characteristics. However, within the casual pattern these disadvantages are also being used to keep the pattern within one identifiable group. This situation means that the attitudes and political consciousness emerging from the power relations must be merged with those arising from ethnic identity if not solidarity. However, Putman (2007) reports increased inter- and intra-ethnic conflict in the USA as diverse communities are forced to cohabit.

The noticeable attitudes and political consciousness of the persons within the casual pattern in the past have been the result of the attempt, not to transform the relations, but to restore personal dignity and to offer some hope of exit (Harrod 1987). The populations then responded to millennialist and messianic movements which are perceived to satisfy these demands. Millennialist movements are often religion based; the adherents to the growing evangelical movement in Brazil are largely the poor. Some aspects of militant Islam also provide solace to those trapped in these relations. Ismail writes about Cairo that 'the mobilization potential of militant Islam seems to lie in its ability to ground its ideological principle in the social antagonisms and the opposition positions that are part of the urban landscape' (Ismail 2000: 393). The Mahdi Army of insurgents in Iraq was likewise recruited from the urban poor. How far the 'new populism' ascendant in Europe (Holman 2004), with immigration posited as the principal cause of social despair, can be set within this tendency needs to be researched. In general most studies overlook the possibility of a collective mentality being derived not only from poverty but from the treatment received when engaged in work and production.

CONCLUSION

The power in production approach thus indicates that if unprotected workers, as described above, form the supposed distinguishable groups of 'urban poor', or the 'underclass', they are unlikely to have a uniform consciousness or world view which many authors and commentators expect they will be mobilized behind for political action. Nor does it seem that poverty alone is a uniting force. Effective mobilization would instead have to come from a coalition of unprotected workers found in different patterns of power relations in production and with accordingly different world views. Their creation and development of 'social space', the appropriation of which is necessary for concerted resistance, would also be mediated by the power relations differences (Davies 2005: Bakker and Gill 2003), as would their attitudes in joining any possible coalitions with organized labour (Stevis 2002).

Attempts at organization and empowerment using spatial, ethnic and gender similarities would likewise have to take account of the diversity of work situations. Those in the self-employment pattern may be suspicious of change and wish only protection from the state as a tax collector, enterprise workers will respond to measures which strengthen labour law against employers, and casual workers may respond to measures which restore a feeling of worth and dignity. Policy, mobilization and organization therefore must be focused on work and production in its broadest sense. Unless the complexities issuing from work and production are acknowledged, all attempts, both liberating and repressive, to control the people affected, will remain ineffective in relation to the urban poor and underclass. Instead eruptions of sporadic, but politically ineffectual violence or movements based on inter-ethnic or religious conflict will continue to prevail.

17. Unfreedom and workers' power: ever-present possibilities

Siobhán McGrath and Kendra Strauss

INTRODUCTION

Trafficking, forced labour and related phenomena have been documented time and again in recent years by advocacy groups, the media and government agencies. The International Labour Organization (ILO) estimates that there are 20.9 million people in some form of forced labour worldwide. The estimate is broken down regionally and sectorally: 11.7 million of these are thought to be in the Asia and Pacific region; and 18.7 million are believed to be in the private economy, among whom 14.2 million are involved in economic activities not related to sexual exploitation. Debt bondage appears to be the most common mechanism of forced labour (cf. ILO 2005; 2012; Andrees and Belser 2009). The prevalence of labour relations characterized by various forms of unfreedom raises critical questions about how the phenomenon fits into the contemporary economy, and therefore about how to address the issue(s) in ways that advance the interests of all exploited workers.

Critical scholarship plays a key role in interpreting the issue(s), often in ways that suggest particular solutions; these solutions, in turn, face real-world problems of implementation and institutionalization. Thus, while there are important debates around the categorization of these phenomena – as forced labour, unfree labour or contemporary 'slavery' – the epistemological and theoretical questions for scholars of political economy do not only relate to definition and interpretation. They are also about understanding how and why particular social, economic and politico-legal regulatory solutions are adopted, and with what implications. In this chapter we explore different approaches to the problematic of unfreedom in contemporary labour relations. In particular we contrast the influential *New Slavery* school with new directions in research on forced and unfree labour, which have emerged out of critiques of the assumed binary between free and unfree labour. Many authors in this emerging school of thought posit that labour relations can instead be understood as falling at various points along a spectrum, or continuum, of exploitation (Skrivankova 2010). The implications of this stance, however, have yet to be fully explored, particularly for the promotion of workers' rights in relation to the actually existing modalities of unfreedom and regulation under conditions of uneven development.

We suggest that a way forward is through examining *unfreedom in labour relations*. We believe that it is important to account for not only *degrees* of unfreedom but *forms* of unfreedom (McGrath 2013a). Building on this, we further propose that workers' (un)freedoms can also be understood in terms of their power vis-à-vis capital. Our approach entails a commitment to viewing extreme levels of unfreedom in labour relations within their political economic context, rather than as a matter of individual relationships. We hold that labour relations must always be understood to include relations of social reproduction. And we see racialization as a key dynamic of capitalist labour relations, which also serves as a dynamic of unfreedom.

We turn to the work of Wright (2000), Silver (2003) and others in providing a structure for thinking through how workers' (un)freedoms might be reinterpreted as part of their power relations with capital. One implication of this is that relations *within* the workplace are connected to but, critically, *cannot be deduced from*, relations within the labour market. This approach demonstrates how our understanding of unfree labour can be enriched by challenging its isolation from other studies of labour. Conversely, studies of work, labour and employment have largely cordoned off unfree labour from their remit, and they in turn can be enriched by attending to unfreedom (Strauss and Fudge 2014). We are therefore calling for a political economy of labour that takes unfreedom seriously. Following Miles (1987), our analysis of unfreedom aims to uncover the ways that capitalism, while producing and reproducing labour relations characterized by (limited) contractual freedom, is also sustained through producing, incorporating and interacting with other forms of labour relations. The implication of this is, for us, profound: we understand unfreedom in labour relations as an ever-present possibility under capitalism.

BINARIES

Trafficking, forced labour, bondage, new slavery, unfree labour: a number of terms exist to describe closely related and often overlapping phenomena. Definitions come from a variety of sources: legal and policy instruments such as the United Nations (UN) Trafficking Protocol or the ILO convention on forced labour can serve as key reference points. Academic and policy discussions of 'new slavery' or forced labour provide another set of definitions. While each definition can be analysed and potentially critiqued in turn, what they generally share is a reliance on a dichotomy in which forced labour and slavery are understood in opposition to a concept of 'free' labour.

For the New Slavery school – or as Choi-Fitzpatrick (2012) calls it, the *field of contemporary slavery studies* – Bales (1999) serves as a foundational text (Bales 2005; 2007; van den Anker 2004; Manzo 2005; Craig et al. 2007; Kara 2009; Batstone 2010; Brysk and Choi-Fitzpatrick 2012). This school insists on a clear distinction between free and unfree labour, in which slavery 'should not be confused' with other forms of exploitative work (Bales 1999: 259). The analytical distinction has political stakes: condemning 'slavery' has proven effective in garnering significant support and resources over the last decade. Brysk and Choi-Fitzpatrick, for example, describe a veritable renaissance of anti-trafficking efforts. Yet they also acknowledge that this has 'done little to reduce the incidence or harm of the phenomenon' (2012: 2). Our argument below is that the reason behind this lack of progress is that interventions focused on criminalization (and to a lesser extent on social inequalities) typically fail to fundamentally change the power relations that underlie exploitation.

The dichotomous approach of the New Slavery school follows Bales' influential framing of 'new' slavery in comparison to 'old' or 'traditional' slavery. The latter category is clearly a representation of the transatlantic slave trade and chattel slavery in the 'New World'. While the accuracy of this representation can be questioned, a broader issue is the choice of a particular time, place, population and set of practices as the baseline against which contemporary forms of 'slavery' are measured. This choice is strategic, drawing an analogy with what is widely seen as a great historical injustice. Yet, both today *and* historically, there have been numerous forms of labour relations which fall significantly short of anything we might call 'free labour'. These include not only chattel slavery but indentured servitude, sharecropping, 'apprenticeships', convict labour, debt bondage, and forced labour enacted by states (particularly in the context of colonialism and/or war), each of which has taken a variety of forms.

Distinctive of the twentieth and twenty-first centuries is the way in which states restrain and/or compel workers' movements, restricting workers' 'freedoms' and providing a source of power for capital through laws, regulations and policies on immigration and emigration. Historical analogies to this are not limited to the transatlantic slave trade but include penal transportation, vagrancy laws, entrapment and Black Codes as part of the convict leasing system, as well as Apartheid pass laws. The New Slavery school seeks inspiration from earlier abolitionist movements against slavery, as is evident in the genre of contemporary slave narratives (e.g. Bok 2003; Cadet 1998; Nazer and Lewis 2005; Sage and Kasten

2006; and Bales and Trodd 2008; see Johnson 2013; Trodd 2013). But if unfreedom has played a more extensive and complex role in relations of production and social reproduction, portrayals of abolitionism as the main conceptual and political foundation of strategies for combating contemporary forms of unfreedom are also called into question (Quirk 2012; see also Kothari 2013; Quirk 2011).

In contrast to the New Slavery school, a hallmark of what we label the *critical studies of unfree labour* school is the questioning of dichotomous definitions and the promotion of alternative, 'continuum'-oriented frameworks. In the introduction to a recent journal special issue representative of this school, for example, Barrientos et al. (2013: 1038) state that 'contemporary labour relations often cannot . . . be positioned on one side or other of a clear dividing line between "free" and "unfree" labour.' Here analytical and political stances are intertwined: the continuum approach highlights how concerns about the 'new slavery' may be met by policy responses which fail to serve the best interests of workers and migrants. It is argued that, underpinned by problematic liberal philosophies (Brace 2010), the 'new slavery' approach has clear pitfalls, particularly in that calls to address trafficking and forced labour often frame the problem(s) as residual (O'Connell Davidson 2010; Lerche 2007). High degrees of exploitation, and indeed forms of unfreedom that fail to meet the threshold of 'forced labour', may be thereby normalized. Worse, those who do not merit the status of 'victims' may be harmed as a result of the policy frameworks grounded in this approach – for example, migrants who are not deemed to be trafficked but are instead seen to 'choose' their employers can be labelled 'illegal' (Anderson 2008; Dottridge et al. 2007). This is exacerbated by popular representations (news stories, materials from advocacy organizations, reports by government agencies, and fictional portrayals such as the 2005 *Human Trafficking* television series or the 2008 film *Taken*), which tend to disproportionately emphasize: trafficking at the expense of other forms of unfreedom; 'women and children' as victims at the expense of other workers; and sex work at the expense of other sectors (Gulati 2012; Ditmore 2003; Anderson and Davidson 2002).

There is of course a rich tradition of Marxist analyses of, and heated debates over, unfree labour, especially in the areas of agrarian and peasant studies, often focusing on the majority world/Global South (e.g. Brass 1999; Brass and van der Linden 1997; cf. Miles 1987 on agriculture in Canada). In contrast to the sparse references to it in the New Slavery school, the *critical studies of unfree labour* school has closer connections to this literature (e.g. Breman et al. 2009) – albeit seeking to avoid what some have characterized as 'formal abstractionism' (LeBaron and Ayers 2013).

For Marxists, free labour is defined by both 'freedom' from ownership or rights over the means of (re-)production, and freedom to enter into a contract to sell one's labour to an employer (and to change employers). The latter freedom, however, is seen as masking the compulsion of the former: for what 'freedom' from the means of (re-)production actually entails is dispossession, forcing workers to sell their labour power in the first place. Unfree labour, then, is understood by Marxists as involving a *double dispossession*, with workers separated from the means of (re-)production but also unable to commodify their own labour power. Marxist interpretations of contemporary forms of unfree labour include those drawing on Marx's notion of primitive accumulation. What Blackburn (1997) terms the process of 'extended primitive accumulation' accompanying capitalism's continued economic expansion is seen as engendering unfree labour relations (Sakamoto 2007; Phillips and Sakamoto 2012). Many 'labour relations involving degrees of unfreedom' (Lerche 2007) appear, however, to be compatible with already-existing capitalist relations (Strauss 2012). In Brass' formulation, this can be understood in terms of a process of deproletarianization resulting from class struggle (Brass 1999). Miles (1987) opens more possibilities. Constructing an articulation of modes of production framework that compares different forms of unfree labour, he examines how capitalism produces, incorporates or interacts with these forms.

If it is clear that the sharp distinction between free and unfree labour made by the New Slavery school (and arguably also in many Marxist writings) can be viewed as problematic, this is reinforced by scholars working on labour who explicitly exclude 'unfree labour' from their remit. As Barrientos et al. (2013: 1038) put it, exploitative forms of labour 'are only rarely integrated' into a framework that includes unfree labour relations, which are instead 'thought to represent a separate and specific category of labour relations [that] need[s] to be viewed through different theoretical and empirical lenses'. Smith (2006: 390), for example, writes that 'the ability to change employers' is 'special to capitalism' so that 'feudalism, slavery and state socialism' can be excluded from the analysis – consequently denying the significance of unfreedom in contemporary labour relations. Castree et al. similarly state that 'en masse . . . firms could never, say, force their workers to labour hard 20 hours each day for little reward (*unless they were wage-slaves. . .*)', thus excluding the problem of unfreedom from their analysis of contemporary labour relations (2004: 36, emphasis added). We suggest that this is because the analysis of power relations between labour and capital is at the heart of many studies of labour, but that 'unfree labour' has been seen as lacking agency, and therefore power. If the question of labour's freedom can be understood as a question of power, then there might be scope for cross-fertilization between scholarship on unfree labour and other studies of labour.

'FREEDOMS' AS POWER

According to Bales, contemporary slavery is characterized by violence, the loss of free will and economic exploitation (2007: 11). This characterization has been broadly followed within the New Slavery school, albeit amended or refined by some authors (Brysk 2012; Choi-Fitzpatrick 2012). What exactly constitutes 'exploitation' is difficult to pin down, but it is the other two elements that concern us here: presumed loss of free will, and necessity of violence. 'Slavery' is also defined in individualized terms as a 'relationship between (at least) two people' marked by the 'violent control of one person by another' (Bales 2005: 8–9). These elements work together to remove 'slavery' from its politico-economic context and obviate any discussion of power beyond individual compulsion. This is because workers who have lost free will can exercise no power at all, and because violence stands in where power might enter. Furthermore, the heavy focus on the sexual exploitation of women and children, especially in trafficking approaches, denies them the status of workers, bolstering approaches that often paradoxically result in 'victims' being criminalized rather than liberated (cf. Chin, this volume).

The relationship between violence and power is a troubled one, with some scholars following Arendt in distinguishing power from violence (Allen 2003). We seek to problematize positions that create binary conceptualizations of power and violence: the threat of violence, when understood as including structural and economic violence or violence perpetrated by state actors, clearly shapes workers' realities in their relations with capital. This is true for 'free' workers (think, for example, of the 2012 Marikana massacre in South Africa), and is particularly the case for 'unfree' workers (O'Connell Davidson 2010). Yet by insisting on violence both as implicitly absent for 'free' workers and as a *necessary* aspect of 'slavery', the *only* mechanism of power exercised, all *other* forms of power recede into the background. As the theorization of labour control has highlighted, threats of violence have been a feature of 'despotic' regimes in ways that are both widespread and context-specific, and following Gramsci, power can simultaneously be exercised through the manufacture of consent in the creation of hegemonic socio-economic orders. The separation of violence from power facilitates problematic 'black and white' definitions of coercion and consent.

Ignoring other forms of power is enabled by the view that 'slaves' are stripped of free will. The position can be objected to in philosophical terms, by starting from a position that human beings are never devoid of free will. This is the position taken by Choi-Fitzpatrick (2012: 23). But beyond this lies the fact that workers can *and do* exercise agency even in the most dire of circumstances. This is what Coe and Jordhus-Lier (2011) refer to as 'constrained agency' (see also Rogaly 2009; Carswell and De Neve 2013). Rogaly (2008: 1438) demonstrates that for workers classified as experiencing forced labour, even 'at the scale of the individual seasonally migrant worker, capital does not have absolute power. There are spaces of negotiability.' We will return to this below.

Choi-Fitzpatrick (2012: 13) identifies an opportunity to 'better theorise the role of *power* in contemporary slavery'. While this is a welcome move, the attempt to grasp this opportunity nonetheless falls short. The problem is still framed as one of 'power exercised by slaveholders' rather than, say, by capital or fractions of capital. The forms of power exercised are described as 'psychological and cultural' but the way in which these form part of the political economy is left largely unexplored. Further, Choi-Fitzpatrick's description of the state as 'a distant and abstract force' in rural India (or alternatively, as corrupt) is only possible by conceptualizing the state as separable from the political economy of labour relations. This is in stark contrast to Rogaly (2008: 1439), who writes of the

> contingency of capital–labour relations in broader sets of power relations involving the state, which is 'omnipresent in the countryside'. State regulation, together with the workings of markets for agricultural outputs, underpins production relations in agricultural workplaces . . . this includes state regulation of landownership, of the relation between traders and producers, of migration, and tie-ups with companies.

Viewing relations of unfreedom as embedded in a broader political economy through which labour relations are regulated, Rogaly concludes that a focus on the 'perpetrators' serves to shift attention away from these broader relations and how they might be challenged.

While Bales further insists that 'race means little in the new slavery' (1999: 10–11), this is due to the tacit use of the transatlantic slave trade as an 'ideal type' against which to measure modern manifestations of 'slavery'. Race is implicitly treated as static and natural, rather than resulting from processes of *racialization*. In our view, understanding the political economy in which (unfree) labour relations are embedded means recognizing that these relations are powerfully shaped by the social construction of categories of difference including race, ethnicity, migrant status, caste and gender. Choi-Fitzpatrick (2012) does refer to caste, class, citizenship and gender as culturally embedded power structures.

Yet we would argue that this should be followed to its logical conclusion: capitalism necessarily entails making use of, reinforcing and/or producing these relations of 'difference' in the construction of labour relations. The process that Miles (1987) refers to as racialization is the prime example of this. As critical scholars of race have pointed out, racialization is not a second-order process; in fact, racial relations are *central to the organization of space-economy under capitalism* (Inwood and Bonds 2013).

POWER IN LABOUR RELATIONS

As alluded to in the preceding section, a key critique of the literature on new slavery and trafficking is that 'victims' are treated as lacking agency and in need of rescue. Choi-Fitzpatrick (2012) seeks to address this critique head on. He attempts to clear new ground by considering empowerment and resistance, thus breaking with the idea of a 'loss of free will'. Yet while the piece begins to explore how there may be forms of power beyond 'overt control' exercised by 'slaveholders', any forms of power exercised by the 'slaves' themselves are not detailed in any depth. We suggest that this may be because 'empowerment' still highlights the agency of outside actors presumed to have the capacity to grant workers power (if not freedom). Further, resistance is a tall order. We propose instead to analyse forms of agency exercised by workers who experience unfreedoms, utilizing Katz's (2004) framework of resilience, reworking and resistance (Coe and Jordhus-Lier 2011; Cumbers et al. 2008). This, we hope, will point to the actual and potential sources of power exercised by workers. In turn, these sources of power can be evaluated, starting from (and building on) the framework of structural and associational power (Wright 2000; Silver 2003).

To be clear, when using the term 'resistance' here we do not necessarily mean resistance to capitalism as a whole, or overt (as opposed to subversive) defiance. Rather, in resistance we include actions which challenge the (unfree) terms and (degrading) conditions of work and/or which insist on the dignity, value and rights of those undertaking work *as workers*. In this sense we are primarily interested in labour resistance, but recognize that struggles for social recognition (against inequality, exploitation and specific oppressions grounded in, for example, race, ethnicity or gender) interact in important ways with struggles against unfreedom. For our purposes, workers who seek to achieve – and insist on their rights to – degrees of mobility approximating 'free' wage labour and decent conditions of employment (in which there are efforts to protect their health and safety) are engaging in resistance.

As discussed above, we also want to rethink (un)freedoms as power. In this sense, we are building on approaches in the critical studies of unfree labour tradition that seek to explore in new ways how relations of production are interrelated with specific modalities of unfreedom (see, for example, Phillips 2013 on adverse incorporation), but in ways that emphasize the relational nature of power vis-à-vis both capital (sectors, firms) and labour. For this task, we start from the framework developed by Olin Wright (2000) and built upon by Silver (2003) to distinguish between associational power – the ability workers have to organize and achieve unity, and structural power – their ability to affect capital. Structural power is further divided into workplace power – the strategic location of workers which enables them to impact the business, and marketplace power – the extent to which there is a tight labour market or shortage of workers. Others, drawing on social movement theory, have added new elements to this framework such as 'symbolic' (normative, or moral) power, a subset of associational power (in that it is a means of building solidarity) and logistical power, a subset of structural power rooted in the increased importance of logistics and distribution (delivery time, flexibility and reliability) (Webster et al. 2008). This demonstrates a conception of power relations as dynamic, in which sources of power are continually identified and/or constructed: for example, whereas the logistics revolution empowered capital in relation to workers, the increased importance of logistics in turn represents a weak point for capital, which workers may be able to exploit strategically.

Finally, Smith (2006) identifies two sources of workers' power: work-effort power – which relates to shop-floor conflicts, and mobility power – which entails the threat of leaving. While Smith is seeking to redress the lack of attention to labour market dynamics within labour process theory, these can be seen as analogous to Silver's workplace and marketplace power. What the piece highlights for us, however, is that these sources of power shape each other. Workers confront exploitation through disciplined, creative, spontaneous or obstructive forms of agency, which both produce, and are produced by, the kinds of resilience, reworking and resistance described by Katz (see also Mann 2007 on struggles over value and the wage). Workers who can make credible threats of leaving are better able to push the boundaries within the workplace, thus identifying and constructing new sources of work-place or work-effort power. These forms of power are always exercised in relation to others (employers, capitalists, other workers, state bodies, etc.) and so we can also use this framework to analyse how others are able to block or remove sources of workers' power.

Here we draw on our previous research, in particular McGrath's qualitative comparative study of Bolivian migrants living and working in small-scale garment workshops in and around São Paulo, Brazil and of internal migrants working in sugar cane in the south-east and centre-west of Brazil. In both of these cases, for which fieldwork was carried out in 2008, there was substantial evidence that severely restricted freedoms and degrading working conditions were not uncommon, confirming a significant incidence of what is referred to in Brazil as 'slave labour'. McGrath previously (2013a) analysed workers' 'freedom' in these cases as broken down into three types: freedom of movement, freedom to change employers and freedom to contest conditions. She argued that workers experienced restrictions on these three types of freedoms in both cases, to different extents and through a variety of mechanisms. However, applying the frameworks outlined above, we can see these as forms of power.

The freedom to change employers, to participate in a labour market, equates to mobility/marketplace power. In the Brazilian cases, the use and manipulation of debt (often involving workers' sense of honour), tied accommodation, the use of labour recruiters and/or network hiring (in which the choice to leave could potentially harm workers' reputations and social networks), and delayed payment of wages (keeping workers on the job in the hopes of recovering wages already earned) were all mechanisms used to remove potential sources of mobility/marketplace power for workers. In the garment case, there were also instances in which workers were not allowed to leave the workplaces or were physically prevented from doing so. In the sugar cane case, there was little evidence of this, but workplaces were sometimes in quite isolated locales. This limited physical mobility means limited labour market mobility, constricting workers' mobility/marketplace power.

In both of these cases, workers had been seeking employment, following in the footsteps of others who had undertaken labour migration for similar jobs in the same destination regions, one of few apparent opportunities for earning a regular income. They were not captured or imprisoned as a means of getting them to work. In some cases the choice of their labour migration and entry into employment was comparatively 'free', while in other cases the recruitment process itself had elements of trafficking (e.g. holding workers' passports, instilling fear of the Brazilian authorities, deception about the employment which would be obtained, and aspects of debt bondage through the charges for recruitment/transportation and means of repaying these). The dichotomous approach described above in which entry is either 'free' or 'unfree', however, has in our view led to an assumption that this in and of itself will determine shop-floor relations. Mobility power, as explained above, will shape and be shaped by workplace power. But the former cannot be read in absolute terms, nor as exclusively determining the latter; the elements of trafficking described above are often effective, but do not *guarantee* shop-floor compliance. If entry and exit are neither entirely 'free' nor completely 'unfree' then the extent to which workers are able to exercise mobility power is likely to interact with workplace power (and other forms of power) in more complex ways.

It is important to recognize that these sources of power emerge from particular politico-economic contexts – and in the Brazilian cases, these contexts are characterized by extreme inequalities. Brazil has the highest GDP in South America while Bolivia has one of the lowest. Within the country, in spite of remarkable progress under Workers' Party governments, Brazil's Gini coefficient of income inequality was still 54.7 in 2009, in part reflective of regional and racial disparities. Further, immigration policy (prior to and during the period of fieldwork) structured the choices for these workers. Garment workers' perceived and actual migrant status is intertwined with a process of racialization. Migrant sugar cane workers are also affected by racialization, which interacts with the fact that in their regions of origin there have been longstanding struggles over land and dispossession from it. Workers are not individually 'vulnerable' due to circumstances, then. Rather their 'vulnerability' is a function of political economic processes and struggles.

SOCIAL REPRODUCTION AND POWER

Above, we have outlined existing frameworks to analyse relations of power between workers and capital, and attempted to incorporate questions of unfreedom into these. Yet any analysis of power and (un)freedom in labour relations must also avoid replicating traditional masculinist frameworks which have too often rendered invisible 'non-productive' labour: unpaid domestic labour, paid domestic and care work, and the ways in which households, communities and societies sustain, perpetuate and challenge forms of social organization over time and in place. Thus while Silver (2003) sees opportunities to withdraw from the labour market – to rely on means of social reproduction outside of waged work – as a subset of workers' marketplace power, our analysis takes this further. We wish to examine the way in which the interrelationship of production and social reproduction is essential to the understanding of the political economy of contemporary forms of unfreedom (Strauss 2013; Strauss and Fudge 2014).

As discussed above, one of Marx's insights is that the 'freedom' of workers in actually existing capitalist economies to commodify their labour is premised on their dispossession from both the means of production and the resources necessary for their subsistence outside of waged work (Marx 1976). Yet the concept of the free wage labourer in Marx is an ambivalent one. While he uses the stylized facts of political economy to characterize the way in which the capitalist and the labourer meet in the process of free contract, his methodology and empirical analyses of the proletariat in England suggest that this freedom needs to be understood in the context of clear and present relations of dispossession (primitive accumulation), oppression and exploitation (Strauss and Fudge 2014). The abstract freedom of liberal individualism is held up against a systemic and materialist analysis that makes the collective relations of production visible.

While the concept of free contract has informed subsequent analyses of the evolution of wage labour and labour markets in ways that have contributed to the perpetuation of a binary conceptualization of free/unfree labour, another equally salient, if less-often acknowledged, binary also underpins dominant epistemologies of unfree labour: the distinction between production and social reproduction (LeBaron and Ayers 2013; Strauss 2013). Feminist political economists use the concept of social reproduction to describe this binary, in which waged work is understood to generate a surplus, the appropriation of which is the basis of capitalist profit and accumulation, while unwaged work in the home and community is understood as non-productive.

Social reproduction has been developed as a conceptual and analytical framework by socialist feminists and feminist political economists to account for: (a) the role, importance and value of the unpaid work performed mostly by women to reproduce the labouring population – typically unacknowledged in production-oriented analyses; (b) 'the activities and attitudes, behaviours and emotions, responsibilities and relationships directly involved in the maintenance of life on a daily basis, and intergenerationally' (Laslett and Brenner 1989: 382); (c) biological reproduction and the tasks and relations of care associated with rearing children; and (d) in capitalist welfare states, pooled risk services and programmes (Bezanson 2006) such as schooling (Bowles and Gintis 1976).

Domestic labour is the exemplar: it is the unwaged work that is done, usually by women, which allows the working class (men and women) to continue to work for wages by providing the conditions for the maintenance of everyday life, from cooking meals and washing clothes to creating time (by the accomplishment of these tasks) for leisure. Domestic work, performed for a wage and outside the home (Braedley and Luxton forthcoming), may replace the domestic labour of family members, which can either be for the purpose of enabling a dual wage-earner household or establishing and reinforcing hierarchy and status differentials. Race, class and gender often intersect (Crenshaw et al. 1995) and/or interlock (see Collins 2000 on the matrix of domination), such that women's labour market participation is shaped by the ways in which they experience their 'place' in the economic order as mediated simultaneously by gender, race, ethnicity, class and sexuality. Racialization, predicated on white privilege, produces labour market segmentation and social sorting that buttresses and reinforces status and hierarchy differentials (for example between housewives and domestic servants). This has been an essential component of the unfreedom associated with domestic servitude.

Social reproduction is also a lens through which to focus on the interrelationship of the social construction of gender and unequal divisions of labour (what feminists have theorized as *inter alia* the sex-gender system and gender order – see Rubin 1975 and Lerner 1986) in the home and workplace, which assume a separate and distinct character under capitalist relations of production (cf. Mitchell et al. 2004). These divisions of labour relate, but are not reducible, to what Carol Pateman (1988) called 'the sexual contract'. The idea of the sexual contract is used to analyse the uneven imbrication (and often fusion) of patriarchal and radical individualist conceptions of natural equality in theories of contract in political philosophy. Thus,

> The contractarian conception of social life implies that there is nothing but contract 'all the way down'; social life is nothing more than contracts between individuals . . . The fact that contractarians treat the employment contract as the exemplary contract suggests that economic institutions provide an example of their ideal . . . Only the postulate of natural equality prevents the original social contract from being an explicit slave contract; or, to put this another way, only the postulate of natural equality prevents *all stories about social contracts from turning into a variety of coercive arrangements* (Pateman 1988: 59–60, emphasis added).

Pateman points out that in this abstracted world the way in which 'the humanity of the slave must necessarily be denied and affirmed, recurs in a variety of dramatic and less dramatic guises in modern patriarchy' (ibid.: 60). Although referring to historical forms of chattel slavery, this argument has implications for understanding degrees of freedom in relations of subordination in contemporary labour markets. Here the social construction of categories of difference, including gender and class but also, vitally, race, ethnicity and citizenship, intersects with, and is constitutive of, related processes of racialization and the production of unfree workers (Sharma 2006). Racialization in relation to labour markets, which describes the interrelationship of the social construction of racial categories with labour market segmentation *on the basis of those racial categories*, is particularly salient for understanding new and evolving forms of unfreedom and 'new slavery' that often involve migrant workers (Miles 1987; Satzewich 1991). Race and ethnicity become entangled with nationality and citizenship: as Miles and Sharma both suggest, racism becomes a social relation of production, which legitimizes the state-sanctioned unfree wage labour of migrant workers, the denial of citizenship rights to those same workers, *and* the ways in which their labour supports the social reproduction of citizens.

There are thus at least two distinct dimensions to the interrelationship of relations of unfreedom and relations of social reproduction in contemporary labour markets, which also influence the discursive and political framing of 'the new slavery' and human trafficking. First, degrees and forms of unfreedom and subordination in labour markets relate to degrees and forms of unfreedom and subordination in other spheres: labour markets are socially constructed and relations and conditions of social reproduction and production are intrinsically (dialectically) related. This manifests itself in a variety of concrete ways, including through wage determination (Picchio 1992) and labour control (see, for example, Burawoy 1985; Jonas 1996), but also through the ways in which some workers, such as sex workers, are legally and politically characterized as victims or criminals but never as those who perform labour (Bernstein 2010; Shamir 2012). Second, because both production and social reproduction are structured by stratified, intersecting social relations such as race and gender (and the interlocking oppressions they produce), what Bakan and Stasiulis (2012) call modalities of unfreedom are also structured by 'hierarchies of desirability' (Mountz 2003) that determine mobility, status and rights.

A well-researched example is illustrated by the relationship between food production, wage determination and the treatment of agricultural workers (Rogaly 2008; 2009; Scott et al. 2012; Strauss 2013). Labour markets, and norms and relations of social reproduction, are inherently but not exclusively local; workers experience them in the context of a globalized political economy that they both shape and must adapt to (Mackinnon et al. 2010; Bedford and Rai 2010). One of the insights of feminist political economy is, contra orthodox economics, that wages are intrinsically related to collectively determined and struggled over norms of social reproduction – rather than being subject, like 'regular' commodities, to asocial market forces of supply and demand (Picchio 1992). Cheapening food has been a strategy, like the expansion of credit, to maintain stability of consumption in the face of real wage stagnation in many minority world/Global North economies. This has in part been possible through the strategic development of new and evolving relations of unfreedom for agricultural labour, much of which is done (in both the minority and majority worlds – Global North and South) by migrant and immigrant workers (Miles 1987; Satzewich 1991).

These strategies of capital and the state, including in Europe and North America, involve the development of guest worker programmes, the use of labour intermediaries, forms of real and de facto debt bondage and forms of assisted migration that can amount to human trafficking. Relations of social reproduction form an integral and complex aspect of capitalist labour relations, which also shape the differential incorporation of workers into labour markets. We view social reproduction as an additional arena in which power relations are played out, not least when these labour relations are characterized by unfreedom(s). Questions of power, agency, resistance and victimhood need to be understood through the interrelationship of production and social reproduction in the political economy of labour markets.

WORKERS' AGENCY AND POWER

The question that arises then is whether, for workers enmeshed in labour relations characterized by unfreedom, it is possible to identify the exercise of power. Rather than seeking to find outright resistance and being disappointed by the lack of evidence for it, we believe that identifying the forms of agency exercised by workers may point towards actual and potential forms of resistance. These are expressed through: demands about food, clean water and accommodation; organizing that takes the form of demands for social recognition; and 'traditional' forms of labour resistance such as strikes (McGrath 2013a). This follows Rowbotham (1994: 188), who writes of the way that reformers in nineteenth- and early twentieth-century Britain often failed to acknowledge the articulation of grievances by homeworkers, painting a picture of these workers as passive and unorganizable. Responses to domination and exploitation from the ruling classes tended to focus on morality rather than economic injustice; it is instructive that both historical responses to the use of women and girls in agricultural gangs (see Strauss 2013 on the regulation of gangmasters in the UK), and in sex work, have tended to emphasize sexual and social rather than labour or economic exploitation, and de-emphasize their agency *as workers*. It also highlights the entanglement of relations of production and social reproduction in relation to 'formal wage labour'. Rogaly makes this point with regard to contemporary discussions of forced labour which obscure 'continual (re)negotiation by workers' over 'apparently small but often meaningful' aspects of workplace arrangements (2008: 1432).

We draw on data from the Bolivian garment workers' case cited earlier, in which they contest the quality and quantity of food/meals. The quality and quantity of food/meals are central to workers' evaluations of the conditions in which they have been employed. For example, when asked if those running one workshop he was employed in were 'good people', Danilo responded '. . . not everybody is good in all things. I used to work in Vila Guilherme [a São Paulo neighbourhood]. There the food was very good; there was plenty, it was very good, there was fruit, everything.' Running his own workshop, Elías stated that he treats people well and mentioned that he doesn't give them 'just any food, no. The best food, that I like, for everybody . . . rice, beans, sausage every day, or eggs, I make a really good meal! Everybody eats the same food that I do, that I like.' Gabriel referred to his initial harsh employment experience during which he sometimes had to mix sugar or salt with water as a means of battling hunger and dehydration. Teófila stated that shortly after leaving a workshop she had been employed in, she sought medical treatment and discovered that she was anaemic.

In one sense, this is an example of reworking, because while overt struggles over wages and working hours rarely erupt, workers do seek to improve their day-to-day experience and well-being while on the job, and feel justified in doing so. Food is open for discussion in a way that wages, hours and the employment relation itself are not. Yet it is also clear that the provision of food is used by workers as symbolic of 'good' or 'bad' treatment. This may also, then, serve as a source of (symbolic, workplace) power for workers, who are able to contest the authority of those running the workshops through reference to the provision of meals.

Individual 'escapes' from the workshop and demands for unpaid wages from (former) employers can be identified as individual acts of resistance. Collective organizing, though, did not appear common. The sewing workers' union had not successfully incorporated migrant workers and their demands. There are, however, some spaces in São Paulo where workers might be able to construct a degree of associational power: migrant support centres founded by the Catholic Church as part of its 'pastoral' mission, drawing on its historically progressive role in Brazil. The centres are effective in identifying issues faced by workers which go beyond traditional 'labour' issues, such as the gendered violence in the garment workshops. This violence is not only perpetrated by employers, but also by workers – yet the combination of living and working space is one factor which contributes to the elevated incidence of this violence. In a context of growing concern over 'slave labour' in the garment workshops, these centres are critical spaces for struggles over migrants' rights. Cultural celebrations among Bolivian workers, for example, some of which are organized through the centres, are a form of resilience. But they also connect to attempts at gaining recognition and shifting perceptions of migrants, constructing associational power by challenging their status as 'clandestine'. In 2009, there was an amnesty for irregular immigrants as well as a Residency Agreement for Nationals of Mercosur, Bolivia and Chile. It seems no coincidence that the first two Bolivian garment workers were liberated from 'slave labour' as a result of a labour inspection in Brazil in the very next year.

To some extent this points toward the varied forms of collaboration and solidarity among diverse groups of working people represented by social movement unionism (Moody 1997; Gordon 2005; Lier 2007a; Wills 2009; Webster et al. 2008). Organizing along the lines of migrant status and identity, however, is complicated in this case by the fact that many small-scale sewing workshops are now often run by Bolivian and other Latin American migrants. Although only a small degree of the value is retained by them, with much of the profits being made further up the supply chain, these migrants are nonetheless in a different position to the regular employees, while still part of the 'community' served by the centres – complicating efforts to challenge working conditions (indeed, opening a workshop is an aspiration for many workers).

Sugar cane workers have an additional source of power: an expectation of support from state and civil society actors. In recent years, migrant sugar cane workers have been incorporated into efforts to combat 'slave labour'. These efforts emerge from complex histories of struggle over land and labour in Brazil. There are more examples of active resistance in this case. Migrant sugar cane workers hold recruiters accountable for conditions, call labour inspectors (or threaten to), engage in work stoppages and strikes, and carry out protests. There are limits to this resistance, and the support received by workers is still counterbalanced by the influence of the rural lobby and the central role of the sugar cane agro-industrial complex in the Brazilian economy, in which the state plays an active role in maintaining (McGrath 2013b; Carstensen and McGrath 2012).

Social reproduction is therefore an integral dynamic of labour relations in the sugar cane case as well. Sugar cane workers often undertake these seasonal migrations for only a certain number of years in order to accumulate enough resources to improve or build a home or run a business. But this is also due to the severe physical toll the work has on workers' bodies. Workers thus also engage in reworking through struggles over their bodily well-being (e.g. the provision of clean drinking water). Further, as discussed elsewhere (McGrath 2013a), those who migrate for this work are expected to do so alone, with employer-provided accommodation often exclusively for men. Constructed as individuals unencumbered by families and communities, the trans-local nature of social reproduction is obscured in the destination regions. Yet their wages are used for the types of projects just discussed, and in turn they are supported by social reproductive work carried out in regions of origin – including care work as well as various forms of agricultural work. To the extent that workers are able to construct these extended forms of social reproduction (for they do not always succeed), this is an example of resilience. Importantly, the fact that couples and families are finding private accommodation and migrating together in spite of expectations that the women stay at 'home' is a form of (symbolic and practical) resistance in the arena of social reproduction.

CONCLUSION: REGULATION AND POWER

To return to our starting point, the different approaches to unfreedom in contemporary labour relations that we have discussed also entail different approaches to the question of action, as well as analysis. How should we not only understand, but also tackle, extreme exploitation in contemporary labour markets? Here, again, there are divergences and we will conclude by considering the politico-legal implications of these in the context of the global political economy.

The New Slavery school has been successful in raising the profile of extreme labour exploitation to the point where it is now being acknowledged and debated in many countries. The school has largely been associated with abolitionist movements grounded in criminalization and human rights frameworks. The former seek to create or bolster frameworks for criminalizing those who traffic or subject workers to slavery, forced labour, domestic servitude or sexual exploitation. The latter tend to produce positive obligations grounded in the recognition of those subject to exploitation as alleged victims of criminal offences and human rights abuses. The politics of the New Slavery has produced shifting alliances among feminists, human rights groups, religious organizations and anti-slavery campaigners (who in some cases have links to historical mobilizations against slavery, particularly the Atlantic slave trade). There are overlapping, complementary and occasionally contradictory relationships with anti-trafficking movements. In spite of the progress made, however, policy responses to the problem of 'new slavery' have often relied on stereotypes (e.g. of the racialized foreign exploiters and powerless victims) rather than addressing root causes. Approaches focusing on criminalization have further been critiqued for failing to produce successful prosecutions or justice for victims (who are often themselves criminalized), while carceral and anti-immigration policies have been framed as combating trafficking even though they may harm the most vulnerable workers in the global political economy.

At the same time, while our approach has suggested building on the *critical studies of unfree labour* school, the model we have proposed not only takes a continuum of unfreedom in labour relations as a starting point, but insists that these forms of exploitation are not exceptional, residual or reducible to extra-economic relations; unfreedom in relations of production and reproduction are resources on which capital draws in order to enhance the extraction of surplus and the process of accumulation. Even more important, however, is the recognition that as long as unfreedom is seen as delinked from 'mainstream' relations of power in labour markets, firms, sectors and policy-makers can condemn (through discursive and juridical means) 'new slavery' while *at the same time* seeking to actively undermine the wages, conditions and protections of 'ordinary' workers. This suggests that despite the welcome attention being paid to the unfreedom of (some) workers, the conditions of their exploitation are a feature of the global political economy. As a question of power as much as freedom, there is no shortcut to abolition.

18. The race to the bottom halted? Passive revolution and workers' resistance in China

Youngseok Jang and Kevin Gray

The transformation of Maoist China from a peasant-based, state-socialist order to an export-oriented mass production economy has come about through a revolution from above. In the absence of an indigenous bourgeoisie, the Chinese state took upon itself the leading role in the reorganization of social relations commensurate with a restoration of capitalism. Seeking a rapprochement with the West in order to stave off what it perceived as a threat from the Soviet Union, China's adoption of capitalist practices allowed its industrial base to expand to record proportions, reciprocating the quest for low-wage locations on the part of transnational capital. The country's emergence as a low-cost production platform in the context of the globalization of the capitalist economy accommodated the supposed 'race to the bottom' elicited by the availability of new sources of labour power.

The present chapter argues that capitalist restoration in China can be fruitfully analysed as a 'passive revolution' in Gramsci's sense, in which changes in the global political economy and the balance of local class forces are dialectically related. However, the period in which Chinese workers were passive victims of this process appears to be drawing to a close. The 2010 strike at the Nanhai Honda plant in Guangzhou will serve as a case in point. We will highlight the important parallels between this strike and the historical pattern of labour struggles elsewhere in East Asia. Whereas strikes by migrant workers in China's coastal manufacturing regions had for the most part been responses to the infringement of workers' individual rights, workers at Nanhai Honda were primarily concerned with a proactive struggle to increase wages and achieve union democracy. The strike demonstrated the incipient development of a class consciousness amongst the second generation of migrant workers, but also reflects the increased structural power accrued to such workers as a result of ongoing changes in China's labour market.

China appears to be at a similar juncture to South Korea and Taiwan in the mid-1980s when industrialization and the transition from an unlimited to a limited labour supply led to the emergence of militant labour movements that eventually went on to challenge authoritarian industrialization and to struggle for democracy in the workplace. The Nanhai Honda strike may therefore be viewed as an instance in a potential transition towards a model of political economy in which higher wages, domestic consumption and a greater protection of labour rights plays a more important role. Given China's central role as the 'workshop of the world', any transition in the country's political economy is likely to have a momentous impact upon reversing any apparent globalization-induced 'race to the bottom' and on the structure of the global political economy generally.

PASSIVE REVOLUTION AND WORKING CLASS AGENCY

The world-historical relationship between labour and global capitalist restructuring can be profitably examined by adopting Antonio Gramsci's concept of passive revolution. This concept denotes, on the one hand, the initiating role of the state in the process of social transformation; on the other, the fact that the particular political, economic and social dynamics of individual social formations and processes of state formation must be analysed within the broader framework of a temporally and spatially differentiated global capitalist economy and the geopolitical inter-states system (Morton 2010). Gramsci's framework is particularly useful for examining the dynamics of China's capitalist restoration since the 1970s. It can help to address the issue of the role of the state in facilitating the restoration of capitalism, and how this 'revolution from above' has been embedded within broader processes of transnational accumulation and inter-state rivalry. Most importantly, it can help to place the analysis of labour and of class struggle more generally at the centre of those processes and examine how the 'optimistic' and 'pessimistic' characteristics of labour movements are interlinked with the spatial and temporal dynamics of global capitalism.

The pre-eminent role of the Chinese state in the process derives from a particular balance of forces in which an ascendant class is still unable to achieve a position of dominance over the old order and a stalemate occurs. In such situations, the state can substitute for the ascendant social class, as (in Gramsci's example) happened with Piedmont in the bourgeois revolution in Italy. Since the Italian bourgeoisie was still too weak to provide leadership over other social groups, the task was conferred on the Piedmont state, which took upon itself the functions of the monarchy (Gramsci 1971: 104–6). Thus passive revolution, as Anne

Sassoon argues, indicates 'the constant reorganization of state power and its relationship to society to preserve control by the few over the many, and maintain a traditional lack of control by the mass of the population over the political and economic realms'. This is achieved through such techniques as Caesarism, in which a strongman steps in to resolve conflicts amongst opposed social forces, and *trasformismo*, where the potential leaders of subaltern groups are deliberately co-opted into ruling elites, which can be seen as common features of non-hegemonic societies (Sassoon 1982: 129; cf. Bradanini, this volume). Passive revolution can thus have two distinct yet complementary aspects. First, it serves as a 'revolution from above' reliant on state-led initiatives to ensure the political rule of capital in a situation in which the bourgeoisie is too weak to achieve such aims itself. Second, passive revolution achieves this through seeking to both forestall and at the same time adopt subaltern demands, yet without bringing those subaltern groups into the ruling historical bloc (Morton 2010).

The Chinese state played this 'Piedmont-type role' through three 'social' interventions from above.

- First, capitalist restoration was achieved through the creation of a nascent capitalist class out of the ranks of the party–state bureaucracy itself. Cadres turned local state and collective enterprises into township enterprises; later, when the state adopted a policy of privatization of small and medium-sized state enterprises, the assets of these companies went directly into the hands of the cadres who managed them.
- Second, the Chinese state sought to bring about a proletarianization of workers through the dismantling of the socialist enterprise system and the creation of a capitalist labour market. From the mid-1990s onwards, the government abandoned its long-held commitment to SOEs as the central anchor of the Chinese economy. This led to the creation of a massive sector of laid-off or 'off-post' (*xiagang*, 下岗) workers.
- Third, the state's de-collectivization of agriculture in the early 1980s played a key role in bringing about the semi-proletarianized workforce for the export-oriented sector in the coastal areas that emerged following the opening of the doors to foreign investment in the early 1980s.

How did the Chinese working class respond to these changes? Gramsci developed the concept of passive revolution precisely in order to refine and elaborate upon the primacy that Marx and Engels ascribed to social being over social consciousness, and to purge those comments of 'every residue of mechanism and fatalism' (Gramsci 1971: 107), tendencies which are equally present in approaches to the study of labour. Too often, the absorption of the effects of capitalist transnationalization have been treated as a residual process, both in areas abandoned by capital and in zones where it appears in force.

Clearly it is not enough to conclude, as Stevis and Boswell (2008: 14) do, that 'it would be surprising if unions were not affected by . . . dynamics [of globalization].' Even notions of an impending Polanyian counter-movement (Munck 2002; Webster et al. 2008), tend to remain tributary to a conception of globalization as a primarily structurally-driven phenomenon, in which agency is insufficiently accounted for. As Samuel Knafo argues,

> Agency . . . tends to be wrongly conflated with resistance and thus reduced to a limited moment of analysis. When agency is discussed, it is generally associated with disadvantaged social forces that are most interested, presumably, in changing society. But, being weaker, they are often seen as struggling to garner the power needed to realize their vision of a different world. For this reason, they always seem to be 'in waiting' for the moment when they will be empowered and finally able to change things (Knafo 2010: 494; cf. Bradanini on the Italian Communist Party, this volume).

The failure to consider the active agency of workers is particularly apparent in the way that China and the role of Chinese workers enter into analyses of globalization. A key argument has been that the 'race to the bottom' has intensified with the emergence of China as the 'workshop of the world'. Rather than representing the latest in the flock of Asian 'flying geese', China has now come to serve as a final production platform for the region's exports market, and earlier industrializers in North-East and South-East Asia have narrowed their industrial bases to the production and trade of parts and components within this broader regional production network. This process also pits different workers in different countries against each other to the benefit of transnational capital and its local subordinates, intensifying competition and uneven development (Hart-Landsberg and Burkett 2006: 13). As such, the so-called 'China price' (Harney 2008) has a devastating impact on the livelihood of workers globally. As William Greider (2001) has argued in *The Nation*,

> The 'giant sucking sound' Ross Perot used to talk about is back, only this time it is not Mexico sucking away American jobs. It is China sucking away Mexico's jobs. And jobs from Taiwan and South Korea, Singapore and Thailand, Central and South America, and even from Japan . . .. In the 'race to the bottom', China is defining the new bottom.

Anita Chan argues that China's role in the race to the bottom is established upon the basis of a comprehensive system of labour exploitation that makes Chinese wages particularly low in comparison with other countries. This system includes the failure of local governments to set minimum wage levels to the stipulated minimum of 40 per cent of the local wage. The structural weakness of Chinese labour and the low wages offered is a result of the fact that the country has an 'almost inexhaustible supply of cheap labour from the countryside' (Chan 2003: 5). Once migrant workers relocate to the urban areas the *hukou* (户口) residency permit system effectively makes migrant workers foreigners in their own country through denying them access to education and government services (Solinger 1999). In the workplace, workers are denied collective rights through strict proscription of free trade unions and denial of the right to strike (Chen 2007). As a result, workers experience a form of 'managerial despotism' at the point of production (Lee 1999) and local authorities fail to enforce labour laws. Furthermore, the prospects for reform of China's labour conditions are not considered to be bright, given that it is precisely this dependence on low wages and the export-oriented manufacturing that has underpinned the country's impressive economic growth in recent years (Morgan 2008: 418). To make matters worse, any concrete measures taken by the central government to improve labour conditions are likely to be ineffectual as a result of the decentralized governance structure and the fact of competition between local governments to attract foreign investment (Hart-Landsberg and Burkett 2006: 25).

RESURGENT LABOUR IN THE EAST ASIAN EXPERIENCE

The static depiction of China's labour regime illustrated above fails to consider countervailing processes that might challenge the country's role in the race to the bottom. In considering the transformative role of workers' struggles in producing 'globalization', it is instructive to examine the historical experience of newly industrializing countries such as South Africa, Brazil, Poland and South Korea. As Beverly Silver (2003 and this volume) has argued, there is a clear historical pattern in which repressive labour regimes are eventually challenged by forces emerging out of the industrialization process itself. Indeed, the integration of coastal China into global production networks can be seen as an outcome of such processes elsewhere in the global political economy.

There is evidence to suggest that similar processes are underway in China. The process of industrialization and accompanying structural changes in the labour market are strengthening the structural power possessed by Chinese workers. Widespread privatization of state-owned enterprises in the 1990s led workers to increasingly engage in collective actions to defend their job security or fight for redundancy compensation, and to seek the punishment of corrupt managers. Since the early 2000s, however, migrant workers in the coastal manufacturing regions have become increasingly militant and prone to collective action as well. Protests have taken the form of strikes, sit-down demonstrations, protests outside government offices, traffic blockades, riots and so on. In 2004, for example, official figures recorded 74 000 mass incidents involving both peasants and workers, up from 10 000 a decade earlier (Macartney 2006). Initially, the majority of these disputes were reactive in character and were aimed at resisting infringements on workers' livelihood such as the non-payment of wages (*China Labour Bulletin* 2007). More recently, however, this increased militancy of labour has been notable both for its scope and its relative shift away from reactive issues such as the infringement of basic labour rights towards a proactive concern with material issues such as wages and union democracy. This suggests a broader transition in workers' class consciousness from a class *in itself* to a class *for itself*.

The reasons for this shift can be found through an examination of the broader East Asian experience. As Deyo (1989) has argued, Taiwan and South Korea's postwar export-oriented industrialization was underpinned by their distinctive systems of labour control. However, the process of industrialization itself conferred upon workers the structural power with which to challenge this system of state-mandated hyper-exploitation. Taiwan in the late 1960s and South Korea in the mid-1970s both experienced Lewisian turning points, in which they underwent a transition from an 'unlimited' to a limited labour supply and thus experienced a rise in industrial wages (Fei and Ranis 1975; Bai 2007). This led to the rise of labour movements in both countries in the 1980s which went on to push for further improvements in wages and working conditions. It was these structural changes and the rise of labour as a social force alongside aggressive US exchange rate policies that led to the relocation of low-wage manufacturing away from Taiwan and South Korea towards South-East Asian and mainland China.

Importantly, as Cai Fang of the Chinese Academy of Social Sciences has argued, China itself may now be approaching or may even have already passed its Lewisian turning point (Cai 2010; see also Das and Diaye 2013). In combination with a clear shift away from the pro-urban bias of the Jiang Zemin years towards an abolition of agricultural taxes and the raising of government procurement prices under the Hu Jintao administration, this has served to slow migration to the cities and cause labour shortages in the urban export-oriented manufacturing sector (Hung 2009: 20). Growing labour shortages have led to a tripling of wages in real terms between 1997 and 2007, though their impact has been felt differentially across the country. They have been highest in the coastal manufacturing regions such as Guangzhou and Shenzhen and the urban centres of Beijing and Shanghai, and have been higher for skilled workers than for the unskilled workers who typically work in manufacturing (Yang et al. 2010).

Given the structural nature of this transition, the government's authoritarian labour policies have become increasingly ineffective in containing labour unrest, and there has been a transition towards a more conciliatory approach on the part of the Chinese government. Whereas the government had traditionally responded to labour unrest with a policy of heavy repression, the Hu Jintao administration which came to power in 2002 adopted a more balanced strategy of coercion and consent under the slogan of the 'harmonious socialist society' (社会主义和谐社会). A key element of this programme was strengthening the legal framework governing industrial relations. Whilst this has not extended as far as ensuring the freedom of association, these reforms have nonetheless involved an implicit recognition of the divergent interests between labour and capital and have provided new avenues whereby workers can address their grievances legally, albeit on an individualized basis.

This has involved the creation of institutions that are able to represent workers more effectively by channelling unrest into bureaucratic forms of dispute resolution (Clarke and Pringle 2009: 93), a key element of which was the passing of the new Labour Contract Law (LCL) in 2008. The LCL sought to compel companies to sign contracts with their workers and stipulated that employees who have been with a company for more than ten years are automatically entitled to contracts, thereby protecting them against dismissal without cause. In addition, the law stipulates that employers must contribute to employees' social security funds and set new wage standards for employees on probation and those working overtime (Cnci.org.cn 2008).

Whilst the primary motivation behind the LCL was the increased social tensions that threatened the rule of the Chinese Communist Party, the task of shifting the balance of class forces towards labour was given added impetus by the global financial crisis. The crisis has exposed the inherent vulnerabilities of the Chinese model of growth and its reliance on developed country markets, and in particular that of the United States. The Chinese government has, as a result, increasingly signalled the need to facilitate a shift away from export-oriented development towards a model oriented more towards domestic consumption. This imperative became more explicit in the recent 12th Five Year Plan, which called for a doubling of workers' wages (*Xinhua News* 2010). In reality, however, central government's measures to deal with the fallout of the global financial crisis appeared to be at cross purposes with its aims of raising domestic consumption. Its US$585 billion stimulus package placed more emphasis on investment in infrastructure than on boosting household spending. As a result, China saw a sharp decrease in the share and consumption in GDP between 2007 and 2010 (Foster and McChesney 2012).

Whilst the fall in China's current account surplus to GDP ratio in 2011 suggests a possible shift in the weight of the economy towards domestic consumption, this was rather a result of high levels of investment, a weak global economy and an increase in the costs of commodity imports (Yu 2012). Furthermore, when China saw its weakest growth for three years in the second quarter of 2012, Premier Wen Jiabao called for greater investment, suggesting again a preference for increasing export capacity rather than a shift towards household consumption (Bradsher 2012).

There were also real weaknesses in the way that the LCL was implemented. As Feng Chen has argued, the law aims to strengthen individual rather than collective labour rights through the provision of mechanisms through which workers as individuals are able to seek redress for their grievances through arbitration commissions and courts. Enforcement of the law's stipulations concerning wages and working conditions remains weak, and without the freedom of association, workers lack an effective means with which to collectively ensure the enforcement of the law (Chen 2007: 63–4). The state-sanctioned All China Federation of Trade Unions (ACFTU) claims to represent all workers in China, but when faced with labour unrest tries to channel grievances into institutional channels through legislation and administration. It plays no role in facilitating collective bargaining and the right to strike was removed entirely from the 1982 constitution.

Despite these manifest weaknesses, the LCL still managed to provoke vocal resistance from foreign business interests in China when it was first proposed. Furthermore, prior to the law's implementation, companies sought to avoid the requirement to offer permanent contracts to workers with over ten years' service by asking workers to 'voluntarily' resign and then offer new temporary contracts (China.org.cn 2007). When the law came into effect, some employers provided workers with contracts in English (a language few could understand), forced them to sign two separate documents with two different company seals, or used other methods to get around the provision of the law (*China Labour Bulletin* 2009: 18–19). Labour administration authorities have also lacked the economic and political incentives to supervise and inspect employers' compliance with the laws. Punitive measures that can be applied for non-compliance are limited to fines, and there is a national shortage of labour inspectors (Zheng 2009: 608).

At the same time, the LCL has done little to reverse trends towards increased labour unrest or of labour shortages that lead to heightened labour costs. Whilst the onset of the crisis saw a brief wave of mass layoffs (Chan 2010: 666–7), anecdotal evidence suggests the return to an upward trend in labour shortages and wage costs. A survey of 200 Hong Kong-based manufacturers operating in the Pearl River Delta found that in the first three months of 2012 alone, labour shortages and stricter enforcement of social insurance contributions had led to an increase in wages of 10 per cent (Standard Chartered 2012).

The global financial crisis also entailed a rapid rise in the number of 'mass incidents' of unrest. Whilst the government stopped releasing official figures after 2005, unofficial reports suggest that 2008 saw as many as 120000 incidents, declining only slightly in 2009 (Friedman 2012: 464). Furthermore, whereas migrant workers had hitherto been relatively quiescent compared to laid-off SOE workers, the crisis saw a marked shift in the locus of workers' struggles towards the coastal manufacturing regions. This grassroots movement for improved living standards led by migrant workers has raised further questions about the social instability generated by China's export-oriented model.

Parallels with the experience of labour reform elsewhere in East Asia suggest that China is on the verge of a significant transformation in the realm of labour relations. In 1984, in the midst of broader structural changes in the labour market comparable to the ones described above for mainland China, the ruling Kuomintang in Taiwan adopted a strategy of pre-emptive labour legislation vis-à-vis increasingly restless social forces through the passing of the Labour Standards Law (LSL). The Kuomintang's strategy of labour reform arose from a concern about a potential alliance between labour and the emerging *dangwai* (党外) political opposition movement. It was aimed at establishing a system of 'state-mandated enterprise paternalism' through binding workers to their employers, thereby obviating the need for increased direct state regulation (Deyo 1989: 133–5). As with China's LCL, Taiwan's LSL suffered from a number of shortcomings and struggled both with sabotage by employers and poor enforcement. The law also failed to provide any actual mechanisms whereby unions could negotiate matters within its remit (Kleingartner and Peng 1991: 430). Nonetheless, it was precisely these shortcomings that led to calls for the proper implementation of the law, a strategy known as 'fight for what the law offers' (顺法斗争) (Chen and Wong 2002: 36).

In Taiwan, therefore, the LSL marked the rise of the independent labour movement. It led to the establishment, for example, of the Taiwan Labour Front, which explicitly sought to raise consciousness by advocating a socialist ideology and labour rights, as well as providing free legal consultation (Yiu 2004). Similarly in China, most labour rights advocates agree that the passing of the LCL has led to workers becoming more aware of the importance of gaining a contract and of the provisions of the new legal regime. The introduction of the laws has seen an upsurge in labour disputes, and in particular, litigation by workers, suggesting that workers are indeed becoming more conscious of their rights (Wang et al. 2009: 492).

Structural labour market changes and historical precedent do not, of course, determine forms of agency and the forms that workers' struggles take and their impact is an empirical question. Silver's analysis of world-historical patterns of labour unrest cites the case of Japan, which, whilst apparently possessing the conditions for the emergence of a strong labour movement, in fact saw the transition towards cooperative labour relations and the subordination of organized labour (Silver 2003: 71–3). Even between South Korea and Taiwan, there are significant differences in terms of the intensity of their respective strike waves in the late 1980s and the degree to which organized labour developed and remained an influential actor in the post-authoritarian politics (Lee 2008). As argued in the next section, however, the 2010 strike wave in China, and in particularly, the workers' struggle at Nanhai Honda suggests a qualitative shift towards a militant workers' consciousness capable of challenging Chinese labour subordination to the degree that notions of the 'race to the bottom', particularly those predicated on the subordination of Chinese labour, should be rethought.

The strike that took place at Nanhai Honda for 17 days in the early summer of 2010 suggests that Chinese labour struggles may be seeing the same qualitative development witnessed in South Korea and Taiwan, namely from a primarily reactive movement aimed at the infringement of workers' rights to a proactive movement aimed at material gains and union democracy. The following section thus provides an analysis of the strike and its implications for understanding possible future directions for Chinese labour relations.

THE NANHAI HONDA STRIKE

Nanhai Honda, a producer of transmissions in Foshan, Guangzhou province, is one of four Honda factories in the Pearl River Delta. The company was established in 2007, and its workers are largely recruited as interns from a small number of technical schools (Chan and Hui 2012: 656). Unhappy with the failure of the company's management to raise wages in line with the Foshan city government's minimum wage, the strike began on the morning of the 17 May as two migrant workers switched off the power in the assembly plant shouting 'wages are too low, so let's stop working!' Around one hundred workers immediately downed tools and congregated in the factory's basketball court (L. Wei 2010). News of the strike was quickly passed by mobile phone on to workers in the other production units. The striking workers elected their representatives and proceeded to compile a list of as many as 108 demands (Qiao 2011: 252).

On the third day into the strike, two rounds of negotiations took place. Each of the factory's five production units elected two worker representatives each, whilst the company was represented by four managers, including the General Manager. Officials from the Nanhai Honda union acted as mediators. Workers made the demand for a wage raise of 800 yuan, and henceforth a yearly wage increase of 15 per cent. The management, however, countered with an offer of a 55 yuan rise for regular workers only, which the workers immediately rejected. This led to a more hardline approach on the part of the management, who announced the following day through the company's internal broadcasting system that the two instigators of the strike would be fired. Management started taking pictures of workers participating in the strike. However, not only did this hard-line approach fail to intimidate the workers, but by this time, around 1800 workers from across the factory had joined the strike (Zhou and Liu 2010). On 24 May, the impasse between labour and management led to attempts by the Nanhai Honda union chairman to act as a mediator in the negotiations. However, this decisive failure of the union to side with the workers and represent labour's interests led to calls for the union's 'reorganization'. Workers also rejected a further proposal by management for a rise of 355 yuan for regular workers and 477 yuan for trainees, countering with a list of demands including: (1) a rise in the basic wage of 800 yuan, bringing the basic monthly wage to 2000 yuan; (2) a subsequent annual wage rise of 15 per cent; (3) payment of an annual subsidy according to seniority; (4) the reinstatement of the two strike instigators and an assurance from management that there would be no retaliation against other workers that had participated in the strike; (5) payment of workers' wages for the period of the strike; (6) 'reorganization' of the company union through election of a new chairman (Qiao 2011: 253).

Nanhai Honda management, however, continued to reject the workers' demands and asked that they sign a pledge stating that henceforth they would not participate in a strike or any other form of collective action. Workers ignored such requests, however, and the impasse with management led to intervention by the local state authorities. The Shisan township authorities sought to bring pressure on the workers by asking principals of the schools that had dispatched trainees to the company to question participants in the strike. This also failed to dissuade striking workers, however (D. Wei 2010). Finally, on 31 May, as riot police stationed outside the factory stood by, around one hundred people wearing yellow hats and 'Shisan union' badges on their chests entered the factory compound and clashed with the striking workers, injuring three in the process. Although the mobilization of violence has been a tried and tested method of labour repression in China, in this instance the violence marked a more positive turning point in the negotiations. The following day, the General Manager of Guangzhou Automobile Industry Group, Zeng Qinghong, along with an official from Nanhai District Department of Human Resources and Social Security (DHRSS) visited the factory to act as mediators in the negotiations. Zeng stated that he was not there to represent the company vis-à-vis the striking workers, but was participating in his capacity as a National People's Congress (NPC) representative. The workers in turn elected 16 new representatives and made demands for an investigation into the previous day's violence (Honda Workers Negotiating Committee 2010). After three rounds of interviews with the workers, officials from the company and from Shisan Township FTU made a formal apology for the violence and announced that there would be no retribution against striking workers (D. Wei 2010).

On 4 June, as management promised to continue negotiations, workers agreed to resume production. Negotiations henceforth took an even more unorthodox format. In addition to labour and management representatives, participants included company union officials, the chairman of Guangzhou City FTU and Deputy Chief of the Guangzhou NPC Committee Chen Weiguang, Zeng Qinghong, Professor Chang Kai, a well-known labour expert from Renmin University, and the official from Nanhai District DHRSS, who acted as chair for the negotiations (L. Wang 2010). The participation of Chang Kai was proposed by a *Caijing* magazine reporter who was covering the strike. After being told that the strike was illegal, it became clear to the workers that they needed their own legal advisor. The *Caijing* reporter offered to introduce Chang to the workers in return for preferential reporting access (K. Wang 2010). When the workers were unable to establish a unified position on wage demands, Chang suggested that the matter should be put to a vote. Chang also advised that the demand for the reorganization of the union was an issue that could not be resolved with the company, and should be dealt with separately from the wage negotiations, a proposal that the workers also accepted. After six hours of negotiations and a vote by workers, a revised proposal was made for a rise of 300 yuan in the basic salary, a bonus and subsidy rise of 66 yuan, and a further rise of 134 yuan, amounting to a total wage rise of 500 yuan. This proposal was accepted and the strike was officially brought to an end.

The strike at Nanhai Honda had an immediate impact on workers' struggles elsewhere in China. As workers at Nanhai Honda downed tools, strikes broke out at other Honda suppliers in Foshan including Atsumitec and Ormon (a supplier to Honda, Ford and BMW) as well as Honda Locks in neighbouring Zhongshan. Workers struck for higher wages at a Toyota-owned parts supplier, Denso Guangzhou Nansha, which also halted production at the final assembly plant in Tianjin (Tabuchi 2010). However, the Nanhai Honda strike was also significant in terms of the manner in which it represents some important departures in the hitherto dominant pattern of Chinese industrial relations.

As noted, the strike suggests an incipient transition from a movement primarily aimed at a reactive protection of workers' rights towards a more proactive movement pursuing its material interests. Resistance had hitherto been largely limited to issues such as the late payment of wages, excessive fines, the non-payment of social insurance contributions, and other such instances in which management had clearly infringed upon the rights of workers. The Nanhai Honda strike, on the other hand, suggests that migrant workers are developing a class consciousness, and that whilst the formal legal framework is lagging behind, Chinese labour relations were in reality moving from individualized to *de facto* collective labour–management relations (Chang 2011). The strike was also distinctive in terms of the measured response adopted by management. Whilst the government had traditionally adopted a strategy of severe repression, more recently the balance of repression and concession has decisively shifted towards the latter. The authorities typically seek to settle disputes as quickly as possible, encouraging workers to return to work through making concessions (Clarke and Pringle 2009: 93). Although management at Nanhai Honda sacked the two strike instigators and the Shisan FTU had mobilized physical force against the workers, there was less repression than has been typical in Chinese industrial relations. The company management did not carry out mass layoffs or enforce a factory lock-out, an apology was made for the violence, and the strike was ultimately resolved peacefully.

The influence of Japanese industrial relations may to some degree have shaped Nanhai Honda management's more moderate response to the strike. Since the oil crisis of the 1970s and the end of the 'miracle growth' era, unions in Japan have become increasing conciliatory and the country's industrial relations have become stable and harmonious (Kume 1988), and it has been decades since Japanese capital has had to deal with militant workforces. Japanese production methods may also have heightened its vulnerability to work stoppages. In contrast to claims that post-Fordist just-in-time (JIT) production techniques lessen the scope for workers' militancy (Jenkins and Leicht 1997: 378–9), the experience at Nanhai Honda shows conversely that JIT production is in fact highly vulnerable to disruptions and can enhance workers' bargaining power based on direct action at the point of production (cf. Ihara, this volume). The strike halted production at three assembly factories in Guangzhou and one in Wuhan. The huge losses incurred caused these companies to place pressure on Nanhai Honda to resolve the strike quickly. As Koji Endo, an analyst at Advanced Research Japan has argued, workers know well that Japanese firms are particularly vulnerable since many of them rely on single suppliers from affiliated companies, making it difficult to find alternatives if production is halted (Reuters 2010).

It is also likely that the Japanese management of Nanhai Honda found it difficult to mobilize Chinese authorities against the striking workers. Amidst intense public scrutiny, historical legacies relating to Japan's imperialist past in China may have made management more sensitive to the likelihood of provoking negative public opinion through repression of the striking workers. It should be noted, however, that the strike wave was not entirely limited to Japanese corporations and strikes for higher wages also took place at a Hyundai auto parts factory in Beijing (Chen 2010). More generally, however, the rise of nationalism in China has meant that foreign corporations, and particularly Japanese corporations, need to tread carefully. This in fact is another aspect of the passive revolution. China's official socialist ideology provides a rhetoric which can easily be mobilized against foreign-invested enterprises engaged in exploitative labour practices. On the other hand, the same ideology provides workers with a vocabulary and a set of norms with which to criticize exploitation of Chinese workers by foreign capital.

In addition to Nanhai Honda management, the local authorities and unions ultimately adopted a conciliatory approach and along with Prof. Chang Kai of Renmin University, acted as independent mediators. The mediating role of the company union was harshly criticized by the workers, and the higher-level unions were even involved in violent acts. Yet their rapid adoption of a more conciliatory stance appears to have been a result of pressure from Zeng Qinghong and the Nanhai District DHRSS. In any case, the resulting stakeholder-type negotiations were in marked contrast to the usual voluntarism of Chinese labour–management negotiations. Though this model was to some extent a reflection of the institutional shortcomings of the Chinese labour dispute resolution mechanism, it suggests a new direction for 'Chinese-style' labour–management negotiations. At other companies too, there is increased evidence of management taking the cue from shifts in government policy to recognize the need to be more accommodating to workers. Foxconn, the Taiwanese OEM manufacturer of the iPhone, is well known for its illegal working hours, low wages, underage workers, worker suicides and strikes (see Chan, Pun and Selden, this volume). However, the company has recently introduced direct union leadership elections for its 1.2 million workers. As Auret van Heerden, chief executive of the Fair Labor Association, which serves as an independent observer of labour conditions at Foxconn, has argued, '[The government is] likely worried about industrial unrest. It's clear they want to get workers [away from protesting in] the courtyard and to the negotiating table' (Hille and Jacob 2013).

CONCLUSION

Clearly the study of labour in the international political economy cannot be reduced to a sociology of labour bureaucracies acting in a 'global civil society', or to isolated incidents of cross-border organization and solidarity, or to the expectation that at some unspecified point in the future workers will play a distinctive transformatory and emancipatory role globally. Studying processes of class formation in the context of passive revolution, which links the realms of state–society contestation and the wider field of international politics, instead offers a perspective on how a changing balance of forces in any domestic context reflects back on the global political economy in its entirety.

Heightened domestic social unrest and the manifest vulnerabilities associated with dependence on external demand has led to the increased recognition by the Chinese government of the need to reorient towards domestic consumption. These dual internal and external pressures have led to new approaches to deal with labour rights and social unrest. As the Chinese government's slogan 'stability is the overriding priority' (稳定压倒一切) suggested, the Jiang Zemin administration saw social stability as a prerequisite for economic growth and regarded the subordination of labour as the primary means by which that goal was to be achieved. However, by the early 2000s, workers' dissatisfaction had already accumulated to such a degree that repression could no longer effectively serve to contain labour unrest. Policymakers have become aware of how repression alone can not only fail to contain labour unrest, but can develop into a threat to the regime itself. The establishment of a more cooperative form of labour–management relations thus requires a more proactive approach, and as such, the Hu Jintao administration thus placed increased emphasis on the establishment of a 'harmonious socialist society'.

The passing of the LCL in 2007 was an attempt by the central government to reform the legal framework governing industrial relations to provide more legal channels for the redress of individual labour grievances. More recently, the government has adopted an explicit policy of seeking to increase wages, and thus, does appear to have at least a rhetorical commitment to increased domestic consumption. However, other policies designed to tackle the GFC appear to be at cross purposes with such aims. Placing the Chinese experience within a broader comparative perspective, however, suggests that structural changes in the nature of the Chinese working class will ultimately be more important in terms of charting the future transition of the Chinese political economy. With increased labour shortages in the coastal areas, the structural power of China's workers is increasing. As the analysis of the 2010 Nanhai Honda strike has suggested, this has been accompanied by important changes in workers' consciousness. Second generation migrants are beginning to develop a class consciousness and are actively pursuing their own rights and material interests. Given these changes in the domestic social underpinnings of China's low-wage labour regime, a labour policy aimed primarily on repression is less and less viable.

The extent to which the Chinese labour relations will continue in this direction is of course not pre-determined and is subject to numerous factors including the balance of class forces within China and changes in the external environment. Nonetheless, as this chapter has argued, the raising of workers' incomes and undermining of labour subordination seems set to reduce the export competitiveness of China's low-wage industries and thereby reduce the US trade deficit. These trends are likely to challenge the uneven US–China relationship that has hitherto underpinned global neoliberalism and will facilitate a shift towards 'global convergence' (Dunford and Yeung 2010) rather than a race to the bottom. Longer-run transformations in the social underpinnings of China's low-wage economy suggest a medium-term shift towards a more domestically focused political economy based on the country's large internal market. In the context of the debate surrounding global imbalances, the case of Nanhai Honda and the broader changes in government labour policies suggest that the global race to the bottom in wages and working conditions is under challenge and the ability of capital to circumvent workers' structural power is becoming constrained. Whilst the more mobile elements of transnational capital may seek to relocate production to the internal regions in China or to other low-wage production sites elsewhere in Asia, the experience suggests again that such fixes to the problem of workers' resistance are likely to be only temporary in scope.

19. Bargaining in the global commodity chain: the Asia Floor Wage Alliance

Anannya Bhattacharjee and Ashim Roy

Within a framework of unequal regional and national development, an unequal and segmented labour market, and transnational companies (TNCs) enjoying the advantage of benefiting from both these factors, labour organizations in Asia have forged the Asia Floor Wage Alliance to address the urgent need for developing new pathways of bargaining on a global scale. This chapter explores these issues in one of the most globalized industries, the garment industry, and explains the strategies of the Asia Floor Wage Alliance.

The global commodity chain has been enabled by varieties of continually evolving transnational corporate structures and capital functions. Capital from the Global North, aided by Northern governments and multilateral institutions, and with acquiescence from Southern governments, creates an environment favouring the operation of such global commodity chains. Gary Gereffi initially put forward the concept of the global commodity chain (GCC) to analyse the shift in global production patterns (Gereffi 1994; Gereffi and Korzeniewicz 1994). It viewed the shift in organizational terms and went beyond the limitations of neoclassical explanations of relative prices to incorporate the concept of market power. It also provided a framework for studying the spatial reorganization of global production. The concept of a 'buyer-driven commodity chain' further located the impetus of this shift in TNCs enjoying immense market power in the Global North. In this buyer-driven chain the TNCs retain their domination as the lead firms in the chain. As such, they have the capacity to foster organizational flexibility, to reduce and externalize production cost, and to secure the highest profit margin in the consumer markets they dominate.

To examine the power dimensions and the structures of the global garment business, we also found the concept of the Global Production Network (GPN) useful (Hess and Yeung 2006). GPN is a term used to describe the contemporary production system, which results from the shift in international trade from exchange based on distant market relationships to one based on closely connected firms. In the past, exchange through trade was limited to the TNCs and their subsidiaries. However, the contemporary process of exchange expands and transforms intra-firm trade to new dimensions. GPN helps us to understand that exchange takes place through a networked structure in which the TNCs do not formally own the overseas subsidiaries or franchisees but outsource production to them, without the burden of legal ownership.

In addition to understanding the power and structure of contemporary TNCs, another aspect, and one equally important to attend to, concerns the role of monopolistic practices. Stephen Hymer, one of the earlier economists examining monopolies, looked at the evolution of transnational corporations as monopolistic structures dominating modern industry (Hymer 1972). In light of the alarmist concern about monopoly in free market capitalism, it is important to understand that in reality the GPN provides the conditions for Global North TNC monopolism in the global economy. The evolution of GPN is the most evident form of global production in the contemporary epoch, and in our understanding, promotes a form of monopolistic structure. This chapter delves into these issues by examining the global garment industry, with particular reference to the growth of the Asia Floor Wage movement and the Asia Floor Wage Alliance.

THE BALANCE OF POWER IN THE GLOBAL PRODUCTION NETWORK

Even in the initial phase of development of GCC as an analytical tool, we in the international trade union movement found it a useful concept as it provided a framework for intervening in the 'social clause' debates in which the issue of corporate labour rights in international trade was raised. We argued, as Global South trade unionists, that the changing nature of the trade and the emergence of global exchange through the buyer-driven commodity chain required new regulatory mechanisms for which the nation-state regulatory framework of the ILO was inadequate. In the absence of an adequate regulatory framework in a world of unequal regional and national development, social clauses would become just another mechanism of wielding power by the TNCs and their home states in the Global North over the Southern economy to force the entry of new investment regimes and restructuring of trade (Roy 1996). Subsequently, the GCC provided a framework to examine the labour dynamics in garment commodity chains both at the industry level and at the firm level, which then helped the Asia Floor Wage Alliance develop a collective bargaining strategy for the global garment industry.

The concepts of buyer-driven GCCs and the GPN together help in understanding the structure, the market powers and the leverage points in global production. The context and conditions for the emergence of GPN became more prominent and politically feasible in the period after the 1980s. The crisis in the Northern economy compelled the inherent tendency in developed capitalism to sustain a high rate of profit to take recourse to further internationalization of production, and hence to facilitate the great global job shift. It became necessary to ensure that the new industrial base that emerged in the post-colonial period in the developing countries, which were primarily domestic focused and state-centric, open up for export-oriented industrialization and allow Northern private capital to expand.

With the dominance of neoliberal thinking in the 1980s the export-oriented industrialization (EOI) in post-colonial countries was established. This allowed for the scaling up of export-oriented production and enabled the formation of the GPN. This export became nothing more than a mechanism to capture low labour cost which was essentially poverty level wages. This is the essential ground within which the GPN needs to be understood. GPN structures built on the fertile ground of EOI became the dominant form of international trade, more particularly so in the sectors of automobiles, electronics and garments.

TNCs from the Global North increasingly transferred segments of value-added tasks of production to geographically dispersed locations. The World Investment Report 2013 by UNCTAD states that:

> Today's global economy is characterized by global value chains (GVCs), in which intermediate goods and services are traded in fragmented and internationally dispersed production processes. GVCs are typically coordinated by TNCs, with cross-border trade of inputs and outputs taking place within their networks of affiliates, contractual partners and arm's-length suppliers. TNC-coordinated GVCs account for some 80 per cent of global trade.

This dispersal pattern of value-added tasks of production in many ways was dependent on the EOI policies of the state and on labour market conditions within the affected countries, in particular what can be called the surplus labour within those economies. The suppliers in the Global South competed for orders from the big buyers in the Global North and this evolved into the key factor in keeping the labour cost down, since this cost was determined by the labour market situation prevalent in those countries.

The GPN framework expresses the organizational linkages that the TNCs use to reorganize production through services and contractual agreements, as an alternative to arm's length transactions in the markets. In fact the GPN is an organizational form that expresses how TNCs from the Global North succeed in linking two distinct aspects of market control within their organizations: one, their dominance in consumer markets in the Global North, and the other, their access to cheap production sites in the Global South. It is our argument that the GPN shifts the market relationship between firms from a trade relationship to a quasi-production relationship without the risks of ownership. The global economy becomes more integrated and the GPN becomes the organizational form of a monopoly capitalism from which the risks have been removed.

The UNCTAD World Investment Report 2013 has called for a 'regulatory framework to ensure joint economic, social and environmental upgrading to achieve sustainable development gains'. In other words, it is asking for a rebalancing of the global production system, in which inequality has reached such overwhelming proportions. This balance can only be brought about by creating a framework in which the bargaining power of local firms in the Global South can be increased. The Asia Floor Wage is a corrective strategy developed to intervene in the GPN from a class perspective, to bring about a more equitable trade framework.

THE GLOBAL RESERVE ARMY OF LABOUR AND GLOBAL ARBITRAGE

The first step towards a corrective intervention is to examine the capital–labour relationship within the GPN. In order to do this, the concept of *circuit of capital* developed by Marxist political economists is particularly helpful. It provides the vantage point from which the GPN can be viewed as a single process consisting of complementary, intersecting but distinct functional capitals, namely, commercial, production and financial capital. These functional circuits result in different types and modes of competition. At the Northern end of the chain competition takes place among commercial (retail) capitals in the consumer market; at stake is market share. At the Southern end, the competition in the newly expanded export-oriented areas is among productive capitals, seeking to supply to global retailers. Finally, there is the vertical competition between the buyers in the Global North and suppliers in the Global South, hence between commercial and productive capital, over the distribution of profit. This vertical, North–South competition has been called 'value capture' in the business literature.

Though the GPN framework is useful to bring out the quasi-production relationships, it needs to be further studied from the perspective of labour-market dynamics. It is important to understand how GPN structures the conditions of work in the chain. The concept of a low-cost production location as a monopolistic tool has been best expressed by Michael Porter when he writes that 'Having a low-cost production yields the firm above average returns in the industry' (Porter 1980: 35). Low-cost production came to be synonymous with a low-wage workforce. The buyers in the Global North compete in their home market on the basis of their share in accessing low-cost production areas, rather than through price competition. Their ability to indiscriminately gain access to low-cost production countries required a dismantling of the Multi-Fibre Agreement quota regime of the textiles industry, the free flow of capital, and a turn to export-oriented industrialization in production countries.

The dual dominance of TNCs from the Global North in their home countries' consumer market and in terms of access to low-cost production countries is absolutely critical. Only thus can they avert the possible competitive threat from firms in the South which otherwise might penetrate the Northern markets on the basis of their exclusive low-cost position in the globalizing economy. This dual dominance has been the result of a coordinated effort between Global TNCs, Global North governments and international multilateral institutions. This strategy for exploiting a low-wage labour force came to be termed in the business world by Stephen Roach of Morgan Stanley as 'global labour arbitrage': as a system of economic rewards derived from gaining monopoly control over the international wage hierarchy, resulting in huge returns (cf. Delgado Wise and Martin, this volume).

The TNCs' monopolistic strategy is made possible by the growth of a global reserve army of labour in the Global South under a neoliberal globalization process, and realized by connecting the GPN into this reserve army. The neoclassical assumption that wages will inevitably adjust to productivity growth and will result in a new global equilibrium, has proved to be empirically wrong. While the global economy grew at an average of 3.3 per cent per year between 1995 and 2007, annual wage growth was at 1.9 per cent every year. The wage share has been declining across the globe. As the ILO's Global Wage Report 2010/2011, sounding the alarm, put it, 'The overall short-term impact of the crisis on wages should be looked at within the context of a long-term decline in the share of wages in total income, a growing disconnect between productivity growth and wages, and widespread and growing wage inequality.'

In a capitalist economy, wages are kept low by the existence of labour reserves in the country. Wage rises are possible when growth is significant enough to exhaust an economy's labour reserve, and to induce tightness in the labour market, in other words, when the growth rate of the economy exceeds the growth of supply in the labour market. However, if a specific sector grows rapidly in terms of output as a result of *capital infusion*, it raises the labour productivity in that sector relative to the rest of the economy, without triggering a wage rise.

The proportion of reserve labour to active labour, then, determines the nature of the labour market. In regions where there is a large section of latent labour in agriculture, the availability of reserve labour is proportionally large. The size of the reserve army of labour is what structures the labour market. Today it is in Asia that we find the largest reserve army of labour. According to Marx a major form of reserve labour is the one that involves extremely irregular employment, or in today's terms, the informal sector. The wages of the workers in this category could be said, according to Marx (1990: 792), to 'sink below the average normal level of the working class' that is, below the value of labour power, its reproduction cost, which in itself is historically determined. Rosa Luxemburg deepened our understanding of the process by the phrase, 'the surplus labour from non-capitalist modes of production' to characterize the reserve army of labour. It is the enormous weight of the relative surplus labour population that tends to pull down the wages below the average value.

Between 1980 and 2007, the global labour force according to the ILO grew from 1.9 billion to 3.1 billion, most of them from the developing countries and with India and China contributing 40 per cent of this rise (cf. Selwyn, this volume). Still according to the ILO, there are 555 million working poor, a significant percentage being female. 'Since the mid-1990s the proportion of people on low pay – defined as less than two-thirds of median wage – has increased in more than two-thirds of countries with available data.' The ILO's *Global Employment Trends 2011* shows that 'the number of workers in vulnerable employment is estimated at 1.53 billion workers globally in 2009, more than half of all workers in the world'.

It is important to note that the global labour force to which these discussions refer is too often viewed as a homogeneous bloc. Of course in reality, this labour force is far from homogeneous. It is highly segmented geographically and its characteristics depend on the poverty level of the region and the country. Asia, the largest recipient of foreign investment, also holds the largest workforce and represents most of the global working poor, among which women comprise an increasingly significant proportion. This is no coincidence because foreign investment seeks out the most pliant, poor and under-valued working class. The garment industry is of course one such labour-intensive industry that absorbs both low and high-skilled workers.

The GPN draws on this new labour in organizing global production. To illustrate, Nike and Reebok rely on their global supply contractors for 100 per cent of their production. In other words, the production workers for Nike and Reebok are all in the developing countries but they are not recognized as workers of these firms. The struggle for an Asia Floor Wage focuses on this global arbitrage – the manifest form of the development of absolute law of capitalist accumulation in the new global phase. In economics, the term 'arbitrage' means the buying of an asset at a low price and then immediately selling it on a different market at a higher price. In other words, a single product, but access to two different markets, is what creates the conditions for profitability, unrelated to the production cost itself. This arbitrage is made possible by an augmentation of the imperialist rent extracted from the South through integration of low-wage, highly exploited workers into the capitalist production. According to Marx (1990: 792), 'The relative surplus population is therefore the background against which the law of demand and supply of labour does its work. It confines the field of action of this law to the limits absolutely convenient to capital's drive to exploit and dominate the workers.'

In the garment industry output has increased but real earnings have not grown at the same rate, though the productivity has increased due to capital infusion in the garment industry in Asia. An important question for the labour movement is the distribution of the enormous and consistent surplus that is generated from arbitrage and higher productivity.

NODES OF INEQUALITY IN THE GLOBAL GARMENT INDUSTRY

The global fashion apparel industry is one of the most important sectors of the economy in terms of investment, revenue, trade and employment generation all over the world. The Asia-Pacific region is home to the largest amount of production and trade in the apparel industry worldwide. Globally there are an estimated 40 million garment workers, with a significant proportion female. The global garment industry's total revenue was estimated to reach a value of US$1782 billion by the end of 2010. The level of garments' sales rarely drops; in fact, research shows that even when prices rise, sales continue. Apparel imports of the United States witnessed an increase of 13.5 per cent in January–April 2011 from the corresponding period of the previous year and amounted to US$23.2 billion. For the same period, US imports of apparel from India increased by 12.7 per cent to US$1313 million against US$1165 million in January–April 2010. US imports from China saw an increase of 8.3 per cent in January–April 2011 over the corresponding period of the previous year and all the other major suppliers, such as Vietnam, Indonesia, Bangladesh and Mexico also witnessed increases of 16.9 per cent, 18.2 per cent, 29.7 per cent and 8.4

per cent, respectively. Among the top six suppliers, Bangladesh registered maximum growth from the previous year of the same period.

Today the largest bulk of garment manufacturing, although spread across all the continents, is found in Asia. Asia manufactures 60 per cent of the world's clothing. In terms of scale of production, size of workforce, access to raw materials, technology, diversity of skills, and labour cost, Asia offers the greatest competitive advantage. Within Asia, garment production takes place in many countries such as China, India, Bangladesh, Sri Lanka, Pakistan, Indonesia, Cambodia, Vietnam and Thailand. In the Global North, multi-goods retail companies and big brands set the standard for the garment global supply chain.

An astonishing phenomenon is that even as prices of most commodities have shot upwards, the prices of garments have *fallen* in the Global North. Yet profits of garment brands have been impressive. This can be explained by the fact that the prices that brands pay to the manufacturers in Asia have decreased, reducing the profit margins of Asian manufacturers, which depresses the poverty wages production workers continue to get. American consumers, despite falling income, can be relied upon to continue buying by depressing prices and pressing down on wages at the production end. 'Much of the emphasis on competitiveness has focused on production costs and, in particular, labour costs. Consumers in affluent nations benefit from low-wage imports when retail prices fall for the goods they purchase' (Heintz 2002).

It is our argument that the surplus produced, through dual and exclusive access of the TNCs to the consumer market in the Global North and low-cost production areas in the Global South, is disproportionately distributed between local/Asian producers and the global buyers via the price mechanism. At one end of the chain, in the consumer market dominated by the large brands, there is a tendency for retail prices to move upwards. At the production end, on the other hand, the expansion of the supplier base in the developing countries (and also because the market for garment manufacturing has become plain commodity production rather than requiring skill-based labour), works to create competitive pressure among the suppliers, leading to a race to the lowest level of production costs. The two components of the GPN thus operate in different competitive structures. The buyer–supplier price mechanism links the two and constitutes the node at which the disproportionate sharing of the surplus takes place. It also provides the possibility of a wage rise in the export sector of the garment sector of production countries, if only the workers could develop this node as a leverage point for a common demand, and build an effective strategy and an organization structure to support it.

Under monopoly capitalism in general, wage rises are always smaller than productivity rises unless there is a labour struggle that can force the wages upwards. As David Harvey says, 'The geographical organization of capitalism internalizes the contradictions within the value form. That is what is meant by the concept of the inevitable uneven development of capitalism' (Harvey 1982: 417).

As contemporary capitalism reorganizes itself by geographical dispersion, assuming the organizational form of a GPN, the question remains as to how both the dependency and the unequal exchange are intertwined within the value analysis of the GPN. It is at the level of the FOB (Freight-on-Board meaning till goods reach the ship's board) price – essentially the transfer price from production area to consumer area – that the unequal exchange in the GPN is hidden. The FOB price is the manifest market mechanism covering the inequality of the price of labour, given equal labour productivity. Such a value transfer can only operate within the GPN, EOI and 'free' capital flow that underpin the globalization of production and consumption.

The FOB price is also the nodal point at which the exchange rate operates. By basing their buying decision on the exchange rate of individual countries, the buyers render opaque this value transfer. To make this transparent one needs to see there is a twofold operation involved here. One concerns the purchasing power exchange that takes place between the Northern consumer market and the Southern production (production task market); the other is the comparative nature of productivity and wages in a regional labour market within the GPN. This becomes possible by calculating both the prevailing wages and the potential living wage, in Purchasing Power Parity (PPP) dollar terms. The wages in national currencies or in exchange rate terms appear far apart. But they can be brought around into a narrow band if calculated in PPP$ terms, a more appropriate measure for comparison. This makes visible the extent of labour exploitation and the undervaluation of the labour price with their regional productivity.

Two realities dominate labour at the global level. One, the GPN that is built on wage arbitrage or the system of imperialist rent; and two, the existence of a massive global reserve army of labour that makes this wage arbitrage possible. It is the super exploitation of labour that is behind the expansion of production in the Global South. The net result is a fall in purchasing power of the majority of people in Asia, over production of goods for which there are not enough consumers and unemployment in the Global North. The purchasing power of working class and poor people in Asia is falling and poverty levels are being pushed down so that few people can be listed below it. This has blocked the majority of today's consumers from the consumer market. As Gary Gereffi has written,

> Unlike producer-driven chains, where profits come from scale, volume and technological advances, in buyer-driven chains profits come from combinations of high-value research, design, sales, marketing and financial services that allow the retailers, designers and marketers to act as strategic brokers in linking overseas factories and traders with product niches in their main consumer markets (Gereffi and Memedovic 2003: 3).

He goes on to say,

> The lavish advertising budgets and promotional campaigns needed to create and sustain global brands, and the sophisticated and costly information technology employed by mega-retailers to develop 'quick response' programmes that increase revenues and lower risks by getting suppliers to manage inventories, have allowed retailers and marketers to displace traditional manufacturers as the leaders in many consumer-goods industries (ibid.: 4).

Any intervention to benefit production workers in this global garment production structure has to simultaneously consider the interlinked factors of low retail prices, brands' huge profits, reduced prices for Asian manufacturers and stagnant wages of Asian workers.

THE ASIA FLOOR WAGE STRATEGY

In a global scenario, where mobility of labour does not exist, it is the localized labour market and the ratio of the active labour force to the reserve labour force in the localized area that determines the character of these labour markets. In the phase of globalization, these labour markets tend to get interlinked. It is our argument that this interlinked labour market takes a regional form. Therefore, the extent of the reserve army of labour in these regions determines the character of the labour market.

From a GPN vantage point the regional character of the labour market, specific to a specific industry, determines the average cost structure of the product, with each country within the region providing the different margin to sustain the average. The threat of relocation of capital or sourcing that the workers face, when unionizing, is confined to the regional labour market and not uniformly spread at a global level. The space for relocation is regional.

The Asia Floor Wage strategy is built on the argument that Asia has the largest reserve labour force in agriculture. It also has more than a third of the world's working poor. So the relocation of garment production, which is labour-intensive and requires masses of labour, from Asia to a different region of the globe is improbable, at least until the reserve labour in Asia has been exhausted. In this context, the threat of relocation that the labour face can be addressed if unions take, as the unit of analysis and action, the region, in this case Asia.

Garment workers in Asia, the majority of whom are women, currently earn around half of what they require to meet their own and their families' basic needs, such as food, water, education and healthcare. A living wage has been a key demand among labour activists in the garment industry for a long time. This demand has been posed to the brands over a long period with very little progress other than rhetorical support. Three main reasons have often been adduced by reluctant brands. One, that there is no common definition of a living wage and no method of calculation; therefore, it is not possible to pay something that is not defined. Two, that any attempt to demand a living wage at a national level results in relocation across the border, and therefore is punitive to national economies. Three, that demand for a living wage is often driven by Northern activists without a collective demand from the Global South.

Trade unions and labour rights organizations in Asia, after years of experience in the garment industry, came together to frame a demand that is bargainable and deliverable, and that is appropriately targeted given the structure and economics of the industry as a whole. The Asia Floor Wage Alliance began as an Asia-focused alliance and grew into a global alliance with Global South and Global North partners. It has been building towards a global movement for an Asia Floor Wage in the global garment industry. The process of building an Asia-centred, union-led, industry-wide initiative has been inspiring and historic.

The Asia Floor Wage movement can be seen to have three phases. The first phase was a bottom-up consensus-building process in Asia to develop the demand concept. The second phase was the presentation of the demand. The third phase, the present one, is struggle and bargaining.

Phase 1: Consensus-based Bottom-up Demand Development

This phase consisted of union meetings in key garment-producing Asian countries on the issue of wages. Workers and worker representatives were frustrated with the statutory poverty level minimum wage as a ceiling in an industry that produces a vast amount of global wealth for global employers; they resented the continual threat of relocation that brands and suppliers imposed on workers, exploiting intra-Asia competition. Dialogue and secondary research confirmed the reality that it is Asia's large labour force, which manufactures most of the world's clothing, that creates the conditions for a recognition of Asian garment workers as a single bargaining bloc or unit. The analysis of the global commodity chain reveals a global subcontracting production chain in which the brand is the principal employer and the Asian supplier factory is a subcontractor. Asian unions held the view that like any other subcontractual relationship, the principal employer must be held accountable for the growing poverty and desperation among garment workers.

The demand for an Asia Floor Wage first began developing in 2006 through a collective consensus-building process among Asian labour organizations. In a segmented global labour market, Asian organizations came to the conclusion that the combination of the scale and the wage level of the workforce made Asian workers the largest workforce producing garments. Moreover, the wage levels of the garment workers in the major garment-producing Asian countries were not too dispersed when compared in terms of purchasing power, and were nearer to the poverty level wage. The prevalence of a legal minimum wage in these countries did not affect these poverty level wages. In fact, in some countries the minimum wage was below the universally accepted poverty level norms! This understanding provided the basis for evolving and establishing the idea of a homogeneous bloc that would act as the 'bargaining unit' in the global garment industrial framework. The AFW Alliance has developed a concrete formulation for a regional living wage. The goal was to have a common regional wage that would raise workers' wages without disturbing the competitive ranking of the Asian countries, thus allowing wages to be taken out as a factor in intra-Asia competition.

The AFW Alliance decided to first conduct a need-based survey in garment-producing countries to determine workers' needs so as to calculate a living wage at the country level. The results of the survey were in local country currencies. The AFW Alliance used data from need-based surveys in India, China, Bangladesh, Sri Lanka and Indonesia as a basis for the AFW formula. The Asia Floor Wage is based on widely accepted norms that are institutionalized in existing policies, laws and practices in Asian countries and on Asian government figures and international research. The Asia Floor Wage is composed of two categories: Food and Non-food. Both categories are estimated at a broad level, the goal being to provide a robust regional formula that can be further tailored by trade unions in different countries, based on their needs and context. In Figure 19.1 the share of expenditure on food in total household expenditure is given for the poorest 10 per cent of households.

The poorer the economy, the more the workers spend on food. In Asia, food cost takes up the most substantial part of a worker's income. The food component of the AFW is expressed in calories rather than food items, in order to provide a common basis. The AFW calorie figure is based on studying calorie intake in the Asia region by governmental and intergovernmental bodies, and the physical nature of work. The AFW

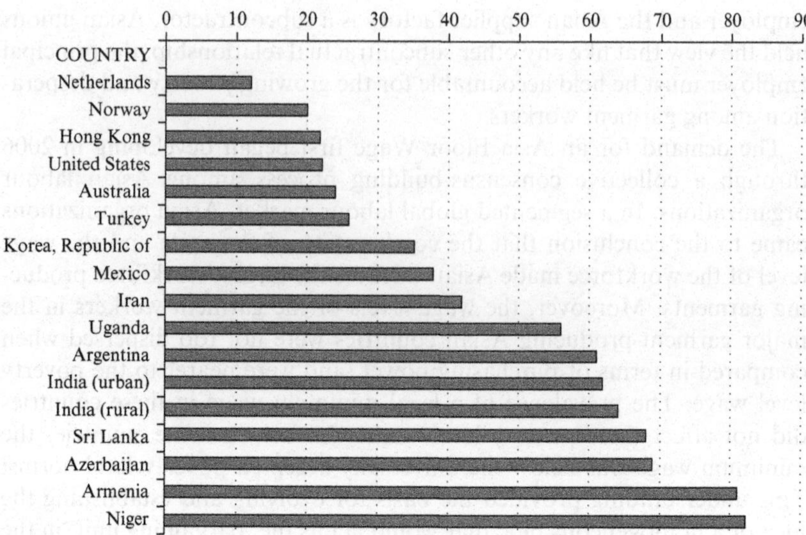

Source: ILO Laborsta.

Figure 19.1 Poorest households' expenditure on food (latest years when data was available, percentage of total expenditure)

Alliance has decided that the Floor Wage should not result in lowering standards in any country. In Indonesia, the standard is set at 3000 calories, and so the Alliance agreed to adopt this as its standard.

The AFW study of the working class population in various countries in Asia shows an average of 50 per cent of household income being spent on food. Therefore non-food costs are taken to be the other half of the income, leaving the details of what comprises non-food to be left to the trade unions in local contexts. The 1:1 ratio of food costs to non-food costs was thus calculated based on the ratio that currently exists for the working class of different Asian garment-producing countries. Since the AFW unions decided to base an AFW on a family, the Alliance studied family sizes in key Asian countries and the ratio of earner to dependents. In order to account for childcare costs, the AFW assumes a single income family, and uses a formula based on three adult consumption units.

The AFW, then, is a basic wage figure prior to benefits. It defines the regular working week as a maximum of 48 hours prior to overtime. AFW's definition of a working week and the assumption that there are no further benefits sends a clear message that workers need to earn a minimum living wage without having to sacrifice humane working conditions. The

Table 19.1 *Asia Floor Wage in local currency on the basis of PPP, 2012–13*

Country name	PPP conversion factor, 2011	Local currency figure for 540 PPP$, 2012	Local currency figure for 725 PPP$, 2013
Bangladesh	35.43	19132	25687
Cambodia	2182.99	1178815	1582668
China	4.32	2333	3132
India	22.40	12096	16240
Indonesia	5583.76	3015230	4048226
Malaysia	2.16	1166	1566
Nepal	39.11	21119	28355
Pakistan	36.38	19645	26376
Sri Lanka	63.68	34387	46168

Source: Asia Floor Wage Alliance.

currency through which the Asia Floor Wage is expressed is the imaginary currency of the World Bank, PPP. The reasoning for choosing the PPP as opposed to exchange rates is that exchange rates are determined by supply and demand for each currency globally, in other words, by the currency market. Exchange rates are highly volatile and fluctuate on a daily basis and are not reflective of national conditions. PPP, on the other hand, is based upon the consumption of goods and services by people within a country; it reflects the standard of living and hence is a more appropriate tool for comparing wages.

The AFW Alliance conducted country-based surveys of monthly food costs for a family in which an adult consumes 3000 calories per day. This cost was doubled to include non-food costs. This AFW in local currency was converted to PPP$ and the result was a comparable spectrum of values in PPP$. The AFW Alliance unions then discussed the spectrum of values and came to a consensus on AFW in PPP$ for the region as a whole. This figure has been adjusted annually to account for inflation and the AFW Alliance conducts fresh food cost surveys every three years to re-establish the base food cost component. Table 19.1 gives the key indicators for the different countries.

Phase 2: Presentation of Demand

The AFW movement entered the second phase of presentation of demand through an International Public Launch on 7 October 2009. The AFW Alliance wrote letters to almost 60 brands demanding meetings for the delivery of AFW. From 2009 onwards, the AFW Alliance has engaged in numerous debates and dialogues with brands and multi-stakeholder initiatives (MSIs); and several meetings with the ILO and Global Union Federations (GUFs). Over two years, the AFW achieved international credibility and legitimacy and began to be used as a benchmark by some brands/MSIs and semi-government agencies, just as it gained currency in ongoing discussions on labour issues worldwide.

The Asia Floor Wage bargaining process targets the brands, the principal employers of the buyer-driven global subcontracting commodity chain, in order to ensure decent wages for workers in the industry. In the global garment industry, global buyers (or brands and retailers) exercise maximum influence over the way that production is organized. They set prices and determine how production takes place. These practices immediately impact the capacity for suppliers to pay a living wage. Scholars have found that brands force supplier companies to operate below production costs, causing wages to be adversely affected. Brands and retailers' sharing a negligible fraction of their profit can dramatically raise millions of workers and families out of poverty.

Central to the demands of the AFW is, therefore, the need for a concerted effort by brands and retailers to address the issue of unfair pricing (the FOB or Freight-on-Board cost), as an important first step towards the implementation of a living wage in the garment industry. The AFW is formulated based on the paying capacity of the *global* industry whereas national wage definitions arise from an analysis of prevailing wages within the country. Global sourcing companies pay approximately the same prices to their supplier factories in Asia: around 25 per cent of the retail price. Garment workers' wages make up a very small proportion of the final retail price for clothes (around 1 to 2 per cent) so substantial wage rises could be achieved without increasing retail prices. The proposed demand is an Asia Floor Wage for Asian garment workers in conjunction with fair pricing that would make Asia Floor Wage possible.

A key finding is that fashion retailers are not engaged in any systematic costing of the labour input into garment manufacture (Miller 2013). The imprecise clarification of 'labour minute values' and factory efficiency is a significant factor in the chronic persistence of factory non-compliance on wages and overtime. It is possible to calculate labour minute values for any garment, which also incorporates a living wage element. It is possible to determine and ring-fence the agreed labour cost and to make this an explicit part of the contractual obligation between the buyer and the supplier, in the same way that fabric is itemized in negotiations. Ring-fencing the labour cost would force brands and suppliers to address the issue of how the factory is operating since the basic minimum wage would be the same regardless of factory efficiency. Labour cost is one of the most suppressed costs of production. Other factors of production include quality of infrastructure, access to raw materials, technology, energy, transportation, quality of management, legal systems and so on. Yet another factor in production costs is the purchasing practices of buyers that include lead time, quantity of order, advanced planning and so on.

The AFW fixes the labour cost and would reduce the tendency of industry and government to compete solely on this human factor and turn their attention to other factors which will bring about efficiency, higher productivity, better production and sourcing systems and so on. An initiative involving labour costing will require a high degree of transparency and openness between sourcing companies and their suppliers. Some buyers insist unilaterally that their suppliers 'open their books' during price negotiations, a practice which some observers see as naked power play in an attempt to drive prices down. In such circumstances, it is argued, suppliers have no other option but to hedge by distorting their figures. A more cooperative 'open book costing' will require integrity measures on the part of buyers such as price increases, long-term supply agreements and the offer of productivity expertise where available. Buyers will also require an assurance that the additional amount of money identified as the living or sustainable wage element in excess of the current prevailing unit labour costs is reaching the workers. The AFW Alliance has shown a willingness to participate in helping brands to develop such mechanisms.

The Asia Floor Wage is a practical implementation of the concept of a 'Minimum Living Wage', the original ILO concept. Although minimum living wage is an important qualitative concept, there exists no concrete quantitative definition. The Asia Floor Wage is a quantitative definition of Minimum Living Wage for garment workers in the global garment industry. The Asia Floor Wage has several other social benefits as well. AFW will help decrease the gender pay gap by raising the floor. Worldwide, women form the vast majority of garment workers. Women are over-represented among low-paid workers and their ability to move into higher wage work is also lower. In fact, some believe that the garment industry, a modern manufacturing industry, has such low wages because its workers are predominantly women (unlike, say the more male automobile industry).

Workers work back-breaking overtime hours to earn a minimum living wage. Workers' family lives, health and basic humanity are lost in the race to earn a minimum living wage. A new generation of children without parental care or education will lead to more child labour. Raising workers out of poverty leads to sustainable communities where new generations can lead a better future. The AFW affirms the principle that the only way to enforce AFW is through unions. The AFW implementation requires the existence of a union, and is not a substitution for unionization. In so far as the AFW is a collective bargaining strategy, the right to 'effective recognition of collective bargaining' is essential, and efforts must be made to secure the necessary legal and institutional framework for this. The ILO makes explicit the link between collective bargaining and wage setting in its Global Report on Wages 2008/09. It notes that 'higher coverage of collective bargaining ensures that wages are more responsive to economic growth, and also contributes to lower wage inequality'.

Since the Asia Floor Wage was made public on 7 October 2009, it has gained recognition as a credible benchmark for a living wage in the industry, in the garment labour movement, and in scholarly discussions. The AFW has become a point of reference for scholarly living wage debates such as by Richard Anker and Daniel Vaughan-Whitehead. It has been adopted as a living wage benchmark by the multi-stakeholder forum, the Fair Wear Foundation, and serves as a point of reference for brand-level associations such as the Fair Labor Association. The German development organization GIZ has acclaimed the value of AFW. The AFW has been adopted by a few brands as a comparative benchmark for wage analysis; its credibility and feasibility continue to act as a pressure point. The Workers' Rights Consortium has used the AFW in a variety of ways in its analysis and benchmarking.

Phase 3: Struggle and Bargaining

The present phase of the Asia Floor Wage Alliance is struggle and bargaining. The AFWAlliance actively supports all minimum wage struggles in garment-producing countries; minimum wage rises are critical steps towards an AFW. The AFW Alliance condemns and resists all employer attacks and resistance to unionization, because unions are central to the implementation of an AFW; the AFW is a demand of unions and cannot be reduced to a Corporate Social Responsibility policy or a discursive tool. The AFW Alliance sees the growth of contract labour or short-term contract workers as an attack on freedom of association; therefore the Alliance calls for the abolition of such contractual labour.

The AFW Alliance has developed the Asia Brand Bargaining Group (ABBG) consisting of Asian unions to enable greater coordination and regional bargaining that complements national priorities and struggles. The ABBG has four common demands for the welfare of garment workers in Asia: Living Wage, Freedom of Association, Abolition/Regulation of Contract Labour, and an End to Gender-based Discrimination. The AFW Alliance has also conducted three National People's Tribunals in

India, Sri Lanka and Cambodia on the issue of Living Wage and Working Conditions in the garment global supply chain. Dozens of women workers have testified. Brands have been asked to testify as well to demonstrate what they have done to deliver a living wage. The jury verdicts that have emerged point to shocking deficits in decent labour standards and dangerously low wages. For example, in Cambodia, the mass fainting of women workers in the workplace was clearly attributed to malnutrition and poverty wages. The juries in all three tribunals have unanimously recommended that a living wage needs to be paid immediately and that any other activity of the TNCs (most popular being further research to learn what is already well known) are only delaying tactics.

The Asia Floor Wage Alliance believes that the Asia Floor Wage must be implemented by brands that possess the political and economic power in the global supply chain. They are the principal employers in the global subcontracting chain. A generalized pricing mechanism can be developed taking into account the unit AFW labour cost of a garment in terms of both FOB and retail costs. AFW would fix the floor for the labour cost so that the FOB costs can be adjusted accordingly through other factors and the price agreed.

The premise of Asia Floor Wage implementation requires freedom of association to be respected and for unionization to occur, since enforcement can only be done effectively with unions and worker representatives as part of the process. Therefore, the right to organize is central to the ultimate success of the Asia Floor Wage campaign. An AFW is possible only in the presence of dynamic workers' struggles. In fact, the AFW campaign unites national struggles into an Asian framework and so complements and adds to the power of bargaining at national levels.

20. Twilight of the machinocrats: creative industries, design and the future of human labour

Alan Freeman[1]

INTRODUCTION

On 13 January 2014, after extensive consultation, the UK Department for Culture, Media and Sport (DCMS) released new data for employment and output in the UK's creative industries (DCMS 2014). These data refined a statistical series first published in 2000 (DCMS 1998; 2001), drawing on an extensive legacy (Deroin 2011) to make DCMS the custodian of a de facto world standard. The 'intensity' approach underlying its revisions (Vaizey 2013) was the fruit of a ten-year collaboration between three leading research centres (Bakhshi et al. 2013a), providing the most authoritative indicators yet available for this new economic sector.

This chapter has three objectives:

- to show that the creative economy constitutes a definite new branch of industry, based on a specific type of labour: creative labour;
- to establish that creative labour is 'non-substitutable': it may not be mechanized or replaced by machinery;
- to explore the implications of non-substitutable labour for the future of modern production.

THE EMPIRICAL REALITY OF THE CREATIVE ECONOMY

The most basic point about the creative economy is that it is growing. Jobs and output are both increasing, in proportions such that value-added per

[1] Among many who have helped, special mention goes to colleagues Hasan Bakhshi, Radhika Desai and Peter Higgs. Carlota Perez has been an inspiration throughout. Special thanks to Geoff Oldham, who suggested to a bedraggled group of Chris Freeman's friends, on the wettest day in Sussex history, that we give the name 'economics of hope' to his contribution to economics. Errors are of course my own.

head is also rising – a phenomenon which the Greater London Authority (GLA) termed a 'benign productivity revolution' (Freeman 2002). It is now growing faster than any other UK production industry, with around 2.5 million employed and accounting for 5.2 per cent of Gross Value Added (NESTA 2014). Between 2004 and 2012, UK creative employment grew at an average annual rate of 2.4 per cent compared with 0.7 per cent overall. Though pedestrian by boom-time standards, it is remarkable in a period which spans the opening years of the current long recession in one of the worst-hit countries.

The creative economy is demonstrably a new and permanent feature of modern industrial capitalism. Its growth dates back to 1992, the first year for which we have reliable data. Nine of the original 11 creative industries which DCMS included within it are growing at such rates. Similar growth has been observed in many countries.

A range of studies, using a variety of definitions, have established the creative industries' distinctive characteristics.

- They produce in small quantities for a well-defined customer base. Aesthetic, intangible or 'cultural' characteristics of their outputs typically add to their value (Hesmondhalgh 2007; Stoneman 2010; Haskel et al. 2009).
- They cluster geographically (Chapain et al. 2010; Freeman 2009; Pratt 2006), forming tight concentrations of identical or interrelated activities, such as advertising in London's West End, broadcasting and video in West London or Shoreditch's 'High-Tech' cluster (Cities Institute 2011).
- They employ distinctive techniques to recoup up-front investment and maintain a competitive advantage, of which Intellectual Property (IP) (Howkins 2013, WIPO) is only one of a battery, including first-mover advantage and unprotected identity based on connoisseurship, loyalty or genre (Frontier Economics 2007).
- They use 'pre-market selection' involving 'gatekeepers' such as gallery owners, buyers, publishers, editors, agents and producers (Caves 2002), and collaborate using 'open innovation' (Chesbrough 2003) and 'motley crew' methods (Caves 2002) to construct teams of specialists for one-off projects.
- They have evolved distinctive contracting techniques to manage uncertainty (rather than 'risk'; Knight 1921; Caves 2002).

We can therefore treat the creative economy, following Bakhshi et al. (2013a), as a *pragmatic reality*: these facts appear to a greater or lesser degree in a wide variety of approaches (UNESCO 2009). The intensity approach integrates all these into a coherent whole by asking how the creative economy really functions, summed up in the conclusion that it is a *new industry*.

CREATION: A BRANCH OF INDUSTRY BASED ON A TYPE OF LABOUR

Many definitions of creativity impose concepts external to the reality of a straightforward commercial activity, instead of simply asking what these industries produce, how they produce it, who buys their products, and why. Yet such questions flow naturally from Adam Smith's approach to the way capitalism functions – by subdividing the economy into branches of the division of labour, now commonly referred to as industries. Anybody who speaks of agriculture, manufacturing or construction is unconsciously referring to industries but, for the most part, simply take them for granted, failing to recognize that economic structures are not fixed, and new industries emerge all the time, beside new products and processes. What, then, defines an industry? The standard manual of procedure (ISIC 2008) offers three criteria:

1. specific inputs, generally material (for example, the extractive industries);
2. specific outputs, also generally material (for example, the construction industries);
3. specific processes of production (for example manufacturing).

Interestingly, the industries we take for granted are surprisingly difficult to pin down (A. Freeman 2008). We might naively suppose agriculture produces food using land – but it also supplies wool, bio-fuels and even wood, whilst factory-farmed animals are lucky to see the sky, never mind the land. For this reason, the statistical authorities take any one of the above criteria as sufficient to define an industry. The creative economy meets all three:

1. The creative industries that comprise it share a common type of input: the creative workforce.
2. Their outputs share common features: they emphasize content, their products are differentiated, a high proportion of their value is intangible, and they sell small quantities to discretionary clients.
3. They have common processes of production. They use pre-market

selection, collaborative uncertainty-management contracts and just-in-time production. They cluster, and they exploit IP, first-mover advantage and brand, to secure returns on their investment.

Let us first consider the special workforce. We can measure it, because DCMS adopted, from the outset, a feature of earlier European studies whose importance it did not at first recognize: it combined employment figures for creative industries with those for occupations. An industry and an occupation are two different things. Not everyone who works in the electrical industries is an electrician. In fact, only 12 per cent of people working in the 'Electricity, Gas, Steam and Air Conditioning Supply' industries are occupied as 'Skilled Metal and Electrical Trades' workers, and a further 7 per cent as 'Skilled Construction and Building'. This compares with 14 per cent who are 'Science and Technology Professionals' and 17 per cent corporate managers (Bakhshi et al. 2013a: 13). Less than half the agricultural workforce consists of agricultural workers, and teachers make up only 45 per cent of the education industry. In the creative industries the levels of occupational specialization are, in contrast, extraordinarily high. 'Creative intensity' denotes the proportion of any given industry's workforce made up of creatively-occupied workers (Table 20.1).

Intensity in the creative industries is not only large, but exceptionally so: on average, 25 times greater than outside them. This holds for all but three of the 11 industries that DCMS now considers creative. This might be thought to arise from a circular definition since these nine industries are chosen using intensity as a criterion; but as we noted in Bakhshi et al. (2013a: 23), similar intensities were observed using DCMS's old definition which did not depend on any such prior supposition.

This unique workforce composition yields a straightforward conclusion: the specialist resource of the creative economy is in fact its creative labour force. What, then, is creative labour? Given their liberal use of the word 'creativity', writers are surprisingly contradictory when it comes to defining it. UNCTAD's (2010) definitive report covers almost every concept possible, without actually adopting any one of them:

> There is no simple definition of 'creativity' that encompasses all the various dimensions of this phenomenon. Indeed, in the field of psychology, where individual creativity has been most widely studied, there is no agreement as to whether creativity is an attribute of people or a process by which original ideas are generated. Nevertheless, the characteristics of creativity in different areas of human endeavour can at least be articulated. For example, it can be suggested that artistic creativity involves imagination and a capacity to generate original ideas and novel ways of interpreting the world, expressed in text, sound and

Table 20.1 Creative intensity of the creative industries, DCMS 2011 definition

Creative sector	Creative occupations	Other occupations	Total occupations	Intensity (creative occupations/total occupations)
Advertising	45 900	69 400	115 300	40%
Architecture	67 800	36 200	103 500	65%
Arts and Antiques	500	8 300	8 800	6%
Design	56 400	42 100	98 500	57%
Designer Fashion	3 700	2 900	6 600	56%
Film, Video and Photography	28 700	29 500	58 200	49%
Music and the Visual and Performing Arts	138 400	52 800	191 300	72%
Publishing	71 300	111 500	182 700	39%
Software/ Electronic Publishing	900	22 300	23 200	4%
Digital and Entertainment Media	2 000	11 200	13 200	15%
TV and Radio	61 700	34 200	96 000	64%
All Creative Industries (2011 definition)	476 800	420 500	897 300	53%

Source: Bakhshi et al. 2013a: 10.

image; scientific creativity involves curiosity and a willingness to experiment and make new connections in problem solving; and economic creativity is a dynamic process leading towards innovation in technology, business practices, marketing, etc., and is closely linked to gaining competitive advantages in the economy.

The confusion arises because of attempts to impose, on a new economic reality, ideal notions drawn only from past experience. Following the pragmatic reality principle, the intensity approach derives its concept of creativity by studying what creative workers really do. Since everyone recognizes musicians, artists, fashion designers, actors and architects as creative, what do their occupations have in common?

Occupation, we should note, is not synonymous with talent, training or qualification, though these may be job requirements. It defines what the worker is employed to do, the 'concrete labour' (cf. Marx 1976: 132–8). Artists who work in McDonald's are not employed for their creative capacities. Despite wide differences, creative occupations share one critical characteristic: they are *non-substitutable* (Krzyzaniak 1973);[2] they are all activities which cannot be replaced by a machine (Bakhshi et al. 2013a: 24). Creative labour is not the only non-substitutable labour: caring is almost certainly non-substitutable, and education has resisted all attempts at mechanization. The characteristic that creative labour shares with these occupations is that human agency is either an essential characteristic of the product – as in relations of caring – or is preferred by consumers, as with handmade artefacts.

A further feature is, however, specific to the creative industries (A. Freeman 2008): they are *non-mechanizable.* Most importantly, they are non-repetitive. Each new assignment differs in one or other vital respect from the preceding one. The output of each creative production run is different, so that the steps involved in it can never be laid down in advance – a new film, a new work of art, a new building or advertising campaign. Creative production is the antithesis of mass production: indeed, industries like fashion make a clear distinction between mass indistinguishable generic products and designer items in which the skills involved are visibly displayed (Newbery 2003). This is the diametrical opposite of the production line, that archetype of modern manufacture, in which every step is specified in the minutest detail. Essential decisions on how to create the product are left to the individual creative worker or team. The complexity of the final product makes it impossible to specify how it should be achieved.

Creative labour shares non-mechanizability with much scientific labour, one of the topics of a forthcoming study (Bakhshi et al. 2014). Scientific labour, however, has a different type of output, being concerned either with the introduction of new knowledge into productive processes, or with the production of new knowledge. The creative economy deploys its specific type of labour in specific creative processes, to produce specific, creative outputs, in a distinctive and truly Smithian industry: a branch of the division of labour. The nature of this labour has immense repercussions for economics and economic theory.

---

[2] Thanks to Nicholas Theocarakis for this reference.

THE SECOND GREAT TRANSFORMATION: GENESIS AND LIMITS OF THE MACHINOCRATIC VIEW

Non-substitutable labour is the antithesis of mechanized labour, with profound macroeconomic consequences for growth, trade and all aspects of economic development because it obliges us to confront the real limits of mechanization.

Mechanization is a method in industrial capitalism for decreasing the labour needed to produce what human society uses in reproducing itself. It combines two moments: the reduction of labour itself to a set of repetitive simple movements, and the deployment of devices that conduct these same movements in place of human labour. The idea that if all human requirements can be met without work, labour will become redundant is cogently explored in Morris-Suzuki's (1984) penetrating article on robots and capitalism, and has been the subject of dystopian movies like *Colossus: The Forbin Project, Robocop* or at its most extreme, *The Matrix*. It suggests that mechanization is heading for a stationary state, not unlike the related 'zero-growth' economy projected in the 'Limits to Growth' debate (Meadows et al. 2004).

However, mechanization cannot eliminate all labour but only substitutable labour. The limit would then be a society in which only non-substitutable labour remains. In any such society, growth does not have to involve the ever-increasing consumption of resources. To the extent that it involves the development of labour – the expansion of its spiritual, mental and cultural capacities – it may co-exist with either a rising, constant or declining use of primary resources. Non-substitutable labour does not mean 'labour without machines'; it depends on a new *relationship* with machines, which has come into being because of ICT, modern transport, the modern city, the modern university and many other systems which rely on highly advanced technology. Without such systems, creative labour could not function as the principal resource of a growing branch of the economy. The present growth path will prove unsustainable regardless of the labour it uses; but if the choice is made to 'resource-decouple' (Swilling 2005; 2011), a materially sustainable growth path placing no limit on the capabilities of labour comes within reach.

Classical growth theory, a product of the mechanical epoch, suggests a search for the appropriate 'balance' between capital and labour (understood as mutually substitutable) along the growth path. But the new imperative is to provide the technology that non-substitutable labour demands for its deployment. Human development then becomes the only option. Equally in terms of trade theory, if non-substitutable labour is dominant or even rising secularly, then development strategies cannot but focus on those resources that will optimize its growth and capabilities. Creative labour obliges developing countries to abandon the cruel illusion that they can achieve an optimum by 'specializing' in labour in some generic sense. The issue is which *type* of labour, and what technology is needed to support it?

The very unpreparedness of economic and social thought for such unexpected problems betrays the mental barriers involved. The common prejudices of both everyday speech and social theory assign pre-eminence to machinery. Labour is treated as a 'lump' with no distinct characteristics; machinery and materials are the locus and target of innovation. Industrial or innovation policies, where they exist, are invariably described in such terms as 'high-tech', 'high-end manufacture' or 'STEM' (Science, Technology, Engineering and Medicine/Mathematics) (DIUS 2009; Hecker 2005; Rothwell 2013). Creativity, as a factor of production, is either absent or conceived of as eccentric science. Ingrained polarities define the concepts we use to talk about production and its antinomies:

production = work = necessity = repetitive identity

versus

creation = leisure = luxury = distinctive individuality

Such counterpositions have their origins in Romantic opposition to industry dating back to the late eighteenth century. The idea that industry is the opposite of art, or manufacture of creation, is the mental product of a specific historical era in which mechanization has been the dominant form of economic and social transformation. As products of a passing age, such mental constructs are plainly inadequate for understanding non-mechanical production and its social and economic transformations. Indeed as Williams (1958) notes, the word 'art', whose derivation from the word 'artisan' betrays its origins in the Latin word for technique or skill, was not widely distinguished from industry or even science until late in the Industrial Revolution. Thus Young (1759:12, cited by Williams 1958: 37), one of the earliest exponents of English Romanticism, states: 'An Original may be said to be of a vegetable nature; it rises spontaneously from the vital root of genius; it grows; it is not made; Imitations are often a sort of manufacture, wrought up by those mechanics, arts and labour, out of pre-existent materials not their own.'

Art and labour are here identified as 'mechanics' and counterposed to origination, or genius. Seventy years passed, with industrialization sweeping the nations of Europe, before Carlyle (1829: 243) voiced the cry that mechanism defines the age:

> were we required to characterise this age of ours by any single epithet, we should be tempted to call it, not an Heroical, Devotional, Philosophical or Moral Age, but, above all others, the Mechanical Age. It is the Age of Machinery, in every outward and inward sense of that word. . . Nothing is now done directly, or by hand; all is by rule and calculated contrivance.

His description is as accurate as it is evocative: 'On every hand, the living artisan is driven from his workshop, to make room for a speedier, inanimate one. The shuttle drops from the fingers of the weaver; and falls into iron fingers that ply it faster.'

The material conditions for the concept of universal creativity were absent. With precious few exceptions – in fact only Marx and Keynes come to mind – critics of mechanism fell back on one of three ideas: the utopian and ultimately reactionary worship of pre-commercial social relations; the idea of entrusting a special group of gifted people ('artists') with oversight of culture; or the view that managing the cultural values of a people is the business of the nation and should be handled by the state. These ideas are also found in all manner of mixtures (Williams 1958) such as Coleridge's 'clerisy', producers of culture who could be entrusted with its public administration, or Carlyle's 'heroes' who could lead the people in advancing their culture. In the UK this has mutated into the Disraelian idea that the educated and wealthy elite per se is the legitimate custodian of cultural virtues.

The common thread is German Romanticism (Elias 1969): cultural production is the special job of a restricted group of exceptional 'men made Gods by genius' (Safranski 2004). If this Romantic view were true – and it dominates modern thinking about creativity – it would set another limit on the creative economy, because there would simply not be enough creative people to resource it.

Machinocratic thinking here too displays the constraints of a quintessentially nineteenth-century conception; in this case, its concept of social reproduction. The counterpart to the cramped idea that economic production uses machines to turn things into other things is a stylized 'culture' occupying a twilight zone which descends when the factory whistle sounds, undertaken by a small group of gifted people drawn, by an inexplicable stroke of fate, from families who can afford to indulge them. But even if not everybody is destined to be a virtuoso artist or athlete, all humans have within themselves the capacity to perform activities which machines cannot, and this capacity is almost tautologically the defining attribute of being human – as testified by aboriginal art, which is problematic in

Western eyes (Smith 2011). Projects such as Venezuela's 'Sistema' have shown how rapid human and creative development can be when the material barriers to participation are removed. The greatest artistic innovation the USA has given the world – jazz – originated in the poorest and most oppressed sector of its early twentieth-century population, in a city now abandoned to Hurricane Katrina.

The mindset just described is entrenched in two factors: the resolute elitism of the middle classes and the pervasive notion that machines are the true essence of production. The result is a *Zeitgeist* that Radhika Desai and I term the 'machinocratic' outlook, by analogy with the pre-classical physiocrats for whom the land was the location of truly productive labour. In the machinocratic outlook, the place of land is taken by machinery, beside which we find the only labour that 'genuinely' produces. Creation, culture, not to mention health, caring or even education are ancillaries that merely recycle: parasitic and derivative, panhandlers on the bleak streets of Wasteville, sitting targets of all attacks on the spendthrift state and the idle poor.

This outlook has material roots in commodity fetishism: relations between humans, in commercial society, are disguised by the workings of the market as relations between things, leading to 'physicalism' (Kliman 2007: 56); the idea that capital is an assemblage of *things* – tangible, alienable objects – instead of a social relation (Merk, this volume). The critical fallacies nurtured by such modes of thought concern service production, to which we now turn.

THE TRANSFORMATION TO A SERVICE ECONOMY

In Adam Smith's day, production was so quintessentially material that he defined productive labour (Smith 1976: 146) as the creation of 'vendible objects'. This made some sense when the vast bulk of commodities were manufactured or cultivated. But industrial capitalism has brought about a long-term change which economics still struggles with. As Figure 20.1 shows, over 80 per cent of labour in the main industrialized economies works in services (cf. Graz, this volume). This is an inexorable trend. Since 1948 it has shown almost no cyclic variation and has hesitated briefly, if at all, on isolated occasions.

The rise of services is the most characteristic technological transformation of the postwar era. Its social and economic effects outstrip all the changes attributed to nuclear power, oil, or the car (cf. Perez 2002). The surge associated with these innovations exhausted itself in the late 1960s and an utterly different type of technological transformation set in, as

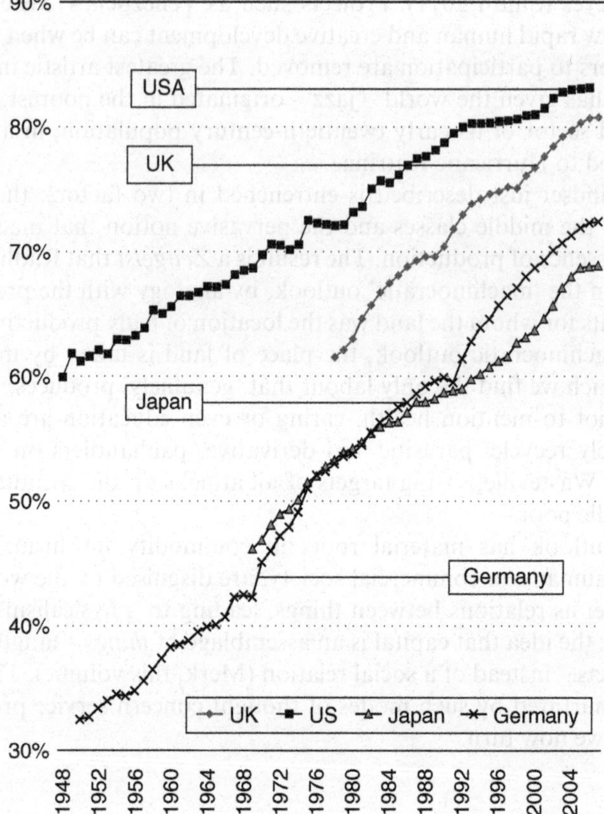

Source: ILO, BLS, author calculations.

Figure 20.1 Share of employment in services, 1948–2007

radical in its consequences as the transition from agriculture to industry. This was not the 'product' of a technological revolution: it *was* a technological revolution. In many profound senses, the paralysis of economic and political thought in the face of the long stagnation that began in the 1970s expresses a radical inability to grasp it, or even respond to it.

The growth in service labour corresponds to a real demand for service outputs, which as we shall see has begun to change the nature of material goods themselves. Figure 20.3 shows how UK household demand has evolved since 1976. Except for a recent brief reversal, the demand for services has risen continuously while the demand for food and clothing has fallen although demand for these has not decreased. Demand for 'leisure

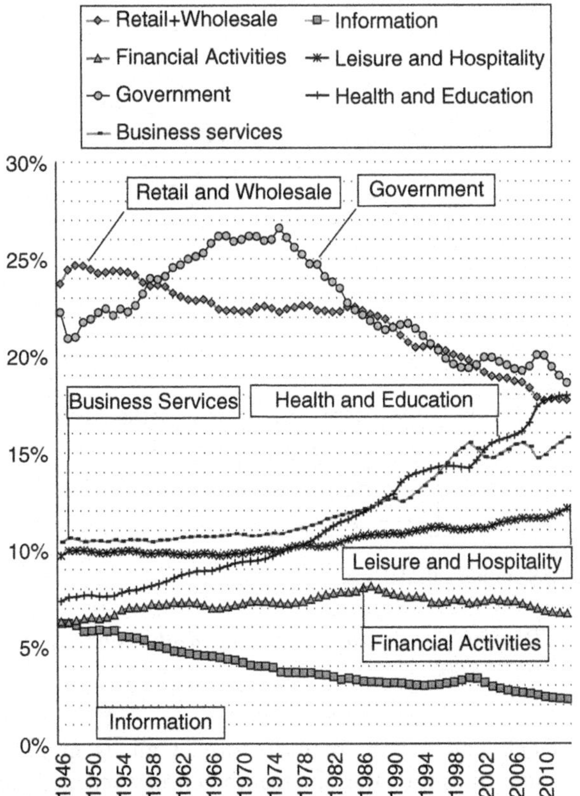

Source: BLS, author calculations.

Figure 20.2 Share of employment in US services, 1946–2013

goods and services' – which includes most creative products – on the other hand almost doubled between 1976 and 2006.

Figure 20.4, showing the 30-year growth rates of the components of UK family spending, emphasizes that leisure and personal service spending have both grown at the expense of food and clothing and also the traditional material 'luxuries', alcohol and tobacco. Businesses too consume an increasing proportion of creative services and an important subgroup – advertising, software and architecture – sells almost entirely to business customers, as Table 20.2 shows.

This is not some kind of service bubble. It is a long-term, irreversible change in the structure of the modern industrial economy, whose evident reality is an antidote to the utopian view that we can simply wind back

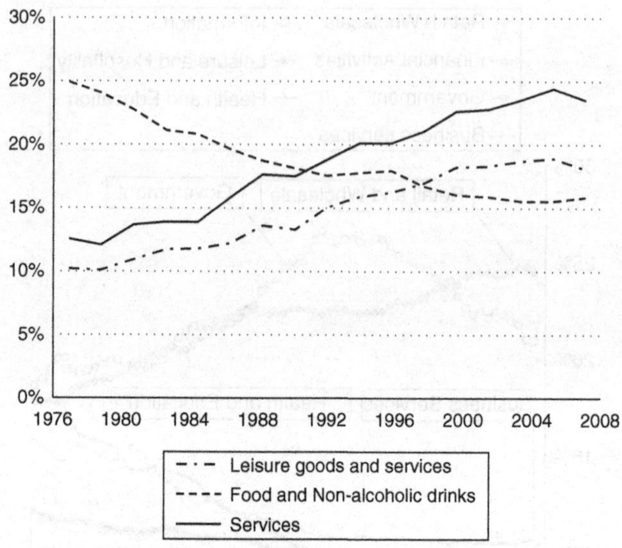

Source: UK FES, author calculations.

Figure 20.3 Demand for leisure and service products by UK families, 1976–2008

the history clock and restore manufacture in all its glory, just as the reactionary romanticism of the nineteenth century yearned for an idyllic pre-industrial age instead of grappling with the real potential, limits and contradictions of industrialization. Otherwise incisive critics like Elliott and Atkinson (2007: 75) thus dismiss the creative economy as an ephemeral fantasy, the illusion that Britain, having lost the role of the workshop of the world, 'can still be the world's creative hub'.

Part of this confusion is due to the inadequacies of the industrial classification system itself. The 'service' sector includes, and once mainly comprised, commerce and finance. This encourages the prejudice that services are inherently unproductive, involving pushing pieces of paper around or selling worthless derivatives. Yet as Figure 20.2 shows, the largest US growth has been in health and education, followed by business services, and then leisure and hospitality. Employment in financial services has never exceeded 9 per cent, and has fallen since 1990 nearly to its 1946 level of 6 per cent. Wholesale and retail employment has fallen since 1948 to its lowest ever level of 18 per cent.

With post-machinocratic illusions out of the way, care is needed to avoid the equally misleading generalizations of the post-industrial litera-

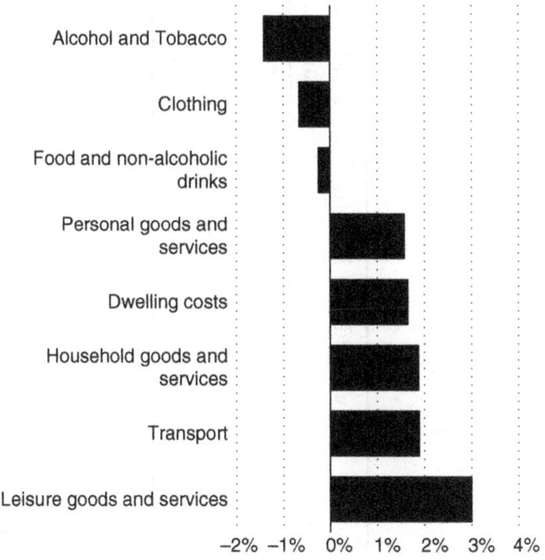

Source: UK FES, author calculations.

Figure 20.4 Annual growth rate of major categories of family expenditure, UK, 1976–2008

ture. Machines have no more disappeared than did landed production in the Industrial Revolution. The new service economy is a particular *mode of deployment* of mechanical devices in which humans use them to deliver services. The drive-in hamburger bar, the modern football stadium, and the cinema alike use sophisticated modern technology to organize a direct relation between human consumers and human producers, whether burger-flippers, actors or soccer stars. It is this direct relation that is paid for; it constitutes the use of what is purchased. Machinery is also deployed ever more extensively in producing other machines and materials, even as the cost of each individual item falls inexorably. These two facts explain why capital – the accumulated value of past labour – continues to increase relative to living labour (Kliman 2012; Freeman 2012b; Maito 2013).

Now services are not creative merely by virtue of being services. On the contrary, we shall see, the biggest obstacle to growth in the service era is the restriction of creative products to luxury consumption. But even when confined to the low-wage and mechanical, service production rises above material production. The output of a burger joint is not the burger, but the serving of it. Economically, this distinguishes the humblest café from the most illustrious jewellery store.

Table 20.2 Demand for creative products

Percent of total demand for creative products	Investment demand	Intermediate demand from business	Government and non-profit	Households	Exports	Total demand
Advertising, Software and Architecture	15%	73%	1%	0%	11%	100%
All other creative	3%	26%	0%	61%	10%	100%
All creative industries	8%	47%	0%	34%	11%	100%

Source: Office for National Statistics, author's calculations.

Finally, material products have not disappeared, but are being transformed by the services which they make possible. Beside the historical transformation of labour and machinery, we see a further transformation in the material commodity, the very essence of capitalist production. Here we may get some appreciation of the magnitude and scope of the reversal under way.

ALL THAT IS SOLID: CREATIVE LABOUR AND THE TRANSFORMATION OF MATERIALITY

Possibly the most important consequence of the service revolution is the transformation of material objects into bearers of services. The conceptual reconsideration it calls for is of critical importance.

The most mysterious attribute of creative products (Hesmondhalgh 2007; Stoneman 2010; Haskel et al. 2009; DCMS 1998; 2001) is their 'aesthetic content'. We don't buy paintings for the use of the canvas but for what the artist has done with it. Their use lies in the concrete form of the artist's labour, which is visible on its exterior. Yet we don't even think of artistic labour as manual; it never occurs to those who lament the passing of 'true manufacture' that Michelangelo subjected his body to more damage when painting the Sistine Chapel than a typical auto worker endures throughout his life. Art sublimed his torment.

The materialization of artistic labour is not confined to art. Fashion clothing is purchased not for warmth or cover but appearance. In 2010, ONS reclassified all publishing as a branch of information: services. The fast-vanishing compact disc, tape or vinyl record is not purchased for its own sake but as the inert medium on which the real product – the service of performance – is inscribed.

This attribute of materiality is transforming erstwhile manufacturing companies. Apple, by 2012, was the largest company in the world in terms of capitalization, but its iPhones sell not for what is in them but what is *on* them; apps, music, Internet access, and occasionally, even phone calls. 'Platform' companies such as Google, Facebook, Spotify or Netflix are dissolving the material substrate of communication into an invisible network of wires and signals in which the service of interaction is the primary product. Even that most solid of industries, auto manufacture, has mutated into a purveyor of 'looks', add-ons, go-faster stripes and opulent designer curves.

Creative labour transforms all it touches into mere signifiers of its activity. Objects become either mere bearers of it, as with the CD or the video tape, or mere symbols of it, as in the cult of authenticity. In live performance this reaches its ultimate limit; artists directly embody their own product, leading to new forms of fetishism like the celebrity, a person who symbolizes an entire branch of collective labour.

This transformation demands a systematic reconsideration of the concept of 'service'. Just as with 'creativity', economists cherry-pick, as suits their purpose, definitions that range (Petit 1987) from the outdated notion that a service must be directly performed by one human for another in the immediate presence of both – eliminating the newspaper, the phone call and the recording from the realm of services – to the diametrically opposed concept of 'capital services' (Harper 1982), wherein 'service' means any use consumed over time, reducing all material production into services.

As with creativity, all attempts to impose outdated or external concepts upon a new reality lead to obfuscation. The real economy is differentiating all products into those whose use is determined by the non-substitutable labour engaged in producing them and those whose materiality determines their use. In line with this change, I suggest the term 'service product' to cover both traditional directly-delivered services, and material objects whose primary function is the delivery of aesthetic content.

This more rigorous concept not only covers most traditional services, but distinguishes rigorously between the two principal types of product now emerging in sphere after sphere of material production. Coffee may be delivered by a machine or by a barista: the former is a material product and the latter a service. Correspondingly, the world of end-user coffee supply divides into makers of vending machines and managers of cafés, formally purveyors of the same material substance but in all practical respects as unlike as chalk and cheese.

What, then, is the *use* of a service product? We will attempt to resolve this question by turning to the second of our criteria for 'industry-hood': the way modern services are produced.

ICT AND THE REVOLUTION IN SERVICE PRODUCTIVITY

The transition to a service economy raises an obvious question which is rarely, if ever, stated clearly: how can the productivity of labour continue to rise, as it apparently did without limit in the mechanical age, once the bulk of it is confined to the delivery of services? Two economic fallacies testify to the obstacles to understanding created by physicalist reasoning. The first arises from Solow's famous remark (Uchitelle 1987) that 'you can see the computer age everywhere but in the productivity statistics'. The second is Baumol's 'paradox' (Baumol and Bowen 1966; Heilbrun 2003) dealing with the 'cost disease' of artistic services which, Baumol argued, cannot increase their output by their very nature. An orchestra cannot 'produce more' by playing faster: therefore, Baumol argued, the public has to fund the arts.

The public should indeed fund the arts, but this is not the reason. The true reason is that there *is* no systematic or rigorous method for measuring the 'quantity' of a service. This is a real problem, not a theoretical quibble: the statisticians don't know how to do it. Five years before Solow's remark, the US Bureau of Labor Statistics (BLS) (Mark 1982) proudly announced: 'Over the last decade, the Bureau of Labor Statistics has been expanding the number of service industries for which it publishes productivity measures, and at present provides measures for 16 industries, representing almost a third of the employment in the sector'.

Since in the same article the BLS recognizes that services provided three-quarters of all employment, valid statistics for real output thus covered precisely half the economy. Solow was technically correct: ICT did not show up in the productivity statistics. Not, however, because ICT had no effect but because the statistics just didn't report them. The implied inference, that productivity has not increased, cannot be drawn.

Critics of Greenspan's 1990s 'productivity miracle' are similarly technically correct but short of the mark. The US Bureau of Economic Analysis (BEA) adjusts real output upwards, using 'hedonic indices' (Gordon 2000; Desai 2013a: 211–15) for improvements in quality. Since other nations use more cautious quality adjustments, US productivity growth was overstated in comparison. But the real problem is deeper.

As we have just seen, three-quarters of the 'real service output' of *all* countries is thin air (cf. Mark 1982). But even physical measures of purely material objects are increasingly uninformative when their primary function is to facilitate a service – even when that service is consumed by the user, like a phone call or text. A computer does not just 'compute'. It serves a multiplicity of purposes whose variety grows almost daily; writing letters, producing accounts, making and watching videos, playing games, or just messing with apps. The electronics industry's output can no longer be measured in tons, yards or units. True, a computer that goes twice as fast does not supply twice as much use – but neither do two computers. In both cases, their usefulness depends on what they are used for.

Baumol's error is the inverse of Solow's: he assumes that the measure of the service is, like some physical object, a pure quantity, the number of performances or the length of one of them. Even by this measure, his conclusion does not stand up: as he wrote, service productivity was already being revolutionized – by ICT, which was dissolving, one by one, the historical constraints on the service relation, all arising from the simple physical need for humans to be next to each other in order to interact. Communication technologies had already removed barriers of distance, whilst recording and reproduction technologies were eradicating barriers of time. Digitization and the Internet have now removed the last barrier of *quantity* allowing humans to interact in any manner they choose. Except where direct personal contact is still needed, as with haircuts, services can be delivered across any distance, in any quantity, and at any time.

An orchestra thus can indeed increase its 'output', measured as the number of people it reaches, by thousands and possibly millions. It can broadcast; it can record; it can just use very large speakers. A well-known rule of thumb in the industry is 'Moore's Law' which states that hardware capacity doubles every year. If we measure either services, or the objects that deliver them, as we do forging ingots or growing corn, we should conclude that ICT has facilitated the greatest continuous output surge in history. However, this actually tells us next to nothing. Something entirely new has happened: ICT has transformed not just the quantitative use of services but their qualitative nature. It is thereby transforming the whole of what we mean by production.

AESTHETICS, DISTINCTION AND THE TRANSFORMATION OF USE

What use is a product? This innocent question divides economics like no other. We will again apply pragmatic reality. What do the consumers of creative products, of other service products and of material products with a service aspect, really do with them?

Figure 20.5 uses data from Will Page, former Chief Economist with the Performing Rights Society (PRS). Since even hotel-lobby music must pay royalties, the PRS administers an extremely well-populated dataset. Page and his colleagues (Page et al. 2011) divided up musical revenues into two parts: the first from sales of recorded material (CDs, discs, tapes and so on) and the second from live performance. When Internet downloading took hold, consumers did not reduce their total spend on music. Instead they used their savings to increase spending on live performance.

This puts the lid on the Baumol fallacy. Consumers have differentiated among forms of the same use: performance. They treat live music as enhanced performance, as performance of greater use value.

This differentiation furthermore does not stop with the live/recorded distinction. Consumers of performance establish a visible hierarchy of uses, with live performance at the top, Spotify in the middle and a ring-

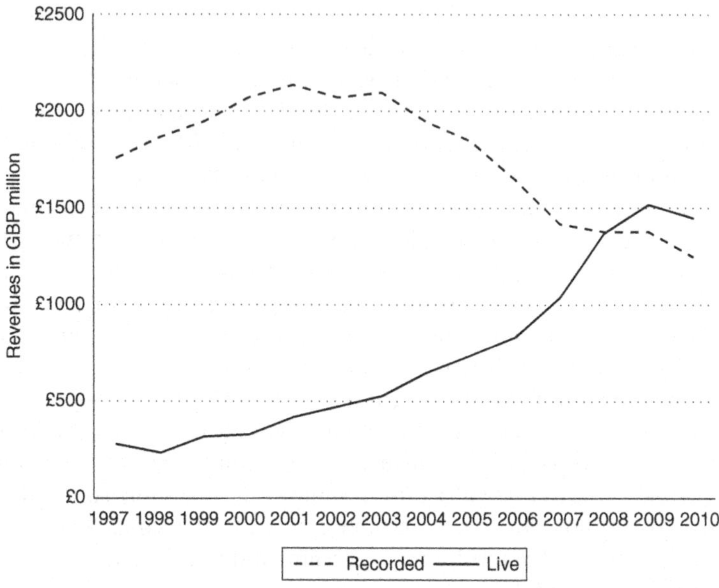

Source: Page et al. (2011).

Figure 20.5 Revenue from recorded and live music in the UK, 1997–2010

tone at the bottom. The same phenomenon is observed across the board; personal contact is simply rated more highly than other interactions. Thus in business circles it is common to describe a meeting as an upgrade for a phone call. This explains the great value that businesses set on 'closeness', first manifested in financial districts and now in the sprouting 'clusters' noted earlier.

'Productivity' can then be increased 'vertically' or 'horizontally'. Producers can simply move upwards along this lattice of socially established uses. Live performance is growing because it is recognized by consumers as 'more useful'. They also differentiate 'sideways': they pursue variety, explaining the characteristic production structure noted earlier: short runs of specific products, short life cycles and so on.

It might be thought that the multiplication of products adds no extra use – if the number of suitcases in the world is a constant, how is their use increased by division into a Gucci and generic bag population? To this we must first respond that the number of shoes in the world is growing faster than the number of feet. Differentiation brings some purely quantitative increase, because consumers buy more of the 'same' item. However, even more decisive is the fact that *distinction itself acquires a use*. A fashionista, a football supporter, a Lady Gaga fan or even the resident of a desirable district pays to be a type of person, to share membership of a definite group that does the same thing. Beside its normal use, every object acquires a second, symbolic use (Hesmondhalgh 2007): it represents the groups and social classes to which the purchaser belongs.

Creative use is fundamentally collective in nature. Live performance is valued not to be close to the players but to be part of a common experience. A play in an empty theatre is not just dismaying for the cast but dispiriting for their audience. The lover of a type of music or art, a collector, or a team supporter finds merit in being 'like' others with similar taste. Distinction, ironically, becomes a uniform: a marker of collectivity.

The machinocratic vision obscures this critical point because it accustoms us to thinking of use as individual. The very idea of 'methodological individualism' rests on the intrinsic 'excludability' of material objects: two people, we automatically think, cannot wear the same shoes. But two wearers of fashion shoes *are*, in effect, wearing the same shoes. To the extent that their value resides in the design, and not the leather, the shoes are no longer excludable.

No concept illustrates the difficulties more than Intellectual Property (IP). Precisely because aesthetic value is consumed collectively, it is also produced collectively. Performance and exhibition are creative acts, so curation, exhibition or even window-dressing are part of creating use alongside script-writing or designing. This is why one of the five criteria for a creative occupation is that of interpretation (Bakhshi et al. 2013a). IP is in contrast not in any real sense 'produced'; it is a title to income. It plays a partitive or allocative role, as do other instruments like tickets, which have no value in themselves but define the collective consumer. Strategies based simply on acquiring or constructing IP, which are probably most dominant in the USA, can easily frustrate creative production if the title is held by non-producing corporate owners by raising the price of their outputs whilst diverting the income away from the real producers.

UNEVEN DEVELOPMENT, CLASS AND THE REAL LIMITS TO GROWTH

The main purpose of this chapter has been to describe the creative economy as it functions today, exhibit some obstacles to understanding it, and suggest how we might overcome them. This would be a scholastic project if it had no implications for action or policy, and these are profound. The mere existence of the creative economy confirms that both economic and social benefits will be generated by policies that speed up and encourage its growth. If further economic growth actually *requires* a major expansion of non-substitutable labour, then there ultimately is no other way forward. Moreover the creative economy is not an unmitigated good; its more damaging effects (see, for example, Freeman 2012a) include precarization, celebritization, and the new fusions of wealth and power seen in figures such as Berlusconi.

The most decisive question is, however, whether the growth is automatic and can be left to the market or its own devices, or whether specific steps are needed to facilitate it. What are the external and internal obstacles to creativity-led growth? One of the biggest is that capitalism finds difficulty in investing in a form of labour, because it cannot retain the investment. This leads to policies which are simply perverse: human capacity, which means education, health, housing, social provision and the real fostering of creative self-expression, is the main target of austerity drives in most industrialized countries.

What may well be yet more decisive is creative demand. Consumption of creative products is a widespread aspiration but it is not a universal fact. The explanation is quite simple: they are not 'necessities' in the economic sense. Even though such traditional necessities as food and drink and housing are a decreasing cost at least to UK families, and although average family spending on creative products has risen, this is distributed highly unevenly. The wealthy spend far more on 'leisure' than low-income families but the differential is much smaller in spending on food. On a world scale, this unevenness is extreme.

There are therefore two interconnected reasons to 'invest in civilization'. One is that this capacity is becoming the *sine qua non* for expanding the productive powers of both industrialized and emerging nations; second, however, it is the necessary source of the new demand required to fuel a major expansion.

In every surge of growth, economic expansion proceeds on the two fronts of supply and demand (Perez 2002). Technological innovations bring what was once prohibitively expensive within reach of great masses of people (cotton goods, railways, cars, electrical power, household gadgets). This is only possible because *spending* rises to facilitate the mass consumption of these things. What was once a luxury, enjoyed only by an elite, becomes a necessity. On this basis a new productive structure arises as the new types of consumption become part of what work 'is'. If mechanical transport stopped tomorrow, most industrial production would cease. And if Victorian wages had stayed below what was needed even to take an annual holiday, the railways would never have been built. In Marx's terms, travel became a 'moral and historical' component of the wage – in effect, a universal entitlement. Establishing such norms went hand in hand with each great wave of industrialization.

A mass demand for the products of creative labour is thus far from a luxury: it is an economic and social necessity, and without it this new sector can never realize its full potential. *This is why inequality constitutes a disastrous obstacle to economic recovery*. There is, however, a further obstacle which is internal to the creative economy itself, and this chapter would be incomplete without mention of it. This obstacle is the function of creative products in the reproduction of classes.

The market in distinction operates in two ways. As Bourdieu (1984) minutely observes in modern times, it provides *markers of class*. Elias (1969), in chronicling the early history of the concept of 'culture' itself, points out that it acquired its modern meaning in the German language as an indicator of human worth, of merit, in a kind of literary struggle against the term 'civilization' which denoted status of birth, marked by customs and 'manners'. Culture signified that which was produced or delivered, and by its use, the emerging German middle classes sought to establish an *entitlement to status*, both political and social, from which they were excluded by the greatly more powerful aristocracy. The signifiers of this entitlement were markers of taste: above all the appreciation of art, which had to be *exhibited* – by attendance, possession and ostentation. In modern times, every object that departs from the merely functional is a candidate for the social function of an external marker of status: the district you live in, the car you drive, the clothes you wear, the events you are seen at define where you sit in the social hierarchy. This is the origin of 'bling' – of all marketing strategies which play to the aspiration of the buyer to move one tiny step up the social ladder. It also sets huge limits on what is really required before society can make adequate use of creative labour, because almost by definition, it confines the demand for aesthetic value to a restricted class of society, when what is really required is a massive extension of that demand, making it part of the normal life and entitlement of every individual.

If snobbery is the 'vertical' direction in which aesthetic value creates social use, then we can term 'horizontal' the second and vital direction of use creation: this is the multiplication of the capacity of humans. Creative production is characterized, in the last instance, by variety. It simply extends the range of things that people can do, and in particular the variety of social experiences they can take part in. The distinctions involved in enthusiasms are genuine preferences, with no necessary payload of status, and really do extend the mental and spiritual capacities of all humans because they extend the range of choices at every person's disposal.

By definition, the first, vertical form of differentiation is its own worst enemy and sets absolute limits on the expansion of creative demand. If the primary use of a creative product is to mark the relative wealth and status of the consumer, then of course it fails to provide this use if everybody can get it. This fact lies behind the persistent and very determined resistance of social elites to the idea that creative production and consumption can become a universal human entitlement. Their true fear is not that the quality of culture will degrade if everyone has access to it, but that it will no longer serve to distinguish them from those below. To this extent, therefore, it is not merely inequality between or within classes, but the very existence of class itself that stands in the way of the full development of human creativity.

It is therefore the second, 'horizontal' function of differentiation – the greatest creativity of the greatest number – which has to be the target of policy. If this lesson is taken to heart, it renders at least theoretically possible, given the political will, the 'many-sided development of humans' which John Maynard Keynes and Karl Marx both envisaged as the ultimate purpose of economic activity, so that art and culture themselves may in principle resume their rightful place as a universal human heritage.

Appendix to Part II: transnational networks of radical labour research

Örsan Şenalp and Mehmet Gürsan Şenalp[1]

During the last three or four decades labour, union, research and advocacy networks have interacted with networks of anti-capitalist or alter-globalist social justice activists (Dominguez 2007; Bond 2007; Waterman 2010; 2012). These interactions have enabled the (self-)organization of working people across production networks linking the Global North and South (Merk 2004; Munck 2002; Bieler et al. 2011; Wallerstein 2013). Especially after the crisis erupted in 2007–08, the process has expanded to include networks of self-employed, unemployed, marginalized and increasingly radicalized knowledge and service workers (Mosco and McKercher 2008). Online social networks such as Facebook, Twitter and Google Plus, but also free, 'libre' and open source software (FLOSS), offer new experiences complementary to traditional forms of organization. Unprecedented opportunities for exchange, communication and collaboration have arisen, with more and more people politicized and organized in the process (Morell 2012; Gerbaudo 2012; Şenalp 2012). The result has been a remarkable convergence among radical social movements, enabled and aggregated by new-generation online tools and applications (Stalder 2013; Bauwens 2011). Public spaces have been opened up and 'occupied' in a series of popular and grassroots uprisings.

This Appendix presents a concise overview of networks constituted around the quest for 'associated social relations of production', or 'peer production communities' (Bauwens 2005; Rigi 2013). Whether labelled *hackers, makers, diggers, guerrilla translators* and so forth, and involving FLOSS and hardware production, collaborative digital, creative, artistic, media, graphic and architecture projects, or Do-it-Yourself (DIY) or Do-it-with-Others (DIWO) practices (Carlsson 2008; Berlinguer 2010), these networks connect highly educated individual knowledge, information, education and service workers. Often left with nothing but their own mental and manual labour to survive, the new 'dispossessed' no longer can be divided into 'doers' and 'thinkers' but are being transformed into a

[1] We are grateful to Peter Waterman and George Por for comments on an earlier version.

single, conscious social force (Waterman 2012). The overview we present is inevitably limited, but similar initiatives and networks operating in other language spheres besides English, Turkish and Dutch can easily be traced (Guiterrez 2014).

A NEW URBAN KNOWLEDGE PROLETARIAT

Neoliberal deregulation and privatization in the Global North have created increasingly project-based, competitive, flexible and insecure working conditions among highly educated workers (Jessop 2008). Consequently, a steady process of politicization has linked radicalized academic workers and students to existing labour research and advocacy networks. This is producing a sizeable body of innovative and emancipatory knowledge that will help to understand the complexities of globalizing capitalism. The Internet allows much easier access to emancipatory knowledge, making it available for 'transformative' political practices (Wainwright 2013). Resurgent resistance in and around university departments, especially in the social and human sciences, art, architecture, political economy, media, communication, informatics, cybernetics and so on has turned the campus once again into a dynamic space of convergence between labour activism, research and art (Ross et al. 2007; Berardi 2010).

Radical knowledge and political practice radiate from university campuses into the surrounding urban spaces; recent debates such as those on 'Empire' and the new imperialism, international historical sociology, global political economy, cultural political economy and governmentality, profit from the persistence of class analysis in academia and a lowering of sectarian barriers. Digital or online projects and journals such as *Processed World, Multitudes, Mute, Meta-Mute, Ephemera, Incognito, Fibre-culture, E-flux, Ad-busters, Alter-Net, New Internationalist*, as well as cultural events organized by/around these journals facilitate the spread of such knowledge. In addition, integral theorists, cyber punk techno-utopians, as well as independent theorists with practitioner, hacker, activist or artistic backgrounds have also been contributing to the innovative analyses of the contemporary contradictions of the capitalist mode of production.

Innovative conceptual tools and notions such as general intellect, collective intelligence, immaterial labour, affective labour, free labour, 'playbour', commons and commoning, peer production, p2p (peer-to-peer), distributed networks, network cultures and techno-politics have drawn in new generations of activists. International mobilizations such as the 'Battle in Seattle' in 1999, the Global Solidarity and Justice movements in its wake, the World Social Forum, and 'anti-summit' and anti-war movements have created further spaces for rethinking production, labour and value creation practices (de Sousa Santos 2006; Waterman 2006). Such perspectives as 'cognitive capitalism', 'communism of capital' and 'techno-politics' have been developed on account of new capitalistic forms in (post-)industrial sites like Silicon Valley or North Italy (Pasquinelli 2014). Inspired by art, design and digital practices, post-autonomist and post-workerist research informed radical political projects such as Uni-Nomad, Edu-Factory and Class War University in which claims and slogans like 'academic workers' and 'disassembling the neoliberal university' are articulated. Other spaces like the Winter Camps organized by the Amsterdam-based Institute of Network Culture (INC) are examples of innovative projects that have been 'networked'.

Other projects such as Cybersalon, Class War Games, Hypermedia and spaces like the *Historical Materialism* conferences and Left Forums, among many others, have been providing important spaces for exchange and interaction to researchers, practitioners and activists, as have research networks such as Transit Labour, OrgNet, Institute of Distributed Creativity, Dynamics of Virtual Work, the IPEG working group in the British International Studies Association, and Critical Labour Studies. Networked Politics and Networked Labour seminars have allowed those outside academia to link up with these networks. New counter-culture philosophies such as cyberpunk, cybernetics and so on, have contributed to the analysis of 'digital labour' and cognitive or informational capitalism. The massive amount of critical and radical knowledge has been mapped, catalogued and made e-accessible by, among others, Michel Bauwens and his P2P Foundation.

The new wave of 'Global Uprisings', starting in late 2010 and early 2011, have seen a new mass army of marginalized and radicalized workers, with high computer literacy and free time (Morell 2012). Relatively small and isolated, but increasingly spreading and connected networks have been the result of intensifying online communication and connectivity (Şenalp 2012). Self-learning and exchange within these communities have been intertwined with various forms of 'co-produced', collaborative or participative politics. Exchanges on discussion (email) lists such as Net-time, Kein.org, Oekonux, WSF-Discussion, and Labour and Globalization have played key roles here (Riemens interview by Casalegno on Net-time e-list 1999), also in stimulating collaborative projects and processes (Morell 2009, 2010; Kostakis et al. 2014).

While the participants of peer production communities have been trapped in the 'capitalist mode', the expansion of transnational social spaces of exchange and sharing allowed them to produce and share use-value in radically different ways than prescribed by capitalism (Kleiner

2010; Rigi 2013). During the 1980s and 1990s early generations of such communities were made up of self-employed hippies and 'kitsch' entrepreneurs, often well-paid waged artists, journalists, architects, coders and system-administrators. Together with amateur hackers, most of the time of Western middle class origin, they formed the basis of the cyberpunk sub-culture (Barbrook and Cameroon 1995; de Ugarte and Boersman 2014).

However, the collapse of the dot.com bubble in the late 1990s brought about the radicalization of these communities, paving the way to the emergence of politicized p2p movements. Projects such as GNU, Copyleft, Free Software Foundation, Linux, Wikipedia, Pirate Bay, WikiLeaks and TOR are examples. Further radicalization of p2p communities came about in the mid 2000s, with the deepening global recession and revival of authoritarian capitalism. The arrival of digital activism or *hacktivism* (think of Anonymous, LulzSec and Pirate Parties) attracted worldwide public attention. Increasingly hacktivism and p2p movements are seen as an inseparable component of the labour and social justice movements of the previous decades (Himanen 2001; Dafermos and Söderberg 2009; O'Connor interview with Kleiner 2013).

Following the global crisis of 2007–08, well-paid knowledge workers were either losing their jobs or becoming low-waged workers with insecure contracts in creative sectors. Defined alternatively as the *knowledge proletariat, cognitariat* or *cybertariat* as a result they are beginning to see themselves as part of an emerging new and broader class, the *precariat* (Barbrook 2006; Berardi 2010; Huws 2001; Standing 2011). In addition, developments in the computer (software and hardware) technologies brought about what Pasquinelli calls 'the division of mental labour' through the increasing simplification of tasks in the production process due to a higher level of computerization. This development has deskilled and alienated larger segments of knowledge workers, whose high expectations evaporated with the promises of the 'knowledge economy' myth, while empowering those employed for designing managerial operations (cf. Huws 2013). Control and socialization mechanisms made possible by software development of course go beyond the creative industries, affecting all workers, but the changes were most dramatic for the knowledge workers.

As a result, in the aftermath of recent uprisings in Spain, the US and UK, Greece, Mexico, North Africa, Turkey, Brazil and a number of other countries, the separate universes of radicalized worker-researchers and radical p2p movements have started to converge (Guiterrez 2013; 2014). Previously self-enclosed hacker groups such as hackatons, sprints, data-jams, un-conferences, hacker camps and so on, now interlocked with social justice or labour activists through projects like Global Revolution TV, OcccupyTheComm, ROAR, Guerrilla Translation, Global Uprisings and many others co-created by hackers, artists, digital media and video activists. This has opened broad channels for large-scale interlocking among the activist networks, among others by joining hacker groups, FLOSS projects or less radical forms of digital activism like *clicktivism* or *slacktivism* (White 2010). During the uprisings, activists built *online spaces* and tools for others' use, in order to link occupations and camps from different localities. Projects such as DRY-International, Global Square, People's Assemblies Network, Take the Square, have been functional in harmonizing the information flow that allowed various networks to link up with each other and expand (Bennett et al. 2014; Castells 2012; Pór 2008). This raises the question to what extent the new forms of collective action have reached traditional working class constituencies.

NETWORKING ACROSS THE GREAT DIVIDE

Workers joining the occupation of Tahrir Square and similar events during the uprising in Wisconsin in the US have signalled the incipient involvement of trade unions in these movements. Through the international MENA Solidarity Network, which connects independent union centres active in Egypt, Tunis, the UK and the US, and elsewhere, and alternative media projects mentioned above, information and symbols expressing the renewal of the labour class struggle have spread far and wide. Other online communication tools like IRC channels (Instant Relay Chat), social network sites (e.g. N-1, Occupii, Crabgrass, InterOccupy) have been utilized to form assemblies and workgroups. These played a key role, for instance in organizing the Oakland, California General Strike, the West Coast Shut Down, the May First (Occupy) General Strike in the US, as well as Critical Blocs, Citizen Ties in Spain and the first ever Europe-wide general strike on 14 November 2012. Debates and workshops took place in Hub Meetings held in Barcelona, Milan and Lubljana; 'Agora99' in Madrid and Rome; 'Firenze 10+10' in Florence, and the World Social Forum in Tunis. These events featured exchanges on 'creative ways of labour organizing' and on ways to link labour unions, NGOs, social justice activists, workplaces and assemblies and develop new methods of action.

Other concrete forms emerging out of the uprisings included labour solidarity groups in Spain, the UK and the US. Collaborating with IWW and other independent unions, the 99 Picket Lines joined the organization of US-wide Wal-Mart walkouts in 2012 and the Making Change at

Wal-Mart campaign. Hackers linked to Occupy Wall Street successfully leaked the official Wal-Mart guide on how to silence workers (Wal-Mart Watch and Baines, this volume). An international protest against TNCs responsible for the death of more than a thousand textile workers employed in the Rana Plaza in Bangladesh, support for minimum wage struggles and a teachers' strike, are evidence of the role of the new networks, which also have connected factories, hospitals, libraries, theatres and other public spaces occupied and run by workers on the basis of a 'Workers' Economy' (Karyotis 2014).

Since 2011, collaborative action-research networks such as Occupy-Hackaton or Global Revolution have been collecting and analysing the large amount of data which came about as the result of the explosion of online interactions and communications. Scholar-activists, independent and radical media, free culture, and art projects such as Interface, Learning from Each Other's Struggles, STIR, ROAR and Global Uprisings, entered into direct collaboration with similar projects focusing specifically on working class formation. Projects like Cyberunions and Social Network Unionism, developed in the rising wave of grassroots uprisings, led to a much higher level of interaction than the LabourNets in the late 1990s (Waterman 2012). Almost in every country one can find union-related work groups that bring thousands of unionists and labour activists together on Facebook pages, allowing people to get and stay in touch and exchange on a daily base (Hall-Jones 2009).

There is also a growing number of 'secure and alternative' social networking tools built by free information activists and hackers, in order to serve those who need security when organizing under repressive conditions, or for those who are critical about using capitalistic products. Riseup and N-1 are only two examples, serving more than 150000 activists and collectives working on various issues by providing email lists and social networking platforms. For example, Riseup email servers host around 500 email lists created and used by labour and union activists, free of charge. The New Unionism Network (NUN) was built in 2007 and has about 700 members from 47 countries and 1800 subscribers to its 'Work in-Progress' online newsletter. The Unionbook project, created by Eric Lee of Labour Start in 2008, is another example. It has brought more than six thousand international unionists together and enabled them to exchange and interact online. Although it is impossible to gauge all such networks currently in existence, it is obvious that powerful steps towards bridging the historical gap between workers and knowledge are being taken.

Computer literacy and the available e-infrastructure, then, have brought knowledge workers into enduring interaction with workers' knowledge (Sen and Waterman 2013). Peter Waterman in this respect has played a unique role as an observer and a reporter. His list of projects has recently been updated with analyses of labour and trade union projects such as Nowtopia, Labour Nets, LabourTech, LabourStart, NetzwerkIT, Networked Politics, Global Labour Institute, SIGTUR and others (as of 2014). Previous labour-related and web-based networking projects, such as the May First/People Link, have developed ties with NGOs and Social Forums as well as organizations like Free Software Foundation (FSF). FSF was founded by Richard Stallman, the creator of the free operating system GNU (GNU is Not Unix). May First/People Link provided online services, for example website and email list hosting on the secure servers they owned collectively, to its members including unions, progressive NGOs, individual activists or hacktivism projects like Riseup. After kick-starting the politicization of the p2p movement in the 1980s, the May First experience became more interesting over time, since their collaboration and service provision has spread out and involved many Occupy and 15M networks, hosting websites and secure email lists of local Occupy encampments and assemblies. In this sense, May First should be seen as a synthetic project that fuses labour organizing, social justice activism and 'free information' or hacker movements (Dafermos and Söderberg 2009).

Another creative labour project in this line has been Cyberunions blog, initiated by South African unionist Walton Pantland. In collaboration with free and open source software-promoting labour activist Stephen Mahood, Cyberunions blog initiated creative and humorous podcasts using sound recording and streaming software. The original motto of the blog was 'Using Technology to Organise', similar to those earlier projects such as LabourTech or Organizing 2.0. Throughout the grassroots uprisings around the world starting in North Africa, the experience and initiatives of Pantland and Stephen Mahood gave birth to the Union Solidarity International (USI) project. Strategically adopting its social media and networking experience to the already existing union context, the small team of USI in a relatively short time managed to expand their outreach through online solidarity campaigns and communication channels. USI has meanwhile become a May First member organization. This has been followed up by an online social network entitled the Organising Network (ON), built by using an alternative codification developed by FLOSS activists and hackers who have taken part in Occupy and 15M assemblies and media teams (Pantland 2014). It was then installed on May First's secure servers, with a FLOSS audio-video conferencing and distance education tool, Big Blue Button, already available for USI and ON members.

Following the debate on Global Unionism in the early 2000s (Harrod and O'Brien 2002), the International Trade Union Federations (ITFs) were rebranded as Global Unions (GUs). Through international mergers larger structures like ITUC and IndustriAll and Workers' Uniting were created in turn. New Unionism Networks' recent debate, Global Labour Institute's Summer Schools, GLU's Global Labour Conferences, and LabourStarts' Global Solidarity Conferences have taken the discussion on Global Unionism further into the world of established unions. Projects such as NetzwerkIT in Germany, Sendika.org in Turkey and LabourTech in the US have all contributed to a more advanced understanding of the practical meaning of knowledge and communication technology for organizing. Compared to the secure online organizing methods developed by NetzwerkIT, or development of the Safe Space by NUN, and online infrastructures employed by network unionists and labour activists at local, national and regional levels, USI's Organising Network in our opinion has a great potential to attract a variety of radical labour projects, unions, activists and NGOs. ON leads the way towards bridging the separate islands of labour and social justice activists and hackers gathering in international meetings such as Chaos Computer Camps (CCC), Oekeunox or De Growth Conferences, Free Culture Forums, Economics and the Commons conferences, or media-digital art biennales. Newer activist networks too have gained significant experience with combining online organizing (through transnational Instant Relay Chat and Mumble conferences) and international grounded assemblies organized by those linked to 15M and Occupy movements.

UNCHAINING THE GENERAL INTELLECT OF THE COLLECTIVE WORKER?

At the CCC congress in Hamburg in December 2013, WikiLeaks founder Julian Assange's keynote speech was titled, 'Systems administrators of the world, unite!' His speech, relayed via Skype, highlighted how capitalism and the rulers have turned the utopia of the Free Internet into an Orwellian dystopia of mass control and surveillance (Assange 2013). The development of collection, storage, analysis and transmission of large amounts of digital (meta-)data has coincided with the global economic crisis and rising authoritarianism. Large-scale investments have poured into projects such as Internet of Things, Industrial Internet, and Internet of Everything projects that share the vision of fully-fledged artificial intelligence (see General Electric 2012; Cisco Systems 2014a; 2014b; Rifkin 2014). Dating from the 1990s, these projects have accelerated in the last few years. In March 2014, GE, IBM, Cisco and AT&T formed the Industrial Internet Consortium (IIC) to work out the protocols and standards for an infrastructure 'to further development, adoption and wide-spread use of interconnected machines, intelligent analytics and people at work' (IIC 2014). The IIC aims at creating an absolute 'general intellect' (IIC 2014; Vercellone 2007), a technology already allowing capital to organize work, production and global commodity chains but also evoking the spectre of a 'collective worker' (Merk, this volume). Thus the capitalist project of total control may give rise to its nemesis in the form of an agency capable of confronting it. Building on the egalitarian and direct democratic organizational forms described above, this might then usher in a realistic and feasible 'economy for all' (Marsh 2013).

LIST OF WEB LINKS OF PROJECTS AND SPACES[2]

Research and Social Justice Activism Networks

Alliance of Progressive Labour: http://www.apl.org.ph/
BISA – IPEG Work Group: http://www.bisa-ipeg.org/
ClassWarU – Class War University: http://classwaru.org/
CPERN – Critical Political Economy Research Network: http://criticalpoliticaleconomy.net/
Critical Labour Studies: http://criticallabourstudies.org.uk/site/
De-Growth Network: http://www.degrowth.org/
Digital Labour: http://digitallabor.org/
Dynamics of Virtual Work: http://dynamicsofvirtualwork.com/
Economics and Commons: http://commonsandeconomics.org/
Edu-Factory: http://www.edu-factory.org/wp/
Free Culture Forum: http://fcforum.net/
Historical Materialism: http://www.historicalmaterialism.org/
Hypermedia Research Centre: http://www.hrc.wmin.ac.uk/
Global Labour Institute, Centre: http://www.global-labour.org/
Global Labour Institute, UK: http://global-labour.net/
Global Labour University: http://www.global-labour-university.org/4.html
Institute of Distributed Creativity: http://distributedcreativity.org/
Institute of Network Cultures: http://networkcultures.org/
MENA Solidarity Network: http://menasolidaritynetwork.com/
Net-time: http://www.nettime.org/
Network for Critical Studies of Global Capitalism: http://netglobalcapitalism.wordpress.com/

2 Longer list on P2P Foundation's wiki page: http://p2pfoundation.net/Category:Labor.

Networked Politics: http://www.networked-politics.info/
Networked Labour: http://www.networkedlabour.net/
Oekonux: http://en.wiki.oekonux.org/Oekonux
Orgnet: http://orgnets.net/
P2P Foundation: http://blog.p2pfoundation.net/
Ruskin College: http://www.ruskin.ac.uk/
Transit Labour: http://transitlabour.asia/
Transnational Institute: http://www.tni.org/
Uni-Nomad: http://www.uninomade.org/
Workers' Control: http://www.workerscontrol.net/

Magazines and Journals

Adbusters: https://www.adbusters.org/
Aternet: http://www.alternet.org/
Communication, Capitalism & Critique (Triple C): http://www.triple-c.at
E-Flux: http://www.e-flux.com/
Ephemera: http://www.ephemerajournal.org/
Fibre culture: http://www.fibreculture.org/
Interface: http://www.interfacejournal.net/
Journal of Peer Production: http://peerproduction.net/
Meta Mute: http://www.metamute.org
Multitude: http://www.multitudes.net/
Neural: http://www.neural.it/
New Internationalist: http://newint.org/
Red Pepper: http://www.redpepper.org.uk/
Rhizome: http://rhizome.org/
Processed World: http://www.processedworld.com/
Telepolis: http://www.heise.de/tp/english/default.html
The Commoner: http://www.commoner.org.uk
Work Organisation, Labour and Globalisation: http://www.analyticapublications.co.uk/

Networks and Spaces of Hackers

Chaos Computer Club: http://www.ccc.de/en/
Crypto-Party: https://www.cryptoparty.in/index
Free Software Foundation: http://www.fsf.org/
GNU: https://www.gnu.org/
Hacker Spaces: http://hackerspaces.org/wiki/
Kein.org: http://kein.org/

Net-time: http://www.nettime.org/info.html
Waag Society: http://waag.org/en

Interlocking Projects and Spaces

16 Beaver: http://www.16beavergroup.org/
99Pickets: http://99pickets.org/
99PicketLines: http://99picketlines.tumblr.com/
CapulTV: http://capul.tv/
Class War Games: http://www.classwargames.net/
CopyLeft: https://www.gnu.org/copyleft/
Crabgrass (Rise-up): https://we.riseup.net/
Cybersalon: http://www.cybersalon.org/
Cyberunions: https://cyberunions.org/
DatAnalysis15M: http://datanalysis15m.wordpress.com/
DeVakBeweging Vrijwillegers [NL]: https://www.facebook.com/groups/devakbewegingvrijwilligers/
Digital Activism #Now: http://www.digitalactivismnow.org/about/
DRY-International: http://international.democraciarealya.es/
Dyne: http://www.dyne.org/
Global Revolution TV: http://globalrevolution.tv/
Global Uprisings: http://www.globaluprisings.org/
EuroMarches: http://www.euromarches.org/
Fly Wheel Collective: http://www.flywheelcollective.com/
Global Guerrillas: http://globalguerrillas.typepad.com/
Global Villages Network: http://www.globalvillages.info/
GNUnion: http://gnunion.wordpress.com/
Guerrilla Translation: http://guerrillatranslation.com/
Home cooked theory: http://homecookedtheory.com/
Institute of Network Cultures: http://networkcultures.org/wpmu/portal/projects/
InterOccupy: http://interoccupy.net/
Keinform.de: http://keinform.de/
LaborNet: http://www.labornet.org/
LabourTech: http://labortech.net/conferences/
Labour Start: http://www.labourstart.org/
Labour Notes: http://www.labourstart.org/2014/
Las Indias: http://english.lasindias.com/
Making Change at Walmart: http://makingchangeatwalmart.org/
May First/People Link: https://mayfirst.org/
Meta-Activism: http://www.meta-activism.org/
N-1: https://n-1.cc/

NaberMedya TV: http://nabermedya.tv/
New Unionism Network: http://www.newunionism.net/join.htm
NetzwerkIT: http://www.netzwerkit.de/
Nowtopia: http://www.processedworld.com/carlsson/nowtopia_web/software.shtml
OccupyData: http://occupydatanyc.org/
Occupy General Strike May Day Directory: http://occupywallst.org/article/may-day/
Occupy The Comms: https://occupythecomms.cc/
Online Creation Communities: http://www.onlinecreation.info/
On the Commons: http://onthecommons.org/
Open Source Ecologies: http://opensourceecology.org/
Organizing 2.0: http://www.organizing20.org/
People's Assemblies Network: http://www.peoplesassemblies.org/
ROAR: http://roarmag.org/
Sendikalİletişim[Tr]:https://www.facebook.com/groups/179911352070114/
Sendika.org: http://www.sendika.org/
Social Media Club FNV [NL]: https://www.facebook.com/groups/socialmediaclubfnv/
Social Network Unionism: http://snuproject.wordpress.com/
Take the Square: http://takethesquare.net/
Telekommunisten: http://telekommunisten.net/
The Organizing Network: https://on.usilive.org/
The Pirate Bay: https://thepiratebay.se/
TOR Project: https://www.torproject.org/
Turkish Unionists [En]: https://www.facebook.com/groups/turkishtradeunions/
Unionbook: http://www.unionbook.org/
Union Solidarity International: http://usilive.org/
WikiLeaks: https://wikileaks.org/
Wikipedia: http://en.wikipedia.org/wiki/Main_Page

Political Alliances Convergence and Networking Spaces

Alter-Summit: http://www.altersummit.eu/
Agora 99: http://99agora.net/
Blockupy: https://blockupy.org/
European Social Forum: http://www.fse-esf.org/
Firenze 10+10: http://www.firenze1010.eu/
Global Solidarity: http://www.labourstart.org/2014/
Global-Square: http://www.global-square.net/
Joint Social Conference: http://www.jointsocialconference.eu/?lang=en

Left Forum: http://www.leftforum.org/
World Social Forum: http://www.fsm2013.org/en
WSF-Discussion: http://www.openspaceforum.net/mailman/listinfo/worldsocialforum-discuss_openspaceforum.net
The Global Square: https://www.facebook.com/theglobalsquare

PART III

PRODUCTION, REPRODUCTION, NATURE

Introduction to Part III: production, reproduction, nature

In this concluding part of the collection, chapters address the most comprehensive scale on which the political economy of production operates, the nexus with reproduction and nature. Where and how people live, their bodies, what they are fed with and the land on which it grows, it all enters into sustaining globalized production, constituting the ultimate limit to capitalist exploitation.

In Chapter 21, Phoebe Moore contrasts the Cartesian body–mind ontology, already criticized by Spinoza and currently in crisis, with the recent 'corporeal' and 'affective' turns in social science. The Quantified Self movement builds on the atomization of workplaces and austerity-related precarity and has given rise to self-imposed, self-tracking devices used for life-logging and ordering workdays and nights in virtual industries. These devices and projects do take the body into account, but only as part of management attempts to restore control of cognitive work and raise productivity. Moore argues that if IPE develops the corporeal and affective aspects of cognitive work, it may assist in challenging managerial hegemony in this domain.

In Chapter 22, Matt Davies looks at production from the perspective of everyday life. Its 'poetics and prosaics' transpire once production is no longer conceived in terms of abstract equivalence and the indifference of market economics. Taking a broad view ranging from Adam Smith and Henri Lefebvre to recent literature, Davies argues that the apparent triviality and randomness of daily life in fact reveals distinct patterns, on which the economy imprints its specific rationality without entirely controlling them – which explains for instance why urban spaces acquire their unique characteristics. Once the diversity and authenticity of the everyday are understood, 'work' proves to be not identical to production but an interface between the economic prescription of tasks and the human reality of their execution.

Matthew Paterson in Chapter 23 elaborates on how a production regime shapes the everyday by focusing on automobility. The automobile constitutes the central node of Fordism and an entire economic and cultural complex built around it. It has moulded the lives of its users by reaching deep into their personalities to activate the desire for speed and the conquest of space. But not only does the automobile, offered on the promise of fast travel, end up in monotonous traffic jams caused by its popularity over alternative modes of transport. It also has survived the crisis of the Fordist class compromise in the sense that whilst the power of car worker unions has been undermined by transnational restructuring of production, the sense of power at the wheel of a car is undiminished. Thus the automobile remains central to the legitimation of the consumer society, whilst simultaneously bringing out its contradictions including its ecological consequences. For the automobile, Paterson writes, 'implicates daily life in the systemic production of environmental degradation'.

In 'Risk capitalism, crisis of socialization and loss of civilization' (Chapter 24) Werner Seppmann argues that social insecurity and income redistribution at the expense of wage-earners in the last few decades has produced a culture of despondency and anxiety among those affected. Contemporary capitalist society as a consequence is being paralysed by a pervasive fear over job loss combined with resignation concerning what the future holds. As a result, alongside poverty and destitution, a trend to social regression and disintegration of the human personality is threatening social cohesion and civilization. Media and scholarly expertise in the process keep serious critique of the power structure off-limits, whilst individualized, anomic aggression dramatizes ongoing processes of social self-destruction.

Taking the disintegration of social cohesion by the economics of supply and demand one step further, Christine Chin in Chapter 25 examines the phenomenon of women's transnational migration for sex work. More and more, women sex workers of diverse nationalities are now active in major cities throughout the world. This is sustained by and sustains inter-city competition and collaboration that continue to create new modes of migration and employment opportunities. In such cities, migrant women perform sexual labour for a range of clientele, from low-wage migrant men to 'global talent' or knowledge workers.

The impact of capitalist rationality on the realm of physical reproduction emerges as a subject for political economy in various forms, including food production. In Chapter 26, Miriam Boyer discusses various biotechnologies from the perspective of how the reproduction of living processes or organisms is reframed in order to produce. Molecular engineering involving micro-organisms to produce food additives or pharmaceuticals has the potential to dramatically transform industrial production as human labour is replaced by the transformative qualities of other living organisms. These organisms are not only powerful productive forces, but also disruptive or even destructive ones.

Yet for all its technological miracles the corporate food regime does not have the field entirely to itself. As Sylvia Kay illustrates in Chapter

27, the challenge to the current world food system and its agnostic model of food security, to be managed by corporate markets, is not just an intellectual one. The alternative paradigm, which she calls the 'peasant principle', and which combines agro-ecological, sustainable, organic and resilient agriculture, is actually being practised by millions of small-scale food producers around the world. Their repertoire of knowledge and skills sustains a system in which production and reproduction are intimately linked and which in a relatively protected environment such as Cuba is actually growing, against the world-wide trend towards agribusiness and genetically modified agriculture.

These contradictory trends lead Ulrich Brand and Markus Wissen in Chapter 28 to argue that key capitalist agencies are refocusing production along the lines of various Green Economy proposals. By employing a Regulationist perspective, the authors venture that at least in the Global North these projects may result in a Green Capitalism. Like the preceding Fordist regime, regulatory practices will then keep the contradictions inherent to capitalism within a certain bandwidth and possibly come to define the coming epoch. Yet in the absence of a fundamental change of production and consumption patterns a Green Capitalism would continue to rely on an external sphere to which it can shift its socio-ecological costs. This will lend it an exclusive character again, with benefits and costs divided unevenly along class, gender and North–South lines.

The latter point is taken further in the Conclusion to the volume, 'Emergent predatory logics'. Here Saskia Sassen argues that capitalism may be leaving the concerns of production behind under the impetus of new forms of financial enrichment. Her claim is that on at least two frontiers, predatory logics have replaced concepts of growth and progress. In the sub-prime mortgage crisis, providing people with a roof over their head has been completely subordinated to the creation, sale and resale of financial instruments using mortgage contracts for security. In the large-scale sequestration of agricultural land for foreign food and biofuel production, a comparable dismissal of the aspect of livelihood is at work. Speculative investment, notably in African arable land, has likewise resulted in the mass expulsion of people from their land and their homes. The features of the process suggest another round of 'primitive accumulation' except that this time, an ensuing, regular production through accumulation seems more remote than ever.

21. Tracking bodies, the 'Quantified Self', and the corporeal turn

Phoebe Moore

The concept of *affect* is still with us although we still have not fully grasped all its implications for working lives and despite over-saturating a good swathe of recent research. This probably started with the post-autonomists (Hardt 1999 and Negri 1991; 1999), who have sought to revive the ontological dispute between Baruch Spinoza and René Descartes. In the seventeenth century these philosophers fundamentally disagreed on whether or not people are subject to an inherent separation of body and mind. The reworking of the concept of affect, sparked by autonomists in the 1960s and 1970s and then again by feminists, geographers and other cross-disciplinary critical theorists more recently, has rekindled this old debate. Today, research on affect is closely linked to the resurgence of *precarity*. It can be empirically linked to the rise in globalizing flexible labour conditions and increasingly exploitative relations of production in so-called post-Fordist conditions, particularly in cognitive and creative work.

Why is it still important to engage with philosophical questions from centuries ago? First, critical scholars continue to challenge the oppressive relations of production that drive the transnationalization of capital and inform practice and outlook of the managerial cadre (van der Pijl 1998; Sklair 2001). However, the accompanying mutation of political economic models into new forms has not displaced the ontology of Descartes, which remains hegemonic. Cartesian thought invades *la vie quotidienne* in various ways, including the assumed separation of the market from society, the split between the economy and politics, the division of private and public and micro-level competition, and tensions between individuals.

A further reason this debate should be sustained is that exploitation and appropriation are being facilitated by particular advances in technology which have the body/mind monism as their presupposition and advocate the health of the body as intimately linked to the health of the mind. This recognition enables the current promotion of self-tracking, self-archiving devices that primarily serve productivity requirements of management. For these reasons it is vital to revisit how the implications of ontology can inform possibilities for revolutionary change, and to identify the techniques of control contained in technological advances which recognize the threat of immanence emerging from networked labour in the cognitive industries and attempt to appropriate these through mind/body self-management software.

This chapter claims that we continue to rely on a dualistic ontology in International Political Economy (IPE) and particularly so in research on work and production. I will present evidence that this is the case by outlining the work done in other disciplines and the revival of the Cartesian/Spinoza debate there, and argue that IPE research will benefit from a similar turn. Then, to show that there exists an organic intellectual movement with an agenda of appropriating these debates, I outline details of the Quantified Self movement, arguing that IPE must become cognizant of these new forms.

WHERE IS THE AFFECTIVE OR CORPOREAL 'TURN' IN INTERNATIONAL POLITICAL ECONOMY?

The affective and corporeal turns emerging from various disciplines rely on a sometimes implicit use of Spinoza and Marx. These two unlikely bedfellows had particular views of the body which are often misrepresented; yet I argue that writers across the social sciences have much to learn from the turns that have occurred in feminist, poststructuralist and religious studies and in geography. An affective turn in political thought was observed and termed as such by Patricia Clough in 2007. Feminist, autonomist and poststructuralist research of Deleuze (1978; 1988; 1992), Hardt (1999), Colman (2008), Colman and McCrea (2005), Goddard (2011), Macherey (1990), Fracchia (2005) and Robinson (2010) consider affect as a '*power to act* that is singular and at the same time universal' (Negri 1999: 85, emphasis added).

The potency of Spinoza's original concept of affect comes from its immanence in corporeal and cognitive dimensions and recognition of the impact that bodies have on one another. This concept has inspired radical thinking around how social change can occur by way of the emergence of a multitude whose power rests within a singularity of affect (Negri 2002). Negri reasons that singularity of affect is defensible because it 'poses action beyond every measure that power does not contain in itself, in its own structure and in the continuous restructurings that it constructs' (Negri 1999: 85). Affect is at the same time universal, because 'affects construct a commonality among subjects' (ibid.). The body has not therefore disappeared, but 'as an entirely Spinozan thematic, we have [as an ontological reference] above all that of the body, and in particular that of the power of the body' (Negri 2002: 41). Action is permitted or inhibited by affect, which is the reason this concept is endowed with revolutionary potential, as well as linked with research on precarity.

The corporeal and affective turns are not as dissimilar as would appear. Importantly, they are both lines of enquiry that seek to resolve the issue of ongoing disembodiment in social research. The corporeal turn is a distinct journey taken in feminist studies in the work of Witz (2000), but preceded by Grosz (1987; 1994) and Brush (1988) who both refer to Foucault's concepts of the body as text and discourse. Federici (2004; 2012; cf. Gunnarsson 2013) argues against a narrow reading of Marx that sees the labour theory of value strictly in terms of work that produces commodities. This overlooks reproductive work; she instead sees sex, subsistence, care and health as areas of struggle as well as the site for revolution. Butler offers insight into the performativity of gender and importantly attempts to deconstruct the divisions between subject and object through demonstrating how bodies and action are ideologically constituted (2011). A corporeal turn in Jewish Studies is reported by Kirshenblatt-Gimblett (2005) and Boyarin (1995); in geography (Longhurst 2012; Cooper 2011; Goldstein 2013; Orzeck 2007; Anderson 2011); in social theory (Tamborino 2002); critical geography (Harvey 2000); and Environmental Studies (Payne and Wattchow 2009). Goldstein (2013) stresses the misunderstanding of a 'first nature' which is, she states, a historically specific product rather than an inherent and transhistorical, a priori separation of nature from the body.

The affective turn, too, has been led by feminist and poststructuralist authors who call for a 'transdisciplinary approach to theory and method that necessarily invites experimentation in capturing the changing co-functioning of the political, the economic, and the cultural, rendering it affectively as change in the deployment of affective capacity' (Clough 2007: 3). Clough invites research in the affective realm that recognizes the effect that technoscientific advancements have had on 'ghosted bodies and . . . traumatised remains of erased histories' emerging from the industrial era, and a consideration of 'self-reflexivity (processes turning back on themselves to act on themselves) in information/communication systems, including the human body' (ibid.). The pieces in *The Affective Turn: Theorising the Social* observe changes in the social sphere and see these as changes in ourselves which have relevance for bodies and subjectivities that are not reducible to the personal or the psychological, and therefore are affective.

With recognition of the impact affect has had on a range of other disciplines, I here set out to investigate research in IPE on work and labour to see whether the claim that this discipline continues to rely on a dualism of mind and body, is justified. In 1998, in the journal *New Political Economy*,

Carnoy gives an account of the changing world of work with regard to technologies. This author emphasizes the need for pedagogies and education curricula to correspond with the changing times. These themes are rarely seen in IPE journals but are similar to my own research concerns (Moore 2010) on the political economy of knowledge in education curricula. However, Carnoy takes as a given that work and work expectations would rapidly change as the IT bubble simultaneously grew at a startling rate from the late 1990s. He makes a hesitant start in identifying the corporeal features of this transformation by stating that people will be expected to shift jobs several times in the course of a working life, to move geographically and 'if necessary, to learn entirely new vocations' (1998: 124). However, the greater part of the analysis relies on an uncritical view of how education *must change* to prepare people for this exhilarating new world of work. This exclusively emphasizes the cognitive side of skills that would be needed, that is, 'creativity, enterprise and scholarship' (Blunkett 1998).

Also in 1998 Gardiner published a piece that looks at the failure of the human capital thesis in economics to take reproductive labour into consideration. Gardiner cites Mill's recognition of the disproportionate share of women in housework: 'women are in the constant practice of passing quickly from one manual, and still more from one mental operation to another' (Mill 1865: 29, cited in Gardiner 1998: 4). Mill was happy to place teachers and doctors in the category of productive human capital but still does not view domestic work as such. In sociology, the 'new spirit of capitalism' (Boltanski and Chiappello 2007) imposes a type of disembodied neoliberal performativity.

Caraway et al. (2012) set out to investigate whether workers' pressure groups have had an impact on IMF loan conditions. Interestingly, this piece reports that labour conditionalities have only been present in a quarter of all IMF programmes since 1987. Governments of countries with strong labour movements suffer fewer impositions affecting workers' interests than those with weak pre-existing representation. Rather than examining specific interests and related pressures on government and IMF decision-making, this article demonstrates that 'countries with stronger labour movements will receive less intrusive, labour related loan conditions than those with weak labour movements' (ibid.). The IMF technically only negotiates with governments and has no direct involvement with domestic interest groups, so the argument of this article, that citizen pressure groups have had an impact on IMF conditionality, is debatable. Furthermore, the almost exclusive reliance on IMF-owned data for proof that interest groups have had an impact on final conditions demonstrates an absence of consultation with people experiencing reforms and the corporeal aspects of rising uncertainties in all post-austerity cases. Corporeal aspects of structural adjustment include the rise in precarity leading to a reduction of specific work spaces, as seen in particular in the computing industry context; forced living conditions such as the rise in young people continuing to live at home and the lack of home-owning channels; the rise in work-related illnesses, and the inability to put food on tables and clothes on bodies resulting directly from loss of wages.

IPE research that begins to fill in the absence of corporeality in understanding work in *New Political Economy* has been published by Barrientos (1996) and Onuki (2009), whose pieces look at, respectively, women working in Latin America and Filipino care workers in Japan. Other research on work, labour and production in this same journal, including Breen (2012), May (2002) and Hudson (2012), rely on policy-based methodologies and ideas-based rationales. In *Review of International Political Economy* research that begins to demonstrate an understanding of the limitations of cognitive or mental and text-based research is the Special Issue on 'Social reproduction in international political economy' edited by Steans and Tepe (2010) including articles by Rickert, Elias, Ferguson, LeBaron and Kunz. However, other pieces in related fields in this journal include Nederveen Pieterse (2002), Lockea and Romis (2010), Raess (2006), Larner (2002), Paczynska (2007), Lipietz (1997), Kong (2006), Scheuerman (2001), Murphy (2013) and Burgoon and Jacoby (2004), pieces which rely on text-based methodologies, policy and organizational analyses, effectively prolonging the absenting of bodies. Published research in widely read scholarly journals thus works to reproduce a particular Cartesian deontological paradigm and set of assumptions.

Research that can challenge the omission of the corporeal includes interventions from or straddles feminist political economy, research on unfree labour, autonomist ideas, the burgeoning literature on precarity and some aspects of neo-Gramscian research. Cameron et al. (2013) put the focus on the body and its relation to the state, a much-needed comment on the oversight in most political research that has taken a turn toward the knowledge/power nexus. Too often, 'arguments ignore the physical materiality inherent to the constitution and daily reproduction of social relationships which require our body to be sold on the labour market in order to receive an income and thus survive; that is, the *compulsion* to be a commodity' (Bruff 2013: 73).

AN ONTOLOGICAL TURN?

What is missing from IPE, then, is research that looks at corporeal dimensions of everyday life in capitalism. This section explores an ontological turn that could resolve this issue by observing the way that affect is currently dealt with in political readings of Spinoza. In the following section I will discuss the technologically inspired management literature and techniques that rely on these insights.

Writers in political studies have recently equated emotion, affect, affection and sentiment with the corporeal, and affect with emotion (Thompson and Hoggett 2012). However, this is a misreading of Spinoza, who was interested in active being in relation to passions, resolved only through the ways that bodies interact. Affect is like the correspondence between a body and a mind, but it is not the same as the knowable volition of emotions, nor the same as saying that a body and a mind can be said to exist as separate entities. Macherey (1997) has investigated Hegel's readings of Spinoza and sees Spinoza's propositions of the difference between substance and attributes as established by intellect, as a forerunner to the materialist dialectic. Negri (2001) also effectively places Spinoza in a materialist chronology between the work of Lucretius and Marx. The dialectic is not about oppositional forces, as it is often interpreted; indeed 'the more you oppose one another, the more you remain in the same framework of thought' (Serres and Latour 1995: 81; cf. Holland 1998). Difference is not identical to opposition. These points have informed advocates of radical democracy who see Spinozan metaphysics as a way to resolve the problems of objectivistic and spatial aspects of materialism.

Marx himself seems to have been heavily influenced by Spinoza though there is no official recognition of this. Nonetheless, Negri's *The Savage Anomaly* (1991) engages with Marx's dialectic cast in a Spinozan frame. Negri is right to spot possible confluence in contemporary discussions of praxis, revolution and solidarity with these philosophers in mind (of course Marx did not call himself a philosopher). The radical perspectives initiated by Marx and Spinoza should be re-investigated if only to ask, what exactly is it about ourselves (as human beings) that allows us to act to make our own histories as Marx postulated? Fracchia asks us to look at the corporeal possibilities for and limitations of how involved we can be in making our own histories in conditions not of our own choosing (Fracchia 2005: 55). Marx's understanding of *use value* and *concrete labour* are vital to the logic of capitalist exploitation and exchange value; to identify the relevance of Spinozan ideas in Marx's work, Fracchia investigates the confluence between absolute and relative surplus value. Workplace exploitation, then, can be detected by identifying 'deformation of the body, the flip side of which is that the free cultivation of bodily attributes and capacities is essential to any historical materialist notion of freedom' (ibid.: 41). This goes against the idealist views of human nature that usually skip, or only give light treatment to the body.

The new materialist shift is associated with the work of May 1968 philosophers such as Foucault, Irigaray, and Deleuze and Guattari. These scholars explore materialist/monist thought and re-think radical ideas found in Spinoza, Bergson, Proust and Kafka (van der Tuin and Dolphijn 2000: 154) and look for a philosophy of the body that can challenge cultural theorists' reliance on linguistic analysis, overcoming a mind/matter and culture/nature divide within transcendental humanist thought. Braidotti and DeLanda, independently of one another, named this shift in an effort to overcome the prioritization of 'mind over matter or culture over nature' seen in cultural theory (ibid.: 156). Braidotti encourages a renewed analysis of 'the embodied structure of human subjectivity after Foucault' (Braidotti 2000: 158, cited in van der Tuin and Dolphijn 2000). Hence it pays to reread the original texts that recognize that, as Spinoza writes in his *Ethics*, 'a human being consists of a mind and a body, and . . . the human body exists, as we are aware of it' (2003, Part II, Prop. 13 Cor.). For Spinoza, the relationship between the body and the mind and vice versa is an organic one and does not have a temporal or a specific spatial context. What all bodies have in common is the capacity for movement, whether this is tangible or symbolic. The role of affect is not the same as the emotive responses to the representations we form based on corporeal experiences. It is seen in the enabling or disabling of our capacity to act, the power to act, *puissance*, as opposed to affections or emotions which are reactions to constituted environments and relations of power (*pouvoir*).

The key unknown as revealed in Spinoza's work is the *exact capability of bodies*: bodies that are influenced by one another; by cognitive responses to stimuli (as is detailed in the emotional labour literature); as well as in relation to affect, which is not identical to these registers. Descartes' dualism leads him to rate the body against the mind and in so doing, locates superiority in the mind. But Giancotti emphasizes this is impossible, since 'in reality and in perfection, in relation to another mind, its object, that is the human body, would have to be known more fully' for this comparison to be accurately made (1997: 58–9). Spinoza wrote that

> In proportion as a body is more capable than others of doing many things at once, or being acted on in many ways at once, so its mind is more capable than others of perceiving many things at once. And in proportion as the actions of a body depend more on itself alone, and as other bodies concur with it less in acting, so its mind is more capable of understanding distinctly' (2003: II, 13, Schol.).

Spinoza goes on to defend the limitations of assuming that the body acts only when nature or the mind tells it to do so, by pointing out the active unconscious body such as a sleepwalker who does things he/she would not dare to do when awake, or the brute, whose actions 'far surpass human sagacity' (III, 2, Schol.). Spinoza claimed that this 'is sufficient to show that the body itself, merely from the laws of its own nature alone, can do many things, at which the mind marvels' (ibid.). He goes on to remark that:

> (III, 6) Everything, in so far as it is in itself, endeavours to persist in its own being.
> (III, 7) The conatus, wherewith everything endeavours to persist in its own being, is nothing else but the actual essence of the thing in question.

In his commentary, Deleuze (1978) maintains that

> Spinoza will be firm in telling us that what counts among animals is not at all the genera or species . . . What counts is the question, of what is a body capable? And thereby he sets out one of the most fundamental questions in his whole philosophy by saying that the only question is that we don't even know what a body is capable of, we prattle on about the soul and the mind and we don't know what a body can do.

He further notes that 'a body must be defined by the ensemble of relations which compose it, or, what amounts to exactly the same thing, by its power of being affected'. This point is taken directly from Spinoza, indicating that bodies are affected and act, but not in a particular sequence nor in a specific spatial context. This is not a moral question, Deleuze tells us, but:

> As long as you don't know what power a body has to be affected, as long as you learn like that, in chance encounters, you will not have the wise life, you will not have wisdom . . . A body has something fundamentally hidden: we could speak of the human species, the human genera, but this won't tell us what is capable of affecting our body, what is capable of destroying it. The only question is the power of being affected. (ibid.)

The affective turn may 'equally be thought to emerge from the technopolitics of late capitalism, and the convergence of cyber, multimedia, information, and science studies with studies of the body, matter, being and time' (White 2008: 181). IPE research would be well advised to begin to recognize these changes, as social movements and governments are simultaneously 'engaged through affective structures in enabling and disabling this Revolutionary Virtual' (Karatzogianni 2012: 57). These are reflected in the analysis of automated self-tracking activities and the appropriation drive of the managerial cadre.

THE ORGANIC 'QUANTIFIED' INTELLECTUAL?

Empirical research of managerial attempts to gain control of cognitive work suggests that tracking one's self-management is the ideal state for a worker. These arguments, which reveal the rationality of an organic intellectual process, actually cross the divide between bodies and minds by the encouragement of such things as wellness and productivity. In *Work, Happiness, and Unhappiness*, Peter Warr (2007) reports that workers' happiness is linked to better productivity. Dan Pink's (2011) *Drive: The Surprising Truth about What Motivates Us* tells us that workers want autonomy, mastery and purpose, and these are intrinsic motivational features that give people 'joy'. So management guru literature has been celebrating a link between productivity and emotional wellbeing for several years, but bringing the body into it is a more recent phenomenon. Physical wellbeing becomes associated with wellbeing and positive states of mind, which are then linked to management expectations of better productivity. These convictions inform the invention of a range of self-tracking products discussed below that produce the idealized Quantified Man such as the individual reported by Finley (2013a). The danger is of course that mainstream management ideas and incentives will thus come to dominate a hegemonic struggle regarding indisputable changes that technology has made in the world of work; potentially serving to overlook the political economy of the accompanying shift toward precarity and the impact this is having on people.

Cognitive work is assumed to happen in creative, project-based, self-managed organizational contexts resembling rhizomatic networks rather than hierarchical structures (Karatzogianni and Robinson 2013). Hence the role of 'the manager' itself has been challenged, and self-management archiving machines seem to provide the answer to this ambivalence. Placing the self in a position as manager, a range of devices have been introduced and represented in the Quantified Self movement. The fourth Quantified Self Europe Conference was held on 11 and 12 May 2013 in Amsterdam and included expert talks entitled 'Tracking my Happiness', 'Tracking Relationships', 'Stress Tracking', 'Habit Tracking', 'Meditation and Brain Function', and even 'Tracking Puns'. This recent movement is a symptom of a hegemonic struggle around ownership of the value of work and production as well as the potential for new types of solidarity in creative industries.

As we do not know what the body is capable of, and as management is fully aware, we cannot deduce that creative and cognitive work only takes place in the mind. Precarity is the evidence of this. While there are problems with the way the 'precariat' has been identified, in particular its inability to develop a homogeneous class consciousness alluded to in Guy Standing's thesis (2011), rates of precarity in the knowledge and high-tech industries are well known. Precarity, legally speaking a condition of dependency that results from tenure without ownership, has been reinterpreted in neoliberal practice to involve flexible 'reciprocity' between workers and management, privatization, and shrinkages in welfare states (Berlant 2011: 192). Management literature is more than happy to overlook the painful corporeal specifics of precarity in this 'reciprocal' relationship, and rather than troubling to find out about and work to prevent the brutality of the everyday and everynight lives of producers who work in cognitive industries, the literature celebrates flexible workers as a privileged elite and even a new creative class (Florida 2004; 2012a), with access to the highest standard of survival and pleasure due to the freedoms of self-management. The literature promotes a view of people whose ability to prosper is unrelated to traditional features of survival under capitalist conditions such as an income and the ability to feed bodies. The precariat cannot apparently then be measured according to conventionally viewed 'standards of living'; it is instead made up of missionaries for an emancipated form of living, celebrated by a series of management gurus like Peter Drucker who claimed in 1990 that 'the best way to predict the future is to create it'.

These management views propagate similar sounding perspectives but tend to be ideologically opposed to the autonomist movement, where ideas of precarity have their origin. Franco (Bifo) Berardi explains the overlap in workerist and autonomist overtures with the new management rhetoric by outlining the way that the capitalist regime has appropriated many of the radical possibilities informing these Italian movements (2009). The *Potere Operaio*'s manifesto involves the refusal of work, but this has been appropriated through a rise in flexibilized work that is claimed to have liberating potentials for all (rather than simply potentials for those who would like it, which actually would better fit a consumerist model); informatization of factories as a way to reduce work has become fractalization or the fragmenting of time-activities whilst the separation of cognitive labour from the body leads to a form of subsumption. This managerial counterattack is part of a cultural counterrevolution that assumed particular force after the spontaneous violent uprising at Bologna University in 1977 that started at a meeting of the fanatic Catholic group called *Communion and Liberation*. The movement quickly turned against unions, political parties, factory management and fundamentalist religion. However, according to Bifo, the movement missed a historic chance in the absence of an explicit alternative to capitalism. Capitalism is very good at re-inventing itself (Berardi 2009: 77) and appropriation of concepts without providing an apparatus of support such as is needed particularly during times of economic crisis and rising unemployment, has implications for the exacerbation of corporeal oversight.

Precarity, then, is a life experience with a physical impact, and gives rise to management's worry that 'affect must be controlled' (Negri 1999: 87). The corporeal measure of the impact of precarity on bodies is appropriated by devices propagated or at least condoned by the Quantitative Self movement. Managers have taken a growing interest in such tools as daily activity tracking software and other wearable digital recording equipment such as Sensecam, Subcam sensecams, automas, memoto and audio-visual recorders. These products are used for first person perspective digital ethnographies, lifelogging, and self-tracking of both mental and physical activities in conjunction with productivity-related measures. This understanding of the utility of self-archiving devices potentially allows a re-interpretation of radical elements of monism endorsed by the affective and corporeal turns. As Chris Dancy claims, 'if you can measure it, someone will, and that somebody should be you'. Mr Dancy, or the 'Quantified Man' (Finley 2013a) is hooked up to several sensors, all day and night, and uses Google Calendar to track all daily activities. His pulse, skin temperature and REM sleep are all measured constantly. He has a sensor in his toilet that looks for patterns between sleep and usage (see Figure 21.1).

A range of recent technologies allow people to self-track aspects of life including mood, sleep and physical activity. An *autom*, for example, is a personal health lifestyle coach robot designed by Intuitive Automata. The robot gains data about its owner's eating habits and customizes responses based on information gathered over time. A worker can also buy 'Daily Activity Tracking Software', which allows one to work as normal in front of a computer terminal with software that monitors any interruptions to work and measures any inactivity at the terminal (Bit Computing). Tracking thus will help workers with productivity levels and promises to help you 'take control of your daily work time'. The Bit Computing software company also sells activity log, timesheet, timekeeping, daily activity tracking, daily time tracking, organization, personal productivity, productivity management, time reporting and overtime calculation tools.

The Citizen Evolutionary Process Organism (CEPO) is a recent initiative whereby employees at Citizen in Portland, Oregon, which designs mobile technologies, upload information to a central database about their daily lives including exactly what they eat, any exercise completed, hours slept, and the like. The experiment is designed to identify whether healthier employees are also 'happier and more productive' (Finley 2013b) and the

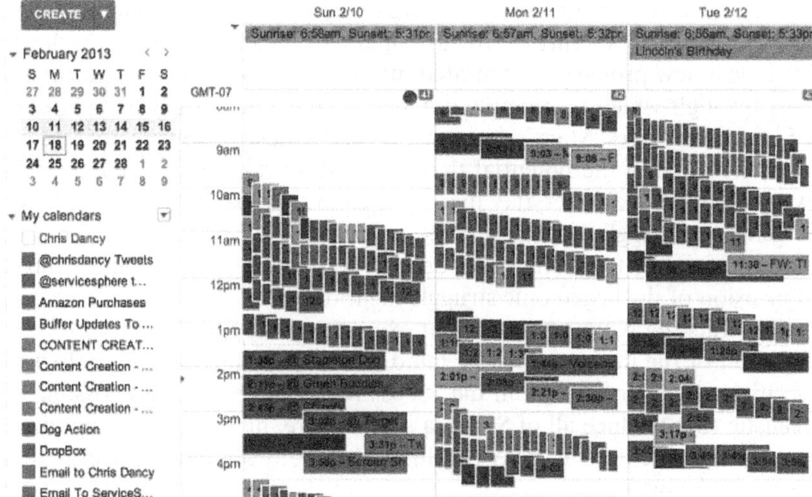

Source: Finley (2013a).

Figure 21.1 Chris Dancy's Google calendar log of daily activities

'ultimate aim is to explicitly show employees how they can improve their work through better personal habits' (ibid.). Darpa is researching ways to track soldiers' health. IBM has a tool to identify unhappy employees. Tesco requires warehouse staff to wear armbands that track productivity: employees receive a score of 100 if tasks are completed on time, and 200 if activities are finished in half the time required, raising obvious questions about health and safety of employees.

Control at work in the information age has taken new forms, but attempts to appropriate the measure of work in this way shifts emphasis from values that can be used to defend workers' rights to measures of physical and emotional aspects of work that prioritize productivity and under the remit of value-added conceptions. These types of software have the potential to subsume workers in the new paradigm of invasive measuring techniques, demonstrating increased recognition of the connection between the mind and body in work. Management techniques to subordinate corporeal functions are a form of control at work that goes beyond the control of the self that I have written about elsewhere (Moore and Taylor 2009).

Hardt's much disputed essay on affective labour in 1999 claims that 'in an earlier era, workers learned how to act like machines both inside and outside the factory. Today as general social knowledge becomes ever more a direct force of production, we increasingly think like computers' (1999: 94, 95). Hardt goes further to say 'interactive and cybernetic machines become a new prosthesis integrated into our bodies and our minds and a lens through which to redefine our bodies and minds themselves' (ibid.: 95). He references Marx's 'general intellect' thesis, showing that Marx was interested in the potential that automation can have for eliminating work from people's everyday lives. The counterargument relevant for the hegemonic struggle is that tracking software could be used to empower and to provide, for example, a defence against unpaid overtime and a dimension of the hegemonic struggle mentioned.

Self-tracking software is a recent example of the appropriation of recognition of the inseparability of mind and body, which is an ontological position taken by Spinoza in the 1600s. While it has not been possible or realistic to introduce all of Spinoza's work here, his main intervention as previously stated was to deny the dualism of body and mind celebrated in Descartes' work.

Descartes relies on a separation of body and mind, and claims that

> There are certain acts that we call 'corporeal', such as size, shape, motion and all others that cannot be thought of apart from local extension; and we use the term 'body' to refer to the substance in which they inhere . . . acts of thought have no relation to corporeal acts, and thought, which is their common concept, is altogether distinct from extension, which is the common concept of the other (Descartes 1999: 176).

Spinoza's rejection of this isolated him as a lone voice, also against Newtonian assumptions that inform most Enlightenment thought. Spinoza's claim that there is one substance or one essence of being, rather than a separation between an immanent deity and the human being violated all religious principles of his time and caused his excommunication from the Jewish faith. Spinoza did not deny the existence of God: what he denies is the separation between God and man; nor does he recognize the separation of mind from body and brain. He points out in the *Ethics* the mistakes of those who perceive God to have the same characteristics of man and who consider God to be a measurable and identifiable body with a mind and passions. Meanwhile, he notes, misguided theorists claim that man has been created *by God*. Spinoza asks: how can this be possible? If God is infinite, as these same theorists also claim, how can he be quantifiable and identifiable in particle form as man is claimed to be? Further, these claims separate the corporeal/extended substance from the divine nature and reaffirm that the former is a creation by God. Yet these binarisms are faulty, Spinoza notes, again not in the tone of an atheist but with the insight of a philosopher who challenges spatial, temporal, quantifiable and otherwise measurable assumptions, common to modernity, about the human experience of life. Spinoza goes further to assert that divisibility is purely a function and characteristic of the imagination and intellect and that, though it is 'very difficult to do', if we fully make use of our intellect, we will see that 'quantity . . . [is] substance . . . infinite, one and indivisible . . . matter is everywhere the same' (*Ethics*, in Morgan 2002: 226).

As we do not know the exact capabilities of bodies, the potential for radical and revolutionary change may be imminent. Work in the cognitive industries has long been unpaid and undervalued (Terranova 2000) and perhaps these tools for self-tracking and self-archiving can be seen as a defensive method of self-management in particular contexts. The hegemonic struggle for ownership of this process is underway and the Quantified Self movement is an indication of this.

TOWARD A CONCLUSION

To overcome the shortage of research that looks at bodies in IPE, scholars can begin by looking at the affective and corporeal turns outlined above, whilst situating our research in the lineage of philosophers and activists who have pushed these lines of argument forward over time and into key international and global questions today. Indeed, I advocate the investigation of Spinoza's and Marx's primary texts and of those approaches across disciplines that have moved away from Cartesian assumptions. Second, research on work that is solely based on policy reports published by intergovernmental organizations and governments lack the depth and breadth required in contemporary IPE research because this work tends to reflect limited interests. It also overlooks the corporeal dimensions of precarity increasingly captured by management rhetoric and advocacy of specific self-management techniques. Thus we should give priority to empirical research that looks at how people actually experience capitalism and, more particularly, the impact of technologies on work and management. These explicit suggestions will help us to overcome Negri's claim that 'political economy has become de-ontological' (Negri 1999: 87).

Much more needs to be done to pry IPE research from the allure of international organizations' policy documents and the assumptions of secondary literature. Molloy (2013) has broken ground with 'Spinoza, Carr, and the ethics of *The Twenty Years' Crisis*', demonstrating that there is a nascent interest in the work of Spinoza in International Relations. Here, I have outlined the way the affective and corporeal turns have influenced research in feminist and critical geography literature and have provided insight into the implications for the type of Quantified Man that self-tracking devices produce, with a call to reinvestigate Spinoza's work to understand this emerging hegemonic struggle. Integrating empirical research with a theoretical challenge, I attempt to motivate a shift in the ontology of most IPE research from one that relies on a dualism of body and mind to one that acknowledges work and social change relating to technological advancements as the site for struggle in contemporary capitalism. Further research should pursue the Spinozan and Marxist threads running through the post-autonomist literature in order to identify its potential for studying non-commodity-producing labour and in particular, labour in the supposed cognitive industries. This is an area in need of extensive research – if only to prevent the mainstream management literature and trends such as the Quantified Self movement from shaping our understanding of these aspects of work in corporeal capitalism entirely.

22. Production in everyday life: poetics and prosaics

Matt Davies

> In the progress of the division of labour, the employment of the far greater part of those who live by labour, that is, of the great body of the people, comes to be confined to a few very simple operations; frequently to one or two. But the understandings of the greater part of men are necessarily formed by their ordinary employments. The man whose whole life is spent in performing a few simple operations, of which the effects too are, perhaps, always the same, or very nearly the same, has no occasion to exert his understanding, or to exercise his invention in finding out expedients for removing difficulties which never occur. He naturally loses, therefore, the habit of such exertion, and generally becomes as stupid and ignorant as it is possible for a human creature to become.
>
> Adam Smith, *The Wealth of Nations* (1998: 429)

INTRODUCTION

After his detailed investigations into how the division of labour across enterprises and across societies serves to increase wealth, Adam Smith, in Book V of *The Wealth of Nations*, appears to come to worry about the brutalizing effects of the 'progress of the division of labour' for workers. For Smith, however, it is less the division of labour that produces these effects as it is the way that the progress of the division of labour establishes a particular kind of routine and routinization of productive activity and distributes them socially. In Smith's argument it is not the division of labour per se, or at least on its own, that robs the worker of the mental challenges needed to cultivate the habits of mind characteristic of civilized society, rather it is the way that the progress of the division of labour allocates the kinds of tasks and ways of performing them that situate the 'great body of the people' in an everydayness of repetition, banality and ultimately stupor. Smith can be said to be putting forward a critique of everyday life – though it is a kind of critique that, as Henri Lefebvre quipped, comes from a class whose lucidity and activeness results from having been elevated above the everyday: in fact, a criticism of other classes (Lefebvre 1991a: 29). Nevertheless, the link Smith intuits between production and everydayness points towards some fundamental political problems.

In the first place, the division of labour separates the mental, conceptual, planning, or 'command and control' functions from the execution of tasks and thus constitutes a social and economic hierarchy in which some productive tasks, and those who perform them, are situated in a dominant power relation in production with regard to those who must merely carry out the assigned tasks. Across the various forms or patterns of power relations in production (Cox 1987; Harrod 1987), the dominant agents in the relation exert their dominance in part through their ability to plan or conceive.

In the second place, the division of labour – or better, the divisions of labour including both the intensive technical divisions that structure particular production processes and the social division that is co-extensive, nationally and internationally, with markets – embodies this separation of mental or intellectual tasks from practical activity. This has at least two politically important consequences: first, solutions to problems that emerge in economies as social systems tend to be defined and addressed in technical terms, that is, in terms of getting the order of things right. This is because thought and reflection are separate and elevated above practical activity, which tends to take on an objective hue. Second, as is evident in Smith's characterization of this everyday practical activity as thoughtless and without mental stimulation, the lived, that is, the organic and integrated character of production and of everyday life is obscured and becomes invisible.

Keeping production and everyday life invisible is necessary in order to preserve the hierarchical distribution of roles and of people affected by the division of labour, in which these roles and tasks can be known on behalf of the people who execute and fulfil them and in which the social can operate as a closed structure. Economically, the production of a surplus may be necessary, but socially and politically, the uses and distributions of the surplus must be prefigured: people must be kept in their place or, if that place is problematic for accumulation or other reasons, the adjustment of that place must be made for them. This is Smith's solution to his perceived stupefaction of the 'great body of the people': the government must intervene to ensure the education and defence of society, and while he argues that the expense of these public goods must be shared across the society as a whole, the nature of these goods and their distributions are givens (Smith 1998: 414–44).

But what happens if production and everyday life are not rendered invisible but made visible and foregrounded in political economic analysis? Can understanding everyday life and production, and the relations between them, help make social order appear not as a technical question but as a political one? Can such an understanding help make the distributions of tasks and of people in power relations appear contingent and changeable rather than given and natural? Can critiques of production and everyday life illuminate the stakes involved in times of international economic disruption and crisis? This chapter will begin to address these questions by examining the importance of everyday life and of production for International Political Economy. The argument will be that to bring the critique of everyday life to bear on IPE, it will be necessary to engage critically with production. Everyday life, as Lefebvre argued, is indeed a way of living that is made everyday by the separation and elevation of thought and reflection, leaving behind the mundane, banal, prosaic – that which is unworthy of reflection. But everyday life is more than this as well: Smith was correct to note the constitutive role of work and production in social life and production as a dimension of everyday life entails something more poetic: making differences.

EVERYDAY LIFE IN INTERNATIONAL POLITICAL ECONOMY

The notion of everyday life began to appear in the field of International Political Economy after having been taken up in recent years in cognate fields such as International Relations and Geography and with reference to relevant topics from globalization (e.g. Ettlinger 2004), to tourism (e.g. Butcher 2008 or Su and Teo 2008), to agriculture and food (e.g. Duruz 2005), amongst others. The 'turn' to the everyday has sought to discover a suitable practical grounding for processes, forces or institutions that appear to operate at different levels or in different idioms. Attentiveness to the everyday has resulted from efforts to find new ways to bring neglected effects, causes and consequences of international processes into view. Can this interest in everyday life help clarify the importance of production for International Political Economy? In what ways can attentiveness to the everyday illuminate production as the 'hidden abode' of political economy?

It must be admitted first that in the turn to the everyday in IPE, everyday life itself goes largely un-theorized. It typically appears either as a target on the receiving end of international or global scale processes, registering the transformations originating from outside the everyday, or it appears as the support or ontological grounding for international or global scale phenomena. This has, largely, to do with the ways we have for theorizing the international, even in critical idioms. Take two important and deservedly influential examples of critical IR theory: Robert Cox's (1987) *Production, Power, and World Order* and Cynthia Enloe's (1990) *Beaches,*

Bananas, and Bases – neither of which set out to theorize the everyday but both of which relied on implicit conceptions of everyday life. For Cox, the social forces in contention that shape world order emerge from the experiences of diverse forms of power relations experienced in the production of the goods and services necessary to sustain life. Having established this premise theoretically, however, his attention turned to world orders and their transformations; he later went so far as to describe the state, intermediating between dominant international forces and subordinate domestic economies, as a 'transmission belt' (Cox 1992). Enloe examined things from the other direction, through a feminist critique of IR that showed how the activities and processes that are typically the concerns of the discipline of IR cannot take place without the productive and reproductive labour of women: in other words, these ordinary labours provide the necessary ground for the 'high' politics of International Relations to take place. Influenced by these two approaches, Michael Niemann and I (Davies and Niemann 2002) set out to find grounding for IPE in work, family life and leisure but we did not manage to overcome the 'givenness' of the everyday: everydayness remained opaque, as it has been in the scholarship that simply takes it for granted.

Two recent books on everyday life in International Political Economy have made signal contributions to the field by self-consciously addressing the need to conceptualize everyday life. Paul Langley's (2008) *The Everyday Life of Global Finance* focuses on financialization from the perspective of the everyday saving, borrowing and planning practices that it entails and that enable it. John Hobson's and Leonard Seabrooke's (2007a) *Everyday Politics of the World Economy*, as its title indicates, seeks to find in the everyday a space for political contestation that the more technically or policy oriented literature on IPE tends to ignore. Langley's focus is on finance and he does not set out to consider production per se, though he does take some pains to provide a conceptually rich account of everyday life. Inspired by a Foucauldian understanding of power, Langley finds in the everyday practices of acquiring and using credit, saving and borrowing, a source and practice of capillary social power that articulates the agents and the possibilities for agency in a financialized economy.

The substantively focused essays in Hobson and Seabrooke's collection examine a range of issues for IPE, though production does not figure prominently for them either: Andrew Herod's contribution on trade unions is primarily interested in the ways that IPE understands the geographies of scale and how these scales focus on the agency of capital, foreclosing IPE's understanding the politics of trade unions (Herod 2007); Michele Ford and Nicola Piper examine the political activism of foreign domestic workers in East Asia (Ford and Piper 2007).

This substantive focus on political activism, rather than on production, stems from the theoretical framing of 'Everyday IPE' given in Hobson and Seabrooke's introduction to the book. As already suggested, their project seeks to recover a capacity for political analysis that they see having been lost in what they call 'Regulatory IPE', that is, the predominant approaches to international political economy that seek to be 'problem solving' in the sense that Robert Cox critiqued. This latter disposition, in Hobson and Seabrooke's view, is regulatory in the sense that it seeks to provide explanations and theory of the international political economy that contribute to its proper functioning; it is, thus, a 'top-down' view that hides its connections to and position in a hierarchical system through neutral technocratic rationality. Against this, they propose the everyday as a site for a 'bottom-up' view, one that acknowledges the agency of 'everyday' actors and thus opens the door for political contestation in a theory of international political economy. For Hobson and Seabrooke:

> Everyday actions are defined as *acts by those who are subordinate within a broader power relationship but, whether through negotiation, resistance or non-resistance, either incrementally or suddenly, shape, constitute and transform the political and economic environment around and beyond them.* This broad definition of everyday actions allows us to include a range of agents from individuals to meso-level groupings (e.g., peasants, migrant labourers, trade unions, small investors, low-income groups), and mega scale aggregations (e.g., peripheral states and peoples) (Hobson and Seabrooke 2007b: 15–16; italics in original).

These actions by subordinate actors are political, according to Hobson and Seabrooke, because they are generated through what they call 'axio-rationality'. This notion is central to both their understanding of the everyday and their conception of the political:

> 'axiorationality' is habit-informed, reason-guided behaviour within which an actor still retains a concept of interest. Axiorational behaviour is neither aimed at purely instrumental goals nor purely value-oriented goals. Rather, axiorational behaviour is where an actor uses reason to reflect upon conventions and norms, as well as the interests they inform, and then chooses to act in ways which are in accordance with broader intersubjective understandings of what is socially legitimate. . . . actors often behave in economically rational ways, but . . . this is in part defined by norms and identities that prevail at any one point in time (Hobson and Seabrooke 2007b: 17).

This conception could be criticized on many grounds. The focus on rationality, especially on economically rational behaviour, goes unquestioned here: neither the genesis of the norms and identities that would classify an interest as rational or non-rational, nor the location of this rationality in individual subjects with the attending reduction of subjectivity to rational behaviour, are brought to bear on their conception of the political. The notion of interest is similarly taken up uncritically from theories of political economy that simply assume that actors know their interests and act accordingly. But more to the point for present purposes, this conception tends to neglect the *everydayness* of the everyday: its banality, its prosaic, repetitive and unreflected character.

THE PROSE OF THE WORLD

To see how a critique of everyday life might contribute to the project of bringing production into focus for political economy, we must first address the question: *what* is everyday life? Efforts to define the terrain of the everyday have emerged from various quarters, from notions of reproduction and *habitus* (Bourdieu 1977), to theories of practice (Certeau 1984), to the microhistory of '*Alltagsgeschichte*' (Lüdtke 1995). Henri Lefebvre's pioneering contributions to philosophy and to critical theory were largely driven by his career-spanning interest in the critique of everyday life – articulated in, among many other books and articles, the three eponymous volumes originally published in 1947 (Lefebvre 1991a), 1961 (Lefebvre 2002) and 1981 (Lefebvre 2008).

For Lefebvre, theory had for far too long neglected the trivial but practical details of life as it is lived. Everyday life, '[in] appearance, . . . is the insignificant and the banal. It is what Hegel called "the prose of the world", nothing more modest' (Lefebvre 1988: 78). Yet despite its triviality, it is necessary: it is the 'soil' in which the 'flowers and trees' of creative human activity grow (Lefebvre 1991a: 87). Because everyday life consists of the banal, routine and repetitive, Lefebvre asserted that it fell outside the attention of philosophical thought and reflection. It is the 'reality without truth', counterpoised to the 'truth without reality' of philosophy (Lefebvre 1984: 14). Indeed, philosophy could reflect on higher concerns precisely because everyday life is banal: it is the routine nature of everyday life that liberates it from thought and reflection and that liberates thought and reflection from everyday concerns. The relationship between reflection and thought, on the one hand, and everyday life, on the other, is hierarchical: as Lefebvre noted in *The Production of Space* (1991b), the conceived tends to dominate the lived. This subordination of the everyday appears as a form of the relation between mental and manual labour, where the separation of the tasks of planning and control from the execution of those tasks defines in part the power relations that structure production (Davies 2010).

Just as everyday life came to be subordinated to planning in terms of the mental–manual division of labour, it also was subjected to the process of commodification. The first volume of Lefebvre's *Critique of Everyday Life* appeared in 1947, in the aftermath of the liberation of France. The moment was one of great optimism concerning the possibilities for 'changing life', and much of the criticism put forward in this first take on the everyday was aimed at the political practices of those, such as Stalinists and sectarian Marxists, who subordinated the concrete analysis of the social and political situation in France to a received elevation of a self-regarding philosophy over a thus neglected sociology. This moment of optimism passed, however, and on the eve of the May 1968 rebellion in France, Lefebvre had come to see everyday life as an object of programming in a 'bureaucratic society of controlled consumption' (Lefebvre 1984).

Despite this highly pessimistic formulation, for Lefebvre everyday life was never reducible either to the entirely passive reproduction of an imposed set of practices or to a space of autonomous, self-regulating behaviour. His final book on 'rhythmanalysis', published posthumously in 1992 (Lefebvre 2004) set out to clarify the methods needed to trace the materiality of everyday life in space and in time, through the observation of the rhythms that govern or express the everyday and their relations (eurhythmia, poly-rhythms, interference and disruption). Everydayness is itself a rhythm: it signals the cyclical recurrence of the daily activities that constitute lived space. Temporalities are very important for the critique of everyday life. We could thus also ask: *when* is the everyday?

The answer to this question is less obvious than it might seem. We might identify it with daily life and the ways that people navigate the rhythms of streets, workplaces, homes or their bodies. However, to locate the everyday at this level of generality and abstraction, as in Hobson and Seabrooke, for whom all actions within subordinate relations are defined as everyday, is very much at odds with Lefebvre's insistence on the materiality of everyday life. Everyday life is peculiar, not general. In terms of time, it requires sufficiently long temporal horizons for the outcomes of daily activities to be adequately predictable, to take place without having to change patterns or disrupt daily routines. Seen from the perspective of international political economy, not everyone can count on enjoying the protection of sustained social reproduction. Foreshortened time horizons are part of what political economy now describes as 'precarity', as precarious workers lack certainty with regard not only to their labour contracts but also with regard to living conditions, health and welfare, and the prospects for both their own and future generations' reproduction.

This particularity of everyday life – that is, a life that can be banal and mundane and that can be lived without being reflected upon because its rhythms reproduce themselves – points to another temporality of the everyday. Everyday life appears as the outcome of a specific historical development, which is usually described as modernity. Modernity, a much abused and complex notion, denotes at least living with constant change: 'all that is solid melts into air' (Marx and Engels). Cyclical rhythms, such as those of the body sleeping and waking or the seasons shaping the productive activities of peasants, encounter and are often subordinated to linear, sequential rhythms such as those of the assembly line. Lefebvre provides an interesting illustration of the conflict between these rhythms and the possibilities that emerge from their encounter in his chapter on 'The media day' (Lefebvre 2004: 46–50). The notion of the media day itself is loaded with antinomies: the media day extends the experience of the day such that the cyclical alternation of day and night is subordinated to the continual provision of media products – television and radio would have been exemplary when Lefebvre wrote this but the development of 'social media' and their worldwide scope has only intensified and accelerated the processes he noted.

Modernity as a process seeks to generalize itself – again, paraphrasing Marx and Engels, 'battering down all Chinese walls'. In doing so, however, it finds resistances and failures, producing uneven development. Cyclical rhythms do not disappear under the relentless pressure of the modern. The 'disenchantment of the world' that Weber noted did not result in the elimination of the small magical rituals and superstitions that govern the daily lives of people – everyday rituals still include, for example, consulting astrologers via horoscopes, now online, or buying lottery tickets (cf. Lefebvre 2002). Everydayness, as Harry Harootunian (2000) notes, provides a 'minimal unity' to these holdovers of the past and the compulsions of the present – which also may point to everyday life as a site of the disruptions of planning and of instrumental or economic rationality.

We can further specify the everyday by inquiring about its place: *where* does everyday life take place? Many observers of the everyday – not only Lefebvre, but also Benjamin, de Certeau, and by the various thinkers surveyed by Harootunian (2000), such as Kracauer (1995), Simmel (2011), Lukács (1971), Arvatov (1997) and Kon Wajirō (cited in Harootunian 2000: 129–31) – link it explicitly with urban life. But the urban, as Lefebvre famously argued, is not merely the city as a place: it is a spatial relationship defined by the centralized dominance of the functions of planning, technocracy and organization over inhabited space. Industrialization concentrates productive forces in space and the management of industry subordinates agricultural production, for example through the textile industries' demand for plant material to be transformed into thread, cloth and clothing, or more generally the organization of the production of food for consumption of workers – and thus the city comes to dominate the countryside.

The predominance of instrumental and economic rationality in industrialization extends to the planning of the use of space in the city as well. Urban planning focuses on programming the use of space to facilitate circulation: from Haussmann's grand boulevards, which cleared away the jumble of Parisian workers' housing to facilitate the movement of troops in order to control the city, to the ongoing dilemmas of planning for car parking that can deliver people to crowded city centres without disrupting the smooth flow of traffic. The emphasis on circulation in urbanism recalls Jacques Rancière's characterization of the police as interpolating people not through stopping them – as in Althusser's 'hey, you!' – but rather through ensuring their circulation – 'move along, nothing to see here' (Rancière 2010: 37). This 'nothing to see' in the everyday can present itself as disruptions, tragedies and accidents but the police function here stops the moment of reflection and ensures the continuity of everyday life.

Urbanism is thus the intensive space of the everyday; however, everyday life also presents itself as an extensive space. The processes that Lefebvre analyses as urban societies do not appear as *faits accomplis* but as practices that tend to produce the results of urbanism. Just as capital and as modernity extend themselves – albeit unevenly – geographically, the centralization of planning and organization becomes a mode of producing and governing space generally. Everyday life is thus an element of the internationalization of political economic arrangements through markets and through production relations.

So-called 'developed' or 'core' countries are therefore not the sole locations of urbanism or urban societies and the critique of everyday life is not the provincial concern of Western cultures. The spatial centralization of planning and organizing functions and practices appears in various national contexts and extends domination over space and territory, creating the conditions where the separation of these 'higher activities' from everyday life and the subordination – and, potentially at least, the 'bureaucratic programming' – of the everyday are not specifically 'Western' phenomena. Everyday life is thus not culture-bound; that is, it is not specifically the result of Westernization or of Americanism. But neither is it a-cultural: it is a way of life shaped by the hierarchical, socially rooted and culturally expressed unity of residual patterns and rhythms of life with emergent and dominant forms of rationality, organization and governance.

Formulations of everyday life that reduce it to notions such as 'consumer society' or 'leisure society' or 'post-industrial society' thus obscure both the spatial generalization of everyday life and its specificity as a way of living peculiar to particular social, temporal and spatial arrangements. The generality of everyday life results from its cultural unboundedness: it can take different forms, patterns and expressions in different circumstances and is not reducible to a form of cultural domination or a particular lifestyle. But even if everyday life is a possible arrangement of modernity and of capital generally, it is also a specific kind of arrangement, not simply the obverse of relations of domination. The banal, mundane, repetitive and prosaic structures of everyday experience are a specific kind of temporality and result from specific kinds of historical processes; they articulate particular kinds of lived spaces and particular spatial relationships. Because it is forms of spaces and times from which reflection and thought have been separated, everyday life can become an object of planning and programming. However, because it provides a ground for planning and for connecting plans to possible outcomes, everyday life also provides those who can inhabit it not only with a certain kind of security but also a condition of the emergence of their subjectivity. To explore these subjective (and political) possibilities, we have to turn to the question of production and how it is related to the everyday.

FROM PROSAIC TO POETIC: PRODUCTION AND EVERYDAY LIFE

To sum up, the notion of everyday life describes a particular condition for living; it is not a general depiction of day-to-day living. Everyday life must therefore be specified as a concept. It has specific temporal characteristics. Intensively, the temporality of everyday life is constituted by repetition, more particularly by patterns of repetition that render it mundane, banal and prosaic – repeated gestures that do not require thoughtful reflection to be enacted and that provide a basis for social reproduction on these unreflected terms. Extensively, these banal patterns of repetition are the outcome of forms of historical development that enact and depend on the separation of thoughtful reflection from everyday activities, an historical development described variously as disenchantment, rationalization or modernization. Everyday life also entails particular kinds of spatial organization. The extensive temporality of everyday life, modernity, is linked to urbanism. Urbanism is not merely life in cities; it refers rather to the concentration in cities of the functions of planning and control, which permits the extended dominance and command of cities over space. Urbanism, and specifically the spatial concentration of command and control, is thus strongly linked to an intensive ordering of space that follows industrialization and consequently the spatial separation and segregation of social functions: thus the household is separate from the workplace, even for the kinds of household where production for market exchange takes place.

This separation and segregation of spatialized functions takes place abstractly. Abstraction thus plays a role in the subordination and consequent invisibility of production. Lefebvre illustrates this process, as well as how it shapes how abstraction can be understood as thought that contributes to the production of space, by considering how the space of work is produced and configured.

> Can the space of work, for example (when indeed it is legitimate to speak of such a space), be envisaged as a void occupied by an entity called work? Clearly not: it is produced within the framework of a global society, and in accordance with that society's constitutive production relations. In capitalist society, the space of work consists of production units: businesses, farms, offices. The various networks which link these units are also part of the space of work. As for the agencies that govern these networks, they are not identical to those that govern work itself, but they are articulated with them in a relatively coherent manner which does not, however, exclude conflicts and contradictions. The space of work is thus the result, in the first place, of the (repetitive) gestures and (serial) actions of productive labour, but also – and increasingly – of the (technical and social) division of labour; the result therefore, too, of the operation of markets (local, national, and worldwide) and, lastly, of property relationships (the ownership and management of the means of production). Which is to say that the space of work has contours and boundaries only for and through a thought which *abstracts*; as one network among others, as one space among many interpenetrating spaces, its existence is strictly relative. (Lefebvre 1991b: 191)

But can we reduce production to a mere social function under modernity, one whose spatial configuration thus merely describes an aspect of everyday life? There can be no doubt that work – both in its locations and in its rhythms – is an element of the everyday, just as everyday life becomes deeply problematic for those subordinate actors for whom work is denied.

So production is not merely an economic – or social – function. To begin to come to terms with production, and thus to illuminate its place in political economic critique, we can again find some help from Henri Lefebvre. In addition to his influential work on the critique of everyday life, Lefebvre is probably best known in the Anglophone world for his work on space, particular his magisterial investigations in *The Production of Space* (Lefebvre 1991b). His rethinking and re-working of the notion of space from an already-given, abstract container of social relations and objects to something that might be *produced* has had an enormous impact on economic geography; less noted, perhaps, is that in order to understand space as produced, Lefebvre also had to think through *production*.

Lefebvre takes up the notion of production in terms of the metabolic relation between the living organism, the body, and the space that the organism produces. He rejects the idea of space as a given or as an empty container into which things can be put. Here, production refers to a general and primordial condition: all change that is associated with the appropriation and discharge of energies or information by the body is productive:

> The fact that a surplus of energy is accumulated before being discharged is thus a defining aspect of the very concept of the 'living body' and its relationship with its space – i.e., with itself, its vicinity, its surroundings, and the world at large. A productive squandering of energy is not a contradiction in terms: an expenditure of energy may be deemed 'productive' so long as some change, no matter how small, is thereby effected in the world. . . . Furthermore, productive energy implies the living organism's relationship with itself, and in this connection takes the form of *reproductive* energy; as such it is characterized by repetition – repetition in the division and multiplication of cells, in actions, in reflexes (Lefebvre 1991b: 179).

Lefebvre suggests that Marx and Engels took up this generalized notion of production and then turned to political economy 'ingenuously' (Lefebvre 1991b: 70), to give the notion a positive content. Thus he identifies a slippage in Marxist thought between an ontological commitment to production as a condition of life, a general conception, and then more particularly production as the programmed and repeated gestures that result in exchangeable products. The point of the critique of political economy is not to refute the latter conception, which evidently describes much of productive activity, but to understand how, and with what consequences, the slippage between the concepts takes place.

The slippage is signalled in part through the distinction between work and products: where work tends to be individual and spontaneous and thus unique – as in a work of art, which indicates production as a general philosophical principle – and products tend to be the result of processes designed to produce identical outputs. However, this distinction is tenuous. Cities illustrate this problem. Lefebvre considers Venice: is it a product or a work? On the one hand, the city's magnificence results in part from its unique expression of the overcoming of the sea by the residents of the city; its grandeur was unplanned. On the other hand, stonemasons and canal diggers and weavers and cooks all occupy particular positions in the technical and social divisions of labour and all perform specific and designated tasks to particular rhythms and according to rules set out in particular hierarchies. The specific and positive meaning of 'production' supplied by political economy is itself a particular condition of the historical development of the forces of production.

This indicates the kernel of truth in the critiques of productivism: 'the concept of production can scarcely be separated out from the ideology of productivism, from a crude and brutal economism whose aim is to annex it for its own purposes' (Lefebvre 1991b: 72). For example, to reduce the analysis of the reproduction of the social relations that underpin international political and economic systems to labour markets and the structure of industrial relations rather obviously neglects the role of consumption in identity formation. But the critique of productivism in the name of consumption is too hasty and it fundamentally misunderstands both production and consumption. The general idea of production demonstrates this: if the living organism is defined by the exchanges, accumulation and discharges of energies, clearly there is no production without consumption and, likewise, no consumption without production. To leave them in separate and unrelated spheres, one of which might dominate the other, is to accept the limiting of production to its positive political economic sense.

Furthermore, such a critique also misunderstands political economy. If political economy can be said to neglect consumption, it is not because it focuses on production. On the contrary, as Marx himself noted in the first volume of *Capital*, the visible face of political economy is not production but rather circulation:

> The consumption of labour-power is completed, as in the case of every other commodity, outside the market or the sphere of circulation. Let us therefore, in company with the owner of money and the owner of labour-power, leave this noisy sphere, where everything takes place on the surface and in full view of everyone, and follow them into the hidden abode of production, on whose threshold there hangs the notice 'No admittance except on business' (Marx 1977: 279–80).

Production, by means of and in a way very similar to the obscuring of everyday life, disappears into the space of work. The subordination of production to circulation in political economic thinking makes work invisible; everyday life becomes invisible through its subordination to the privilege of reflective thought. In both cases, the process of separation and subordination is a process of abstraction. The abstraction of philosophical reflection, technical planning, and reflective thinking more generally from everyday life, as discussed in the previous section, runs parallel to the abstraction from particular use values to exchange values as expressed in quantitative terms as money. In the sphere of circulation, difference is hidden or at least reduced to quantities that can be exchanged because the qualities they express are suspended. This is to say that the sphere of circulation becomes a *zone of indifference*.

For commodities, including the commodity of labour power, to be exchanged in the market, they must encounter each other as embodiments of abstractly equivalent values. To the extent that political economy is a study or science of the functioning of markets, it is strictly indifferent to the particular qualities of the different commodities. This is not to say that the differences are not important; rather, they are important but only outside of the sphere of circulation, in the processes of consuming and producing. These processes thus become private matters, about which political economy has strictly nothing to say. For every particular need to find a supply or every particular capacity to find a demand, the market must be functioning properly. The correct functioning of the market, which came to be the focus of political economic thought, thus becomes a technical problem rather than a political one. The indifference of the sphere of circulation, in other words, is anti-political.

Production, in contrast to circulation, is precisely a matter of difference. In the general philosophical meaning of production elaborated by Lefebvre, production is seen in the changes effected in the metabolic relation between an organism or body and the space it produces. Life, in this perspective, is defined in terms of making differences. Circulation cannot be so easily abstracted from the accumulation, exchange or discharge of energies that bodies enact as they produce and reproduce themselves and their space. Furthermore, this is not only a matter of the production of space. As Marx famously noted: 'Men [sic] make their own history but they do not make it as they please. . .' (Marx 1852). Production in this general sense as the altering of material and of circumstances also refers to time.

A political economy perspective on production gives specific meaning to these processes and changes. When workers produce, they are exercising brain and muscle power to effect changes in material. The general metabolic relation takes on the specific characteristics of accumulating energies and ideas and discharging them into a product. Effecting these changes and making these differences in the social and material world involves overcoming the social and material resistances and constraints presented in the production process. As Christophe Dejours notes, 'there is always a gap between the prescriptive and the concrete reality of the situation. This gap is found at all levels of analysis between task and activity, or between the formal and informal organisation of work. *Working* thus means *bridging the gap* between prescriptive and concrete reality' (Dejours 2007: 72, emphasis in the original). Overcoming the gap between plans or ideas and the material (social or concrete) worked on involves the subjectivity of the worker as well. Classical political economy recognized this: not only in Marx but as we saw in Adam Smith, for whom the brutalizing circumstances of labour were likely to make brutes out of workers: 'The torpor of his mind renders him not only incapable of relishing or bearing a part in any rational conversation, but of conceiving any generous, noble, or tender sentiment, and consequently of forming any just judgment concerning many even of the ordinary duties of private life' (Smith 1998: 429).

We might reject Smith's prognosis but it is striking how much a market-orientated, technocratic political economy has lost by abandoning his concern with subjectivity as situated in the production process. Thanks to the technical and social divisions of labour, this process is not merely individual and biological but rather social. Where the market is the ruling mechanism for the distribution of goods and services, the social division of labour is co-extensive with the market. The difference realized in the product through the production process is important because that is where the value added to the product is manifest. Difference among workers is also important as their different skills and talents and their different positions are allocated through the divisions of labour. Because labour is thus divided, people are distributed across tasks by the market – thus the sphere of production is subordinated to the sphere of circulation. When political economy takes cognizance of production, however, the sphere of circulation is no longer merely a technical problem; people are not only distributed across different tasks but the tasks, and the people, are organized in hierarchical relations in which the subjectivity of some – the planners, the technocrats – is required to flourish while that of others, as argued by Smith, withers. Production and the focus on difference that it enables thus become a key to understanding the politics of international political economy. They also give the critique of everyday life better analytical purchase on IPE.

CONCLUSION

Production and everyday life are linked both extensively and intensively through the way they produce and configure temporalities and the way they are engaged in the production of space. Just as everyday life is constituted through intensive and extensive temporalities and spaces, production also embraces both general, extensive, conditions for living and specific, intensive, operations determined and distributed through the division of labour. A kind of living that can be described in terms of everyday life, with both the minimal security and predictability that can occasion forms of subjective involvement with living and the banality that constrains that subjectivity along the lines signalled by Smith, is made possible through the structure of production relations and the 'progress of the division of labour'. The fragmenting of the production process generates the fragmenting of subjectivity along with the socialization of labour (Lefebvre 1991a: 39).

A focus on production also helps to demonstrate the limits to everyday life. Lefebvre was surely correct to note that everyday life entails its own spontaneous critique (Lefebvre 1991a: 29). For his time, this critique originated in an element of everyday life itself: leisure and private life, as the expressions of a critique of the externally imposed fragmentation and alienation experienced in production relations, were both separated from production in time (e.g. weekends) and space (e.g. holidays) and also united with production as recovery and reproduction. Such a view will appear dated today. Work is both scarce enough to no longer display the everyday character that informed Lefebvre's discussions in the 1950s and, for some at least, more central to the identity of workers who are compelled through managing the course of their working lives to diffuse the boundaries between work and leisure (see Moore 2010 and this volume). If everyday life remains a common sense, regulative norm or at least aspiration for workers, it has also become more clear how tenuous the connection is between such a mode of life and the possibilities for workers confronted by multiple and ongoing crises.

IPE has tended to take up an interest in the everyday for its own purposes and not enough as a critique of either everyday life or of international political economy itself. In the tracks of classical and neoclassical debates in political economy, which defined their field in terms of the circulation of commodities and subordinated and hid production, various theorists of IPE have sought to restore a political vision to the field. Everyday life was a reasonable place to turn for such theorists as it could either be examined for the scars it bears in its encounters with the red teeth and claws of marketization, structural adjustment and austerity, or as it could provide a sociologically concrete source of agency for international political economy.

But these versions of everyday life remain too amorphous, too undetermined. Recovering the intuition of classical political economy's worry about how the structures of production or the 'progress of the division of labour' produce an alienating and stupefying everydayness begins to provide a useful antidote to this even if its demeaning of the everyday is one-dimensional and shallow. Restoring production to the practical and theoretical armoury of critical political economy is both enabled by a turn to everyday life and provides a theoretical ground for the critique of everyday life. By showing how the hierarchical and social distributions of people are not merely a distribution of their supposedly innate – and thus private – characteristics but are the contingent partitioning of roles and rewards through the division of labour, the critique of production can expose a symbolic and practical order that elevates technocratic approaches and renders politics obscure. This involves shifting theoretical effort away from the abstract indifference of circulation and towards a concrete embrace of difference. This enables a political critique by highlighting the stakes of subjective engagements with the disruptions of everyday life by international economic crises: making production and everyday life visible makes the possibilities for different ways of living more evident.

23. Automobility: culture, (re-)production and sustainability

Matthew Paterson

INTRODUCTION

The production, consumption, regulation and cultural valorization of automobiles have been central to the reproduction of capitalist development since at least the 1930s. This chapter elaborates what we can learn from focusing on the automobile – as one particular technology, a culture, a production regime, and a social institution of twentieth-century capitalism. It has been central also to the regime of accumulation known often simply as Fordism (cf. Desai, this volume); it has been a crucial component of the transnationalization of production; and finally, it has been a critical site for the unfolding of various contradictions within Fordism and in ongoing attempts to stabilize (or undermine) capitalism.

At the same time, the regime of accumulation centred on automobility has engendered very particular and highly destructive socio-ecological impacts. At the largest scale it has been integral to the systemic generation of steadily growing greenhouse gas emissions that threaten specific livelihoods across the globe and risk global civilizational collapse. In part, this is precisely because of automobility's spectacular success in shaping twentieth-century capitalism – its contribution to the growth in productivity, as well as its role in generating a model of redistributive politics that integrated much of the working class in the West into capitalist development, and thus in securing capitalist legitimacy. So at the same time as it entails various contradictions between capital and labour, it also generates novel dilemmas in terms of contradictions between a particular productivist model and the socio-ecological conditions of capitalist reproduction.

BEYOND PRODUCTION: AUTOMOBILITY

To claim that automobiles have been absolutely central to capitalist life, in particular to the organization of production and reproduction, from the early twentieth century onwards is not a particularly startling proposition. The automobile sector has been central to a range of debates in political economy, from Harry Braverman's (1974) account of the labour process in sociology, to accounts of Fordism from Gramsci (1971) onwards through to Aglietta's account of it as a regime of accumulation (1976), to various pieces of work on the transnationalization of production (Dicken 1998; Held et al. 1999: 262–3), or the economic basis for US global power (Rupert 1995), to name but four prominent debates. Much of the language concerning the political economy of production has been developed precisely out of analyses of the automobile sector. This section outlines some of these principal debates.

One of the limitations of starting solely with production is that it seems almost arbitrary that the innovations in the production process that triggered the dramatic transformation of capitalism in the twentieth century occurred in the automobile sector – it could have happened in chemicals, consumer goods, military manufacturing, or any other manufacturing sector in principle. However, the advantage of extending our ambit in thinking about automobility as an integrated phenomenon is that it helps us understand why it was that innovation in the automobile sector was so critical to this transformation. To do this we need to start by conceptualizing automobility more clearly.

Sudhir Chella Rajan (1996) refers to this concept as 'automobile use and everything that makes it possible – roads, highways, parking structures, and traffic rules'. In other words it is simultaneously a particular product, the things that go into making that product, and the myriad other institutions, technologies and daily practices that are involved. These extend all the way from primary resource extraction through to healthcare systems to deal with the daily injuries and deaths produced by cars, the insurance sector, or all of the accessories available for use specifically within the car. There are then of course all of the activities that are made possible by automobility itself, my favourite example being the discussion of the emergence of golf in the 1920s as having widespread car availability as its condition of possibility (Flink 1975: 166). John Urry (2004) describes the 'system of automobility' as having a number of features. For Urry, automobility involves 'the quintessential *manufactured object* produced by the leading industrial sectors and the iconic firms within twentieth-century capitalism'; 'the *key concepts* . . . employed in understanding the development of . . . the trajectory of contemporary capitalism'; 'the major item of individual *consumption*'; 'a *machinic complex*'; 'the single most important *environmental issue*'; 'the predominant form of *quasi private mobility*'; and 'the dominant *culture* [which] sustained major discourses of what constitutes the good life' (Urry 2000: 57–8; see Paterson 2007: 25–6 for a fuller elaboration).

Understood this way, it is possible to see why this centrality of the automobile to twentieth-century capitalism is not contingent or accidental. Rather it was central not only because of the transformation of production relations that occurred first within that sector, but because of the massively extensive chain of economic effects it helped enable, stimulating economic activity more or less across the entire economy, in ways that no other sector arguably could have done. Second, it was central because it managed to become a product that was both produced by alienated labour under capitalism but that also became the symbol, perhaps uniquely so, of liberation from a variety of dominating forces within capitalism. The symbolisms of the car, its association with freedom in particular, are both banal and exceptionally powerful, and reproduced ubiquitously in advertising, popular culture and political discourse. These help to explain to a large extent the continued popularity of the car and its global spread, even while the manifest contradictions I explore below are becoming ever more apparent.

The cultural dimensions of automobility have had important consequences for the production of automobiles. Perhaps the most obvious way of understanding this is in relation to the dynamics of 'consumer choice'. Henry Ford was famous for stating that you could have your car any colour as long as it was black. Some of the developments of Toyotism were designed to respond to cultural shifts resistant to this sort of homogenization by enabling more rapid turnover of production such that the features of any individual car could be varied much more easily, from the colour, to the design, internal features such as seats, and so on (cf. Ihara, this volume). Flexibilization of production was thus in part driven by the internal cultural logic of the automobile itself – promising freedom while enforcing homogeneity has its own contradictions, which played out with these effects (Paterson 2007: ch.5; also Gartman 1994).

Another important dimension here is the way that automobility, in the terms of Urry's useful phrase, 'coerces people into an intense flexibility' (2004: 28). The dominance of the automobile, which had been achieved by the 1930s in many parts of the US, and followed later and less completely in other societies, effected a radical transformation of urban life specifically through its spatial structure. While a certain amount of suburbanization had occurred in the United States via the tramway and the train, the automobile both enabled and increasingly required the development of low-density, suburban development. Politically, this usually entailed the development of close relations between property developers and construction companies. The former realized that housing construction on the edges of cities was often far more profitable than within dense city centres, while the construction companies benefited from the investment by public authorities in new roads, electricity, water, telephone and other sorts of urban infrastructure that were significantly more intensive with low-density development than in older urban cores. Occasionally, as in the famous National City Lines case (Paterson 2007: 73–4; Davies 1975; Dunn 1998; St Clair 1988), it entailed direct strategies by consortia of car manufacturers (General Motors), tyre manufacturers (Firestone) and oil companies (Standard Oil of California), which bought up tramlines, closed down the trams and converted them to buses, with the effect that ridership declined dramatically in favour of the automobile.

The effects of these shifts are such that we now can describe the situation in many cities with the phrase that the automobile enjoys a 'radical monopoly', in the sense that car ownership and almost daily use is more or less compulsory (Illich 1974). This has profound effects for the organization of production, since production in more or less the entire economy is dependent on continued investment in automobile-dominated infrastructure and is vulnerable to breakdowns in it. Beyond this contradiction, it of course generates the enormously complicated politics of dealing with automobility's many social and ecological contradictions that I return to below.

These observations should be understood to transform our account of political economy as a field of study. What automobility has been able to do is to make the daily practices of consumption which are integral to the economic cycles of accumulation, simultaneously the means of legitimation of contemporary capitalist life. While the origins of this can be traced analytically to attempts by corporations and states to generate this sort of economic regime, it is overly reductive to regard the widespread cultural valorization of cars as simply an epiphenomenon, with the task of a cultural critique simply to show people that they have been duped.

SPEED AND MOBILITY AT THE HEART OF AUTO-HEGEMONY

The rise of the car as a means of transport has been explained by many an economist or business historian as a natural process. Thus the automobile is portrayed in terms of the natural advantages it has over other forms of transport, and the affinity it has to inherent forces in human psychology, such as the desire to move freely, something that a baby already feels. 'Waiting for a bus or a train', on the other hand, supposedly 'unleashes hidden, unconscious fears of abandonment' (Moxton and Wormald 1995: 33).

Generally among such justifications of car use, the idea that the rapid growth of automobility can have no other explanation than that it must have obeyed profound drivers in the human psyche, is central. But for Ford, such landmark innovations as the five-dollar-a-day were both tactical manoeuvres, a means to pursue labour peace by compensating for the deskilled work and thus reduction in work satisfaction, but also strategic, in that he saw it both as a means to forestall socialism politically and create consumers for his products economically. The new production regime meant that accumulation was now much more based upon gains in labour productivity. But the new regime also engendered its own contradictions: to the extent that it dramatically increased labour productivity, it also increased the potential for underconsumption crises. Indeed, many of the crises of the first half of the twentieth century can be interpreted as an effect of this disjuncture: while productivity increased, there was not a concomitant increase in consumer demand, because of the prevailing distribution of income (Lipietz 1987).

In the postwar welfare states and Keynesian economic management regimes, these contradictions were temporarily overcome. But as the *trente glorieuses* drew to a close and car manufacturers sought to evade the power of car sector unions through transnationalization and flexibilization of production, the contradictions resurfaced (Aglietta 1999). Still the car sector is understood by many state elites as central to economic prosperity (as witnessed by the bailouts of car firms during the crisis of 2008–09), even while its role in economic growth globally is radically reduced compared to the mid-twentieth century. The car culture, however, is as alive as ever. What André Gorz (1980) called the 'social ideology of the motor-car' is deeply entrenched in individual and collective identities. Such an ideology has been able to become so deep-rooted because of the way its manufacturers have been able to link it to pervasive ideologies and widely valorized themes. 'The alliance of those whose livelihood depends on a robust automobile-centred culture . . . also feed on the cultural symbolism of the automobile: freedom, individualism, mobility, speed, power, and privacy' (Tiles and Oberdiek 1995: 137). Such symbolic connections are ubiquitous in a variety of cultural arenas, from pop music, to film, to twentieth-century novels, where cars are widely valorized (Baird 1998: 28–35).

Of these six themes of 'freedom, individualism, mobility, speed, power, and privacy', I focus here on the notions of speed and mobility. In many accounts, speed, and acceleration in particular, are taken as perhaps the primary feature of late modernity. In Freund and Martin's terms, 'Speed *is* the premier cultural icon of modern societies' (1993: 89). Berman makes this explicit in his account of modernity. While for him the central feature is that 'all that is solid melts into air', in the twentieth century this continual change is effected through continuous acceleration brought about by new transportation technologies, primarily the car. Berman quotes Siegfried Giedion, Le Corbusier's most famous disciple (Berman's term) in architecture and urban design, relating this explicitly to the automobile. 'The space-time feeling of our period can seldom be felt so keenly as when driving', Giedion wrote in 1938–39 (Giedion 1949, quoted in Berman 1982: 302). Berman also quotes Le Corbusier himself when he noted that 'on that 1st of October, 1924, I was assisting in the titanic rebirth of a new phenomenon. . . traffic. Cars, cars, fast, fast! One is seized, filled with enthusiasm, with joy. . . the joy of power' (Berman 1982: 166).

The association is then one of modernity and modernization, with notions of progress built in (which are so valorized that they cannot be resisted), with acceleration and increasing speed. Thus the car becomes a primary symbol of modernity itself. The driving experience becomes itself an end, not simply a means. As a US car ad in 1993 suggested, 'Illogical as it may seem, the simple act of motoring down the boulevard, exhaust burbling, that's what Viper ownership is all about. Only behind the wheel does it all make perfect sense' (quoted in Freund and Martin 1993: 3).

Speed has been one of the main motifs underlying popular constructions of the car. At times, it has been a central part of advertising strategies, which focus, for example, on the time taken to accelerate from 0 to 60 mph. Whilst regulations may have worked to curtail the straightforward propagation of speed in car advertisements due to safety concerns, it remains a popular theme outside them. *Top Gear*, the hugely popular UK TV programme about cars, focuses heavily on speed in the way it portrays cars. Its most prominent presenter, Jeremy Clarkson, is well-known for glamorizing the speed of cars demonstrated in the programme. In one episode of *Top Gear*, he drove a Jaguar XJR above 100 mph, proclaiming that it was 'bonkers fast. . . rockets from nought to 60 [mph] in five seconds' (quoted in Baird 1998: 187; Clarkson's reply to those questioning the size of his carbon footprint is that as a car driver he does not have a footprint).

Nigel Thrift also makes speed a central feature in his account of changes in contemporary societies (Thrift 1996). Thus he groups together three themes – speed, light and power – under the collective term 'mobility', to characterize such changes in ways similar to Berman's account of 'modernity'. Thrift suggests that the three 'have been crystallised by considerations of a commonplace, even banal, image; an urban landscape at night through which runs a river of headlight' (ibid.: 257).

Like Berman, Thrift focuses on nineteenth- and twentieth-century change in terms of the mobility produced by transport and communication technologies. In the nineteenth century, the consequences of the adoption of such technologies (confining ourselves to speed and transport here) were fourfold (Thrift 1996: 265ff). First, they produced a 'change in the consciousness of time and space', involving increased attention paid by people to smaller distinctions in time (leading to the development of a market for watches), the emergence of travelling to work as a social practice, and the increasing experience of landscape from a moving rather than stationary vantage-point. Second, there was the way that literary texts paid attention to speed either in terms of celebration of machine-driven acceleration or as protests against the increasingly hurried nature of life. Third, there was a change in the nature of subjectivity, involving an 'increasing sense of the body as an anonymised parcel of flesh which is shunted from place to place' (ibid.: 266). Finally, prevalent social metaphors emerged reflecting the preoccupation with speed, notably 'circulation' and 'progress'. Speed thus culturally became understood as causally connected to progress. 'Whatever was part of circulation was regarded as healthy, progressive, constructive; all that was detached from circulation, on the other hand, appeared diseased, medieval, subversive, threatening' (Schivelsbusch 1986: 195, quoted in Thrift 1996: 266). Travel thus became an end in itself. By the late twentieth century such a conception became deeply embedded: 'Travel is now thought to occupy 40 per cent of available "free time"' (Urry 1990: 6, as quoted in Thrift 1996: 280).

In the twentieth century, Thrift suggests that speed continued as a predominant social theme, but that through at least the 1960s, there was little qualitatively different about the consciousness of space and time from the nineteenth century. The car emerged, however, as the 'most important device', the 'avatar of mobility' (Thrift 1996: 272), which has helped to entrench the notion of a society where the 'only truly profound pleasure [is] that of keeping on the move' (ibid.: 273, quoting Baudrillard 1988: 52–3).

But the importance of the way cars could be linked to freedom through notions of speed and mobility has also had a context in the way that industrial societies have become increasingly regimented and bureaucratized to serve the needs of industrial production. 'More than any other consumer good the motor car provided fantasies of status, freedom and escape from the constraints of a highly disciplined urban, industrial order' (McShane 1994: 148; also Ling 1990: 4–5). This fantasy was particularly important since even in the US, the most motorized country in the world, no one was actually able to commute or even, apart from a very tiny number, travel far (on holiday, for instance), until after the Second World War (ibid.: 125–7).

The association of cars with speed, and with speed as their main legitimizing motif, is widely recognized in contemporary accounts (e.g. Ross 1995: 21; McShane 1994: 114; Wolf 1996: chapter 13). This can perhaps be best seen in the way that many critiques of the car focus on the notion of speed and mobility. They focus on the fact that in many cities, average speeds are now often no faster than they were before the car's emergence, with London averaging 7 mph, Tokyo 12 mph and Paris 17 mph in the rush hour (Wajcman 1991: 127). The critiques in popular accounts, such as Ben Elton's *Gridlock* (1991) focus, among other things, on the irony and frustration produced by the car. The myth of the car is centred on speed and mobility, but since it simultaneously produces congestion on a scale never previously seen, it is simple (at least in Elton's fictional account) for political elites to manipulate this and produce a total gridlock of London, in order to justify further road-building.

A classic critique of this is in Ivan Illich's *Energy and Equity* (1974). Illich calculated that:

> the typical American male devotes more than 1,600 hours a year to his car. He sits in it while it goes and while it stands idling. He parks it and searches for it. He earns the money to put down on it and to meet the monthly instalments. He works to pay for petrol, tolls, insurance, taxes, and tickets. He spends four of his sixteen waking hours on the road or gathering his resources for it (Illich 1974: 30).

On this basis, Wolf suggests that speed is a myth, not in the sense of an organizing social motif, but as something false and to be debunked. He calculates that taking all these factors which Illich discusses, the 'real' speed of car transport averages at approximately 20 km/h, about the same speed travelled by a 'very fit cyclist' (1996: 187). The modernization of which the car was the ultimate expression is therefore deeply embedded in individual identities. However, the way this is embedded in those identities seems to me not best expressed in Gorz's terms. For Gorz (1980) ideology is used in the sense of something which masks reality. All that is required is to unmask this ideological cloak and social change becomes possible. Similarly, Wolf (1996) and Gartman (1994) both treat the way that cars are embedded in identities as primarily a psychological reaction to alienation in the capitalist labour process; a means by which capitalism displaces the alienation it inevitably produces. The car for Wolf is then a 'substitute satisfaction' (1996: 192), or for Gartman, an '*ersatz* satisfaction' for the degradation of work under Fordist mass production (1994: 12). But the notion of false consciousness which underlies these interpretations is deeply problematic. While not wishing to dispute the 'facts' they present (Gorz's argument about the impossibility of everyone owning a car, Wolf's concerning the myth of speed, both drawing on Illich), it seems to me more useful to take seriously the reality and depth of the identities produced around the car. They should not be dismissed as false consciousness, but should be understood as deeply embedded. As Gartman argues, 'rather than see the needs appealed to by consumer ads as false needs engineered by the culture industry, my formulation conceptualizes them as true needs for self-determining activity channelled by class conflict into the only path compatible with capital – commodity consumption' (1994: 11). However, Gartman still relies on viewing mass consumption, notably of the car, as a displacement from the alienation produced by capitalist mass production.

Berman again seems to understand the relationship and contradiction here better: 'This strategy [of the promoters of the "expressway world"] was effective because, in fact, the vast majority of modern men and women do not want to resist modernity: they feel its excitement and believe in its promise, even when they find themselves in its way' (1982: 313).

As Berman quotes Allen Ginsberg, the forms of identity produced in this process are not false, imposed purely to meet someone else's interests; they are more like 'Moloch, who entered my soul early' (Berman 1982: 291). The car is partly constitutive of who it is to be us, not something externally imposed on us through deceit. Understanding the relationship in terms of notions of the cyborg developed in general by Haraway (1991), and invoked in relation to the car by Thrift (1996) or Luke (1996), for example, gets closer to the complexities of the relationship between human identities and the machines through which such identities are shaped. The transformation of those identities cannot be achieved by simply showing their 'false' nature. This takes us to actual nature.

AUTOMOBILITY AND ECOLOGICAL CONTRADICTIONS OF CAPITALISM

The environmental effects of the dominance of the car are widely documented, and relatively easy to understand and demonstrate (for useful sources see those cited in Paterson 2007: 36–40). They include, just to name the most obvious and extensive, the role of widespread car use in generating climate change, acid rain, urban pollution, lead pollution, and water pollution from run-off from road surfaces. Each of these problems generates a number of direct effects, from direct health effects to widespread ecological change. They also include the role of the car in generating depletion of non-renewable resources such as oil, iron and various rare metals. This latter is of course the flipside of why automobiles have been so economically successful.

When treated cumulatively, these problems point to the crucial role of automobility in the current unsustainable course of the global political economy. Any one of them individually, we might imagine fixing with some technology or other, but when combined it becomes clearer that the problem is the system as a whole. A transition to a mobility regime not premised on the car becomes the objective rather than piecemeal adaptation of the car system to deal with particular problems.

But the problems generated by automobility are not only environmental in the narrow sense. They are broadly socio-ecological in character. That is, many of the environmental effects of cars are intertwined with social impacts of automobility that also serve to reproduce the regime of automobility in contradictory ways. So for example, to take the way that the car has produced large-scale urban spatial change, this is associated with a whole set of health impacts that are both because of the paradoxical immobility of individuals in car-dominated environments and because of the pollution generated by the large number of cars being driven daily. Commentators on this dynamic refer to low-density urban environments, which have engendered automobile dependence, as 'obesogenic' (e.g. Lake and Townshend 2006). Automobile dependence means that levels of exercise embedded in daily life are so low, and in many instances the quality of nutrition is so poor (for those living in what are known as 'food deserts', or parts of cities with very little access to good quality grocery stores), that ideal conditions are produced for the generation of systemic obesity. These problems then intertwine with other health-related impacts of automobility such as urban air pollution, which aggravate problems felt by those living in such obesogenic environments.

The other aspect of the socio-ecological character of automobility is in the way that it implicates daily life in the systemic production of environmental degradation. This occurs across the range of activities involved in automobility, both production and consumption, as well as a range of other related activities (investment, government regulation, advertising, and so on). Precisely because automobility was tremendously successful in integrating individual subjectivities with capitalist development, many of the activities that generate environmental degradation are simultaneously those that give enormous meaning to daily life for large numbers of people. The ecological problem of automobility is therefore not simply one of the power of large corporations and the capture of the state by the interests of those companies, but a much more complicated one where the resistance to ecological action is as likely to come from union members, car drivers, and many of those who depend on cars even if they don't drive.

Political economy approaches to environmental destruction tend still to couch their arguments in productivist terms. That is, they start either with some version of James O'Connor's notion of the 'second contradiction of capital' (O'Connor 1991), with Alan Schnaiberg's notion of the 'treadmill of production' (Schnaiberg et al. 2002), or perhaps with the notion of the 'metabolic rift' (Foster 1999; Clark and York 2005; Introduction, this volume). The first of these understands ecological problems as a result of the contradiction between the combined relations and forces of production and the conditions of production, which refer to the background conditions of ecological reproduction that all societies depend on (reasonably stable climate, access to fresh water, clean air and the like, and access to a range of resources on which economic activity depends). The second refers to capitalist development as a 'treadmill', in other words a self-reproducing system which inexorably produces environmental degradation – this is a sort of Marxist version of Weber's iron cage. The third refers to the key transformation that industrial capitalism effected from the early nineteenth century onwards, which is a shift from cyclical flows (of soil, water, energy) to linear flows. To take the example of energy, it means shifting from renewable sources, both from water and wind as well as from animals (human and others), to non-renewable resources, specifically fossil fuels. This 'metabolic rift' is precisely what has enabled capitalist development to produce such spectacular growth in the last two centuries, but at the same time to produce the profound contradiction between that growth and the reproduction of basic systems on which human and other life depends.

None of these approaches adequately enables us to grasp the difference between the politics of ecological problems and those of the typical problems for which Marx and other classical political economists developed their theories. Specifically, they tend to assume or assert that class-centric analyses will be adequate for thinking through how we might overcome these sorts of contradictions. Thinking briefly about the politics of automobility and its relationship to ecological degradation should be instructive about the limits of this analysis. Even while class is clearly going to be important to shaping various aspects of this politics, there are clearly areas where organized labour and individual workers exist themselves in a contradictory relationship to the pursuit of sustainability. They have not only narrow economic interests but much more deeply embedded identities both as workers involved in car manufacturing and production, with a long heritage of being relatively privileged within the world of manufacturing work and regarded as leaders within the trade union movement, but also in large parts of the world as consumers of automobiles themselves, as deeply embedded in the world of compulsory automobility as anybody else. It is thus no surprise that for example on questions of environmental change, unions like the United Auto Workers in the US have very frequently taken the same position as their employers.

ECOLOGY AND THE POLITICS OF PRODUCTION AND PRODUCTIVISM

Automobility thus points to a complicated relationship between environmental politics and a politics of production. From an ecological point of view it is reasonably clear that the pursuit of sustainability and global social justice entails a radically reorganizing production away from automobiles. But large parts of the global labour movement regard threats to the auto sector as precisely part of the neoliberal onslaught on union power and workers' prosperity. Attempts to chart a path away from car dependence to deal with environmental problems can be interpreted as such a threat. While there are many attempts on both sides of this apparent divide to build alliances and work more creatively (see for example Nugent 2011), the underlying contradictions nevertheless still exist (e.g. Hrynyshyn and Ross 2011).

Correspondingly, what we see in many places is an attempt to reframe environmental policy and politics precisely in terms of a transformation of those sectors of the economy that will become central. If we turn to climate change specifically, where the transformational logic is the most obvious since it entails a 'decarbonization' of the global economy, in other words the abandoning of fossil fuels as the principal source of energy for the global economy, we can see a number of places where the issue was framed as one of generating novel sorts of production regime around something other than sectors so dependent on fossil fuels.

One hint of this was contained in the stimulus packages that were developed from the early phase of the financial crisis 2007 onwards. While it is true that these packages certainly contained elements in some countries, notably the United States and Canada, that were really directed to shoring up the car industry's position, many other elements in these packages pointed to an attempt to redirect investment towards new economic sectors that might replace the car industry as key drivers of growth. The *Financial Times* produced data showing that large numbers of countries had significant elements in their stimulus packages that would be regarded as investments in 'green' infrastructure developments (Bernard et al. 2009). Notably, many of the countries with the most significant investments in sectors that might transform the economy away from automobile dependence were in emerging countries without long established car industries. According to the *Financial Times*, South Korea had the highest component of 'green' investment, focused in particular on advanced technologies in public transport, while China also had a very significant environmental component to its package (see also Barbier 2010).

While the stimulus packages were nevertheless rather ambivalent in this regard, since then a whole discourse of 'green growth' and more recently 'global green growth' has emerged as a principal frame to understand responses to environmental problems, notably climate change (see notably the Global Green Growth Institute at www.gggi.org, and Brand and Wissen, this volume). This framework builds on but also goes beyond existing frames within environmental discourse, notably those of sustainable development (e.g. WCED 1987) and ecological modernization (e.g. Mol 1996), by focusing very specifically on strategies that generate growth in sectors that would radically reduce environmental impacts in order to replace the importance of sectors, such as the automobile sector, that have been environmentally so problematic. Green growth thus represents a highly focused strategy for integrating questions of sustainability into the core process of economic planning. Thus it can be understood in political economy terms as an attempted hegemonic project for reframing the interests of capital-in-general in relation to environmental change, and/or an attempt to think through the problem of environmental change as the pursuit of a specific sort of regime of accumulation. It has been integrated into a number of countries' economic strategies, notably in countries that had high environmental components in their stimulus packages (on Korea, for example, see Kang et al. 2012).

The most advanced set of developments that can be interpreted as a key part of this emerging regime (if that is indeed what it might become) are in the demand for carbon markets (see Paterson 2010 for an elaboration of this argument). For a time in the 2000s, these were the fastest-growing financial markets in the world. While the growth in the value of the transactions within carbon markets has slowed during the recession, the volume of trades has continued to grow, and if there have been some setbacks, for example with the 2013 general election in Australia, the policy initiatives that aim to create such markets continue apace, with new markets having recently been established in California, Quebec, some municipalities and one province in China, and set to start in South Korea in 2015.

Carbon markets essentially create a commodification of either rights to emit carbon into the atmosphere or of promises not to emit such carbon. The former refers to emissions trading systems or 'cap and trade' systems, where an authority issues allowances to the actors to be regulated (governments, corporations, etc.). Those actors then have to limit their emissions to the number of allowances that they have within a given time frame, and if they cannot do so must try to buy surplus allowances in the marketplace. The logic is thus that, if there is scarcity in the allowance market, emissions will be reduced by the actors that find it cheapest to do so, who then have an incentive to raise money by selling surplus allowances. But what of course is created is a set of property rights that generate the possibility of all sorts of financial strategies by both the holders of the allowances (who have an asset they can profit from or need to hedge against price volatility), and the range of financial intermediaries who can try to benefit from conducting the transactions that regulated actors feel the need to engage in. So beyond the direct trade in allowances, there is a reasonably well established, if relatively simple, set of derivative instruments (futures, options, swaps, notably).

The second type of carbon market is what is known as an offset market. Here, the commodity is produced by a bureaucratic process that approves the creation of credits on the basis of claims made by developers concerning the emissions that would be reduced by a project (compared to some baseline projection). In this sort of market there is no innate scarcity; value is generated by something that creates demand for the credits. In the main such market, the Clean Development Mechanism (CDM, within the Kyoto Protocol), the demand is generated by the obligations that industrialized countries have to reduce their emissions, and more concretely, by the way that European Union countries enabled private companies regulated under their cap and trade system, the European Union Emissions Trading Scheme (EU ETS), to purchase credits in the CDM and count them against their obligations under the EU ETS. In other offset markets, mostly known under the label of 'voluntary carbon markets', the driver of demand is mostly the search by corporations for 'green PR'.

These markets are widely regarded as highly dangerous and problematic for a number of reasons, notably the injustices they produce and their potential to distract from rather than generate action to reduce emissions (see in particular Lohmann 2006; Reyes and Gilbertson 2010; Newell and Paterson 2010). Nevertheless they have become a dominant part of responses to climate change in many countries, and can be understood precisely as attempts to generate investment in sectors that would benefit from climate policy and to generate patterns of economic growth not dependent directly on fossil fuel extraction. Whether they could become part of an 'ecological regime of accumulation' really depends on whether or not the financialized strategies in fact also generate investment in new, low carbon economic sectors beyond the financial industry. This is an open question.

Finally, we can see this dynamic play at more micro levels. One policy development that is instructive in this regard is the emergence of a feed-in tariff in the electricity system in Ontario, Canada. The provincial government introduced this in 2009 to provide incentives to invest in renewable energy, particularly wind and solar (see Yatchew and Baziliauskas 2011 for a general overview). At one level, they were simply importing policy developed from elsewhere, notably Germany, based on the demonstrated success of that policy in generating investment in renewables. The policy certainly recreated this success, generating applications to install capacity equivalent to 43 per cent of current Ontario generating capacity. But Ontario added a distinct twist to the policy. In January 2010 they signed a $7bn deal with Samsung where Samsung would invest in wind and solar photovoltaic manufacture within Ontario, in return for a guaranteed access to the feed-in tariff benefits (ibid.). Historically, Ontario has been the heartland of car manufacture in the Canadian economy, mostly because of its proximity to the Detroit area, and the Ontario government has engaged intensively in the sort of subsidies to the car industry that will attract investment in high-paying and relatively high-skill jobs. The deal with Samsung can be understood as an extension of this sort of logic to generate similar sorts of jobs in an industry that is growing rapidly (solar photovoltaics are the most rapidly growing source of electricity generation in the world) as opposed to those in relative decline, and articles on the initiative have focused on the job creation and financial benefits as much as the environmental benefits (e.g. Branker and Pearce 2010).

These examples and others can be thought of in terms of regulation theory as attempts to try to imagine some sort of stable regime of growth which has at least some of the features that Fordism-automobility had: a relationship between productivity growth and the means of consumption of those products, a pattern of relations between states, business and organized labour, that could sustain capital accumulation over time (Brand and Wissen, this volume). It is an open question whether any of these could succeed, individually or combined; and then they of course will generate their own contradictions in turn. Those contradictions associated with carbon markets are particularly obvious (Lohmann 2006; Reyes and Gilbertson 2010; Newell and Paterson 2010). But they only illustrate that the task for thinking ecologically about production and political economy will generate provocative questions about the transformation of capitalist production in ways that are far from easy or comfortable.

CONCLUSION

I have tried to show in this chapter how in order to understand the relationship between ecology and production politics, we need to think about not only production itself and the social relations involved, but the relationship between production and consumption and the broad cultures that sustain both. The case of automobility is perhaps an exceptionally good vehicle for exploring such an argument, and the centrality of automobility to the reproduction of twentieth-century capitalism means that the illustration goes to the core of how capitalism and ecological degradation are systemically intertwined. However, in principle such a cultural political economy analysis could be used to explore many economic sectors and their relationship to environment degradation (Paterson 2007; Best and Paterson 2009; for a different account see Jessop 2010; Sum and Jessop 2013). What it provokes is first to think more systemically about what is being produced in the production process and its range of connections to the use of resources, the generation of a range of pollutants, the social exploitation involved in both of those, and to the system of consumption of those products, by individuals, corporations and states. It is by understanding this systemic character of production that we will be able to grasp the nature of the ecological contradictions associated with capitalist development.

24. Risk capitalism, crisis of socialization and loss of civilization[1]

Werner Seppmann

Neoliberal transformation has dramatically changed the social conditions prevailing in the West, and in a remarkably short time at that. The speed with which social contradictions thought to have been overcome are spreading also in countries with a tradition of 'social partnership' would have been inconceivable three decades ago, even for radical critics of capitalism. The downward spiral in the developed capitalist world has reached a point reminiscent of Third World conditions. Unlike the prosperous capitalism of the postwar period, nowadays if someone gets drawn into the vortex of social degradation it is increasingly difficult to find a way out. Even those living above the poverty line cannot rest on their laurels; they too are at constant risk. Minor reasons (an additional child, long-term illness or unemployment of one's partner) suffice to break one's stride.

It took a conservative politician, the long-term Prime Minister of Luxembourg and current President of the European Commission, J.-C. Juncker, to put his finger on what is the heart of the matter when he characterized the neoliberal transformation as a 'process of de-civilization' with far-reaching negative consequences in the social and cultural spheres. One aspect of this regressive development is the disappearance of social mobility – as Juncker also pointed out, he himself would not have been able to go to university if his father, a steelworker, had been unemployed. Today, however, marginalization is increasingly hereditary.

In this chapter I discuss some of the psycho-social effects of the current crisis of socialization (*Vergesellschaftungskrise*), the consequent loss of civilization, and the formation and propagation of a neoliberal consciousness.

EXPLOITATION AND MARGINALIZATION

Forms of capitalism differ in various countries, but all of them display the same basic tendency: broad layers of the population are experiencing

---

[1] This chapter has been translated from the German by Hannes Fellner, Vienna.

declining living standards. Fundamental principles of labour relations and legal social protection are consistently being reversed. This economic decline is accompanied by targeted political reforms contributing to the growing social rift (cf. Butterwegge 2009). As the priority of profit maximization is upheld with brutal consistency, the wage-earning population is subjected to ever-intensifying pressures and forced to adjust psychologically to the new requirements of accumulation. For years now, the income of almost all those dependent on selling their labour power to make a living has been decreasing (Delgado Wise and Martin, this volume); consumption patterns of broad strata of the population have been depressed, from 'bread to acorns' to use Voltaire's phrase. Hard-won occupational and social positions can no longer be regarded as secure and a lot of vital energy goes into the effort of holding on to one's social status. If one does not want to fall back or be weeded out as an employer, one has to strive consistently to achieve ever more and ever better. 'Your rivals never rest!' is the name of the game, and abiding by that rule takes its daily toll on everyone.

The fear of social decline and concern to be excluded from 'social security' has become the signature of the epoch, since 'the terrifying aspect of the system is constantly growing (competitive constraints are intensifying, threat of social decline and exclusion is increasing. . .), whilst the promise [of social status and security] is fading away' (Rosa 2009: 111). Once a career path has been interrupted, workers are forced to accept steadily deteriorating labour conditions and ever-shorter phases of active employment. It becomes more and more apparent that the times of the postwar 'prosperity' and 'economic miracle' were only a special development phase of capitalism and can no longer be viewed as typical. Reforms of existing welfare state regulations, begun in Germany under Social Democratic Chancellor Schröder, are exerting an 'extortionist pressure' (Castel 2000) to force the wage-dependent population into precarious and ever more ruinous employment relationships. Former Vice-Chancellor Joschka Fischer in a press talk in 2004 remarked that the kind of radical changes of labour laws backed by his Green Party normally would 'only be possible to implement in wartime' (cf. Holman, this volume).

The coercive mechanisms driving this social decline 'not only cause poverty by law, but can psychologically be viewed as a way of disfranchisement through law' (Bianchi 2011: 14). The marginalized of today have little in common with traditional misfits. Unlike Parisian *clochards* of old, the new lower class is the product of government policy aimed at enforcing concepts of neoliberal transformation with the intention of redefining the norms of dependent labour (cf. Seppmann 2013a). The sole purpose of this reorganization of the social fabric is the fortification and intensification of a regime of inequality. Clearly class relations were in existence prior to the neoliberal offensive but they now appear more pronounced due to the expanding zones of socio-cultural deprivation. In Germany, a highly unequal distribution regarding opportunities in life has become firmly entrenched. Heinz Steinert accurately labels this 'class politics' because it aims at the 'creation and regulation of inequality which is correlated with the needs of production and the reproduction of capital and labour force' (Steinert 2010: 185).

Resistance to these changes has so far been scant since the intimidating (and ideologically disorienting) social development typically spawns conformist attitudes and behaviour (Seppmann 2011). Thus the creation of a 'precariat' has become 'part of a new form of rule that is based on the permanent condition of uncertainty, with the goal of forcing the employee to accept his/her exploitation' (Bourdieu 1997: 100). These mechanisms are part of comprehensive frameworks of integration into the system that at first glance present a mode of 'silent' adaptation. In reality, however, 'they constitute a truly violent process. . . . It is a process of deformation and forceful adjustment: physiologically, psychologically, mentally. It is a process of de-subjectivization that ends with the destruction of the human body, soul and reason' (Metscher 2009: 40). Although the French social scientist Robert Castel is correct in seeing these tendencies of regression as a fundamental part of today's industrial system, his designation of 'unemployment and precarization of labour' as 'current dynamics of modernization' (Castel 2000: 350) by its neutral language underestimates the violence involved.

More and more marginalized people have abandoned the hope of escaping this situation. A contemporary study on Germany (Neugebauer 2007) was met with surprise from the general public which was largely unaware of this stratum of the population (about 8 per cent) that comprises long-term unemployed, people dependent on social welfare, people working in precarious jobs, 'working poor', failed self-employed persons, relatively young people who are unable to achieve integration into the working system, chronically ill persons, and persons with psychological problems. However, the structural stabilization of unequal opportunities in life is but one aspect of socio-political decline, and not even the most severe one. It is also accompanied by a range of phenomena signalling decay in the sphere of everyday culture. So the marginalized not only suffer from poverty, but also no longer see any chance of 'reintegration' into the working world's 'normal zones'. This often causes them to become mentally unstable and their lack of perspective is characterized by a paralysing resignation to fate.

All this reflects the fact that precarization not only means a daily struggle on the breadline, but it also entails the loss of personal stability and the increasing erosion of self-respect. With their consequences for psychological stability and life satisfaction, unemployment and marginalization represent an acute form of structural violence. Because of unemployment people suffer from 'massive mental instability, the threat of losing their personhood and identity, enormous self-doubts, fear of humiliation, feelings of guilt, fear of failure, and depression' (Bianchi 2011: 13). Decay of everyday culture is connected with these crises and processes of psycho-social destabilization: in extreme cases it leads to complete self-abandonment, as well as the neglect of children. It is also worth noting that marginalized people rapidly lose the socially acquired abilities to handle time in an organized fashion and to motivate themselves. Since the outsiders lack the structure of gainful employment in their everyday life they are confronted with 'a dangerous void' (Dahrendorf 2000: 1065). Under these circumstances material deprivation goes hand in hand with mental disorientation and psychological regression since they are usually connected with the exclusion from vital spheres of social life (cf. Wacker 1976). Let me now investigate the consequences of this regression in greater depth.

CRISIS OF SOCIALIZATION AND LOSS OF CIVILIZATION

Social marginalization is frequently accompanied by forms of intellectual and emotional impoverishment. Since the marginalized are constantly concerned with the question of how to go on, their life is characterized by the permanent feeling of anxiety. This anxiety 'permeates people's everyday life in the same way as deregulation seizes life's foundations and the bastions of civilization are falling' (Bauman 2008: 29).

The social afflictions, mental destabilization and the ubiquity of existential anxiety leave their marks, especially on children: they lag behind in their mental, emotional and physical development. Fine and gross motor skills show deficits, power of speech and everyday orientational knowledge are fragmented. Children growing up in social distress attract attention in gym classes at school because they have problems exercising for more than a couple of minutes and coordinating the moves of their bodies. However, 'it is not only exercise that these pupils are lacking. Rarely does anyone read to them, take them outside to play or make music with them. Furthermore, the teachers state that there is not much conversation in their pupils' homes – much less concerning emotions' (Friedrichs et al. 2009: 128). In Germany, 'middle class children have a lexicon twice the size of children coming from lower class families' (Kloepfer 2008: 171).

The social lethargy of their environment has a negative impact on the children and so their perceptual horizon deteriorates massively. It means in effect that their life is surrounded by invisible walls. The widespread withdrawal of unemployed adults into their narrowest social environment is paralleled by geographical immobility and, in children, loss of curiosity towards the world. People who went through phases of poverty during their childhood suffer more often and more intensively from illness in their later lives than people who grew up under secure circumstances.

The experience of marginalization not only shapes the mental states of children and adolescents by 'consolidating' resignation and deep-rooted insecurity. It also has long-term consequences right up to impact on neuronal structures (cf. Bauer 2011). The principles of this *negative socialization* are damaging to the child's psyche:

> At the time of pre-adolescence this system is particularly vulnerable since the brain is being transformed for the requirements of becoming an adult. Billions of neurons are dying off (pruning) and billions of differentiated neurons are developing. For kids whose pruning-phase is disturbed by chronic stress factors this means that the brain will not acquire the optimal state of differentiation for the relevant neurons necessary for higher cognitive functions and emotional performance. This can lead to an imbalance of the subcortical mesolimbic dopamine and serotonin systems with high risk of depression, schizophrenia, addiction and personality disorder. The maturation of the aforementioned functions is crucial for the development of ego functions, the social self, sexuality, autonomy and emancipation from one's family' (Wiebel and Pilenko 2011: 66).

The development potential for personality traits such as self-esteem and self-confidence, which are important for the formation of a self-determining conduct of life, are being restricted. A person crippled by resignation and beset with self-doubts will barely be able to show initiative, let alone dissent and nonconformity. Since self-esteem is low in persons experiencing marginalization they lack the basis for taking control of their life and actively putting up a fight against their exclusion.

These consequences of the social divide and the increasing social insecurity illustrate how deeply they are connected with symptoms of civilizational decay (cf. Berman 2000). The reason for this is not only that poverty evokes fatalism and resignation and frequently is accompanied by the aforementioned tendencies of mental and emotional regression (cf. Lewis 1961), but also the fact that as a consequence of these, socio-cultural destabilization has become intensified in the same way as the mechanism of societal stabilization has become suspended.

SELF-DAMAGING COMPULSION AND THE DYNAMICS OF CIVILIZATIONAL DECAY

The aforementioned tendencies of civilizational regression are but one aspect of a *dynamic of social self-destruction* by which the current capitalist system may be characterized. Not only does it destroy nature and the worker, as Marx argued, but also it demolishes its own social and cultural bases of existence. Current risk capitalism reproduces itself in a mode of self-destruction which has its cause in the growing erosion of personal identity. Capital increasingly turns people into objects and damages their subjectivity in its drive for ever better conditions of realizing profits. This undermines society's ability of self-stabilization. Socio-cultural cohesion diminishes to the point of decay since the rhythms of private life are more and more subjugated to the requirements of the economic sphere. The dominance of purely economic considerations also destroys identity-establishing contexts of life experience that are traditionally responsible for providing personal stability and social competence.

These processes of *de-socialization* (the flipside of which is constituted by *de-solidarization*) are essentially characterized by the fact that 'current wage labour is structured according to the principle that only the ones without concrete responsibilities towards others are flexible and mobile enough to dedicate themselves fully to the strategies of their companies' (Nowack 2007: 63). However, it is not only performance and mobility that are called for in professional life, but also unscrupulousness and ruthlessness – towards others, but also towards oneself. Here structural a-sociality is combined with destructive compulsions leading to emotional and mental deficits and self-damaging behaviour (cf. Ehrenberg 2009), in addition to an antisocial disposition.

The spread of depression and the rising intake of antidepressants, like the increase of alcohol, drug and pill addiction, are best understood as the flipside of the development of a society under capitalist conditions in which self-objectification and instrumentalization have become the rule. The intensification of exploitation in the name of neoliberalism not only urges the wage-dependent population to push their performance to the limit, but more and more forces them to go beyond it. There have been waves of suicides among employees of French companies resulting from systematic excessive demand. Death by overwork is a frequent phenomenon in Japan (cf. Ihara, this volume). Heart attack due to stress more generally has become one of the most common causes of death in the 'developed industrial societies'. The long lines of people seeking help from a psychotherapist because they are overwhelmed by the pressure to perform and burned out by their work, are a symptom of an exploitation that increasingly impairs the mental capacities of the employees – to the point of disintegration of their personal stability.

Even if the common diagnosis of 'burnout' is a makeshift solution; the problems it is reflecting cannot be overlooked, especially since this disorder is more severe than the fashionable expression 'burnout' is able to convey (cf. Neckel and Wagner 2013). More and more physicians believe that the feeling of being burned out is in reality a symptom of depression.

The increasing pressure on those still integrated into the world of work (with its destructive consequences for mental stability and physical health) corresponds to processes of personal destabilization and emotional burden among the unemployed and people who have completely dropped out of working life. According to one psychiatrist there are two major groups of patients she has to take care of: 'The ones who are unable to stand the stress of their jobs and the ones who do not have a job anymore' (Steinrücke 2005: 198). The need for consultation among the latter is not surprising given the fact that everyday life, for people who have been found dysfunctional for the employment system, 'is characterized by discrimination, exclusion, lack of participation, isolation, and the lack of hope and perspective. A lot of people give up and become depressive because of that. The numbers of people suffering from depression are increasing year by year' (Ossendorff 2011: 135).

The growing incidence of mental disorders and other psychological malfunctions is an aspect of the advancing pathologization of society due to the destruction of human resources and cultural 'commodities' by risk capitalism. This means that it is almost impossible for the individual to get by without suffering mental defects. Living a life deprived of emotional engagement as a consequence of being weighed down by insecurity and permanent exertion, stress and exhaustion, makes it increasingly difficult not to slip into a condition of chronic anxiety.

The regressive transformations and their psychological manifestations are consequences of the fact that the negative developments of working and living conditions increasingly force individuals to optimize (and discipline) themselves (cf. Moore, this volume). This frequently results in a deformation of the personality due to the social-functional character of self-optimization and disciplining at the expense of emotional balance. This is the reason why 'this development is met with increasing approval since what is neurotic in the individual might be normal in capitalism and desirable for the working of society' (Braverman 1977: 78); ruthlessness and absolute will to succeed, as well as willingness to accept abstract principles instead of concrete vital interests, would be examples of this.

The instrumentalization of the self leads to the burdensome, but not easily understandable feeling of not having accomplished enough despite all efforts. This can be interpreted as the operation of a 'bad infinity' (*schlechte Unendlichkeit*) in the sense of Hegel. It prevents one from reaching one's goal since in every domain of the so-called 'modern world of work' there is an absence of repose, there are no pauses – whilst what is considered to be a superior performance today will be the required, normal performance level tomorrow.

The universality of this systematic pressure has the consequence that the dissolution of boundaries in the sphere of economy and the ambivalences in everyday working life are corresponding to feelings of powerlessness and anxiety. These in turn lead to the destruction of mental capabilities of dissent and the decay of mechanisms for self-stabilization.

> The tectonic quakes that have been caused by the processes of modernization and globalization not only shake the backbone of society, but also the traditional forms of social integration, sending shock waves down to the innards of man. More and more people are forced to develop fragmentary identities due to the imperative of 'flexible capitalism' not to be too attached to anything and to promptly react to the shifting tides of the market (Eisenberg 2002: 32).

The fragmentation and instrumentalization of subjects, then, lead to processes of decay. These are in turn dangerous for the cohesion of the whole system since 'the current crisis of erosion has the effect that masses of people are in danger of reverting to simple mechanisms of mental regulation' (Eisenberg 2002: 32). Via different intermediate steps (which I have analysed elsewhere, cf. Seppmann 2012), these processes entail socio-dysfunctional consequences for individuals whilst at the level of society as a whole they are symptoms and causes of a general barbarization and increasing loss of civilization. The tendencies of regression are accompanied by the advance of irrationalism as a functional element of late-capitalist societies. But irrationalism should not be seen as a deviation from a prior social norm; it goes to the heart of the social process itself. This can be illustrated by the fact that people who are integrated into the employment system are forced to work ever harder and longer, while a considerable part of the unemployed workforce is sentenced to involuntary 'idleness' – an absurdity by any standard.

It is this exclusion of a major group of society from the elementary social reproduction cycle that causes the aforementioned anti-civilizational effects, effects that have consequences for society as a whole. This is because 'the outsourcing, detachment, division and fragmentation which constitutes and nourishes the lower ranks of society's broken and destroyed biographies . . . rapidly penetrate the centre of society and are able to challenge the cohesion of its totality' (Negt 2001: 255). Not only are the victims of the crisis destabilized mentally; their social consciousness is also narrowing. In these circumstances irrationality is around the corner, not least in the form of a rise of right-wing extremism. The victims of the crisis become susceptible to politically irrational interpretive systems like neo-fascism, racism and nationalism (cf. Bathke and Hoffstadt 2013).

The everyday praxis of capitalist life, with its contradictions, paradoxes, humiliations and threats, directly contradicts the normative commitments of bourgeois society, which once upon a time championed the cause of general welfare and the rationality of social conditions. It also produces a level of socio-cultural antagonism with enormous destructive power, since given the particular structure of economy and society prevailing today, individual gain can only be achieved in ways detrimental to others. Financial speculation or the exorbitantly profitable hedge-fund strategies of buying and asset-stripping companies, with their attendant destruction of jobs, are only the more conspicuous examples of the economic self-negation of current capitalism. Strategies for social action often (and inevitably) lead to antisocial consequences due to the permanent pressure to succeed, which entails a brutalization of behaviour and the barbarization of cultural standards. The aggressive juvenile who beats up his classmate lying on the ground is only the mirror image of the 'successful' manager who earned a tremendous bonus for destroying a particularly large number of jobs. 'Cynicism and amorality of the big predators trickle down from the top of the [social] pyramid to its lower levels' (Ziegler 2003: 85).

The prevalent principles of socialization prove to be less and less appropriate for the current problems of society. They are nevertheless being kept on life support even if they exacerbate existing contradictions. The inability to adequately react to the existential problems of society sustains a vicious circle of alienation and self-alienation that affects both those who rule and those being ruled in the developed capitalist societies. Since the struggle for existence is absorbing more and more intellectual and mental power, the socio-cultural ability to shape stable social relations (*Gestaltungskompetenz*) cannot emerge to the extent needed. There is a growing normative and emotional void because ever-more intellectual and mental energy is needed to block or downplay the elementary contradictions of society (cf. Seppmann 2013b), or in the phrase of Hölderlin, 'What does the shipwreck of the world concern me, I know nothing but my blessed island'.

Repression and ignorance have become key principles of existence and survival for the ruling bloc, since its conceptual horizon is primarily characterized by egoistic (profit) interests. It is shackled to it because of the foreboding that any substantive strategy towards solving the problems of society might challenge the system as a whole. Thus the ruling bloc is condemned to a paralysing inability to think beyond day-to-day business and develop any kind of longer-term perspective. 'One is unable to think about the whole because one becomes desperate thinking about changing it' (Adorno 1972: 52).

Because the option of change is taboo, the tendency of societal decay gains momentum and leads to an erosion crisis. If the possible and necessary change is postponed, the fundamentals of civilization disintegrate and the totality of society becomes destabilized. The processes of disintegration are usually not immediately recognized; they work like an 'odorless gas' (Packer 2011) but as a result acquire only greater destructiveness. One of the most conspicuous consequences of the virulent irrationalization is people going berserk, which occurs with increasing frequency. These have to be viewed as manifestations of civilizational regression, as symptoms of the decay of mechanisms of social stabilization which have been damaged by the tearing apart of the fabric of society. There is an obvious correlation between the occurrence of people running amok and the implementation of neoliberal organizational principles in the economy, culture and society (cf. Milzner 2010). Living in conditions which undermine one's identity thus leads one to take revenge on a society which as a result becomes subject to self-destruction.

> Not unlike a mental patient unveiling the truth about his family . . . the person running amok reveals the repressed truth about current society. Far from being merely the expression of adjustment processes that have gone astray at the individual level – which certainly is also the case – running amok testifies to the indifference and coldness that has been implemented in practice by the deregulators and modernizers as the prevalent social climate (Eisenberg 2000: 98).

People in this state are trying to call attention to themselves by desperate means; their acts of violence are aimed at showing that they still exist. The analysis of dozens of outbreaks of random violence in Germany in the last couple of years reveals remarkable similarities: the perpetrators grew up in bourgeois households in an atmosphere of emotional coldness and silence. Since they were not able to fulfil the requirements of life (including the requirements of education) they suffer from fear of failure and are struggling with the feeling of a lack of recognition and lack of perspective. They react to this mental pressure with fantasies of violence and increasing fits of rage and aggression. In the retreat from a world that supposedly poses a threat to them, they often find solace behind the computer screen, with violent games taking up more and more of their time. Next they begin to distance themselves from their social environment, which only makes it easier to combine their virtual (computer) world and their fantasies of violence and murder. Almost all of those who ran amok had a predilection for weapons because possession gives them the feeling of power and the ability to act – feelings they are unable to marshal otherwise.

Whilst much more can be said about this than there is space for here, we are obviously dealing with a glaring deficit in the development of socialization. At first sight it might seem this is a matter of 'normal' problems of socialization among male juveniles, and if viewed in isolation they most certainly are. However, within a neoliberal system of pressure and deformation (especially if these occur in mutually escalating combinations) what would otherwise be regular if often already extreme features of adjustment to adulthood can lead to dramatic consequences. For even though incidents of people running amok mainly involve juveniles, it also happens to adults. International comparisons reveal that humiliation in the workplace and unemployment are the main causes for such destructive behaviour in adults. And so we come full circle from the analysis of socio-political regression and everyday marginalization which have become characteristic of neoliberal 'enhanced' living conditions in the last decades.

The everyday person living in a supposedly 'second modernity' as propagated by Giddens, Beck and others (Beck et al. 1996) no longer has the competence (which arises from the full constitution of the self) promised to her/him by the mythology of individualization, because s/he is divided and fragmented in his/her personality structure, just as the social environment surrounding her/him is schizophrenic. These people lack the reliable tools for social orientation which are the necessary prerequisites for a self-determined way of life. Thus they are chased and controlled by objective impositions, facing a hostile society to which in their mind they are only able to react with powerless resignation or desperate anger.

This takes us to the question of how power is exerted on this fragmented society from the outside, as dominant ideology.

NEOLIBERAL CONSCIOUSNESS AS MONOCULTURE

The decades in which neoliberalism became hegemonic appear as a classic phase of restoration. The edifice of postwar social security constructed over a century and consolidated at a time of relative strength of a variety of progressive forces right after World War II, was steadily dismantled again, workers' rights were revised and new, rigorous conditions of exploitation introduced. However, the protagonists of neoliberalism also understood the necessity of developing an active programme of shaping popular consciousness to accompany the social restructuring and make it palatable, neutralizing any resistance in the process. They have taken to heart the lesson of historical experience that the establishment of comprehensive social conditions in which capital operates successfully 'is not possible without a dedicated [popular] mobilisation' (Kurz 1999: 539).

Thus the neoliberal restructuring was accompanied by a media offensive aimed at undermining resistance and sidelining all serious intellectual reflection. For a protracted period even a timid questioning of the keywords of neoliberal propaganda was treated as if a dangerous taboo was being violated. Instead a truncated way of thinking from which the obvious reservations were removed by declaring them illegitimate, accompanied the tearing down of social security and the institutionalization of the unrelenting pressure to perform, with the crippling physical and mental consequences referred to above. 'Privatization', 'flexibilization' and 'international competitiveness' were presented as universally valid; 'deregulation' and 'individual responsibility' likewise. Thus the isolation of the 'superfluous' and the reduction of the level of participation of the majority of the population were legitimated by introducing a vocabulary in which there was no meaning left to them. The entire programme was transmitted without restraint, without even the veneer of critical distance by the media, as if it concerned not rational consideration but articles of faith.

In a climate in which references to solidarity and equal opportunities, or just to rudimentary forms of justice and social responsibility, were being denounced as expressions of stupidity and political adventurism, it became effectively impossible for contrary positions to reach the public sphere any longer. Even the slightest attempt at serious social stocktaking was made suspect. Thus the insight that a policy in the interest of the well-off was in the general interest was disseminated to the population at large. That society had to be geared to international competitiveness and required the mobilization of the population as if for economic warfare, was presented as the overriding challenge of the epoch. This war would only be won, and won soonest, if

> the nation understands itself as a capitalist enterprise: hierarchically structured, dedicated to economic goals, subdivided into profit-making centres, functioning smoothly and efficiently, led along authoritarian lines, with core and auxiliary personnel, limited co-determination rights, and loyal circles of innovation, production and quality (Hirsch 1995: 109).

Consent was not just organized by exploiting the objective insecurity of people, but also by rolling out an equally one-dimensional and corrupt 'scholarly expertise'. Thus, with only few exceptions, politics, scholarship and the media began to function as PR agencies of capital, displaying a historically unparalleled unanimity in the process. The notion of enforced conformity (German *Gleichschaltung*) captures the process best

(Schimmeck 2010). Even the *critique* of power slipped into a posture that had the effect of closing off an analysis of how the process of propagating a neoliberal consciousness is connected with the intensification of exploitation and marginalization by capital.

There is no doubt that power and rule in late-capitalist societies are being perpetuated across various levels and intermediations through 'micro-practices' situated in the everyday structures of social relations (Foucault 1992: 38). Yet it is not enough to remain focused on the routine practices via which the consciousness industry performs its functions in the reproduction of rule. It is necessary to enlarge this with a concrete critique of power and deal with economic relations of dominance and dispositional power over the means of production. This cannot be achieved if the *forms* in which power appears in daily life are understood as the basis of power. Such a stylized representation would be inadequate to understanding its reproduction. Narrowing the perspective in this way entails the obfuscation of the conditions under which the system of power is constituted in the first place, just as it removes from view the agency involved in the process. Yet this is just what Foucault demands explicitly: when investigating power, we must avoid (this is his express instruction) 'identifying definite institutions, groups, classes, or elites as its bearers' (Foucault 2005: 245). But confining oneself to the mediation of power and not penetrating its social foundations leaves one with an incomplete picture in which the integral reality of power remains hidden behind the separate episodes of its imposition and reproduction.

In this reductionist cosmos of thought there is no place for the actual processes of rule, which express themselves in the hegemonic strategies of capital. Even less will there be a recognition of their destructive, socially deforming structural power, as discussed above. In fact we are looking at a pseudo-philosophy which, starting from a particular 'epistemological and ethical cowardice, seeks refuge in facile resignation' (Saña 1997: 99). By ruling out the 'demystification of ideologically distorted systems of opinion' (Fraser 1994: 32) as a valid strategy of investigation, we merely perpetuate an obvious reductionism, since one of the conditions of a dialectical reflection on reality concerns the critique of ideology and the political positions associated with it. Thus the entire tradition of critical social theory, including Marx's critique of political economy, ends up on the scrapheap of the history of thought. Those who intellectually follow Foucault will suffer the fate of the dissident in Orwell's *1984*, who joins a subversive group in the hope of giving his desire to resist a concrete form. However, the people he teams up with have already become influenced by the ruling thought long ago. Their 'discourses' are organized in such a way as to lead the new arrival back into the system without realizing it. The group's language seems radical enough, and their posture rebellious. But that is just what is needed to achieve conformity in the end; its dissent remains a façade and only serves to hide the fundamental compliance.

> Even the promising announcement of Foucault to investigate the imbrication of techniques of rule and techniques of the self with the help of the concept of 'governmentality' . . . is not fulfilled. Since neither Foucault himself nor governmentality studies. . . take seriously the distinctions between rule and power, socialization through others or by oneself, the neoliberal action rhetoric of the management literature is replicated by empathy and duplicated in theory (Rehmann 2008: 19).

AN IDEOLOGY BEYOND ITS EXPIRY DATE?

The ideological offensive that accompanied the introduction of neoliberalism might still be explained from a growing concern among the protagonists of the capitalist order about the loss of economic vitality in the late 1970s and 1980s and from the conviction that the welfare state had to be restructured to meet a perceived international competition. However, with the consolidation of neoliberalism and the growing evidence of its socially destructive consequences, the situation has changed fundamentally. Even after the neoliberal articles of faith and conceptual frameworks had already lost the semblance of plausibility, they were stubbornly adhered to, and increasingly, the ideological clichés peddled by the media and propagandistic scholarly 'expertise' were replaced by 'selective truth', if not actual lies.

A ruling ideology in the sense of distorted thinking which fails to account for reality or does so incompletely, necessarily involves false consciousness. Only thus are people enabled to function in antagonistic relations. Because alienated thought is correlated to alienated relations, the subjects can accommodate to their daily life only if there is a consistency in lived and thought experience. This also applies to the messages of professional ideologues in the media and the scientific-bureaucratic complex. They reproduce distorted mental content, because the social relations that bring it about are being accepted unquestionably. Neither should we underrate the pressure to conform that these ideologues must assimilate if they want to avoid seeing their institutional positions deteriorate. Given their social and ideological preparation, they will normally believe what they say: whoever pursues a career as an economist will know that one must reproduce what has been learned, and thus for instance ignore the value-creating role of labour; as a consequence 'exploitation' will appear as a demagogic concept that can be dismissed. The 'serious' economist will view, counterfactually but consistently, every human action as an expression of abstract self-interested rationality; egoism as a fundamental determinant of human existence. In the media world too, as a rule only those who have interiorized the dominant outlook functional for existing power, will be able to establish themselves (Bourdieu 1977).

Yet once reality no longer corresponds in any sense to the prevalent conceptual grid, as is already the case for the main theses of neoliberal ideology, the limits of self-delusion will become apparent. This is the situation where the 'subjective lie', as Ernst Bloch has called it, mutates into the 'objective lie' in order to master the otherwise unbridgeable contradictions through 'interpretation' and to be able to make counterfactual statements concerning socio-economic matters. When that becomes the rule, it expresses 'especially strong signs of decay' (Bloch 1980: 67). The lie under these circumstances becomes a constant and develops its own language through the use of which images of reality become systematically distorted, as when for instance the destruction of systems of social security is being presented as 'stabilization', or when militarily supported hegemonic strategies are explained as 'peace missions' (Losurdo 2011). These linguistic inversions are 'acts of intentional disinformation' that become part of what Thomas Metscher calls the 'compulsion towards extensive ideological reproduction'. They are

> part of a system of conscious manipulation that is produced by imperialist society in order to reproduce its rule. The unprecedented force and latent dynamics of its inner contradictions force this society to develop strategies of manipulative integration which enlarge and simultaneously cover . . . the economic, social and cultural mechanism of integration – or perish (Metscher 2009: 49).

Meanwhile those affected by neoliberal restructuring strategies, including the supporting 'scientific expertise' propagated by the media apparatus, do not readily abjure the neoliberal gospel. Socially insecure and largely cut off from alternative outlooks, many victims of the crisis (if only to give it one last chance) are paradoxically willing to lend credence to the neoliberal promises that 'reforms' will protect their pensions or that by lowering social security expenditure, rising corporate profits will make jobs secure once again. Hence wage-dependent workers are ready to accept concepts from which any attempt to hide that they are directed against the interests of the majority of the population, has been dropped. Compounding the distorting psychological effects of over-exploitation and marginalization discussed earlier in this chapter, a neoliberal consciousness organized around counterfactual quasi-'truths' is actively disseminated among the population at large. It is as if the ruling bloc has in mind Voltaire's ironic comment that just as cattle-drivers prefer the herd to be passive, the rulers have an interest in keeping the people ignorant.

In the early modern age, social degradation on the basis of lies and deceit also preceded the German Peasant Wars. Pressure on the peasants was being intensified, economic crisis and hardship was invoked to bring down the legal and social status of the weak, and simultaneously an attempt was made to justify the entire process as the expression of 'God's will'. What today is the doubtful expertise of economic competence and its misleading claims that breaking down social security will be the precondition of new welfare ('rising corporate profits secure jobs'), in the late Middle Ages was the fictitious legal document used by the nobility and the clergy. By invoking 'old charters' that had been falsified, the tribute imposed on the peasants was increased and their legal status downgraded. Even then, 'privatization' already played a big role in the form of changing common property into lordly possessions. Just as in the late fifteenth century the manipulation of legal documents served to downscale peasants to sharecroppers and sharecroppers to serfs, today the permanently employed skilled worker is being made redundant to be employed again as a temporary labourer, under qualitatively worse conditions.

For all the similarities, the one that perhaps is most relevant today is the time that it took for the peasants to begin to contest and resist the social degradation imposed on them. This happened only after they had begun to see through the lies and machinations of the lords, which they hitherto had accepted under the influence of the theological auxiliaries of the landowners. This demonstrates that social resistance needs a period of incubation, just as the spirit of revolt will depend on a jolt to become a reality. What is needed is the questioning of the old thinking and a steadily growing radicalization of the collective mood if a real will to resist is to come about. Fury, as it is certainly in evidence today, is not sufficient because it mostly feeds on desperation. Even so its existence need not be a drawback: as Pope Gregory, later named 'the Great', formulated it in the seventh century, 'the mind can withstand evil with greater force, if anger sustains it'.

25. Servicing the world: women, transnational migration and sex work in a neoliberal era

Christine B.N. Chin

In this chapter, I examine the relationship between women, transnational migration and sex work. My analysis demonstrates why and how this relationship is directly relevant to the study of International Political Economy (IPE), as it also sustains some of the major structures and processes characterizing neoliberal globalization.

For the past three decades or so, feminist scholars have explicitly and implicitly challenged the marginalization of gender in IPE. Two of the most salient research trajectories focus respectively on the feminization of labour in transnational production, and a mutually dependent relationship between transnational production and reproduction. Both, importantly, incorporate and highlight women's internal and cross-border migrations, for example, from women's urban in-migration for factory work (see, for example, Ong 1987; Wolf 1992; Wright 2006; C. Freeman 2000; Nash and Kelly 1983) to women's cross-border migration for domestic work (see, for example, Chin 1998; Constable 1997; Parreñas 2001). Research has brought to light key ways and consequences in which neoliberal restructuring processes exacerbate rather than eliminate low-wage gendered labour performed by women in sending and receiving contexts. As such, local and transnational migrant women's low-wage work constitutes and is constituted by a 'capitalist interior infrastructure of service and servitude' (Hart 2005: 5).

Still, the gender and reproductive dimensions remain largely tangential to mainstream conceptualizations and analyses of what are considered the major drivers of contemporary economic restructuring processes. At best, reproductive labour such as domestic and care work performed predominantly by women is considered the purview of 'lower circuits' of capital. Reproductive labour is conceptually and empirically divorced from the more masculinized productive labour and 'upper circuits' of capital such as trade, manufacturing, investment and finance (Agathangelou 2004: 7). The dominance of this gendered production–reproduction binary (and related dyads of public–private, global–local, formal–informal economies) camouflages a mutually inextricable relationship between production and reproduction and obscures as well the structural forces that shape women's experiences and lives (Peterson 1996; Bedford and Rai 2010; Beloso 2012; Griffin 2007a). Thus, there exists a vicious cycle in which the reproductive dimension of women's labour remains a separate self-contained issue area, unconnected to the major drivers of neoliberal globalization.

A salient example is ascertained from responses to the contemporary phenomenon of women who migrate for sex work. Since the late twentieth century, transnational migrant women's presence in sex sectors (Lim 1998) or industries of major cities in the world has garnered extensive global attention (e.g. Nigerian women in Bangkok, Chinese women in Rio de Janeiro and French women in Dubai). It is assumed that the women are sex trafficked by criminal organizations, otherwise they must be illegal (even immoral) aliens who flout immigration and employment laws by selling their bodies in exchange for cash. Receiving states focus their efforts on curbing criminal organizations and rescuing sex trafficked victims while detaining and deporting other migrant women who willingly engage in the illicit activity. The phenomenon is largely perceived and addressed as an issue of criminality and illegality.

Underlying states' responses is the entrenched belief of a sacrosanct 'private sphere of sexuality' (Smith 2010: 532) that is segregated from the public sphere. Sex trafficking groups violate this by deceiving women, transporting them across borders and coercing them into indentured sex work or even sexual slavery. It is assumed, concurrently, that women would neither want to nor should they be encouraged to exchange their sexual labour for income. Most women, when given options, will engage in other types of labour, that is, socially-approved remunerated work based on their ascribed gendered traits (e.g. working in households, factories and service industries of sending and receiving economies) as opposed to a socially disapproved and stigmatized activity that, in an overwhelming majority of contexts, is not legally recognized as work.

The above framings, however, neither acknowledge nor are able to examine complex structural connections between women, transnational migration, sex work and neoliberal restructuring processes. Conversely, structural connections may be reduced to that of patriarchal power: given the exigencies elicited by sex trafficking reports, the culpable are men who traffic women for sex and men who pay for sex. Marginalized in either case are analyses of entangled structures and the embeddedness of women's commercialized sexual labour in the new global political economy.

This chapter offers an analysis of structural forces that shape the relationship between women, transnational migration and sex work. The first section briefly discusses the manner in which women's paid and unpaid sexual labour became essential to the political economy of colonialism.

Their performance of sexual labour was shaped by interlocking structures and attendant hierarchies of race, gender, class and sexuality. The second section examines the globalized commercialization of women's sexual labour, particularly that of contemporary sex work performed increasingly by transnational migrant women in global or world cities. This chapter argues that, in the present as in the past, the reproductive dimension is firmly enmeshed with the productive dimension: they are mutually constitutive of and dependent on one another. Subsequently, migrant women's placement in specific tiers and spaces of sex work in global cities evinces the resilience of entangled structures and their contextualized hierarchies that sustain and are sustained by neoliberal economic restructuring processes.

COLONIAL SEXUAL SERVING CLASSES

During the colonial era, women migrated internally and across borders to provide paid and unpaid sexual labour (Pierce 2004; McClintock 1995; Tagliacozzo 2008; White 1990). As slaves, concubines, indentured and free sex workers, and entertainers, they met the sexual needs of colonial administrators, soldiers, explorers, traders, migrant workers and so forth. The colonies, indeed, were sites of colonial administration, trade and exploration, including sexual exploration and liberation from strict European moral codes. Notably, men did not just travel to the colonies for expressly non-sexual activities but they combined these activities with the consumption of women's sexual labour.

Women were recruited via formal and informal schemes involving the colonial state, families, friends, acquaintances and/or strangers. Recruiters were not exclusively men: former sex workers also actively participated in the process. While some women were deceived, transported, sold and then forced to provide sexual labour against their will, others arrived as free and indentured workers. In the Straits Settlements, for example, Singapore became the destination and transit site for women and girls en route to the peninsula, and other colonies and countries in the region. The British initially placed no restrictions on the entry of self-declared prostitutes so long as they migrated of their 'own free will' (Lai 1986: 28; see also Warren 1990).

Women performed sexual labour in a variety of capacities, work conditions and spaces (e.g. plantations, brothels, entertainment venues, military bases, home and so forth) in the colonies. Significantly, women were exoticized and racialized in the process. For example, Black women slaves in the Caribbean were ascribed specific animalistic characteristics that represented them as closer to nature: 'the Black woman was described as naturally "hot constitution'd," and sensuous in an animal-like way, lacking all the qualities that defined "decent" womanhood or women of "purity of blood"' (Kempadoo 2000: 5). In Asia, the Dutch and French initially encouraged their men to take native concubines (since they initially forbade married European men and single women to migrate to the colonies). Colonial intent was to recreate sexual and economic stability associated with the family, albeit without emotional commitments and legal responsibilities.[1] Over time and with the arrival of European women, concubinage had to be outlawed in order to clarify racial boundaries, and to prevent the emergence of an impoverished European class of mixed-race children. The decline of concubinage fuelled the growth of prostitution.

Women's paid and unpaid sexual labour was considered so crucial to the British's dual goals of managing the growing migrant men population while increasing revenue sources in the colonies that, whenever possible, the state directly managed their in-migration and work environments. Licensed brothels, in particular, became highly racialized and classed spaces, for example, brothels for elite clientele who preferred women with certain traits ascribed by the conflation of skin colour, country of origin and culture (Chin 2013; Manderson 1997; Dunne 1994; Warren 1990). At the same time, what is known today as military or base prostitution would be institutionalized for personnel's 'rest and rehabilitation' (eventually also known as 'intercourse and intoxication'): 'the specific construction of militarized masculinity demands heterosexual sex on a regular basis' (Kempadoo 2001: 31; see also Enloe 2000; Moon 1997). Collectively, the long colonial histories of Asian women's sexual labour performed in a variety of capacities is aptly summarized by Prasso's 'Asian mystique' or 'fantasy of the exotic, indulging, decadent, sensual Oriental who will indulge you and delight you with the decadence and servility that no women in your culture could' (2005: 5).

Gradually toward the end of the nineteenth century and at the height of Victorian morality, the British implemented a series of legislation (e.g. Contagious Diseases Ordinances, and Women and Girls Protection Ordinances) that first regulated and then banned brothels, enforced medical examinations for women, and prohibited the in-migration of indentured women as well as under-age girls. The initial impetus for doing so arose from racist discourses in which native and foreign women were

---

[1] On the island of Java, the Dutch urged new European men arrivals to 'find local companions as a prerequisite for quick acclimatization, as insulation from the ill-health that sexual abstention, isolation and boredom were thought to bring' (Stoler 1989: 637; see also Stoler 2006).

represented and treated as vectors of diseases, while European men were victims of the licentious women (Levine 2003). This was similarly the case in some French colonies (Dunne 1994).

Meanwhile, transatlantic public outcries over 'white slavery' or the abduction and transport of white women for sexual slavery led to a series of 'white slave conventions' cementing a relationship between prostitution and sex trafficking. A white slave was 'a white woman, victim of animal lusts of the dark races' (Doezema 1998: 44). Josephine Butler, who helped campaign for the Contagious Diseases Ordinances, argued that there could be no distinction between 'innocent victims and immoral prostitutes':

> Butler and other 'abolitionists' argued that men were responsible for prostitution, placing the blame for prostitution squarely on the shoulders of unbridled male lust. No women could be said to truly consent to prostitution: if a woman appeared 'willing', this was merely the result of the power that men held over her (Doezema 2002: 22).

Prostitution was conceptualized as men's sexual control of, and violence against, women. Women's consent, from this perspective, was irrelevant. Today, the privileging of patriarchal power over that of class relations remains a dominant stance of 'abolitionists' who insist that the elimination of prostitution is fundamental to the elimination of sex trafficking (Barry 1995; Hughes 2000; Raymond 2004).

It is important to underscore here that women's sexual labour in the colonies was shaped by more than European patriarchal structures transposed onto existing native structures. At the outset, it can be said (and indeed, this was the case evinced from colonial discourses) that women's sexual labour was perceived to have palliative functions. Since men had natural sexual urges and demands, regardless of where they were in the world, colonial states either directly managed and/or oversaw private interests that arranged for native and foreign women to meet such needs.

Inscribed in a functionalist approach toward sex as a palliative, then, was the fundamental need to ensure social order in the colonies: 'private' acts of sexual relations between women and men from various backgrounds were fused to 'public' goals of political control, capital accumulation and racio-cultural boundary construction and maintenance (see especially Stoler 2006; Levine 2003). Women emerged as the colonial sexual serving classes via what can be called sexation processes that 'socially constructed and mapped race, gender, class and sexuality to imbrications of economic production, social reproduction, identity maintenance and security' (Chin and Persaud 2013: 8). In this complexly synthesized way, reproduction was central to the political economy of colonialism.

During the colonial era then, the economy was not separate from but deeply intertwined with governance and culture, production with reproduction, and the public with the private–domestic domains. Race, gender and sexuality also were not subordinated to class, that is, they were 'not additive elements to the economic and political structures of the capitalist-world system, but an integral, entangled and constitutive part of the broad entangled "package" called the European modern/colonial capitalist/patriarchal world system' (Grosfoguel 2007: 217). Phrased simply, the entangled structures beget complex stratified orders in the colonies.

GLOBAL SEXUAL SERVING CLASSES

Colonialism's demise did not put an end to women as the sexual serving classes. On the contrary, women have become the global sexual serving classes in a new global political economy characterized still by entangled structures, albeit with localized expressions. Global or world cities are the most salient sites from which to discern and analyse the relationship between women, migration and the commercialization of sexual labour.

By the mid to late twentieth century, economic crises that affected countries in the Global North and South prompted a gradual sustained adoption of policies (especially the triadic liberalization, deregulation and privatization policies) promoting states' retreat from their economies. A main objective was to establish or deepen free market operations with accompanying emphasis, for example, on efficiency and transparency in governance. This formally signalled neoliberalism as the foundational ideology for the new global political economy (Harvey 2005).

Neoliberal restructuring processes 'de-territorialized' or freed capital to flow around the world in search of profits (Scholte 2000). 'Re-territorialized' capital continues to bring about new spatial configurations ranging from offshore tax havens and free trade zones, to growth triangles and global or world cities. Of these new configurations, global cities promulgate and intensify the phenomenon of women's transnational migration for sex work.

Global cities in the twenty-first century are akin to 'one-stop shops' for transnational firms. As firms' coverage and operations take on a global scale, such cities have emerged to facilitate their ease of access to specialized services such as accounting, legal and finance. These cities 'possess capabilities for serving the global operations of firms and markets, for organizing enormous geographic dispersal and mobility, and for maintaining centralized control over that dispersal' (Sassen 2008c: 57).

Global cities thus are the command posts or centres for managing a globalized world economy. These cities are known for offering 'advanced producer services' performed by 'highly skilled professionals', 'knowledge workers' or most euphemistically referred to as 'global talent'.

Global cities, however, are not alike. Although New York, London and Tokyo typically are hailed as archetypes, cities differ in their specializations, characteristics and functions: 'differences [are] rooted in cultural, geography, and institutional dynamics' (Shatkin 2007: 2). States are deeply implicated in the emergence and growth of their global cities via policies pertaining to foreign investments, land use, public services, governance, urban (re)development, tourism marketing and so forth.

In their key role as strategic sites for the management and coordination of the new global economy, cities are connected to one another within and beyond regions. These interconnections can be likened to metaphorical multi-lane global and regional highways (land, air, sea and e-infrastructure) for the movement of goods, services, information and capital. More and more, states sign 'open skies' bilateral air service agreements linking far-flung cities in an ever-growing interconnected web (Fu et al. 2010; Grubesic et al. 2008).

Importantly, some of these highways are migratory pathways. The most celebrated and in-demand category is that of global talent or transnational migrants with professional skill sets. More often than not, they are represented by male professionals from the Global North and South in the highly 'masculine worlds of finance, banking, insurance and law, seeing these are more "skilled occupations" and more important in driving the world economy' (Hubbard 2011: 295).

Overemphasis and valorization of predominantly male professionals has tended to obscure equally important categories of mostly low-wage transnational migrant workers or temporary, contract-based men and women workers from the Global South. Besides jobs in receiving economies' manufacturing and agricultural sectors, migrants are also employed in 'personal/support services' of global cities. Many of these are gendered jobs, for example, men as taxi drivers and parking valets, and women as domestic workers, elderly care aides and restaurant servers. These global 'serving classes', too, travel on migratory pathways: some are participants of formal recruitment schemes authorized by bilateral agreements between sending and receiving states, as others become undocumented workers (Sassen 2002: 262). Empirical studies demonstrate that migrants' insertion in segmented labour markets of receiving cities affirm or modify existing racialized, gendered and classed hierarchies (see, for example, Cordero-Guzmán et al. 2001; Thukral 2010; Man 2007). From this perspective global cities are the contemporary versions of colonial-era contact zones, that is, the spaces 'where disparate cultures meet, clash, deal with each other, often in highly asymmetrical relations of domination and subordination' (Pratt 2008: 4).

Within the global serving classes is the subcategory of the global sexual serving classes represented increasingly by transnational migrant women. The women, to be sure, cater to global talent since cities offer spaces wherein 'transnational elites can cement friendships with business contacts and work colleagues at the same time they pursue sexual pleasures' (Hubbard 2011: 296; see also Jeffreys 2010). Global cities' sustained economic growth also means that there are heightened demands by men from all classes and nationalities for migrant women sex workers.

Depending on the global city, migrant women are differentially positioned in sex work hierarchies. European women in Dubai are the highest paid, top tier sex workers, followed by women from other nationalities. They are based primarily in luxury hotels, whereas Black African women are relegated mainly to street-based sex work (Mahdavi 2010). In Kuala Lumpur's hierarchy, Russian and Central Asian women (who exhibit Caucasian features) are at the highest tier, followed by fair-skinned Chinese women. They work in luxury hotels, serviced apartments and private homes. At the middle tiers are some Chinese and South-East Asian women who work in health and beauty spas, hotels, retail malls and housing developments. At the lowest tiers are darker-skinned South and South-East Asian women who work out of massage parlours, entertainment outlets, budget inns and even construction sites. Most Black African women, however, occupy a special niche catering to high-end clientele (Chin 2013). In Geneva, the nexus of race–nationality–immigration status characterizes women's placement in specific spaces, for example, Eastern European women in strip clubs, African women in champagne bars and Latin American and Asian women in massage parlours (Chimienti 2010). In Seoul, 'Russian blondes' occupy the top tiers of sex work occurring in elite spaces (Kim and Fu 2008). In some major cities of the Mediterranean, white women work in the top tiers whereas Latin American and African women are at the bottom (Agathangelou 2004). Global cities' hierarchies thus expose colonial-like racialized orders as they encapsulate how women's performance of commercialized sexual labour is mediated by the race–nationality–class–spatial nexus.

It can be said that although colonial administrations have long disappeared, their legacies of entangled structures and attendant hierarchies persist. This is ascertained from 'Third World migrants' inscription in the racial/ethnic hierarchy of metropolitan global cities. 'In this sense, there is periphery outside and inside of the core zones and there is a core inside and outside the peripheral regions' (Grosfoguel 2007: 219–20). Global cities in the North are becoming 'microcosms of empire' that reproduce 'the racial/ethnic [and sexual] hierarchies of the old colonial empires' (Grosfoguel and Georas 2000: 98): peripheries now exist in the core. Similarly, core zones also exist in the periphery, that is, hierarchies in global cities of the South.

Hierarchies emerging from entangled structures of race, gender, class and sexuality are affirmed, modified or transformed, but they cannot be eliminated entirely. As women and men move from one global city to another for work, cities become 'turnstiles' as opposed to more permanent destinations:

> [It is] a mistake to think of these destinations as sites of permanent settlement. A more accurate metaphor may be that of a turnstile, where immigrants enter for a period of time and then leave for other cities in a transnational network. Thus a Nigerian immigrant may migrate to Seville, then to London or New York, and then return back to Lagos. . . . Urban economies are increasingly reliant upon new and large flows of foreign-labour for distinct segments of the labour market. (Price and Benton-Short 2007: 104)

Hierarchies help give meaning, thus order, to constantly in-flux environments that inevitably elicit questions such as the types of jobs that are seen to be appropriate for women or men migrants from different nationalities; why others should not be allowed to enter; who or what rightly constitutes the nation and so forth.

State Responses to Migrant Women

Over time, transnational migration for employment has been subsumed under the category of national security in receiving contexts: the September 11, 2001 terrorist attacks hastened processes of securitizing migration. For receiving states, a major challenge is keeping immigration doors open to specific categories of transnational migrants while closing them to others. This is a paradox arising from the pursuit of neoliberal restructuring policies designed to create an integrated global economy within the broader context of an existing inter-state system. Although barriers continue to disappear with regard to the movement of goods, capital and information, they nevertheless remain for the movement of people.

Officially sanctioned or authorized migratory pathways are not neutral: they are shaped by a variety of factors from interstate relations and sectoral demands to domestic politics. In general, immigration policies and regulations are designed to attract and retain credentialed professionals: they enjoy favourable entry requirements that include spouses and children, attractive benefit packages, as well as longer term employment contracts with the possibility of acquiring permanent residency. Those governing low-wage workers are much more restrictive, for example, entry of family members is prohibited as is marriage to citizens in receiving countries; the provision of short-term contracts with little to no worker protection and benefits; and the stipulation of official approval for switching employers or sectors. Receiving states' migrant worker management strategies legitimize practices of differential inclusion (Andrijasevic 2009: 391) that, depending on the context, may explicitly or implicitly be informed also by the politics of normative heterosexuality (Griffin 2007b).

The majority of receiving states expressly refuse to recognize sex work as a legal immigration and work category. Yet, there exist different types of sex markets (e.g. legal-formal and illegal-informal) in global cities, and transnational migrant women (more so than men) are visibly involved in them (Sanders 2008). The dominant assumption is that if migrant women are not sex trafficking victims, then they must be irregular migrants engaged in an illicit-immoral activity. State adoption of the Palermo Protocol (the United Nationals Protocol to Prevent, Suppress, and Punish Trafficking in Persons) and its '3P' approach of preventing trafficking, protecting victims and prosecuting traffickers, then is complemented by the '3D' approach of detaining, disempowering and deporting irregular migrants whenever deemed necessary (USTIP 2010).[2]

Receiving states, however, remain culpable despite their injurious claims of being under siege by human and sex traffickers, smugglers and irregular migrants. In the case of migrant women sex workers, they can travel to and enter global cities via additional migratory pathways created by ongoing state liberalization of the services sectors.[3] Tourism and education liberalization policies, in particular, offer institutionalized migratory pathways for sex work: these policies serve as front and back doors for doing so. Categorized as tourists, hospitality workers, or as international students, migrant women can enter for work in global cities' sex industries. They then work alongside women who moonlight to supplement their income from authorized employment, those who have been deceived by labour brokers, those who have been sold into sexual slavery, and so forth.

Sex industries have directly and indirectly become part of global cities'

---

[2] In tandem, these approaches stretch the meanings and practices of border control to internal spaces and places of the nation such as those ascertained from 'petit apartheid' practices (Georges-Abeyie 2001) carried out by the authorities and even citizenry to mitigate perceived threats respectively posed by migrant women and men (see, for example, Chin 2008; Romero 2008; Bigo and Guild 2005).

[3] Implemented in 1995 following the Uruguay Round on trade agreements, the General Agreement on Trade in Services (GATS) provides the overall framework for states to liberalize 12 specific services sectors. Liberalization of services is expected to generate more revenue sources while enhancing global cities' and countries' brands or identities.

distinctive brands and identities in tourism promotion. It is not that cities explicitly promote their sex industries but that marketing and branding campaigns invoke specific images and stereotypes, for example 'the presence of foreign sex workers in South Korea today underscores the fact that they are not merely meeting demand for sexual labour but that the demand for exotic, foreign women is actively created through marketing, promotion, and sales' (Kim and Fu 2008: 507). In this light, highly publicized immigration and vice raids signify states' occasional withdrawal of tacit approval for migrant women's participation in sex industries.

As states, NGOs, communities, international financial institutions and other key actors in tourism development aim to promote the distinctiveness of Global South destination cities and countries, they often affirm a 'representational loop' by resurrecting imperial-colonial images of the exotic 'Other' (Sturma quoted in Echtner and Prasad 2003: 662). An outcome of intercity and interstate competition for tourism revenue is the construction of 'the foundation for globally structured, though geographically localized, sex tourism' (Wonders and Michalowski 2001: 565). Although some men (and even women) travel exclusively for domestic or international sex tourism, many others combine their desire to consume migrant women's commercialized sexual labour with other activities such as business and leisure travel.

A key difference between the present and past is that the selection of available 'exotic' women in one site has expanded greatly. Besides their more mobile counterparts, local men from all classes now have access to transnational migrant women sex workers. Cyberspace plays an integral role in promoting and augmenting men's corporeal experiences: there are websites dedicated to the exchange of information on their experiences (such as who, where, how much and how long) in global cities. The absence of a clearly demarcated red-light district in a global city, then, does not automatically imply the absence of a vibrant sex industry. Sex work has become more deeply 'domesticated' or obscured from public view. Encouraged by and in addition to cyberspace, sex work occurs in many more commercial and residential spaces (Löw and Ruhne 2009).

Of the two additional migratory pathways, the education route is much more recent as states and their global cities in the South are beginning to compete with traditional education hubs in the North. Education liberalization policies are expected to generate additional revenue, and train the next generation of international student/young professionals while enhancing cultural–public diplomacy efforts. The most prominent examples are Doha's Education City and Singapore's Global Schoolhouse Initiative known for branch campuses established by renowned institutions of higher education from the North, and local–international partnership and exchange agreements. Women, with the help of facilitating groups, may obtain student visas or permits only to pursue full-time sex work; they may enter as international students but then find themselves performing part-time sex work to help pay for education and living expenses; and they may enter as tourists with the intent to pursue sex work but also take the opportunity to enrol in certification and degree programmes (Chin 2013: 13–14).

Not all women's decisions to migrate for sex work are driven exclusively by the economic survival imperative. Their decisions range from the need to help support families financially while escaping patriarchal home environments, to the desire for material goods or for some type of education while being able to travel the world (see especially Chin 2013; Mahdavi 2010; Andrijasevic 2009; Agustin 2007). For some migrant women, sex work offers relatively higher wages and more control over work conditions than many authorized and unauthorized low-wage jobs open to them. This is not to say that no migrant woman is exploited and abused in sex work. Empirical studies reveal that although women knowingly migrate for sex work, they may not always be able to fully anticipate working conditions. The point here is that women are acutely aware of the legally recognized yet bondage-like conditions of other jobs in receiving contexts. For example, Baoyan, a Chinese sex worker in Kuala Lumpur insisted that if it is morally wrong for women to be sex workers, then it must be morally wrong also to pay women very low wages for long hours of work in restaurants ('I was always exhausted and I did not earn enough to even survive'). From Baoyan's perspective, there are two types of coercion with regard to migrant women and sex work. The first concerns physical violence: women who are 'threatened, beaten and forced by men to work as a "Miss" [euphemism for sex worker]. . .should be "saved".' The second concerns structural forces that shape women's employment and life chances. In the latter case, there should be no moral distinctions given women's limited choices. As Baoyan asserts: 'washing dishes by the roadside, picking up people's trash, taking care of their children, or working in a factory for little pay must be the same [as women who are "coerced" into sex work by their need to feed children and take care of their family]' (Chin 2013: 105). Compared to low-wage gendered jobs such as the live-in domestic worker, elderly care assistant or restaurant server, some migrant women view sex work as a relatively quicker way of earning income in less exploitative environments which then allows them to achieve their goals in life (see also Lim 1998; Kitiarsa 2008; Agustin 2006).

States' complicity in encouraging women's transnational migration for sex work is particularly obvious with regard to women who are given 'entertainer' visas, for example, Russian women in Seoul and other cities as a result of bilateral political, economic and cultural relations between South Korea and Russia (Kim and Fu 2008). In the case of Chinese women sex workers in Yaoundé, the capital of Cameroon, the Chinese state overtly encouraged women's migration specifically to service Chinese construction workers (Ndjio 2009). Jeffreys' point of states as 'pimps' is appropriately made here (2009).

Facilitating Groups

Women's transnational migration for sex work inevitably brings up the issue of facilitating groups or syndicates. These can be very small groups comprised of a few individuals or very large groups; they may be locally based or have transnational ties; and they may specialize in some or all phases, from recruitment to employment. The larger groups (comprised of men and women) often have domestic and transnational alliances (e.g. those based on diaspora ties) controlling all phases and dimensions of transnationalized sex work (from labour recruitment, finance and transportation, to housing, security, marketing and assignment of migrant women). Such groups not only meet but shape the demands for migrant women sex workers of different nationalities and races.

These large facilitating groups' operations divulge the fact that formal circuits of capital in neoliberal globalization generate and strengthen 'counter-circuits' (Sassen 2002: 256) of 'shadow globalization', that is, 'activities made possible by global flows of information, technology, finance and people, that are taking place in informal and illegal ways, but in the shadows in terms of otherness' (Penttinen 2007: 7). In sex trafficking literature, these groups are most often identified as criminal organizations (Shelley 2003; Turner and Kelly 2009; UNODC 2010). Not all of them, however, specialize in the sex trafficking of women. There are Asian groups with transnational ties that, in return for agreed-upon fees and taxes on monthly earnings, arrange women's travel documents, board and lodging, personal security, clients and even forward journeys to other global cities (Chin 2013; Chin and Finckenauer 2011). Nuanced distinctions between trafficking and contract-based groups, however, are eliminated by the subsumption of the latter into the former. This is paralleled by the subsumption of migrant women sex workers into the sex trafficked category despite a range of migration modes, and living and working conditions:

> The relationship involving women who live inside sex establishments and rarely leave until they are moved to another place without being consulted receives the media's usual attention, it being taken for granted that this represents a

> total loss of freedom. In many cases, however, migrant workers prefer this situation, for any of a number of reasons: if they don't leave the premises they don't spend money; if they don't have working papers, they feel safer inside in a controlled situation; if someone else does the work of finding new venues and making arrangements, they don't have to do it; or having come on a three-month tourist visa they want to spend as much time as possible making money (Agustin 2006: 36).

Collectively, groups with transnational alliances and domestic networks are becoming major anchors of migration–ancillary industries for commercial sex work in global cities. It can be said that they are the informal economies' version of the formal economies' one-stop shop for the production and consumption of migrant women's commercialized sexual labour (Chin 2013: 143). Significantly, groups' operations straddle formal–informal economies and recruitment schemes as they organize major participants ranging from other facilitating groups, travel agents, employment agencies, state agencies, airlines, consulates, banks, retail and entertainment outlets, to direct and indirect 'profiteers' (Samarasinghe 2009: 40–41) such as family members, acquaintances, friends, pimps, 'mamees' (former sex workers responsible for taking care of and guiding migrant women), drivers, hotel concierges and the authorities (Chin 2013, Chapter 5 *passim*). Embedded in a global context that valorizes free market operations and exchanges, this kind of network assemblage cannot but help ensure the endurance of the global sexual serving classes.

CONCLUSION

The contemporary relationship between women, transnational migration and sex work is neither an unintended consequence nor a side-effect of neoliberal economic restructuring processes. This relationship has its roots in the colonial era. As the sexual serving classes, native and foreign women were indispensable to the political economy of colonialism that was built from, and characterized by, entangled structures. Women's paid and unpaid sexual labour deeply intertwined colonial governance, economic production, social stability and racio-cultural boundary construction and maintenance in the colonies.

Colonial-era legacies find their expressions in the postcolonial era as the scope and scale of commercializing women's sexual labour have expanded greatly: transnational migrant women are now the global sexual serving classes. Global cities' web-like interconnections accord women institutionalized migratory pathways for moving from one city to the next. In the cities, women are placed in racialized-classed hierarchies, and concomitant spaces for sex work. The mutually constitutive relationship between reproduction and production persists amid entangled structures that are affirmed, modified or transformed by ongoing neoliberal restructuring processes.

Although seldom acknowledged, global cities have become main nodes for management of a global sex frontier. They are the sites for agglomeration of personal services, including sexual services demanded by all classes and nationalities of male clientele, and performed increasingly by transnational migrant women. Instead of serving the colonial administrator, soldier, explorer, trader, plantation owner and migrant worker, migrant women serve the highly skilled professional who travels the world plying his knowledge, the guest worker in factories, construction sites, hotels and agroplantations, the businessman, the politician, the police, the tourist, and so forth.

As discussed, there is neither one causal factor nor a universal outcome of women's decisions to migrate for sex work. Decisions are shaped by women's understandings of and responses to structural constraints and opportunities. Whether women migrate independently, with the help of their personal–social networks or directly contract with facilitating groups, they 'have found a way to navigate networks of migration for their own benefit' (Berman 2003: 46).

Facilitating groups with transnational and local ties are the informal–illicit economy's version of one-stop shops managing every phase from recruitment and transportation to housing and security. Whether or not some groups treat women as commodities to be bought and sold or as clients who remunerate their services, their networks give order to, while strengthening, the integration of informal and formal economies. Bluntly put, facilitating groups help organize and manage a global sex frontier distinguished by entangled structures of class, gender, race and sexuality. On this global sex frontier, there are a range of profit-generating activities, women's migratory modes as well as outcomes from the sex slave to the indentured and independent sex worker: 'forms of unfree labour not only survive, but are reproduced and even expanded while the capitalist mode of production (and thus free wage labour) becomes dominant' (Munck 2008: 1235).

Women's transnational migration for sex work is a hidden-in-plain sight phenomenon. Until the structural embeddedness of this phenomenon is recognized fully and addressed accordingly, the existing 3P and 3D approaches adopted by states can only have 'band-aid' effects at best. So, too, will remain elusive the quest for women's human and worker rights.

26. Molecular biotechnologies: insights on production through the lens of reproduction

Miriam Boyer

INTRODUCTION

In recent years, the life processes of various organisms, rationalized through molecular engineering, have acquired a new and increasingly important role in production. In the social sciences these transformations have been captured, on the one hand, by analyses that speculate on large-scale social transformations claimed to entail 'a new face and a new phase of capitalism' (Sunder Rajan 2006: 3); and on the other, by a number of studies of intellectual property regimes and resource appropriation – that is, essentially of political relations and institutions (Kinchy 2012; McAffee 2003; Pechlander and Otero 2008; Zeller 2008). Existing studies of production based on molecular biotechnologies tend to focus on economic sectors and the rise of new capitals (Cooper 2008; Parry 2004; Sunder Rajan 2006; Zeller 2010), but have largely left unaddressed how the materiality of production has been transformed, that is, *how we produce differently* as a result of the molecular transformation of living organisms.

Clarifying this material dimension of production sheds light on the concrete processes that redefine our practical relationship with nature. While this is the case for all production, from mining to microelectronic processing, in the case of all biotechnologies the relationship is uniquely important in that nature is a dynamic element related to the immediate productive process. How we produce is intricately connected to how living organisms *re*produce: from cultivating a crop of maize to a bacterium molecularly engineered to produce human insulin, the production process largely coincides with the reproductive or living processes of the organism in question. Living nature is therefore a transformative force whose changing material qualities must be accounted for in order to understand the characteristics of a new way of producing.

The fact that social and nature processes are deeply interwoven and therefore should be studied jointly has been recognized by contemporary approaches in the social sciences. In particular, 'social nature' (Castree

2001; Smith 2008) and Actor Network theories have argued that we must acknowledge the intricate ties between society and nature or otherwise face a choice 'between two catastrophic solutions . . . naturalization on the one hand, [and] socialization on the other' (Latour 2004). Characteristic of this scholarship, however, is the assumption that the inextricability between nature and society that is recognized empirically should also hold at the analytical level. Yet a focus on 'hybrids', 'actants' or the claim that nature is increasingly 'produced' makes it difficult to discern the non-social materialities whose qualities are distinctly different from, and therefore play a unique role in transforming social relations such as production. Distinguishing between empirical and analytic dimensions is no different from the basic approach we otherwise take in the social sciences. For instance, empirically, it is impossible to say 'where' gender relations 'begin' and class relations 'end', yet our basic approach is largely based on establishing such distinctions. Similarly, when studying living nature, it is also useful to distinguish between production and reproduction because it allows us to gain greater analytical depth in integrating living nature as a key dimension that is acknowledged but only rarely actively analysed.

In the following I take this approach to address several issues regarding the changing materiality of production in the context of molecular engineering. First, I discuss the role of reproduction in agriculture, arguing that molecular engineering of agricultural plants has not brought about a transformation in production as did classical genetics breeding in the early twentieth century. I argue that this should not be seen primarily as a question of technological sophistication but is better understood as the result of a specific way of reframing reproduction in order to produce. I then focus on the transformations in the material productive process beyond agriculture, taking the example of vanilla flavour in molecularly engineered yeast. The goal is to bring attention to new qualities in the productive process itself and to the 'fluid' relationship between the transformative living processes of humans (labour) and non-humans that makes these organisms attractive to industrial processing. Although we cannot foresee the outcome of the various social struggles that are currently shaping the role of molecular biotechnologies as part of larger productive relations, exploring what this way of producing entails materially is an important step in clarifying what this new kind of production entails and how it differs from other types of production. Last but not least, distinguishing analytically between production and reproduction can help not only to clarify the new qualities that make these transformations productive – but also to identify what makes them potentially disruptive or even destructive.

PRODUCTION DEFINED AS REFRAMING REPRODUCTION

To appreciate what is novel about the transformations to the productive process brought about by molecular engineering, it is helpful to briefly look back at the relationship between production and reproduction in agriculture. Agricultural production is also biotechnological in that it relies on the life processes of plants and animals as a transformative force. To be incorporated productively, living processes are harnessed or *practically reframed in particular ways* that define how reproduction becomes production, that is, how it becomes a new use-value.

In peasant agricultural production, the living processes of plants were productively reframed by selecting (the seeds of) particular plants over many life cycles, thereby repeatedly encouraging particular material qualities in relation to a wider ecosystem. For example, tomato plants with larger fruits, or maize plants that grow well in particular soil or climate conditions might be chosen over others. However, the explosion of new use-values created in this process was not only the product of human intervention in the environment through selection, but also of relying on much wider reproductive or living processes that were not reframed or manipulated directly. This can be seen clearly in the characteristic practice of peasant systems based on polycultures in which the production of maize or tomatoes is inseparable from the reproduction of a number of other cultivated and non-cultivated species in the agro-ecosystem (Plucknett and Smith 1986, cf. also Kay, this volume). But it can also be seen in the fact that agriculture did not take place without the insects that pollinated the flowers; the microbes in the soil that supplied nutrients to the plants; or the weedy relatives that the crops periodically intermixed with. Thus, against the common-sense notion of agriculture as a social practice and as a specific technology acting upon nature, it is important to recognize that producing with nature entails *both* transforming but also relying on a particular reproductive context as an important part of the productive transformation. In peasant systems, the result was an ensemble of new use-values (including various crops, but in many cases also animals such as insects, livestock or fish) whose (re)production was materially different from, yet also relied on the historical life cycles of the cultivated plants as part of an agro-ecosystem.

An important aspect of all of this worth noting for the discussion below is that practically reframing reproduction in a particular way should not be seen as mechanistically 'corresponding' to a new type of production. In fact, seed selection was also used productively in contexts that were no longer peasant, including plantation-based colonial production systems, and it even played a central role in the first phases of the industrialization of agriculture in the nineteenth century. What rendered it productive in non-peasant contexts was that reproduction through selection was now being carried out at a global scale and organized institutionally via states that exploited differences among ecosystems through a coordinated, sometimes centralized effort, and at an unprecedented speed. This type of production often greatly simplified the reproductive context of the agro-ecosystem in an effort to produce individual use-values – a single variety of cacao; the production of one type of particularly hardy wheat – rather than the interrelated multiplicity of use-values that characterize peasant agriculture. Yet it was a type of production whose defining practice continued to be reframing the reproduction of plant ecosystems through seed selection (cf. Boyer 2013).

This particular way of framing reproduction only changed significantly in the late nineteenth century with a new definition of reproduction made available through the science of biology. In contrast to prior scholarly approaches that understood relationships among living beings from the optic of natural history, the development of modern biology practically reframed reproduction in terms of individual 'functions' of organisms through scientific experimentation (Coleman 1977; Weber 2005). Mendelism, in particular, used cross- and self-fertilization of plants to redefine agricultural (re)production as a composite materiality consisting of *discrete* character 'traits': peas that were, as Mendel himself put it, green *or* yellow, wrinkled *or* smooth; whose flowers were positioned near the stem *or* at its end, and so on (Mendel 1865: 4f.). Like peasant transformations, however, achieving new changes in the material qualities that could be produced was based on two materially distinct transformative forces: on the one hand, intervening in the reproductive process, in this case by deliberately pollinating individual plants in particular combinations corresponding to the observation of particular traits; and on the other, by relying on the sexual reproduction of plants much more widely defined: the fertilization of the cell, the creation of a seedling and a mature plant, and so on. Empirically, production and reproduction are of course one and the same process, but in order to understand *how* new forms of production unfold, it is important to recognize that producing differently entails a practical redefinition of reproduction but that there are also dimensions of reproduction that are not directly intervened in yet remain crucial for bringing about the productive transformations in question.

At the turn of the twentieth century, the Mendelian definition of (re-) production in terms of discrete traits was especially welcomed by agricultural entrepreneurs who recognized that the new way of practically reframing reproduction could lead to qualitatively new ways of producing, in particular because self-fertilizing the plants created a high degree of homogeneity for a given trait. Within a few decades it became the dominant way of harnessing the reproduction of agricultural plants (and animals) in industrial centres such as the United States and Europe. This approach provided a solution to a longstanding search for rationalizing production away from the complex interrelationships of agro-ecosystems and populations of plants and towards the production of discrete, trait-defined use-values: barley grains with a stable nitrogen content (for the brewing industry to create a product of standard quality); maize plants with stiff stalks (facilitating mechanical harvesting); or rice with short stems (facilitating the application of nitrogen fertilizer to be utilized by the plant for increased production of grains rather than stem height). Beyond the transformations in the productive process, the contours of Fordist agriculture as new production relations are of course the result of a wider set of social transformations – including the development of particular political institutions that have been the subject of most of the social science contributions to the Fordist transformation of agriculture (Friedmann and McMichael 1989; Kloppenburg 2004). But at the level of the process of production, new use-values obtained through the Mendelian approach to reproduction created the characteristic materiality of Fordist agricultural production: mechanization; the use of chemical inputs; crop homogeneity; and so on.

MOLECULAR ENGINEERING: A NEW WAY OF PRODUCING?

The molecular transformation of agricultural plants since the 1980s follows a similar pattern to that of Mendelian transformations in that it is based on reframing reproductive processes discretely – albeit no longer in terms of traits, but of molecules. Conceptually, it is anchored in what was once the 'central dogma' of molecular biology, according to which a living process originates in a specific segment or segments of the DNA molecule that are exclusively associated with reproducing a discrete (protein) molecule. Although this way of defining reproduction at the molecular level has long become obsolete in molecular biology as a science, it became enshrined in the conceptual approach and practice of molecular engineering (Álvarez-Buylla et al. 2013: 112; Commoner 2002). As in peasant and Mendelian transformations of agriculture, reframing reproduction to achieve a new productive quality has two dimensions: directly modifying the DNA of a given organism through various techniques such as transferring a segment of this molecule to another organism, or deploying particular enzymes to modify particular DNA sequences, among many others. At the same time, production also relies on much larger reproductive transformations involving not just a few molecules, but the entirety of the living cell in order to (re)produce the targeted substance.

Since the 1970s, this redefinition of reproduction at the sub-cellular level by manipulating the DNA molecule has made it possible to produce a number of new use-values. For example, plants such as maize, canola or cotton have been altered to (re)produce toxins of the soil bacterium, *B. thuringensis* (*Bt*) with insecticidal properties; potatoes have been engineered to remove the segments of DNA associated with the production of amylose, one of the two kinds of starch molecules found in all plants, thereby making it easier to process the starch for industrial uses; and monoclonal antibodies have been produced in the leaves of tobacco plants, among many others. But an important question is whether these new redefinitions of reproduction have also led to a transformation in the materiality of agricultural production more broadly. On the one hand, molecular engineering has in fact played a role in the new reorganization of agriculture (in terms of *who* is producing, i.e., a change in capital; *where* production takes place; in some cases also *what* is being produced (cf. Otero 2008; Pechlander and Otero 2008). All of this does not, however, appear to be primarily the result of new material qualities in the productive process but of the monopolization of breeding techniques and of the plants (or parts thereof) through new privatization schemes which have led to changes in political power and a new division of labour in agriculture (Burch and Lawrence 2009). However, in terms of how agriculture has unfolded as a transformative process, the transformations in the materiality of agricultural production/farming remain unchanged. Unlike the changes that took place in how agricultural production processes unfolded as a result of the Mendelian redefinition of reproduction, the molecular redefinition of production has not brought about a change in the process of agricultural production.

To be clear, this is not to argue that these changes to reproduction via molecular engineering do not affect productive processes at all nor that they do not bring about other important consequences. As discussed throughout, production and reproduction are categories that describe one and the same material process and as such we can expect that there are important consequences to production when reproduction is altered, as I discuss below. The point is that by considering production and reproduction as distinct sources of productive transformations, we can analytically ‘disaggregate’ the diverse social relations and gain more clarity about which dimensions of society–nature relations are being transformed and how. Thus, we can see that in the specific case of agriculture, it has been possible to radically transform living or reproductive processes without immediately translating into a transformation in the materiality of the agricultural production process, for example, how a crop of maize is farmed.

The misleading impression that the 'how' of agricultural production has been directly transformed as a result of molecularly modified crops is magnified, first of all, by the fact that the molecular transformations have indeed radically changed the reproductive processes of the plants, as underlined by the many unexpected outcomes suggesting that these transformations may entail a major departure from the plants' evolutionary history, whether at the level of molecules, cells, organisms or ecosystems (cf. Álvarez-Buylla et al. 2013; Filipecki and Malepszy 2006; Lu and Yang 2009; *Nature Biotechnology* 2006). I will return to this point below. Second, it is evoked by the fact that almost 20 years since being grown commercially, molecularly modified crops occupy a sizeable area of agricultural production. In 2012, 170 million hectares or 12 per cent of total arable land (not including land for livestock or forestry) was farmed to these crops, above all engineered soybeans, maize, cotton and canola (FAO 2010; ISAAA 2012). Yet over 99 per cent of molecularly engineered crops currently grown commercially have been bred to exhibit only two use-values as defined by molecularly (re)producing two types of substances: bacterial enzymes that grant the plants 'resistance' to various herbicidal chemicals and the *Bt* toxin mentioned earlier that has insecticidal properties. In other words, the new use-values created through molecular techniques do not represent new qualities in the agricultural production process including the general labour process, the ensemble of other technologies used to carry it out, and beyond it, the process of value-creation. Far from this, the new use-values may be molecularly (re)produced but they tend to reinforce production qualities and productive processes that became dominant during the Second Food Regime/Fordism, in particular the widespread use of chemical inputs as a replacement for labour (cf. Benbrook 2012).

Moreover, even more significantly, all the most important qualities affecting the materiality of current agricultural production, such as higher-yielding strains; stiff or shorter stalks/stems (to facilitate mechanized harvesting and/or the use of nitrogen fertilizer); homogeneity in shape or the stability of these qualities over time are qualities that continue to be (re)produced by Mendelian techniques rather than molecular ones. The latter have been notably poor in achieving these types of qualities and according to plant breeders in favour of molecular techniques, 'the most important limitation [for improving on classical plant breeding through molecular engineering] is the complexity of the plant biological processes and agricultural traits of interest, which has been found to be higher than expected' (Molina 2010: 182). While it may be argued that what may seem a complex task in molecular engineering today may become simple tomorrow, the issue of molecular simplicity versus complexity should not only be understood as an issue that can be resolved if, and to the extent that, molecular engineering becomes more sophisticated (for such an argument see Murphy 2007: 162). Rather, it should be seen as a basic difference arising from two different ways of (re)producing (Mendelian vs. molecular); that is, as a difference related to *two distinct ways of practically reframing reproduction in order to produce*.

As discussed above, molecular engineering is an approach whose central 'innovation' is based on abstracting from the complexity of the cell, redefining reproduction as discrete DNA segments corresponding to the reproduction of discrete molecular substances. By the same token, it is also an approach whose strength is not in reproducing the myriad substances orchestrated by the combinations of perhaps hundreds of discrete molecularly defined processes that would have to be manipulated directly to recreate, by molecular means, a typical Mendelian plant trait such as 'tolerance to frost', or many other qualities important to farming. Put differently, molecular transformations have a hard time 'competing' with the Mendelian approach to (re)producing plants that, despite its narrow emphasis on discrete traits, relies on very old and well-probed historical living processes of plants in order to carry out many of the use-values it seeks without having to redefine them through a direct manipulation. From this perspective, the material advantages and disadvantages of molecular transformations would suggest that they are not necessarily an advantageous (re)productive force for creating many of the basic 'agronomic' or farming qualities that have been essential to agriculture. It is therefore not surprising that molecular engineering does not seem to be transforming the 'how' of agricultural production – at least not directly – a point that I will return to below.

TRANSFORMATIONS IN PRODUCTION: 'DE NOVO' PROCESSING

In contrast to agricultural production with molecularly engineered plants there are other molecular transformations of living organisms that do entail important changes to how productive processes unfold, in particular for industrial production. New and characteristic about them is that they tend to blur the difference between primary and secondary production. For example, instead of growing the sweet wormwood tree (primary production) and chemically processing its leaves (secondary production) to produce an anti-malarial substance, artemisinin, the precursor of the same molecule has been produced by molecularly engineering yeast, processing it minimally thereafter (Peplow 2013; Ye and Bhatia 2012). What is noteworthy about this is that it brings the plants and other organisms into a new role in which the importance of the use-values produced is not primarily as either goods, or raw materials for production, but as the central productive forces in various production processes, from energy, to pharmaceuticals, to food additives. In the following, I illustrate this with the example of vanilla flavour produced by molecularly engineered yeast.

To produce 1 kg of true vanillin as an extract of the orchid, *Vanilla planifolia*, 500 kg of vanilla pods are needed, meaning that 40 000 orchid flowers are pollinated, harvested and cured by hand in countries such as Indonesia or Madagascar. Today, this type of plant-based production corresponds to only 40 tons of the total vanilla aroma produced worldwide, or 0.25 per cent of the global market of this popular food aroma (Hansen et al. 2009; Priefert et al. 2001). The rest of vanilla flavouring is derived from a chemically processed molecule that has a similar aroma but has been produced, since the mid-1930s, from fermented lignin, a carbohydrate found in woody plant cells and obtained as a residue of the paper industry. Chemical processing is less laborious than hand-pollinating the orchid flowers and curing the pods, but producing it nevertheless entails substantial additional processing: it begins with the leftover material of paper pulping, sulphite pulping liquor, which is fermented in several stages. This is then oxidated with air at a certain temperature and pressure, followed by several steps of mechanical and chemical transformation. It is then purified with various chemicals and filtered. Finally, to obtain food-grade purity, the substance must be crystallized and vacuum-distilled (Hocking 1997).

A new and less laborious alternative to both producing vanilla flavour through plant fermentation and the chemical modification of lignin is molecularly engineering the yeast strains, *S. pombe* (African beer yeast) or *S. cerevisiae* (baker's yeast) (Hansen et al. 2009). Through various kinds of alterations to the yeast that include inserting DNA segments of fungal plant and animal origin, vanilla aroma can be produced *de novo* – that is, the yeast (re)produces the final vanilla aroma molecule without requiring further processing. Production takes place in a medium of table sugar (0.30 USD/kg) in addition to the similarly low cost of the nutrients that keep the yeast strains alive, a mixture of sugars, amino acids and yeast extracts (Treco and Lundblad 1994). On the one hand, the new molecule would provide a novel use-value to future consumers (e.g. various food industries) in that the molecule and therefore the aroma is said to be closer to the cured orchid pods than the chemically processed vanilla of the twentieth century.[1] But perhaps the most important use-value motivating this type of *de novo* production in industries such as food processing, pharmaceuticals and energy is the potential advantage from the point of view of changes in the production process itself, in particular regarding the labour process. This shift in the relationship between living processes of humans and non-human organisms in achieving productive transformations is worth looking at more closely.

By molecularly engineering the yeast strains, the labour used to produce vanilla according to the other two methods is replaced by transformations carried out by the altered metabolism of the yeast. This type of transformation is novel in that it breaks with a longstanding pattern in which human living labour is replaced by what Karl Marx referred to as 'dead' labour, that is, by machines (Marx 1962: 446), and is instead supplanted by another living force. However, this rather 'fluid' relationship between the two living, transformative, qualities of humans on the one hand and plants on the other, is actually not something new in our productive relationship with plants. This is illustrated well by plant scientists' description of the process of peasant plant domestication in agriculture as one in which farmers 'took over' the living processes of plants through their labour: for example, early peasant farmers often selected plants without the toxins frequently produced by the latter to protect them against predator insects in their habitat. In a sense, therefore, by selecting plants without the toxins, farmers' labour replaced a living process – the toxin that defended the plant from falling prey to insects – with their own farming labour (Jordan 2002).

While the example just given is of human labour as a living process replacing that of plants, the vanilla-producing yeast is an example of the same materially 'fluid' relationship but in the opposite direction, in which the living process of the plant replaces part of the human labour process. The latter is, however, not unique to molecular engineering. For example, as part of twentieth-century Mendelian breeding, 'male-sterility' in maize (plants that did not produce viable pollen) was a sought-after trait that reduced the need for removing the pollen-bearing male flowers

[1] The vanilla flavouring produced in yeast is currently not marketed although it is expected to be commercially available in 2014. However, yeast that has been molecularly engineered to produce similar industrial chemicals is currently marketed, including orange and grapefruit aromas used by the cosmetic industry. The market price of these 'fine chemicals' can be as high as $10 000 per kilogram with an overall market worth US$20 000 million (cf. Hayden 2014: 598).

by hand in the process of cross-fertilizing for commercial seeds known as 'hybrids'. As a result, the seed industry in the United States was able to save US$10 million annually and replace the annual labour of 125000 workers who had previously removed the pollen-bearing flowers by hand (Hobbelink 1991). At the same time, an important difference between this and the vanilla-producing yeast is that, as discussed above, the yeast replaces human labour not only in agriculture, but also as part of processes that have, until now, been part of what is considered the 'secondary' or processing sector, that is, processes in which, unlike agriculture, living organisms have not been a source of productive transformations.

Underlining the ability to 'stretch' or recalibrate the living processes of non-humans, the new role of living organisms in production has been captured with the analogy of a 'formal' versus 'real' subsumption of nature, parallel to Marx's distinction between a formal/real subsumption of labour. The analogy is less interesting as a distinction between production with living versus non-living materials (cf. Boyd et al. 2001). Rather, following Marx's attention to labour as a material quality of the living human body, it is interesting as a recognition of how a living process can be harnessed in qualitatively different ways to optimize production – in the case of human labour, by intensifying it, by using tools, or through a division of labour; in the case of the yeast, by altering the cell's metabolism via its DNA. The comparison does not seek to downplay the important qualitative differences among the living processes of yeast and humans in how they are engaged productively. Indeed, as I emphasize below, these are important differences that by no means make this type of replacement of one living process with another materially identical or unproblematic. But my point here is to highlight how they are being treated as 'fluid' replacements by an industry that can exploit them similarly because as living forces both have transformative material qualities that can be inserted into the productive process.

There are several qualities of the molecular transformations that make them attractive from the perspective of rationalizing living organisms for industrial processing. First, molecular engineering has the potential to effect recurrent changes that go beyond a single (re)productive cycle and this makes them different from previous transformations of living organisms. In both peasant production and Mendelian breeding, plant transformations were short-lived unless human labour intervened at each life cycle. If a domesticated plant is no longer farmed, the crop reverts to the materiality of a wild plant, usually becoming a weed (Li 1969: 256). Likewise, if a plant is no longer reproduced according to Mendelian practices of cross- and self-fertilization, the stability of the 'traits' is quickly lost, often within a single generation. In both cases, the plant cannot be used productively without labour intervention at each life cycle. By contrast, one of the particularities of transformations via changes to the DNA molecule is that, from the transformation of the first initial cell, with each replication the new DNA and the targeted transformation with which it is associated, also continue to be reproduced. Thus, if the substance in question is reproduced accurately one cycle after another, human labour could potentially decrease substantially beyond the initial engineering of the yeast.

The question of exactly how much labour decreases in these types of production may be potentially great, but it is an open question that needs to be researched, taking into account how it may change when this kind of production process unfolds at an industrial scale and over many production cycles. But beyond the transformation of labour, the papers that describe how the yeast was transformed to produce the vanilla flavour emphasize various other material advantages that the molecular transformations present from the perspective of industrial processing. For example, it is described how the metabolism of the yeast can be altered to produce the vanilla in greater quantities by 'knocking out' (rather than adding) particular DNA segments. Another transformation entails adding a sequence of the mustard weed, *A. thaliana*, to the yeast's DNA, changing the cells' metabolism in such a way that accumulating high concentrations of the vanillin (re)produced by the yeast cells is no longer toxic to the yeast itself, a condition that would otherwise ruin the production process (Hansen et al. 2009: 2765). These examples illustrate, from the perspective of industry, the potential advantages presented by the molecular manipulations in 'recalibrating' organisms to produce new use-values for the productive process with a high degree of flexibility.

The processes just described in which (mostly single-celled) organisms are modified to produce new substances is often referred to as 'synthetic biology' (Carlson 2010; Endy 2005; Hayden 2014). The distinction between molecular engineering and what is being called 'synthetic biology' is not always clear (Morange 2009), as both seek to transform discrete living processes of organisms by reorganizing DNA sequences. But from the perspective of the transformation to the productive process made possible through the practical reframing of reproduction, the shift in emphasis makes sense: what is being expressed with the notion of 'synthesis' is often an engineering approach to creating 'parts' or 'building pieces' that could potentially be used in a number of different organisms (Tucker and Zilinskas 2006). From a production perspective, synthetic biology could therefore be described as a search for a type of 'flexible specialization' based on the advantages or disadvantages of the different (re)productive qualities of humans versus plants versus animals versus fungi, and so on.

For example, given that molecular engineering usually transforms living organisms by targeting single cells, from an industrial perspective it may be more advantageous to rely on single-celled organisms such as bacteria or yeast because their functioning is less complex than that of plants or animals and therefore often easier to transform. The well-studied bacterium, *E. coli*, whose reproduction at a molecular level is better understood than other organisms, currently (re)produces about 30 per cent of the molecularly engineered proteins used in pharmaceuticals (Martínez et al. 2012: 695). On the other hand, a small and comparatively 'simple' cell such as *E. coli* may be unable to reproduce larger and more complex molecules, presenting a disadvantage if the unfinished substances it produces require further chemical processing. As an alternative, molecular engineers may seek to produce the same substance in more complex cells such as those of plants so that the targeted protein can be 'harvested' in a specific cell organelle, and because the great amount of biomass produced by the plant makes it less expensive to produce even despite low 'yields' of the targeted proteins (Masumura et al. 2006; Sourrouille et al. 2009). In other cases, algal cells are seen as particularly advantageous 'productive platforms', for in addition to being single-celled and reproducing quickly, they can 'source' much of the energy for the (re)productive process through photosynthesis or by fixing atmospheric carbon (Laursen 2011).

A similar advantage based on photosynthesis plus the capacity to (re-) produce more complex molecules than algae is achieved by culturing colonies of individual plant cells in a liquid suspension of nutrients, a method currently used to produce paclitaxel, the compound for the anticancer drug 'taxol' (Lim and Bowles 2012: 272). This example of plant or animal cells suspended in nutrients to produce these substances most vividly underscores that what is sought is *a rationalization of production that takes advantage of some of the living qualities* – here, the ability to photosynthesize, the complexity of the plant cell versus a more simple bacterial cell, etc. – *but at the same time that seeks to abstract from other dimensions of the living organism*, the particularities and complexities of organisms, populations of organisms and their ecosystems that can be seen as disturbing a fully rationalized process. This tension, in which the complexity of living processes is at the same time encouraged and also repressed is a contradictory process that affects both production and reproduction. By looking at it more closely we can see an important explanation as to why production with molecular engineering has the potential to create not only powerful productive forces – as the industries that seek out this type of production recognize – but also powerfully disruptive or even destructive ones. I address this key issue in the final section of this chapter.

PRODUCTION AS AN ABSTRACTION FROM REPRODUCTION: FROM PRODUCTIVE TO DESTRUCTIVE FORCES

As discussed throughout, producing or creating new use-values with living organisms entails practically reframing their reproduction. It also means (de)limiting the material contours of processes that, throughout the evolution of life, have been deeply and extensively interwoven with one another. And yet an important qualitative difference between the three types of biotechnological production reviewed here – peasant, Mendelian and molecular – is the high degree of abstraction involved in how the latter two, Mendelian and molecular approaches, delimit reproduction in order to produce. The abstraction is created when reproduction is redefined in highly discrete terms. Of interest is the reproduction of particular traits, in one case; and particular substances, in the other, in abstraction of the other living dimensions that have historically been a part of the life process in question: the living cell and the ensembles of living cells in relation to one another as an organism; the other living entities in the organism's environment, such as microbes, fungi, plants, humans and other animals; or even the interaction of these with the non-living environment such as rainfall patterns, sunlight and so on, that have historically framed how living processes unfold.

By contrast, in the peasant reproduction of plants (and animals) a major difference is that selection is always in relation to the organism's wider environment, so that the production of the use-values is based on the management and reproduction of complex agro-ecosystems (Francis 1990; Plucknett and Smith 1986). While peasant reproduction certainly redefined ecosystems and even radically transformed them (Harlan 1992), it is a way of reframing reproduction that does not abstract away from it, but on the contrary, it is a system in which a very broad and complex definition of reproduction is an explicit source of its productivity. The redefinitions of reproduction in both Mendelian as well as molecular ways of reframing reproduction take a radically different approach which is not one of degree (a more or less narrow redefinition of reproduction) but of *kind*. Their very ingenuity and productivity – epitomized in Mendel's radically different approach to plants as either 'yellow *or* green', 'smooth *or* wrinkled'; or the reductionist approach of early molecular biology epitomized in the 'central dogma' – is based on breaking with the complexity of life processes and redefining them *in abstraction* of that complexity. In the case of molecular engineering, redefinitions of reproduction go as far as defining it in abstraction even of the cell, the most basic reproductive 'unit'. These abstractions are crucial for molecular engineering because they are no more and no less the very source of the specific use-values it creates.

At the same time, these abstractions are also highly contradictory because, as emphasized earlier in the chapter, producing with nature entails both transforming and also relying on a wider reproductive context to achieve a particular transformation. For this reason, the abstraction can only be approximated: even as myriad dimensions of life are abstracted from, they continue to be present in the wider (re)productive process and are even essential to it. Thus, the engineered yeast not only (re) produces the vanilla aroma but also myriad other life processes that keep the yeast alive and without which, moreover, the production of the targeted use-value would not even take place. In Mendelian production also, while a plant may be bred to produce a handful of traits such as 'short stems', 'stiff stalks', 'tolerance to frost', the plant continues to reproduce countless of other living processes, whether they are defined in terms of molecules, of other traits, or however else we may choose to approach them. As a result, while Mendelian or molecular definitions of production tend to only consider their intervention into a particular life process as if it had clearly discernible borders, its effects and repercussions are usually much broader, affecting a much wider constellation of living processes than foreseen.

In the case of Mendelian production, the effects of this narrow redefinition of reproduction have largely been captured as a loss of the diversity of cultivated plant species as a result of the reproduction of a very limited number of discrete traits in abstraction of undesired ones, and more generally, in abstraction of the ecosystems that created them. For example, according to the UN Food and Agriculture Organization, only 20 per cent of maize varieties that existed in Mexico in the 1930s were still known in 1997. In the United States, out of over seven thousand varieties of apple documented as having been in use between 1804 and 1904, approximately 86 per cent have been lost. The same is true of 95 per cent of cabbage, 91 per cent of maize, 94 per cent of peas and 81 per cent of tomatoes once (re) produced in that country through peasant methods (FAO 1997: 34).

In the case of the molecular reproduction of plants, the very narrow definition of reproduction in which molecules are transformed as if apparently nothing beyond the molecular level were altered, has taken the form of a number of similarly 'unexpected consequences'. These range from mutations, the production of toxic substances, to negative impacts on other organisms that were not a target of the molecular transformation, to health damage to a range of organisms, including humans (Álvarez-Buylla et al. 2013; Kuruganti 2013; Saxena and Stotzky 2001). The negative impacts of these 'unexpected consequences' loom particularly large for the type of production described in this chapter, in which yeast, algae but also other organisms such as plants and animals, are being used to produce pharmaceuticals, fuels, adhesives, plastics and so on. Reproduction defined as a discrete DNA segment leading to the production of a discrete molecular substance such as vanilla in yeast or a vaccine in a maize plant is a productive abstraction that, however, does not continue to exist as such in society–nature relations more widely defined. We are reminded or, indeed, admonished of this in cases in which molecularly engineered crops that produce substances such as pharmaceuticals have already contaminated the fields of crops grown for food. In 2001 the company ProdiGene hired farmers to grow genetically engineered maize producing an animal vaccine in open fields in Iowa and Nebraska in the United States. The result was the contamination of other non-genetically engineered fields of maize.

Moreover, if one produces in a way that abstracts from the way that living processes have reproduced/evolved historically, the risk is to negatively affect not only the stability and viability of the reproductive process, but over the longer run, also that of production itself. In the case of the Mendelian abstraction, diversity loss also means a loss of many of the use-values previously associated with peasant reproduction, with negative consequences for the production process. Consider the many cases of plagues that have seriously undermined the homogeneous crops, from maize to oranges, that have been bred according to only a handful of traits, incurring losses in the thousands of millions of dollars as a result of their material homogeneity (Kloppenburg 2004; Liston 2013). Another example is the development of 'superweeds' that have become a major problem associated with plants molecularly engineered to resist certain herbicides, but which have now exchanged DNA with the surrounding plants, resulting in weeds that are also resistant to the herbicide that was meant to destroy them. In all countries in which genetically engineered herbicide-resistant crops have been grown, these 'superweeds' currently present serious problems for industrial farming, decreasing production output and raising costs (cf. Gillam 2011). In the United States, in the past three years alone the surface area covered by weeds that are no longer affected by the herbicide glyphosate, has nearly doubled, from 32.6 million to 61.2 million acres, according to an agricultural consulting agency (Stratus Research 2013). Regarding the production of industrial substances, from vanilla to vaccines, which is only beginning, it is not difficult to imagine a situation in which the unintended exchange of DNA among several engineered organisms may not only cause serious disruptions to reproduction but may also render these organisms useless to anyone who wants to produce with them, whether for food or for industrial processing.

Studying production from the lens of reproduction allows us to capture the tension between how various ways of redefining production have led to the production of new use-values but also how these stand in tension with how production unfolds more broadly, based on very complex interconnections at the molecular, cellular, organism and ecosystem levels. On the one hand, this allows us to gain a more sophisticated analytic grip over social interactions with living nature that are otherwise captured in terms of 'environmental consequences'. Yet it is important that we recognize them not simply as 'environmental', that is, as caused by a social action but remaining unintelligible to social theory, but that using these two categories and the distinctions they allow we can integrate them into theorizing on nature–society relations. The possibilities related to viewing production from the lens of reproduction are many and can be applied fruitfully to a wide range of studies of living nature in the social sciences.

Furthermore, viewing production from the lens of reproduction underlines that it is simply impossible to have one's cake and eat it too: given a historical process of reproduction that is the material basis for all social relations including production, it is not plausible to produce according to increasingly narrow definitions of living organisms and forget that one is at the same time reproducing with them. In other words, it is a major problem to produce with living nature as if it were a discrete entity and assume that affecting life processes according to this highly narrow definition will have no impact on that same life process and the others it has been connected to through millions of years of reproductive history. Yet our interaction with living nature and our responsibility as scholars goes far beyond analysing what has been or what can be (re)produced and how. We must also deal with the wider issue that is currently the object of major social contention involving farmers, industrial capital, scientists, consumers, social movements, political institutions and so on who are seeking answers to define *how we want to produce* and whether we will continue to do so according to increasingly narrow definitions of reproduction. It is perhaps one of the greatest questions we face, for our very reproduction – our life – depends on it.

27. Alternatives to agribusiness: agro-ecology and the peasant principle

Sylvia Kay[1]

Following decades of political neglect and declining investment, the problem of structural hunger has once again come to the fore as the era of cheap food was brought to a dramatic end by rapid food price inflation. Yet solutions from within the existing corporate food regime based on the spread of global value chains should be met with a high degree of scepticism. Answers from agribusiness fail to convince: with 1 billion of the world's population 'starved', another 1.3 billion 'stuffed' and 1 billion malnourished it is clear that capitalism doesn't know where the hungry are nor how to feed them (Patel 2007; ETC 2009).

This chapter argues that a mode of agrarian capital accumulation which ignores the imperatives for social reproduction and which destroys the natural resource base upon which agriculture depends, is fundamentally flawed. Instead of the extractive logic of global value chains, it examines various examples of agricultural production that conform to an alternative logic, also termed the 'peasant principle' (Van der Ploeg 2008). This peasant principle is defined by a set of practices that differentiate it from other capitalist and entrepreneurial styles of farming: 'pluri-varied' activity, instead of specialization; family labour instead of wage labour; working with rather than against natural regeneration cycles; and so on. In resisting the increasing commodification of nature and the undemocratic control of the world food system by 'food empires', the peasant principle is above all an emancipatory notion.

Rather than the disappearance of the peasantry under conditions of global capitalism, this chapter argues that the growing spread of these types of farming practices point towards a powerful trend of 're-peasantization' (ibid.). This trend, rooted in the peasant style of farming, is increasingly being channelled into new forms of politics, agrarian mobilization, and state–society interaction at local, national and transnational levels. This points to the possibility of an 'alternative peasant way' grounded in the transformational projects of food justice and food sovereignty.

---

[1] The author is grateful for exchanges with Jan Douwe van der Ploeg and Philip McMichael which helped shape this chapter.

THE AGRIBUSINESS MODE OF PRODUCTION: THE RISE OF THE CORPORATE FOOD REGIME

The rise of the 'corporate food regime'[2] has its origins in the transition from the era of developmentalism to the era of globalization. With the onset of world recession following the 1973 oil crisis, it became clear that states could no longer police the international relations of food production nor expect to develop agriculture through national regimes of capital accumulation fortified by mercantilist trade policies. This was to mark a radical restructuring of agriculture away from state-led development programmes towards the primacy of the market. In terms of agricultural investment, the 1980s and 1990s witnessed a dramatic reduction of public support to the point where 'by the late 1980s, the state had been so drastically downsized that, in the rural areas, it had become almost irrelevant' (De Schutter 2011: 511). The scaling back of public extension services, subsidized inputs and credit saw many small-scale farmers caught in a vicious cycle of debt (Rosset 2000; Desmarais 2007). The dismantling of domestic price supports and national grain boards meanwhile set off a wave of 'second green revolutions' involving the production of animal feed, luxury foods and more generally a switch in investment priorities away from staple food crops towards commercial crops destined for export (DeWalt 1985).

The globalization of agriculture was consummated by the signing of the World Trade Organization's Agreement on Agriculture. While the official discourse emphasized the importance of market access, competition and free trade, the outcome has been an extraordinary degree of market concentration, oligopolistic behaviour, and subsidization and/or protectionism for the agricultural sectors of the global North. The increasing specialization and integration of world food production encouraged by a global division of agricultural labour has allowed transnational corporations to insert themselves strategically in between the buyers and sellers of food as consumer-driven value chains have decoupled world market prices from production costs (Friedmann 1993).

The scale of market concentration is truly astounding. According to latest figures provided by the Berne Declaration and EcoNexus (2013), the state of 'agropoly' is such that the top corporations control the market to the following degrees:

---

[2] Philip McMichael (2012: 101) defines a food regime as '. . . a conceptual tool to define periods or projects of rule based in particular forms of agriculture, social diets and power relations on a geopolitical scale . . . Each food regime has pivoted on a particular agrarian question'.

- the top 10 animal feed corporations, 15.5 per cent;
- the top 4 livestock breeding corporations, 99 per cent;
- the top 10 seed corporations, 75 per cent;
- the top 11 pesticide corporations, 97.8 per cent;
- the top 4 food trading corporations, 75 per cent;
- the top 10 food processing corporations, 28 per cent;
- the top 10 food retail corporations, 10.5 per cent.

One of the starkest impacts of this transformation has been a substantial decline in the value-added captured by primary producers. A dramatic fall in net farm incomes in many countries around the word has precipitated a steep decline in the relative farming population (Desmarais 2007). This rural exodus is an expression of the crisis of social reproduction prevalent in many rural areas, where 70 per cent of the world's very poorest live despite the global urban population now outnumbering the rural population (IFAD 2010).

Yet as the world food crisis tipped the number of hungry and undernourished to over one billion, the dominant response by agribusiness, international policy makers, the donor community and other philanthrocapitalist ventures has been to continue with business as usual. This is reflected in the growing rise of global value chain sourced agricultural commodities along with the outsourcing of responsibilities that were once the provenance of the state to the purveyors of agro-inputs. As with the previous Green Revolution, these initiatives are likely to produce a situation 'where a sub-set of consumers and producers prosper (for a time) without altering the incidence and/or geography of hunger' (McMichael 2013c). To understand why, it is necessary to examine in more depth the agribusiness mode of production and its preferred business model: the global value chain.

GLOBAL VALUE CHAINS AS 'TECHNOLOGIES OF CONTROL'

Value chains have become a globalized model for producing any number of commodities, both agricultural and non-agricultural (cf. Selwyn, this volume).[3] Agribusiness holdings present the rise of value chain agriculture

---

[3] The value chain is an economic model for organizing the flow of agricultural commodities 'from farm to fork'. The idea is that along each link in the chain, value is added – through for example processing, packaging, and branding and marketing activities. In agriculture, value chains are closely associated with contract farming arrangements.

as a demand driven expansion, a response to the growing need for investment and technology transfer. While undoubtedly encouraged by governments eager to bridge investment deficits, their rise has as much to do with the global sourcing strategies of the world's leading agribusiness companies. As the instability in agricultural commodity prices and the ongoing 'supermarket revolutions' have forced food suppliers to conform to ever tighter delivery schedules of high-quality, high-volume produce, agribusiness companies have looked to exert greater control over the production process through greater vertical integration along the value chain.

However, the claim that contract farming acts as new vector of smallholder development must be more closely interrogated. Although benefits have been observed with some contracting arrangements – including higher incomes and increased access to credit and inputs – this must be set against the commanding position occupied by the company to set all the terms and conditions regarding pricing, product quality, delivery schedules, payment, and so on. Debt is often a point of leverage in this relationship as upfront payments, delayed payments, or non-payment in case of rejected produce are also a common feature, 'constituting the chain through which such new contract farming is activated, reproduced and, in some cases, dispossessed' (McMichael 2013c: 672).

Furthermore, despite the rhetoric of 'the smallholder', the operation of inclusion thresholds means that most companies prefer to transact with better-off farmers. This is of course nothing new. The history of the first Green Revolution shows how implicit assumptions guided the roll-out of the new technology and its focus on the so-called 'progressive farmer' (Griffin 1979; Pearse 1980). Although it was never explicitly stated that this signified the well-endowed farmer, in reality it proved to be code for the farmer who 'owned a medium or large farm, was better educated, had already adopted some of the elements of the new technology, and had sufficient resources and financial backing to accept the risks involved in experimentation' (Pearse 1980: 175). It was these more commercially minded farmers, whose real cost of innovation was lower compared to that of the more resource-poor, risk-averse, small producer, who were identified as the appropriate targets for adoption of the new technology package (Griffin 1979).

Similar assumptions underpin the global sourcing strategies of today's agribusiness corporations, which prefer to deal with the 'entrepreneurial farmer' with a more commercial outlook. This is evidenced in the increasing patterns of class differentiation that have accompanied the growth of contract farming. The spectacular growth of Chile's non-traditional agricultural export sector for example was made possible in large part due to agribusiness-led contract farming. While certainly a success in terms of growth figures and export earnings, this depended to a large extent on the ability of the new capitalist firms to tap into cheap rural labour from the peasantry's reserve army of labour – the ranks of which were greatly increased by the agro-export model (Kay 2002a). As Cristobal Kay (2002a: 480–81) explains with respect to the growth of Chile's fruit export sector,

> The fruit export boom encouraged land concentration as capitalist entrepreneurs bought land from peasant farmers who generally did not have the capital to shift from crop cultivation to fruit farming. In the few instances where peasant farmers did manage to engage in fruit production, a significant proportion later sold part, or all, of their land to capitalist farmers or fruit agro-industries as they could not repay their accumulated debts resulting from their initial investment in fruit trees.

The result of this transformation was that as agricultural exports surged, so did rural poverty, rising to 53.5 per cent in 1987 from a comparatively low 25 per cent in 1970 (Kurtz 2001). Philip McMichael (2013b) documents a similar case of supermarket contracts for fresh fruit and vegetables in Kenya. Here, the capital requirements put the supermarket option beyond the reach of the vast majority of smallholders. Instead, some end up working as wage labour on the supermarket chain controlled farms. The disappearance or 'transformation' of the peasantry is a real possibility, depending on the speed with which land concentration progresses and the 'relative profitability and feasibility of converting grain, bush and pasture land as the medium farmers now do, coupled with the transaction costs of assembling tracts of land by purchases from many small farmers with fragmented plots' (Neven, Odera et al. in McMichael 2013b: 683–4).

Far from being 'a benign facilitator of agricultural productivity and rural income', the value chain must be seen as leading to – at best – contradictory outcomes (McMichael 2013c). At worst, value chains are actively reproducing the conditions for dispossession and the complete subsumption of agriculture by capital in the form of 'an agro-industrial sector unable to self-reproduce, being entirely dependent on agro-chemical and/or biotechnical inputs' (ibid.). This is also reflected in the shift in the distribution of land area operated in favour of better-off farmers. Small-scale farmers, who were either forced to give up their land due to debt and impoverishment or who could not expand their holdings sufficiently to guarantee survival, have had to rely increasingly on wage labour.

The point is not that poverty and inequality persist *in spite* of the rise of contract farming and export-led agriculture but that the one actively produces the other. As Andrew Pearse (1980: 172) argues,

> Rich and poor do not simply coexist. The accumulation of land by the rich creates a demand for labour, which the poor are obliged to satisfy because of their land-poverty or landlessness; moreover, the entrepreneurial success of the rich is made possible by the hunger and importunity of the poor cultivator, who is obliged to surrender his bargaining freedom and even to pledge his future labour at a reduced price in order to sustain his family and meet current obligations.

Class formation in the countryside can of course not just be laid at the hands of contract farming. The example of Chile is particularly interesting as it shows how the rise of the contract farming-based agro-export model interlocks with unequal public investment and policy biases that significantly accelerate processes of class differentiation. Kurtz (2001) describes how public efforts to adjust to trade opening – key to the take-off and success of Chile's non-traditional agricultural exports – were disproportionately geared towards larger capitalist farms. A full 95 per cent of subsidies for irrigation organized under Law 18450 of 1985, for instance, were captured by large producers. Together with the active dismantling of state support for peasant cooperatives and public marketing boards, this meant that 'an important potential source of export production was lost, leading to increasing concentration of landholdings, rising poverty and inequality, and the decapitalization and marginalization of an important economic sector' (Kurtz 2001: 7).

Discussions around value chains and agribusiness sourcing strategies can therefore not be disconnected from broader state objectives and policy agendas. This does not mean, however, that no conclusions can be drawn about the agribusiness mode of production based on contract farming. Although the governance of each chain will vary, all value chains adhere to a similar logic of value creation, extraction and capture. In this relationship, the 'battle for the capture of added value' (Van der Ploeg 2008) is undoubtedly won by the contracting party – in this case an agribusiness holding – who has the power to set the terms and conditions of the arrangement while food producers occupy the link in the chain where the least value resides. This is not only an attack on the 'territory of self-determination' (McMichael 2013b). It is also to question the broader development claims that are made for the value chain model when these chains are structured and reproduced by conditions of debt, deployed in this model as a subordinating mechanism or 'technology of control' to discipline classes of (rural) labour according to the exigencies of commodity exchange (McMichael 2013c).

AGRARIAN QUESTIONS IN THE TWENTY-FIRST CENTURY

As struggles *for* the land connect with struggles *on* the land, the shape of contemporary agrarian questions is ever changing. Henry Bernstein (2009: 251) argues that the spread of global capitalism today means that 'popular struggles over land are driven by experiences of the fragmentation of labour' as rural classes of labour become increasingly differentiated according to the pursuit of their means of reproduction. That is, forms of primitive accumulation have, under conditions of global capitalism, now become generalized and have intensified as commodity relations deepen in the countryside. The result is that we can today identify rural classes of labour who must pursue their reproduction, either directly or indirectly, through the sale of their labour power.

This is reflected in the increasing numbers of rural subjects who must combine petty commodity production with wage employment and informal sector work, often as Bernstein notes, 'across different sites of the social division of labour including urban and rural, agricultural and non-agricultural, wage employment or self-employment'. The outcome is that 'land struggles more generally today are generated by the semi-proletarian condition' (ibid.: 252). The failure of the capitalist order to guarantee a living wage as it fills the ranks of a global proletariat generates a 'crisis of reproduction' and forms for Bernstein and others working in the Marxist political economy vein, the essence of the agrarian question of labour in the twenty-first century.

What does this mean for those struggling for a more just food system? One based not on profit but on the principles of 'food sovereignty', articulated by the global peasant movement *La Via Campesina* as 'the right of people to define their own agriculture and food policies' through 'safe, healthy and ecologically sustainable production' (McMichael 2009). Bernstein and others make no bones about their scepticism of such a project, arguing that food sovereignty amounts to a form of 'agrarian populism' that proclaims the moral superiority of the peasantry (often called upon as a unified collective) while suffering from an under-developed political economy analysis and underplaying the notable achievements of the productive forces of capitalism (Bernstein 2013).

Bernstein's criticism of the food sovereignty movement is certainly well taken. There are, however, also limitations that a pure capital accumulation lens runs up against. These concern principally an overly economistic understanding of the values which guide peasant societies and modes of reproduction and hence an implicit justification of the order that capitalism imposes. As Jan Douwe van der Ploeg (2008: 19) comments, 'peasant-like ways of farming often exist as practices without theoretical representation . . . . Hence they cannot be properly understood, which normally fuels the conclusion that they do not exist or that they are, at best, some irrelevant anomaly.'

While the starting point for Marxist political economists is the capitalist system, with peasant agriculture counterposed as 'capitalism's other' (Bernstein 2013), for proponents of food sovereignty, the relationship is inverted. Industrial agriculture functions as the alternative to an analytical norm deriving from existing food cultures, practices and investments that are based on a healthy logic of reproduction of social and ecological relations. For Philip McMichael (2013a) the great agrarian question of the twenty-first century concerns therefore the notion of 'value'. While capitalist value relations seek to reduce everything to the commodity form, the food sovereignty movement stresses the importance of other values – cultural and agro-ecological – which guide the decisions of small-scale farming communities. Crucially, by historicizing and de-naturalizing capital, the possibility of transcendence is opened up as the fetishism of the exchange-value calculus can be overcome. The first step towards this transcendence is to understand and make visible the values, practices and investments that define the 'peasant principle'.

THE 'PEASANT PRINCIPLE' AND THE POLITICS OF REPRESENTATION

Investments made by small-scale farmers are often based on what has been called the 'peasant pedagogy' (Rosset et al. 2011) or the 'peasant principle' (Van der Ploeg 2008). These notions refer to the ability of small-scale family farmers to harness locally derived knowledge about agriculture and natural systems in order to build up forms of ecological, social and cultural capital which allow for the reproduction of the peasant condition. It is intimately connected to the (re)assertion of peasant autonomy and control over land and other productive resources in order to construct a 'farmer road to development' based on the principles of food sovereignty, agrarian reform and human rights (Rosset 2006; Desmarais 2007).

In resisting the increasing commodification of nature and the undemocratic control of the world food system by 'food empires', the peasant principle is above all an emancipatory notion (Van der Ploeg 2008). It is perhaps best understood not through an academic definition but through an examination of concrete examples and practices of this principle in action. In what follows, three examples of 'resistance' are given that are based on this principle. Resistance here is understood as 'a wide range of heterogeneous and increasingly interlinked *practices* through which the peasantry constitutes itself as *distinctively different*' to the ordering principles set by agribusiness and the corporate food regime (Van der Ploeg 2008: 265, emphasis in the original). These examples show that peasants across the world are mobilizing as well as differentiating (McMichael 2013b). Together, they also represent instances of 're-peasantization', understood as both an increase in the number of peasants and a qualitative shift in the mode of production towards a peasant style of farming that enlarges autonomy and distance from conventional markets (Van der Ploeg 2008).

The Farmer-to-Farmer Agro-ecology Movement

A powerful example of this form of peasant-driven development is the agro-ecological movement. Agro-ecology combines insights from both agronomy and ecology in order to generate an agro-ecological systems approach to the management of natural landscapes. This management is based on five key ecological principles[4] which advance a form of low-external input, sustainable agriculture based on farming systems which are resource-conserving, resilient and highly biodiverse (De Schutter and Vanloqueren 2011). Agro-ecology does not involve just the technical aspects of farming. Since the ecological principles underpinning agro-ecology are adapted to best suit local circumstances, agro-ecological systems are highly reliant on local, traditional and indigenous knowledge of farming techniques. Agro-ecology is thus strongly aligned with processes of re-peasantization and the strengthening of small-scale agriculture. This forms perhaps the key difference with other sustainable agriculture initiatives, such as organic agriculture, which simply involve forms of input-substitution. Agro-ecological systems meanwhile emphasize food, technological and energetic sovereignty, which ensures that agro-ecology does not end up becoming subsumed by corporate controlled agriculture (Altieri and Toledo 2011).

Cuba's agro-ecological revolution provides one of the best examples that alternative agriculture can succeed. The novelty and strength of this revolution is derived from the fact that small farmers were at the forefront of Cuba's transition from a form of high-input, export-oriented, industrial

---

[4] De Schutter and Vanloqueren (2011) detail the five key ecological principles as follows: (1) recycling biomass and balancing nutrient flow and availability; (2) securing favourable soil conditions for plant growth through enhanced organic matter; (3) minimizing losses of solar radiation, water and nutrients by way of microclimate management, water harvesting and soil cover; (4) enhancing biological and genetic diversification on cropland; (5) enhancing beneficial biological interactions and minimizing the use of pesticides.

agriculture towards agro-ecological farming. Beginning with the activities of small farmers on the ground, whose knowledge and use of organic fertilizers, biological forms of pest control, and animal traction made them remarkably adept at responding to the Cuban economic crisis, these practices were to become transformed into a grassroots agro-ecological social movement known as the *Campesino*-to-*Campesino* Agro-ecology Movement, or MACAC (Rosset et al. 2011). The success of this movement, which is spearheaded in Cuba by the National Association of Small Farmers, ANAP, is reflected in its rapid growth in membership. From just over 200 families in 1999, MACAC has expanded to encompass 110000 families – a third of the total peasant sector – in 2009. In 2008, MACAC registered more than 2 million participants, including families, promoters, facilitators and coordinators, involved in over 60000 projects and activities (ibid.).

The success of MACAC in Cuba can be attributed to a number of factors. By far the most important is the fact that MACAC relies strongly on the 'peasant pedagogy' (Rosset et al. 2011). By harnessing the power of peasants, MACAC re-developed a form of 'horizontal communication' in which farmers themselves were the main agents in the dissemination of agro-ecological techniques (ibid.). This involved peasant families with proven success in particular agro-ecological farming methods, linking up with other peasant families in the country through the support of facilitators, promoters and coordinators, to demonstrate these agro-ecological practices. This farmer-to-farmer exchange offers considerable advantages over conventional forms of extension which can be top-down and demobilizing. In the blueprint set out by MACAC, farmers themselves are the main actors in both the generation and dissemination of agricultural knowledge and technology.

MACAC would not have succeeded, however, had the benefits of agro-ecological over industrial agriculture not materialized. Bolstered by the Cuban government's national food sovereignty policy, the creation of farming cooperatives and the transfer of 80 per cent of formerly state-owned farmland to cooperative and individual farmers, Cuban food production rapidly rebounded after its collapse following the end of the Soviet trade bloc (Rosset 1998). By mid-1995, Cuba's food shortage had been overcome and in the 1996–97 growing season Cuba recorded its highest-ever production levels for 10 of the 13 basic food items in the Cuban diet. Between 1996 and 2005, Cuba posed the highest food production scores in Latin America and the Caribbean with an annual growth in per capita food production of 4.2 per cent compared to a regional average of 0 per cent (Altieri and Funes-Monzote 2012). These production increases (which are highest on farms with the greatest degree of agro-ecological integration) have allowed Cuba to achieve high levels of food, energetic and technological sovereignty (Altieri and Toledo 2011; Rosset et al. 2011). Cuba now imports only 16 per cent of its food while the use of agricultural chemicals declined by 72 per cent between 1988 and 2007 (Altieri and Funes-Monzote 2012).

The spread of the agro-ecology movement in Cuba has been accompanied by a growth in the total value of peasant production in Cuban agriculture and in the number of small-scale farmers (Rosset et al. 2011). As the transition from conventional agriculture to simple input substitution to agro-ecological farming raised the total productivity of both land and labour, farmers' incomes relative to other sectors of society increased (Tharamangalam 2008). This has sparked a process of re-peasantization, with former urban workers, especially from the eastern part of Cuba, moving back to the countryside (Enrique 2003). It has also contributed to an unprecedented growth in urban agriculture (Rosset 1998; Altieri and Funes-Monzote 2012). The movement of non-agricultural to agricultural labour challenges the fundamental premise of the agrarian transition paradigm, while the growth in urban agriculture holds out 'the potential of creating a rural–urban continuum that will reduce the gap between rural, agricultural life on the one hand and urban non-agricultural life on the other' (Tharamangalam 2008). In many respects Cuba thus represents a truly alternative model for the role of agriculture in society.

Can Cuba's agro-ecological revolution be replicated elsewhere? Some sceptics argue that Cuba's unique characteristics and historical experience make it an unlikely model for emulation.[5] This is, however, to miss the opportunities for spreading agro-ecological knowledge and practices presented by the *campesino-a-campesino* social process methodology. Considering that 'in the typical case, in most countries most of the time, there are abundant and productive ecological farming practices "on offer", but low adoption of them is the norm, because what is lacking is a methodology to create a social dynamic of widespread adoption' (Rosset et al. 2011: 168), MACAC's decentralized, non-hierarchical process of innovation and diffusion based on the 'peasant pedagogy' offers significant advantages over the 'project based' nature of many NGOs

[5] The 'Cuban exceptionalism' thesis argues that the confluence of factors which induced Cuba's switch to agro-ecological farming does not exist in conjunction elsewhere. These include: (i) the economic crisis engineered by the collapse of the Soviet trading bloc which imposed extraordinarily high 'scarcity costs' for imported agricultural inputs; (ii) an agrarian reform which had placed land in the hands of an organized peasantry; and (iii) a supportive state committed to the renewal of peasant farming. See Rosset et al. (2011) for further discussion.

(Holt-Gimenez 2006) and the 'cyclical mindset' of state authorities (Altieri and Funes-Monzote 2012).

Having initially spread in a capillary fashion throughout Mesoamerica and the Caribbean (Holt-Gimenez 2006), MACAC is now increasingly being consolidated as a global movement for social change, in large part due to the championing of agro-ecology by the worldwide peasant movement, *La Via Campesina* (LVC). According to Rosset et al. (2011), 'The past three to five years have seen virtually every organization in LVC around the world attempt to strengthen, initiate, or begin to plan its own program for promoting, to varying extents, the transition to agro-ecological farming among their members'. Agro-ecology is consistently being recognized as a new approach to rural development and features prominently in the report of The International Assessment of Agricultural Knowledge, Science and Technology for Development (IAASTD 2009) and in the work of the UN Special Rapporteur on the Right to Food, Olivier de Schutter (2010). It will be through the continued work on all these fronts that the new agro-ecological paradigm will take hold.

Seed Sovereignty and the (Re)assertion of Farmers' Rights

The seed represents perhaps the ultimate battleground symbol between two different visions for the future of farming. Jack Kloppenburg (1988), in his seminal work on the politics of seed, describes how the introduction of high-yielding seed varieties is a way for capital to overcome a fundamental obstacle to its penetration of agriculture: the fact that in planting traditional seed varieties farmers also reproduce a critical part of their means of production collecting, storing and re-planting the seeds from last season's crop. High-yielding seed varieties, which are not self-reproducing and which need to be bought every year from commercial seed suppliers, remove this 'plant back option'. The development of hybrid seeds – which serve no agronomic function – is therefore intended to further the corporate dominance of agriculture. As a form of agricultural expropriation, Kloppenburg (2010) calls this a process of 'accumulation by dispossession'.

Much of the history of the Green Revolution can be read as the steady erosion of 'seed sovereignty' as the introduction of high-yielding varieties displaced traditional varieties that had often been cultivated over generations. This displacement is, however, also being actively resisted. In her overview of the European context, Elisa Da Via (2012) documents a plethora of seed networks bringing together family farmers, collectives, farmers' movements, researchers, agronomists and NGOs that are exchanging locally adapted seeds in Spain, Italy, France, Austria,

Portugal, Switzerland, Hungary, Germany, Bulgaria, Romania and Scotland. According to Da Via, the emergence of these seed networks 'politicizes the relationship between peasant autonomy and agro-ecology beyond the level of the individual farm unit, thus redefining the social, cultural and ecological roles of farming and farmers' rights as a source of both food sovereignty and environmental sustainability' (ibid.: 231).

One of the iconic examples is that of the cooperative *La Verde*, in Villamartin, Spain. Founded in 1987, the cooperative has pioneered organic agriculture in Southern Andalucia based on the reproduction of locally adapted seeds. Encompassing six families working on 14 hectares of land, it has now grown to become the largest bank of farm-saved seeds in the country. Following the principles of agro-ecology, *La Verde* adopts a holistic approach to the on-farm selection, storage and multiplication of seeds. Through its involvement in different forms of farmer-to-farmer exchange, participatory breeding and experimental programmes, as well as its integration into the Spanish seed network, *Red de Semillas, La Verde* ensures the free flow of genetic materials. Local food retailers and consumers are also mobilized in this network as *La Verde*'s cooperative members supply their horticultural produce to local organic shops, markets and consumer groups. Last but not least, *La Verde* functions as a 'knowledge hub', acting as a training centre for young researchers and producers, hosting visitors, organizing workshops, and arranging participatory trials on the selection and management of farmers' seeds.

Da Via highlights *La Verde* within a growing European-wide context of 'everyday practices of resistance that build upon seed autonomy and pave the way for alternative forms of production and consumption as de facto expressions of food sovereignty rights' (ibid.: 236). These practices, she argues, are translating into a new form of politics that emanates directly from the fields and which can be considered an important example of re-peasantization in the rural areas of Europe. The growing links between different seed networks throughout Europe have, for example, led to the creation of the European Coordination of Farmers' Seeds 'aimed at developing common positions for the implementation of farmers' rights to save, use, exchange and sell farm-saved seeds in accordance with Articles 5, 6, and 9 of the International Treaty on Plant Genetic Resources for Food and Agriculture' (ibid.: 234). The Coordination has been active in the review of EU seed legislation, protecting farmers' seeds from appropriation and contamination. Such politicization of the seed issue demonstrates the importance of de-commodified circuits of exchange and means of reproduction in paving the way for peasant alternatives.

New Markets and Struggles for Autonomy: Towards a New Rural Development Paradigm?

The construction of new market spaces in which alternative modes of production, exchange and value creation can flourish is often the outcome of intense social struggle. Yet it is within these spaces that new synergies and investment opportunities are visible, pointing towards a new model of agrarian political economy. Brazil is an interesting example of how new markets have come into being through the interactions of different social actors including farmers' organizations, trade unions, rural NGOs, social movements and various government ministries. Some have identified in this constellation of forces a new emergent Brazilian rural development paradigm centred on land reform, agro-ecology, food security and support for small-scale farmers (Schneider et al. 2010; Van der Ploeg et al. 2010). Rural development is, however, a contested notion and the ability to steer it in any one direction is often compromised by conflicting interests and power agendas. The state often reveals itself to be a contradictory and uneven actor in this process. This is reflected in the evolution of Brazilian rural development policy in the past two decades.

On the one hand, the Brazilian government has enacted policies and mobilized resources in support of small-scale farmers. In 1994, the government established the National Programme for the Enhancement of Family Farming, PRONAF. Over the years, the size of its financial resources and the number of its beneficiaries has steadily grown. Between 1996 and 2008, PRONAF extended more than 14.5 million loans worth around $31 billion (Schneider et al. 2010). Family farming has grown as a result, with a 10 per cent increase between 1995/96 and 2006 in the number of family farm units as well as in their gross value of production. The agro-ecology movement is also supported by the Brazilian government through its PROAMBIENTE policy which promotes environmental conservation and agro-ecological practices by providing farmers with technical assistance, investment and credit, making direct payments for environmental services, and enabling market access for sustainably produced products.

The Brazilian state has also been adept at using public policy tools to open up new market spaces for poor, small-scale producers through its School Meals Programme and the Government Food Procurement Programme (PAA). Under the School Meals programme, each Brazilian municipality receives a daily subsidy for each student enrolled for 200 days a year with the requirement that 70 per cent of the municipalities' procurements should be staple, non-processed foods and 30 per cent of the food purchased should come from local family farms. The PAA programme meanwhile involves the public procurement of food, either by the state or by institutions such as schools, hospitals and restaurants, produced by small-scale farmers grouped together in associations and registered with the National Supply Company. This is set to benefit over 300000 poor family farmers – about 10 per cent of the total number of family farmers in Brazil (Schneider et al. 2010).

On the other hand, these investments occur against the backdrop of the huge expansion of Brazilian agri-business, accelerating land and resource grabs, continued deforestation and environmental degradation, and vast inequalities in the distribution and ownership of land. The state is often directly implicated in these processes. The National Bank for Economic and Social Development (BNDES) is, for example, the largest source of credit for sugar ethanol production, one of the major drivers of large-scale land appropriations in Brazil (Sauer and Leite 2012). Indeed, while the Brazilian government has recently responded to concerns of 'land grabbing' by banning foreign land ownership, it actively facilitates other mechanisms (foreign-domestic partnerships, processes of land regularization, failure to secure the territorial rights of indigenous groups) through which land can be controlled by large-scale corporate capital. In this way the dynamics of the 'global land grab' are perhaps subverted but not overturned by the Brazilian state (Oliveira 2011), in large part due to the government's belief that increasing competition for agro-fuels and agricultural commodities represents a 'window of opportunity' for Brazil in 'assuming technological leadership in a globally dynamic sector' (Wilkinson and Herrera in Sauer and Leite 2012).

This tension at the heart of Brazilian politics serves as a reminder that 'enlightened' public policy has only come about through significant grass-roots struggle. Following its founding in 1994, PRONAF was expanded in 1996 in large part due to political pressure from rural workers' unions which organized one-day marches which were to become consolidated into an annual national protest event, the 'Shout of the Brazilian Land' (Schneider et al. 2010). In a similar vein, it is largely thanks to the activism of social movements such as the Brazilian Landless Movement (MST) that land reform has received any attention in policy circles at all (Stedile 2002). The National Forum for Agrarian Reform (FNRA) – a nationwide network gathering together over 40 different agrarian movements, rural organizations and NGOs – led a national land-ceiling campaign in 2010 calling for a maximum limit of 35 fiscal units to be set for all rural property (Schneider et al. 2010). Although this has not been taken up by the Brazilian government, it has forced the issue of land concentration onto the national political debate.

Reflecting on the trajectory of Brazil's rural development policies thus reveals many contradictions. This is in part due to the context in which rural development programmes operate. Where neoliberalism has reified markets and rendered state intervention unthinkable, rural development policies prevaricate between the adoption of the ordering principles of global capital accumulation and more redistributive social policies which seek to regulate the free flow of capital. *This makes it clear that rural development should not be a state-led project*. This is not to say that public investment has no role to play. On the contrary, in an age where capitalist agriculture mobilizes many vectors of rural dispossession (Li 2009), states have a crucial role to play in guaranteeing the right to a living wage, enforcing labour legislation and protecting the Right to Food (De Schutter 2009). This should include opening up new market spaces for small-scale farmers, either through public procurement or through other policy tools. Against decades of government neglect of agriculture based on 'let die' rather than 'make live' interventions (Li 2009), it is time for states to foreground small-scale agricultural alternatives in official policy making and investment.

AN ALTERNATIVE 'PEASANT WAY'?

This chapter has sought to challenge the underlying values and assumptions that guide the capitalist teleology for agrarian relations. By explicitly politicizing the corporate food regime and its agnostic model of food security structured through global value chains, it has shown how flows of capital, food and people are intimately linked to normative assumptions on the role of agriculture in development. Rather than accepting the modernization narrative which views agriculture as a mere input-output process and a mechanism for 'releasing' people from the land, this chapter has shown that an extractive form of agrarian accumulation which degrades farming livelihoods, ignores the imperatives for social reproduction, and consigns ever larger populations to dwell in a 'planet of slums' (Davis 2006) is fundamentally flawed.

Instead of 'agropoly' whereby a handful of transnational agribusiness companies control the world food system, this chapter has argued in favour of a more just and democratic form of food governance rooted in the everyday practices of the world's small-scale food producers. The examples provided – from the agro-ecology movement in Latin America and the Caribbean, to the farmer-based seed networks in Europe, to the new markets and rural development paradigms emerging in Brazil – aim to make visible, in concrete form, the strategies of peasant populations to de-commodify farming practices and stem the rural exodus through acts of 're-peasantization'. In all these examples, food is not simply understood as a commodity, but also as a source of social solidarity, political identity and substantive rights.

Do these examples, however, point to an alternative 'peasant way'? In other words, to an alternative ordering principle that can exist beyond the local and which can bring together diverse constituencies of both food producers and consumers who can coalesce under the umbrella of 'food sovereignty'? Or as McMichael puts it (2009), 'How can a peasant politics make sense in a world-historical conjuncture overwhelmingly dominated by capital?'. While sympathetic to its critique of corporate agriculture, the Marxist agrarian scholar Henry Bernstein (2013) is sceptical of the broader political aspirations of the food sovereignty project, arguing that its central claims remain 'under-theorised' and 'insufficiently evidenced' with an 'over-emphasis on certain "emblematic" cases of small farmer practice that become taken as the norm'.

In particular, Bernstein criticizes food sovereignty proponents for lacking an adequate political economy analysis that would allow them to appreciate the contradictions of rural communities and the attendant class dynamics. Bernstein argues that the commodification of subsistence has proceeded to such an extent, that it is better to speak of petty commodity producers and classes of labour rather than to use the outdated language of the 'peasantry'. Bernstein's provocation that 'there are no peasants in the world of contemporary capitalist globalisation' is a tantalizing one. This of course recalls the earlier discussion of how one defines 'peasants', which will not be repeated here. Rather, in what remains, this chapter will look at how the 'peasant principle' and food sovereignty can work as a political project.

More than just an alternative mode of production, the 'peasant principle' also represents a new form of politics that links different levels of 'resistance', from the micro-level in the form of farming in a particular way, to the meso-level in the form of farmer-to-farmer networks and direct producer-to-consumer food chains, to the macro-level in the form of national and transnational agrarian movements. This resistance plays out in different spaces, from the farm-level, to the local and regional 'community of food practice' (Friedmann 2007), to international arenas such as the Committee on World Food Security (CFS) where social movement representatives from a diverse range of constituencies can parlay their field activism into high-level negotiating and lobbying work. Together, this multi-layered counter-movement against corporate capture shows that peasant forces are mobilizing as well as differentiating (McMichael 2013b). To be sure, this mobilization includes an element of class-based struggle and is imbued with tensions as well as expressions of solidarity. To a great extent though, it is also a politics that practises an open, democratic and participatory approach to issues of food governance.

The scope for this form of peasant politics is actively being redefined and reconstituted through various agrarian mobilizations. The international peasant movement, *La Via Campesina*, is perhaps the most well known example but these mobilizations encompass a whole range of actors, practices and encounters that are altering the nature of rural politics. In the struggle for progressive agrarian change, the state is often regarded with a high degree of suspicion. This is not surprising given that many rural livelihoods have been overturned throughout history by states pursuing 'high modernist' visions of development and progress (Scott 1998). Indeed, the very success of the peasant mode of production rests at least in part on the 'art of not being governed' (Scott 2009). Scholars such as Henry Bernstein (2013) are therefore sceptical as to how food sovereignty can work as a political project, noting that no state in history has so far fulfilled the conditions required by the proponents of food sovereignty.

The state, however, is not a monolithic actor and power resources in society are not statically distributed. Jonathan Fox (1993) captures this dynamic situation in his 'state–society interactive approach'. This approach looks at how progressive change can come about through political interaction between pro-reform forces in state and society. When the interaction between pro-reform forces is mutually reinforcing, Fox argues, then the 'boundaries of the politically possible' can be changed. Although the emphasis of this chapter has been on peasant autonomy and emancipation, it has also detailed some moments of positive state–society interaction, whether in the formation of 'new markets' or in up-scaling agro-ecological knowledge and techniques. The potential for maximizing these synergies and expanding the space for agricultural alternatives through public policies and public investments is great (see Kay 2014).

The problem for realizing this potential lies in the 'adverse environment' that the new peasant way must contend with (Van der Ploeg 2013). From the state of 'agropoly', to the extraordinary 'cost–price squeeze', to the roll-out of neoliberal structural adjustment programmes and austerity politics, the room for peasant alternatives and progressive public policies is narrowing. In a context wherein public investment is considered ideologically impossible and investments based on the peasant principle are made invisible, agribusiness and value-chain farming presents itself as the solution to the problem of structural hunger and malnutrition. This chapter has argued that it is only through forms of 'resistance' rooted in the peasant principle and translated into a new form of politics that positive rural futures can be realized. Against a state–capital alliance, the interaction between pro-reform forces within the state and society may lead to unexpected political outcomes and open the door for (re)distributive policies and an alternative peasant way.

28. Strategies of a Green Economy, contours of a Green Capitalism

Ulrich Brand and Markus Wissen[1]

INTRODUCTION

In recent years, a re-politicization of the ecological crisis has taken place in the Global North. The chief actors in this process are not primarily social movements, but state apparatuses, scientific institutions and private companies. Certainly their various initiatives are being undertaken on the ground prepared by the arguments of the social movements. Yet they are also moving the goalposts by concentrating on warnings of a scarcity of resources and 'sinks' (the systems that absorb a quantity of a particular pollutant larger than they discharge into their environment themselves, such as forests and oceans in the case of CO_2). It is in response to those scarcities that new economic opportunities are being discovered: electric mobility, agro-fuels and other renewable energy sources, all promising fields for business.

This is not just a matter of environmental policy, or the growth of an eco-industry. Far from representing an isolated sub-section of society, the re-politicization of the ecological crisis reveals a comprehensive quest to reorient the existing production and consumption patterns in their entirety, in the context of a transformation towards a Green Economy. The Green Economy, coupled with the call to halt the degradation of the natural basis of life by eco-capitalist modernization, constitutes a conceptual field in its own right. Like the theme of 'sustainable development' twenty years ago, Green Economy has become the norm for what is politically possible and plausible; at the same time, as in the case of sustainable development, it works to either obscure alternatives or make them seem unviable and irrational.

It is our argument in this chapter that the various strategies pursued under the Green Economy umbrella are in the process of establishing what may develop into a new capitalist formation, potentially taking the place

1 Our thanks to Roland Atzmüller, Lukas Oberndorfer and Thomas Sablowski for their useful comments, to Stefan Armborst and Marisa García Mareco for the translation into English and to Etienne Schneider for research assistance.

of the crisis-ridden post-Fordist, neoliberal formation. For this eventual formation we propose the label of Green Capitalism (Kaufmann and Müller 2009; Wallis 2010; Koch 2012; Newell 2012).

The question, then, is how the processes of change set in motion by Green Economy strategies, and potentially leading to a Green Capitalism, can be understood and explained. Which strategies are politically, economically and culturally feasible, and under which conditions can they be expected to be successful? We are primarily interested in those processes that may result from a 'historical chance discovery', a profound mutation that redefines socioeconomic, cultural and political practices, structures and power relations but which in its unfolding will necessarily remain highly uneven, both temporally and spatially. In adopting a long-term view, we ask ourselves also how these developments can be evaluated from a socio-ecological and radical democratic viewpoint.

Our theoretical frame is critical political economy – Regulation theory, Gramscian hegemony and critical state theory – supplemented by Political Ecology. The premise is that such a broad theoretical perspective will allow us to address the problems associated with this issue most effectively. Initial research along these lines has addressed the extent to which a green project is feasible and whether a 'green power bloc' and potentially forms of 'green corporatism' are being established (Kaufmann and Müller 2009; Haas and Sander 2013). But beyond that, any social science research seeking to understand the current dynamics of social and socio-ecological transformation must also look at the contradictory socioeconomic, political, cultural and subjective social conditions which, in their mutual correlation, will have to be stabilized for a certain period of time to make the project viable. By 'stabilization' we do not mean a static economy and society, but the dialectics of constructive and destructive capitalist dynamics which take place under more or less stable conditions.

Our approach provides the conceptual grid in which these different conditions, as a contradictory totality, can yet be brought into a relatively, and temporary, viable and manageable social structure. Indeed its specific contribution resides in the exploration of the socioeconomic, the politico-cultural and also, in a sense, the biophysical 'functionalities' of a potentially emerging Green Capitalism. Functionality here is measured by the extent to which norms of production and consumption are being adjusted in a way that avoids ever-larger crises of overproduction or under-consumption and instead puts in place mechanisms allowing for the externalization of crisis, be it through spatial, material and/or sectoral displacement, in order to stabilize capital accumulation over a certain period of time. Enlarging the analysis by taking the state and hegemony into account will in turn allow the identification of complementary social and political functionalities. A Green Capitalism after all must also be brought into accordance with people's way of life – their practices, aspirations and norms – and be safeguarded at the state and institutional levels. In addition, the formal, money-mediated and 'market-shaped' areas of production and reproduction need to be harmonized with other mechanisms and sectors of social (re)production. Finally, it is important to consider the prevention, the effective management or the spatio-temporal displacement of manifest socio-ecological crisis.

Once we examine the Green Economy as a *strategy* (or series of strategies) pursued by relevant social actors, and Green Capitalism (its outcome from a Regulation-theoretical perspective) as a potentially hegemonic capitalist *project* (see also Brand 2012; Wissen 2012), we are back in the debate concerning the relationship between critical political economy – we refer especially to Regulation theory – and Political Ecology.

The Regulationist debate has mainly centred on the extent to which the five structural features of a mode of regulation – the wage relation, the form of competition, monetary constraint, the state form and the form in which a given national economy is integrated into the world market (Becker 2002: 102, referring to Boyer 1990: 37ff; Desai, this volume) – should be complemented by a sixth, namely the so-called 'ecological constraint'. This points to the fact that the capitalist production is subject not only to monetary, but also to physical-material constraints (see Becker and Raza 2000, Raza 2003, and critically, Görg 2003b).

Here, in contrast, we are concerned with exploring the potential of the Regulation approach for a better diagnosis of time, rather than with developing it further conceptually (although it would in due course also necessitate further conceptual development). Our conviction is that Regulation theory possesses an evident potential with regard to socio-ecological transformation processes. This derives from its interest in the spatially and temporally variegated concretizations of the capitalist mode of production, which it analyses by means of its intermediate categories (mode of regulation, regime of accumulation). These include the possibility of an exacerbation of the ecological contradictions as well as their management.

In the following we will take a critical look at the concept of the Green Economy as it is being developed in the relevant documents. We then outline a theoretical perspective on socio-ecological questions, from which we derive an outline of the contours of Green Capitalism as a possible (albeit not at all necessary) new capitalist formation. Obviously, given the highly dynamic conjuncture in which this will play out we acknowledge the many uncertainties our diagnosis faces. Therefore, the following considerations are best understood as a research programme.

THE REGULATION OF DESTRUCTIVE SOCIETY–NATURE RELATIONS: THEORETICAL CONSIDERATIONS

Our approach to critical political economy is based on Regulation theory, which we propose to enlarge by materialist state theory and Gramsci's theory of hegemony. Combined with insights of Political Ecology this will serve to guide our understanding of the current quest for a Green Capitalism and more specifically, for the assessment of its social, ecological, economic and democratic implications. Moreover, we will show that political practices in the sense of the voluntaristic Green Economy interpretations form part of a much more complex process of regulation. We argue that historically, the contradictions of capitalism, manifested unequally as a consequence of the varied, contingent outcomes of social conflict, yet will be stabilized over time in such a way that a context of relative stability permits the process of capital accumulation to proceed as a relatively predictable process over a certain period. Or as Alain Lipietz defines it, regulation of a social relation is 'the way in which this relation is reproduced despite and through its conflictual and contradictory character' (Lipietz 1988: 11).

Society as a structured totality thus is reproduced through the actions of individuals and groups pursuing quite different strategies and possessing very dissimilar resources, both in terms of allocation and in terms of authority. For this reason this reproduction always remains a precarious process, and yet a degree of reliability of planning and an internal dynamism can arise nevertheless because social relations congeal into a temporary pattern. This pattern will also tend to hold in times of crisis, even though its stability will obviously be reduced and the capacity for compromise among the ruling forces diminishes once capital accumulation stagnates and authority and the capacity for repression are put to the test.

Regulation theory provides us with the concept of an accumulation regime. An accumulation regime denotes a package of social forms of organizing production, cycles of capital valorization, demand, but also the relationship with non-capitalist forms of production (Lipietz 1988: 23). The regime of accumulation itself is articulated with the mode of regulation: the wage and money relation, state, competition between companies and integration into the world market (see Aglietta 1979; Boyer 1990; Becker 2002). Additionally, whilst the concept of the technological paradigm and the industrialization model has been gradually lost sight of in current debates, it is obvious that it has to be revisited in an analysis of the Green Economy and Green Capitalism.

A mode of regulation, then, refers to the institutional embeddedness of macro-economic coherence. This refers, again in Lipietz's words, to the 'totality of institutional forms, networks, explicit and implicit norms that all guarantee the compatibility of modes of conduct within the framework of a regime of accumulation, corresponding to social conditions as well as transcending their conflictual properties' (Lipietz 1988: 24). Achieving a relative permanency of social conditions (not excluding the crystallization of temporary adjustments into institutions of their own) also means stabilizing the expectations underlying individual and collective (e.g. trade unionist) everyday practices. Here an important role is played by social discourse and knowledge (Demirovic 1992). A more or less stable mode of development, in which limited social struggles may occur – they may actually be large-scale as long as they do not lead to any fundamental transformation of the social order – allows the formation of a historic bloc. Everyday socioeconomic, technological, political and cultural conditions, as well as class and gender relations and relationships with nature, are actively reproduced (see Davies, this volume). That Fordism was the pre-eminent theoretical subject of Regulation theory is not in doubt; but the extent to which a specific post-Fordist or neoliberal mode of development has emerged remains contested (Demirovic et al. 1992; Brand and Raza 2003; Ihara, this volume).

State policies and systems of governance are a structural feature of modern societies. Unsustainable dynamics of development are not simply a socioeconomic problem which can be solved politically by the state; they are anchored in state apparatuses themselves, in their staff and rules, their ways of functioning and knowledge, their modes and practices. Certain interests are more easily served than others and state policies or governance tend to reinforce the dominant social conditions (Poulantzas 1978; Jessop 2007; Bretthauer et al. 2006; Wissen 2011).

The aforementioned contradiction between the capitalist mode of production and the biophysical reproduction of the conditions of life has been highlighted by Alain Lipietz, who has addressed the ecological crisis early on and who distinguishes the Regulation approach from, for example, eco-Marxism. Our own approach goes beyond eco-Marxism, which focuses on the fundamental ecological incompatibility of the capitalist mode of production with the preservation of the biosphere. It derives this assessment from an analysis of the dominance of exchange value, and pays less or no attention to the changing modes of development of capitalism and the ecological contradictions inherent in each of them. Hence it attaches a low probability to the management of this complex of contradictions (cf. Lipietz's critique of O'Connor, Lipietz 1998, 67–8; Zuindeau 2007). A Political Ecology informed by Regulation and hegemony theory on the other hand helps to explain how and why capitalism is different in each country, and 'how and why capitalism in the late 19th century differs from the current capitalism' (Goodwin and Painter 1997: 16). Hence it rejects the blanket designation as 'capitalist' of these different periods, or of countries such as Japan, the United States and Brazil.

A key strength of the proposed perspective is that it allows a more precise determination of what needs to be ecologically modernized or transformed. The Regulation approach focuses its research less on such objects as 'environment', 'environmental space', 'planetary boundaries' and over-exploited resources and sinks, and more on *social relations* structured by power (including society–nature relations, *gesellschaftliche Naturverhältnisse*). These constitute the material and symbolic forces that drive forward the social context of reproduction. The theory also casts light on how these relations are reproduced and transformed in a complex manner, through social forms of division of labour, production and consumption, as well as gender relations and racialized social relations, subjectivities and political conditions. Thus the social forms of the appropriation of nature are becoming apparent in a well-defined manner: the ways in which basic social needs, such as food and housing, mobility, communication, health and reproduction are satisfied materially and symbolically (see Becker et al. 2011; Görg 2003a). This also involves the social division of labour, the development of prices, structural political conditions, what constitutes an 'attractive life', and so on.

Hence a closer look at socioeconomic structures and processes will make it possible to understand how capitalist societies can organize the appropriation of nature in production and reproduction in such a way as to make their inherent ecological contradictions temporarily manageable. A social regulation of the contradictory society–nature relations is therefore possible, and is in fact taking place already (Lipietz 1998; Görg 2003a; Brand et al. 2008; Brand and Wissen 2012). In other words, regulation does not imply the end of the tendentially destructive appropriation of nature; nor the suppression of social rule. *What it does is to defuse the threat of a destruction of nature as a problem of capitalist development as a whole, by postponing hazardous negative consequences into the future or externalizing them across space.* A perfect example of this is climate change: in spite of all existing uncertainty, its consequences, from the perspective of the Global North, will take place in the future and will affect, directly or by active displacement, vulnerable places (in the Global South). In this way the risk that the ecological crisis will call into question the basic structures and developmental dynamics of capitalism, is neutralized (Altvater 1993; Koch 2012).

As to resource scarcity, expectations regarding its impact and strategies for the commodification and valorization of nature are being combined into new forms of the regulation of the exploitation of nature. Extracting energy from tar sands or natural gas deposits contained in deep shale rock by hydraulic fracturing thus is combined across different locales with generating fuel from biomass, which in turn relies on control over and use of land, and with a partial transition towards solar energy. It would therefore be inexact to translate biophysical scarcities into a question of the continuation of capitalism. Under capitalist conditions, scarcities and related problems can be managed through a mix of domination and repression, and through spatial and temporary externalization; all formulated and enforced by the dominant political and economic groups. Historical experience demonstrates that responding to ecological threats in such a way as to neutralize their politicization may be successful too. Examples may be taken from the development of environmental technologies to handle the ecological consequences of Fordist production and consumption patterns, or the formal institutionalization of environmental policy in state apparatuses at the national, supranational and international levels. As Christoph Görg states with regard to the post-Fordist regulation of biological diversity, the result may be characterized as a 'strategy of dominating nature which is partly shaped by reflexivity' (Görg 2003c: 130).

CURRENT GREEN ECONOMY PROPOSALS

Along a broad front, the Green Economy is being proclaimed as the approach to overcome the multiple crises of the present period. For all their differences concerning the proposed instruments and envisaged protagonists of the transformation process, the arguments put forward all agree that the Green Economy constitutes a social, ecological and economic 'win–win' situation. Thus the United Nations Environment Programme (UNEP), alongside opportunities for environmental improvements and economic growth, more particularly predicts the possibility of reduced poverty and of greater equity between the Global North and the Global South. Growth can be reconciled with environmental and social objectives: 'the greening of economies is not generally a drag on growth but rather a new engine of growth; . . . it is a net generator of decent jobs, and. . . it is also a vital strategy for the elimination of persistent poverty' (UNEP 2011b: 3). The Organisation for Economic Co-operation and Development (OECD 2011) in turn considers the greening of the economy a 'double strategy of innovation and crisis prevention' (Jänicke 2011: 5). A study conducted for the German Federal Environment Ministry, finally, indicates that because of induced investments (e.g. in the construction sector), an ambitious climate policy would even give rise to a higher growth rate than a policy of business-as-usual (Jaeger et al. 2011).

These proposals closely correspond with an approach that for a long time has been around in the social science debate under the name of *ecological modernization* (Huber 2011; Mol et al. 2009). But the problems they pose are also similar. For one thing, nearly all presuppose a strong political steering capacity of the state, or at least an effective governance. Thus in the Green Growth Strategy of the OECD (2011:10) for example, we find the statement that 'good economic policy lies at the heart of any strategy for green growth'. The ecological modernization strategies also emphasize in most cases the importance of international cooperation through multilateral environmental agreements such as the Kyoto Protocol of the UNFCCC (see UNEP 2011b: 33ff). What is missing is a reflection on the systematic limits of the state's steering capacity, and on the current crisis of multilateral environmental policy (Wissen 2010). Even the German federal government's Scientific Advisory Council on Global Environmental Change (WBGU), which at first sight appears to be less state-centred and acknowledges the crisis of global governance (whilst identifying the interests opposing a 'great transformation', which it projects may be overcome by 'pioneers of change' emerging from civil society), yet places its hopes in a strong state role in initiating structural change. It would then be up to the international community of states to provide the impetus for a transformation (WBGU 2011).

In the majority of studies in the ecological modernization lineage, there is hardly any definition of the real social content of the problems and crises that should be managed. If we just sum up, these would include the earth's overexploited natural systems, such as land surface, subterranean natural resources, the atmosphere and the oceans. Diagnosis instead is confined mainly to the problem of the overexploitation of resources and sinks, especially those of the atmosphere, caused by excessive CO_2 emissions. Again the German government's WBGU study, conducted by the Scientific Advisory Council on Global Environmental Change on the necessity of a 'New Great Transformation', stands out with its analytically substantial and strategically far-reaching nature. Yet it does not go beyond mentioning the 'mega-trends' such as climate change, urbanization or natural resource scarcity and does not refer them to the dynamics of capitalist socialization either.

This in our view is a step back. As Rainer Rilling rightly concludes, the WBGU wishes 'to change capitalism – but only one half of it: it targets manufacturing including its energetic basis, but not its political economy' (Rilling 2011: 16). Likewise Elmar Altvater, in a discussion in 1996 of a study by the Wuppertal Institute for Climate, Environment and Energy entitled *Sustainable Germany*, already asked 'whether it is admissible to talk about ecological sustainability and remain silent about capitalism; to call for an ecological revolution – because the reduction scenarios require exactly that – and to leave nearly everything as it is, politically, economically and socially' (Altvater 1996: 84). The key to understanding the Green Economy debate and the socioeconomic and political outlook underpinning it, is hidden in exactly such omissions. What we need instead is to delineate the possible and plausible routes along which the current quest to resurrect a capitalist dynamism might proceed. These would then add up to a *passive revolution* in the sense used by Gramsci, that is, a transformation towards a Green Capitalism from above, induced by the dominant forces in society.

From what has been argued so far, the strengthening of Green Economy strategies, the possible evolution towards a Green Capitalism, and the assessment of its social, ecological, economic and democratic political implications can be put in perspective. In particular our analysis rules out the inappropriate, voluntaristic optimism that has predominated in Green Economy approaches. These approaches tend to situate political regulatory practices, defined as intentional political steering, within the context of an overarching process of regulation. Regulation is then defined as a complex way of dealing with social contradictions of which the contingent and non-intentional aspects are central. Our claim, however, is that whilst intentional political regulatory measures are indeed being taken, they are necessarily inscribed in social power relations and structures; without taking these into account, the specific contents, forms and consequences of intentional policies cannot be understood.

CONTOURS OF A GREEN CAPITALISM

On the basis of the Regulationist political economy perspective developed so far it becomes possible not only to examine social conditions and dynamics in hindsight, once they have solidified, or assess the differentially coherent modes of development *ex post*, or even in the hour of their crisis. It is equally feasible to analyse the potential moments of a certain stabilization prospectively, as they evolve on the basis of historical chance discoveries. For this purpose, strategies, concrete actions and (changing) structures have to be taken into account. This is less a matter of perspectives or scenarios (e.g. Raskin et al. 2010) than of an enquiry into the conditions of feasibility of a particular regime of accumulation and, understood more comprehensively, a mode of development.

In order to outline the realm of the possible as far as a Green Capitalism is concerned, we must look more closely at the current structures and developments and, more precisely, at the crisis of the post-Fordist, neoliberal formation of capitalism. Certainly from a regulationist perspective, the exact definition of this formation has always been controversial. But this has not ruled out a consensus on the significance of neoliberal power constellations and institutions designed along neoliberal lines such as central banks operating under a monetarist monetary policy (Plehwe et al. 2006). Likewise the central position of financial capital as a chief characteristic of the post-Fordist accumulation regime has been generally accepted (see Sablowski 2009). With regard to the physical–material dimensions, we are concerned with the emergence of 'post-Fordist society–nature relations' (Brand et al. 2008; Wissen 2011), because only this would allow an appropriation of nature without the accompanying, rampant destruction as we are seeing today (e.g. in the case of biotechnologies). Yet to a considerable extent we will have to face a continuity and even expansion of resource-intensive, fossil-fuel-based, Fordist patterns of production and consumption. Clearly automobility (see Paterson, this volume) and industrial agriculture (Boyer, Kay, this volume) will not easily be displaced or discontinued.

Yet precisely these features (the finance-led regime of accumulation and the fossil-fuel patterns of production and consumption) are currently in a state of deep crisis. The crisis of finance-led accumulation reveals a crisis of over-accumulation, whilst the crisis of production and consumption patterns manifests itself mainly in the complex of problems related to resource supply and environmental sinks. It is obviously further intensified by the rise of newly industrializing nations.

These specifics of the crisis have to be taken into account for a full comprehension of what the Green Economy can realistically be expected to achieve. Not only is this crisis the starting point in the search process for a new capitalist formation, but in a certain way it also structures the quest for such an economy in advance. This quest is characterized by an intensified *valorization* of nature on the one hand, and the *economization* of ecological crisis management on the other. This latter aspect in particular may be credited with opening up new growth potentials, even though they must be expected to be socially and spatially extremely exclusive, uncertain and, with respect to some regions of the world, entirely crisis-driven.

The Green Economy strategy suggests that the valorization of nature can be a significant constituent of crisis management, and thus generate a capitalist formation that is new, for the very reason that it is located at the intersection of a range of crisis phenomena. Central among these is one key aspect of the ecological crisis, the resource crisis, in particular of energy and other mineral resources, but also of food. This crisis generates responses that promise to have the potential to overcome the economic crisis by commodifying scarce resources (e.g. land which could be used for food or agro-fuel production, or the potential of forests to absorb CO_2). As one fund manager puts it, 'The single best recession hedge of the next 10 or 15 years is an investment in farmland . . . Demand is going up very strongly on a global basis' (quoted in Zeller 2009: 10). One may add the increased valorization of sinks, which can serve as a counterbalance to strategies to contain climate change, in a way that creates, through artificial scarcity, new profit opportunities (Brand et al. 2013; Cooper 2010; Fairhead et al. 2012; Newell 2012).

This development is made even more salient by the rapid spread of Northern production and consumption patterns amongst the middle and upper classes in countries such as China or India. As a result the demand for fossil fuels, biomass, metals and emission sinks is increasing considerably (UNEP 2011a; cf. the recent debate about 'resource extractivism' as a new-old development model in many countries of the Global South). From this perspective, the aforementioned exploratory processes, in which the Green Economy strategy is playing such an important role, are turned into constitutive moments of a newly emerging capitalist formation, the one that we refer to as Green Capitalism. The quest for a new regime of accumulation based on society–nature relations of a new type is taking place in a situation in which the old formation, neoliberal, finance-led capitalism, has run aground and struggles to overcome a profound and multiple crisis.

We have already mentioned the significance of single, non-simultaneous social formations existing next to each other. Especially in countries like Germany and Austria, green-capitalist development models might be carried forward in the medium term, in particular in spheres like power or food production, provided that a range of social forces converge in support of this project, and there is some evidence for this. These forces comprise, amongst others, what may be called the 'green fractions of capital', as well as sections of the civil service, trade unions and environmental and consumer associations. All of them obtain representation through political parties and are, for the moment, actually present in certain state apparatuses.

Under the pressures of capitalist globalization, the consent of wage-earners and trade unions to accept these departures as part of a new class compromise may be almost taken for granted. In China state anti-crisis policies indicate that the interests behind an ecological modernization are increasing (UNEP 2013), and even in the United States this is obviously the case. In Great Britain, on the other hand, the Green Economy debate remains closely linked to the finance sector and to the issue of financial services, for example in the emissions trading sector (Carbon Tracker Initiative 2012; on emission trading in general, see Kill et al. 2010; Brand et al. 2013).

However, measured against the requirements formulated in the strategy papers cited above, the current green-economic strategies are still quite insufficient. They still face resistance from 'brown' capital fractions and fossil-economy 'normality', with automobility again the obvious reference point. In the energy sector in particular, competing strategies are being pursued along different lines of conflict. Thus, the promotion of renewable energies is competing – and also sometimes co-existing – with the use of fossil resources from 'unconventional' sources, that is, fuel from deepwater oil fields or tar sands, or 'fracked' gas. The latter are accessible as a result of technological advances, and due to rising energy prices, their exploitation becomes profitable. There are still a range of objectives that remain controversial amongst the protagonists of a Green Economy themselves, such as the relative desirability of electric automobility vis-à-vis the expansion of public transport, the viability of the agro-fuel option, or the future interrelation between centralized and decentralized forms of energy supply.

A Green Capitalism will therefore be the outcome of the particular mix of Green Economy strategies that prevail in these various domains. Likewise, it will depend on the spatially differentiated power relations between 'green' and 'brown' fractions of capital, as well as on the degree to which fossil-fuel consumption patterns remain the reference in popular common sense and everyday life practices. The future design of the relationship between finance and productive capital will equally and even more fundamentally determine a new regime of accumulation. If the creation of new financial instruments will continue to be the preferred route to the quest of overcoming the ecological crisis, extended reproduction is not likely. The example would be emissions trading and comparable climate policy instruments, which have so far mainly generated investments in hot air. Should this become the dominant trend, we will hardly be able to speak of a new regime of accumulation, but instead face a mainly presentational 'greening' of the old finance-dominated one.

On the other hand, developments in recent years have effectively produced a real increase, not only in the ecological efficiency of industrial production, but also in the development of new energy-saving products. This in turn has stimulated investment in the agriculture, biomass and food sectors. At present it is still impossible to fully appreciate the importance of these investments. Fossil fuels have turned out to be not as scarce as projected in the 1970s. Given the current consumption and known reserves, statistics suggest that conventional oil will be available for 42 more years, gas for 59 years and coal for 139 years (Enquête-Kommission 2013: 386–8). Even with unconventional fossil fuels becoming available it is probable that prices for fossil fuels are going to rise (making investments in renewables more attractive); but this is not certain. The required supply might also lead to an intensification of biomass extraction, parallel to the use of fossil fuels. Biomass was the main energy source in pre-industrial times (Fischer-Kowalski et al. 1997). Increased reliance on it in the current circumstances would make investment in land a crucial anticipatory strategy. The valorization of nature would then become a fundamental axis of ecological and economic crisis management within the framework of a green-capitalist project. But it would also rekindle the entire complex of conflicts associated with 'land grabbing' and 'green grabbing', such as enclosures and the marginalization of local communities (Fairhead et al. 2012; Peluso and Lund 2012; and Sassen, this volume).

This in turn raises other questions. For any project in the sense of a mode of development depends not only on technological and economic factors or economic policy to become a real possibility. Its feasibility also critically depends on social power relations as well as on the multiple practices of everyday life (see Davies, this volume). This concerns both how daily life is intended and how it is experienced, beginning with the various forms of the division of labour and the determining separation between a formal production sector and that of reproduction. Green-capitalist projects might also be established in authoritarian varieties against the interests of ordinary people, or, as in countries such as Germany or Austria, in the form of a green corporatism that seeks to integrate the majority of the wage-earners and their interest groups. Within such a green corporatism people would be directed to orient themselves towards rather narrow economic interests again (in terms of profits, income and economic growth); they would also be led to believe that 'green innovations' will bring growth, prosperity and jobs. But this would reproduce relations of domination and subordination too (Bauriedl and Wichterich 2013).

As noted above, such a development may be understood in terms of Gramsci's concept of passive revolution (1971: 104–6; cf. Candeias 2011; Sassoon 2001; and Jang and Gray, this volume). Passive revolution implies that the way in which crises are settled must not be allowed to jeopardize the fundamental preconditions of the capitalist mode of production and the power relations on which it is premised. This conformity is ensured (abstracting from local and temporal specificities) either by the co-optation or conversion of key political personalities or groups belonging to the leadership of the subordinated class; and/or by the marginalization of the forces which deliberately resist the dominant development or oppose them for other reasons. A successful passive revolution may then lead to a modernization of the capitalist mode of production as part of a new hegemonic project. The Green Economy strategy and Green Capitalism project can be seen in this light, except that we do not see passive revolution as being followed automatically by social progress, as Gramsci does in his analysis of Italy and in his analysis of Fordism. In fact modernization can be partial and selective, and will not necessarily result in an improvement of living conditions for the majority. In this spirit Sassoon (2001) analyses neoliberal globalization as a passive revolution.

The enforcement of a pattern allowing the elements of a Green Capitalism to be brought into some sort of stable social structure is itself a conflictive process. Clearly the role of the state, the political dimension and the question of hegemony are prominently involved here, given that the issues and the various forms of conflict management are broadly accepted by the different actors. In the process, the power relations in which 'green' actors, or the increasingly green orientations of 'traditional' actors, are involved, are being stabilized in a variety of ways by making them compatible with capitalist imperatives such as economic growth and competitiveness. Simultaneously these complex relations are restructured to ensure compatibility with the distributive possibilities of enterprises and state institutions. All this is to be accomplished through a selective management of the ecological crisis, which is what makes it possible to remain within the parameters of the capitalist mode of production in the first place.

From a perspective of the maintenance of the world's oligarchic structure of wealth and power, the externalization of ecologically burdensome aspects of the reproduction of our way of life, and the mechanisms to make it possible, dictate a degree of 'green' adjustment in the Global North. Relocating 'dirty industries' to other countries and waste shipments to Eastern Europe and to Africa are examples. Here the concept of the 'externalization shadow' of a way of life (Biesecker et al. 2012) and of externalization as a principle of a capitalist social formation open up important avenues for further research.

However, in light of the increasing attractiveness, around the world, of an 'imperial way of life' (Frosini et al. 2012; Brand and Wissen 2012), there is no guarantee that such a perspective would gain much social resonance. The experience today is that the production and consumption patterns hegemonic in the Global North are being generalized across the globe in a 'capillary', disjointed and refracted manner, whilst there are obviously considerable time-spatial differences involved as well. This is not just a matter of particular business strategies, commerce and investment policies, or of geopolitics. Hegemonic production and consumption patterns resonate unevenly in every society as they become diffused through the world market; it then depends on the available purchasing power, its distribution, and the definition of what constitutes an attractive way of life, whether and how they catch on. Specific class and gender relations, ethnic and ethno-constitutive fault-lines all enter into the equation in each concrete case. Hence its spatial development is profoundly uneven. 'Generalization' here does not mean that everybody lives in the same way either; particular ideas about what constitutes a 'good life' and when social development is considered adequate, rest on different prior experiences and are deeply anchored in tradition. So beyond spatial heterogeneities and temporal lags in the formation of an imperial way of life, for example between the Global South and the Global North, there also exist substantial social differences of various kinds within particular societies (for details, Brand and Wissen 2012).

The generalization of an imperial way of life does not contradict the possibility of a green-capitalist project. Our argument, however, is that such a project would entail spatial and social exclusion on a vast scale. Even if a Green Capitalism would increase resource efficiency and reduce the sink pollution per unit of GDP, a complete decoupling of economic growth from environmental consumption is most improbable (see UNEP 2011a; Haberl et al. 2011). In addition, Green Capitalism requires an externalization of its social-ecological costs through what might be called an 'environmental fix' (Castree 2008; Wissen 2010). This means that it is an exclusive project which cannot be generalized and which therefore, again and again, has to be contractually or militarily protected against newcomers from the Global South.

OUTLOOK

Obviously the significance of Green Economy strategies, as a process evolving over a longer period, and the possible contours of a Green Capitalism that will result from one or several of these strategies in the given circumstances, remains replete with questions. Its historical outcome is inevitably uncertain. Our purpose in this chapter has rather been to demonstrate that they can still have a significant influence in shaping structural changes. Even if the aforementioned strategies fail to meet their own postulated standards (in particular the substantial transformation of the energetic and resource-specific base), one may project a number of effects that will shape even the unintended consequences of these strategies. What is ultimately at stake is always the question of the democratic organization of social relationships, including, critically, society–nature relations. Hence we may ask,

- Which democratic forms exist to control the access and the use of natural resources?
- Which struggles have been and are still necessary to put them into practice, and to which conflicts will they lead?
- How can these become institutionally contained and stabilized?
- What are the requirements for a comprehensive democratic structuring of society–nature relations?
- To what extent are concrete Green Economy strategies beneficial, and to what extent are they counterproductive?
- Which problems and contradictions, struggles and experiences, proposals and practices do already point to post-capitalist ways of socialization, i.e. different socioeconomic and cultural forms of (re-) production and related forms of politics; and which of these might become important on a larger scale?

It is with these questions in mind that the social-ecological dimensions of the demands raised by the various protest movements, insurgencies and comparable struggles worldwide must be analysed, and the transformation processes they have set in motion, or which may emerge as they develop further, be assessed. In some countries in Latin America, such as Bolivia and Ecuador, socio-ecological questions are clearly on the agenda; in Argentina, Brazil and probably also in North Africa, the situation on the other hand is dominated by a classical development consensus. Such a development consensus must be taken into account when we reflect on the concrete forms of an emerging green-capitalist mode of production and way of life.

Conclusion: emergent predatory logics

Saskia Sassen

The end of the Cold War launched one of the most brutal economic phases of the modern era. But its brutalities are, in some ways, less visible than the degradations described by Marx and Engels about the new industrial era in their time-space. Today's visual order of glamorous global cities, the luxuries of high-tech research campuses, the impressive engineering of state-of-the-art transport systems, are just some of the visible conditions in our current epoch that can keep us from seeing the devastations and miseries on which they rest. Following a period of Keynesian-led relative redistribution in developed market economies, the United States became the driving force for a radical reshuffling of capitalism.

Two logics organize this reshuffling. One is systemic, and in the 1990s and onwards got wired into the economic and (de)regulatory policies of most countries. Eventually deregulation, privatization, and specific fiscal and monetary policies were implemented near universally and came to affect key economic sectors, albeit with variable degrees of intensity. The effect was to open up ground for new or sharply expanded modes of profit extraction even in unlikely places and through unlikely instruments. The second logic is the actual material transformation of extreme zones for the enactment of that systemic logic, no matter the cost in lives and the environment. Global cities and the spaces for outsourced work stand out among these zones.

Critical to both these logics is the invention of extremely complex organizational and financial instruments to engage in what are, ultimately, new forms of primitive accumulation (Sassen 2008a; 2014). Many of the key components of the post-1989 global economy were already present and under development in the early 1980s. Just as the silent revolutions of 1989 are the iconic representation of a political process that had been building for a long time, so the corporate globalizing that took off in the late 1980s started many years earlier. But 1989 did make a major difference, most notably in giving these innovations the run of the world via the legitimating aura of market triumphalism. The outcome was the formation of a new kind of global economy, one with strong capture at the top and major losses in significant components of national economies (e.g. IMF 2013; Jubilee Debt Campaign 2013; McKinsey 2008).

Here I can only examine a few aspects of the dominant economic tendencies of the last decades and their deeply destructive character. The first section focuses on the capacity of key international institutions to impose particular logics across economic sectors and across the world. I argue that the equivalent of today's austerity policies in the Global North began in the 1980s in the Global South, weakening their economies and their governments. The financialization of more and more domains marks the ascendance of a new organizing logic in advanced capitalism. This is not just a matter of the volume of finance, but, more importantly, of its getting wired into more and more economic sectors across the globe.

A NEW PHASE OF ADVANCED CAPITALISM

The geographic expansion and systemic deepening of capitalist relations of production over the last 20 years have led to a brutal sorting of winners and losers. Since its origins and across its diverse phases, capitalism has been marked by violence, destruction and appropriation. But it has also been partly shaped by the making of the regulatory state, a victory for the struggling working classes and the expanding middle classes.

Much attention in the development scholarship has gone to the destruction of pre-capitalist economies via their incorporation into capitalist relations of production. The post-1980s period makes visible yet another variant of this appropriation via incorporation: the appropriation of traditional capitalisms to further the deepening of *advanced* capitalism (e.g. Harvey 2003). I use the term 'advanced' to capture a phase dominated by a financial logic (Sassen 2008a: Chapters 4 and 5; Arrighi 1994). Built into this proposition is the fact of diverse phases of capitalist development and hence the possibility that in today's global phase the extension of capitalist relations has its own distinct mechanisms and that these need to be distinguished from older national and imperial phases. One key mechanism is the capacity of today's financial system to financialize more and more components of economies. This has led to an appropriation of advanced capitalist economic sectors into a yet more advanced form of capitalism. It is this that I mean by the notion of new forms of primitive accumulation inside advanced capitalism itself, a thesis I develop at length elsewhere (Sassen 2010; 2008a; 2014).

Thus I find that the organizing logic of this post-Keynesian period is now making legible its shape. An extreme component of this logic diverges sharply from the earlier systemic 'valuing' of people as workers and as consumers. To put it starkly, it is a phase marked by the expulsion of people and the destruction of the 'advanced' capitalisms of the mid-twentieth century in order to feed today's emergent forms of advanced capitalism shaped by the logics of high finance – its need to financialize more and more sectors, from used car loans to gold.

One of these instances is the structural adjustment project implemented by global regulatory institutions, notably the IMF and the World Bank starting in the 1980s, joined by WTO in the 1990s. My argument here is that beyond the much-noted extraction of billions of dollars from Global South countries in the form of debt servicing, the key is the work of systemic conditioning that took place. Debt servicing was the instrument for this disciplining: it weakened the governments of those countries by forcing them to pay growing shares of national revenue for interest on their debts rather than engaging in economic development; further, it made them susceptible to signing unfavourable deals with global firms in extractive industries rather than furthering mass manufacturing by national firms.

The second instance is the sub-prime mortgage crisis that began in the early 2000s and exploded in 2007. Most of the attention has gone, and rightly so, to the massive losses for the individuals and families who were sold these mortgages, losses that are continuing. But beyond the logics of extraction in the form of mortgage payments and mortgage agents' fees, here too we can detect a more foundational emergent dynamic: the use of a contract on a material asset (the mortgage) as one ingredient for making a complex investment instrument for high finance, with a willingness to sacrifice the basic livelihoods of what have become over ten million households in the US, and over two million (and growing) in Europe.

Central to my analysis is that inside capitalism itself we can characterize the relation of advanced to traditional capitalism as one marked by predatory dynamics rather than merely evolution, development or progress (Sassen 2010; 2014). At its most extreme this can mean immiseration and exclusion of growing numbers of people who cease being of value as workers and consumers. But it also means that traditional petty bourgeoisies and traditional national bourgeoisies cease being of value. I see the latter as part of the current systemic deepening of capitalist relations. One brutal way of putting it is to say that the natural resources of much of Africa and good parts of Latin America count more than the people on those lands count as consumers and as workers. This is part of the systemic deepening of advanced capitalist relations of production. We have left behind the varieties of Keynesian periods that thrived on the accelerated expansion of prosperous working and middle classes – though not in today's emergent economies, especially in Asia. Keynesianism's valuing of people as workers and consumers was critical for the deepening of capitalism.

In what follows, the emphasis is on the *making* of capitalist relations of production, whether those of early or of advanced capitalism. I focus on two instances that are easily described as familiar resource-extraction. While extraction is indeed a major feature, it is critical to go deeper so as to recover the making of a systemic transformation – how older forms of 'advanced' capitalist economies are being destroyed or incorporated into the operational space of a new type of advanced capitalism.

SYSTEMIC DEEPENING: THE DEBT NEXUS AS A LOGIC OF EXTRACTION

The extraction of value from the Global South and the implementation of restructuring programmes at the hands of the IMF and the World Bank, have had the effect of 'reconditioning' the terrain represented by these countries for an expansion of new forms of advanced capitalism. This includes its explicitly criminal forms. Throughout the Global South we see the rise of extremely rich elites along with the devastation of vast sectors of their economies and populations. More concretely, many of the poor countries subjected to this regime now have richer and larger elites than they used to have, along with larger shares of their population in desperate poverty and less likely to enter the capitalist circuit via consumption than they did even 20 years ago. Many of the sub-Saharan countries had functioning health and education systems and economies, and less destitution than today. Systemically governments have been weakened and corrupted; even resource-rich countries have had expanded shares of their people become destitute, with Nigeria the most noted case. The dominant dynamic at work for these populations is, to a good extent, the opposite of the Keynesian period's valuing of people as workers and as consumers. This expulsion has given expanded space to criminal networks, greater access to land and underground water resources to foreign buyers, whether firms or governments. Systemically, the role of rich donor countries has also shifted: overall they give less in foreign aid for development than 30 years ago. As a result, the remittances sent by low-income immigrants are larger than foreign aid. Philanthropies now enter the realm once almost exclusive to governments.

These systemic shifts contribute to explaining a complex difference that can be captured in a set of simple numbers (Sassen 2010). For much of the 1980s and onwards indebted poor countries were asked to pay a share of their export earnings toward debt service. This share tended to hover around 20 per cent, which is far higher than that asked from other instances of country indebtedness. For instance, in 1953, the Allies cancelled 80 per cent of Germany's war debt and only insisted on 3 to 5 per cent of export earnings for debt service. And they asked only

8 per cent from Central European countries in the 1990s. In comparison, the debt service burdens on today's poor countries have wound up being extreme, as I discuss below. It does suggest that the aim regarding Germany was re-incorporation into the capitalist world economy of the time, and incorporation into today's advanced capitalism with regard to Central Europe.

In contrast, the aim vis-à-vis the countries of the Global South in the 1980s and 1990s was more akin to a disciplining regime, starting with forced acceptance of restructuring programmes and of loans from the international system, measures that helped large extractive firms enter these economies on favourable terms. After 20 years of this regime, it became clear that it did not deliver on the basic components for healthy development (see e.g. Jubilee Debt Campaign 2013; IMF 2013; IAEG 2009). The discipline of debt service payments was given strong priority over infrastructure, hospitals, schools and other people-oriented development goals. The primacy of this extractive logic became a mechanism for systemic transformation that went well beyond debt service payment – the devastation of large sectors of traditional economies, including small-scale manufacturing, the destruction of a good part of the national bourgeoisie and petty bourgeoisie, the sharp impoverishment of the population and, in many cases, the impoverishment and thereby corruptibility of the state.

DEBT AS A DISCIPLINING REGIME

Debt and debt servicing problems have long been a systemic feature of the developing world. But it is the particular features of IMF negotiated debt rather than the fact of debt per se that concerns me here. For the gradual destruction of traditional economies prepared the ground, literally, for some of the new needs of advanced capitalism, among which are the acquisitions of vast stretches of land – for agriculture, for underground water tables and for mining. Precisely at a time of extreme financialization and systemic crisis, the growing demand for those material resources has ascended in importance and visibility. Along with the new survival economies of the impoverished middle classes and of the poor, all of this is familiar and has happened before, but they are now part of a new organizing logic that changes their valence and their interaction.

Even before the economic crises of the mid-1990s that hit a vast number of countries as they implemented neoliberal policies, the debt of poor countries in the South had grown from US$507 billion in 1980 to US$1.4 trillion in 1992. Debt service payments alone had increased to $1.6 trillion, more than the actual debt. From 1982 to 1998, indebted countries paid four times their original debts, and at the same time, their debt stocks went up by four times. These countries had to use a significant share of their total revenues to service these debts. For instance, Africa's payments reached $5 billion in 1998, which means that for every $1 in aid, African countries paid $1.40 in debt service in 1998. Debt to Gross National Product (GNP) ratios were especially high in Africa, where they stood at 123 per cent in the late 1990s, compared with 42 per cent in Latin America and 28 per cent in Asia. By 2003, debt service as a share of exports only (not overall government revenue) ranged from extremely high levels for Zambia (29.6 per cent) and Mauritania (27.7 per cent) to significantly lowered levels compared with the 1990s for Uganda (down from 19.8 per cent in 1995 to 7.1 per cent in 2003) and Mozambique (down from 34.5 per cent in 1995 to 6.9 per cent in 2003). As of 2006, the poorest 49 countries (i.e. 'low-income countries' with less than $935 per capita annual income) had debts of $375 billion. If to these 49 poor countries we add the 'developing countries', in 2011 this total of 144 countries had a debt of over $4.9 trillion and paid $620 billion in interest on their debts in 2011 (Jubilee Debt Campaign UK 2013).

The IMF, World Bank and other such programmes establish the criteria and process these debts, thereby functioning as a global disciplining regime. The Highly Indebted Poor Country initiative (HIPC) was set up in 1996 by the World Bank and IMF to assist countries with debts equivalent to more than one and a half times their annual export earnings as part of an IMF and World Bank programme. In order to be eligible, countries have to have been compliant to the IMF for at least three years. The HIPC process begins with a 'decision point' document. This sets out eligibility requirements, among which is the development of a Poverty Reduction Strategy Paper (PRSP), that replaces the earlier Structural Adjustment Programmes (SAPs). PRSPs describe 'the macroeconomic, structural, and social policies and programs' that a country is required to pursue in order to be eligible for debt relief (IMF 2009a). As of 1 July 2009, 26 countries had completed HIPC, and had 'passed the decision point' (IMF 2009b; see also IMF 2013). Finally, the Multilateral Debt Relief Initiative (MDRI) went into full force in July 2006. It was intended to address many of the criticisms of the HIPC initiative. MDRI promised cancellation of debts to the World Bank (incurred before 2003), IMF (incurred before 2004), and African Development Fund (incurred before 2004) for the countries that completed the HIPC initiative. The major debt cancellation schemes (HIPC and MDRI initiatives) together cancelled $130 billion in debt by 2011 (Jubilee Debt Campaign UK 2013).

The debt burden that built up in the 1980s, and especially the 1990s, has had substantial repercussions on state spending composition (see IAEG 2009; IMF 2013; 2009a; 2009b; Oxfam 1999). Zambia, Ghana and Uganda, three countries that global regulators (notably the World Bank and the IMF) saw as cooperative, responsible and successful at implementing SAPs, illustrate some of the issues even when held in high esteem by global regulators. A few examples of expenditure levels paint a troubling picture about how they achieved this high esteem. At the height of these programmes in the early to mid-1990s, Zambia's government paid $1.3 billion in debt but only $37 million for primary education; Ghana's social expenses, at $75 million, represented 20 per cent of its debt service; and Uganda paid $9 per capita on its debt and only $1 for healthcare. In 1994 alone, these three countries remitted $2.7 billion to bankers in the North. When the new programmes became an option, these three countries benefited from HIPC and MDRI programmes and conceded to the attendant PRSP requirements. Thus, while in 1997 Zambia spent 18.3 per cent of income on exports of goods and services on debt service, by 2007 this was reduced to 1.3 per cent (IAEG 2009). For Ghana these figures are 27.1 and 3.1 per cent respectively. For Uganda they are 19.7 and 1.2 per cent (IAEG 2009).

Generally, IMF debt management policies from the 1980s onwards can be shown to have worsened the situation for the unemployed and poor (UNDP 2005; 2008). Much research on poor countries documents the link between hyper-indebted governments and cuts in social programmes. These cuts tend to affect women and children in particular through cuts in education and health care, both investments necessary to ensuring a better future (for overviews of the data, see UNDP 2005; 2008; World Bank 2005; 2006). There is by now a large body of literature on this subject, including a vast number of limited circulation items produced by various activist and support organizations. Older literature on women and debt also documents the disproportionate burden that these programmes put on women during the first generation of SAPs in the 1980s in several developing countries in response to growing government debt (Beneria and Feldman 1992; Bose and Acosta-Belen 1995; Bradshaw et al. 1993; Tinker 1990; Jubilee Debt Campaign UK 2007).

Unemployment of women themselves but also, more generally, of the men in their households has added to the pressure on women to find ways to ensure household survival (Buechler 2007; Lucas 2005; Rahman 1999; Safa 1995; see also Ratha et al. 2009). Subsistence food production, informal work, emigration and prostitution have all become survival options for women and, by extension, often for their households. For instance, when there is a shortage of basic healthcare women usually take on the extra burden of caring for the sick. When school fees are introduced or spending is cut, sons' education is prioritized over daughters'. Water privatization can reduce access to water and increase the water-gathering burden placed on women. When families grow cash crops for export, women's work produces money, which men usually control, rather than food (Jubilee Debt Campaign UK 2007).

One question concerns the option of not becoming part of the IMF debt-servicing disciplining regime and forgoing the help it is meant to provide. The so-called adjustment programmes of the 1980s and 1990s destroyed many traditional economies, leaving many countries only with major debts. At that point, becoming part of the debt cancellation programme launched in 2006 has probably been preferable. The evidence suggests that once a country has been pushed into debt, cancellation can, in principle, help a country allocate more government revenue for general social and development questions. This has been the case with Ghana, Uganda and a few others which have seen the growth of middle classes – along with continuing abject poverty. On the other hand, Angola, which was not accepted for debt cancellation, spent 6.8 per cent of GDP on debt service payments and only 1.5 per cent of GDP on health in 2005; it continues to spend about $2.2 billion each year on external debt payments (Jubilee Debt Campaign UK 2008). But the Angola case also points to another combination of elements. Its elites have become wealthy on the vast mining resources, mostly for export, and this arrangement can now continue without much interference. The vast poverty continues and so does the mining for export. One cannot help but ask, who are the other beneficiaries of this situation?

The above is part of a larger history in the making. In my reading it includes as one key element a repositioning of much of Africa and good parts of Latin America and Central Asia in a new, massively restructured global economy. Weakened governments and the destruction of traditional economies have launched a new phase of extraction by powerful states and firms and a new phase of survival economies by the impoverished middle classes and the long-term poor (for a more detailed analysis see Sassen 2008a; 2008b and 2014).

THE RISE OF FOREIGN LAND ACQUISITIONS: EXPANDING THE OPERATIONAL SPACE OF ADVANCED CAPITALISM

The weakening and corrupting of Global South governments described above enables the rapid and sharp increase in foreign land acquisitions that took off in 2006. While this can be seen merely as a continuation of an old practice, the available evidence points to significant change in the curve describing the size of overall acquisitions (cf. Anseeuw et al. 2012; Margulis et al. 2013; Cotula 2011; Land Matrix 2014; FAO 2010; De Schutter 2011: 257; and Borras et al. 2012). From 2006 to 2011 over 200 million hectares of land were acquired by foreign governments and foreign firms, especially in Africa, Latin America and particular regions of Asia; this figure includes only acquisitions of a minimum of 200 hectares. What concerns me here is this sharp change in the curve of acquisitions: it points to a break in a long-term trend of acquisitions, for example Japan's acquisitions of land in Asia and Brazil beginning in the 1960s (Sassen 1991: Chapter 4) and prior imperial phases. But since most territory in the world today is part of *formally* independent sovereign countries, the recent sharp rise in land acquisitions might indicate a larger structural transformation in an old practice.

It is a well-known and generally accepted fact that the key reason for this growth is rapid development in several parts of the world that has generated a demand for industrial crops, food crops, wood, water, metals and more (e.g. Land Matrix 2012). The larger context within which this growth takes place is characterized by changes in the global economy and in financial markets, and, at a deeper level, changes in the inter-state system, still the basic frame for cross-border transactions. Further, the financialization of commodities has brought new potentials for profit-making to the primary sector, from food to minerals and metals, thus stimulating speculative investments in land.

The issue here is not one of nationalism versus globalism, but one of complexity: where once there was a prospect of democratic decision-making, now there is an expansion of opaque transnational networks that control the land. These massive foreign land acquisitions re-position that acquired land for their own aims. This also brings with it a shift of that acquired land from 'national sovereign territory' to the commodity 'land' for the global market – in other words, a weakening of a complex category that *at its best* brought with it a formal enabling of the state's authority and inhabitants' rights to make the state accountable (Sassen 2008a; 2014: Chapter 2). While the much-reported explosion in food demand and in its prices was certainly a key factor in this new phase of land acquisitions, it is biofuels that account for most of the acquisitions. Food commodification and the financializing of these commodities is a major growth sector. *The Economist* index of food prices began to rise sharply in the mid-2000s; in 2007 it rose 78 per cent, and particular crops (soy beans and rice) soared more than 130 per cent (*Economist* 2009). Cross-referenced data from the Land Matrix show biofuel production accounts for 40 per cent of land acquired. In comparison, food crops account for 25 per cent of cross-referenced deals, followed by 3 per cent for livestock production, and 5 per cent for other non-food crops. Farming broadly understood accounts for 73 per cent of cross-referenced acquisitions. The remaining 27 per cent of land acquired is for forestry and carbon sequestration, mineral extraction, industry and tourism.

A second major pattern is the massive concentration of foreign acquisitions in Africa. Of the publicly reported deals, 948 land acquisitions totalling 134 million hectares are located in Africa; 34 million of these hectares have been cross-referenced (information available from more than one source). This compares with 43 million hectares reported for Asia (of which 29 million hectares have been cross-referenced) and 19 million hectares in Latin America (of which 6 million hectares have been cross-referenced). The remainder (5.4 million hectares reported and 1.6 million hectares cross-referenced) is in other regions, particularly Eastern Europe and Oceania.

In an analysis of 180 large land acquisitions in Africa, Friis and Reenberg (2010) categorize major investors into four main groups: (1) oil-rich Gulf States (Saudi Arabia, United Arab Emirates, Qatar, Bahrain, Oman, Kuwait and Jordan); (2) populous and capital-rich Asian countries such as China, South Korea, Japan and India; (3) Europe and the US; (4) private companies from around the world. Investors are mostly energy companies, agricultural investment companies, utility companies, finance and investment firms and technology companies. The top six African land sellers are Ethiopia, Madagascar, Sudan, Tanzania, Mali and Mozambique – all sub-Saharan, and all, except Mali, in East Africa. In all these countries both private investors and government agencies have acquired land. Just considering investment capital, three countries dominate: the United States, United Kingdom and Saudi Arabia together account for 25 per cent of all investments in these six African countries, and each has investments in four.

Overall Friis and Reenberg (2010) find a total of 47 different country origins among investors in these six countries. Among the countries with the most diverse group of investors by country of origin are Madagascar, with 24 foreign investors from 15 countries, and Ethiopia, with 26 investors from 12 countries. Asian countries (China, South Korea, India and Japan) make up almost 20 per cent of investors, as distinct from investments, in these six countries. Middle Eastern Countries (Saudi Arabia, UAE, Egypt, Jordan, Qatar, Lebanon and Israel) account for almost 22 per cent of investors. European countries (UK, Sweden, Netherlands, Germany, Italy, Denmark and France) account for 30 per cent of investors. African countries (South Africa, Mauritius, Libya and Djibouti) account for about 10 per cent of investors. The remaining investors are from Australia, Brazil and the United States.

These investments in land have crowded out investments in mass manufacturing and other sectors that can generate good jobs and feed the growth of a middle class. The rise in such investments happened at a time when several countries of the Global South were beginning to experience significant growth in mass manufacturing, and much foreign direct investment was in this sector (Sassen 2014: Chapter 2). This is the type of development that can contribute to the growth of a middle class and a strong working class. If we just consider Africa, for instance, the data show a sharp decline in foreign direct investment in manufacturing. South Africa and Nigeria, Africa's top two FDI recipients accounting for 37 per cent of FDI stock in Africa by 2006, have both had a sharp rise in FDI in the primary sector and a sharp fall in the manufacturing sector (UNCTAD 2008). This is also the case in Nigeria, where foreign investment in oil has long been a major factor: the share of the primary sector in inward FDI stock stood at 75 per cent in 2005, up from 43 per cent in 1990. Other African countries have seen similar shifts. Even in Madagascar, one of the few (mostly small) countries where manufacturing FDI inflows began to increase as recently as the 1990s and onwards, this increase was well below that of the primary sector. Overall, the current phase of land acquisitions dwarfs investments in manufacturing.

THE LAUNCH OF A NEW FINANCIAL ERA: DEBUNKING THE NOTION OF THE POST-1997 'GLOBAL STABILITY'

The 1980s opened a new financial phase that became yet another disciplining mechanism, not through structural adjustment programmes but through financial adjustment crises. Since the 1980s there have been several financial crises, some famous, such as the 1987 New York stock market crisis and the 1997 Asian Crisis, and some obscure, such as the individual country financial crises that happened in over 70 countries in the 1980s and 1990s as they deregulated their financial systems, mostly under pressure from global regulators aiming at facilitating the globalizing of financial markets.

Conventional data show the post-1997 financial crisis period to be a fairly stable one, until the 2008 crisis explodes. One element in this picture is that after a country goes through an 'adjustment' crisis, 'stability' (and prosperity!) follows. This then produces a representation of considerable financial stability, except for a few major global crises, such as the dot. com crisis. A much-mentioned fact regarding the current 2007–2008 crisis intended to show that the system is fine, is that in 2006 and 2007, 124 countries had a GDP growth rate of 4 per cent a year or more, which is much higher than that of previous decades. The suggestion is then that the 2007–2008 crisis is precisely that – an acute momentary event, but the system is fine.

But behind this supposed post-1997 stability lies a making of winners and losers, and the fact that it is easier to track winners than to track the slow sinking of households, small firms and government agencies (such as health and education) that are not part of the new glamour sectors (finance and trade). The miseries these adjustment crises brought to the middle sectors in each country and the destruction of often well-functioning economic sectors is largely an invisible history to the global eye. These individual country adjustment crises only intersected with global concerns and interests when there were strong financial links, as was the case with the 1994 Mexican crisis and the 2001 Argentine crisis, or when members of the traditional middle class took part in food riots in Buenos Aires (and elsewhere) in the mid-1990s – after adjustment! – something unheard of in Argentina.

Besides the very partial character of post-adjustment stability and the new 'prosperity' much praised by global regulators and global media, there is the deeper fact that 'crisis' is a structural feature of deregulated, interconnected and electronic financial markets. These same features also fed the sharp growth of finance, partly based on the financializing of non-financial economic sectors, leading to overall extreme financial deepening. The financial deepening of economies has become one of the major dynamics characterizing advanced economies. The number of countries where financial assets exceed the value of their gross national product more than doubled from 33 in 1990 to 72 in 2006 (McKinsey 2008). Securitizing a broad range of types of debt is a key vehicle for this financial deepening. The extension of securitization into consumer debt, including mortgages, took off in the 1980s in the US.

Thus, if crisis is a structural feature of current financial markets, then crisis becomes a feature of non-financial economic sectors through their financialization, a subject I have developed elsewhere (Sassen 2014: Chapter 3; 2008a: 355–65). The overall outcome is an extreme potential for instability even in strong and healthy (capitalist) economic sectors, particularly in countries with highly developed financial systems and high levels of financialization, such as the US and the UK. What stands out in this phase that begins in the 1980s is that global and adjustment crises had the effect of securing the conditions for globally linked financial markets and the ascendance of a financial logic organizing larger and larger sectors of the economy in the Global North. In this process large components of the non-financial economy in these countries were ruined. Against this background, the 2007–2008 financial crisis is yet another step in this trajectory. One question is whether it spells the exhaustion of this trajectory, or rather the beginning of its decay.

THE GLOBAL NORTH HAS ITS OWN VERSIONS: A NEW FRONTIER FOR FINANCE

In what follows I argue that the specific way of using the sub-prime mortgage in the 2001–2007 period makes it a dangerous instrument that is likely to be used worldwide over the next decade. It is a mistake to see this instrument as having to do with providing modest-income households with housing. It has rather to do with a structural condition of high finance marked by the combination of a growing demand for asset-backed securities given extremely high levels of speculative investments. This structural condition is at the heart of the actual event that momentarily brought the system to a (partial) standstill – the credit-default swap crisis of September 2008 – which in turn suggests an even keener interest in asset-backed securities, and hence in the speculative use of sub-prime mortgages. I see this as one of the new global frontiers for finance, specifically, the billions of modest-income households worldwide. The effect could be yet another brutal sorting, with expulsions from more traditional economies, not unlike the consequences of the structural adjustment crises in the Global South discussed in the first half of this chapter.

Much has been made, especially in the US media, of the sub-prime mortgage crisis as a source of the larger crisis. Modest-income families unable to pay their mortgage were often represented as irresponsible for having taken on these mortgages. But the facts show another pattern. The overall value of the sub-prime mortgage loss was too small to bring this powerful financial system down. What triggered the crisis was a far more complex financial innovation. The key was the growing demand for asset-backed securities by investors, in a market where the outstanding value of derivatives was \$630 trillion, or 14 times the value of global GDP. The total value of financial assets (which is a form of debt, but unlike derivatives represents actual money) in the US stood at almost five times (450 per cent) the value of its GDP in 2006, before the crisis was evident. The UK, Japan and the Netherlands, all had a similar ratio (McKinsey 2008: 11). From 2005 to 2006 the total value of the world's financial assets grew by 17 per cent (in nominal terms, 13 per cent at constant exchange rates), reaching \$167 trillion. This is not only an all-time high value; it also reflects a higher growth rate in 2006 than the annual average of 9.1 per cent since 1980. This points to growing financial deepening. The total value of financial assets stood at $12 trillion in 1980, $94 trillion in 2000 and $142 trillion in 2005.

This is the context within which the demand for asset-backed securities became acute (see Sassen 2008a: Chapters 4 and 7, esp. 352–65; Sassen 2014: Chapter 3). To address this demand, even sub-prime mortgage debt could be used as an asset. Sellers of these mortgages needed vast quantities of them to make it work for high finance: 500 such sub-prime mortgages was a minimum. As the demand for asset-backed securities grew, so did the push by sub-prime mortgage sellers to have buyers sign on, regardless of capacity to pay the mortgage. This combination of demand and increasingly low-quality assets meant mixing slices of poor quality mortgages with high-grade debt. Out came an enormously complex instrument that was also enormously opaque: nobody could trace what was there. When the millions of foreclosures came, beginning in 2006 (see Table C.1), investors had a crisis of confidence: it was impossible to tell what the toxic component was in their investments.

Sub-prime mortgages can be valuable instruments to enable modest-income households to buy a house. But what happened in the US over the last few years was an abuse of the concept. The small savings or future earnings of modest-income households were used to develop a financial instrument that could make profits for investors even if those households in the end could not pay the mortgages and thereby lost both their home and whatever savings and future earnings they had put into it – a catastrophic and life-changing event for millions of these households. This becomes clear in the microcosm that is New York City. Whites, who have a far higher average income than all the other groups in New York City, were far less likely to have sub-prime mortgages than all other groups. Thus 9.1 per cent of all people that got sub-prime mortgages in 2006 were

Table C.1 US home foreclosures, 2006–10

Year	No. of foreclosures	% Rise from past year	Relative incidence
2006	1.2 million	up 42% from 2005	1 in 92 US households
2007	2.2 million	up 75% from 2006	
2008	3.1 million	up 81% from 2007	
2009	3.9 million	up 120% from 2007 (2 yrs)	1 in 45 US households
2010	2.9 million		
Total:	13.3 million		

Source: RealtyTrac, Federal Reserve.

Table C.2 Rate of sub-prime lending by ethnic group in New York City, 2002–06

	2002	2003	2004	2005	2006
White	4.6%	6.2%	7.2%	11.2%	9.1%
Black	13.4%	20.5%	35.2%	47.1%	40.7%
Hispanic	11.9%	18.1%	27.6%	39.3%	28.6%
Asian	4.2%	6.2%	9.4%	18.3%	13.6%

Source: Furman Center for Real Estate & Urban Policy.

whites, compared with Asians (13.6 per cent), Hispanics (28.6 per cent) and blacks (40.7 per cent). If we consider the most acute period, 2003 to 2005, the number more than doubled for whites, but basically tripled for Asians and Hispanics and quadrupled for blacks (see Table C.2). A big majority of those who had sub-prime mortgages went into foreclosure and lost their homes eventually.

There were, then, two very separate crises: the crisis of the people who had taken on these mortgages and the crisis of confidence in the investor community. The millions of home foreclosures were a signal that something was wrong, but in itself, it could not have brought down the financial system. There is a profound irony in this crisis of confidence: the brilliance of those who make these financial instruments became the undoing of a large number of investors (besides the undoing of the modest-income families who had been sold these mortgages). The toxic link was that for these mortgages to work as assets for investors, vast numbers of mortgages were sold regardless of whether these homebuyers could pay their monthly fee. The faster these mortgages could be sold, the faster they could be bundled into investment instruments and sold off to investors. Overall, sub-prime mortgages more than tripled from 2000 to 2006, and accounted for 20 per cent of all mortgages in the US in 2006. This premium on speed also secured the fees for the sub-prime mortgage sellers and reduced the effects of mortgage default on the profits of the sub-prime sellers. In fact, those sub-prime sellers that did not sell off these mortgages as part of investment instruments went bankrupt eventually, but not before having secured fees. In brief, the financial sector invented some of its most complicated financial instruments to extract the meagre savings of modest households in order to produce an 'asset': the mortgage on a house.

The complexity of the financial innovation was a series of products that de-linked sub-prime sellers' and investors' profits from the creditworthiness of consumer home mortgage-buyers. Whether the mortgage is paid matters less than securing a certain number of loans that can be bundled up into 'investment products'. The crisis of homebuyers was not a crisis for financial investors, even though millions of middle and working class families now live in tents in the US. For finance it was a crisis of confidence. But it showed the importance of the systems of trust that make possible the speed and orders of magnitude of this financial system. The crisis of homeowners (valued at a few hundred billion dollars) was the little tail that dented the enormous dog of trust in the financial system. In other words, this type of financial system has more of the social in it than is suggested by the technical complexity of its instruments and electronic platforms (Sassen 2008a: 355–65; 2014: Chapter 3).

The critical component that brought the financial system to a momentary standstill was more of an old-fashioned speculation gone wrong: the $62 trillion dollar credit-default swap crisis that exploded on the scene in September 2008, a full year after the sub-prime mortgage of August 2007. This was more than the combined domestic product of all countries in the world, $54 trillion. These credit-default swaps grew from about $1 trillion in 2001 to $62 trillion by 2007; this is an extremely sharp growth over an extremely short period of time. Credit-default swaps could not have grown so fast and reached such extreme values if they had been sold as insurance, which would have been the lawful way. None of the financial firms had the capital reserves they would have needed to back $60 trillion in insurance. Because they were recoded as derivatives, they could have an almost vertical growth curve beginning as recently as 2001. While much attention has gone to sub-prime mortgages as causes of the financial crisis, the $62 trillion in swaps in mid-2008 is what really got the financial crisis going. Declining house prices, high foreclosure rates, declining global trade, rising unemployment, all alerted investors that something was not right. This, in turn, led those who had bought credit-default swaps as a sort of 'insurance' to want to cash in. But the sellers of these swaps had not expected this downturn or the demand to cash in from those whom they had sold these credit swaps. They were not ready, and this catapulted much of the financial sector into crisis. Not everybody lost. Among the winners are also those who 'shorted' sub-prime mortgage securities. Betting against is not new. A familiar case is that of Soros two decades ago when he made over $3 billion on the British pound's fallout from the European Exchange Rate Mechanism (ERM).

These credit-default swaps are part of what has come to be referred to as the shadow banking system. According to some analysts this shadow banking system accounted for 70 per cent of banking at the time that the crisis exploded. The shadow banking system is not informal, illegal or clandestine. Not at all: it is in the open, but it has thrived on the opaqueness of the investment instruments. The complexity of many financial instruments is such that nobody can actually trace all that is bundled up in some of these financial instruments. Eventually this meant that nobody knew exactly or could understand the composition of their investments, not even those who sold the instruments. Developed countries with multiple financial circuits, such as the US and the UK, clearly show that compared to other types of loans, mortgages are a relatively small share of all loans, even if most households have mortgages. It is important to note that the same low level of mortgage loans to total loans in economies marked by a small elite of super rich individuals has a different meaning in the US and UK: hence, Russia's extremely low incidence of residential to total loans in the economy is an indication of a narrow mortgage market (mostly for the rich and very rich) and the fact that there are vast financial circuits centred on other resources.

It is important to emphasize that the viral infection of sub-prime mortgages originated in the United States but spread to other countries via the globalization of financial markets. This spread was helped by the fact that non-national investors are, as a group, the single largest buyers of some of the weakest types of mortgage instruments. Together with banks, non-national mortgage buyers are over a third of all sub-prime mortgage holders. Foreign ownership strengthens the potential for spill-over effects well beyond the United States. An important question raised by these developments is the extent to which developed and developing countries will follow this troublesome 'development' path (Sassen 2008b). It has become another way of extracting value from individuals, in this case, through home mortgages that even very poor households are invited to buy, partly because the sellers are merely after the contract that represents an asset, in order to bundle them up and sell the package to an investor, thereby passing on the risk and removing an incentive to care whether the home owner manages to pay the mortgage.

CONCLUSION: EXPELLING PEOPLE AND INCORPORATING TERRAIN

The potential for global replication of the financial innovation that destroyed many millions of households in the US, thereby devastating whole neighbourhoods, is the systemic equivalent, albeit on a much smaller scale, of the Global South countries devastated by an imposed debt and debt servicing regime which took priority over all other state expenditures. These are two manifestations of a systemic deepening of advanced capitalism, one marked by its potential to spread globally and the other marked by its full enactment in the Global South.

Both cases can be seen as part of a much larger process of financial deepening, one of today's major dynamics characterizing advanced capitalist economies. Financial deepening requires specific mechanisms, which can be extremely complex, as in the case of the type of sub-prime mortgage examined in this chapter, or they can be quite elementary, as in the debt servicing regime that took off in the 1990s. I examine these two cases through a specific lens: the transformative processes that expand the operational space of current advanced capitalism. Particular attention went to the assemblages of specific processes, institutions and logics that get mobilized in this systemic transformation/expansion/consolidation.

The result is an expulsion of people from their land and livelihood both in the Global South and in the North, even as it incorporates rural and urban land into new organizing logics. The devastated economies of the Global South subjected to a full decade or two of debt servicing are now being incorporated into the circuits of advanced capitalism through the accelerated acquisition of millions of hectares of land by foreign investors – to grow crops and extract water and minerals, all for the capital-investing countries. This also holds for such a radically different instance as the sub-prime mortgage crisis, a largely Global North dynamic. I see the sub-prime mortgage as extending the domain for high finance but in a way that de-links the financial circuit from the actual material entity that is the house, and hence from the neighbourhood, and from the people who got the mortgage.

This also means that the land and the devastated neighbourhoods I examined here are expelled from what are, strictly speaking, traditional circuits of capital. It is akin to wanting only the horns of the rhino, and throwing away the rest of the animal. Or using the human body to harvest some organs, and seeing no value in all the other organs, let alone the full human being – it can all be discarded. But unlike the clear realignments we see in vast stretches of the Global South, it is not clear how these devastated urban spaces in the Global North will be incorporated into the circuits of advanced capitalism.

Bibliography

Abarca, H. 1943. 'Por un plan económico general'. *Principios*, 24, 2ª epoca: 13–14.

Abbott, Andrew. 2001. *Chaos of Disciplines*. Chicago: University of Chicago Press.

Abbott, Andrew and DeViney, Stanley. 1992. 'The welfare state as transnational event: Evidence from sequences of policy adoptions'. *Social Science History*, 16 (2) 245–74.

Abegglen, J. 1958. *The Japanese Factory: Aspects of its Social Organization*. Glencoe, IL: Free Press.

Abegglen, J. 1970. *Business Strategies for Japan*. Tokyo: Sophia University in cooperation with Encyclopædia Britannica.

Adelman, Jeremy. 1991. 'Against essentialism: Latin American labour history in comparative perspective: A critique of Bergquist'. *Labour*, 27: 175–84.

Adler, P.S. 2007. 'The future of critical management studies: A Paleo-Marxist critique of labour process theory'. *Organization Studies*, 28 (9) 1313–45.

Adler-Milstein, S., Champagne, J. and Haas, T. 2014. 'The right to organize, living wage, and real change for garment workers'. In S. Garwood, S. Croeser and C. Yakinthou, eds. *Lessons for Social Change in the Global Economy: Voices from the Field*. Plymouth: Lexington Books.

Adorno, Th.W. 1972. 'Zur Logik der Sozialwissenschaften'. In Th.W. Adorno, R. Dahrendorf, H. Pilot et al., eds. *Der Positivismusstreit in der Deutschen Soziologie*. Darmstadt: Luchterhand.

Agathangelou, A.M. 2004. *The Global Political Economy of Sex: Desire, Violence, and Insecurity in Mediterranean Nation States*. New York: Palgrave Macmillan.

Aglietta, Michel. 1976. *Régulation et Crises du Capitalisme: L'expérience des États-unis*. Paris: Calman-Lévy.

Aglietta, Michel. 1979[1976]. *A Theory of Capitalist Regulation. The US Experience* [trans. D. Fernbach]. London: Verso.

Aglietta, Michel. 1999. 'La globalisation financière'. In CEPII, eds. *L'économie Mondiale 2000*. Paris: La Découverte for the Centre d'études Prospectives et d'informations Internationales.

Agustín, L.M. 2006. 'The disappearing of a migration category: Migrants who sell sex'. *Journal of Ethnic and Migration Studies*, 32 (1) 29–47.

Agustín, L.M. 2007. *Sex at the Margins: Migration, Labour Markets and the Rescue Industry*. London: Zed Books.

Allen, John. 2003. *Lost Geographies of Power*. Oxford: Blackwell.

Allen, K. and MacLennan, M. 1971. *Regional Problems and Policies in France and Italy*. London: Verso.

Alnasseri, Sabah. 2003. 'Ursprüngliche Akkumulation, Artikulation und Regulation. Aspekte einer Globalen Theorie der Regulation'. In Ulrich Brand and Werner Raza, eds. *Fit für den Postfordismus? Theoretisch-politische Perspektiven des Regulationsansatzes*. Münster: Westfälisches Dampfboot.

Alnasseri, Sabah, Brand, Ulrich, Sablowski, Thomas and Winter, Jens. 2001. 'Space, regulation and the periodization of capitalism'. In Robert Albritton, Makoto Itoh, Richard Westra and Alan Zuege, eds. *Phases of Capitalist Development. Booms, Crises and Globalizations*. London: Macmillan.

Altieri, M.A. and Funes-Monzote, F.R. 2012. 'The Cuban agriculture's paradox: The persistence of the agroecological paradigm the emergence of biotechnology'. *Monthly Review*, 63 (8) 16–26.

Altieri, M.A. and Toledo, V.M. 2011. 'The agroecological revolution in Latin America: Rescuing nature, ensuring food sovereignty and empowering peasants'. *The Journal of Peasant Studies*, 38 (3) 587–612.

Altvater, Elmar. 1993. *The Future of the Market*. London: Verso.

Altvater, Elmar. 1996. 'Der Traum vom Umweltraum. Zur Studie des Wuppertal Instituts über ein "zukunftsfähiges Deutschland"'. *Blätter für Deutsche und Internationale Politik*, 41 (1) 82–91.

Álvarez-Buylla, Elena, Piñeyro Nelson, Alma, Turrent, Antonio, Nieto-Sotelo, Jorge, Wegier, Ana, Alavez, Valeria, Milán, Leonora, Traavik, Terje and Quist, David. 2013. 'Incertidumbre, riesgos y peligros de la liberación de maíz transgénico en México'. In Elena Álvarez-Buylla and Alma Piñeyro Nelson, eds. *El Maíz en Peligro ante los Transgénicos. Un Análisis Integral sobre el Caso de México*. Mexico DF: Universidad Nacional Autónoma de México.

Amato, G. 1992. 'Il mercato nella costituzione'. *Quaderni Costituzionali*, 1: 7–19.

Amoore, Louise. 2001a. 'Work, production and social relations: Repositioning the firm in the international political economy'. In J. Harrod and R. O'Brien, eds. *Global Unions: Theory and Strategy of Organised Labour in the Global Political Economy*. London: Routledge.

Amoore, Louise. 2001b. 'Globalisation at work: Unheard voices and invisible agency'. Paper presented at Annual Convention, International Studies Association.

Amoore, Louise. 2002. *Globalisation Contested: An International Political Economy of Work*. Manchester: Manchester University Press.

Amyot, G. 2004. *Business, the State and Economic Policy: The Case of Italy*. London: Routledge.

Anderson, B. 2011. 'Population and affective perception: Biopolitics and anticipatory action in US counterinsurgency doctrine'. *Antipode*, 43 (2) 205–36.

Anderson, Bridget. 2008. '"Illegal immigrant": Victim or villain?'. *COMPAS Working Paper WP-08–64*. Oxford: COMPAS.

Anderson, Bridget and O'Connell Davidson, Julia. 2002. *Trafficking: A Demand-Led Problem? A Multi-Country Pilot Study*. Stockholm: Save the Children.

Anderson, Perry. 1976. *Considerations on Western Marxism*. London: Verso.

Andrees, Beate and Belser, Patrick. eds. 2009. *Forced Labour: Coercion and Exploitation in the Private Economy*. London: Lynne Rienner.

Andreff, Wladimir. 2009. 'Outsourcing in the new strategy of multinational companies: Foreign investment, international subcontracting and production relocation'. *Papeles de Europa*, 18: 5–34.

Andrijasevic, R. 2009. 'Sex on the move: Gender, subjectivity and differential inclusion'. *Subjectivity*, 29: 389–406.

Andrijasevic, Rutvica and Sacchetto, Devi. 2013. 'China may be far away but Foxconn is on our doorstep'. *Open Democracy*. 5 June. Available at: http://www.opendemocracy.net/rutvica-andrijasevic-devi-sacchetto/china-may-be-far-away-but-foxconn-is-on-our-doorstep.

Angell, Alan. 2010. 'Social class and popular mobilisation in Chile: 1970–1973'. *A Contra Corriente*, 7 (2) 1–51.

Anseeuw, Ward, Boche, Mathieu, Breu, Thomas, Giger, Markus, Lay, John, Messerli, Peter and Nolte, Kerstin. 2012. *Transnational Land Deals for Agriculture in the Global South: Analytic Report based on the Land Matrix Database International Land Coalition*. Bern: CDE/CIRAD/GIGA. Available at: http://www.landcoalition.org/publications/transnational-land-deals-agriculture-global-south.

Antón, Philip S., Silberglitt, Richard and Schneider, James. 2001. *The Global Technology Revolution: Bio/Nano/Materials Trends and their Synergies with Information Technology by 2015*. Santa Monica, CA: RAND.

Aoki, M. 1988. *Information, Incentives, and Bargaining in the Japanese Economy*. Cambridge: Cambridge University Press.

Appelbaum, R. and Lichtenstein, N. 2006. 'A new world of retail supremacy: Supply chains and workers' chains in the age of Wal-Mart'. *International Labor and Working Class History*, 70: 106–25.

Appelbaum, Richard P. 2008. 'Giant transnational contractors in East

Asia: Emergent trends in global supply chains'. *Competition and Change*, 12 (1) 69–87.

Apple. 2011. 'Apple launches iPad 2'. 2 March. Available at: http://www.apple.com/pr/library/2011/03/02Apple-Launches-iPad-2.html.

Apple. 2012a. 'Reclassified summary data: Product summary'. Available at: http://files.shareholder.com/downloads/AAPL/2228807434x0x630364/ad8fe602–72bb-4a3a-bcaf-0e4d2a300fb2/Reclassified_Summary_Data.pdf.

Apple. 2012b. 'Annual report for the fiscal year ended September 29, 2012'. Available at: http://investor.apple.com/secfiling.cfm?filingID=1193125–12–444068&CIK=320193.

Apple. 2012c. 'New iPad tops three million'. 19 March. Available at: http://www.apple.com/pr/library/2012/03/19New-iPad-Tops-Three-Million.html.

Apple. 2012d. 'Apple supplier responsibility: 2012 progress report'. Available at: http://images.apple.com/supplier-responsibility/pdf/Apple_SR_2012_Progress_Report.pdf.

Apple. 2012e. 'Apple Supplier Code of Conduct'. Available at: http://images.apple.com/supplierresponsibility/pdf/Apple_Supplier_Code_of_Conduct.pdf.

Appy, Christian. 1993. *Working Class War: American Combat Soldiers in Vietnam*. Chapel Hill, NC: University of North Carolina Press.

Aquanno, S. 2009. 'US power in the international bond market: Financial flows and the construction of risk value'. In L. Panitch and M. Konings, eds. *American Empire and the Political Economy of Global Finance*, 2nd edn. London: Palgrave.

Arrighi, Giovanni. 1994. *The Long Twentieth Century*. London: Verso.

Arrighi, Giovanni. 2007. *Adam Smith in Beijing. Lineages of the Twenty-First Century*. London: Verso.

Arrighi, Giovanni and Silver, Beverly J. (with I. Ahmed, K. Barr, S. Hisaeda, P.K. Hui, K. Ray, T. Reifer, M. Shih and E. Slater). 1999a. *Chaos and Governance in the Modern World System*. Minneapolis: University of Minnesota Press.

Arrighi, Giovanni and Silver, Beverly J. 1999b. 'Hegemonic transitions: A rejoinder'. *Political Power and Social Theory*, 13: 310.

Arvatov, Boris. 1997. 'Everyday life and the culture of the thing'. *October*, 81: 119–28.

Asanuma, B. 1985. 'The organization of parts purchases in the Japanese automotive industry'. *Japanese Economic Studies*, 13 (4) 32–53.

Asanuma, B. 1989. 'Manufacturer–supplier relationships in Japan and the concept of relation-specific skill'. *Journal of the Japanese and International Economies*, 3 (1) 1–30.

Aschoff, N. 2009. *Globalization and Capital Mobility in the Automobile Industry*. Doctoral Dissertation, Johns Hopkins University.

Aschoff, N. 2011. 'A tale of two crises: Labour, capital and restructuring in the US auto industry'. *Socialist Register 2012*, London: Merlin.

Ascoly, N. and Zeldenrust, I. 1999. *The Code Debate in Context: A Decade of Campaigning for Clean Clothes*. Amsterdam: Clean Clothes Campaign.

Asian Development Bank. 2008. *Emerging Asian Regionalism: A Partnership for Shared Prosperity*'. Manila: ADB.

Assange, J. 2013. 'SysAdmins of the world, unite!', speech at Chaos Computer Congress 30C3 in Hamburg, 29 December. Available at: https://www.youtube.com/watch?v=hzhtGvSflEk.

Austin, J.E. and Aguilar, F. 1988. *Nike in China. Case 386–065*. Cambridge, MA: Harvard Business School.

Babson, S. 1995. 'Whose team?: Lean production at Mazda U.S.A.'. In S. Babson, ed. *Lean Work*. Detroit: Wayne State University Press.

Baccaro, L. 1999. 'Il sistema italiano di concertazione sociale: Problemi aperti e prospettive di evoluzione'. Working Paper, Weatherhead School of Management, Case Western Reserve University, Cleveland, OH.

Backer, Larry. 2007. 'Economic globalization and the rise of efficient systems of global private law making: Wal-Mart as global legislator'. *Connecticut Law Review*, 39 (4) 1739–84.

Bai, M-K. 2007. 'The turning point in the Korean Economy'. *The Developing Economies*, 20 (2) 117–40.

Baidakov, M. and Gromyko, Y. 2013. 'Cresci, Eurasia, cresci! Verso il G 20 in Russia, l'idea di un nuovo polo di sviluppo per generare ricchezza sociale. Contromano. Memoria. Attualità'. *Futuro*, 1: 44–6.

Baidakov, M., Bassanini, F., Gromyko, Y., Zyukov, V., Raimondi, P., Reviglio, E. and Tennenbaum, J. 2012. *Trans-Eurasian Belt of Development* (ed. Y. Gromyko). Moscow: Praxis.

Baidakov, Michail, Gromyko, Yury and Raimondi, Paolo. 2011. 'The next technological and industrial revolution: the case of Russia'. *World Affairs: Journal of International Issues*, 15 (4) 76–103.

Bair, J. 2005. 'Global capitalism and commodity chains: Looking back, going forward'. *Competition and Change*, 9 (2) 153–80.

Baird, Nicola. 1998. *The Estate We're In: Who's Driving Car Culture?* London: Indigo.

Bakan, Abigail B. and Stasiulis, Daiva. 2012. 'The political economy of migrant live-in caregivers: A case of unfree labour'. In P.T. Lenard and C. Straehle, eds. *Legislated Inequality: Temporary Labour Migration in Canada*. Toronto: McGill-Queens University Press.

Baker, A. 2006. *The Group of Seven: Finance Ministries, Central Banks and Global Financial Governance*. London: Routledge.

Bakhshi, H., Freeman, A. and Higgs, P. 2014. *A Regional Dynamic Mapping of the UK's High Technology and Creative Economies*. London: NESTA.

Bakhshi, H., Freeman, Alan and Higgs, Peter. 2013a. *A Dynamic Mapping of the Creative Industries in the UK*. London: NESTA. Available at: https://www.academia.edu/5538116/A_Dynamic_Mapping_of_the_UKs_Creative_Industries.

Bakhshi, H., Hargreaves, Ian and Mateos-Garcia, Juan. 2013b. *A Manifesto for the Creative Economy*. London: NESTA. Available at: nesta.org.uk/publications/manifesto-creative-economy.

Bakker, Isabella and Gill, Stephen, eds. 2003. *Power, Production and Social Reproduction*. London: Palgrave.

Bales, Kevin. 1999. *Disposable People: New Slavery in the Global Economy*. Berkeley, CA: University of California Press.

Bales, Kevin. 2005. *Understanding Global Slavery: A Reader*. Berkeley, CA: University of California Press.

Bales, Kevin. 2007. *Ending Slavery: How We Free Today's Slaves*. Berkeley, CA: University of California Press.

Bales, Kevin and Trodd, Zoe, eds. 2008. *To Plead Our Own Cause: Personal Stories by Today's Slaves*. Ithaca: Cornell University Press.

Balfour, Frederik and Culpan, Tim 2010. 'Everything is Made by Foxconn in Future Evoked by Gou's Empire'. *Bloomberg*. 10 September. Available at: http://www.bloomberg.com/news/2010–09–09/everything-is-made-by-foxconn-in-future-evoked-by-terry-gou-s-china-empire.html.

Balkenende, Jan Peter. 2005. Presentation by the Prime Minister, Dr J.P. Balkenende, Bilderberg Conference of the Stichting NCW, 'Op eigen kracht; van verzorgingsstaat naar participatiemaatschappij'. Oosterbeek, 22 January.

Banaji, J. 1977. 'Modes of production in a materialist conception of history'. *Capital and Class*, 3: 1–42.

Banjo, Shelly. 2012. 'Wal-Mart to pay $4.8 million in back wages, damages'. *Wall Street Journal*. Online edn. http://online.wsj.com/article/SB10001424052702304868004577378381606731206.html.

Baran, Paul A. and Sweezy, Paul M. 1968[1966]. *Monopoly Capital. An Essay on the American Economic and Social Order*. Harmondsworth: Penguin.

Barba, A. 2011. 'La redistribuzione del reddito nell'Italia di Maastricht'. In L.Paggi, ed. *Un'altra Italia in un'altra Europa*. Roma: Carocci.

Barbier, E. 2010. 'How is the global green new deal going?' *Nature*, 464 (7290) 832–3.

Barboza, D. 2010. Foxconn increases size of raise in Chinese factories.

New York Times. Available at: www.nytimes.com/2010/06/07/business/global/07foxconn.html.
Barbrook, R. 2006. *The Class of the New*. London: OpenMute.
Barbrook, R. and Cameroon, A 1996[1995]. 'The Californian ideology'. *Science as Culture*, 26: 44–72.
Barefoot, K. and Mataloni Jr, R. 2010. 'US multinational companies'. Washington, DC: Bureau of Economic Analysis.
Barrientos, S. 1996. 'Social clauses and women workers in Latin America'. *New Political Economy*, 1 (2) 274–8.
Barrientos, S. 2001. 'Gender, flexibility and global value chains'. *IDS Bulletin*, 32 (3) 83–93.
Barrientos, S. and Smith, S. 2007. 'Do workers benefit from ethical trade? Assessing codes of labour practice in global production systems'. *Third World Quarterly*, 28 (4) 713–29.
Barrientos, S., Gereffi, G. and Rossi, A. 2011. 'Economic and social upgrading in global production networks: A new paradigm for a changing world'. *International Labour Review*, 150 (3–4) 319–40.
Barrientos, Stephanie, Kothari, Uma and Phillips, Nicola. 2013. 'Dynamics of unfree labour in the contemporary global economy'. *Journal of Development Studies*, 49 (8) 1037–41.
Barrow, Clyde W. 1990. *Universities and the Capitalist State. Corporate Liberalism and the Reconstruction of American Higher Education, 1894–1928*. Madison, WI: University of Wisconsin Press.
Barry, K.L. 1995. *The Prostitution of Sexuality: The Global Exploitation of Women*. New York: New York University Press.
Barstow, David. 2012. 'Vast Mexico bribery case hushed up by Wal-Mart after top-level struggle'. *New York Times*. Onlinc edition. http://www.nytimes.com/2012/04/22/business/at-wal-mart-in-mexico-a-bribe-inquiry-silenced.html?pagewanted=alland_moc.semityn.
Bartley, T. 2003. 'Certifying forests and factories: States, social movements, and the rise of private regulation in the apparel and forest products fields'. *Politics and Society*, 31 (3) 433–64.
Basker, Emek. 2007. 'The causes and consequences of Wal-Mart's growth'. *Journal of Economic Perspectives*, 21 (3) 177–98.
Bassanini, Franco and Reviglio, Edoardo. 2010. 'New regulatory framework and instruments for European long term investments after the crisis'. Available at: http://www.ltic.org/IMG/pdf/Working_Paper_Bassanini_Reviglio_Venice_Forum2010.pdf.
Bathke, P. and Hoffstadt, A. eds. 2013. *Die neuen Rechten in Europa. Zwischen Neoliberalismus und Rassismus*. Cologne: PapyRossa.
Batstone, David. 2010. *The Return of the Global Slave Trade – And How We Can Fight It*. New York: HarperCollins.

Battelle. 2012. *2013 Global RandD Funding Forecast*, Columbus, Ohio: Battelle. Available at: http://www.rdmag.com/sites/rdmag.com/files/GFF2013Final2013_reduced.pdf.

Baudrillard, Jean. 1988. *America*. London: Verso.

Bauer, J. 2011. *Schmerzgrenze. Vom Ursprung alltäglicher und globaler Gewalt*. Munich: Blessing.

Bauman, Z. 2008. *Flüchtige Zeiten. Leben in der Ungewissheit*. Hamburg: Hamburger Edition.

Baumol, W.J. and Bowen, W.G. 1966. *Performing Arts, the Economic Dilemma: A Study of Problems Common to Theater, Opera, Music, and Dance*. New York: Twentieth Century Fund.

Bauriedl, Sybille and Wichterich, Christa. 2013. 'Gender, Nachhaltigkeit und kapitalistische Verwertung. Anknüpfungspunkte für sozial-ökologische Transformation. Expertise für die Rosa-Luxemburg-Stiftung'. Unpublished Manuscript.

Bauwens, M. 2005. 'The political economy of peer production'. *C-theory Journal*. http://www.ctheory.net/articles.aspx?id=499.

Bauwens, M. 2011. 'The first social cyberwar as the class warfare of the 21st cy: On the convergence of hacktivism with social movements'. Available at: http://blog.p2pfoundation.net/the-first-socialcyberwar-as-the-class-warfare-of-the-21st-cy-on-the-convergence-of-hacktivism-with-socialmovements/2011/06/22.

Becattini, G. 2000. *Il distretto industriale. Un nuovo modo di interpretare il cambiamento economico*. Turin: Rosenberg and Sellier.

Beck, U., Giddens, A. and Lash, U. 1996. *Reflexive Modernisierung*. Frankfurt: Suhrkamp.

Becker, Egon, Hummel, Diana and Jahn, Thomas. 2011. 'Gesellschaftliche Naturverhältnisse als Rahmenkonzept?' In Matthias Groß, ed. *Handbuch Umweltsoziologie*. Wiesbaden: Verlag für Sozialwissenschaften.

Becker, Joachim. 2002. *Akkumulation, Regulation, Territorium. Eine Kritische Rekonstruktion der Französischen Regulationstheorie*. Marburg: Metropolis.

Becker, Joachim and Raza, Werner. 2000. 'Theory of regulation and political ecology: an inevitable divorce?' *Économie et Sociétés*, 56 (11) 55–70.

Bedford, K. and Rai, M.R. 2010. 'Feminists theorize international political economy'. *Signs*, 36 (1) 1–18.

Bell, Daniel. 1960. *The End of Ideology*. New York: The Free Press.

Bell, Daniel. 1974. *The Coming of Post-Industrial Society*. New York: Harper Colophon Books.

Bello, Walden. 2005. *Dilemmas of Domination: The Unmaking of the American Empire*. New York: Metropolitan Books.

Beloso, B.M. 2012. 'Sex, work, and the feminist erasure of class'. *Signs*, 38 (1) 47–70.

Benbrook, Charles M. 2012. 'Impacts of genetically engineered crops on pesticide use in the U.S.: the first sixteen years'. *Environmental Sciences Europe*, 24: 24. Available at: http://www.enveurope.com/content/24/1/24.

Beneria, L. and Feldman, S., eds. 1992. *Unequal Burden: Economic Crises, Persistent Poverty, and Women's Work*. Boulder, CO: Westview.

Bennett, W.L., Segerberg, A. and Walker, S. 2014. 'Organization in the crowd: Peer production in large-scale networked protests'. *Information, Communication & Society*, 17 (2) 232–60.

Berardi, Bifo F. 2010. 'Cognitarian subjectivation'. *E-Flux Journal*, 20, November. Available at: http://www.e-flux.com/journal/cognitarian-subjectivation.

Berardi, F. 2009. *Precarious Rhapsody*. New York: Minor Compositions.

Berger, Allen N. 2003. 'The economic effects of technological progress: Evidence from the banking industry'. *Journal of Money, Credit, and Banking*, 35 (2) 141–76.

Berger, A., Kashyap, A. and Scalise, J. 1995. 'The transformation of the US banking industry'. *Brookings Papers on Economic Activity*, No. 2.

Bergquist, Charles. 1986. *Labor in Latin America: Comparative Essays on Chile, Argentina, Venezuela, and Colombia*. Stanford, CA: Stanford University Press.

Berlant, L. 2011. *Cruel Optimism*. Durham, NC: Duke University Press.

Berlinguer, E. 1977. *Austerità, occasione per trasformare l'Italia*. Rome: Editori Riunti.

Berlinguer, M. 2010. 'The effects of the open source movement on the development of politics and society', *Transform!* (6). Available at: http://transform-network.net/journal/issue-062010/news/detail/Journal/knowledge-is-a-common-good.html.

Berman, I. Morris. 2000. *The Twilight of American Culture*. New York: W.W. Norton.

Berman, J. 2003. '(Un)popular strangers and crises (un)bounded: Discourses of sex-trafficking, the European political community and the panicked state of the modern state'. *European Journal of International Relations*, 9 (1) 37–86.

Berman, Marshall. 1982. *All That is Solid Melts into Air: the Experience of Modernity*. London: Verso.

Bernard, S., Asokan, S., Warrell, H. and Lemer, J. 2009. 'Which country has the greenest bail-out?' *Financial Times*. 2 March.

Berne Declaration and EcoNexus. 2013. *Agropoly: A Handful of*

Corporations Control World Food Production. Zurich: Berne Declaration and Oxford: EcoNexus.

Bernhardt, T. and Milberg, W. 2011. 'Does economic upgrading generate social upgrading? Insights from the horticulture, apparel, mobile phones and tourism sector'. Capturing the Gains Working Paper 07, University of Manchester.

Bernstein, E. 2010. 'Militarized humanitarianism meets carceral feminism: The politics of sex, rights, and freedom in contemporary antitrafficking campaigns'. *Signs*, 36 (1) 45–71.

Bernstein, H. 2009. 'Agrarian questions from transition to globalization'. In A.H. Akram-Lodhi and C. Kay, eds. *Peasants and Globalization: Political Economy, Rural Transformation and the Agrarian Question*. London: Routledge.

Bernstein, H. 2013. 'Food sovereignty: A sceptical view'. Paper presented at Conference *Food Sovereignty: A Critical Dialogue*, 14–15 September. Yale University. Available at: http://www.yale.edu/agrarianstudies/foodsovereignty/papers.html.

Besser, T. 1996. *Team Toyota: Transplanting the Toyota Culture to the Camry Plant in Kentucky*. Albany: State University of New York Press.

Best, Jacqueline. 2012. 'Bureaucratic ambiguity'. *Economy and Society*, 41 (1) 84–106.

Best, Jacqueline and Paterson, Matthew. 2009. *Cultural Political Economy*. London: Routledge.

Bevir, M. 1999. 'Foucault, power and institutions'. *Political Studies*, 47 (2) 345–59.

Bezanson, Kate. 2006. *Gender, the State, and Social Reproduction: Household Insecurity in Neoliberal Times*. Toronto: University of Toronto Press.

Bhaduri, Amit. 1973. 'A study in agricultural backwardness under semi-feudalism'. *The Economic Journal*, 83 (329) 120–37.

Bhattacharjee, A. and Roy, A. 2012. 'Asia floor wage and global industrial collective bargaining'. *International Journal of Labour Research*, 4 (4) 67–84.

Bianchi, R. 2011. 'Psychosoziale Destruktion im Neoliberalismus aus der Perspektive der Relationalen Psychologie'. In B. Wiebel, A. Pilenko and G. Nintemann, eds. *Mechanismen psycho-sozialer Zerstörung. Neoliberales Herrschaftsdenken, Stressfaktoren der Prekarität, Widerstand*. Hamburg: VSA.

Bianco, Anthony. 2006. *The Bully of Bentonville: How the High Cost of Wal-Mart's Everyday Low Prices is Hurting America*. New York: Currency Doubleday.

Bianco, Anthony and Anderson Forest, Stephanie. 2003. 'Outsourcing war: An inside look at Brown and Root, the kingpin of America's new military–industrial complex'. *Business Week Online*, 15 September.

Bieler, A. and Lindberg, I. eds. 2008. *Global Restructuring, Labour and the Challenges for Transnational Solidarity*. Abingdon: Routledge.

Bieler, A., Lindberg, I. and Pillay, D., eds. 2011. *Labour and the Challenges of Globalisation: What Prospects for Transnational Solidarity?* London: Pluto.

Biesecker, Adelheid, Wichterich, Christa and von Winterfeld, Uta. 2012. 'Feministische Perspektiven zum Themenbereich Wachstum, Wohlstand, Lebensqualität', background paper for the Expert Commission 'Growth, Well-Being and Quality of Life' of the German Bundestag, Material 17–26–3. Berlin.

Bigo, D. and Guild, E. eds. 2005. *Controlling Frontiers: Free Movement into and within Europe*. Aldershot: Ashgate.

Bit Computing. 'Daily Activity Tracking Software. Automated & Accurate'. Available at: http://www.bitcomputing.com/software/daily-activity-tracking-software/.

Bizzari, K. and Burton, A. 2013. 'A brave new transatlantic partnership. The proposed US–EU transatlantic trade and investment partnership (TTIP/TAFTA), and its socio-economic and environmental consequences'. Brussels: Seattle to Brussels Network.

Blackburn, Robin. 1997. *The Making of New World Slavery: From the Baroque to the Modern 1492–1800*. London: Verso.

Blind, Knut. 2004. *The Economics of Standards. Theory, Evidence, Policy*. Cheltenham, UK and Northampton, MA, USA: Edward Elgar Publishing.

Bloch, Ernst. 1980. *Abschied von der Utopie? Vorträge*. Frankfurt: Suhrkamp.

Block, Fred. 2008. 'Swimming against the current: The rise of a hidden developmental state in the United States'. *Politics & Society*, 36 (2) 169–206.

Bloomberg Businessweek. 2010. 'The Tao of Gou'. Available at: http://images.businessweek.com/mz/10/38/1038foxconn65.pdf.

Blunkett, D. 1998. *The Learning Age*. Cm 3790. The Stationery Office Lifelong Learning summary. Available at: http://www.lifelonglearning.co.uk/greenpaper/summary.pd.

Blyth, Mark. 2013. *Austerity. The History of a Dangerous Idea*. Oxford: Oxford University Press.

Boccara, Paul. 2008. *Transformations et Crise du Capitalisme Mondialisé. Quelle Alternative?* Pantin: ESPERE/Le Temps des Cerises.

Boden, Mark and Miles, Ian. 2000. 'Conclusions: Beyond the services economy'. In Mark Boden and Ian Miles, eds. *Services and the Knowledge-Based Economy*. London: Continuum.

Bois, Guy. 1985. 'Against the neo-Malthusian orthodoxy'. In T.H. Ashton and C.H.E. Philpin, eds. *The Brenner Debate*. Cambridge: Cambridge University Press.

Boittin, J.A., Firpo, C. and Church, E.M. 2011. 'Hierarchies of race and gender in the French colonial empire, 1914–1946'. *Historical Reflections–Reflexions Historiques*, 37 (1) 60–90.

Bok, Francis. 2003. *Escape from Slavery: The True Story of My Ten Years in Captivity and My Journey to Freedom in America*. New York: St Martin's Griffin.

Boltanski, L. and Chiapello, E. 2007[1999]. *The New Spirit of Capitalism*. London: Verso.

Bonacich, Edna and Hamilton, Gary G. 2011. 'Global logistics, global labor'. In G.G. Hamilton, M. Petrovic and B. Senauer, eds. *The Market Makers: How Retailers are Reshaping the Global Economy*. Oxford: Oxford University Press.

Bond, P. 2007. 'Linking below, across and against: World Social Forum weaknesses, global governance gaps, and the global justice movement's strategic dilemmas'. *Development Dialogue*, 49: 81–95.

Borras, Saturnino M. Jr and Franco, Jennifer C. 2012. 'Global land grabbing and trajectories of agrarian change: A preliminary analysis'. *Journal of Agrarian Change*, 12 (1) 34–59.

Bose, C.E. and Acosta-Belen, E. eds. 1995. *Women in the Latin American Development Process*. Philadelphia, PA: Temple University Press.

Boston Review. 2013. 'Forum: Can global brands create just supply chains?' 21 May. Available at: http://www.bostonreview.net/forum/can-global-brands-create-just-supply-chains-richard-locke.

Bourdieu, Pierre. 1977. *Outline of a Theory of Practice*. Cambridge: Cambridge University Press.

Bourdieu, Pierre. 1984. *Distinction: A Social Critique of the Judgement of Taste*. Cambridge, MA: Harvard University Press.

Bourdieu, Pierre. 1997. *Gegenfeuer. Wortmeldungen im Dienste des Widerstandes gegen die neoliberale Invasion*. Konstanz: Universitäts-Verlag.

Bowles, Samuel and Gintis, Herbert. 1976. *Schooling in Capitalist America: Educational Reform and the Contradictions of Economic Life*. New York: Basic Books.

Boyarin, D. 1995. *Carnal Israel: Reading Sex in Talmudic Culture*. London: University of California Press.

Boyd, William, Prudham, Scott W. and Schurman, Rachel. 2001. 'Industrial dynamics and the problem of nature'. *Society and Natural Resources*, 14: 555–70.

Boyer, Miriam. 2013. *Transforming Nature: A Brief Hiatus in Space and Time*. PhD Dissertation, Columbia University/Freie Universität Berlin.

Boyer, Robert. 1990. *The Regulation School: A Critical Introduction*. New York: Oxford University Press.

Brace, Laura. 2010. 'Slavery and its opposites: Contract, freedom and labour'. Keynote lecture: *Human Rights, Victimhood and Consent workshop*. Uni Rokkan Centre, Bergen, 10–12 June.

Bradanini, D. 2012. *Common Sense and 'National Emergency': Neoliberal Hegemony in 1990s Italy*. PhD thesis, IMT (Institutions-Markets-Technologies) Lucca.

Bradanini, Davide. 2014. 'Common sense and "national emergency": Italian labour and the crisis'. *Global Labour Journal*, 5 (2) 176–95.

Bradshaw, Y., Noonan, R., Gash, L. and Buchmann, C. 1993. 'Borrowing against the future: Children and third world indebtedness'. *Social Forces*, 71 (3) 629–56.

Bradsher, K. 2012. 'Facing a slowing economy, China turns to American exports'. *New York Times [Online]*. Available at: http://www.nytimes.com/2012/07/14/business/global/chinese-exports-to-us-surge-as-the-domestic-economy-cools.html.

Braedley, Susan and Luxton, Meg. Forthcoming. 'Foreword'. In Katie M. Meehan and Kendra Strauss, *Precarious Lives: Contested Geographies of Social Reproduction*. Athens, GA: University of Georgia Press.

Brancaccio, E. and Passarella, M. 2012. *L'austerità è di destra*. Milan: Il Saggiatore.

Brand Finance. 2013. 'Brandirectory: Ranking the world's most valuable brands'. Available at: http://brandirectory.com/league_tables/table/global-500–2013.

Brand, Helmut et al. 2013. 'Austerity policies in Europe: Bad for health'. *British Medical Journal*, 346: f3716.

Brand, Ulrich. 2006. 'The World Wide Web of anti-neoliberalism: Emerging forms of post-Fordist protest and the impossibility of global Keynesianism'. In Dieter Plehwe, Bernhard Walpen and Gisela Nuenhoeffer, eds. *Neo-Liberal Hegemony: A Global Critique*. New York: Routledge.

Brand, Ulrich. 2012. 'Green economy and green capitalism: Some theoretical considerations'. *Journal für Entwicklungspolitik*, 28 (3) 118–37.

Brand, Ulrich and Raza, Werner, eds. 2003. *Fit für den Postfordismus? Theoretisch-politische Perspektiven der Regulationstheorie*. Münster: Westfälisches Dampfboot.

Brand, Ulrich and Wissen, Markus. 2012. 'Global environmental politics and the imperial mode of living. Articulations of state–capital relations in the multiple crisis'. *Globalizations*, 9 (4) 547–60.

Brand, Ulrich, Görg, Christoph, Hirsch, Joachim and Wissen,

Markus. 2008. *Conflicts in Global Environmental Regulation and the Internationalization of the State. Contested Terrains*. London: Routledge.

Brand, Ulrich, Lötzer, Ulla, Müller, Michael and Popp, Michael. 2013. *Big Business Emission Trading. Against the Financialization of Nature*. Policy Paper No. 2/2013, Berlin: Rosa Luxemburg Foundation.

Branford, Sue. 2011. 'The great global land grab'. In Marcin Gerwin, ed. *Food and Democracy. Introduction to Food Sovereignty*. Krakow: Polish Green Network.

Branigan, Tania. 2011. 'Workers killed in blast at China plant of iPad maker Foxconn'. *The Guardian*. 20 May. Available at: http://www.guardian.co.uk/technology/2011/may/20/foxconn-apple-blast-china.

Branker, K. and Pearce, J.M. 2010. 'Financial return for government support of large-scale thin-film solar photovoltaic manufacturing in Canada'. *Energy Policy*, 38 (8) 4291–303.

Brass, Tom. 1999. *Towards a Comparative Political Economy of Unfree Labour: Case Studies and Debates*. London: Frank Cass.

Brass, Tom and Van der Linden, Marcel, eds. 1997. *Free and Unfree Labor: The Debate Continues*. Bern: Peter Lang.

Braverman, H. 1974. *Labor and Monopoly Capital: The Degradation of Work in the Twentieth Century*. New York: Monthly Review Press.

Braverman, H. 1977. *Die Arbeit im Modernen Produktionsprozeß*. Frankfurt: Campus.

Breen, K. 2012. 'Production and productive reason'. *New Political Economy*, 17(5) 611–32.

Breman, Jan, Guérin, Isabelle and Prakash, Aseem. eds. 2009. *India's Unfree Workforce: Of Bondage Old and New*. New Delhi: Oxford University Press.

Brenke, Karl, Rinne, Ulf and Zimmermann, Klaus F. 2011. *Short-Time Work: The German Answer to the Great Recession*. IZA Discussion Paper Series No. 5780. Bonn: Forschungsinstitut zur Zukunft der Arbeit.

Brenner, Robert. 1977. 'The origins of capitalist development: A critique of neo-Smithian Marxism'. *New Left Review*, 104: 25–92.

Brenner, Robert. 1998. 'The economics of global turbulence'. *New Left Review*, 229: 1–265.

Brenner, Robert. 2002. *The Boom and the Bubble: The U.S. in the World Economy*. London: Verso.

Brenner, Robert. 2009. 'What is good for Goldman Sachs is good for America: The origins of the current crisis'. Prologue to the Spanish edition of *The Economics of Global Turbulence: The Advanced Capitalist Economies from Long Boom to Long Downturn, 1945–2005*. London: Verso. Available at: http://www.sscnet.ucla.edu/issr/cstch/papers/BrennerCrisisTodayOctober2009.pdf.

Brenner, Robert and Glick, Mark. 1991. 'The regulation approach: Theory and history'. *New Left Review*, 188: 45–119.

Bresnahan, T.F. and Trajtenberg, M. 1995. 'General purpose technologies: "Engines of Growth"'. *Journal of Econometrics*, 65 (1) 83–108.

Bresser-Pereira, L. 2007. 'Method and passion in Celso Furtado'. In E. Pérez and M. Vernego, eds. *Ideas, Policies and Economic Development in the Americas*. London: Routledge.

Bretthauer, Lars et al. 2006. *Poulantzas Lesen*. Hamburg: VSA-Verlag.

Brewer, A. 1980. *Marxist Theories of Imperialism*. London: Routledge and Kegan Paul.

Brick, H. 2006. *Transcending Capitalism: Visions of a New Society in Modern American Thought*. Ithaca: Cornell University Press.

Brie, Michael. 2009. 'Ways out of the crisis of neoliberalism'. *Development Dialogue*, 51: 15–31.

Brighton Labour Process Group. 1977. 'The capitalist labour process'. *Capital and Class*, 1: 3–22.

Brody, David. 1980. *Workers in Industrial America*. New York: Oxford University Press.

Brookes, B. and Madden, P. 1995. *The Globe-trotting Sports Shoe*. London: Christian Aid.

Brown, Garrett. 2010. 'Global electronics factories in spotlight'. *Occupational Health and Safety*. 4 August. Available at: http://ohsonline.com/articles/2010/08/04/global-electronics-factories-in-spotlight.aspx.

Bruff, Ian. 2010. 'Germany's Agenda 2010 reforms: Passive revolution at the crossroads'. *Capital and Class*, 34 (3) 409–28.

Bruff, Ian. 2013. 'The body in capitalist conditions of existence: A foundational materialist approach'. In A. Cameron, J. Dickinson and N. Smith, eds. *Body/State*. Farnham: Ashgate.

Brush, P. 1988. 'Metaphors of inscription: Discipline, plasticity and the rhetoric of choice'. *Feminist Review*, 58: 22–43.

Brysk, Alison. 2012. 'Rethinking trafficking: Human rights and private wrongs'. In A. Brysk and A. Choi-Fitzpatrick, eds. *From Human Trafficking to Human Rights: Reframing Contemporary Slavery*. Philadelphia, PA: University of Pennsylvania Press.

Brysk, Alison and Choi-Fitzpatrick, Austin, eds. 2012. *From Human Trafficking to Human Rights: Reframing Contemporary Slavery*. Philadelphia, PA: University of Pennsylvania Press.

Brzezinski, Matthew. 2003. 'The unmanned army'. *The New York Times*, 18 April.

Brzezinski, Zbigniew. 1997. *The Grand Chessboard. American Primacy and its Geostrategic Imperatives*. New York: Basic Books.

Buechler, S. 2007. 'Deciphering the local in a global neoliberal age: Three favelas in Sao Paulo, Brazil'. In S. Sassen, ed., *Deciphering the Global: Its Scales, Spaces, and Subjects*. New York: Routledge.

Bulmer-Thomas, Victor. 2003. *The Economic History of Latin America Since Independence*. Cambridge: Cambridge University Press.

Burawoy, Michael. 1985. *The Politics of Production: Factory Regimes under Capitalism and Socialism*. London: Verso.

Burch, David and Lawrence, Geoffrey. 2009. 'Towards a third food regime: Behind the transformation'. *Agriculture and Human Values*, 26: 267–79.

Burgoon, B. and Jacoby, W. 2004. 'Patch-work solidarity: Describing and explaining US and European labour internationalism'. *Review of International Political Economy*, 11 (5) 849–79.

Burke, Edmund. 1934. *Reflections on the Revolution in France* [1790] in Vol. IV of the *Works of Edmund Burke*. Oxford: Oxford University Press and London: Humphrey Milford.

Butcher, Jim. 2008. 'Ecotourism as life politics'. *Journal of Sustainable Tourism*, 16 (3) 315–26.

Butler, J. 2011. *Bodies That Matter: On the Discursive Limits of Sex*. Oxford: Routledge.

Butollo, Florian and ten Brink, Tobias. 2012. 'Challenging the atomization of discontent: Patterns of migrant-worker protest in China during the series of strikes in 2010'. *Critical Asian Studies*, 44 (3) 419–40.

Butterwegge, Ch. 2009. *Armut in Einem Reichen Land*. Frankfurt: Campus.

Byres, T.J. 1991. 'The Agrarian Question and differing forms of capitalist transition: An essay with reference to Asia'. In J. Bremen and S. Mundle, eds. *Rural Transformations in Asia*. Delhi: Oxford University Press.

Cadet, Jean-Robert. 1998. *Restavec: From Haitian Slave Child to Middle-Class American*. Austin: University of Texas Press.

Cai, F. 2010. 'Demographic transition, demographic dividend, and Lewis turning point in China'. *China Economic Journal*, 3 (2) 107–19.

Calleo, David. 1987. *Beyond American Hegemony: The Future of the Western Alliance*. New York: Basic Books.

Cameron, A., Dickinson, J. and Smith, N., eds. 2013. *Body/State*. Farnham: Ashgate.

Cameron, Angus and Palan, Ronen. 2004. *The Imagined Economies of Globalization: Mapping Transformations in the Contemporary State*. London: Sage.

Cameron, M. 1992. 'Micro and macro logics of political conflict: The informal sector and institutional change in Peru and Mexico'. In A. Ritter, M. Eron and D. Pollock, eds. *Latin America to the Year 2000:*

Reactivating Growth, Improving Equity, Sustaining Democracy. New York: Praeger.

Cammack, P. 2002. 'Attacking the poor'. *New Left Review*, 2nd series, (13) 125–34.

Candeias, Mario. 2011. 'Interregnum: Molekulare Verdichtung und organische Krise'. In A. Demirovic, J. Dück, F. Becker and P. Bader, eds. *VielfachKrise im Finanzdominierten Kapitalismus*. Hamburg: VSA.

Caraway, T.L., Rickard, S.J. and Anner, M.S. 2012. 'International negotiations and domestic politics: The case of IMF labor market conditionality'. *International Organization*, 66 (1) 27–61.

Carbon Tracker Initiative. 2012. *Unburnable Carbon – Are the world's financial markets carrying a carbon bubble?* London. Available at: http://www.carbontracker.org/carbonbubble.

Cárdenas, Enrique, Ocampo, Jose Antonio and Thorp, Rosemary. 2000. 'Introduction'. In E. Cárdenas, J.A. Ocampo and R. Thorp, eds. *An Economic History of Twentieth Century Latin America*. Vol. 3: *Industrialization and the State in Latin America: The Postwar Years*. Basingstoke: Palgrave.

Carlson, Robert. 2010. *Biology is Technology: The Promise, Peril, and New Business of Engineering Life*. Cambridge, MA: Harvard University Press.

Carlsson, C. 2008. *Nowtopia: How Pirate Programmers, Outlaw Bicyclists, and Vacant-lot Gardeners are Inventing the Future Today*. Oakland: AK Press.

Carlyle, T. 1829. 'Signs of the times' ['The mechanical age']. *Edinburgh Review*. xlix: 439.

Carnoy, M. 1998. 'The changing world of work in the information age'. *New Political Economy*, 3 (1) 123–8.

Carnoy, M. 2001. 'Work, society, family and learning for the future'. In OECD, ed. *What Schools for the Future?* Paris: OECD.

Carpenter, M. and Jefferys, S. 2000. *Management, Work and Welfare in Western Europe: A Historical and Contemporary Analysis*. Cheltenham, UK and Northampton, MA, USA: Edward Elgar Publishing.

Carr, Edward Hallet. 1945. *Nationalism and After*. London: Macmillan.

Carrieri, M. 1997. *Seconda Repubblica – senza sindacati?* Rome: Ediesse.

Carstensen, Lisa and McGrath, Siobhán. 2012. 'The national pact to eradicate slave labour in Brazil: A useful tool for unions?' *Global Labour Column*, 117. Available at: http://www.global-labour-university.org/fileadmin/GLU_Column/papers/no_117_Carst_McGraith.pdf.

Carswell, Grace and De Neve, Geert. 2013. 'Labouring for global markets: Conceptualising labour agency in global production networks'. *Geoforum*, 44: 62–70.

Casalengo, F. 1999. 'Communitarian dynamics, electro-electives affinities and networked memories in the contemporary cyberculture: the nettime list: Interview with Patrice Riemens'. Available at: http://web.media.mit.edu/~federico/living-memory/english/interview_riemens.html.

Casey, Bernard H. and Gold, Michael. 2005. 'Peer review of labour market programmes in the European Union: What can countries really learn from one another?' *Journal of European Public Policy*, 12 (1) 23–43.

Casey, W. 1973. 'Memo for George Shultz from Wm. J. Casey, Under Secretary of State for Economic Affairs', in William Simon Papers, I, 14:46, 9 May 1993.

Castel, R. 2000. *Die Metamorphosen der Sozialen Frage*. Konstanz: Universitäts Verlag.

Castells, M. 2012. *Networks of Outrage and Hope: Social Movements in the Internet Age*. Cambridge: Polity Press.

Castillo, Sandra. 2009. *Cordones Industriales: Nuevas Formas de Sociabilidad Obrera y Organizacion Politica Popula*. Concepción: Escaparte Ediciones.

Castree, Noel. 2001. 'Socializing nature: Theory, practice and politics'. In Noel Castree and Bruce Brown Castree, eds. *Social Nature: Theory, Practice and Politics*. Oxford: Blackwell.

Castree, Noel. 2008. 'Neoliberalising nature: The logics of deregulation and reregulation'. *Environment and Planning A*, 40 (1) 131–52.

Castree, N., Coe, N., Ward, K. and Samers, M. 2004. *Spaces of Work: Global Capitalism and Geographies of Labour*. London: Sage.

Castree, N., Featherstone, D. and Herod, A. 2008. 'Contrapuntal geographies: The politics of organizing across sociospatial difference'. In K.R. Cox, M. Low and J. Robinson, eds. *The Sage Handbook of Political Geography*. Los Angeles, CA: Sage.

Caves, R. 2002. *Creative Industries: Contracts between Art and Commerce*. Cambridge, MA: Harvard University Press.

CAW-CANADA Research Group on CAMI 1993. *The CAMI Report: Lean Production in a Unionized Auto Plant*. Willowdale: CAW.

CEN/Cenelec Management Centre. 2009. *Consolidated Report on the Feasibility Study in Response to EU Mandate M/ 371. CEN's Horizontal European Services Standardization Strategy*. CHESSS Consortium, July.

CEPAL. 1962. *La Industria Textil en América Latina 1: Chile*. New York: Publicaciones de Las Naciones Unidas.

Ceracchi, Andrea. 2013. 'Factory of the future'. Interview for *eRazviti*, September. Available at: http://erazvitie.org/en/article/fabrica-budushego.

Cerny, P.G. 1990. *The Changing Architecture of Politics: Structure, Agency, and the Future of the State*. London: Sage.

Certeau, Michel de. 1984. *The Practice of Everyday Life*. Berkeley: University of California Press.

Chakrabortty, Aditya. 2013. 'Austerity? Call it class war – and heed this 1944 warning from a Polish economist', *The Guardian*, 14 January. Available at: http://www.theguardian.com/commentisfree/2013/jan/14/deepening-mess-words-polish-economist.

Chalmers, John. 2012. 'Thousands in Bangladesh demonstrate after deadly blaze', *Reuters*, 26 November. Available at: http://www.reuters.com/article/2012/11/26/us-bangladesh-fire-idUSBRE8AP05T20121126.

Chaminade, C. and Vang-Lauridsen, J. 2008. 'Globalisation of knowledge production and regional innovation policy: Supporting specialized hubs in the Bangalore software industry', *Working Papers*, Lund University.

Chan, Anita. 2003. 'A "Race to the Bottom": Globalisation and China's labour standards'. *China Perspectives*, 46: 1–12.

Chan, Anita. 2011. *Wal-Mart in China*. Ithaca: Cornell University Press.

Chan, Anita and Kaxton, Siu. 2010. 'Analyzing exploitation'. *Critical Asian Studies*, 42 (2) 167–90.

Chan, C.K-C. and Hui, E.S-I. 2012. 'The dynamics and dilemma of workplace trade union reform in China: The case of the Honda workers' strike'. *Journal of Industrial Relations*, 54 (5) 653–68.

Chan, Jenny. 2013. 'A suicide survivor: The life of a Chinese worker'. *New Technology, Worker and Employment*, 28 (2) 84–99; and *The Asia-Pacific Journal*, 11 (31/1). Available at: http://www.japanfocus.org/-Jenny-Chan/3977.

Chan, Jenny and Pun Ngai. 2010. 'Suicide as protest for the new generation of Chinese migrant workers: Foxconn, Global Capital, and the State'. *The Asia-Pacific Journal* 37–2-10, 13 September. http://japanfocus.org/-Jenny-Chan/3408.

Chan, Jenny, Pun Ngai and Selden, Mark. 2013. 'The politics of global production: Apple, Foxconn and China's new working class'. *New Technology, Work and Employment*, 28 (2) 100–15; and *The Asia-Pacific Journal*, 11 (32/ 2). Available at: http://www.japanfocus.org/-Jenny-Chan/3981.

Chan, K.W. 2010. 'The global financial crisis and migrant workers in China: "There is no future as a labourer; Returning to the village has no meaning"'. *International Journal of Urban and Regional Research*, 34 (3) 659–77.

Chang, Ha-Joon. 2002. *Kicking Away the Ladder: Development Strategy in Historical Perspective*. London: Anthem.

Chang, K. 2011. 'From individualised labour relations to collective labour relations' [Cong gebie laodong guanzi dao jiti laodong guanxi]. In *Third*

Annual Meeting of the Chinese Sociological Association Professional Committee on Labour and Work [Zhongguo shehui kexue laodong shehuixue zhuanye weiyuanhui disanjie nianhui].

Chapain, C., Clarke, Phil, de Propis, Lisa, MacNeill, Stewart and Mateos-Garcia, Juan 2010. *Creative Clusters and Innovation*. London: NESTA.

Chen, F. 2007. 'Individual rights and collective rights: Labor's predicament in China'. *Communist and Post-Communist Studies*, 40 (1) 59–79.

Chen, Hsin-Hsing. 2011. 'Field report: Professionals, students, and activists in Taiwan mobilize for an unprecedented collective-action lawsuit against a former top American electronics company'. *East Asian Science, Technology and Society*, 5 (4) 555–65.

Chen, X. 2010. 'Labor woes spread to Beijing Hyundai'. *Global Times* [Online]. http://www.globaltimes.cn/auto/auto-china/industry/2011–03/537155.html.

Chen, Y. and Wong, M. 2002. *New Bondage and Old Resistance: Realities of the Labour Movement in Taiwan*. Hong Kong: Hong Kong Christian Industrial Committee.

Cheng, L.L. 1996. *Embedded Competitiveness: Taiwan's Shifting Role in International Footwear Sourcing Networks*. Ph.D. thesis, Duke University.

Chengdu Weekly. 2011. 'Chengdu factory's iPad capacity to reach 100 million units in 2013'. 2 January. Available at: http://www.chengduhitech.co.uk/Trends/News.asp.

Chesbrough, H.W. 2003. *Open Innovation: The New Imperative for Creating and Profiting from Technology*. Cambridge, MA: Harvard Business Review Press.

Chesbrough, H.W. 2008. 'Open innovation: A new paradigm for understanding industrial innovation'. In H. Chesbrough, W. Vanhaverbeke and J. West, eds. *Open Innovation: Researching a New Paradigm*. Oxford: Oxford University Press.

Chimienti, M. 2010. 'Selling sex in order to migrate: The end of the migratory dream?' *Journal of Ethnic and Migration Studies*, 36 (1) 27–45.

Chin, Christine B.N. 1998. *In Service and Servitude: Foreign Female Domestic Workers and the Malaysian 'Modernity' Project*. New York: Columbia University Press.

Chin, Christine B.N. 2008. '"Diversification" and "Privatisation": Securing insecurities in the receiving country of Malaysia'. *The Asia Pacific Journal of Anthropology*, 9 (4) 285–303.

Chin, Christine B.N. 2013. *Cosmopolitan Sex Workers: Women and Migration in a Global City*. New York: Oxford University Press.

Chin, Christine B.N. and Persaud, Randolph B. 2013. 'Dispersed submission: Political economy of sex work', Paper presented at the International Studies Annual Convention, San Francisco.

Chin, K.L. and Finckenauer, J.O. 2011. 'Chickenheads, agents, mommies, and jockeys: The social organization of transnational commercial sex'. *Crime, Law and Social Change*, 56 (5) 463–84.

China Digital Times. 2011. 'Directives from the "Ministry of Truth"'. 20 May. http://chinadigitaltimes.net/2011/06/directives-from-the-ministry-of-truth-may-1–31–2011/.

China Labour Bulletin. 2007. 'Standing up: The workers movement in China, 2000–2004'. Available at: http://www.clb.org.hk/en/content/standing-workers-movement-china-2000–2004.

China Labour Bulletin. 2009. 'Going it alone: the workers' movement in China 2007–2008'. Available at: http://www.china-labour.org.hk/en/files/share/File/research_reports/workers_movement_07–08_print_final.pdf.

China.org.cn. 2007. 'Huawei urges thousands of employees to resign'. http://www.china.org.cn/english/news/230662.htm.

China's National Bureau of Statistics. 2010. 'Monitoring and investigation report on the rural migrant workers in 2009'. [In Chinese]. Available at: http://www.stats.gov.cn/tjfx/fxbg/t20100319_402628281.htm.

Choi-Fitzpatrick, Austin. 2012. 'Rethinking trafficking: Contemporary slavery'. In A. Brysk and A. Choi-Fitzpatrick, eds. 2012. *From Human Trafficking to Human Rights: Reframing Contemporary Slavery*. Philadelphia, PA: University of Pennsylvania Press.

Chorev, N. 2007. *Remaking US Trade Policy: From Protectionism to Globalization*. Ithaca: Cornell University Press.

Christopherson, Susan. 2006. 'Challenges facing Wal-Mart in the German market'. In S. Brunn, ed. *Wal-Mart World*. New York: Routledge.

Christopherson, Susan. 2007. 'Barriers to "US style" lean retailing: The case of Wal-Mart's failure in Germany'. *Journal of Economic Geography*, 7 (4) 451–69.

Chuang, Ming-Ling, Donegan, James, Ganon, Michele and Wei, Kan. 2011. 'Wal-Mart and Carrefour experiences in China: Resolving the structural paradox'. *Cross Cultural Management*, 18 (4) 443–63.

Chumer, Mike, Hull, Richard and Prichard, Craig. 2000. 'Introduction: Situating discussions about "knowledge"'. In C. Prichard, R. Hull, M. Chumer and H. Willmott, eds. *Managing Knowledge. Critical Investigations of Work and Learning*. Basingstoke: Macmillan.

Ciampi, C.A. 1996. *Un Metodo per Governare*. Bologna: Il Mulino.

Cisco Systems. 2014a. 'Internet of everything: How more relevant and valuable connections will change the world', by Dave Evans. Available at: http://www.cisco.com/web/about/ac79/innov/IoE.html.

Cisco Systems. 2014b. 'What is the Internet of things?'. Available at: http://www.cisco.com/web/solutions/trends/iot/overview.html.

Cities Institute. 2011. 'Mapping the digital economy: Tech City and the university'. Cities Institute, London Metropolitan Business School. Available at: http://www.citiesinstitute.org/fms/MRSite/Research/cities/Publications%202011/Mapping_the_Digital_Economy_90520112.pdf.

Citigroup 2005. *Nike Inc.* [Company Report] 22 December. New York: Citigroup.

Clark, B. and York, R. 2005. 'Carbon metabolism: Global capitalism, climate change, and the biospheric rift'. *Theory and Society*, 34 (4) 391–428.

Clark, R. 1979. *The Japanese Company*. New Haven: Yale University Press.

Clarke, S. and Pringle, T. 2009. 'Can party-led trade unions represent their members?' *Post-Communist Economies*, 21 (1) 85–101.

Clayton, K. 1981. 'US agriculture in the 1980s, economic perceptions', Economic Research Service, US Department of Agriculture. Available at: http://ageconsearch.umn.edu/.

Clough, P.T. with J. Halley. 2007. *The Affective Turn: Theorising the Social*. Durham NC: Duke University Press.

Cnci.org.cn, 2008. 'Labor contract law of the People's Republic of China'. Available at: http://en.cnci.gov.cn/Law/LawDetails.aspx?ID=6079&p=1.

Coatsworth, John. 2005. 'Structures, endowments, and institutions in the economic history of Latin America'. *Latin American Research Review*, 40 (3) 126–44.

Coe, N., Dicken, P. and Hess, M. 2008. 'Global production networks: Realizing the potential'. *Journal of Economic Geography*, 8 (3) 271–95.

Coe, Neil M. and Jordhus-Lier, David C. 2011. 'Constrained agency? Re-evaluating the geographies of labour'. *Progress in Human Geography*, 35 (2) 211–33.

Coenen, Christopher, Rader, Michael and Fleischer, Torsten. 2004. 'Of visions, dreams and nightmares: The debate on converging technologies', *Technologiefolgenabschätzung – Theorie und Praxis*, 13 (3) 118–25.

Cohen, S. 2003. 'Alienation and globalization in Morocco: Addressing the social and political impact of market integration'. *Comparative Studies in Society and History*, 45 (1) 168–89.

Cole, R. 1981. 'Nihon Jidosha Sangyo, Sono Tsuyasa no Himitsu: Zeninsankagata no Hinshitsukanri'. *The Economist*, 59 (2) 50–56.

Coleman, William. 1977. *Biology in the Nineteenth Century. Problems of*

Form, Function and Transformation. Cambridge: Cambridge University Press.

Collins, Patricia Hill. 2000. *Black Feminist Thought: Knowledge, Consciousness, and the Politics of Empowerment*, 2nd edn. New York: Routledge.

Colman, F. 2008. 'Affective vectors: icons, Guattari, and art'. In S. O'Sullivan and S. Zepke, eds. *Producing the New: Deleuze, Guattari and the Production of the New*. London: Continuum.

Colman, F. and McCrea, C. 2005. 'The digital maypole'. *Fibreculture Journal*, 6: 1–5.

Commoner, Barry. 2002. 'Unraveling the DNA myth. The spurious foundation of genetic engineering'. *Harper's Magazine*, February.

Competitiveness Advisory Group. 1997. 'Competitiveness for employment'. Report to the President of the Commission and the Heads of State and Government, November. Reprinted in Peter Muntigl et al., eds. 2000. *European Union Discourses on Un/employment*. Amsterdam: John Benjamins.

Competitiveness Advisory Group. 1999. 'Sustainable competitiveness'. Report to the President of the Commission and the Heads of State and Government. September.

Constable, N. 1997. *Maid to Order in Hong Kong: An Ethnography of Filipina Workers*. Ithaca: Cornell University Press.

Cooper, D. 2011. 'Theorising nudist equality: An encounter between political fantasy and public appearance'. *Antipode*, 43 (2) 326–57.

Cooper, Frederick. 1996. *Decolonization and African Society: The Labour Question in French and British Africa*. Cambridge: Cambridge University Press.

Cooper, Melinda. 2008. *Life As Surplus: Biotechnology and Capitalism in the Neoliberal Era*. Seattle: University of Washington Press.

Cooper, Melinda. 2010. 'Turbulent worlds. Financial markets and environmental crisis'. *Theory, Culture & Society*, 27 (2–3) 167–90.

Cordero-Guzmán, H.R., Smith, R.C. and Grosfoguel, R. 2001. *Migration, Transnationalization, and Race in a Changing New York*. Philadelphia: Temple University Press.

Cotula, Lorenzo. 2011. *The Outlook on Farmland Acquisitions*. Rome: International Land Coalition.

Cotula, Lorenzo and Vermeulen, Sonja. 2009. 'Deal or no deal: The outlook for agricultural land investment in Africa'. *International Affairs*, 85 (6) 1233–47.

Cowhey, P. and Aronson, J. 2009. *Transforming Global Information and Communication Markets: The Political Economy of Innovations*. Cambridge, MA: MIT Press.

Cowie, Jefferson. 2001. *Capital Move: RCA's Seventy-Year Quest for Cheap Labor*. New York: The New Press.

Cox, Robert W. 1971. 'Approaches to the futurology of industrial relations'. *International Institute of Labour Studies Bulletin*, 8: 139–64.

Cox, Robert W. 1981. 'Social forces, states, and world orders: Beyond international relations theory'. *Millennium – Journal of International Studies*, 10 (2) 126–55.

Cox, Robert W. 1987. *Production, Power, and World Order: Social Forces in the Making of History*. New York: Columbia University Press.

Cox, Robert W. 1992. 'Global perestroika'. In R. Miliband and L. Panitch eds. *New World Order? Socialist Register 1992*. London: The Merlin Press, pp. 26–43.

Cox, Robert W. with Timothy Sinclair (ed.). 1996. *Approaches to World Order*. Cambridge: Cambridge University Press.

Craig, Gary, Gaus, Aline, Wilkinson, Mick, Skrivankova, Klara and McQuade, Aidan. 2007. *Contemporary Slavery in the UK: Overview and Key Issues*. York: Joseph Rowntree Foundation.

Crenshaw, Kimberle, Gotanda, Neil, Peller, Gary and Thomas, Kendall. 1995. *Critical Race Theory: The Key Writings that Formed the Movement*. New York: The New York Press.

Crescentini, C. Rustichini, A. and Rumiati, R. 2012. 'Equality versus self-interest in the brain: Differential roles of anterior insula and medial prefrontal cortex'. *NeuroImage*, 62: 102–12.

Crinis, V.D. 2004. 'The silence and fantasy of women and work'. Doctoral Dissertation, University of Wollongong, Australia.

Críticas de la Economía Política. 1979. *El Intercambio Desigual*, no. 10 Latin American edition, Mexico: El Caballito.

Crosland, C.A.R. 1956. *The Future of Socialism*. London: Jonathan Cape.

Crouch, Colin. 2011. *The Strange Non-Death of Neoliberalism*. Oxford: Polity.

Crozier, Michel, Huntington, Samuel P. and Watanuki, Joji. 1975. *The Crisis of Democracy. Report on the Governability of Democracies to the Trilateral Commission*. New York: New York University Press.

Cumbers, Andy, Nativel, Corinne and Routledge, Paul. 2008. 'Labour agency and union positionalities in global production networks'. *Journal of Economic Geography*, 8 (3) 369–87.

Curiel, E. 1973. *Scritti*. Roma: Editori Riuniti.

Cutler, A.C., Haufler, V. and Porter, T. 1999. *Private Authority and International Affairs*. New York: SUNY Press.

Cyranoski, G., Ledford, H., Nayar, A. and Yahia, M. 2011. 'The PhD factory. The world is producing more PhDs than ever before. Is it time to stop?' *Nature*, 472, April, 21.

D'Aquili, E. and Newberg, A.N. 1999. *The Mystical Mind: Probing the Biology of Religious Experience*. Minneapolis: Fortress Press.

Da Via, E. 2012. 'Seed diversity, farmers' rights, and the politics of re-peasantization'. *International Journal of Sociology of Agriculture and Food*, 19 (2) 229–42.

Dafermos, G. and Söderberg, J. 2009. 'The hacker movement as the continuation of the labour struggle'. *Capital and Class*, 33 (1) 53–73.

Dahrendorf, R. 2000. 'Die globale Klasse und die neue Ungleichheit'. In H. Merkur, K. Dörre, S. Lessenich and H. Rosa, eds. *Soziologie – Kapitalismus – Kritik*. Frankfurt: Suhrkamp.

Danford, A. 1999. *Japanese Management Techniques and British Workers*. London: Mansell.

Das, M. and Diaye, P.N. 2013. 'Chronicle of a decline foretold: Has China reached the Lewis turning point?'. Available at: http://www.imf.org/external/pubs/ft/wp/2013/wp1326.pdf.

Davies, J.B., Sandström, S., Shorroks, A. and Wolff, E.N. 2008. 'The world distribution of household wealth'. In James B. Davies, ed. *Personal Wealth from a Global Perspective*. Oxford: Oxford University Press.

Davies, Matt. 2010. 'Work, products, and the division of labor'. In Jacqueline Best and Matthew Paterson, eds. *Cultural Political Economy*. Abingdon: Routledge.

Davies, Matt and Niemann, Michael. 2002. 'The everyday spaces of global politics: Work, leisure, family'. *New Political Science*, 24 (4) 557–77.

Davies, Matthew. 2005. 'The public spheres of unprotected workers'. *Global Society*, 19 (2) 131–54.

Davies, R.O. 1975. *The Age of Asphalt: The Automobile, the Freeway, and the condition of Metropolitan America*. Philadelphia: J.B. Lippincott and Co.

Davis, Mike. 1978. '"Fordism" in crisis: A review of Michel Aglietta's *Régulation et crises: L'expérience des Etats-Unis*'. *Review*, 2 (2) 207–69.

Davis, Mike. 2006. *Planet of Slums*. London: Verso.

DCMS. 1998. *Creative Industries Mapping Document 1998*. London: DCMS. Available at: webarchive.nationalarchives.gov.uk/+/http://www.culture.gov.uk/reference_library/publications/4740.aspx.

DCMS. 2001. *Creative Industries Mapping Document 2001*. London: DCMS. Available at: gov.uk/government/publications/creative-industries-mapping-documents-2001.

DCMS. 2013. *Classifying and Measuring the Creative Industries: Consultation on Proposed Changes*. London: DCMS. Available at: gov.uk/government/uploads/system/uploads/attachment_data/file/203296/Classifying_and_Measuring_the_Creative_Industries_Consultation_Paper_April_2013-final.pdf.

DCMS. 2014. *Creative Industry Estimates*. London: DCMS. Available at: https://www.gov.uk/government/publications/creative-industries-economic-estimates-january-2014.

De Cecco, M. 2004. 'L'Italia grande potenza: La realtà del mito'. In P.Ciocca and G. Toniolo, eds. *Storia Economica d'Italia. 3. Industrie, Mercati, Istituzioni*. Bari: Editori Laterza.

De Schutter, O. 2009. *Agribusiness and the Right to Food*. New York: United Nations.

De Schutter, O. 2010. *Agro-ecology and the Right to Food*: Report Presented at the 16th Session of the United Nations Human Rights Council. New York: United Nations.

De Schutter, O. 2011. 'The green rush: The global race for farmland and the rights of land users'. *Harvard International Law Journal*, 52 (2) 503–59.

De Schutter, O. and Vanloqueren, G. 2011. 'The new green revolution: How twenty-first-century science can feed the world'. *Solutions*, 2 (4) 33–44.

De Sousa Santos, B. ed. 2006. *Another Production is Possible: Beyond the Capitalist Canon*. London: Verso.

De Ugarte, D. and Boersman, C. 2014. 'Phyles and the new Communalism'. Available at: http://english.lasindias.com/phyles-and-the-new-communalism.

Deal, T. and Kennedy, A. 1982. *Corporate Cultures: Symbolic Managers*. Reading, MA: Addison-Wesley.

Deane, Phyllis and Cole, W.A. 1962. *British Economic Growth, 1688–1959*. Cambridge: Cambridge University Press.

Dedrick, Jason and Kraemer, Kenneth L. 2011. 'Market making in the personal computer industry'. In Gary G. Hamilton, Misha Petrovic and Benjamin Senauer, eds. *The Market Makers: How Retailers are Reshaping the Global Economy*. Oxford: Oxford University Press.

Dejours, Christophe. 2007. 'Subjectivity, work, and action'. In J-P. Deranty, D. Petherbridge, J. Rundell and R. Sinnerbrink, eds. *Recognition, Work, Politics: New Directions in French Critical Theory*. Leiden: Brill.

Deleuze, Gilles. 1978. 'Spinoza's concept of affect', *Cours Vincennes*. 24 January. Available at: http://www.webdeleuze.com/php/texte.php?cle=14andgroupe=Spinozaandlangue=2.

Deleuze, Gilles. 1988. *Spinoza: Practical Philosophy*. San Francisco: City Lights Books.

Deleuze, Gilles. 1992. *Expressionism in Philosophy*. New York: Zone Books.

Deleuze, Gilles and Guattari, Félix. 2004a[1972]. *Anti-Oedipus*. Vol. 1 of

Capitalism and Schizophrenia, 2 vols; trans. R. Hurlet, M. Seem and H.R. Lane. London: Continuum.

Deleuze, Gilles and Guattari, Félix. 2004b[1980]. *A Thousand Plateaus*. Vol 2 of *Capitalism and Schizophrenia*, 2 vols; trans. B. Massumi. London: Continuum.

Delgado Wise, Raúl. 2013. 'The migration and labor question today: Imperialism, unequal development, and forced migration'. *Monthly Review*, 65 (2) 25–38.

Delgado Wise, Raúl and Cypher, J. 2007. 'The strategic role of Mexican labour under NAFTA: Critical perspectives on current economic integration'. *The Annals of the American Academy of Political and Social Science*, 615, 120–42.

Delgado Wise, Raúl and Márquez, Humberto. 2007. 'The reshaping of Mexican labour exports under NAFTA: Paradoxes and challenges'. *International Migration Review*, 41 (3) 656–79.

Delgado Wise, Raúl, Márquez, Humberto and Rodríguez, Héctor. 2009. 'Seis tesis para desmitificar el nexo entre migración y desarrollo'. *Migración y Desarrollo*, 6 (12) 27–52.

Della Sala, Vincent. 2004. 'Maastricht to modernization: EMU and the Italian social state'. In Andrew Martin and George Ross, eds. *Euros and Europeans. Monetary Integration and the European Model of Society*. Cambridge: Cambridge University Press.

Demirovic, Alex. 1992. 'Regulation und Hegemonie. Intellektuelle Wissenspraktiken und Akkumulation'. In A. Demirovic, H-P. Krebs and Th. Sablowski, eds. *Hegemonie und Staat. Kapitalistische Regulation als Projekt und Prozess*. Münster: Westfälisches Dampboot.

Demirovic, Alex, Krebs, Hans-Peter and Sablowski, Thomas, eds. 1992. *Hegemonie und Staat. Kapitalistische Regulation als Projekt und Prozess*. Münster: Westfälisches Dampboot.

Department of Trade and Industry. 2002. 'New dimensions for manufacturing. A UK strategy for nanotechnology'. Available at: http://www.dti.gov.uk/innovation/nanotechnologyreport.pdf.

Deppe, Frank. 1997. *Fin de Siècle. Am Übergang ins 21. Jahrhundert*. Cologne: PapyRossa.

Derber, Milton. 1967. *Research in Labor Problems in the United States*. New York: Random House.

Deroin, V. 2011. 'European statistical works on culture: ESSnet-Culture Final report, 2009–2011'. Available at: culturecommunication.gouv.fr.

Desai, Radhika. 2009. 'Keynes redux: World money after the 2008 crisis' in Wayne Anthony and Julie Guard, eds. *Bailouts and Bankruptcies*. Winnipeg: Fernwood Press.

Desai, Radhika. 2010. 'Consumption demand in Marx and in the current crisis'. *Research in Political Economy*, 26: 101–41.

Desai, Radhika. 2011. 'The New Communists of the commons: 21st Century Proudhonists'. *International Critical Thought*, 1 (2) 204–23.

Desai, Radhika. 2013a. *Geopolitical Economy: After US Hegemony, Globalization and Empire*. London: Pluto.

Desai, Radhika. 2013b. 'Has quantitative easing had its day?', *The Guardian*, 11 January.

Desai, Radhika. 2013c. 'Individualism and actually existing capitalism'. Keynote Address, closing plenary of the Association of Heterodox Economics conference, London, June. Available from author on request.

Desai, Radhika and Freeman, Alan. 2009. 'Keynes and the crisis: A case of mistaken identity', *Canadian Dimension*, July.

Desai, Radhika and Freeman, Alan. 2011. 'Value and crisis theory in the great recession', *World Review of Political Economy*, 2 (1) 35–47.

Descartes, R. 1999. *The Philosophical Writings of Descartes*. [trans R. Stootoff and D. Murdoch]. Cambridge: Cambridge University Press.

Desmarais, A.A. 2007. *La Via Campesina: Globalization and the Power of Peasants*. London: Pluto Press.

DeWalt, B.R. 1985. 'Mexico's second green revolution: Food for feed'. *Mexican Studies*, 1 (1) 29–60.

Deyo, F.C. 1989. *Beneath the Miracle: Labor Subordination in the New Asian Industrialism*. Berkeley, CA: University of California.

Dicken, P. 1998. *Global Shift*, 3rd edn. London: Paul Chapman.

Dicken, P. 2003. *Global Shift: Reshaping the Global Economic Map in the 21st Century*. New York: Guilford Press.

Dinges, Thomas. 2010. 'Foxconn rides partnership with Apple to take 50 percent of EMS [Electronics Manufacturing Services] Market in 2011'. iSuppli. 27 July. Available at: http://www.isuppli.com/Manufacturing-and-Pricing/News/Pages/Foxconn-Rides-Partnership-with-Apple-to-Take-50-Percent-of-EMS-Market-in-2011.aspx.

Dinges, Thomas. 2011. 'Electronics contract manufacturing market growth slows in 2011'. iSuppli. 24 January. Available at: http://www.isuppli.com/Manufacturing-and-Pricing/News/Pages/Electronics-Contract-Manufacturing-Market-Growth-Slows-in-2011.aspx.

Ditmore, Melissa. 2003. 'Hysterical policy: Morality in new policies addressing trafficking and sex work'. *Women Working to Make a Difference: IWPR's Seventh International Women's Policy Research Conference*. Capital Hilton, Washington, DC, 22–24 June.

DIUS. 2009. 'The demand for science, technology, engineering and mathematics (STEM) skills'. London: Department for Innovation Universities and Skills.

DIW. 1996. *Employment and Social Policies under International Constraints*. Berlin: Deutsches Institut für Wirtschaftsforschung.
DMG (Deutsche Morgan Grenfell). 1998. *Adidas-Salomon AG: Fit for the Market*. 9 March.
Doezema, J. 1998. 'Forced to choose: Beyond the voluntary vs. forced prostitution dichotomy'. In K. Kempadoo and J. Doezema, eds. *Global Sex Workers: Rights, Resistance and Redefinition*. London: Routledge.
Doezema, J. 2002. 'Who gets to choose? Coercion, consent, and the UN trafficking protocol'. *Gender and Development*, 10 (1) 20–27.
Dominguez, R.E. 2007. 'Transnational class and gender networking between the North and the South: Overcoming diversity or reproducing dependency'. In Marjorie Griffen-Cohen and Janine Bodie, eds. *Remapping Gender in the New Global Order*. London: Routledge.
Dore, R. 1973. *British Factory, Japanese Factory: The Origins of National Diversity in Industrial Relations*. Berkeley: University of California Press.
Dossani, Rafiq. 2006. 'Globalization and the offshoring of services: The case of India'. In Lael Brainard and Susan M. Collins, eds. *Brookings Trade Forum 2005: Offshoring White-Collar Work*. Washington, DC: Brookings Institution Press.
Dottridge, Mike, ed. 2007. *Collateral Damage: The Impact of Anti-Trafficking Measures on Human Rights Around the World*. Bangkok: GAATW (Global Alliance Against Traffic in Women).
Dräger, Klaus. 2011. 'Sado-monetarism rules ok?! EU economic governance and its consequences'. An analysis and reflection paper, Cologne. Available at: http://www2.euromemorandum.eu/uploads/background_paper_draeger_sado_monetarism_rules_ok_eu_economic_governance_and_its_consequences.pdf.
Drexler, K. Eric. 1986. *Engines of Creation*. New York: Anchor Books.
Dreyfuss, Bob. 2009. 'Chongqing: Socialism in one city'. *The Nation*. 18 November. Available at: http://www.thenation.com/blog/chongqing-socialism-one-city#axzz2YfFB86Pn.
Drucker, P. 1971. 'What we can learn from Japanese management'. *Harvard Business Review*, 49 (2) 110–22.
Dryden, S. 1995. *Trade Warriors: USTR and the American Crusade for Free Trade*. New York: Oxford University Press.
Du Tertre, Christian. 2013. 'Configurations productives de services et internationalisation: Une approche régulationniste'. In Jean-Christophe Graz and Nafi Niang, eds. *Services sans Frontières. Mondialisation, Normalisation, et Régulation de l'économie des Services*. Paris: Presses de Science Po.
Dubofsky, Melvyn. 1983. 'Abortive reform: The Wilson administration and organized labour'. In C. Siriani and J. Cronin, eds. *Work,*

Community and Power: The Emergence of Labour in Europe and America, 1919–1925. Philadelphia, PA: Temple University Press.

Duhigg, Charles and Barboza, David. 2012. 'In China, human costs are built into an iPad'. *The New York Times*. 25 January. Available at: http://www.nytimes.com/2012/01/26/business/ieconomy-apples-ipad-and-the-human-costs-for-workers-in-china.html?pagewanted=all&_r=0.

Duménil, Gérard and Lévy, Dominique. 2011. *The Crisis of Neoliberalism*. Cambridge, MA: Harvard University Press.

Duménil, Gérard, Glick, Mark and Rangel, J. 1987. 'The rate of profit in the United States'. *Cambridge Journal of Economics*, 11 (4) 331–59.

Dunford, M. and Yeung, G. 2010. 'Towards global convergence: Emerging economies, the rise of China and western sunset?' *European Urban and Regional Studies*, 18 (1) 22–46.

Dunn, B. 2005. *Global Restructuring and the Power of Labour*. Basingstoke: Palgrave Macmillan.

Dunn, J.A. 1998. *Driving Forces: The Automobile, Its enemies and the Politics of Mobility*. Washington, DC: Brookings Institution.

Dunne, B.W. 1994. 'French regulation of prostitution in nineteenth-century colonial Algeria'. *The Arab Studies Journal*, 2 (1) 24–30.

Duruz, Jean. 2005. 'Eating at the borders: Culinary journeys'. *Environment and Planning D: Society and Space*, 23 (1) 51–69.

Echtner, C.M. and Prasad, P. 2003. 'The context of third world tourism marketing'. *Annals of Tourism Research*, 30 (3) 660–82.

Economic Report of the President. 2002. Washington: US Government Printing Office. Available at: http://www.presidency.ucsb.edu/economic_reports/2002.pdf.

Economist, The. 2009. 'Economic and financial indicators: Food', 23 May.

Economist, The. 2011. 'Print me a Stradivarius. How a new manufacturing technology will change the world'. 12–18 February. Available at: http://www.economist.com/node/18114327.

Economist, The. 2012. 'Apple in China'. 16 February. Available at: http://www.economist.com/node/21547884.

Edwards, R. 1979. *Contested Terrain: The Transformation of the Workplace in the Twentieth Century*. New York: Basic Books.

Egan, Michelle. 2001. *Constructing a European Market. Standards, Regulation, and Governance*. Oxford: Oxford University Press.

Ehrenberg, A. 2009. *The Weariness of the Self: Diagnosing the History of Depression in the Contemporary Age*. Montreal: McGill-Queens University Press.

Eisenberg, G. 2000. *Amok – Kinder der Kälte. Über die Wurzeln von Wut und Haß*. Reinbek: Rowohlt.

Eisenberg, G. 2002. *Gewalt, die aus der Kälte kommt. Amok – Pogrom – Populismus*. Gießen: Psychosozial Verlag.

Elam, M.J. 1990. 'Puzzling out the post-Fordist debate: Technology, markets and institutions'. *Economic and Industrial Democracy*, 2 (1) 9–37.

Elger, Tony. 1979. 'Valorisation and deskilling. A critique of Braverman'. *Capital and Class*, 7: 58–99.

Elger, Tony and Schwarz, Bill. 1980. 'Monopoly capitalism and the impact of Taylorism: Notes on Lenin, Gramsci, Braverman and Sohn-Rethel'. In T. Nichols, ed. *Capital and Labour: A Marxist Primer*. Glasgow: Fontana.

Elias, J. 2010. 'Making migrant domestic work visible: The rights based approach to migration and the "challenges of social reproduction"'. *Review of International Political Economy*, 17 (5) 840–59.

Elias, N. 1969 (vol. 1) and 1982 (vol. 2). *The Civilizing Process*. Oxford: Blackwell.

Elliott, L. and Atkinson, Dan. 2007. *Fantasy Island: Waking up to the Incredible Economic, Political and Social Illusions of the Blair Legacy*. London: Constable.

Elton, Ben. 1991. *Gridlock*. London: Sphere.

Emmanuel, Arghiri. 1972[1969]. *Unequal Exchange. A Study of the Imperialism of Trade* [additional comments Charles Bettelheim, trans. B. Pearce]. New York: Monthly Review Press.

Empereur, Jean-Claude. 2007. 'Avant-garde et souveraineté technologique', in H. de Grossouvre, ed. *Pour une Europe Européenne: Une Avant-garde pour sortir de l'impasse. France, Allemagne, Belgique, Luxembourg, Hongrie, Autriche*. Paris: Xenia.

Empereur, Jean-Claude. 2008. 'Pour une Europe souveraine'. Available at: http://apres-le-non.forum-carolus.org/archive/2008/03/index.html.

Endo, K. 2004. 'Are personnel assessments fair?' In M. Nomura and Y. Kamii, eds. *Japanese Companies: Theories and Realities*. Melbourne: Trans Pacific Press.

Endy, Drew. 2005. 'Foundations for engineering biology'. *Nature*, 438: 449–53.

Engels, F. 1880. 'Socialism: Utopian and scientific'. Available at: http://www.marxists.org/archive/marx/works/1880/soc-utop/ch03.htm.

Enloe, Cynthia. 1990. *Beaches, Bananas, and Bases: Making Feminist Sense of International Politics*. Berkeley: University of California Press.

Enloe, Cynthia. 2000. *Beaches and Bases: Making Feminist Sense of International Politics*, Updated edn. Berkeley: University of California Press.

Enquête-Kommission. 2013. *Wachstum, Wohlstand, Lebensqualität*. Final Report. Deutscher Bundestag, Document 13/300. Berlin.

Enrique, L.J. 2003. 'Economic reform and repeasantization in post-1990 Cuba'. *Latin American Research Review*, 38 (1) 202–18.

ERT. 1996. *Benchmarking for Policy-Makers. The Way to Competitiveness, Growth and Job Creation*. Brussels: European Round Table of Industrialists.

Espinosa, Juan and Zimbalist, Andrew. 1978. *Economic Democracy: Workers' Participation in Chilean Industry*. London: Academic Press.

Essex, J. 2007. 'Getting what you pay for: Authoritarian statism and the geographies of US trade liberalization strategies'. *Studies in Political Economy*, 80: 75–103.

ETC. 2003a. 'The Little BANG Theory'. Available at: http://www.etcgroup.org/documents/comBANG2003.pdf.

ETC. 2003b. 'The big down: Atomtech – Technologies converging at the nanoscale'. Available at: http://www.etcgroup.org/documents/TheBigDown.pdf.

ETC. 2005a. 'The potential impact of nano-scale technologies on commodity markets: The implications for commodity dependent developing countries'. Available at: http://www.southcentre.org/publications/researchpapers/ResearchPapers4.pdf.

ETC. 2005b. 'Nanotech's "second nature" patents: Implications for the Global South'. Available at: http://www.etcgroup.org/sites/www.etcgroup.org/files/publication/54/02/com8788specialpnanomar-jun05eng.pdf.

ETC. 2009. 'Who will feed us? Questions for the food and climate crises'. *Communiqué*, 102. Available at: http://www.etcgroup.org/content/who-will-feed-us.

Ettlinger, Nancy. 2004. 'Toward a critical theory of untidy geographies: The spatiality of emotions in consumption and production'. *Feminist Economics*, 10 (3) 21–54.

EU Crisis. 2014. http://europa.eu/newsroom/highlights/financial-crisis/index_en.htm.

European Commission. 1995. Press Release on the Competitiveness Advisory Group – IP/95/141. Brussels, 15 February.

European Commission. 2001. Report to the European Council meeting Stockholm in March. Available at: http://eur-lex.europa.eu/.

European Commission. 2004a. *Towards a European Strategy for Nanotechnology*. Luxembourg: Office for Official Publications of the European Communities.

European Commission. 2004b. 'R&D is key to mastery of nanotechnologies'. Available at: http://ec.europa.eu/research/industrial_technologies/articles/article_800_en.html.

European Commission. 2005. 'Nanosciences and nanotechnologies: An action plan for Europe 2005–2009'. COM2005 243 final. Available at: ftp://ftp.cordis.europa.eu/pub/nanotechnology/docs/nano_action_plan2005_en.pdf.

European Commission. 2012. *Employment and Social Developments in Europe 2012*. Brussels: Directorate-General for Employment, Social Affairs and Inclusion.

European Commission. 2013. *EU Employment and Social Situation.* Brussels: Social Europe, Quarterly Review, June.

European Council. 1997. *Presidency Conclusions. Extraordinary European Council meeting on Employment*. Luxembourg, 20 and 21 November.

European Council. 2000. *Presidency Conclusions. European Council meeting*. Lisbon, 23 and 24 March.

Eurostat. 2012. 'Unemployment rate, 2001–2012'. Available at: http://epp.eurostat.ec.europa.eu/statistics_explained/index.php?title=File:Unemployment_rate,_2001–2012_%.png.

Evans, Peter. 2010. 'Is it labor's turn to globalize? Twenty-first century opportunities and strategic responses'. *Global Labour Journal*, 1 (3) 352–79. Available at: http://digitalcommons.mcmaster.ca/globallabour/vol1/iss3/3/.

Fair Labor Association (FLA). 2010a. 'FLA Statement on Nike – GGT Agreement regarding Hugger and Vision Tex'. Available at: http://www.fairlabor.org/report/hugger-and-vision-tex-factories-honduras.

Fair Labor Association (FLA). 2010b. 'Hugger and Vision Tex factories in Honduras', 28 July. Available at: http://www.fairlabor.org/report/hugger-and-vision-tex-factories-honduras.

Fair Labor Association (FLA). 2013. 'Second Foxconn verification status report'. Available at: http://www.fairlabor.org/sites/default/files/documents/reports/second_foxconn_verification_status_report_0.pdf#overlay-context=.

Fairhead, James, Leach, Melissa and Scoones, Ian. 2012. 'Green grabbing: a new appropriation of nature?' *The Journal of Peasant Studies*, 39 (2) 237–61.

FAO. 1997. *The State of the World's Plant Genetic Resources for Food and Agriculture*. Rome: FAO.

FAO. 2009. 'CROPWAT 8.0 Decision Support System'. Available at: www.fao.org/nr /water/infores_databases_cropwat.html.

FAO. 2010. *FAO Statistical Yearbook – Land use*. (Excel) Rome: FAOSTAT, p. A4.

Federici, S. 2002. 'Prostitution and globalization'. Paper presented at Annual Convention, International Studies Association.

Federici, S. 2004. *Caliban and the Witch: Women, the Body and Primitive Accumulation*. New York: Autonomedia.

Federici, S. 2012. *Revolution at Point Zero: Housework, Reproduction, and Feminist Struggle*. Brooklyn/Oakland: PM Press/Common Notions/ Autonomedia.

Feeley, D. 2008. 'Everything's on the line at AAM'. *Against the Current*, 134. Available at: http://www. solidarity-us.org/current/node/1472.

Fei, J.C.H. and Ranis, G. 1975. 'A model of growth and employment in the open dualistic economy: The cases of Korea and Taiwan'. *The Journal of Development Studies*, 11 (2) 32–63.

Feldman, Gerald. 1966. *Army, Industry and Labour in Germany, 1914–1918*. Princeton, NJ: Princeton University Press.

Ffrench-Davis, Ricardo, Muñoz, Oscar, Benavente, José and Crespi, Gustavo. 2000. 'The industrialization of Chile during protectionism, 1940–1982'. In E. Cárdenas, J.A. Ocampo and R. Thorp, eds. *An Economic History of Twentieth Century Latin America*. Vol. 3: *Industrialization and the State in Latin America: The Postwar Years*. Basingstoke: Palgrave.

Filipecki, Marcin and Malepszy, Stefan. 2006. 'Unintended consequences of plant transformation: A molecular insight'. *Journal of Applied Genetics*, 47 (4) 277–86.

Financial Times. 2010. 'Global 500, 2010, market value by country and sector'. Available at: http://www.ft.com/reports/ft500–2010.

Finanza, La. 2013. 'Il dibattito su una visione alternativa per l'economia mondiale. Un nuovo paradigma o un nuovo crash'. *La Finanza*, 3 (3) 10–18.

Fine, B. 2006. 'The New Development Economics'. In K.S. Jomo and B. Fine, eds. *The New Development Economics: After the Washington Consensus*. London: Zed.

Fine, B., Petropoulos, A. and Sato, H. 2005. 'Beyond Brenner's investment overhang thesis: The case of the steel industry'. *New Political Economy*, 10 (1) 43–64.

Fingleton, Eamonn. 1999. *In Praise of Hard Industries: Why Manufacturing, not the Information Economy is the Key to Future Prosperity*. Boston: Houghton Mifflin.

Fingleton, Eamonn. 2008. *In the Jaws of the Dragon: America's Fate in the Coming Era of Chinese Hegemony*. New York: St. Martin's Press.

Fink, Marcel. 2011. 'Ideas, institutions and interests in European and National reforms of employment and social policy: The case of flexicurity'. In Ipek Eren Vural, ed. *Converging Europe*. Farnham: Ashgate.

Finley, K. 2013a. 'The quantified man: How an obsolete tech guy rebuilt himself for the future'. *Wired*, 22 February. Available at: http://www. wired.com/wiredenterprise/2013/02/quantified-work/.

Finley, K. 2013b. 'What if your boss tracked your sleep, diet, and exercise?' *Wired*, 18 April. Available at: http://www.wired.co.uk/news/archive/2013-04/18/quantified-work-citizen.

Fischer-Kowalski, Marina, Haberl, Helmut, Hüttler, Walter, Payer, Harald, Schandl, Heinz, Winiwarter, Verena and Zangerl-Weisz, Helga. 1997. *Gesellschaftlicher Stoffwechsel und Kolonisierung von Natur. Ein Versuch in sozialer Ökologie*. Vienna: Facultas.

Flanagan, Mike. 2012. 'The Flanarant: Olympics signal new scrutiny in apparel sourcing'. 10 August. Available at: http://www.just-style.com/comment/olympics-signal-new-scrutiny-in-apparel-sourcing_id115217.aspx.

Fleck, S., Glaser, J. and Sprague, S. 2011. 'The compensation–productivity gap: A visual essay'. *Monthly Labour Review*, January.

Fleetwood, S. 2002. 'What is Marx's theory of value? A critical realist inquiry'. In A. Brown, S. Fleetwood and J.M. Roberts, eds. *Critical Realism and Marxism*. London: Routledge.

Flink, J. 1975. *The Car Culture*. Cambridge, MA: MIT Press.

Florida, Richard. 2004. *The Rise of the Creative Class and How it's Transforming Work, Leisure, Community and Everyday Life*. New York: Basic Books.

Florida, Richard. 2012a. *The Rise of the Creative Class*, 2nd edn. New York: Basic Books.

Florida, Richard. 2012b. 'The 66%: America's growing underclass'. Available at: http://www.theatlanticcities.com/jobs-and-economy/2012/10/66-americas-growing-underclass/3618/.

Flyvbjerg, Bent, Bruzelius, Nils and Rothengatter, Werner. 2003. *Megaprojects and Risk: An Anatomy of Ambition*. Cambridge: Cambridge University Press.

Fodor, G. 2004. 'Le grandi scelte del dopoguerra'. In P. Ciocca and G. Toniolo, eds. *Storia Economica d'Italia 3. Industrie, Mercati, Istituzioni*. Bari: Editori Laterza.

Ford, Michele and Piper, Nicola. 2007. 'Southern sites of female agency: Informal regimes and female migrant labour resistance in East and Southeast Asia'. In J.M. Hobson and L. Seabrooke, eds. *Everyday Politics of the World Economy*. Cambridge: Cambridge University Press.

Fortune Global 500. 2014. 'Hon Hai Precision Industry [Foxconn Technology Group]'. Available at: http://fortune.com/global500/hon-hai-precision-industry-32/.

Foster, John Bellamy. 1999. 'Marx's theory of metabolic rift: Classical foundations for environmental sociology'. *American Journal of Sociology*, 105 (2) 366–405.

Foster, John Bellamy. 2010. 'The financialization of the capitalist class:

Monopoly-finance capital and the new contradictory relations of ruling class power'. In H. Veltmeyer, ed. *Imperialism, Crisis and Class Struggle: The Enduring Verities and Contemporary Face of Capitalism*. Leiden: Brill Publishers.

Foster, John Bellamy. 2013. 'Marx and the rift in the universal metabolism of nature'. *Monthly Review*, 65 (7) 1–19.

Foster, John Bellamy and McChesney, R.W. 2012. 'The global stagnation and China'. *Monthly Review*, 63 (9). Available at: http://monthlyreview.org/2012/02/01/the-global-stagnation-and-china.

Foster, John Bellamy, McChesney, R.W. and Jonna, J. 2011a. 'The internationalization of monopoly capital'. *Monthly Review*, 63 (2) 3–18.

Foster, John Bellamy, McChesney, R.W. and Jonna, J. 2011b. 'The global reserve army of labour and the new imperialism'. *Monthly Review*, 63 (6) 1–15.

Foucault, Michel. 1975. *Surveiller et Punir: Naissance de la Prison*. Paris: Gallimard.

Foucault, Michel. 1986[1976]. 'Disciplinary power and subjection' in S. Lukes, ed. *Power*. Oxford: Blackwell.

Foucault, Michel. 1991. 'Governmentality', in Graham Burchell, Colin Gordon and Peter Miller, eds. *The Foucault Effect: Studies in Governmentality*. New York: Harvester Wheatsheaf.

Foucault, Michel. 1992. *Überwachen und Strafen*. Frankfurt: Suhrkamp.

Foucault, Michel. 2004. *Sécurité, territoire, population. Cours au Collège de France (1977–1978)* [ed. M. Senellart]. Paris: Gallimard-Seuil.

Foucault, Michel. 2005. *Analytik der Macht*. Frankfurt: Suhrkamp.

Fox, J. 1993. *The Politics of Food in Mexico. State Power and Social Mobilization*. Ithaca: Cornell University Press.

Foxconn Technology Group. 2009. 'Corporate Social and Environmental Responsibility Annual Report 2008'. Available at: http://ser.foxconn.com/ViewAnuReport.do?action=showAnnual.

Foxconn Technology Group. 2010a. 'Foxconn is committed to a safe and positive working environment'. 11 October. Available at: http://regmedia.co.uk/2010/10/12/foxconn_media_statement.pdf.

Foxconn Technology Group. 2010b. 'Corporate Social and Environmental Responsibility Annual Report 2009'. Available at: http://ser.foxconn.com/ViewAnuReport.do?action=showAnnual.

Foxconn Technology Group. 2011. 'Corporate Social and Environmental Responsibility Annual Report 2010'. Available at: http://ser.foxconn.com/ViewAnuReport.do?action=showAnnual.

Fracchia, J. 2005. 'Beyond the human–nature debate: Human corporeal organisation as a "first fact" of historical materialism'. *Historical Materialism*, 13 (1) 33–61.

Francis, C.A. 1990. 'Potential of multiple cropping systems'. In Miguel Hecht and Susanna B. Altieri, eds. *Agroecology and Small Farm Development*. Boca Raton: CRC Press.

Fraser, N. 1994. *Widerspenstige Praktiken. Macht, Diskurs, Geschlecht*. Frankfurt: Suhrkamp.

Freeman, Alan. 2002. *Creativity: London's Core Business*. London: GLA. Available at: ideas.repec.org/p/pra/mprapa/52548.html.

Freeman, Alan. 2007. *London's Creative Sector: 2007 Update*. London: Greater London Authority.

Freeman, Alan. 2008. *Culture, Creativity and Innovation in the Internet Age*. Available at: http://ideas.repec.org/p/pra/mprapa/9007.html.

Freeman, Alan. 2009. *London's Creative Workforce: 2009 Update*. London: Greater London Authority.

Freeman, Alan. 2010. 'Marxism without Marx: A note towards a critique'. *Capital and Class*, 34 (1) 84–97.

Freeman, Alan. 2012a. 'Ushering in the creative age'. *Chicago Policy Review*, February. Available at: http://chicagopolicyreview.org/2012/02/27/ushering-in-the-creative-age-alan-freeman/.

Freeman, Alan. 2012b. 'The profit rate in the presence of financial markets'. *Journal of Australian Political Economy*, 70: 167–92.

Freeman, Alan. 2014. 'Schumpeter's theory of self-restoration: A casualty of Samuelson's Whig Historiography of science'. *Cambridge Journal of Economics*, 38 (3) 663–79.

Freeman, C. 2000. *High Tech and High Heels in the Global Economy: Women, Work, and Pink-Collar Identities in the Caribbean*. Durham NC: Duke University Press.

Freeman, Richard B. 2000. 'The feminization of work in the USA: A new era for (man)kind?' in Siv S. Gustaffson and Daniele E. Meulders, eds. *Gender and the Labour Market: Econometric Evidence of Obstacles to Achieving Gender Equality*. New York: Macmillan.

Freeman, Richard B. 2006. *The Great Doubling: the Challenge of the New Global Labor Market*. Available at: http://emlab.berkeley.edu/users/webfac/eichengreen/e183_sp07/great_doub.pdf.

Freeman, Richard B. 2008. 'The new global labor market'. *Focus*, 26 (1) 1–6.

Freund, Peter and Martin, George. 1993. *The Ecology of the Automobile*. Montreal: Black Rose Books.

Freyssenet, M., Shimzu, K. and Volpato, G. 2003. *Globalization or Regionalization of the European Car Industry?* London: Palgrave.

Frias, Patricio, Echeverría, Magdalena, Herrera, Gonzalo and Larraín, Christian. 1987a. *Industria Textil y del Vestuario en Chile*, Vol. II.

Evolución Económica y Situación de los Trabajadores. Santiago: Academia de Humanismo Cristiano: Programa de Economía del Trabajo.

Frias, Patricio, Echeverría, Magdalena, Herrera, Gonzalo and Larraín, Christian. 1987b. *Industria Textil y del Vestuario en Chile*, Vol. III. *Organizacion Sindical: Historia y Proyecciones*. Santiago: Academia de Humanismo Cristiano: Programa de Economía del Trabajo.

Friedman, E. 2012. 'Getting through the hard times together? Chinese workers and unions respond to the economic crisis'. *Journal of Industrial Relations*, 54 (4) 459–75.

Friedman, Eli and Ching Kwan Lee. 2010. 'Remaking the world of Chinese labour: A 30-year retrospective'. *British Journal of Industrial Relations*, 48 (3) 507–33.

Friedman, Thomas L. 2009. *Hot, Flat and Crowded. Why the World needs a Green Revolution – and How we can Renew our Global Future*. New York: Picador.

Friedmann, Harriet. 1993. 'The political economy of food: A global crisis'. *New Left Review*, 197: 29–57.

Friedmann, Harriet. 2007. 'Scaling up: Bringing public institutions and food service corporations into the project for a local, sustainable food system in Ontario'. *Agriculture and Human Values*, 24: 389–98.

Friedmann, Harriet and McMichael, Philip. 1989. 'Agriculture and the state system. The rise and decline of national agricultures, 1870 to the present'. *Sociologia Ruralis*, 29 (2) 93–117.

Friedrichs, J., Müller, E.. and Baumholt, B. 2009. *Deutschland dritter Klasse. Leben in der Unterschicht*. Hamburg: Hoffmann und Campe.

Friis, Cecilie and Reenberg, Anette. 2010. *Land Grab in Africa: Emerging Land System Drivers in a Teleconnected World*. GLP Report No. 1. Copenhagen: GLP International Project Office.

Frontier Economics. 2007. *Creative Industry Spillovers – Understanding their Impact on the Wider Economy*. London: DCMS. Available at: www.culture.gov.uk/images/publications/CreativeIndustry_Spillovers2007.pdf.

Frosini, Fabio, Wille, Christian, Schnabel, Annette, et al. 2012. 'Lebensweise, Lebensbedingungen'. In *Historisch-kritisches Wörterbuch des Marxismus*, vol. 8/I. Hamburg: Argument Verlag.

Fu, X., Oum, T.H. and Zhang, A. 2010. 'Air transport liberalization and its impacts on airline competition and air passenger traffic'. *Transportation Journal*, 49 (4) 24–41.

Fucini, J. and Fucini, S. 1990. *Working for the Japanese: Inside Mazda's American Auto Plant*. New York: Free Press.

Fudge, Judy and Strauss, Kendra, eds. 2014. *Temporary Work, Agencies and Unfree Labour*. New York: Routledge.

Fumagalli, A. 2006. *Lavoro – Vecchio e Nuovo Sfruttamento*. Milan: Punto Rosso.

Furman Center for Real Estate and Urban Policy. 2007. 'New housing data continue to show signs of danger for New York City's homeowners, Furman Center analysis Concludes', 15 October. New York: New York University. Available at: http://furmancenter.org/files/FurmanCenterHMDAAnalysis_000.pdf.

Galama, T. and Josek, J. 2008. *U.S. Competitiveness in Science and Technology*. Santa Monica: RAND Corporation.

Gallagher, K. and Zarsky, L. 2007. *The Enclave Economy: Foreign Investment and Sustainable Development in Mexico's Silicon Valley*. Cambridge, MA: MIT Press.

Gallagher, Mary E. 2005. *Contagious Capitalism: Globalization and the Politics of Labor in China*. Princeton, NJ: Princeton University Press.

Gallo, Ernesto. 2009. 'Italy and Spain: Different patterns of state/society complexes in the contemporary era'. *Journal of Contemporary European Studies*, 17 (2) 255–70.

Gammon, Earl. 2008. 'Affect and the rise of the self-regulating market'. *Millennium. Journal of International Studies*, 37 (2) 251–78.

Gardener, D. 2012. 'Workers' rights and corporate accountability: The move towards practical, worker-driven, change for sportswear workers in Indonesia'. *Gender and Development*, 20 (1) 49–65.

Gardiner, J. 1998. 'Beyond human capital: Households in the macroeconomy'. *New Political Economy*, 3 (2) 209–21.

Garrahan, P. and Stewart, P. 1992. *The Nissan Enigma: Flexibility at Work in a Local Economy*. London: Mansell.

Gartman, D. 1994. *Auto Opium: A Social History of American Automobile Design*. London: Routledge.

Gaudichaud, Frank. 2005. 'Construyendo "Poder Popular": El movimiento sindical, la CUT y las luchas obreras en el periodo de la Unidad Popular'. In J. Pinto Vallejos, ed. *Cuando Hicimos Historia: La Experiencia de la Unidad Popular*. Santiago: LOM Ediciones.

General Electric. 2012. 'Industrial Internet: Pushing the boundaries of minds and machines'. P.C. Evans and M. Annunziata. Available at: http://www.ge.com/docs/chapters/Industrial_Internet.pdf.

Georges-Abeyie, D.E. 2001. Foreword. 'Petit apartheid in criminal justice: "The more 'things' change, the more 'things' remain the same"'. In D. Milovanovic and K.K. Russell, eds. *Petit Apartheid in the U.S. Criminal Justice System: The Dark Figure of Racism*. Durham, NC: Carolina Academic Press.

Gerbaudo, P. 2012. *Tweets and Streets: Social Media and Contemporary Activism*. London: Pluto Books.

Gereffi, Gary. 1994. 'The organization of buyer-driven global commodity chains: How U.S. retailers shape overseas production networks'. In Gary Gereffi and Miguel Korzeniewicz, eds. *Commodity Chains and Global Capitalism*. Westport, CT: Praeger.

Gereffi, Gary. 1999. 'International trade and industrial upgrading in the apparel commodity chain'. *Journal of International Economics*, 48 (1) 37–70.

Gereffi, Gary and Christian, Michelle. 2009. 'The impacts of Wal-Mart: The rise and consequences of the world's largest retailer'. *The Annual Review of Sociology*, 35: 573–91.

Gereffi, Gary and Korzeniewicz, Miguel, eds. 1994. *Commodity Chains and Global Capitalism*. Westport, CT: Praeger.

Gereffi, Gary and Memedovic, Olga. 2003. *The Global Apparel Value Chain: What Prospects for Upgrading by Developing Countries*. Durham, NC: Duke University, and Vienna: UNIDO, Strategic Research and Economics Branch.

Gereffi, Gary, Humphrey, J. and Sturgeon, T. 2005. 'The governance of global value chains'. *Review of International Political Economy*, 12 (1) 78–104.

Ghai, D. 2006. 'Decent work: Universality and diversity'. In D. Ghai, ed. *Decent Work: Objectives and Strategies*. Geneva: International Institute for Labour Studies.

Ghiani, E. and Binotti, A.M. 2011. 'La "questione dei bassi salari" in Italia: l'interazione tra rigidità salariale reale e political monetaria. Ipotesi interpretativa e verifica empirica per il periodo 1970–1977'. *Studi e Note di Economia*, 16 (2) 171–98.

Giancotti, E. 1997. 'The birth of modern materialism in Hobbes and Spinoza'. In W. Montag and T. Stolze, eds. *The New Spinoza*. Minneapolis: University of Minnesota Press.

Gibbon, P. and Ponte, S. 2005. *Trading Down: Africa, Value Chains, and the Global Economy*. Philadelphia: Temple University Press.

Gibbon, P., Bair, J. and Ponte, S. 2008. 'Governing global value chains: An introduction'. *Economy and Society*, 37 (3) 315–38.

Giddens, Anthony. 1987. *The Nation-State and Violence*. Berkeley, CA: University of California Press.

Giddens, Anthony. 1990. *The Consequences of Modernity*. Cambridge: Polity.

Giedion, Siegfried. 1949. *Space, Time and Architecture: The Growth of a New Tradition*. Cambridge, MA: Harvard University Press.

Gill, R.C. and Pratt, A. 2008. 'In the social factory? Immaterial labour, precariousness and cultural work'. *Theory, Culture and Society*, 25 (7–8) 1–30.

Gill, Stephen, ed. 1993. *Gramsci, Historical Materialism, and International Relations*. Cambridge: Cambridge University Press.

Gill, Stephen. 1995. 'Globalisation, market civilisation and disciplinary neoliberalism'. *Millennium: Journal of International Studies*, 25 (3) 399–423.

Gill, Stephen. 1996. 'Globalization, democratization, and the politics of indifference'. In J. Mittelman, ed. *Globalization: Critical Reflections*. London: Lynne Rienner.

Gill, Stephen. 2003. *Power and Resistance in the New World Order*. Basingstoke: Palgrave Macmillan.

Gillam, Carey. 2011. 'Analysis: Super weeds pose growing threat to U.S. crops'. Reuters. Available at: http://www.reuters.com/, accessed 15 January 2014.

Gilpin, Robert. 1975. *U.S. Power and the Multinational Corporation. The Political Economy of Foreign Direct Investment*. New York: Basic Books.

Gilpin, Robert. 1987. *The Political Economy of International Relations*. Princeton: Princeton University Press.

Glick, Mark. 1987. 'The current crisis in light of the Great Depression', in R. Cherry et al., eds. *The Imperiled Economy*. New York: Union for Radical Political Economics.

Goddard, M. 2011. 'From the multitudo to the multitude: The place of Spinoza in the political philosophy of Antonio Negri'. In P. Lamarche, M. Rosenkrantz and D. Sherman, eds. *Reading Negri: Marxism in the Age of Empire*. Chicago: Carus Publishing.

Golden, M. 1988. *Labor Divided: Austerity and Working Class Politics in Contemporary Italy*. Ithaca: Cornell University Press.

Golding, T. 2001. *The City: Inside the Great Expectations Machine*. London: Pearson Education.

Goldman, R. and Papson, S. 1998. *Nike Culture, the Sign of the Swoosh*. London: Sage.

Goldstein, J. 2013. 'Terra economica: Waste and the production of enclosed nature'. *Antipode*, 45 (2) 357–75.

Gompers, P. and Lerner, J. 1999. *The Venture Capital Cycle*. Cambridge, MA: MIT Press.

Goodwin, Mark and Painter, Joe. 1997. 'Concrete research, urban regimes, and regulation theory'. In L. Mickey, ed. *Reconstructing Urban Regime Theory. Regulating Urban Politics in a Global Economy*. Thousand Oaks: Sage.

Gootenberg, Paul. 2004. 'Between a rock and a softer place: Reflections on some recent economic history of Latin America'. *Latin American Research Review*, 39 (2) 239–57.

Gordon, Jennifer. 2005. *Suburban Sweatshops: The Fight for Immigrant Rights*. Cambridge, MA: Harvard University Press.

Gordon, Robert J. 2000. 'Does the "New Economy" measure up to the great inventions of the past?' *The Journal of Economic Perspectives*, 14 (4) 49–74.

Gordon, Robert J. 2012. 'Is US economic growth over?' *Center for Economic Policy Research Policy Insight*, No. 62. September.

Gordon, S.C. 1990. 'From slaughterhouse to soap-boiler: Cincinnati's meat packing industry, changing technologies, and the rise of mass production, 1825–1870'. *IA. The Journal of the Society for Industrial Archeology*, 16 (1) 55–67.

Görg, Christoph. 2003a. *Regulation der Naturverhältnisse. Zu einer Kritischen Theorie der Ökologischen Krise*. Münster: Westfälisches Dampfboot.

Görg, Christoph. 2003b. 'Gesellschaftstheorie und Naturverhältnisse. Von den Grenzen der Regulationstheorie'. In U. Brand and W. Raza, eds. *Fit für den Postfordismus? Theoretische und Politische Perspektiven des Regulationsansatzes*. Münster: Westfälisches Dampfboot.

Görg, Christoph. 2003c. 'Nichtidentität und Kritik. Zum Problem der Gestaltung der Naturverhältnisse'. In G. Böhme and A. Manzei, eds. *Kritische Theorie der Technik und der Natur*. Munich: Wilhelm Fink Verlag.

Gorz, André. 1980. *Ecology as Politics*. London: Pluto Press.

Gorz, André. 2010. *The Immaterial. Knowledge, Value, and Capital*. London: Seagull Books.

Gough, J. 1992. 'Where's the value in "Post-Fordism"?' In N. Gilbert, R. Burrows and A. Pollert, eds. *Fordism and Flexibility: Divisions and Change*. Basingstoke: Macmillan.

Gough, J. 2003. *Work, Locality and the Rhythms of Capital: The Labour Process Reconsidered*. London: Continuum.

Graham, F. 2003. *Inside the Japanese Company*. London: RoutledgeCurzon.

Graham, F. 2005. *A Japanese Company in Crisis: Ideology, Strategy and Narrative*. London: RoutledgeCurzon.

Graham, L. 1995. *On the Line at Subaru-Isuzu: The Japanese Model and the American Worker*. Ithaca: ILR Press.

Grahl, John. 2001. 'Globalized finance: The challenge to the Euro'. *New Left Review*, 2nd series (8) 23–47.

Grahl, John. 2004. 'The European Union and American power'. *The Empire Reloaded, Socialist Register 2005*, London: Merlin.

Grahl, John and Teague, Paul. 1990. *1992 – The Big Market: The Future of the European Community*. London: Lawrence and Wishart.

Gramsci, Antonio. 1949. *Il Risorgimento*. Turin: Einaudi.

Gramsci, Antonio. 1971. *Selections from the Prison Notebooks* [ed. and trans Q. Hoare and G. Nowell-Smith]. London: Lawrence and Wishart.

Gramsci, Antonio. 1972. 'La situazione italiana e i compiti del PCI'. In *La Costruzione del Partito Comunista 1923–1926*. Turin: Einaudi.

Graz, Jean-Christophe. 2006a. 'Hybrids and regulation in the global political economy'. *Competition and Change*, 10 (2) 230–45.

Graz, Jean-Christophe. 2006b. 'International standardisation and corporate democracy'. In K-G. Giesen and K. van der Pijl, eds. *Global Norms in the Twenty-First Century*. Newcastle: Cambridge Scholars Press.

Graz, Jean-Christophe. 2011. 'International standards and the service economy'. In Christian Joerges and Josef Falke, eds. *Globalisation and the Potential of Law in Transnational Markets*. Oxford: Hart.

Graz, Jean-Christophe and Niang, Nafi. 2012. 'Connecting India: The rise of standards in service offshoring'. *The Service Industries Journal*, 32 (14) 2287–305.

Graz, Jean-Christophe and Niang, Nafi, eds. 2013. *Services sans Frontières. Mondialisation, Normalisation et Régulation de l'économie des Services*. Paris: Presses de Sciences Po.

Graziani, A. 1989. *L'economia Italiana dal 1945 a Oggi*. Bologna: Il Mulino.

Graziani, A. 1998. *Lo Sviluppo dell'economia Italiana: Dalla Ricostruzione alla Moneta Europea*. Turin: Bollati Boringhieri.

Gregg, Paul and Manning, Alan. 1997. 'Labour market regulation and unemployment'. In D.J. Snower and G. de la Dehesa, eds. *Unemployment Policy. Government Options for the Labour Market*. Cambridge: Cambridge University Press.

Greider, William. 2001. 'A new giant sucking sound'. *The Nation*. Available at: http://www.thenation.com/article/new-giant-sucking-sound#.

Griffin, K.B. 1979. *The Political Economy of Agrarian Change: An Essay on the Green Revolution*. London: Macmillan.

Griffin, P. 2007a. 'Refashioning IPE: What and how gender analysis teaches international global political economy'. *Review of International Political Economy*, 14 (4) 719–36.

Griffin, P. 2007b. 'Sexing the economy in a neo-liberal world order: Neoliberal discourse and the reproduction of heteronormative heterosexuality'. *The British Journal of Politics and International Relations*, 9 (2) 220–38.

Grimes, W. 2001. *Unmaking the Japanese Miracle: Macroeconomic Politics, 1985–2000*. Ithaca: Cornell University Press.

Gromyko, Yury. 2012. *Klass Razvitie*. Moscow: Praxis.

Gromyko, Yury. 2013. 'Investire nel corridoio transeuroasiatico "Razvitie"'. Available at: http://smdp.ru/arh/miroporyadok/43–2010–06–04–08–39–31/192-krizis.html.

Grosfoguel, R. 2007. 'The epistemic decolonial turn: Beyond political economy paradigms'. *Cultural Studies*, 21 (2/3) 211–23.

Grosfoguel, R. and Georas, C.S. 2000. '"Coloniality of power" and racial dynamics: Notes toward a reinterpretation of Latino Caribbeans in New York City'. *Identities*, 7 (1) 85–125.

Grosz, E. 1987. 'Notes toward a corporeal feminism'. *Australian Feminist Studies*, 2 (5) 1–16.

Grosz, E. 1994. *The Body as an Inscriptive Surface*. Bloomington: Volatile Studies.

Grubesic, T.H., Matisziw, T.C. and Zook, M.A. 2008. 'Global airline networks and nodal regions'. *GeoJournal*, 71 (1) 53–66.

Guiterrez, B. 2013. 'Spain's micro-utopias: The 15M movement and its prototypes'. *Guerrilla Translation!*. Available at: http://guerrilla-translation.com/2013/05/16/spains-micro-utopias-the-15m-movement-and-its-prototypes/.

Guiterrez, B. 2014. 'Theory Thursday: It is not a revolution, it is a new networked renaissance', *OccupyWallStreet*, available at: http://occupy-wallst.org/article/theory-thursday-it-not-revolution-it-new-networked/.

Gulati, Girish J. "Jeff". 2012. 'Representing trafficking: Media in the United States, Great Britain and Canada'. In A. Brysk and A. Choi-Fitzpatrick, eds. *From Human Trafficking to Human Rights: Reframing Contemporary Slavery*. Philadelphia: University of Pennsylvania Press.

Gunnarsson, L. 2013. 'The naturalistic turn in feminist theory: A Marxist-realist contribution'. *Feminist Theory*, 14 (3) 3–19.

Haas, Tobias and Sander, Hendrik. 2013. '*Grüne basis'. Grüne Kapitalfraktionen in Europa – Eine Empirische Untersuchung*. Berlin: Rosa-Luxemburg-Stiftung.

Haberl, Helmut, Fischer-Kowalski, Marina, Krausmann, Fridolin, Martinez-Alier, Juan and Winiwarter, Verena. 2011. 'A socio-metabolic transition towards sustainability? Challenges for another great transformation'. *Sustainable Development*, 19 (1) 1–14.

Habermas, Jürgen. 1971. *Technik und Wissenschaft als 'Ideologie'*. Frankfurt: Suhrkamp.

Halbfinger, David M. and Holmes, Steven A. 2003. 'Military mirrors working class America'. *The New York Times*. 30 March.

Hale, A. and Wills, J. 2005. *Threads of Labour Garment Industry Supply Chains from the Workers' Perspective*. Malden, MA: Blackwell.

Hall, Stuart and Jacques, Martin, eds. 1989. *New Times: The Changing Face of Politics in the 1990s*. London: Lawrence and Wishart.

Hall-Jones, P. 2009. 'Precariat meet'n'greet', New Unionism blog, available at: http://newunionism.wordpress.com/2009/11/22/precariat/.

Hansen, E.H., Møller, B.L., Kock, G.R., Bünner, C.M., Kristensen, C.M., Jensen, O.R., Okkels, F.T., Olsen, C.E., Motawia, M.S. and Hansen, J. 2009. 'De novo biosynthesis of vainillin in Fission Yeast (*Saccharomyces cerevisiae*) and Baker's Yeast (*Schizosaccharomyces pombe*)'. *Applied and Environmental Microbiology*, 75: 2765–74.

Hansen, F. 2005. 'Business focus: Global labour arbitrage resets wages', *Business Finance*, 1 April: 7–10, available at: http://businessfinancemag.com/hr/economic-amp-business-focus-global-labor-arbitrage-resets-wages.

Haraway, Donna. 1991. *Simians, Cyborgs and Women: The Reinvention of Nature*. New York: Routledge.

Hardt, M. and Negri, A. 2004. *Multitude: War and Democracy in the Age of Empire*. New York: Penguin.

Hardt, Michael. 1999. 'Affective labour'. *Boundary 2*, 26 (2) 89–100.

Harlan, Jack R. 1992. *Crops and Man*. Madison: American Society of Agronomy.

Harney, A. 2008. *The China Price: The True Cost of Chinese Competitive Advantage*. London: Penguin.

Harootunian, Harry. 2000. *History's Disquiet: Modernity, Cultural Practice, and the Question of Everyday Life*. New York: Columbia University Press.

Harper, M.J. 1982. 'The measurement of productive capital stock, capital wealth, and capital services'. Bureau of Labor Statistics Working Paper No. 128. Available at: http://www.bls.gov/osmr/pdf/ec820020.pdf.

Harris, Paul and Franklin, Jonathan. 2003. 'Bring us home: GIs flood US with war-weary emails', *The Observer*, 10 August.

Harrison, Bennett. 1997. *Lean and Mean: The Changing Landscape of Corporate Power in the Age of Flexibility*. New York: The Guilford Press.

Harrod, Jeffrey. 1987. *Power, Production and the Unprotected Worker*. New York: Columbia University Press.

Harrod, Jeffrey. 1989. 'Lech, Lula and Kwon: Industrialisation, productivity and multiple power relations'. Scribd, available at: http://www.scribd.com/doc/23829533/Lech-Lula-and-Kwon.

Harrod, Jeffrey. 1997. 'Social forces and international political economy: Joining the two IR's'. In S. Gill and J.H. Mittelman, eds. *Innovation and Transformation in International Studies*. Cambridge: Cambridge University Press.

Harrod, Jeffrey. 1999. 'The end of opposition?: Market power as a rationality or diverting the egalitarian neurological imperative?' Paper presented at the Annual Convention, International Studies Association. Available at: www.ciaonet.org/isa/har01.

Harrod, Jeffrey. 2001a. 'Global realism: Unmasking power in the international political economy'. In R. Wyn-Jones, ed. *Critical Theory in World Politics*. London: Lynne Rienner.

Harrod, Jeffrey. 2001b. 'Power, production and the unprotected worker: Rationalities, world views and global change'. Paper presented at the Annual Convention, International Studies Association, 20–24 February.

Harrod, Jeffrey. 2003. 'The new politics of economic and social rights'. In K. Arts and P. Mihyo, eds. *Responding to the Human Rights Deficit*. The Hague: Kluwer.

Harrod, Jeffrey. 2004. 'Global unions: Constraints in an age of the politics of the underclass'. In B. Unfried and M. van der Linden, eds. *Labor and New Social Movements*. Vienna: ITH.

Harrod, Jeffrey. 2007. 'The global poor and global politics: Neomaterialism and the sources of political action'. In M. Ryner and M. Davies, eds. *Poverty and Production and the Production of World Politics: Unprotected Workers in the Global Political Economy*. Basingstoke: Palgrave Macmillan.

Harrod, Jeffrey. 2008. 'The International Labour Organisation and the world labour force: From "peoples of the world" to "informal sector"'. Scribd, available at: http://www.scribd.com/doc/2389635/.

Harrod, Jeffrey. 2012. 'Sabotage, organisation, conformity and adjustment: Reactions to workplace pressures'. Paper presented at Joint BISA-ISA Joint Conference, Edinburgh, 20–22 June.

Harrod, Jeffrey and O'Brien, R. 2002. *Global Unions: Theory and Strategies of Organized Labour in the Global Political Economy*. London: Routledge.

Hart, Gill. 1986. 'Interlocking transactions: Obstacles, precursors or instruments of agrarian capitalism'. *Journal of Development Economics*, 23 (1) 177–203.

Hart, J. 1992. *Rival Capitalists: International Competitiveness in the United States, Japan, and Western Europe*. Ithaca: Cornell University Press.

Hart, M. 2005. 'Women, migration, and the body-less spirit of capitalist patriarchy'. *Journal of International Women's Studies*, 7 (2) 1–16.

Hart-Landsberg, M. and Burkett, P. 2006. 'China and the dynamics of international accumulation: Causes and consequences of global restructuring'. *Historical Materialism*, 14 (3) 3–43.

Harvey, David. 1982. *The Limits to Capital*. London: Verso.

Harvey, David. 1990. *The Condition of Postmodernity. An Enquiry into the Origins of Cultural Change*. Cambridge, MA: Blackwell.

Harvey, David. 2000. *Spaces of Hope*. Cambridge: Cambridge University Press.

Harvey, David. 2001. *Spaces of Capital: Towards a Critical Geography*. Edinburgh: Edinburgh University Press.

Harvey, David. 2003. *The New Imperialism*. Oxford: Oxford University Press.

Harvey, David. 2005. *A Brief History of Neoliberalism*. New York: Oxford University Press.

Harvey, David. 2006[1982]. *The Limits to Capital*, rev. edn. London: Verso.

Harvey, David. 2007. 'Neoliberalism as creative destruction'. *The Annals of the American Academy of Political and Social Science*, 610: 21–44.

Harvey, David. 2010. *The Enigma of Capital and the Crises of Capitalism*. New York: Oxford University Press.

Haskel, J., Clayton, Tony, Goodridge, Peter, Pesole, Annarosa, Barnett, David, Chamberlain, Graham, Jones, Richard, Khan, Khalid and Turvey, Alex. 2009. 'Innovation, knowledge spending and productivity growth in the UK'. London: NESTA. Available at: http://www.nesta.org.uk/library/documents/growth-accounting.pdf.

Hayden, Erika Check 2014. 'Synthetic-biology firms shift focus. Switch to food and fragrances risks consumer rejection'. *Nature*, 505: 598.

Hecker, D. 2005. 'High-technology employment: A NAICS-based update'. *Monthly Labour Review*, July, 57–72.

Heilbrun, J. 2003. 'Baumol's cost disease'. In R. Towse, ed. *A Handbook of Cultural Economics*. Cheltenham, UK and Northampton, MA, USA: Edward Elgar Publishing.

Heintz, James. 2002. 'Low-wage manufacturing exports, job creation, and global income inequalities'. Political Economy Research Institute. Working Paper Series, (Revised version).

Held, D., McGrew, A., Goldblatt, D. and Perraton, J. 1999. *Global Transformations*. Cambridge: Polity.

Helleiner, Eric and Pagliari, Stefano. 2011. 'The end of an era in international financial regulation? A postcrisis research agenda'. *International Organization*, 65 (1) 169–200.

Henderson, J., Dicken, P., Hess, M., Coe, N. and Yeung, H.W-C. 2002. 'Global production networks and the analysis of economic development'. *Review of International Political Economy*, 9 (3) 436–64.

Henderson, Jeffrey and Nadvi, Khalid. 2011. 'Greater China, the challenges of global production networks and the dynamics of transformation'. *Global Networks*, 11 (3) 285–97.

Her Majesty's Government. 2005. *Science & Innovation Investment Framework 2004–2014*. London: The Stationery Office.

Hernández, J. 1954. 'La lucha contra la política impuesta por el imperialismo yanqui'. *Principios*, 25: 1–5.

Herod, A. 2001. 'Implications of Just-in-Time production for union strategy: Lessons from the 1998 General Motors–United auto workers dispute'. *Annals of the Association of American Geographers*, 90 (3) 521–47.

Herod, Andrew. 2007. 'The agency of labour in global change: Reimagining the spaces and scales of trade union praxis within a global economy'. In J.M. Hobson and L. Seabrooke, eds. *Everyday Politics of the World Economy*. Cambridge: Cambridge University Press.

Hesmondhalgh, D. 2007. *The Cultural Industries*, 2nd edn. London: Sage.

Hess, M. 2008. 'Governance, Value Chains and Networks: An Afterword'. *Economy and Society*, 37 (3) 452–9.

Hess, M. and Yeung, H.W-C. 2006. 'Whither global production networks in economic geography? Past, present, and future'. *Environment and Planning A*, 38 (7) 1193–204.

Hettne, B. 1995. 'Introduction: The international political economy of transformation'. In B. Hettne, ed. *International Political Economy: Understanding Global Disorder*. London: Zed Press.

Heyes, Jason. 2013. 'Flexicurity in crisis: European labour market policies in a time of austerity'. *European Journal of Industrial Relations*, 19 (1) 71–86.

Hibbs, Douglas. 1978. 'On the political economy of long-run trends in strike activity'. *British Journal of Political Science*, 8 (2) 153–75.

Hibou, Béatrice. 2012. *La Bureaucratisation du Monde à l'ère Néolibérale*. Paris: La Découverte.

Higgs, P., Cunningham, S. and Bakhshi, H. 2008. 'Beyond the creative industries: Mapping the creative economy in the United Kingdom'. London: NESTA. Available at: www.eprints.qut.edu.au/archive/00012166/01/beyond_creative_industries_report_NESTA.pdf.

Higgs, P., Cunningham, Stuart, Hearn, Geoff, Adkins, B. and Barnett, K. 2005. 'The ecology of Queensland design'. Technical Report, CIRAC, Queensland University of Technology. Available at: http://eprints.qut.edu.au/ archive/00002410.

Hille, K. and Jacob, R. 2013. 'China wary amid push for workers' union poll'. *Financial Times*. Available at: http://www.ft.com/cms/s/0/3ee205de-6c5a-11e2-b774-00144feab49a.html#axzz2OGgXekAU.

Himanen, P. 2001. *The Hacker Ethic and the Spirit of the Information Age*. New York: Random House.

Hines, Alice and Miles, Kathleen. 2012. 'Wal-Mart strike hits 100 cities, but fails to distract Black Friday shoppers'. *Huffington Post*. Online Edition, 23 November. Available at: http://www.huffingtonpost.com/2012/11/23/Wal-Mart-strike-black-friday_n_2177784.html.

Hirsch, Joachim. 1978. 'The state apparatus and social reproduction: Elements of a bourgeois state'. In John Holloway and Sol Picciotto, eds. *State and Capital: A Marxist Debate*. London: Edward Arnold.

Hirsch, Joachim. 1995. *Der nationale Wettbewerbsstaat. Staat, Demokratie und Politik im globalen Kapitalismus*. Berlin: Id-Verlag.

Hobbelink, Henk. 1991. *Biotechnology and the Future of World Agriculture*. London: Zed Press.

Hobsbawm, Eric J. 1968. *Industry and Empire*. Harmondsworth: Penguin.

Hobsbawm, Eric. 1994. *The Age of Extremes*. New York: Vintage.

Hobson, J.A. 1965[1902]. *Imperialism, a Study*. Ann Arbor: University of Michigan Press.

Hobson, John M. and Seabrooke, Leonard, eds. 2007a. *Everyday Politics of the World Economy*. Cambridge: Cambridge University Press.

Hobson, John M. and Seabrooke, Leonard. 2007b. 'Everyday IPE: Revealing everyday forms of change in the world economy'. In John M. Hobson and Leonard Seabrooke, eds. *Everyday Politics of the World Economy*. Cambridge: Cambridge University Press.

Hocking, Martin B. 1997. 'Vanillin: Synthetic flavoring from spent sulfite liquor'. *Journal of Chemical Education*, 74 (9) 1055–9.

Hofstadter, Richard. 1955. *The Age of Reform. From Bryan to F.D.R.*. New York: Vintage.

Holland, E. 1998. 'Spinoza and Marx'. *Cultural Logic*, 2 (1). Available at: http://clogic.eserver.org/2-1/2-1index.html.

Holman, Otto. 1996. *Integrating Southern Europe. EC Expansion and the Transnationalisation of Spain*. London: Routledge.

Holman, Otto. 2004. 'Asymmetrical regulation and multidimensional governance in the European Union'. *Review of International Political Economy*, 11 (4) 714–35.

Holman, Otto. 2006. 'Transnational governance without supranational government: The case of the European employment strategy'. *Perspectives on European Politics and Society*, 7 (1) 91–107.

Holmes, J. 1992. 'The continental integration of the North American automobile industry: From the Auto Pact to the FTA and beyond'. *Environment and Planning A*, 24 (1) 95–119.

Holt-Gimenez, E. 2006. *Campesino a Campesino: Voices from Latin America's Farmer to Farmer Movement for Sustainable Agriculture*. Oakland: Food First Books.

Honda Workers Negotiating Committee. 2010. 'An open letter from the Negotiation Committee of Foshan Honda's striking workers to all workers and other sections of society' [Foshan bentian bagong gongren tanpan daibiao zhi quanti gongren he shehui gejie de gongkaixin]. Available at: http://www.ideobook.com/29/open-letter-by-foshan-honda-workers/.

Hoogvelt, Ankie and Yuasa, Masae. 1994. 'Going lean or going native? The social regulation of "lean" production systems'. *Review of International Political Economy*, 1 (2) 281–304.

Hopkins, Michael. 2007. *Corporate Social Responsibility and International Development: Is Business the Solution?* Bath: Bath Press.

Hopkins, Terence K. and Immanuel Wallerstein. 1986. 'Commodity chains in the world-economy prior to 1800'. *Review* (Fernand Braudel Center), 10 (1) 157–70.

Hounshell, D. 1985. *From the American System to Mass Production, 1800–1932: The Development of Manufacturing Technology in the United States*. Baltimore, MD: Johns Hopkins University Press.

Howard, M.C. and King, J.E. 1992. *A History of Marxian Economics*, Vol. II. Basingstoke: Macmillan.

Howkins, J. 2013. *The Creative Economy: How People Make Money from Ideas*. London: Penguin.

Hrynyshyn, D. and Ross, S. 2011. 'Canadian autoworkers, the climate crisis, and the contradictions of social unionism'. *Labor Studies Journal*, 36 (1) 5–36.

Hubbard, P. 2011. 'World cities of sex'. In B. Derudder, ed. *International Handbook of Globalization and World Cities*. Cheltenham, UK and Northampton, MA, USA: Edward Elgar Publishing.

Huber, Joseph. 2011. 'Ökologische Modernisierung und Umweltinnovation'. In Matthias Groß, ed. *Handbuch Umweltsoziologie*. Wiesbaden: VS Verlag.

Hudson, R. 2012. 'Critical political economy and material transformation'. *New Political Economy*, 17 (4) 373–97.

Hughes, D.M. 2000. 'The "Natasha" trade: The transnational shadow market of trafficking in women'. *Journal of International Affairs*, 53 (2) 625–51.

Humphrey, J. and Schmitz, H. 2002. 'How does insertion in global value chains affect upgrading in industrial clusters?' *Regional Studies*, 36 (9) 1017–27.

Hung, Ho-fung. 2009. 'America's head servant?: The PRC's dilemma in the global crisis'. *New Left Review*, 2nd series (60) 5–25.

Hung, Ho-fung. 2013. 'Labor politics under three stages of Chinese capitalism'. *The South Atlantic Quarterly*, 112 (1) 203–12.

Husson, Michel. 2001. 'The Regulation School: A one-way ticket from

Marx to the Saint-Simon Foundation?'. Available at: http://www2.cddc.vt.edu/digitalfordism/fordism_materials/Husson.pdf.

Huws, Ursula. 2001. 'The making of a cybertariat: Virtual work in a real world'. *Socialist Register*, 1–23.

Huws, Ursula. 2013. 'Working online, living offline: Labour in the internet age'. *Work Organisation, Labour and Globalisation*, 7 (1) 1–11.

Hymer, Stephen. 1972. 'The multinational corporation and the law of uneven development'. In J. Bhagwati, ed. *Economics and World Order from the 1970s to the 1990s*. London: Collier Macmillan.

IAASTD. 2009. *Agriculture at a Crossroads*. Washington, DC: International Assessment of Agricultural Knowledge, Science and Technology for Development IAASTD.

IAEG Inter-Agency and Expert Group on MDG Indicators, United Nations Statistics Division. 2009. *Millennium Development Goals Indicators: Debt Service as a Percentage of Exports of Goods and Services and Net Income*, last updated 14 July. Available at: http://mdgs.un.org/unsd/mdg/SeriesDetail.aspx?srid1/4655.

IDG News. 2011. 'Watchdog group cites continued Foxconn abuses'. 7 May. Available at: http://www.pcworld.com/businesscenter/article/227306/watchdog_group_cites_continued_foxconn_abuses.html.

Ietto-Gillies, G. 2002. *Transnational Corporations: Fragmentation Amidst Integration*. London: Routledge.

IFAD. 2010. *Rural Poverty Report 2011*. Rome: IFAD.

Ihara, Ryoji. 2007. *Toyota's Assembly Line: A View from the Factory Floor*. Melbourne: Trans Pacific Press.

Ihara, Ryoji. 2012. 'Syokuba wo torimaku Kankyo no Henka to "Utsubyo" no Hiromari'. *Gendai Shiso*, 39 (2) 228–45.

Ihara, Ryoji. 2013. 'Rodo ni matsuwaru Shi no Henka to Mondai no Shozai: Shisyo, Karoshi kara Jisatsu he'. *Gendai Shiso*, 41 (7) 110–28.

Illich, I. 1974. *Energy and Equity*. London: Calder and Boyars.

Illich, I. 2001[1973]. *Tools for Conviviality*. London: Marion Boyars Publishing.

ILO. 1999. *Decent Work. Report of the Director-General to the 89th Session of the International Labour Conference*. Geneva: International Labour Organization.

ILO. 2005. *A Global Alliance Against Forced Labour*. Geneva: International Labour Organization.

ILO. 2008a. *Declaration on Social Justice and Fair Globalization*. Geneva: International Labour Organization.

ILO. 2008b. *The Global Employment Challenge*. By Ajit K. Ghose, Nomaan Maji and Christoph Ernst. Geneva: International Labour Organization.

ILO. 2010. *Global Wage Report 2010/11. Wage Policies in Times of Crisis*. Geneva: International Labour Organization.

ILO. 2011. *Global Employment Trends 2011: The Challenge of a Jobs Recovery*. Geneva: International Labour Organization.

ILO. 2012. *ILO Global Estimate of Forced Labour: Results and Methodology*. Geneva: International Labour Office, Special Action Programme to Combat Forced Labour SAP-FL.

Imai, M. 1986. *Kaizen: The Key to Japan's Competitive Success*. New York: Random House.

Independent Evaluation Office. 2011. *IMF Performance in the Run-up to the Financial and Economic Crisis, IMF Surveillance 2004–7*. Washington, DC: Independent Evaluation Office of the International Monetary Fund.

Industrial Internet Consortium. 2014. 'Accelerating innovation in connected, intelligent machines and processes'. Available at: http://blog.iiconsortium.org/.

International Labour Office. 1972. *Employment, Incomes and Equality: A Strategy for Increasing Productive Employment in Kenya*. Geneva: International Labour Organization.

International Monetary Fund (IMF). 2009a. *Factsheet: Poverty Reduction Strategy Papers* (PRSP), 14 August. Available at: https://www.imf.org/external/np/exr/facts/prsp.htm.

International Monetary Fund (IMF). 2009b. *Factsheet: Debt Relief Under the Heavily Indebted Poor Country (HIPC) Initiative*, 22 September. Available at: http://www.imf.org/external/np/exr/facts/hipc.htm.

International Monetary Fund (IMF). 2011. *Regional Economic Outlook. Europe. Strengthening the Recovery*. Washington, DC: International Monetary Fund.

International Monetary Fund (IMF). 2013. *World Economic Outlook Database*. April. Available at: http://www.imf.org/external/pubs/ft/weo/2013/01/weodata/index.aspx.

International Organization for Standardization. 2013. *The ISO Survey of Management System Standard Certifications – 2012*. October. Geneva: ISO.

Inwood, Josh and Bonds, Anne. 2013. 'On racial difference and revolution'. *Antipode*, 45 (3) 517–20.

ISAAA. 2012. *Pocket K No.16: Global Status of Commercialized Biotech/GM Crops in 2012*. Ithaca: International Service for the Acquisition of Agri-Biotech Applications.

ISIC. 2008. *International Standard Industrial Classification of All Economic Activities*, Revision 4. United Nations Department of Economic and Social Affairs, Statistics Division. Available at: unstats.un.org/unsd/publication/seriesM/seriesm_4rev4e.pdf.

Ismail, S. 2000. 'The popular dimensions of contemporary militant Islamism: Socio-spacial determinants in the Cairo urban setting'. *Comparative Studies in Society and History*, 42 (2) 363–93.

Istat. 2003. 'Salari, inflazione e conflitti di lavoro'. In *Istat, Rapporto Annuale. La Situazione del Paese nel 2002*. Rome: Istat.

Jacobi, Lena and Kluve, Jochen. 2006. *Before and After the Hartz Reforms: The Performance of Active Labour Market Policy in Germany*. Discussion paper 2100, Bonn: Forschungsinstitut zur Zukunft der Arbeit. Available at: http://ssrn.com/abstract=900374.

Jacobsson, L.S. 2013. 'Play fair: A campaign for decent sportswear'. Report 66. Swedwatch. Available at: http://www.swedwatch.org/en/reports/play-fair-—campaign-decent-sportswear.

Jacoby, S. 2005. *The Embedded Corporation: Corporate Governance and Employment Relations in Japan and the United States*. Princeton, NJ: Princeton University Press.

Jaeger, Carlo C. et al. 2011. *A New Growth Path for Europe. Generating Prosperity and Jobs in the Low-Carbon Economy. Synthesis Report*. A study commissioned by the German Federal Ministry for the Environment, Nature Conservation and Nuclear Safety. Potsdam: European Climate Forum.

Jameson, Fredric. 1991. *Postmodernism, or the Cultural Logic of Late Capitalism*. Durham, NC: Duke University Press.

Jänicke, Martin. 2011. *"Green Growth". Vom Wachstum der Öko-Industrie zum Nachhaltigen Wirtschaften*. FFU-Report 06–2011. Berlin: Freie Universität, Forschungszentrum für Umweltpolitik.

Jeffreys, S. 2009. *The Industrial Vagina: The Political Economy of the Global Sex Trade*. New York: Routledge.

Jeffreys, S. 2010. 'The sex industry and business practice: An obstacle to women's equality'. *Women's Studies International Forum*, 33: 274–82.

Jenkins, J.C. and Leicht, K.T. 1997. 'Class analysis and social movements: A critique and reformulation'. In J.R. Hall, ed. *Reworking Class: Cultures and Institutions of Economic Stratification and Agency*. Ithaca: Cornell University Press.

Jessop, Bob. 1990. *State Theory. Putting the State in its Place*. Cambridge: Polity Press.

Jessop, Bob. 1991. 'On articulate articulation'. In René B. Bertramsen, Jens P. Thomsen Frølund and Jacob Torfing, eds. *State, Economy and Society*. London: Unwin Hyman.

Jessop, Bob. 2002. *The Future of the Capitalist State*. Cambridge: Cambridge University Press.

Jessop, Bob. 2007. *State Power: A Strategic-Relational Approach*. Cambridge: Polity.

Jessop, Bob. 2008. 'A cultural political economy of competitiveness and its implications for higher education'. In B. Jessop, N. Fairclough and R. Wodak, eds. *Education and the Knowledge-Based Economy in Europe*. Rotterdam: Sense Publishers.

Jessop, Bob. 2010. 'Cultural political economy and critical policy studies'. *Critical Policy Studies*, 3 (3–4) 336–56.

Jessop, Bob and Sum, Ngai-Ling. 2006. *Beyond the Regulation Approach. Putting Capitalist Economies in their Place*. Cheltenham, UK and Northampton, MA, USA: Edward Elgar Publishing.

Johnson, Chalmers. (unpublished). 'The real casualty rate from America's Iraq war', manuscript.

Johnson, Kelli Lyon. 2013. 'The new slave narrative: Advocacy and human rights in stories of contemporary slavery'. *Journal of Human Rights*, 12 (2) 242–58.

Jonas, Andrew. 1996. 'Local labour control regimes: Uneven development and the social regulation of production'. *Regional Studies*, 30 (4) 323–38.

Jopson, Barney. 2012. 'Wal-Mart slows international expansion'. *Financial Times*. Online edition. Available at: http://www.ft.com/cms/s/0/876f65a4-e79d-11e1-86bf-00144feab49a.html#axzz27FTwF4g4.

Jordan, Carl F. 2002. 'Genetic engineering, the farm crisis, and world hunger'. *BioScience*, 52 (6) 523–29.

Jubilee Debt Campaign UK. 2007. *Debt and Women*. Available at: http://www.jubileedebtcampaign.org.uk/Debt%20and% 20Womenþ3072.twl.

Jubilee Debt Campaign UK. 2008. *Angola, Country Information*. Available at: http://www.jubileedebtcampaign.org.uk/ Angolaþ4038.twl.

Jubilee Debt Campaign UK. 2009a. *How big is the debt of poor countries?* Available at: http://www.jubileedebtcampaign.org.uk/ 2%20How%20big%20is%20the%20debt%20of%20poor%20countries%3Fþ2647.twl.

Jubilee Debt Campaign UK. 2009b. *Hasn't All the Debt been Cancelled?* Available at: http://www.jubileedebtcampaign.org.uk/4%20Hasn%27t%20all%20the%20debt%20been%20cancelled%3Fþ2651.twl.

Jubilee Debt Campaign, London. 2013. *How Big Is the Debt of Poor Countries?* Available at: http://jubileedebt.org.uk/faqs-2/how-big-is-the-debt-of-poor-countries.

Judt, T. 2011. *Guasto è il mondo*. Bari: Laterza.

Kaindl, Ch., ed. 2007. *Subjekte im Neoliberalismus*. Marburg: BdWi.

Kaiser, Mario and Kurath, Monika. 2007. 'Nano visions: Implications for technology assessment, communication and regulation'. *Technologiefolgeabschätzung – Theorie und Praxis*, 16 (1) 118–22.

Kalecki, Michal. 1943. 'Political aspects of full employment'. *Political Quarterly*, 14 (4) 322–31.

Kamata, S. 1983. *Japan in the Passing Lane: Insider's Account of Life in a Japanese Auto Factory*. New York: Pantheon Books.

Kang, S.I., Oh, J. and Kim, H. 2012. *Korea's Low-Carbon Green Growth Strategy*. Working Paper No. 310. Paris: OECD.

Kaplinsky, R. 2005. *Globalization, Poverty and Inequality: Between a Rock and a Hard Place*. Cambridge: Polity.

Kaplinsky, R. and Morris, M. 2001. *A Handbook for Value Chain Research*. Brighton: IDS. Available at: http://www.ids.ac.uk/ids/global/.

Kapsos, S. 2007. *World and Regional Trends in Labour Force Participation. Methodologies and Key Results*. Geneva: ILO.

Kara, Siddarth Ashok. 2009. *Sex Trafficking: Inside the Business of Modern Slavery*. New York: Columbia University Press.

Karanikolos, Marina et al. 2013. 'Financial crisis, austerity, and health in Europe'. *The Lancet*, 381 (9874) 1323–31.

Karatzogianni, A. 2012. 'Wikileaks affects: Ideology, conflict and the revolutionary ideal'. In A. Karatzogianni and A. Kuntsman, eds. *Digital Cultures and the Politics of Emotion: Feelings, Affect and Technological Change*. Basingstoke: Palgrave.

Karatzogianni, A. and Robinson, A. 2013. *Power, Resistance and Conflict in the Contemporary World*. London: Routledge.

Karyotis, G. 2007. 'European migration policy in the aftermath of September 11: The security–migration nexus'. *Innovation: European Journal of Social Sciences*, 20 (1) 1–17.

Karyotis, T. 2014. 'Report from the *Workers' Economy* international meeting', 31 January–1 February, occupied factory of Fralib, Marseille. Available at: http://www.autonomias.net/2014/02/report-from-workers-economy.html.

Kato, T. and Steven, R. 1993. 'Is Japanese capitalism post-Fordist?' In T. Kato and R. Steven, eds. *Is Japanese Management Post-Fordism?* Tokyo: Mado-sha.

Katz, Cindi. 2004. *Growing Up Global: Economic Restructuring and Children's Everyday Lives*. Minneapolis: University of Minnesota Press.

Katz, D. 1994. *Just Do It. The Nike Spirit in the Corporate World*. Holbrook: Adams.

Katz, R. 1998. *Japan: The System that Soured: The Rise and Fall of the Japanese Economic Miracle*. Armonk, NY: M.E. Sharpe.

Katzenstein, Peter J., Keohane, Robert O. and Krasner, Stephen D. 1998. 'International Organization and the study of world politics'. *International Organization*, 52 (4) 645–85.

Kaufmann, Stefan and Müller, Tadzio. 2009. *Grüner Kapitalismus. Krise, Klimawandel und kein Ende des Wachstums*. Berlin: Dietz.

Kawahara, A. 1997. *The Origin of Competitive Strength: 50 Years of the Auto Industry in Japan and the US*. Kyoto: Kyoto University Press.

Kay, C. 2002a. 'Chile's neoliberal agrarian transformation and the peasantry'. *Journal of Agrarian Change*, 2 (4) 464–501.

Kay, C. 2002b. 'Why East Asia overtook Latin America: Agrarian reform, industrialisation and development'. *Third World Quarterly*, 23 (6) 1073–102.

Kay, Sylvia. 2012. *Positive Investment Alternatives to Large-Scale Land Acquisitions or Leases*. Amsterdam: Transnational Institute.

Kay, Sylvia. 2014. *Reclaiming Agricultural Investment: Towards Public–Peasant Investment Synergies*. Amsterdam: Transnational Institute.

Keeley, J.F. 1983. 'Cast in concrete for all time? The negotiation of the auto pact'. *Canadian Journal of Political Science*, 16 (2) 281–98.

Kempadoo, K. 2000. 'Gender, race and sex: Exoticism in the Caribbean', paper delivered at the Simpósio Internacional O Desafio da Diferença: Articulando Gênero, Raça e Classe, Salvador, Bahia, Brasil. Available at: http://www.desafio.ufba.br/gt5–003.html.

Kempadoo, K. 2001. 'Women of color and the global sex trade: Transnational feminist perspectives'. *Meridians*, 1 (2) 28–51.

Kempadoo, K. 2004. *Sexing the Caribbean: Gender, Race, and Sexual Labor*. New York: Routledge.

Kenney, M. and Florida, R. 1993. 'Beyond mass production: Production and the labor process in Japan'. In T. Kato and R. Steven, eds. *Is Japanese Management Post-Fordism?* Tokyo: Mado-sha.

Keohane, R.O. and Nye, J.S. Jr. eds. 1973[1971]. *Transnational Relations and World Politics*. Cambridge, MA: Harvard University Press.

Kessler, Oliver. 2012. 'World society, social differentiation and time'. *International Political Sociology*, 6: 77–94.

Kiely, Ray. 1998. 'Globalization, post-Fordism and the contemporary context of development'. *International Sociology*, 13 (1) 95–111.

Kill, Jutta, Ozinga, Saskia, Pavett, Steven and Wainwright, Richard. 2010. *Trading Carbon: How it Works and Why it is Controversial*. Brussels: FERN. Available at: http://www.fern.org/sites/fern.org/files/tradingcarbon_internet_FINAL.pdf.

Kim, J.K. and Fu, M. 2008. 'International women in South Korea's sex industry: A new commodity frontier'. *Asian Survey*, 48 (3) 492–513.

Kinchy, Abby J. 2012. *Seeds, Science, and Struggle: The Global Politics of Transgenic Crops*. Cambridge, MA: MIT Press.

Kindleberger, C. 1970. *The International Corporation: A Symposium*. Cambridge: Cambridge University Press.

Kirshenblatt-Gimblett, B. 2005. 'The corporeal turn'. *The Jewish Quarterly Review*, 95 (3) 447–61.

Kitiarsa, P. 2008. 'Thai migrants in Singapore: State, intimacy and desire'. *Gender, Place and Culture: A Journal of Feminist Geography*, 15 (6) 595–610.

Klein, L., Saltzman, C. and Duggal, V. 2003. 'Information, technology and productivity: The case of the financial sector'. *Survey of Current Business*, August.

Klein, Naomi. 2000. *No Logo*. London: Flamingo.

Kleiner, D. 2010. *The Telekommunist Manifesto*, Network Notebooks 03, Institute of Network Cultures, Amsterdam.

Kleingartner, A. and Peng, H. (Shara). 1991. 'Taiwan: An exploration of labour relations in Transition'. *British Journal of Industrial Relations*, 29 (3) 427–45.

Kliman, Andrew. 2007. *Reclaiming Marx's Capital: A Refutation of the Myth of Inconsistency*. Lanham, MD: Lexington Books.

Kliman, Andrew. 2012. *The Failure of Capitalist Production*. London: Pluto.

Kloepfer, I. 2008. *Aufstand der Unterschicht*. Hamburg: Hoffmann und Campe.

Kloppenburg, Jack Ralph, Jr. 1988. *First the Seed: The Political Economy of Plant Biotechnology, 1492–2000*. New York: Cambridge University Press.

Kloppenburg, Jack Ralph, Jr. 2004[1988]. *First the Seed: The Political Economy of Plant Biotechnology 1492–2000*, 2nd edn. Madison, WI: The University of Wisconsin Press.

Kloppenburg, Jack Ralph, Jr. 2010. 'Impeding dispossession, enabling repossession: Biological open source and the recovery of seed sovereignty'. *Journal of Agrarian Change*, 10 (3) 367–88.

Knafo, Samuel. 2010. 'Critical approaches and the legacy of the agent/structure debate in international relations'. *Cambridge Review of International Affairs*, 23 (3) 493–516.

Knight, F. 1921. *Risk, Uncertainty, and Profit*. Boston: Houghton and Mifflin.

Knight, G. and Greenberg, J. 2002. 'Promotionalism and subpolitics: Nike and its labor critics'. *Management Communication Quarterly*, 15: 541–70.

Knights, D. and Collinson, D. 1987. 'Disciplining the shopfloor: A comparison of the disciplinary effects of managerial psychology and financial accounting'. *Accounting, Organizations and Society*, 12 (5) 457–77.

Koch, Max. 2012. *Capitalism and Climate Change*. London: Palgrave Macmillan.

Koike, K. 1983. 'Internal labor markets: Workers in large firms'. In T. Shirai, ed. *Contemporary Industrial Relations in Japan*. Wisconsin: University of Wisconsin Press.

Kondo, D. 1990. *Crafting Selves: Power, Gender, and Discourses of Identity in a Japanese Workplace*. Chicago: The University of Chicago Press.

Kong, T.Y. 2006. 'Labour and globalization: Locating the Northeast Asian newly industrializing countries'. *Review of International Political Economy*, 13 (1) 103–28.

Korzeniewicz, M. 1994. 'Commodity chains and marketing strategies: Nike and the global athletic footwear chain'. In G. Gereffi and M. Korzeniewicz, eds. *Commodity Chains and Global Capitalism*. Westport, CT: Praeger.

Kose, M.A., Prasad, E., Rogoff, K. and Wei, S. 2006. 'Financial globalization: A reappraisal', National Bureau of Economic Research, Working Paper No. 12484.

Kostakis, V., Niaros, V. and Giotitsas, C. 2014. 'Production and governance in hackerspaces: A manifestation of Commons-based peer production in the physical realm?'. *International Journal of Cultural Studies* (forthcoming).

Kothari, Uma. 2013. 'Geographies and histories of unfreedom: Indentured labourers and contract workers in Mauritius'. *Journal of Development Studies*, 49 (8) 1042–57.

Kozul-Wright, R. and Rayment, P. 2004. 'Globalization reloaded', UNCTAD Discussion Paper No. 167, January.

Kracauer, Siegfried. 1995. *The Mass Ornament: Weimar Essays*. Cambridge, MA: Harvard University Press.

Kraemer, Kenneth L., Linden, Greg and Dedrick, Jason. 2011. 'Capturing value in global networks: Apple's iPad and iPhone'. Available at: http://pcic.merage.uci.edu/papers/2011/Value_iPad_iPhone.pdf.

Krasner, Stephen D. 1985. *Structural Conflict. The Third World Against Global Liberalism*. Berkeley, CA: University of California Press.

Krugman, Paul. 1997. 'In praise of cheap labor: Bad jobs at bad wages are better than no jobs at all'. Available at: http://web.mit.edu/krugman/www/smokey.html#Bio.

Krugman, Paul. 2007. 'Introduction' to John Maynard Keynes, *The General Theory of Employment, Interest and Money*. New York: Palgrave Macmillan.

Krugman, Paul. 2012. *New York Times* blog, 16 November. Available at: http://krugman.blogs.nytimes.com/2013/11/16/secular-stagnation-coalmines-bubbles-and-larry-summers/?_php=true&_type=blogs&_r=0.

Krupnov, Yuri. 2013. 'Siberia becomes the center of Russia' [in Russian]. Available at: http://krupnov.livejournal.com/572236.html.

Krzyzaniak, M. 1973. 'Benefit–cost and incidence study of transfers, financed by taxes on profits, in a growing neoclassical economy with two labor inputs'. *Public Finance = Finances Publiques*, 28 (2) 151–77.

Kumazawa, M. 1996. *Portraits of the Japanese Workplace*. Boulder, CO: Westview Press.

Kume, I. 1988. 'Changing relations among the government, labor, and business in Japan after the oil crisis'. *International Organization*, 42 (4) 659–87.

Kuntz Ficker, Sandra. 2005. 'From structuralism to the New institutional Economics: The impact of theory of the study of foreign trade in Latin America'. *Latin American Research Review*, 40 (3) 145–62.

Kurtz, M. 2001. 'State developmentalism without a developmental state: The public foundations of the "Free Market Miracle" in Chile'. *Latin American Politics and Society*, 43 (2) 1–26.

Kuruganti, Kavitha. 2013. 'Adverse impacts of transgenic crops/foods. A compilation of scientific references with abstracts'. New Delhi: Coalition for a GM-Free India.

Kurz, R. 1999. *Schwarzbuch Kapitalismus. Ein Abgesang auf die Marktwirtschaft*. Frankfurt: Eichborn-Verlag.

Laclau, Ernesto and Mouffe, Chantal. 1985. *Hegemony and Socialist Strategy: Towards a Radical Democratic Politics*. London: Verso.

LaFeber, W. 1999. *Michael Jordan and the New Global Capitalism*. New York: W.W. Norton.

Lai, A.E. 1986. *Peasants, Proletarians and Prostitutes: A Preliminary Investigation into the Work of Chinese Women in Colonial Malaya*. Singapore: Institute of Southeast Asian Studies.

Lake, A. and Townshend, T. 2006. 'Obesogenic environments: Exploring the built and food environments'. *The Journal of The Royal Society for the Promotion of Health*, 126 (6) 262–7.

Land Matrix. 2014. The Online Public Database on Land Deals. Available at: http://land portal.info/landmatrix.

Langley, Paul. 2008. *The Everyday Life of Global Finance: Saving and Borrowing in Anglo-America*. Oxford: Oxford University Press.

Lapavitsas, Costas. 2009. 'Financialised capitalism: Crisis and financial expropriation'. *Historical Materialism*, 17 (2) 114–48.

Lapavitsas, Costas, Kaltenbrunner, A., Labrinidis, G., Lindo, D., Meadway, J., Mitchell, J., Panceira, J.P., Pires, E., Powell, J., Stenfors, A., Teles, N., and Vatikiotis, L. 2012. *Crisis in the Eurozone*. London: Verso.

Larner, W. 2002. 'Globalization, governmentality and expertise: Creating a call centre labour force'. *Review of International Political Economy*, 9 (4) 650–74.

Lashinsky, Adam. 2012. *Inside Apple: The Secrets Behind the Past and Future Success of Steve Jobs's Iconic Brand.* London: John Murray.

Laslett, Barbara and Brenner, Johanna. 1989. 'Gender and social reproduction: Historical perspectives'. *Annual Review of Sociology*, 15: 381–404.

Latour, Bruno. 2004. *Politics of Nature. How to Bring the Sciences into Democracy*. Cambridge, MA: Harvard University Press.

Laursen, Lucas. 2011. 'Monsanto dips into Algae'. *Nature Biotechnology*, 29 (6) 473.

Lazzarato, M. 1996. 'Immaterial labor'. In M. Hardt and P. Virno, eds. *Radical Thought in Italy: A Potential Politics*. Minneapolis: University of Minnesota Press.

LeBaron, Genevieve and Ayers, Alison J. 2013. 'The rise of a "New Slavery"? Understanding African unfree labour through neoliberalism'. *Third World Quarterly*, 34 (5) 873–92.

Lebowitz, Michael. 1992. *Beyond Capital: Marx's Political Economy of the Working Class*. Basingstoke: Macmillan.

Lebowitz, Michael. 2003[1992]. *Beyond Capital: Marx's Political Economy of the Working Class*. 2nd edn. Basingstoke: Macmillan.

Lecuyer, C. 2006. *Making Silicon Valley: Innovation and the Growth of High Tech, 1930–1970*. Cambridge: MIT Press.

Lee, C.K. 1999. 'From organized dependence to disorganized despotism: Changing labour regimes in Chinese factories'. *The China Quarterly*, 157: 44–71.

Lee, Ching Kwan. 2007. *Against the Law: Labor Protests in China's Rustbelt and Sunbelt*. Berkeley: University of California Press.

Lee, Ching Kwan. 2010. 'Pathways of labor activism'. In Elizabeth J. Perry and Mark Selden, eds. *Chinese Society: Change, Conflict and Resistance*, 3rd edn. London: Routledge.

Lee, Ching Kwan and Hsing, You-tien. 2010. 'Social activism in China: Agency and possibility'. In You-tien Hsing and Ching Kwan Lee, eds. *Reclaiming Chinese Society: The New Social Activism*. London: Routledge.

Lee, Ching Kwan and Zhang, Yonghong. 2013. 'The power of instability: Unraveling the microfoundations of bargained authoritarianism in China'. *American Journal of Sociology*, 118 (6) 1475–508.

Lee, Joonkoo and Gereffi, Gary. 2013. 'The co-evolution of concentration in mobile phone value chains and its impact on social upgrading in developing countries'. *Capturing the Gains Working Paper* No. 25. Available at: http://www.capturingthegains.org/pdf/ctg-wp-2013-25.pdf.

Lee, Y. 2008. 'Divergent outcomes of labor reform politics in democratized Korea and Taiwan'. *Studies in Comparative International Development*, 44 (1) 47–70.

Lefebvre, Henri. 1984. *Everyday Life in the Modern World*. New Brunswick, NJ: Transaction Publishers.

Lefebvre, Henri. 1988. 'Toward a Leftist cultural politics: Remarks occasioned by the centenary of Marx's death'. In Cary Nelson and Lawrence Grossberg, eds. *Marxism and the Interpretation of Culture*. London: Macmillan.

Lefebvre, Henri. 1991a. *The Critique of Everyday Life*, vol. 1: *Introduction*. London: Verso.

Lefebvre, Henri. 1991b. *The Production of Space*. Oxford: Blackwell Publishers.

Lefebvre, Henri. 1998. 'Towards a Leftist cultural politics: Remarks occasioned by the centenary of Marx's death'. In Cary Nelson and Laurence Greenberg, eds. *Marxism and the Interpretation of Culture*. Urbana: University of Illinois Press.

Lefebvre, Henri. 2002. *The Critique of Everyday Life*, vol. 2: *Foundations for a Sociology of the Everyday*. London: Verso.

Lefebvre, Henri. 2004. *Rhythmanalysis: Space, Time, and Everyday Life*. London: Continuum.

Lefebvre, Henri. 2008. *The Critique of Everyday Life*, vol. 3: *From Modernity to Modernism. Towards a Metaphilosophy of Daily Life*. London: Verso.

Lerche, Jens. 2007. 'A global alliance against forced labour? Unfree labour, neo-liberal globalization and the International Labour Organization'. *Journal of Agrarian Change*, 7 (4) 424–5.

Lerche, Jens. 2012. 'Labour regulations and labour standards in India: Decent work?' *Global Labour Journal*, 3 (1) 16–39.

Lerner, Gerda. 1986. *The Creation of Patriarchy*. Oxford: Oxford University Press.

Lett, E. and Bannister, J. 2009. 'China's manufacturing employment and compensation costs: 2002–2006'. *Monthly Labour Review*, US Department of Labor, April.

Letwin, Michael. 2003. 'Growth of labour anti-war action tied to Bush's anti-worker moves'. *Labour Notes*. April, 11–13.

Levine, P. 2003. *Prostitution, Race and Politics: Policing Venereal Diseases in the British Empire*. New York: Routledge.

Levy, D. 2008. 'Political contestation in global production networks'. *Academy of Management Review*, 33: 943–62.

Levy, Jack. 1989. 'The diversionary theory of war: A critique'. In M. Midlarsky, ed. *Handbook of War Studies*. London: Allen and Unwin.

Levy, Jack. 1998. 'The causes of war and the conditions of peace'. *Annual Review of Political Science*, 1: 139–65.

Lewis, O. 1961. *The Children of Sànchez. Autobiography of a Mexican Family*. New York: Random House.

Li, Hui-Lin. 1969. 'The vegetables of Ancient China'. *Economic Botany*, 23 (3) 253–60.

Li, T.M. 2009. 'To make live or let die? Rural dispossession and the protection of surplus populations'. *Antipode*, 41 (Special Issue, 1) 66–93.

Lichtenstein, Nelson. 2002. *State of the Union: A Century of American Labour*. Princeton, NJ: Princeton University Press.

Lichtenstein, Nelson. 2006. 'Wal-Mart: A template for twenty-first century capitalism'. In N. Lichtenstein, ed. *Wal-Mart: The Face of Twenty-First Century Capitalism*. New York: The New Press.

Lichtenstein, Nelson. 2009. *The Retail Revolution: How Wal-Mart Created a Brave New World of Business*. New York: Metropolitan Books.

Lier, David C. 2007a. 'Overcoming difference, confronting hegemony: The unruly alliances of social movement unionism in Cape Town'. *Politikon: South African Journal of Political Studies*, 34 (1) 35–52.

Lier, David C. 2007b. 'Places of work, scales of organising: A review of labour geography'. *Geography Compass*, 1 (4) 814–33.

Liguori, G. and Voza, P. 2009. *Dizionario Gramsciano 1926–1937*. Rome: Carocci.

Liker, J. 2003. *The Toyota Way: 14 Management Principles from the World's Greatest Manufacturer*. New York: McGraw-Hill.

Lim, Chong Y. 1990. 'The Schumpeterian road to affluence and communism'. *Malaysian Journal of Economic Studies*, 27 (1–2) 213–23.

Lim, Eng-Kiat and Bowles, Dianna. 2012. 'Plant production systems for bioactive small molecules'. *Current Opinion in Biotechnology*, 23: 271–7.

Lim, L.L. 1998. *The Sex Sector: The Economic and Social Bases of Prostitution in Southeast Asia*. Geneva: International Labour Organization.

Lincoln, E. 2001. *Arthritic Japan: The Slow Pace of Economic Reform*. Washington, DC: Brookings Institution.

Ling, Peter J. 1990. *America and the Automobile: Technology, Reform and Social Change*. Manchester: Manchester University Press.

Lipietz, Alain. 1987. *Mirages and Miracles: The Crisis of Global Fordism*. London: Verso.

Lipietz, Alain. 1988. 'Accumulation, crises, and ways out. Some methodological reflections on the concept of "regulation"'. *International Journal of Political Economy*, 18 (2) 10–43.

Lipietz, Alain. 1990. 'The rise and fall of the Golden Age: An historical analysis of post-war capitalism in the developed market economies'. In

S. Marglin and J. Schor, eds. *The Golden Age of Capitalism*. Oxford: Clarendon Press.

Lipietz, Alain. 1992. *Towards a New Economic Order: Postfordism, Ecology and Democracy*. New York: Oxford University Press.

Lipietz, Alain. 1997. 'The post-Fordist world: Labour relations, international hierarchy and global ecology'. *Review of International Political Economy*, 4 (1) 1–41.

Lipietz, Alain. 1998. 'Die politische Ökologie und die Zukunft des Marxismus'. In A. Lipietz, *Nach dem Ende des "Goldenen Zeitalters". Regulation und Transformation Kapitalistischer Gesellschaften*. Hamburg: Argument.

Lipietz, Alain. (n.d.). 'Rebel sons: The Regulation School'. Interview with Jane Jenson. Available at: http://lipietz.net/IMG/article_PDF/article_750.pdf.

Lipschutz, R. 2005. *Globalization, Governmentality and Global Politics: Regulation for the rest of us?* London: Routledge.

Lipsey, Richard, Carlaw, Kenneth I. and Bekar, Clifford T. 2005. *Economic Transformations: General Purpose Technologies and Long Term Economic Growth*. New York: Oxford University Press.

Liston, Barbara. 2013. 'Florida counts on experimental trees to fight orange plague'. Reuters. Available at: http://www.reuters.com/article/2013/10/14/us-usa-citrus-florida-idUSBRE99D0NC20131014.

Litzinger, Ralph A. 2013. 'The labor question in China: Apple and beyond'. *The South Atlantic Quarterly*, 112 (1) 172–8.

Livingston, James. 2009. 'Their great depression and ours'. *Challenge*, 52 (3) 34–51.

Locke, R., Kochan, T., Romis, M. and Qin, F. 2007. 'Beyond corporate codes of conduct: Work organization and labour standards at Nike's suppliers'. *International Labour Review*, 146 (1–2) 21–40.

Locke, Richard M. 2013. *The Promise and Limits of Private Power: Promoting Labor Standards in a Global Economy*. Cambridge: Cambridge University Press.

Locke, R.M. and Romis, M. 2010. 'The promise and perils of private voluntary regulation: Labor standards and work organization in two Mexican garment factories'. *Review of International Political Economy*, 17 (1) 45–74.

Loeppky, Rodney. 2004. 'International restructuring, health and the advanced industrial state'. *New Political Economy*, 9 (4) 493–513.

Loeppky, Rodney. 2005. *Encoding Capital. The Political Economy of the Human Genome Project*. London: Routledge.

Lohmann, L. 2006. 'Carbon Trading: A critical conversation on climate change, privatization and power'. *Development Dialogue*, 48: 1–356.

Longhurst, R. 2012. 'Becoming smaller: Autobiographical spaces of weight loss'. *Antipode*, 44 (3) 871–88.

López, Isidro and Rodríguez, Emmanuel. 2011. 'The Spanish model'. *New Left Review*, 2nd series, 69: 5–29.

Lösch, Andreas. 2006. 'Means of communicating innovations. A case study for the analysis and assessment of nanotechnology's futuristic visions'. *Science, Technology & Innovation Studies*, 2: 103–25.

Losurdo, D. 2011. *Die Sprache des Imperiums: Ein historisch-philosophischer Leitfaden*. Cologne: PapyRossa.

Loth, Wilfried. 1988. *The Division of the World, 1941–1955*. London: Routledge.

Lotman, Y.M. 2001. 'Letter to B.A. Uspenskiy, 19 March 1982'. *Semiosphera* (St. Petersburg: Art-SPb). pp. 683–4.

Louv, Jason. 2013. *Monsanto vs. The World. The Monsanto Protection Act, GMOs and our Genetically Modified Future*. Ultraculture Press.

Low, N. and Gleeson, B. 2000. 'Ecosocialisation and environmental justice'. Paper presented at: Conference of the International Critical Geography Group, 10–13 August. University of Taegu.

Löw, M. and Ruhne, R. 2009. 'Domesticating prostitution: Study of an interactional web of space and gender'. *Space and Culture*, 12 (2) 232–49.

Löwy, Michael. 2013. *La Cage d'acier. Max Weber et le Marxisme Wébérien*. Paris: Stock.

Lu, Bao-Rong and Yang, Chao. 2009. 'Gene flow from genetically modified rice to its wild relatives: Assessing potential ecological consequences'. *Biotechnology Advances*, 21 (27) 1083–91.

Lucas, L. ed. 2005. *Unpacking Globalisation: Markets, Gender and Work*. Kampala: Makerere University Press.

Lüdtke, Alf. 1995. 'Introduction: What is the history of everyday life and who are its practitioners?' In A. Lüdtke, ed. *The History of Everyday Life: Reconstructing Historical Experiences and Ways of Life*. Princeton, NJ: Princeton University Press.

Lukács, Georg. 1971. *History and Class Consciousness: Studies in Marxist Dialectics*. Cambridge, MA: The MIT Press.

Luke, Timothy W. 1996. 'Liberal society and cyborg subjectivity: The politics of environments, bodies, and nature'. *Alternatives*, 21 (1) 1–30.

Luther, Wolfgang ed. 2004. *Industrial Applications of Nanomaterials: Chances and Risks – Technological Analysis*. Düsseldorf: Futures Technologies Division of VDI Technologiezentrum GmbH.

Lüthje, Boy. 2006. 'The changing map of global electronics: Networks of mass production in the new economy'. In Ted Smith, David A. Sonnenfeld and David Naguib Pellow, eds. *Challenging the Chip: Labor*

Rights and Environmental Justice in the Global Electronics Industry. Philadelphia: Temple University Press.

Lüthje, Boy, Hürtgen, Stefanie, Pawlicki, Peter and Sproll, Martina. 2013. *From Silicon Valley to Shenzhen: Global Production and Work in the IT Industry*. Lanham, MD: Rowman and Littlefield.

Macartney, J. 2006. 'China admits social unrest threatens party's iron grip'. *The Times*, p. 49. Available at: http://www.timesonline.co.uk/tol/news/world/asia/article665095.ece.

Macherey, P. 1990. 'Spinoza, la fin de l'histoire et la ruse de la raison'. In E. Curley and P-F. Moreau, eds. *Spinoza: Issues and Directions: The Proceedings of the Chicago Spinoza Conference*. Leiden: E.J. Brill.

Macherey, P. 1997. 'The problem of the attributes'. In W. Montag and T. Stolze, eds. *The New Spinoza*. Minneapolis: University of Minnesota Press.

MacKinnon, Danny, Cumbers, Andrew, Featherstone, David, Ince, Anthony and Strauss, Kendra. 2011. *Globalisation, Labour Markets and Communities in Contemporary Britain*. York: Joseph Rowntree Foundation.

Maddison, Angus. 2001. *The World Economy: A Millennial Perspective*. Paris: OECD Publishing.

Maddison, Angus. 2006. *The World Economy*, 2 Vols. Paris: OECD Publishing.

Madrick, Jeff. 1998. 'Computers: Waiting for the revolution'. *New York Review of Books*, 26 March.

Mahdavi, P. 2010. 'The "Trafficking" of Persians: Labor, migration, and traffic in Dubayy'. *Comparative Studies of South Asia, Africa and the Middle East*, 30 (3) 533–46.

Maito, E. 2013. 'Distribución del ingreso, rotación del capital y niveles rentabilidad en Chile (1964–2009), Japón (1955–2008), Países Bajos (1964–2009) y Estados Unidos (1960–2009)'. *Jornadas de Economia Politica* VI. Available at: https://www.academia.edu/4177784/Maito_Esteban_Ezequiel_-_Distribucion_rotacion_del_capital_y_niveles_de_rentabilidad_en_Chile_Japon_Paises_Bajos_y_Estados_Unidos_1964–2009_.

Majone, Giandomenico. 2001. 'Two logics of delegation: Agency and fiduciary relations in EU governance'. *European Union Politics*, 21: 103–21.

Malenkov, Y.A. 2008. *Strategic Management* [in Russian]. St. Petersburg: Prospekt.

Malenkov, Y.A. 2011. 'Cause–effect models in the strategic planning' [in Russian]. *Vestnik Sankt-Peterburgskogo Universiteta*, 5 (2) 116–29.

Mallorquín, C. 2007. 'The unfamiliar Raúl Prebish'. In E. Pérez and M. Vernego, eds. *Ideas, Policies and Economic Development in the Americas*. London: Routledge.

Mamic, I. 2004. *Business and Code of Conduct Implementation: How Firms use Management Systems for Social Performance*. New York and Geneva: International Labor Organisation.

Man, G. 2007. 'Racialization of gender, work, and transnational migration: The experience of Chinese immigrant women in Canada'. In S. Hier and B. Singh, eds. *Race and Racism in 21st-Century Canada: Continuity, Complexity, and Change*. Peterborough: Broadview Press.

Mandel, Ernest. 1974. *Der Spätkapitalismus. Versuch einer Marxistischen Erklärung*. Frankfurt: Suhrkamp.

Mandel, Ernest. 1975[1972]. *Late Capitalism*. London: New Left Books.

Manderson, L. 1997. 'Migration, prostitution and medical surveillance in early twentieth-century Malaya'. In L. Marks and M. Worboys, eds. *Migrants, Minorities and Health: Historical and Contemporary Studies*. London: Routledge.

Mania, R. and Orioli, A. 1993. *L'accordo di S.Tommaso*. Rome: Ediesse.

Mann, Geoff. 2007. *Our Daily Bread: Wages, Workers and the Political Economy of the American West*. Chapel Hill: The University of North Carolina Press.

Mann, Michael. 1988. *States, Wars and Capitalism*. Malden, MA: Blackwell.

Mansbridge, M. and Morris, A., eds. 2001. *Oppositional Consciousness: The Subjective Roots of Social Protest*. Chicago: Chicago University Press.

Manzo, Kate. 2005. 'Modern slavery, global capitalism and deproletarianisation in West Africa'. *Review of African Political Economy*, 10: 521–34.

Mao, Tse-Tung. 1964[1926, 1927]. 'Analysis of the classes in Chinese society' and 'Report on the investigation of the peasant movement in Hunan'. In *Selected Works of Mao Tse-Tung*, Vol. 1. Peking: Peoples Publishing House.

Marglin, Stephen and Schor, Juliet, eds. 1990. *The Golden Age of Capitalism: Reinterpreting the Postwar Experience*. Oxford: Clarendon Press.

Margulis, Matias E., McKeon, Nora and Borras, Saturnino M. 2013. 'Land grabbing and global governance: Critical perspectives'. *Globalizations*, 10 (1) 1–23.

Mark, J. 1982. 'Measuring productivity in the service industries'. *Monthly Labor Review*, June. Available at: http://www.bls.gov/opub/mlr/1982/06/art1full.pdf.

Marketplace (American Public Media). 2012. 'The people behind your iPad'. 12 April. Available at: http://www.marketplace.org/topics/world/apple-economy/people-behind-your-ipad-bosses.

Markoff, John. 1996. *Waves of Democracy: Social Movements and Political Change*. Thousand Oaks, CA: Pine Forge Press.

Márquez, H. and Delgado Wise, R. 2011a. 'Signos vitales del capitalismo neoliberal: Imperialismo, crisis y transformación social'. *Estudios Críticos del Desarrollo*, 1 (1) 11–50.

Márquez, H. and Delgado Wise, R. 2011b. 'Una perspectiva del sur sobre capital global, migración forzada y desarrollo alternativo'. *Migración y Desarrollo*, 9 (16) 3–42.

Marsh, H. 2013. *Binding Chaos: Mass Collaboration on a Global Scale*. CreateSpace Independent Publishing Platform. Available at: http://georgiebc.wordpress.com/2013/05/24/binding-chaos/.

Marshall, A.J. 2007. *Vilfredo Pareto's Sociology: A Framework for Political Psychology*. Aldershot: Ashgate.

Martin, John P. and Scarpetta, Stefano. 2012. 'Setting it right: Employment protection, labour reallocation and productivity'. *De Economist*, 160 (2) 89–116.

Martin, R. 2000. 'Reading capital for the socializing politics of globalization'. *Environment and Planning D: Society and Space*, 18 (1) 37–51.

Martinez Lucio, M. and Stewart, P. 1997. 'The paradox of contemporary labour process theory: The rediscovery of labour and the disappearance of collectivism'. *Capital and Class*, 62 (2) 49–78.

Martínez, J., Liu, L., Petranovic, D. and Nielsen, J. 2012. 'Pharmaceutical protein production by yeast: Towards production of human blood proteins by microbial fermentation'. *Current Opinion in Biotechnology*, 23: 965–71.

Marx, Karl; see also *MEW* (*Marx–Engels Werke*).

Marx, Karl. *Economic and Philosophical Manuscripts of 1857–1859*, in K. Marx and F. Engels, *Works* [Russian ed.]. Vol. 46, parts 1–2.

Marx, Karl. 1852. *The Eighteenth Brumaire of Louis Bonaparte*. In Karl Marx and Friedrich Engels, Marxists Internet Archive. Available at: http://www.marxists.org/archive/marx/works/1852/18th-brumaire/index.htm.

Marx, Karl. 1962[1867]. *Das Kapital, Kritik der Politischen Ökonomie*, Vol. I. Berlin: Dietz Verlag.

Marx, Karl. 1965[1867] *Capital: A Critique of Political Economy*, Vol. I. Moscow: Progress Publishers.

Marx, Karl. 1969[1865]. *Value, Price and Profit*. New York: International Co.

Marx, Karl. 1971. *Un Chapitre Inédit du Capital* [intro. and trans. R. Dangeville]. Paris: Ed. Générales 10/18.

Marx, Karl. 1973. *Grundrisse, Foundations of the Critique of the Political Economy*. Rough Draft [trans. M. Nicolaus]. Harmondsworth: Penguin.

Marx, Karl. 1976. *Capital: A Critique of Political Economy* [trans. Ben Fowkes]. Vol. I. Harmondsworth: Penguin.

Marx, Karl. 1977. *A Contribution to the Critique of Political Economy*. Moscow: Progress Publishers. Available at: http://www.marxists.org/archive/marx/works/1859/critique-pol-economy/index.htm.

Marx, Karl. 1978. *Capital: A Critique of Political Economy*. Vol. II. London: Penguin.

Marx, Karl. 1979. *Theories of Surplus Value*. Vol. III. London: Lawrence and Wishart.

Marx, Karl. 1981[1894]. *Capital: A Critique of Political Economy*. Vol. III. London: Penguin.

Marx, Karl. 1990[1867]. *Capital: A Critique of Political Economy* [trans. Ben Fowkes]. Vol. I. London: Penguin.

Massey, D. and Pren, K. 2012. 'Origins of the new Latino underclass'. *Race and Social Problems*, 4: 5–17.

Massumi, B. 2002. *Parables for the Virtual: Movement, Affect, Sensation*. Durham, NC: Duke University Press.

Masumura, Takehiro, Morita, Satoshi, Miki, Yoshiyuki, Kurita, Akihiro, Morita, Shigeto, Shirono, Hiroyuki, Koga, Junichi and Tanaka, Kunisuke. 2006. 'Production of biologically active human interferon-a in transgenic rice'. *Plant Biotechnology*, 23: 91–7.

Matusitz, Jonathan and Reyers, Anne. 2010. 'A Behemoth in India: Wal-Mart and glocalisation'. *South Asia Research*, 30: 233–53.

Matusitz, Jonathan and Minei, Elizabeth. 2011. 'Cultural adaptation of an MNC in Mexico: A success story'. *Transitional Studies Review*, 18: 418–29.

Maurin, E. 2004. *Le Ghetto Français*. Paris: Le Seuil.

May, C. 2002. 'The political economy of proximity: Intellectual property and the global division of information labour'. *New Political Economy*, 7 (3) 317–42.

Mayer, F. and Pickles, J. 2011. 'Re-embedding governance: Global apparel value chains and decent work'. Capturing the Gains Working Paper 01, University of Manchester.

Mayer, Frederick and Gereffi, Gary. 2010. 'Regulation and economic globalization: Prospects and limits of private governance'. *Business and Politics*, 12 (3) 1–25.

Mayes, David. 1995. 'Introduction: Conflict and cohesion in the Single European Market: A reflection'. In Ash Amin and John Tomaney, eds. *Behind the Myth of European Union. Prospects for Cohesion*. London: Routledge.

Mazzetti, G. 2012a. *Contro i sacrifici: Governo di Tecnici o Congrega di Maldestri Stregoni?* Trieste: Asterios Editore.

Mazzetti, G. 2012b. *Ancora Keynes?! Miseria o Nuovo Sviluppo?* Trieste: Asterios Editore.

McAffee, Kathleen. 2003. 'Plants, power, and intellectual property in the new global governance regimes'. In Rachel Schurman and Dennis Takahashi Kelso, eds. *Engineering Trouble: Biotechnology and its Discontents*. Berkeley: University of California Press.

McClintock, A. 1995. *Imperial Leather: Race, Gender and Sexuality in the Colonial Contest*. London: Routledge.

McCulloch, R. 1991. 'Why corporations are buying into US business'. *Annals of the American Political Science Association*, 516: 76–90.

McDowell, L., Batnitzy, A. and Dyer, S. 2009. 'Precarious work and economic migration: Emerging immigrant divisions of labour in Greater London's service sector'. *International Journal of Urban and Regional Research*, 33: 3–25.

McGrath, Siobhán. 2013a. 'Many chains to break: The multi-dimensional concept of slave labour in Brazil'. *Antipode*, 45 (4) 1005–28.

McGrath, Siobhán. 2013b. 'Fuelling global production networks with slave labour? Migrant sugar cane workers in the Brazilian ethanol GPN'. *Geoforum*, 44: 32–43.

McGrath-Champ, S., Herod, A. and Rainnie, A., eds. 2010. *Handbook of Employment and Society: Working Space*. Cheltenham, UK and Northampton, MA, USA: Edward Elgar Publishing.

McInerney, Claire and LeFevre, Darcy. 2000. 'Knowledge managers: History and challenges'. In C. Prichard, R. Hull, M. Chumer and H. Willmott, eds. *Managing Knowledge. Critical Investigations of Work and Learning*. Basingstoke: Macmillan.

McIntyre, R. 2007. 'The perplexities of worker rights'. *The Good Society*, 16 (2) 49–56.

McIntyre, R. 2008. *Are Worker Rights Human Rights?* Ann Arbor: University of Michigan Press.

McKay, Steven C. 2006. *Satanic Mills or Silicon Islands? The Politics of High-Tech Production in the Philippines*. Ithaca, NY: Cornell University Press.

McKeown, A. 2012. 'How the box became black: Brokers and the creation of the free migrant'. *Pacific Affairs*, 83 (1) 21–45.

McKinsey and Company. 2008. *Mapping Global Capital Markets*. Fourth Annual Report, McKinsey Global Institute, January. Available at: http://www.mckinsey.com/mgi/reports/pdfs/Mapping_Global/MGI_Mapping_Global_full_Report.pdf.

McKinsey Global Institute. 2012. *The World at Work: Jobs, Pay, and Skills for 3.5 billion People*. McKinsey and Co. June. Available at: http://www.mckinsey.com/insights/employment_and_growth/the_world_at_work.

McMichael, Philip. 2009. 'Food sovereignty, social reproduction and the agrarian question'. In A.H. Akram-Lodhi and C. Kay. *Peasants and Globalization. Political Economy, Rural Transformation and the Agrarian Question*. London: Routledge.

McMichael, Philip. 2012. 'Food regime crisis and revaluing the agrarian question. Rethinking agricultural regimes'. In R. Almas and H. Campbell, eds. *Research in Rural Sociology and Development*. London: Emerald.

McMichael, Philip. 2013a. *Food Regimes and Agrarian Questions*. Halifax: Fernwood.

McMichael, Philip. 2013b. 'Historicizing food sovereignty: A food regime perspective'. Paper presented at *Food Sovereignty: A Critical Dialogue*. International Conference. 14–15 September, Yale University. Available at: http://www.yale.edu/agrarianstudies/foodsovereignty/papers.html.

McMichael, Philip. 2013c. 'Value-chain agriculture and debt relations: Contradictory outcomes'. *Third World Quarterly*, 34 (4) 671–90.

McNeill, William. 1982. *The Pursuit of Power: Technology, Armed Force and Society Since A.D. 1000*. Chicago: University of Chicago Press.

McShane, Clay. 1994. *Down the Asphalt Path: The Automobile and the American City*. New York: Columbia University Press.

Meadows, Donella H., Meadows, Dennis L., Randers, Jørgen and Behrens, William W. 1972. *The Limits to Growth. A Report for the Club of Rome's Project on the Predicament of Mankind*. New York: New American Library.

Meadows, Donella H., Randers, Jorgen and Meadows, Dennis L. 2004. *Limits to Growth: The 30-Year Update*. White River Junction, VT: Chelsea Green Publishing Company.

Meek, Ronald. 1972[1956]. 'The marginal revolution and its aftermath'. In E.K. Hunt and Jesse G. Schwartz, eds. *A Critique of Economic Theory*. Harmondsworth: Penguin.

Meeus, Marius. 1989. *Wat Betekent Arbeid? Over het ontstaan van de Westerse Arbeidsmoraal*. Assen: Van Gorcum.

Melamed, L. 1992. *Leo Melamed on the Markets*. New York: Wiley.

Mendel, Gregor. 1865. 'Experiments in plant hybridization'. In *Brünn Natural History Society Meetings*, 8 February and 8 March.

Merez, S. 2008. 'Germ form theory: Peer production in historic perspective'. Available at: http://oekonux.org/texts/GermFormTheory.html#the-historic-potential-of-peer-production.

Merk, Jeroen. 2004. 'Regulating the global athletic footwear industry: The collective worker in the product chain'. In K. van der Pijl, L. Assassi and D. Wigan, eds. *Global Regulation: Managing Crises After the Imperial Turn*. Basingstoke: Palgrave Macmillan.

Merk, Jeroen. 2007. 'The private regulation of labour standards: The case of the apparel and footwear industries'. In J-C. Graz and A. Nölke, eds. *Transnational Private Governance and its Limits*. Oxford: Blackwell.

Merk, Jeroen. 2008. 'Restructuring and conflict in the global athletic footwear industry: Nike, Yue Yuen and labour codes of conduct'. In M. Taylor, ed. *Global Economy Contested: Finance, Production and the International Division of Labour*. New York: Routledge.

Merk, Jeroen. 2009. 'Jumping scale and bridging space in the era of corporate social responsibility: Cross-border labour struggles in the global garment industry'. *Third World Quarterly*, 30 (3) 599–615.

Merk, Jeroen. 2011. 'Production beyond the horizon of consumption: Spatial fixes and anti-sweatshop struggles in the global athletic footwear industry'. *Global Society*, 25 (1) 71–93.

Metscher, Th. 2009. *Imperialismus und Moderne*. Essen: Neue Impulse.

MEW: Marx–Engels Werke. 35 vols. Berlin: Dietz, 1956–71. Vols. 23–25 contain *Capital*, I–III.

Michelini, L. 2008. *La Fine del Liberismo di Sinistra*. Florence: Il Ponte Editore.

Milberg, W. and Winkler, D. 2010. 'Economic and social upgrading in global production networks: Problems of theory and measurement'. 'Capturing the Gains' Working Paper, University of Manchester.

Miles, Robert. 1987. *Capitalism and Unfree Labour: Anomaly or Necessity*. London: Tavistock.

Milios, John and Sotiropoulos, Dimitris P. 2009. *Rethinking Imperialism. A Study of Capitalist Rule*. Basingstoke: Palgrave Macmillan.

Millán, J., Congregado, E. and Concepción, C. 2010. 'Employers vs. own-account workers: Success and failure'. Available at: http://www.uhu.es/emilio.congregado/materiales/employerspersistence.pdf.

Miller, Doug. 2009. 'Business as usual? Governing the supply chain in clothing – post MFA phase-out: The case of Cambodia'. *International Journal of Labour Research*, 1 (1) 9–33.

Miller, Doug. 2013. 'Towards sustainable labour costing in the UK fashion retail: Some evidence from UK fashion retail'. Social Science Research Network, University of Northumbria at Newcastle, February.

Miller, J. 2005. 'Commodity fetishism: A concept for organizing against sweatshop labor and neoliberal globalization'. Paper presented at Union for Radical Political Economics Summer Workshop. Available at: http://mrzine.monthlyreview.org/2005/miller121105.html.

Milling and Baking News. 1999. 'Five largest US supermarkets now account for 40% of industry sales'. 7 September, 12.

Milzner, G. 2010. *Die Amerikanische Krankheit. Amoklauf als Symptom einer Zerbrechenden Gesellschaft*. Gütersloh: Bertelsmann.

Minor, M. 1994. 'The demise of expropriation as an instrument of LDC policy, 1980–1992'. *Journal of International Business Studies*, 25 (1) 177–88.

Mitchell, Katharyne, Marston, Sallie A. and Katz, Cindi. 2004. 'Life's work: An introduction, review and critique'. In K. Mitchell, S.A. Marston and C. Katz, eds. *Life's Work: Geographies of Social Reproduction*. Oxford: Blackwell.

Miyamura, S. 2012. 'Emerging consensus on labour market institutions and implications for developing countries: From the debates in India'. *Forum for Social Economics*, 41 (1) 97–123.

Mol, Arthur. 1996. 'Ecological modernisation and institutional reflexivity: Environmental reform in the late modern age'. *Environmental Politics*, 5 (2) 302–23.

Mol, Arthur, Sonnenfeld, David and Spaargaren, Gert, eds. 2009. *The Ecological Modernisation Reader. Environmental Reform, Theory and Practice*. London: Routledge.

Molina, Antonio. 2010. 'Plant biotechnology. Editorial overview'. *Current Opinion in Biotechnology*, 21: 182–4.

Molloy, S. 2013. 'Spinoza, Carr and the ethics of *The Twenty Years' Crisis*'. *Review of International Studies*, 39 (2) 251–72.

Molot, Maureen, ed. 1993. *Driving Continentally: National Policies and the North American Auto Industry*. Ottawa: Carleton University Press.

Monden, Y. 1983. *Toyota Production System: Practical Approach to Production Management*. Norcross, GA: Industrial Engineering and Management Press.

Moody, Kim. 1997. *Workers in a Lean World: Unions in the International Economy*. London: Verso.

Moon, K.H.S. 1997. *Sex among Allies: Military Prostitution in US.–Korea Relations*. New York: Columbia University Press.

Moore, Phoebe. 2005. 'Revolutions from above: Worker training as *Trasformismo* in South Korea'. *Capital and Class*, 86: 39–72.

Moore, Phoebe. 2006. 'Global knowledge capitalism, self-woven safety nets, and the crisis of employability'. *Global Society*, 20 (4) 453–73.

Moore, Phoebe. 2007. *Globalisation and Labour Struggle in Asia: A Neo-Gramscian Critique of South Korea's Political Economy*. London: I.B. Tauris.

Moore, Phoebe. 2009. 'UK education, employability, and everyday life'. *Journal of Critical Education Policy Studies*, 7 (1) 243–73.

Moore, Phoebe. 2010. *The International Political Economy of Work and Employability*. Basingstoke: Palgrave Macmillan.

Moore, Phoebe. 2011. 'Subjectivity in the ecologies of P2P production'

The Journal of Fibreculture FCJ-119. Available at: http://seventeen.fibreculturejournal.org/fcj-119-peer-to-peer-production-a-revolutionary-or-neoliberal-mode-of-subjectivation/.

Moore, Phoebe. 2012. 'Where is the study of work in critical International Political Economy?' *International Politics*, 49 (2) 215–37.

Moore, Phoebe and Taylor, P.A. 2009. 'Exploitation of the self in community-based software production: Workers' freedoms or firm foundations?' *Capital and Class*, 97: 99–120.

Moran, M. 1994. 'The state and the financial services revolution: A comparative analysis'. *West European Politics*, 17 (3) 158–77.

Morange, Michel. 2009. 'A critical perspective on synthetic biology'. *HYLE: International Journal for Philosophy of Chemistry*, 15 (1) 21–30.

Morell, M.F. 2009. 'Politics of technology and participation at the Social Forum Process'. Paper presented at the 5th General Conference of ECPR, University of Potsdam, 9–12 September.

Morell, M.F. 2010. 'Participation in online creation communities: Ecosystemic participation?' In S.W. Shulman and C.M. Schweik, eds. *Conference Proceedings of JITP 2010: The Politics of Open Source*. Available at: http://scholarworks.umass.edu/jitpc2010/1.

Morell, M.F. 2012. 'Composition of 15M mobilization in Spain: Free culture movement a layer of 15M ecosystem movement', *Social Movement Studies: Journal of Social, Cultural and Political Protest* (Occupy! special issue) 11 (3–4) 386–92.

Moretti, E. 2013. *The New Geography of Jobs*. Boston: Mariner Books.

Morgan, J. 2008. 'China's growing pains: Towards the (global) political economy of domestic social instability'. *International Politics*, 45 (4) 413–38.

Morgan, Michael L. 2002. *Spinoza, Complete Works*. [trans. S. Shirley]. Indianapolis: Hackett.

Moriguchi, C. and Ono, H. 2006. 'Japanese lifetime employment: A century's perspective'. In M. Blomstroem and S. La Croix, eds. *Institutional Change in Japan*. Abingdon: Routledge.

Morris-Suzuki, T. 1984. 'Robots and capitalism'. *New Left Review*, 147: 109–21.

Morton, Adam David. 2010. 'Reflections on uneven development: Mexican revolution, primitive accumulation, passive revolution'. *Latin American Perspectives*, 37 (1) 7–34.

Mosco, V. and McKercher, C. 2008. *The Labouring of Communication: Will Knowledge Workers of the World Unite?* Lanham: Lexington Books.

Mosco, V., McKercher, C. and Huw, U. eds. 2010. 'Getting the Message: Communications Workers and Global Value Chains'. Theme issue, 4 (2) of *Work, Organisation, Labour and Globalisation*.

Moseley, Fred. 1995. 'Capital in general and Marx's logical method: A response to Heinrich's critique'. *Capital and Class*, 56: 15–48.
Moulian, Tomás. 2006. *Fracturas: De Pedro Aguirre Cerda a Salvador Allende 1938–1973*. Santiago: LOM Ediciones.
Moulian, Tomás. 2009. *Contradicciones del Desarrollo Político Chileno: 1920–1990*. Santiago: LOM Ediciones.
Mountz, A. 2003. 'Human smuggling, the transnational imaginary, and everyday geographies of the nation-state'. *Antipode*, 35 (3) 622–44.
Moxton, Graeme and Wormald, John. 1995. *Driving over a Cliff? Business Lessons from the World's Car Industry*. Reading, MA: Addison-Wesley.
Munck, R. 2000. 'Dependency and imperialism in Latin America'. In R. Chilcote, ed. *The Political Economy of Imperialism*. Lanham, MD: Rowman and Littlefield.
Munck, R. 2002. *Globalisation and Labour: The New Great Transformation*. London: Zed Books.
Munck, R. 2008. 'Globalisation, governance and migration: An introduction'. *Third World Quarterly*, 29 (7) 1227–46.
Murphy, Craig and Yates, JoAnne. 2009. *The International Organization for Standardization ISO: Global Governance through Voluntary Consensus*. London: Routledge.
Murphy, Denis J. 2007. *Plant Breeding and Biotechnology: Societal Context and the Future of Agriculture*. Cambridge: Cambridge University Press.
Murphy, Hannah. 2013. 'The World Bank and core labour standards: Between flexibility and regulation'. *Review of International Political Economy*, 21 (2) 399–431.
Murray, C. 1997. 'The underclass revisited'. *American Enterprise Institute: Papers and Studies*. Available at: www.aei.org/ps/psmurry.
Nadvi, K. and Wältring, F. 2002. 'Making sense of global standards'. *INEF Report No 58*. Duisburg: Institut für Entwicklung und Frieden der Gerhard-Mercator-Universität Duisburg.
Nash, J. and Kelly, P.F. eds. 1983. *Women, Men, and the International Division of Labor*. Albany: State University of New York Press.
Nasr, V. 2000. 'International politics, domestic imperatives, and identity mobilization: Sectarianism in Pakistan, 1979–1988'. *Comparative Politics*, 32 (2) 171–90.
National Science Board. 2012. *Science and Engineering Indicators Digest*. Arlington: The National Science Board.
National Science Foundation. 2010. *Science and Engineering Indicators 2010*. Washington, DC: NSF.
Nature Biotechnology. 2006. 'Consequences' (Editorial), 24 (4) 368.
Nazer, Mende and Lewis, Damien. 2005. *Slave: My True Story*. New York: Public Affairs.

Ndjio, B. 2009. 'Shanghai beauties and African desires: Migration, trade and Chinese prostitution in Cameroon'. *European Journal of Development Research*, 21 (4) 606–21.

Neckel, S. and Wagner, G. 2013. *Leistung und Erschöpfung: Burnout in der Wettbewerbsgesellschaft*. Berlin: Suhrkamp.

Nederveen Pieterse, J. 2002. 'Globalization, kitsch and conflict: Technologies of work, war and politics'. *Review of International Political Economy*, 9 (1) 1–36.

Negrelli, S. 2000. 'Social pacts in Italy and Europe: Similar strategies and structures: Different models and national stories'. In G. Fajertag and P. Pochet, eds. *Social Pacts in Europe – New Dynamics*. Brussels: European Trade Union Institute.

Negri, A. 1991. *The Savage Anomaly: The Power of Spinoza's Metaphysics and Politics*. Minneapolis: University of Minnesota Press.

Negri, A. 1999. 'Value and affect'. *Boundary 2*, 26 (2) 77–88.

Negri, A. 2001. *Kairos, Alma Venus, Multitude: Neuf Leçons en Forme d'exercices*. Paris: Calmann-Lévy.

Negri, A. 2002. 'Approximations: Towards an ontological definition of the multitude' ['Pour une définition ontologique de la multitude', trans. A. Bove]. *Multitudes*, 9: 36–48.

Negt, O. 1997. 'Machtpolitischher Kampfplatz zweier "Ökonomien"'. In Loccumer Initiative, ed. *Ökonomie ohne Arbeit – Arbeit ohne Ökonomie?* [preface P. von Oertzen and J. Perels]. Hannover: Offizin Verlag.

Negt, O. 2001. *Arbeit und Menschliche Würde*. Göttingen: Steidl.

Neilson, Jeffrey and Pritchard, Bill. 2007. 'The final frontier? The global roll-out of the retail revolution in India'. In D. Burch and G. Lawrence, ed. *Supermarkets and Agri-food Supply Chains*. Cheltenham, UK and Northampton, MA, USA: Edward Elgar Publishing.

NESTA. 2014. 'How big are the UK's creative industries?' NESTA blog, 14 February. Available at: http://www.nesta.org.uk/blog/how-big-are-uk%E2%80%99s-creative-industries-part-3.

Neugebauer, G. 2007. *Politische Milieus in Deutschland*. Bonn: Dietz.

Newbery, M. 2003. 'A study of the UK designer fashion sector'. DTI. Available at: http://webarchive.nationalarchives.gov.uk/+/http://www.dti.gov.uk/support/textiles/pdfs/designer.pdf.

Newell, Peter. 2012. *Globalization and the Environment: Capitalism, Ecology and Power*. Cambridge: Polity.

Newell, Peter and Paterson, Matthew. 2010. *Climate Capitalism: Global Warming and the Transformation of the Global Economy*. Cambridge: Cambridge University Press.

Nichiporuk, B. 2000. *The Security Dynamics of Demographic Factors*. Santa Monica, CA: The Rand Corporation.

Nike. 2005. *Nike's 2004 CSR Report*. Available at: Http://www.nikebiz.com/responsibility/documents/Nike_FY04_CR_report.pdf.

Nitzan, Jonathan and Bichler, Shimshon. 2000. 'Capital accumulation: Breaking the dualism of "economic" and "politics"'. In R. Palan, ed. *Global Political Economy: Contemporary Theories*. London: Routledge.

Nitzan, Jonathan and Bichler, Shimshon. 2009. *Capital as Power: A Study of Order and Creorder*. New York: Routledge.

Nomura, M. 2004. 'A critical analysis of Koike Kazuo's skill theory'. In M. Nomura and Y. Kamii, eds. *Japanese Companies: Theories and Realities*. Melbourne: Trans Pacific Press.

Nonaka, I. and Konno, N. 1998. 'The Concept of "*Ba*": Building a foundation for knowledge creation'. *California Management Review*, 40 (3) 40–55.

Nonaka, I. and Takeuchi, H. 1995. *The Knowledge-Creating Company: How Japanese Companies Create the Dynamics of Innovation*. New York: Oxford University Press.

Norman, Al. 2007. 'Hey, we cut Wal-Mart in half!' *Huffington Post*. Online edn. Available at: http://www.huffingtonpost.com/al-norman/hey-we-cut-Wal-Mart-in-hal_b_69834.html.

North, Douglass. 1995. 'The New Institutional Economics and third world development'. In J. Hariss, J. Hunter and C. Lewis, eds. *The New Institutional Economics and Third World Development*. London: Routledge.

Nowack, I. 2007. 'Von mutigen Männern und erfolgreichen Frauen. Work–Life-Balance in prekarisierten Verhältnissen'. In Ch. Kaindl, ed. *Subjekte im Neoliberalismus*. Marburg: BdWi.

NSET/ NSTC. 2003. 'The National Nanotechnology Initiative. Research and Development Supporting the next Industrial Revolution. Supplement to the President's FY 2004 Budget'. Arlington: National Nanotechnology Coordination Office.

NSTC/ NSET. 2013. 'The National Nanotechnology Initiative. Supplement to the President's 2014 Budget'. Available at: http://www.whitehouse.gov/sites/default/files/microsites/ostp/nni_fy14_budgetsup.pdf.

Nugent, J.P. 2011. 'Changing the climate: Ecoliberalism, green new dealism, and the struggle over green jobs in Canada'. *Labor Studies Journal*, 36 (1) 58–82.

O'Connell Davidson, Julia. 2010. 'New slavery, old binaries: Human trafficking and the borders of "freedom"'. *Global Networks*, 10 (2) 244–61.

O'Connor, James. (1991). 'On the two contradictions of capitalism'. *Capitalism, Nature, Socialism*, 2 (3) 107–109.

O'Connor, K. 2013. 'Interview with Dmytri Kleiner'. Available at: http://c-realm.blogspot.nl/2013/12/interview-with-dmytri-kleiner-venture.html.

O'Neill, W.M. 1968. *The Beginnings of Modern Psychology*. Harmondsworth: Penguin.

OECD. n.d. International Trade Balance. Available at: http://stats.oecd.org/index.aspx?queryid=166.

OECD. 1973. *Manpower Policy in Japan*. Paris: OECD.

OECD. 2000. *The Service Economy*. Paris: OECD, Directorate for Science, Technology and Industry.

OECD. 2008. *Open Innovation in Global Networks*. Copenhagen: OECD. Available at: http://www.oecd.org/sti/openinnovationinglobalnetworks.htm.

OECD. 2011. *Towards Green Growth*. Paris: OECD.

OECD. 2013. 'Protecting jobs, enhancing flexibility: A new look at employment protection legislation'. In *OECD Employment Outlook 2013*. Paris: OECD.

Ogasawara, Y. 1998. *Office Ladies and Salaried Men: Power, Gender, and Work in Japanese Companies*. Berkeley, CA: University of California Press.

Ohno, T. 1988. *Toyota Production System: Beyond Large-Scale Production*. New York: Productivity Press.

Olegrio, R. 1997. 'IBM and the two Thomas J Watsons'. In T. McCraw, ed. *Creating Modern Capitalism: How Entrepreneurs, Companies, and Countries Triumphed in Three Industrial Revolutions*. Cambridge, MA: Harvard University Press.

Olive, David. 2004. 'Hitting the wall'. *Toronto Star*, 29 August, E1.

Oliveira, G. 2011. 'Land regularization in Brazil and the global land grab: A statemaking framework for analysis'. *International Conference on Global Land Grabbing*. University of Sussex, Brighton: LDPI.

Ong, A. 1987. *Spirits of Resistance and Capitalist Discipline: Factory Women in Malaysia*. Albany: State University of New York Press.

Onuki, H. 2009. 'Care, social reproduction and global labour migration: Japan's "special gift" toward "innately gifted" Filipino workers'. *New Political Economy*, 14 (4) 489–516.

Orhangazi, O. 2008. *Financialization and the US Economy*. Cheltenham, UK and Northampton, MA, USA: Edward Elgar Publishing.

Ortega, Luiz, Norambuena, Carmen, Pinto, Julio and Bravo, Guillermo. 1989. *Corporación de Fomento de la Producción: 50 años de realizaciones 1939–1989*. Santiago: Departamento de Historia, Facultad de Humanidades, Universidad de Santiago de Chile.

Ortiz, Carlos. 2010. *Private Armed Forces and Global Security*. Santa Barbara, CA: Praeger.

Orzeck, R. 2007. 'What does not kill you: Historical materialism and the body'. *Environment and Planning D: Society and Space*, 25(3) 496–514.

Osipov, G., Sadovnichiy, V. and Yakunin, V. 2013. *Integrative Eurasian Infrastructural System as the Priority of National Country Development* [in Russian]. Moscow: ISPI RAN.

Ossendorff, K. 2011. 'Die Situation Hartz-IV-Betroffener im Neoliberalismus'. In B. Wiebel, A. Pilenko and G. Nintemann, eds. *Mechanismen Psycho-sozialer Zerstörung. Neoliberales Herrschaftsdenken, Stressfaktoren der Prekarität, Widerstand.* Hamburg: VSA.

Otero, Gerardo. 2008. *Food for the Few: Neoliberal Globalism and Biotechnologies in Latin America.* Austin: University of Texas Press.

Ouchi, W. 1981. *Theory Z: How American Business Can Meet the Japanese Challenge.* Reading, MA: Addison-Wesley.

Overbeek, Henk, ed. 2003. *The Political Economy of European Employment. European Integration and the Transnationalization of the Unemployment Question.* London: Routledge.

Oxfam International. 1999. *Oxfam International Submission to the Heavily Indebted Poor Country (HIPC) Debt Review.* Available at: http://policy-practice.oxfam.org.uk/publications/oxfam-international-submission-to-the-heavily-indebted-poor-county-hipc-debt-re-114964.

Packer, George. 2011. 'The broken contract. Inequality and American decline'. *Foreign Affairs*, 90 (6) 20–31.

Paczynska, A. 2007. 'Confronting change: Labor, state, and privatization'. *Review of International Political Economy*, 14 (2) 333–56.

Page, W., Carey, Chris, Haskel, Jonathan and Goodridge, Peter. 2011. 'Wallet share'. *Economic Insight*, 22, 18 April. Available at: http://prsformusic.com/creators/news/research/Documents/Economic%20Insight%2022%20Wallet%20Share.pdf.

Paggi, L. 2003. 'La strategia liberale della seconda repubblica. Dalla crisi del PCI alla formazione di una destra di governo'. In F. Malgeri and L. Paggi, eds. *L'Italia Repubblicana nella Crisi degli Anni Settanta. Partiti e Organizzazioni di Massa.* Soveria Mannelli: Rubbettino e Editore.

Paggi, L. and D'Angelillo, M. 1986. *I Comunisti Italiani e il Riformismo.* Turin: Einaudi.

Palan, Ronen. 2003. *The Offshore World. Sovereign Markets, Virtual Places, and Nomad Millionaires.* Ithaca, NY: Cornell University Press.

Palan, Ronen and Abbott, Jason. 1996. *State Strategies in the Global Political Economy* [with Phil Deans]. New York: Pinter.

Palloix, Christian. 1976. 'The labour process: From Fordism to neo-Fordism'. In R. Panzieri, A. Sohn-Rethel, C. Palloix, S. Bologna and M. Tronti. *The Labour Process and Class Strategies.* London: CSE.

Palma, Gabriel. 2000a. 'Trying to "tax and spend" oneself out of the "Dutch Disease": The Chilean economy from the war of the Pacific to the Great Depression'. In E. Cárdenas, J.A. Ocampo and R. Thorp, eds. *An Economic History of Twentieth Century Latin America*. Vol. 1. *The Export Age: The Latin American Economies in the Late Nineteenth and Early Twentieth Centuries*. Basingstoke: Palgrave.

Palma, Gabriel. 2000b. 'From an export-led to an import-substituting economy: Chile 1914–1939'. In R. Thorp, ed. *An Economic History of Twentieth Century Latin America*, Vol. 2. *Latin America in the 1930s: The Role of the Periphery in the Crisis*. Basingstoke: Palgrave.

Palpacuer, F. 2008. 'Bringing the social context back in'. *Economy and Society*, 37 (3) 393–419.

Panitch, Leo and Gindin, Sam. 2012. *The Making of Global Capitalism: The Political Economy of American Empire*. London: Verso.

Pantland, W. 2014. 'Karl Marx on Facebook: What is the ideology of your social network?'. Available at: https://cyberunions.org/every-social-network-has-an-ideology/.

Parker, M. and Slaughter, J. 1988. *Choosing Sides: Unions and the Team Concept*. Boston: South End Press.

Parreñas, R.S. 2001. *Servants of Globalization: Women, Migration and Domestic Work*. Stanford: Stanford University Press.

Parry, Brownwyn. 2004. *Trading the Genome: Investigating the Commodification of Bio-information*. New York: Columbia University Press.

Parthasarathi, A. 2002. 'Tackling the brain drain from India's information and communication technology sector: The need for a new industrial, and science and technology strategy'. *Science and Public Policy*, 29 (2) 129–36.

Partnership for a New American Economy. 2012. 'Patent pending. How immigrants are reinventing the American economy'. Report from the partnership for a new American economy. Available at: http://www.renewoureconomy.org/patent-pending.

Pascale, R. and Athos, A. 1981. *The Art of Japanese Management*. New York: Simon and Schuster.

Pasquinelli, M. 2014. 'Italian Operaismo and the Information Machine'. *Theory, Culture & Society* (forthcoming).

Patel, R. 2007. *Stuffed and Starved: Markets, Power and the Hidden Battle for the World Food System*. London: Portobello.

Pateman, Carol. 1988. *The Sexual Contract*. Stanford, CA: Stanford University Press.

Paterson, Matthew. 2000. *Understanding Global Environmental Politics: Domination, Accumulation, Resistance*. Basingstoke: Palgrave Macmillan.

Paterson, Matthew. 2007. *Automobile Politics: Ecology and Cultural Political Economy*. Cambridge: Cambridge University Press.

Paterson, Matthew. 2010. 'Legitimation and accumulation in climate change governance'. *New Political Economy*, 15 (3) 345–68.

Patomäki, H. 2003. 'Problems of democratizing global governance: Time, space and the emancipatory process'. *European Journal of International Relations*, 9 (3) 347–76.

Payne, P.G. and Wattchow, B. 2009. 'Phenomenological deconstruction, slow pedagogy, and the corporeal turn in wild environmental/outdoor education'. *Canadian Journal of Environmental Education*, 14 (1) 15–32.

Paz, Andre de, Nunes, Rodrigo, Padula, Raphael and Wexell Severo, Luciano. 2011. *Americo do Sul. Integracao e infrastructure*. [Organizacao Darc Costa]. Rio de Janeiro: Capax Dei.

PCAST. 2012. 'Report to the President and Congress on the Fourth Assessment of the National Nanotechnology Initiative'. Available at: http://www.whitehouse.gov/sites/default/files/microsites/ostp/PCAST_2012_Nanotechnology_FINAL.pdf.

Pearse, A.C. 1980. *Seeds of Plenty, Seeds of Want: Social and Economic Implications of the Green Revolution*. Oxford: Clarendon Press for United Nations Research Institute for Social Development.

Pechlander, Gabriela and Otero, Gerardo. 2008. 'The third food regime: Neoliberal globalism and agricultural biotechnology in North America'. *Sociologia Ruralis*, 48 (4) 351–71.

Peluso, Nancy Lee and Lund, Christian. 2012. 'New frontiers of land control: Introduction'. *The Journal of Peasant Studies*, 39 (2) 667–81.

Penttinen, E. 2007. *Globalization, Prostitution and Sex Trafficking: Corporeal Politics*. New York: Routledge.

Peoples, J. and Sugden, R. 2000. 'Divide and rule by transnational corporations'. In C. Pitelis and R. Sugden, eds. *The Nature of the Transnational Firm*. London: Routledge.

Peplow, Mark. 2013. 'Malaria drug made in yeast causes market ferment. Synthetic biology delivers combination therapies into an uncertain market'. *Nature*, 494: 160.

Perez, Carlota. 2002. *Technological Revolution and Financial Capital: The Dynamic of Bubbles and Golden Ages*. Cheltenham, UK and Northampton, MA, USA: Edward Elgar Publishing.

Perez, Carlota. 2006. 'Re-specialisation and the deployment of the ICT Paradigm'. In 'The future of the information society in Europe: Contributions to the debate', European Commission: IPTS-DG JRC. Available at: http://www.carlotaperez.org/downloads/pubs/Perez%20Respecialisation%20in%20IPTS%20book,%20EU%20Sevilla%202006.pdf.

Perrons, D. 2004. *Globalization and Social Change: People and Placed in a Divided World*. London: Routledge.

Peters, T. and Waterman, R. 1982. *In Search of Excellence: Lessons from America's Best-Run Companies*. New York: Harper and Row.

Peterson, S.V. 1996. 'Shifting grounds: Epistemological and territorial remapping in the context of globalization'. In E. Kofman and G. Youngs, eds. *Globalization: Theory and Practice*. London: Continuum.

Petit, P. 1987. 'Services'. *The New Palgrave: A Dictionary of Economics*, Vol. 4. New York: Palgrave Macmillan, 314–15.

Phillips, Nicola. 2013. 'Unfree labour and adverse incorporation in the global economy: Comparative perspectives on Brazil and India'. *Economy and Society*, 42 (2) 171–96.

Phillips, Nicola and Sakamoto, Leonardo Moretti. 2012. 'Global production networks, chronic poverty and "slave labour" in Brazil'. *Studies in Comparative International Development*, 47 (3) 287–315.

Picchio, Antonella. 1992. *Social Reproduction: The Political Economy of the Labour Market*. Cambridge: Cambridge University Press.

Pick, Adam. 2006. 'Foxconn takes number one rank in EMS [Electronics Manufacturing Services]'. iSuppli. 30 May. Available at: http://www.emsnow.com/npps/story.cfm?ID=19523.

Pierce, S. 2004. 'Prostitution, politics, and paradigms'. *Journal of Colonialism and Colonial History*, 5 (3) 230–46.

Pink, D. 2011. *Drive: The Surprising Truth about What Motivates Us*. New York: Riverhead Books.

Pinto, A. 1945. 'Anotaciones sobre los efectos de guerra en nuestra economía'. *Principios*, 49: 7–20.

Piore, M. and Sabel, C. 1984. *The Second Industrial Divide: Possibilities for Prosperity*. New York: Basic Books.

Pizarro, Cristosomo. 1986. *La Huelga Obrera en Chile, 1890–1970*. Santiago: Ediciones Sur.

Plehwe, Dieter, Neunhöffer, Gisela and Walpen, Bernhard, eds. 2006. *Neoliberal Hegemony. A Global Critique*. London: Routledge.

Plucknett, D.L. and Smith, N.G.H. 1986. 'Historical perspectives on multiple cropping'. In C.A. Francis, ed. *Multiple Cropping Systems*. New York: Macmillan.

Polanyi, Karl. 1957[1944]. *The Great Transformation. The Political and Economic Origins of Our Time*. Boston: Beacon.

Polaski, S. 2003. 'Protecting labour rights through trade agreements: An analytical guide'. *Journal of International Law and Policy*, 10: 13–25.

Pór, G. 2008. 'Collective intelligence and collective leadership: Twin paths to beyond chaos'. Sprouts: Working Papers on Information Systems. University of Amsterdam, Netherlands. Available at: http://sprouts.aisnet.org/8-2.

Porter, M., Takeuchi, H. and Sakakibara, M. 2000. *Can Japan Compete?* Basingstoke: Macmillan.

Porter, Michael E. 1980. *Competitive Strategy*. New York: Free Press.

Porter, Tony. 2004. 'Private authority, technical authority, and the globalisation of accounting standards'. Paper presented at Inaugural Workshop of the Amsterdam Research Centre for Corporate Governance Regulation. Department of Political Science, Vrije Universiteit, Amsterdam.

Portes, A., Castells, M. and Benton, L. 1989. *The Informal Economy: Studies in Advanced and Less Developed Countries*. Baltimore: Johns Hopkins University Press.

Postone, M. 1996. *Time, Labor, and Social Domination; A Reinterpretation of Marx's Critical Theory*. Cambridge: Cambridge University Press.

Poulantzas, Nicos. 1973 [1971]. *Political Power and Social Classes*. London: Sheed and Ward.

Poulantzas, Nicos. 1978. *State, Power, Socialism*. London: New Left Books.

Prasso, S. 2005. *The Asian Mystique: Dragon Ladies, Geisha Girls, and Our Fantasies of the Exotic Orient*. New York: Public Affairs.

Pratt, A.C. 2006. 'Advertising and creativity, a governance approach: A case study of creative agencies'. *Environment and Planning A*, 38 (10) 1883–99.

Pratt, M.L. 2008. *Imperial Eyes: Travel Writing and Transculturation*. New York: Routledge.

Prebisch, R. 1986[1950]. 'El desarrollo económico en América Latina y alguno de sus principales problemas'. *Desarrollo Económico*, 26 (103) 479–502.

Prestowitz, Clyde. 2010. *The Betrayal of American Prosperity: Free Market Delusions, America's Decline, and How We Must Compete in the Post-Dollar Era*. New York: Free Press.

Price, M. and Benton-Short, L. 2007. 'Immigrants and world cities: From the hyper-diverse to the bypassed'. *GeoJournal*, 68 (2–3) 103–17.

Priefert, H., Rabenhorst, J. and Steinbüchel, A. 2001. 'Biotechnological production of vanillin'. *Applied Microbiology and Biotechnology*, 56: 296–314.

Pringle, Tim. 2013. 'Reflections on labor in China: From a moment to a movement'. *The South Atlantic Quarterly*, 112 (1) 191–202.

Projekt Klassenanalyse@BRD. 2007. *Mehr Profit – mehr Armut. Prekarisierung und Klassenwiderspruch. Beiträge zur Klassenanalyse*. Vol. IV [eds. E. Lieberam and W. Seppmann]. Essen: Neue Impulse.

Pruett, D. 2005. *Looking for a Quick Fix: How Weak Social Auditing is Keeping Workers in Sweatshops*. Amsterdam: Clean Clothes Campaign.

Pun Ngai and Chan, Jenny. 2012. 'Global capital, the state, and Chinese workers: The Foxconn experience'. *Modern China*, 38 (4) 383–410.

Pun Ngai and Chan, Jenny. 2013. 'The spatial politics of labor in China: Life, labor, and a new generation of migrant workers'. *The South Atlantic Quarterly*, 112 (1) 179–90.

Pun Ngai, Shen Yuan, Guo Yuhua, Huilin Lu, Chan, Jenny and Selden, Mark. 2014. 'Worker-intellectual unity: Trans-border sociological intervention in Foxconn'. *Current Sociology*, 62 (2) 209–22.

Putnam, R. 2007. 'E pluribus unum: Diversity and community in the twenty-first century'. *Scandinavian Political Studies*, 30 (2) 137–74.

Qiao, J. 2011. 'Employees' conditions in 2010: A call for an equal share in the benefits of economic development and for collective rights' [2010nian zhigong zhuangkuang: huhuan gongxiang jingji fazhan chengguo he jiti laoquan]. In X. Ru, X. Lu and P. Li, eds. *Analysis of the Situation and Forecast for Chinese Society in 2010 [2010nian Zhongguo shehui xingshi fenxi yu yuce]*. Beijing: Social Sciences Academic Press [Shehui Kexue Wenxian Chupanshe].

Quan, K. 2008. 'Use of global value chains by labor organizers'. *Competition and Change*, 12 (1) 89–104.

Quirk, Joel. 2011. *The Anti-Slavery Project: From the Slave Trade to Human Trafficking*. Philadelphia: Pennsylvania University Press.

Quirk, Joel. 2012. 'Uncomfortable silences: Contemporary slavery and the "lessons" of history'. In A. Brysk and A. Choi-Fitzpatrick, eds. *From Human Trafficking to Human Rights: Reframing Contemporary Slavery*. Philadelphia: University of Pennsylvania Press.

Raess, D. 2006, 'Globalization and why the "time is ripe" for the transformation of German industrial relations'. *Review of International Political Economy*, 13 (3) 449–79.

Rahman, A. 1999. 'Micro-credit initiatives for equitable and sustainable development: Who pays?' *World Development*, 27 (1) 67–82.

Rainnie, A., Herod, A. and McGrath-Champ, S. 2011. 'Review and positions: Global production networks and labour'. *Competition and Change*, 15 (2) 155–69.

Rajan, S.C. 1996. *The Enigma of Automobility: Democratic Politics and Pollution Control*. Pittsburgh: University of Pittsburgh Press.

Rancière, Jacques. 2010. 'Ten theses on politics'. In J. Rancière, *Dissensus: On Politics and Aesthetics*. London: Continuum.

Rand Corporation. 2008. *U.S. Competitiveness in Science and Technology*. Santa Monica, CA: Rand Corporation.

Raskin, Paul D., Electris, Christi and Rosen, Richard A. 2010. 'The century ahead: Searching for sustainability'. *Sustainability*, 2 (8) 2626–51.

Ratha, D., Mohapatra, S. and Silwal, A. 2009. 'Migration and

Development Brief 11: Migration and Remittance Trends 2009: A Better-than-expected Outcome for Migration and Remittance Flows in 2009, but Significant Risks Ahead', 3 November, Washington, DC: World Bank, Migration and Remittances Team, Development Prospects Group. Available at: http://siteresources.worldbank.org/INTPROSPECTS/Resources/334934–1110315015165/MigrationAndDevelopmentBrief11.pdf.

Raymond, J.G. 2004. 'Prostitution on demand: Legalizing the buyers as sexual consumers'. *Violence Against Women*, 10 (10) 1156–86.

Raza, Werner. 2003. 'Politische Ökonomie und Natur im Kapitalismus. Skizze einer regulationstheoretischen Konzeptualisierung'. In U. Brand and W. Raza, eds. *Fit für den Postfordismus? Theoretisch-politische Perspektiven des Regulationsansatzes*. Münster: Westfälisches Dampfboot.

Read, J. 2003. *The Micro-Politics of Capital: Marx and the Prehistory of the Present*. Albany: State University of New York Press.

Recalcati, M. 2010. *L'uomo senza Inconscio. Figure della Nuova Clinica Psicoanalitica*. Milan: Raffaello Cortina Editore.

Regalado, Antonio. 2004. 'Nanotechnology patents surge as companies vie to take claim'. *Wall Street Journal*, 18 July.

Regalia, I. and Regini, M. 2004. 'Collective bargaining and social pacts in Italy'. In H. Katz, W. Lee and J. Lee, eds. *The New Structure of Labor Relations*. Ithaca: Cornell University Press.

Rehmann, Jan. 2008. *Einführung in die Ideologietheorie*. Hamburg: Argument-Verlag.

Reich, S. 1989. 'Roads to follow: Regulating direct foreign investment'. *International Organization*, 43 (4) 543–84.

Reischauer, Edwin O. 1977. *The Japanese*. Cambridge, MA: Harvard University Press.

Reisenbichler, Alexander and Morgan, Kimberley J. 2012. 'From "sick man" to "miracle": Explaining the robustness of the German labor market during and after the Financial Crisis 2008–09'. *Politics and Society*, 40 (4) 549–79.

Reuters. 2010. 'Workers strike at another auto parts plant in China'. Available at: http://www.reuters.com/article/2010/07/21/china-labour-idUSSGE66K0CK20100721.

Reyes, O. and Gilbertson, T. 2010. 'Carbon trading: How it works and why it fails'. *Soundings*, 45: 89–100.

Rhodes Forum. 2013. Plenary session. 'Alternative visions of the world. Geo-Economics'. Available at: http://www.inafran.ru/sites/default/files/news_file/rhodes_forum.pdf.

Rhodes, M. 1997. 'Southern European welfare states: Identity, problems

and prospects for reform'. In M. Rhodes, ed. *Southern European Welfare States – Between Crisis and Reform*. London: Frank Cass.
Rifkin, Jeremy. 2011. *The Third Industrial Revolution: How Lateral Power is Transforming Energy, the Economy, and the World*. New York: Palgrave Macmillan.
Rifkin, Jeremy. 2014. *The Zero Marginal Cost Society: The Internet of Things, the Collaborative Commons, and the Eclipse of Capitalism*. New York: Palgrave Macmillan.
Rigi, J. 2012. 'Peer 2 Peer Production as the alternative to capitalism: A new communist horizon'. *Journal of Peer Production*. 1 (1). Available at: http://snuproject.wordpress.com/2012/08/02/.
Rigi, J. 2013. 'Peer production and Marxian Communism: Contours of a new emerging mode of production'. *Capital and Class*, 37 (3) 397–416.
Rilling, Rainer. 2011. 'Wenn die Hütte brennt. . . "Energiewende", green New Deal und grüner Sozialismus'. *Forum Wissenschaft*, 27 (4) 14–18.
Rinehart, J., Huxley, C. and Robertson, D. 1995. 'Team concept at CAMI'. In S. Babson, ed. *Lean Work*. Detroit: Wayne State University Press.
Rinehart, J., Huxley, C. and Robertson, D. 1997. *Just Another Car Factory? Lean Production and its Discontents*. Ithaca: ILR Press.
Roach, Stephen. 2000. 'How global labour arbitrage will shape the world economy'. *Global Agenda Magazine*. Available at: http://ecocritique.free.fr.
Roberts, Bryan and Berg, Natalie. 2012. *Walmart: Key Insights and Practical Lessons from the World's Largest Retailer*. Philadelphia: Kogan.
Roberts, G. 1994. *Staying on the Line: Blue-Collar Women in Contemporary Japan*. Honolulu: University of Hawaii Press.
Robinson, A. 2010. 'Symptoms of a new politics: Networks, minoritarianism and the social symptom in Žižek, Deleuze and Guattari'. *Deleuze Studies*, 4 (2) 206–33.
Robinson, W.I. 2004. *A Theory of Global Capitalism: Production, Class, and State in a Transnational World*. Baltimore: Johns Hopkins University Press.
Roccas, M. 2004. 'Le esportazioni nell'economia italiana'. In P. Ciocca and G. Toniolo, eds. *Storia Economica d'Italia 3. Industrie, Mercati, Istituzioni*. Bari: Editori Laterza.
Roco, Michail C. 2003. 'Broader societal issues of nanotechnology'. *Journal of Nanoparticle Research*, 5: 181–9.
Roco, Michail C. 2007. 'National nanotechnology initiative: Past, present, future'. In William A. Goddard, Donald Brenner, Sergey E. Lyshevski and Gerald J. Iafrate, eds. *Handbook of Nanoscience, Engineering, and Technology*. Boca Raton: CRC Press.

Roco, Michail C. 2008. 'National Nanotechnology Investment in the FY 2009 budget request'. In Intersociety Working Group, eds. *Research and Development FY 2009, AAAS Report XXXIII*. Washington, DC: American Association for the Advancement of Science.

Rogaly, Ben. 2008. 'Migrant workers in the ILO's global alliance against forced labour report: A critical appraisal'. *Third World Quarterly*, 29 (7) 1431–47.

Rogaly, Ben. 2009. 'Spaces of work and everyday life: Labour geographies and the agency of unorganised temporary migrant workers'. *Geography Compass*, 3 (6) 1975–87.

Rohlen, T. 1974. *For Harmony and Strength: Japanese White-Collar Organization in Anthropological Perspective*. Berkeley: University of California Press.

Romero, M. 2008. 'Crossing the immigration and race border: A critical race theory approach to immigration studies'. *Contemporary Justice Review: Issues in Criminal, Social and Restorative Justice*, 11 (1) 23–37.

Rosa, H. 2009. 'Kapitalismus als Dynamisierungsspirale – Soziologie als Gesellschaftskritik'. In H. Merkur, K. Dörre, S. Lessenich and H. Rosa, eds. *Soziologie – Kapitalismus – Kritik*. Frankfurt: Suhrkamp.

Ross, A. 2008. 'The new geography of work: Power to the precarious?' *Theory, Culture and Society*, 25 (7–8) 31–49.

Ross, A., Krause, M., Palm, M. and Nolan, M. 2007. *The University Against Itself: The NYU Strike and the Future of the Academic Workplace*. Philadelphia: Temple University Press.

Ross, Andrew. 2006. *Fast Boat to China: Corporate Flight and the Consequences of Free Trade – Lessons from Shanghai*. New York: Pantheon Books.

Ross, Kirstin. 1995. *Fast Cars, Clean Bodies: Decolonization and the Reordering of French Culture*. Cambridge, MA: MIT Press.

Ross, R. and Trachte, K. 1990. *Global Capitalism: The New Leviathan*. Albany: State University of New York Press.

Rosset, P.M. 1998. 'Alternative agriculture works: The case of Cuba'. *Monthly Review*, 50 (3) 137–46.

Rosset, P.M. 2000. 'Lessons from the green revolution'. Available at: http://www.foodfirst.org/media/opeds/2000/4-greenrev.html.

Rosset, P.M. 2006. 'Moving forward: Agrarian reform as a part of food sovereignty'. In P.M. Rosset, R. Patel and M. Courville, *Promised Land: Competing Visions of Agrarian Reform*. Oakland: Food First Books.

Rosset, P.M., Machin Sosa, B. et al. 2011. 'The *Campesino*-to-*Campesino* agroecology movement of ANAP in Cuba: Social process methodology in the construction of sustainable peasant agriculture and food sovereignty'. *The Journal of Peasant Studies*, 38 (1) 161–91.

Rothwell, J. 2013. 'The hidden STEM economy'. Washington, DC: Brookings Institution Metropolitan Program.

Rowbotham, Sheila. 1994. 'Strategies against sweated work in Britain'. In Sheila Rowbotham and Swasti Mitter, eds. *Dignity and Daily Bread: New Forms of Economic Organising Among Poor Women in the Third World and the First*. London: Routledge.

Rowthorn, R. 1997. 'Manufacturing in the world economy', *Economie Appliquée*, 4: 63–96.

Roxborough, Ian. 1984. 'Unity and diversity in Latin American studies'. *Journal of Latin American Studies*, 16 (1) 1–26.

Roy, Ashim. 1996. 'Labour standards in multilateral trade agreements: An overview'. In J. John and Anuradha M. Chenoy, eds. *Labour, Environment and Globalisation*. New Delhi: Centre for Education and Communication.

Royal Society/ Royal Academy of Engineering. 2004. *Nanoscience and Nanotechnologies: Opportunities and Uncertainties*. Plymouth: Latimer Trend.

Rubin, Gayle. 1975. 'The traffic in women: Notes on the "political economy" of sex'. In R. Reiter, ed. *Towards an Anthropology of Women*. New York: Monthly Review Press.

Ruggie, John G. 2012. 'Working conditions at Apple's overseas factories'. *The New York Times*. 4 April.

Ruigrok, Winfried and van Tulder, Rob. 1995. *The Logic of International Restructuring*. London: Routledge.

Rupert, M. 1995. *Producing Hegemony: The Politics of Mass Production and American Global Power*. Cambridge: Cambridge University Press.

Ruttan, Vernon. 2006. *Is War Necessary for Economic Growth?: Military Procurement and Technology Development*. New York: Oxford University Press.

Ryner, Magnus. 2002. *Capitalist Restructuring, Globalisation and the Third Way*. London: Routledge.

Sablowski, Thomas. 2009. 'Die Ursachen der neuen Weltwirtschaftskrise'. *Kritische Justiz*, 41 (2) 116–31.

Safa, H. 1995. *The Myth of the Male Breadwinner: Women and Industrialization in the Caribbean*. Boulder, CO: Westview.

Safranski, Rüdiger. 2004. *Schiller oder Die Erfindung des Deutschen Idealismus*. Munich: Hanser.

Sage, Jesse and Kasten, Liora. 2006. *Enslaved: True Stories of Modern Day Slavery*. New York: Palgrave Macmillan.

Sakamoto, Leonardo Moretti. 2007. *Os Acionistas da Casa-grande: A*

Reinvenção Capitalista do Trabalho Escravo no Brasil Contemporâneo. PhD dissertation. São Paulo: Universidade de São Paulo.

Salazar, Gabriel and Pinto, Julio. 2010. *Historia Contemporanéa de Chile III, La economía: Mercados, Empresarios y Trabajadores*, 5th edn. Santiago: LOM Ediciones.

Samarasinghe, V. 2009. '"Two to Tango". Probing the demand side of female sex trafficking'. *Pakistan Journal of Women's Studies: Alam-e-Niswan*, 16 (1–2) 33–54.

Saña, H. 1997. *Die Zivilisation frisst ihre Kinder. Die abendländische Weltherrschaft und ihre Folgen.* Hamburg: Rasch und Röhring Verlag.

Sánchez Taylor, J. 2001. 'Dollars are a girl's best friend? Female tourists' sexual behaviour in the Caribbean'. *Sociology*, 35 (3) 749–64.

Sanders, T. 2008. 'Selling sex in the shadow economy'. *International Journal of Social Economics*, 35 (10) 704–16.

Santa Lucia, Patricia. 1976. 'The industrial working class and the struggle for power in Chile'. In P. O'Brien, ed. *Allende's Chile*. London: Praeger.

Sardoni, C. 1997. 'Keynes and Marx'. In G.C. Harcourt and P. Riach, eds. *A 'Second Edition' of The General Theory*. London: Routledge.

Sargent, John F. 2013. 'The national nanotechnology initiative: Overview, reauthorization, and appropriations issues'. Report by the US Congressional Research Service. Available at: http://nanotech.lawbc.com/uploads/file/00123314.PDF.

Sassen, Saskia. 1988. *The Mobility of Labor and Capital.* Cambridge: Cambridge University Press.

Sassen, Saskia. 1991. *The Global City: New York, London, Tokyo.* Princeton, NJ: Princeton University Press.

Sassen, Saskia. 2002. 'Women's burden: Counter-geographies of globalization and the feminization of survival'. *Nordic Journal of International Law*, 71 (2) 255–74.

Sassen, Saskia. 2007. *The Sociology of Globalization.* New York: W.W. Norton and Company.

Sassen, Saskia. 2008a. *Territory, Authority, Rights: From Medieval to Global Assemblages*, revised 2nd edn. Princeton: Princeton University Press.

Sassen, Saskia. 2008b. 'Two stops in today's new global geographies: Shaping novel labor supplies and employment regimes'. *American Behavioral Scientist*, 52 (3) 457–96.

Sassen, Saskia. 2008c. 'Nurturing Asia's world cities'. *Far Eastern Economic Review*, May, 57–9.

Sassen, Saskia. 2010. 'A savage sorting of winners and losers: Contemporary versions of primitive accumulation'. *Globalizations*, 7 (1–2) 23–50.

Sassen, Saskia. 2013. 'Land grabs today: Feeding the disassembling of national territory'. *Globalizations*, 10 (1) 25–46.

Sassen, Saskia. 2014. *Expulsions: Brutality and Complexity in the Global Economy*. Cambridge, MA: Harvard University Press/Belknap.

Sassoon, Anne Showstack. 1982. 'Passive revolution and the politics of reform'. In A.S. Sassoon, ed. *Approaches to Gramsci*. London: Writers and Readers.

Sassoon, Anne Showstack. 2001. 'Globalisation, hegemony and passive revolution'. *New Political Economy*, 6 (1) 5–17.

Satariano, Adam and Burrows, Peter. 2011. 'Apple's supply-chain secret? Hoard lasers'. *Bloomberg Businessweek*, 3 November.

Satzewich, Vic. 1991. *Racism and the Incorporation of Foreign Labour: Farm Labour Migration to Canada since 1945*. London: Routledge.

Sauer, S. and Leite, S.P. 2012. 'Agrarian structure, foreign investment in land, and land prices in Brazil'. *Journal of Peasant Studies*, 39 (3–4) 873–98.

Saxena, D. and Stotzky, G. 2001. 'Bt-corn has a higher lignin content than non-Bt corn'. *American Journal of Botany*, 88 (9) 1704–6.

Saxenian, A.L. 1996. *Regional Advantage: Culture and Competition in Silicon Valley and Route 128*. Boston: Harvard University Press.

Saxenian, A.L. 2002. *Local and Global Networks of Immigrant Professionals in Silicon Valley*. San Francisco: Public Policy Institute of California.

Saxenian, A.L. 2006. *The New Argonauts: Regional Advantage in a Global Economy*. Boston: Harvard University Press.

Sayer, A. 1995. *Radical Political Economy: A Critique*. Oxford: Blackwell.

Scheuerman, W.E. 2001. 'False humanitarianism?: US advocacy of transnational labour protections'. *Review of International Political Economy*, 8 (3) 359–88.

Schimmeck, T. 2010. *Am Besten nichts Neues: Medien, Macht und Meinungsmache*. Frankfurt: Westend-Verlag.

Schivelsbusch, W. 1986. *The Railway Journey: Trains and Travel in the Nineteenth Century*. Oxford: Blackwell.

Schmél, F. 1997. *Professional Training in the Leather-based Industries*. Vienna: UNIDO.

Schmidt, Vivien A. and Thatcher, Mark, eds. 2013. *Resilient Liberalism in Europe's Political Economy*. Cambridge: Cambridge University Press.

Schnaiberg, A., Pellow, D.N. and Weinberg, A. 2002. 'The treadmill of production and the environmental state'. *Research in Social Problems and Public Policy*, 10: 15–32.

Schneider, S., Shiki, S. et al. 2010. 'Rural development in Brazil: Overcoming inequalities and building new markets'. *Rivista di Economia Agraria*, 65 (2) 225–59.

Scholte, J.A. 2000, *Globalization: A Critical Introduction*. Basingstoke: Palgrave Macmillan.

Scholz, T. ed. 2012. *Digital Labour: Internet as Playground and Factory*. New York: Routledge.

Schulten, Thorsten. 2013. 'Europäischer Tarifbericht des WSI – 2012/2013'. *WSI-Mitteilungen*, 66 (8) 588–97.

Schummer, Joachim. 2004. '"Societal and ethical implications of nanotechnology": Meanings, interest groups, and social dynamics'. *Techné*, 8 (2) 56–87.

Schumpeter, Joseph A. 1934. *Theory of Economic Development: An Inquiry into Profits, Capital, Credit, Interest and the Business Cycle*. Cambridge, MA: Harvard University Press.

Scott, J.C. 1992. *Domination and the Arts of Resistance: Hidden Transcripts*. New Haven: Yale University Press.

Scott, J.C. 1998. *Seeing Like a State. How Certain Schemes to Improve the Human Condition Have Failed*. New Haven: Yale University Press.

Scott, J.C. 2009. *The Art of Not Being Governed: An Anarchist History of Upland Southeast Asia*. New Haven: Yale University Press.

Scott, Sam, Craig, Gary and Geddes, Alistair. 2012. *Experiences of Forced Labour in the UK Food Industry*. York: Joseph Rowntree Foundation.

Seidman, G. 1994. *Manufacturing Militance: Workers' Movements in Brazil and South Africa, 1970–1985*. Berkeley: University of California Press.

Seidman, Gay W. 2007. *Beyond the Boycott: Labor Rights, Human Rights, and Transnational Activism*. New York: Russell Sage Foundation.

Selden, Mark and Perry, Elizabeth J. 2010. 'Introduction: Reform, conflict and resistance in contemporary China'. In Elizabeth J. Perry and Mark Selden, eds. *Chinese Society: Change, Conflict and Resistance*, 3rd edn. London: Routledge.

Seligman, Brad. 2006. 'Patriarchy at the checkout counter: The Dukes v. Wal-Mart Stores, Inc., Class Action Suit'. In N. Lichtenstein, ed. *Wal-Mart: The Face of Twenty-First Century Capitalism*. New York: The New Press.

Selin, Cynthia. 2007. 'Expectations and the emergence of nanotechnology'. *Science Technology Human Values*, 32 (2) 196–220.

Selwyn, Ben. 2007. 'Labour process and workers' bargaining power in export grape production, North East Brazil'. *Journal of Agrarian Change*, 7 (4) 526–53.

Selwyn, Ben. 2008. 'Bringing social relations back in: Reconceptualising the "bullwhip effect" in global commodity chains'. *International Journal of Management Concepts and Philosophy*, 3 (2) 156–75.

Selwyn, Ben. 2012a. 'Beyond firm-centrism: Re-integrating labour and capitalism into global commodity chain analysis'. *Journal of Economic Geography*, 12 (1) 205–26.

Selwyn, Ben. 2012b. *Workers, State and Development in Brazil: Powers of Labour, Chains of Value*. Manchester: Manchester University Press.

Selwyn, Ben. 2013. 'Social upgrading and labour in global production networks: A critique and an alternative conception'. *Competition & Change*, 17 (1) 75–90.

Semmel, Bernard. 1993. *The Liberal Ideal and the Demons of Empire: Theories of Imperialism from Adam Smith to Lenin*. Baltimore: Johns Hopkins University Press.

Sen, J. and Waterman, P. eds. 2013. *World Social Forum: Critical Explorations*. New Delhi: Open Word Books.

Şenalp, Ö. 2012. 'The dramatic rise of peer-to-peer communication within the emancipatory movements: Reflections of an international labour, social justice and cyber activist'. Available at: http://wp.me/p1jry0-VU.

Sennett, Richard. 1998. *The Corrosion of Character. The Personal Consequences of Work in the New Capitalism*. New York: W.W. Norton.

Seppmann, Werner. 2011. *Risiko-Kapitalismus. Krisenprozesse, Widerspruchserfahrungen und Widerstandsperspektiven*. Cologne: PapyRossa.

Seppmann, Werner. 2012. *Dialektik der Entzivilisierung. Krise, Irrationalismus und Gewalt*, 2nd edn. Hamburg: Laika.

Seppmann, Werner. 2013a. *Ausgrenzung und Herrschaft. Prekarisierung als Klassenfrage*. Hamburg: Laika.

Seppmann, Werner. 2013b. 'Krise und Utopie'. In H. Kopp, ed. *Wovon wir Träumen Müssen Marxismus und Utopie*. Hamburg: Laika.

Seppmann, Werner. 2013c. 'Dynamik der Entzivilisierung. Über die Gewalt, die aus den gesellschaftlichen Funktionsprinzipien resultiert'. In Peter Bathke and Anke Hoffstadt, eds. *Die Neuen Rechten in Europa. Zwischen Neoliberalismus und Rassismus*. Cologne: PapyRossa.

Sergeev, Y., Chausov, I. and Tretyakov, A. 2012. *Trans-Eurasian Corridor of Razvitie. Concrete Instruments and Approaches. Research Platform of the Schiffers Institute of Advanced Studies* [ed. Y. Gromyko]. Moscow: Praxis.

Serres, M. and Latour, B. 1995, 'Third conversation: Demonstration and interpretation'. In M. Serres with B. Latour, *Conversations on Science, Culture, and Time*. Ann Arbor: University of Michigan Press.

Sewell, G. 1998. 'The discipline of teams: The control of team-based industrial work through electronic and peer surveillance'. *Administrative Science Quarterly*, 43: 397–428.

Shamir, H. 2012. 'A labor paradigm for human trafficking'. *UCLA Law Review*, 60 (1) 76–136.

Shamir, R. 2010. 'Capitalism, governance, and authority: The case of corporate social responsibility'. *The Annual Review of Law and Social Science*, 6: 531–53.

Shamsavari, A. 1991. *Dialectics and Social Theory: The Logic of Capital*. Braunton: Merlin.

Sharma, Nandita. 2006. *Home Economics: Nationalism and the Making of 'Migrant Workers' in Canada*. Toronto: University of Toronto Press.

Shatkin, G. 2007. 'Global cities of the South: Emerging perspectives on growth and inequality'. *Cities*, 24 (1) 1–15.

Shchedrovitskiy, G.P. 2005. *Thinking. Understanding. Reflection* [in Russian]. Moscow: Nasledie MMK.

Shelley, L. 2003. 'Trafficking in women: The business model approach'. *Brown Journal of World Affairs*, 10 (1) 119–31.

Shingo, S. 1989. *A Study of the Toyota Production System*. New York: Productivity Press.

Shirai, T. 1983. 'A theory of enterprise unionism'. In T. Shirai, ed. *Contemporary Industrial Relations in Japan*. Wisconsin: University of Wisconsin Press.

Shultz, G. 1974. 'Statement of Secretary Shultz to the Commission on the Organization of the Government for the Conduct of Foreign Policy'. *William Simon Papers*, IV, 32: 22.

Siegmann, K.A., Merk, J. and Knorringa, P. 2013. 'Labour in Global Value Chains: Beyond voluntary initiatives'. Paper presented at the International Labour Process Conference ILPC, Rutgers School of Management and Labor Relations, New Brunswick, March, 18–20.

Sigmund, Paul. 1977. *The Overthrow of Allende and the Politics of Chile 1964–1976*. Pittsburgh: Pittsburgh University Press.

Silver, Beverly J. 2003. *Forces of Labor: Workers' Movements and Globalization since 1870*. Cambridge: Cambridge University Press.

Silver, Beverly J. and Arrighi, Giovanni. 2001. 'Workers North and South', in *Socialist Register, 2001*. London: Merlin.

Silvia, Stephen J. 1999. 'Every which way but loose: German industrial relations since 1980'. In Andrew Martin and George Ross, eds. *The Brave New World of European Labor: European Trade Unions at the Millennium*. New York: Berghahn.

Silvia, Stephen J. 2009. 'Keynes in Lederhosen: Assessing the German response to the financial crisis'. *AICGS Transatlantic Perspectives*. Available at: http://www.aicgs.org/site/wp-content/uploads/2011/10/silvia.atp09.pdf.

Simmel, Georg. 2011. *The Philosophy of Money*. London: Routledge Classics.

Simon, W. 1975. 'Statement of the Honorable William E. Simon Secretary of the Treasury before the Commission on the Organization of the

Government for the Conduct of Foreign Policy'. *William Simon Papers*, IV, 32: 22.

Singer, H. 1975. *The Strategy of International Development. Essays in the Economics of Backwardness*. London: Macmillan.

Skidelsky, Robert. 2009. *Keynes: The Return of the Master*. London: Penguin.

Sklair, L. 2001. *The Transnational Capitalist Class*. Oxford: Blackwell.

Skrivankova, Klara. 2010. 'Between decent work and forced labour: Examining the continuum of exploitation'. JRF programme paper: Forced Labour. York: Joseph Rowntree Foundation.

Smith, A., Rainnie, A., Dunford, M., Hardy, J., Hudson, R. and Sadler, D. 2002. 'Networks of value, commodities and regions: Reworking divisions of labour in macro-regional economies'. *Progress in Human Geography*, 261: 41–63.

Smith, Adam. 1976[1776]. *An Inquiry into the Nature and Causes of the Wealth of Nations*. Chicago: University of Chicago Press.

Smith, Adam. 1998. *The Wealth of Nations*. Oxford: Oxford University Press.

Smith, Chris. 2006. 'The double indeterminacy of labour power: Labour effort and labour mobility'. *Work, Employment and Society*, 20 (2) 389–402.

Smith, Chris and Meiksins, Peter. 1995. 'System, society and dominance effects in cross-national organisational analysis'. *Work, Employment and Society*, 2 (9) 241–67.

Smith, N.J. 2010. 'The International Political Economy of sex work'. *Review of International Political Economy*, 18 (4) 530–49.

Smith, Neil. 2008 (1984). *Uneven Development: Nature, Capital and the Production of Space*. Athens, GA: The University of Georgia Press.

Smith, T. 2011. 'Creating value between cultures: Contemporary Australian Aboriginal art'. In D. Throsby and Michael Hutter, eds. *Beyond Price – Value in Culture, Economics, and the Arts*. Cambridge: Cambridge University Press.

Smith, Ted, Sonnenfeld, David A. and Naguib Pellow, David, eds. 2006. *Challenging the Chip: Labor Rights and Environmental Justice in the Global Electronics Industry*. Philadelphia: Temple University Press.

Sohn-Rethel, Alfred. 1970. *Geistige und Körperliche Arbeit: Zur Theorie der Gesellschaftlichen Synthesis*. Frankfurt: Suhrkamp.

Sohn-Rethel, Alfred. 1976. 'The dual economics of transition'. In R. Panzieri et al. *The Labour Process and Class Strategies*. London: CSE.

Solinger, D.J. 1999. *Contesting Citizenship in Urban China: Peasant Migrants, the State and the Logic of the Market*. Berkeley: University of California Press.

Sourrouille, Christophe, Marshall, Brian, Liénard, David and Faye, Loïc. 2009. 'From Neanderthal to nanobiotech: From plant potions to pharming with plant factories'. In Loïc Faye and Veronique Gomord, eds. *Recombinant Proteins from Plants. Methods and Protocols*. New York: Humana Press.

Spencer, David. 2009. *The Political Economy of Work*. London: Routledge.

Spinoza, B. 1994. *Spinoza Reader*: The Ethics *and Other Works* [ed. and trans. E. Curley]. Princeton: Princeton University Press.

Spinoza, B. 2003[1677]. *The Ethics* [trans. R.H.M. Elwes 1951]. A Public Domain Book.

St Clair, D.J. 1988. *The Motorization of American Cities*. New York: Praeger.

Stalder, F. 2013. *Digital Solidarity*. PML Books and Mute.

Standard & Poor's. 2011. *RatingsDirect on the Global Credit Portal*. 13 October, London, 2.

Standard Chartered. 2012. 'China – More than 200 clients talk wages in the PRD'. *Global Research*, March. Available at: https://research.standardchartered.com/configuration/ROWDocuments/China_%E2%80%93_More_than_200_clients_talk_wages_in_the_PRD_05_03_12_05_52.pdf.

Standing, G. 2011. *The Precariat: The New Dangerous Class*. London: Bloomsbury Academic.

Stanford, J. 2010. 'The geography of auto globalization and the politics of auto bailouts'. *Cambridge Journal of Regions, Economy and Society*, 3 (3) 383–405.

Starosta, Guido. 2010. 'The outsourcing of manufacturing and the rise of giant global contractors: A Marxian approach to some recent transformations of global value chains'. *New Political Economy*, 15 (4) 543–63.

Statistisches Bundesamt. 2013. 'Fast jede sechste Person war 2011 armutsgefährdet'. Press release No. 361, 25 October. Wiesbaden.

Steans, J. and Tepe, D. 2010. 'Introduction – Social reproduction in international political economy: Theoretical insights and international, transnational and local sitings'. *Review of International Political Economy*, 17 (5) 807–15.

Stedile, J.P. 2002. 'Landless batallions: The Sem Terra Movement of Brazil'. *New Left Review*, 2nd series, 15: 77–104.

Stedman-Jones, Gareth. 1975. 'Class struggle and the Industrial Revolution'. *New Left Review*, I/90, 35–69.

Steinert, H. 2010. 'Das Prekariat: Begriffspolitik und Klassenpolitik'. In H-G. Thien, ed. *Klassen im Postfordismus*. Münster: Westfälisches Dampfboot.

Steinrücke, I.M. 2005. 'Soziales Elend, als psychisches Elend'. In F. Schultheis and K. Schulz, eds. *Gesellschaft mit Begrenzter Haftung*.

Zumutungen und Leiden im Deutsche Alltag. Konstanz: Universitäts Verlag.

Stevis, D. 2002. 'Globalising social justice all the way down? Agents, subjects, objects and phantoms in international labour'. Paper presented at the Annual Convention of International Studies Association, New Orleans.

Stevis, D. and Boswell, T. 2008. *Globalisation & Labour: Democratising Global Governance*. Lanham: Rowman and Littlefield.

Stirati, A. and Levrero, S. 2002. 'La leva del salario'. *Rivista del Manifesto*, 32: 21–5.

Stohl, Michael. 1980. 'The nexus of civil and international conflict'. In Ted Gurr, ed. *Handbook of Political Conflict: Theory and Research*. New York: The Free Press.

Stoler, A.L. 1989. 'Making empire respectable: The politics of race and sexual morality in 20th-Century colonial cultures'. *American Ethnologist*, 16 (4) 634–60.

Stoler, A.L. 1995. *Race and the Education of Desire: Foucault's History of Sexuality and the Colonial*. Durham, NC: Duke University Press.

Stoler, A.L. 2006. *Carnal Knowledge and Imperial Power: Race and the Intimate in Colonial Rule*. Berkeley: University of California Press.

Stoneman, P. 2010. *Soft Innovation: Economics, Product Aesthetics, and the Creative Industries*. Oxford: Oxford University Press.

Strange, Susan. 1972. 'The dollar crisis 1971'. *International Affairs*, 48 (2) 191–216.

Strange, Susan. 1996. *The Retreat of the State. The Diffusion of Power in the World Economy*. Cambridge: Cambridge University Press.

Stratus_Research. 2013. 'Glyphosate resistant weeds – intensifying'. Available at: http://stratusresearch.com/blog/glyphosate-resistant-weeds-intensifying/. Retrieved 20 April 2014.

Strauss, Kendra. 2012. 'Coerced, forced and unfree labour: Geographies of exploitation in contemporary labour markets'. *Geography Compass*, 6 (3) 137–48.

Strauss, Kendra. 2013. 'Unfree again: Social reproduction, flexible labour markets and the resurgence of gang labour in the UK'. *Antipode*, 45 (1), 180–97.

Strauss, Kendra and Fudge, Judy. 2014. 'Temporary work, agencies and unfree labour: Insecurity in the new world of work'. In J. Fudge and K. Strauss, eds. *Temporary Work, Agencies and Unfree Labour*. New York: Routledge.

Streeck, Wolfgang. 1997. 'Citizenship under regime competition: The case of the European works councils'. *European Integration Online*, 1 (5) 1–19.

Streeck, Wolfgang. 2011. 'The crises of democratic capitalism'. *New Left Review*, 2nd series (71) 5–29.

Stuckler, David et al. 2011. 'Effects of the 2008 recession on health: A first look at European data'. *The Lancet*, 378 (9786) 124–5.

Students and Scholars Against Corporate Misbehavior. 2011a. 'The truth of the Apple iPad'. June. (Video clip 6m 33s).

Students and Scholars Against Corporate Misbehavior. 2011b. 'Foxconn and Apple fail to fulfill promises: Predicaments of workers after the suicides'. 6 May. Available at: http://sacom.hk/wp-content/uploads/2011/05/2011–05–06_foxconn-and-apple-fail-to-fulfill-promises1.pdf.

Sturgeon, T.J. 2003. 'What really goes on in Silicon Valley? Spatial clustering and dispersal in modular production networks'. *Journal of Economic Geography*, 3 (2) 199–225.

Sturgeon, T., Van Biesebroeck, J. and Gereffi, G. 2008. 'Value chains, networks and clusters: Reframing the global automotive industry'. *Journal of Economic Geography*, 8 (3) 297–321.

Sturgeon, Timothy, Humphrey, John and Gereffi, Gary. 2011. 'Making the global supply base'. In Gary G. Hamilton, Misha Petrovic and Benjamin Senauer, eds. *The Market Makers: How Retailers are Reshaping the Global Economy*. Oxford: Oxford University Press.

Su, Xiaobo and Teo, Peggy. 2008. 'Tourism politics in Lijiang, China: An analysis of state and local interactions in tourism development'. *Tourism Geographies*, 10 (2) 150–68.

Sultany, N. 2012. 'Forum: The making of an underclass: The Palestinian citizens of Israel'. *Israel Studies Review: An Interdisciplinary Journal*, 27 (2) 190–200.

Sum, Ngai-Ling and Jessop, Bob. 2013. *Towards a Cultural Political Economy*. Cheltenham, UK and Northampton, MA, USA: Edward Elgar Publishing.

Summers, Larry. 2013. Speech at the IMF's Fourteenth Annual Research Conference in Honor of Stanley Fischer. 8 November. Available at: http://larrysummers.com/imf-fourteenth-annual-research-conference-in-honor-of-stanley-fischer/.

Sunder Rajan, Kaushik. 2006. *Biocapital. The Constitution of Postgenomic Life*. Durham, NC: Duke University Press.

Swilling, M. 2005. *Growth, Resource Decoupling and Productivity*. Stellenbosch University and UNEP. Available at: www.learndev.org/dl/BtSM2011/Africa%20Policy%20Brief.pdf.

Swilling, M. 2011. *Just Transitions: Explorations of Sustainability in an Unfair World*. Stellenbosch: Stellenbosch University Press.

Tabuchi, H. 2010. 'With strike, Toyota idles auto plant in China'. *New*

York Times. Available at: http://www.nytimes.com/2010/06/23/business/global/23strike.html?_r=0.

Tacconelli, Wance and Wrigley, Neil. 2009. 'Organizational challenges and strategic responses of retail TNCs in post-WTO-entry China'. *Economic Geography*, 85 (1) 49–73.

Tagliacozzo, E. 2008. 'Morphological shifts in Southeast Asian prostitution: The long twentieth century'. *Journal of Global History*, 3 (2) 251–73.

Tamborino, J. 2002. *The Corporeal Turn: Passion, Necessity, Politics*. Lanham, ML: Rowman and Littlefield.

Tarrow, S. 1990. 'Maintaining hegemony in Italy: The softer they rise, the slower they fall!' In T.J. Pempel, ed. *Uncommon Democracies. The One-Party Dominant Regimes*. Ithaca: Cornell University Press.

Taylor, Alan. 1998. 'On the costs of inward-looking development: Price distortions, growth and divergence in Latin America'. *Journal of Economic History*, 58 (1) 1–28.

Taylor, Frederick Winslow. 1947[1911, 1939]. 'Testimony before the Special House Committee' [1912], reprinted in Taylor, *Scientific Management* [Preface, H.S. Person]. New York: Harper and Row.

Taylor, M.C. 2001. *The Moment of Complexity, Emerging Network Culture*. Chicago: University of Chicago Press.

Taylor, Marcus. 2007. 'Rethinking the global production of uneven development'. *Globalizations*, 4 (4) 529–42.

Taylor, P. 2010. 'The globalization of service work: Analysing the transnational call centre value chain'. In P. Thompson and C. Smith, eds. *Working Life: Renewing Labour Process Analysis*. Basingstoke: Palgrave Macmillan.

Taylor, P. and Bain, P. 2008. 'United by a common language? Trade union responses in the UK and India to call centre offshoring'. *Antipode*, 40 (1) 131–54.

Tennenbaum, Jonathan. 2001. 'Von Kepler Weltenharmonie zu Wernadskijs Noosphäre'. In *Der Kampf um das Gemeinwohl der Bürger und Nationen*. Wiesbaden: Böttinger.

Tennenbaum, Jonathan, Burdmann, Mary and Komp, Lothar. 1997. *The Eurasian Land-Bridge. The "New Silk Road" – Locomotive for Worldwide Economic Development*. Washington, DC: Executive Intelligence Review Special Report.

Terranova, T. 2000. 'Free labor: Producing culture for the digital economy'. *Social Text*, 63, 18 (2) 33–58.

Tharamangalam, J. 2008. 'Can Cuba offer an alternative to corporate control over the world's food system?'. Paper presented at the 20th Conference of North American and Cuban Philosophers and Social Scientists. Havana.

Therborn, Göran. 1976. *Science, Class and Society. On the Formation of Sociology and Historical Materialism*. London: Verso.

Thompson, E.P. 1968[1963]. *The Making of the English Working Class*. Harmondsworth: Penguin.

Thompson, S. and Hoggett, P. 2012. *Politics and the Emotions: The Affective Turn in Contemporary Political Studies*. London: Continuum.

Thorp, Rosemary. 1992. 'A reappraisal of import-substituting industrialisation 1930–1950'. *Journal of Latin American Studies*, 24: 81–195.

Thorp, Rosemary. 1998. *Progress, Poverty and Exclusion: An Economic History of Latin America in the 20th Century*. Baltimore: Johns Hopkins University Press.

Thrift, Nigel. 1996. 'Inhuman geographies: Landscapes of speed, light and power'. In N. Thrift, *Spatial Formations*. London: Sage.

Thukral, J. 2010. 'Race, gender, and immigration in the informal economy'. *Race/Ethnicity: Multidisciplinary Global Contexts*, 4 (1) 65–71.

Tiles, Mary and Oberdiek, Hans. 1995. *Living in a Technological Culture: Human Tools and Human Values*. London: Routledge.

Tilly, Charles. 1990. *Coercion, Capital and European States, A.D. 990–1990*. Malden, MA: Blackwell.

Tilly, Chris. 2007. 'Wal-Mart and its workers: *NOT* the same all over the world'. *Connecticut Law Review*, 39 (4) 1805–24.

Tinker, I., ed. 1990. *Persistent Inequalities: Women and World Development*. New York: Oxford University Press.

Toffler, Alvin. 1970. *Future Shock*. New York: Bantam.

Toffler, Alvin. 1990. *Powershift. Knowledge, Wealth and Violence at the Edge of the 21st Century*. New York: Bantam.

Toledo Obando, Pabla. 1948. 'La industria textil'. Master's thesis. Facultad de Ciencias Juridicas y Sociales, Universidad de Chile.

Townley, B. 1994. *Reframing Human Resource Management: Power, Ethics and the Subject at Work*. London: Sage.

Treco, Douglas A. and Lundblad, Victoria. 1994. 'Preparation of yeast media'. In F.M. Ausubel, R. Brent, R.E. Kingston, D.D. Moore et al., eds. *Current Protocols in Molecular Biology*. Hoboken, NJ: John Wiley & Sons.

Trentin, U. 1980. *Il Sindacato dei Consigli*. Rome: Editori Riuniti.

Trichet, J-C. 2011. Introductory statement of Jean-Claude Trichet to the press conference on 6 October, Berlin. Available at: http://www.ecb.europa.eu/press/pressconf/2011/html/is111006.en.html.

Trodd, Zoe. 2013. 'Am I still not a man and a brother? Protest memory in contemporary antislavery visual culture'. *Slavery and Abolition: A Journal of Slave and Post-Slave Studies*, 34 (2) 338–52.

Tronti, L. 2005. 'Concertazione e crescita economica: L'occasione perduta'.

Available at: http://www.aiel.it/bacheca/MODENA/PAPERS/Tronti.pdf.

Tucker, Jonathan and Zilinskas, Raymond. 2006. 'The promise and perils of synthetic biology'. *The New Atlantis*, Spring: 25–45.

Turner, J. and Kelly, L. 2009. 'Trade secrets: Intersections between diasporas and crime groups in the constitution of the human trafficking chain'. *The British Journal of Criminology*, 49 (2) 184–201.

Tyler, Imogen. 2013. 'The riots of the underclass? Stigmatisation, mediation and the government of poverty and disadvantage in neoliberal Britain'. *Sociological Research Online*. Available at: http://eprints.lancs.ac.uk/id/eprint/61145.

Uchitelle, L. 1987. 'The Solow productivity paradox: What do computers do to productivity?' *Canadian Journal of Economics*, 32 (3) 309–34.

UNCTAD (United Nations Conference on Trade and Development). 2001. *World Investment Report 2001*. Geneva: United Nations.

UNCTAD. 2004. *World Investment Report. The Shift Towards Services*. Geneva: United Nations.

UNCTAD. 2008. *World Investment Directory*. Volume X: Africa. New York: United Nations.

UNCTAD. 2009. *World Investment Report 2009*. Geneva: United Nations.

UNCTAD. 2010. *World Investment Report 2010*. New York: United Nations.

UNCTAD. 2011. *World Investment Report 2011: Non-Equity Modes of International Production and Development*. New York: United Nations.

UNCTAD. 2013. *World Investment Report 2013: Global Value Chains: Investment and Trade for Development*. Geneva: United Nations.

UNCTADSTAT, Statistics. Available at: http://unctad.org/en/Pages/Statistics.aspx.

UNDP (United Nations Development Programme). 1999. *Human Development Report*. New York: Oxford University Press.

UNDP (United Nations Development Programme). 2005. *A Time for Bold Ambition: Together we can Cut Poverty in Half*, UNDP Annual Report. New York: UNDP.

UNDP (United Nations Development Programme). 2008. *Human Development Report 2007–2008*. New York: UNDP.

UNDP (United Nations Development Programme). 2013. *Human Development Report 2013*. New York: UNDP.

UNEP (United Nations Environmental Programme). 2011a. *Decoupling Natural Resource Use and Environmental Impacts from Economic Growth*. A Report of the Working Group on Decoupling to the International Resource Panel. Nairobi and Paris: UNEP.

UNEP (United Nations Environmental Programme). 2011b: *Towards a Green Economy: Pathways to Sustainable Development and Poverty Eradication*. UNEP. Available at: www.unep.org/greeneconomy.

UNEP (United Nations Environmental Programme). 2013. *China's Green Long March*. Nairobi: UNEP.

UNESCO. 2009. *Framework for Cultural Statistics*. UNESCO Institute for Statistics. Available at: http://www.uis.unesco.org/culture/Pages/framework-cultural-statistics.aspx.

Unfried, Berthold, Van der Linden, Marcel and Schindler, Christine, eds. 2004. *Labour and New Social Movements in a Globalizing World System*. Vienna: Akademische Verlagsanstalt.

UNODC. 2010. *The Globalization of Crime: A Transnational Organized Crime Threat Assessment*. New York: United Nations Office on Drugs and Crime.

Urry, John. 1990. *The Tourist Gaze*. London: Sage.

Urry, John. 2000. *Sociology Beyond Societies: Mobilities for the Twenty-First Century*. London: Routledge.

Urry, John. 2004. 'The "system" of automobility'. *Theory, Culture and Society*, 21 (4) 25–39.

US Bureau of Labor Statistics. 2012. 'International labor comparisons'. Available at: http://www.bls.gov/fls/#laborforce.

US Survey of Current Business. 2012. Washington: Bureau of Economic Analysis.

USTIP. 2010. *Annual US Trafficking in Persons Report*. Washington, DC: United States Department of State. Available at: http://www.state.gov/g/tip/rls/tiprpt/2010/index.htm.

Utting, P. 2000. *Promoting Socially Responsible Business in Developing Countries: The Potential and Limits of Voluntary Initiatives*. Report of the UNRISD Workshop. 23–24 October. Geneva.

Vahrenkamp, R. 1976. 'Taylors Lehre – ein Mittelklassentraum'. *Kursbuch*, 43: 14–26.

Vaitilingam, R. 2010. *Research for our Future: UK Business Success through Public Investment in Research*. October. Research Council United Kingdom. Available at: http://www.rcuk.ac.uk/RCUK-prod/assets/documents/publications/researchforourfuture.pdf.

Vaizey, E. 2013. 'Britain's creative industries really do lead the world. Don't they?'. DCMS Blog. 29 April. Available at: http://blogs.culture.gov.uk/main/2013/04/britains_creative_industries_r.html.

Van Apeldoorn, Bastiaan. 2002. *Transnational Capitalism and the Struggle over European Integration*. London: Routledge.

Van Apeldoorn, Bastiaan. 2004. 'Theorizing the transnational: A historical materialist approach'. *Journal of International Relations and Development*, 7 (2) 142–76.

Van den Anker, Christien, ed. 2004. *The Political Economy of New Slavery*. New York: Palgrave Macmillan.

Van der Pijl, Kees. 2012[1984]. *The Making of an Atlantic Ruling Class*. London: Verso.

Van der Pijl, Kees. 1998. *Transnational Classes and International Relations*. London: Routledge.

Van der Pijl, Kees. 2004. 'Two faces of the transnational cadre under neo-liberalism'. *Journal of International Relations and Development*, 7 (2) 177–207.

Van der Pijl, Kees. 2006. *Global Rivalries from the Cold War to Iraq*. London: Pluto.

Van der Pijl, Kees, Holman, Otto and Raviv, Or. 2011. 'The resurgence of German capital in Europe: EU integration and the restructuring of Atlantic networks of interlocking directorates after 1991'. *Review of International Political Economy*, 18 (3) 384–408.

Van der Ploeg, J.D. 2008. *The New Peasantries: Struggles for Autonomy and Sustainability in an Era of Empire and Globalization*. London: Earthscan.

Van der Ploeg, J.D. 2013. *Peasants and the Art of Farming. A Chayanovian Manifesto*. Halifax: Fernwood Publishing.

Van der Ploeg, J.D., Jingzhong, Y. et al. 2010. 'Rural development reconsidered: Building on comparative perspective from China, Brazil and the European Union'. *Rivista di Economia Agraria*, 65 (2) 163–90.

Van der Tuin, I. and Dolphijn, R. 2000. 'The transversality of new materialism'. *Women: A Cultural Review*, 21 (2) 153–71.

Vance, Sandra and Scott, Roy. 1994. *Wal-Mart: A History of Sam Walton's Retail Phenomenon*. New York: Twayne Publishers.

Vanderbilt, T. 1998. *The Sneaker Book: Anatomy of an Industry and an Icon*. New York: New Press.

Vargas Llosa, Mario. 2003. 'This is not good, sir!' *The Guardian*. 5 September.

Veltmeyer, H. 2013. 'The political economy of natural resource extraction: A new model or extractive imperialism?' *Canadian Journal of Development Studies*, 34 (1) 79–95.

Vercellone, C. 2007. 'From formal subsumption to general intellect: Elements for a Marxist reading of the thesis of cognitive capitalism'. *Historical Materialism*, 15 (3) 13–36.

Vernadskiy, Vladimir I. 1998. *The Biosphere*. New York: Copernicus.

Vernon, Raymond. 1973[1971]. *Sovereignty at Bay. The Multinational Spread of US Enterprises*. Harmondsworth: Penguin.

Vianello, F. 1979. *Il Profitto e il Potere – una Raccolta di Saggi*. Turin: Rosenberg and Sellier.

Vitale, Luis. 2011. *Interpretación Marxista de la Historia de Chile: Volumen III Tomos V y VI*. Santiago: LOM Ediciones.

Vogel, David. 1995. *Trading Up. Consumer and Environmental Regulation in a Global Economy*. Cambridge, MA: Harvard University Press.

Vogel, Ezra. F. 1979. *Japan as Number One: Lessons for America*. Cambridge, MA: Harvard University Press.

Volcker, P. and Gyohten, T. 1993. *Changing Fortunes: The World's Money and the Threat to American Leadership*. New York: The Crown Publishing Group.

Vollmer, Gerhard. 2013. 'Wieso können wir die Welt erkennen?' In Luc Saner, ed. *Studium Generale. Auf dem Weg zu einem Allgemeinen Teil der Wissenschaften*. Wiesbaden: Springer Spektrum.

Wacker, A. 1976. *Arbeitslosigkeit. Soziale und Psychologische Voraussetzungen und Folgen*. Frankfurt am Mein: Europäische Verlagsanstalt.

Wainwright, H. 2013. 'Transformative power: Political organisation in transition'. *Socialist Register 2013: Question of Strategy*. 137–58.

Wajcman, Judy. 1991. *Feminism Confronts Technology*. Cambridge: Polity.

Wallerstein, I. 2013. 'End of the road for runaway factories?' Available at: http://www.iwallerstein.com/road-runaway-factories/.

Wallerstein, Immanuel. 2001[1991]. *Unthinking Social Science. The Limits of Nineteenth-Century Paradigms*, 2nd edn. Philadelphia: Temple University Press.

Wallis, Victor. 2010. 'Beyond "green capitalism"'. *Monthly Review*, 61 (9) 32–47.

Wang, H. et al. 2009. 'China's New Labour contract law: Is China moving towards increased power for workers?' *Third World Quarterly*, 30 (3) 485–501.

Wang, K. 2010. 'Changes in the consciousness of Chinese workers and collective actions: The 2010 strikes in the car industry and their influence' [Chungguk nodongjaŭi ŭishik byŏnhwawa tanch'e haengdong: 2010nyŏn chadongch'asanŏpŭi p'aŏp mit yŏnghyangnyŏk]. *International Labour Briefing [Gukjenodong bŭrip'ing]*, 8 (8) 3–15.

Wang, L. 2010. 'Specialists say that the Nanhai Honda strike was a result of no clear means for the representation of interests' [Zhuanjia cheng nanhaibentian tinggong yuanyu liyidaibiao qudao butongyang]. *Sina.com*. Available at: http://dailynews.sina.com/gb/chn/chnpolitics/sinacn/20100919/18281846979.html.

Wang, Shuguang and Zhang, Yongchang. 2006. 'Penetrating the Great Wall, conquering the Middle Kingdom: Wal-Mart in China'. In S. Brunn, ed. *Wal-Mart World*. New York: Routledge.

Warr, P. 2007. *Work, Happiness, and Unhappiness*. E-book: Lawrence Erlbaum Associates.

Warren, J. 1990. 'Prostitution in Singapore society and the *Karayuki-San*'. In P.J. Rimmer and L.M. Allen, eds. *The Underside of Malaysian History: Pullers, Prostitutes, Plantation Workers*. Singapore: Singapore University Press.

Waterman, Peter. 2006. 'Emancipating labour internationalism'. In Boaventura de Sousa Santos, ed. *Another Production is Possible: Beyond the Capitalist Canon*. London: Verso.

Waterman, Peter. 2010. 'Alternative international labour communication by computer after two decades'. *Interface: A Journal for and about Social Movements*, 2 (2), 241–69.

Waterman, Peter. 2012. 'An emancipatory global labour studies is necessary! On rethinking the global labour movement in the Hour of Furnaces'. *Interface: A Journal for and about Social Movements*, 4 (2) 317–68.

WBGU. 2011. *World in Transition. A Social Contract for Sustainability*. Berlin: Wissenschaftlicher Beirat der Bundesregierung Globale Umweltveränderungen.

WCED. 1987. *Our Common Future – Report of the World Commission on Environment and Development*. Oxford: Oxford University Press.

Weber, Marcel. 2005. *Philosophy of Experimental Biology*. Cambridge: Cambridge University Press.

Weber, Max. 1976[1921]. *Wirtschaft und Gesellschaft. Grundriss der Verstehenden Soziologie*, 5th rev. edn. Tübingen: J.C.B. Mohr.

Weber, Max. 1995. *Economie et Société. 1. Les Catégories de la Sociologie*. Paris: Pocket.

Weber, Max. 2004. 'Parlement et gouvernement dans l'Allemagne réorganisée. Contribution à la critique politique du corps des fonctionnaires et du système des partis'. In Max Weber, *Oeuvres Politiques*. Paris: Albin Michel.

Webster, Edward, Lambert, Rob and Bezuidenhout, Andries. 2008. *Grounding Globalization: Labour in the Age of Insecurity*. Malden, MA: Blackwell.

Wei, D. 2010. 'Labour management negotiations at Honda continue' [Nanhai bentian laozi tanpan jixu]. *Caixin*. Available at: www.business.sohu.com/20100601/n272509555.shtml.

Wei, L. 2010. 'Honda workers' oral account: what did we do?' [Bentian bagongshe koushushilu: women zuole shenme?]. *Economic Observer* [*Jingji Guancha*]. Available at: http://finance.jrj.com.cn/biz/2010/06/0113167560626.shtml.

Weir, Bill. 2012. 'A trip to the iFactory'. *ABC News*. 21 February. Available at: http://abcnews.go.com/International/trip-ifactory-nightline-unprecedented-glimpse-inside-apples-chinese/story?id=15748745#.UZPCY0r_mSo.

White House, The. 2000. 'National nanotechnology initiative: Leading to the next industrial revolution'. Press release 21 January. Available at: http://clinton4.nara.gov/WH/New/html/20000121_4.html.

White, L. 1990. *The Comforts of Home: Prostitution in Colonial Nairobi.* Chicago: University of Chicago Press.

White, M. 2010. 'Clicktivism is ruining leftist activism'. *The Guardian*, 12 August. Available at: http://www.theguardian.com/commentisfree/2010/aug/12/clicktivism-ruining-leftist-activism.

White, M.A. 2008. 'Review essay: Critical compulsions: On the affective turn'. *Topia*, 19: 181–8.

Whyte, William H. 1963[1956]. *The Organization Man.* Harmondsworth: Penguin.

Wiebel, B. and Pilenko, A. 2011. 'Gehirn und Gesellschaft – Mechanismen neoliberaler Dekonstruktion'. In B. Wiebel, A. Pilenko and G. Nintemann, eds. *Mechanismen Psycho-sozialer Zerstörung. Neoliberales Herrschaftsdenken, Stressfaktoren der Prekarität, Widerstand.* Hamburg: VSA.

Williams, R. 1982[1958]. *Culture and Society*. London: Hogarth Press.

Williams, William A. 1969. *The Roots of the Modern American Empire: A Study of the Growth and Shaping of Social Consciousness in a Marketplace Society.* New York: Random House.

Wills, J. 2009. 'Subcontracted employment and its challenge to labour'. *Labor Studies Journal*, 34 (4) 441–60.

Winn, Peter. 1986. *Weavers of the Revolution: The Yarur Workers and Chile's Road to Socialism.* Oxford: Oxford University Press.

Winn, Peter. 1994. 'A worker's nightmare: Taylorism and the 1962 Yarur strike in Chile'. *Radical History Review*, 58: 4–34.

WIPO website: http://www.wipo.int/portal/en/index.html.

Wissen, Markus. 2010. 'Klimawandel, Geopolitik und "imperiale Lebensweise". Das Scheitern von "Kopenhagen" und die strukturelle Überforderung internationaler Umweltpolitik'. *Kurswechsel*, 24 (2) 30–38.

Wissen, Markus. 2011. *Gesellschaftliche Naturverhältnisse in der Internationalisierung des Staates. Konflikte um die Räumlichkeit staatlicher Politik und die Kontrolle natürlicher Resourcen.* Münster: Westfälisches Dampfboot.

Wissen, Markus. 2012. 'Post-neoliberale Hegemonie? Zur Rolle des Green-Economy-Konzepts in der Vielfachkrise'. *Kurswechsel*, 26 (2) 28–36.

Witz, A. 2000. 'Whose body matters? Feminist sociology and the corporeal turn in sociology and feminism'. *Body and Society*, 6 (2) 1–24.

Wohl, J. 2012. 'Wal-Mart says it has best Black Friday ever despite protests, crowds'. *Reuters through Huffington Post*, 23 November. Available at: http://www.huffingtonpost.com/2012/11/23/Wal-Mart-best-black-friday_n_2178541.html?ir=Business.

Wolf, D.L. 1992. *Factory Daughters: Gender, Household Dynamics, and Rural Industrialization in Java*. Berkeley: University of California Press.

Wolf, Winfried. 1996. *Car Mania: A Critical History of Transport*. London: Pluto Press.

Wolfe, Joel. 2002. 'The social subject versus the political: Latin American labour studies at a crossroads'. *Latin American Research Review*, 37 (2) 244–62.

Womack, J., Jones, D. and Roos, D. 1990. *The Machine that Changed the World: Based on the Massachusetts Institute of Technology 5-million Dollar 5-Year Study on the Future of the Automobile*. New York: Rawson Associates.

Wonders, N.A. and Michalowski, R. 2001. 'Bodies, borders, and sex tourism in a globalized world: A tale of two cities – Amsterdam and Havana'. *Social Problems*, 48 (4) 545–71.

Wood, Ellen. 1995. *Democracy Against Capitalism: Rewriting Historical Materialism*. Cambridge: Cambridge University Press.

World Bank. 1995. *Workers in an Integrating World*. New York: World Bank.

World Bank. 1997. *World Development Report, The State in a Changing World*. Washington, DC: World Bank.

World Bank. 2004. Databank. Available at: http://data.worldbank.org/indicator/BX.KLT.DINV.CD.WD.

World Bank. 2005. 'Increasing aid and its effectiveness'. In *Global Monitoring Report: Millennium Development Goals: From Consensus to Momentum*. Washington, DC: World Bank. Available at: http://siteresources.worldbank.org/INTGLOBALMONITORING/Resources/ch5_GMR2005.pdf.

World Bank. 2006. *Global Economic Prospects: Economic Implications of Remittances and Migration*. Washington, DC: World Bank.

World Bank. 2008. *Migration and Remittances: Top Ten*. March. Available at: http://econ.worldbank.org.

World Bank. 2011. *Migration and Remittances Factbook 2011*. Washington, DC: The World Bank.

World Bank. 2012a. *Turn Down the Heat: Why a 4°C Warmer World must be Avoided*. Washington, DC: World Bank. Available at: http://documents.worldbank.org/curated/en/2012/11/17097815/turn-down-heat-4%C2%B0c-warmer-world-must-avoided.

World Bank. 2012b. *World Development Report 2013: Jobs*. Washington, DC: World Bank.

World Bank. 2013. *GDP Per Capita Current US$*. Available at: http://data.worldbank.org/indicator/NY.GDP.PCAP.CD?page=1.

World Trade Organization. 2012. *World Trade Report 2012. Trade and Public Policies: A Closer Look at Non-tariff Measures in the 21st Century*. Geneva: WTO.

World Watch Institute. 2011. 'State of the World 2011 Report'. Available at: http://www.upi.com/Business_News/Energy-Resources/2011/07/27/Land-grabs-threaten-African-food-security-says-World-Watch/UPI-86781311802560/#ixzz2rJYYYVMJ. Accessed 24 January 2014.

Wright, Erik Olin. 1996. 'The continuing relevance of class analysis – comments'. *Theory and Society*, 25 (5) 693–716.

Wright, Erik Olin. 2000. 'Working-class power, capitalist-class interests, and class compromise'. *American Journal of Sociology*, 105 (4) 957–1002.

Wright, M.W. 2006. *Disposable Women and Other Myths of Global Capitalism Perspectives on Gender*. New York: Routledge.

Wullweber, Joscha. 2006. 'Der Mythos Nanotechnologie. Die Entstehung und Durchsetzung einer neuen Inwertsetzungstechnologie'. *Peripherie*, 101/102, 99–118.

Wullweber, Joscha. 2010. *Hegemonie, Diskurs und Politische Ökonomie. Das Nanotechnologie-Projekt*. Baden-Baden: Nomos.

Wullweber, Joscha. 2014a. 'Theories of IPE, global politics, and the socio-economic construction of technology'. In Maximilian Mayer, Mariana Carpes and Ruth Knoblich, eds. *International Relations and the Global Politics of Science and Technology*. Berlin: Springer.

Wullweber, Joscha. 2014b. 'Global politics and empty signifiers: The political construction of high-technology'. *Critical Policy Studies*, DOI: 10.1080/19460171.2014.918899.

Xing, Y. and Kolstad, C. 2002. 'Do lax environmental regulations attract foreign investment?' *Environmental and Resource Economics*, 21 (1) 1–22.

Xinhua News. 2010. 'CPC sets targets for 12th Five-Year Program'. China.org.cn. Available at: http://www.china.org.cn/china/2010–10/27/content_21214648.htm.

Yanarella, E. and Green, W. 1996. 'Introduction: Building other people's cars: Organized labor and the crisis of Fordism'. In W. Green and E. Yanarella, eds. *North American Auto Unions in Crisis: Lean Production as Contested Terrain*. New York: State University of New York Press.

Yang, D.T., Chen, V.W. and Monarch, R. 2010. 'Rising wages: Has China lost its global labor advantage?' *Pacific Economic Review*, 15 (4) 482–504.

Yashiro, N. 2011. 'Myths about Japanese employment practices: An increasing Insider–Outsider conflict of interests'. *Contemporary Japan*, 23 (2) 133–55.

Yatchew, A. and Baziliauskas, A. 2011. 'Ontario feed-in-tariff programs'. *Energy Policy*, 39 (7) 3885–93.

Ye, Victor M. and Bhatia, Sujata K. 2012. 'Metabolic engineering for the production of clinically important molecules: Omega-3 fatty acids, artemisinin, and taxol'. *Biotechnology Journal*, 7 (1) 20–33.

Yilmaz, Bediz. 2008. 'Underclass in Turkey: From poverty in turns to perpetual poverty'. *Toplum ve Bilim*, 113: 127–45.

Yiu, C. 2004. 'Pioneer labor activists celebrate 20 years' work'. *Taipei Times*. Available at: http://www.taipeitimes.com/News/taiwan/archives/2004/05/30/2003157505.

Young, E. 1759. *Conjectures on Original Composition*. E.J. Morley, eds. 1918. Manchester: Manchester University Press and London: Longman.

Yu, Y. 2012. 'China's rebalancing act: between exports and domestic demand'. *East Asia Forum*. Available at: http://www.eastasiaforum.org/2012/10/24/chinas-rebalancing-act-between-exports-and-domestic-demand/.

Zadek, S. 2004. 'The path to corporate responsibility'. *Harvard Business Review*, 82 (6) 125–32.

Zapata, Fransisco. 1968. *Estructura y Representividad del Sindicalismo en Chile*. Santiago: Instituto Latinoamericana de Planificación.

Zarembka, Paul. 2002. 'Rosa Luxemburg's *Accumulation of Capital*: Critics try to bury the message'. *Research in Political Economy*, 21: 3–45.

Zeitlin, Jonathan and Pochet, Philippe, eds. 2005. *The Open Method of Co-ordination in Action. The European Employment and Social Inclusion Strategies*. Brussels: Peter Lang.

Zeller, Christian. 2008. 'From thc gene to the globe: Extracting rents based on intellectual property monopolies'. *Review of International Political Economy*, 15 (1) 86–115.

Zeller, Christian. 2009. 'Die Gewalt der Rente: Die Erschliessung natürlicher Resourcen als neue Akkumulationsfelder'. *Schweizerische Zeitschrift für Soziologie*, 35 (1) 31–52.

Zeller, Christian. 2010. 'The pharma-biotech complex and interconnected regional innovation arenas'. *Urban Studies*, 47 (13) 2867–94.

Zheng, Y.L. 2009. 'It's not what is on paper, but what is in practice: China's new labor contract law and the enforcement problem'. *Washington University Global Studies Law Review*, 8 (3) 1–24.

Zhou, Z. and Liu, Z. 2010. 'Nanhai Honda restarts production, workers achieve a partial victory' [Nanhai bentian fugong, gongrenqude 'jubuxing' shengli]. *China News Weekly* [*Zhongguo Xinwen Zhoukan*]. Available at: http://www.letscorp.net/archives/5149.

Ziegler, J. 2003. *Die neuen Herrscher der Welt und ihre globalen Widersacher*, 5th edn. Munich: Bertelsmann.

Zook, Matthew and Graham, Mark. 2006. 'Wal-Mart nation: Mapping the reach of a retail colossus'. In S. Brunn, ed. *Wal-Mart World*. New York: Routledge.

Zuindeau, Bertrand. 2007. 'Regulation school and environment: Theoretical proposals and avenues of research'. *Ecological Economics*, 62 (2) 281–90.

Index